Seventh Edition

Essay Essentials

with Readings

Rhonda Dynes

Sarah Norton

Brian Green

NELSON

NELSON

Essay Essentials with Readings, Seventh Edition

by Rhonda Dynes, Sarah Norton, and Brian Green

VP, Product Solutions, K–20:
Claudine O'Donnell

Publisher:
Lenore Taylor-Atkins

Executive Marketing Manager:
Amanda Henry

Content Manager:
Lisa Berland

Photo and Permissions Researcher:
Karen Hunter

Senior Production Project Manager:
Natalia Denesiuk Harris

Production Service:
MPS Limited

Copy Editor:
Kelli Howey

Proofreader:
Thulasi, MPS Limited

Indexer:
May Hasso

Design Director:
Ken Phipps

Higher Education Design PM:
Pamela Johnston

Interior Design:
Brenda Barratt

Interior Design Modifications:
Ken Cadinouche

Cover Design:
Ken Cadinouche

Cover Image:
Mactrunk/Depositphotos.com

Compositor:
MPS Limited

Printed in Canada
1 2 3 4 21 20 19 18

For more information contact Nelson Education Ltd., 1120 Birchmount Road, Toronto, Ontario, M1K 5G4. Or you can visit our Internet site at nelson.com

Credits for recurring images:
Cozy Home/Shutterstock.com (orange shoes on cobblestones); Pressmaster/Shutterstock.com (overhead of students working at table); Africa Studio/Shutterstock .com (books flying off shelves); Billion Photos/Shutterstock.com (laptop on desk); Jacob Lund/Shutterstock.com (people in meeting room); Graeme Dawe/Shutterstock.com (old books on shelf); Monkey Business Images/ Shutterstock.com (man addressing group of people); Digital Vision/ Shutterstock.com (woman reading book on floor); Unuchko Veronika/ Shutterstock.com (vintage book with fanned pages)

Library and Archives Canada Cataloguing in Publication

Norton, Sarah, author
Essay essentials with readings / Rhonda Dynes, Sarah Norton, Brian Green. — Seventh edition.

Includes index.
Revision of: Essay essentials with readings / Sarah Norton, Brian Green, Rhonda Dynes. Sixth enhanced edition.

Issued in print and electronic formats.
ISBN 978-0-17-672128-2 (softcover).
—ISBN 978-0-17-679882-6 (PDF)

1. Essay—Authorship—Textbooks. 2. Report writing—Textbooks. 3. English language—Rhetoric—Textbooks. 4. College readers. I. Dynes, Rhonda, author II. Green, Brian, author III. Title.

PE1471.N69 2018 808'.042
C2017-906973-X
C2017-906974-8

ISBN-13: 978-0-17-672128-2
ISBN-10: 0-17-672128-2

Brief Contents

Contents

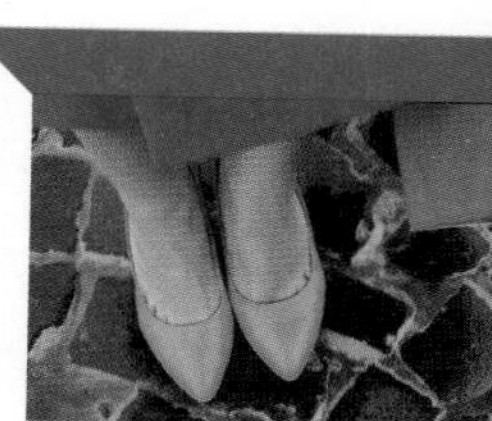

Preface: To the Instructor

Essay Essentials with Readings, Seventh Edition, is designed for all Canadian post-secondary students who are learning to write academic and professional prose. The book has been substantially revised and expanded to inclusively fit the needs of students who want to succeed at school and who require the ability to bring their developed writing skills to the workplace.

New to the Seventh Edition

The most significant change in the seventh edition is a revision to the structure of the book to accommodate courses that focus on integrating the study of writing with detailed information on critical thinking and innovative ideas about relating to audiences effectively in reading, thinking, writing, and presenting. Other highlights of the new edition include the following:

- Two new chapters on academic presentations, posters, and portfolios (Chapters 21 and 22) have been added.
- An expansion of the chapter on writing the main points and the thesis statement (Chapter 5) addresses the struggles students have with the process.
- Further discussion about critical thinking and the process involved in using the steps to analyze articles has resulted in the inclusion of a published article and an outline and draft of an analysis for students to use as a model for their own work.
- New readings focus on current and innovative topics. More readings will be available on the Instructor Resource Centre in MindTap. (See the section on MindTap, which starts on the next page, for more information.)
- For a stronger emphasis on student essay writing, four student essays are included as models for students to critically consider in light of their own work.
- Many of the exercises in the Workbook (Chapters 23–26) are new or have been revised and updated to allow students at a variety of skill levels to increase their understanding of grammar and mechanics.
- A fully online learning solution, MindTap offers further readings and supplements, allowing for more instructor choice and providing more content about writing than could be included in the printed version of the text.

Essay Essentials with Readings is divided into nine parts. Parts 1 through 7 explain, exemplify, and provide practice in planning, drafting, and revising transactional prose, as well as in researching and writing properly formatted and documented essays and workplace material, including presentations and academic posters and portfolios. Because most adults learn better and with more satisfaction when they work with other learners, many of the exercises are interactive.[1] Some involve the whole class, but most are designed to be done in pairs or groups, either in class or online.[2]

The questions following the essays and readings in Part 8 are designed to provoke thinking and discussion as well as to promote students' understanding of structure and development. Teachers will find suggested answers to these questions in the Instructor's Manual available on the *Essay Essentials* website at nelson.com/instructor.

Part 9, the Workbook, reviews the basics of syntax, grammar, punctuation, and spelling. Many students will be required to work through this workbook on their own; answers to the asterisked exercises are provided in Appendix B. Answers to the Mastery Tests are provided in the Instructor's Manual and on the Instructors' page of the website. The four chapters of the Workbook can be covered in any order, but the information within each chapter is interdependent and should be studied sequentially; competency in later parts of each chapter often depends on mastery of the earlier material.

Appendix A provides a revised glossary containing all the words found in bold throughout the text. These provide easy reference for students looking for definitions and clarification of terms.

Inside the front cover is a Quick Revision Guide. We encourage students to use it as a checklist to consult as they revise and edit their work. It also provides an overall summary of the entire book and lists how each chapter illustrates the main process of essay writing. Instructors can duplicate the guide, attach a copy to each student's paper, and mark ✓ or ✗ beside each item in the guide to identify the paper's strengths and weaknesses. This strategy provides students with specific feedback in a consistent format. It also saves hours of marking time.

MindTap

MindTap for *Essay Essentials*, Seventh Edition, is a personalized teaching experience with relevant exercises that guide students to practise and master their writing skills. This allows instructors to measure skills and promote better outcomes with ease. A fully online learning solution, MindTap combines all student learning tools—readings, multimedia, activities, and assessments—into a single Learning Path that guides the student through the curriculum. Instructors personalize the experience by customizing the presentation of these learning tools to their students, even seamlessly introducing their own content into the Learning Path.

[1] Answers to exercises marked with an asterisk are provided in Appendix B.

[2] These group exercises can be adapted to individual assignments if the instructor prefers or the course requires.

Acknowledgments

I would like to thank the following reviewers who helped us with the content of this edition:

Janet Bertsch, Northern Alberta Institute of Technology
Bernett Cody, Kwantlen Polytechnic University
Rashmi Jyoti, MacEwan University
Brigid Kelso, George Brown College
Julie Morris, Sheridan College
Karen Pike, Conestoga College
Mary Ann Pruyser, North Island College

I am thankful for the emphasis that the Communications professors in the Liberal Studies Department of Mohawk College have placed on teaching critical thinking, as that work helped me to realize the value of critical thinking and reading skills to the development of the sound writing skills we focus on here.

I am grateful to the publishing team at Nelson Education Ltd. Lenore Taylor-Atkins is a wonderful and kind editor. Lisa Berland saw this book through some serious reconditioning and has been my rock for years! Amanda Henry and the sales team are always available for quick pick-me-ups. Jillian Kerr is always available for chats and deep life discussions. For all of this, I am truly grateful.

Finally, thanks to my partner, Mark Dynes, for endless support and administrative miracles as I try to balance myriad tasks with so few hours in the day! Thank you, thank you, thank you!

Rhonda Dynes

Introduction: Why We Learn to Write

Writing is a rewarding and career-enhancing skill. Unlike most of the skills you acquire in a career program, however, writing is not job-specific. **The writing skills you learn from this book will be useful to you not only in all your college or university courses but also in every job you hold throughout your working life.** Prospective employers will assume that you, as a college or university graduate, are able to write quickly and skillfully. As you progress through your career and climb higher on the organizational ladder, you will write more, and your writing tasks will become more complex. In any job, evaluations of your performance will be based in part on your communication skills. *Essay Essentials with Readings* will teach you to write standard English prose, the kind you can apply to any writing task.

The word *essay* comes from the French *essayer*, to try or attempt. Broadly speaking, an essay is an attempt to communicate information, opinion, or emotion. In college or university, an essay is an exercise that requires students to explore and explain their own and others' thoughts about a subject. In the larger world, essays appear in print and online newspapers and magazines as editorials, reviews, opinion pieces, and commentaries on news and public affairs. In the workplace, an essay structure can be used for any email, memo, letter, or report. It can even form the backbone of a Prezi or PowerPoint presentation.

Thinking, organizing, and researching are fundamental to all practical writing tasks. From this book, you will learn how to find and organize thoughts, to develop ideas in coherent paragraphs, and to express yourself clearly, correctly, and concisely. Once you've mastered these basics, you will have no difficulty adapting your skills to fit the needs of your work environment to create business or technical reports, instructions, proposals, memoranda, sales presentations, commercial scripts, legal briefs, or websites. Those who can write competently are in high demand.

You can learn to write well through practice, perseverance, and a willingness to believe that writing skills develop over time.

We have designed this book to guide you through focused learning and practice to develop better writing skills. Because it is more fun and more efficient to learn with others than to struggle alone, we have included many group-based exercises. To make the writing process even more relevant to the workplace, we have also introduced some applicable readings and useful examples of professional writing. Part 8, our interactive editing workbook, provides handy tools, rules, and exercises to boost your sentence-writing skills and grammar. **We strongly encourage you throughout your study to keep a list of the errors that you make most frequently.** Only by recognizing your writing weaknesses can you develop them into writing strengths. If you follow the guidelines in this text, you will produce effective essays in school and creditable communications in your career.

Online Supplements

Stay organized and efficient with **MindTap**—a single destination with all the course material and study aids you need to succeed. Built-in apps leverage social media and the latest learning technology. They also help to make the working and writing field more equitable. It's important to understand that we all learn in different ways. *Essay Essentials* with MindTap is designed to be used along with accessible technologies for students learning writing. For example,

- ReadSpeaker will read the text to you.
- You can highlight text and make notes in your MindTap Reader. Your notes will flow into Evernote, the electronic notebook app that you can access anywhere when it's time to study for the exam.
- Self-quizzing allows you to assess your understanding.
- Digital versions of many of the activities are available on MindTap, as are the exercises.

What the Symbols Mean

This symbol in the margin beside an exercise means the exercise is designed for two or more students working together. Read the directions that introduce the exercise carefully to find out how many students should participate and what task is to be performed. Often you are instructed to begin work in a pair or group, then to work individually on a writing task, and finally to regroup and review your writing with your partner(s).

This symbol means "note this." We've used it to highlight writing tips, helpful hints, hard-to-remember points, and information that you should apply whenever you write, not just when you are dealing with the specific principle covered in the paragraph marked by the icon.

This icon attached to an exercise means that the exercise is a mastery test designed to check your understanding of the section of the chapter you have just completed. The answers to these exercises are not in the back of the book; your instructor will provide them.

The Process of Writing

> Writing is a three-step process consisting of
> 1. planning or prewriting
> 2. writing (sometimes called *drafting*)
> 3. revising

The majority of this book explains the approach to writing that you will take when you have already been told what to write about, called the *conceptual approach*. The conceptual (or top-down) approach is the one you choose when you know what you want to say before you begin to write. You identify your subject and main points, and draft a thesis statement (a statement that provides your readers a preview of the content of your paper). Research papers, business reports, and essay questions on exams are examples of writing that requires a conceptual approach.

The experimental (bottom-up) approach is also useful and should be used when you do not know ahead of time what you want to say. You discover your thesis gradually, incrementally, through trial and error, and through several drafts. Experimental writers often rely on prewriting strategies such as brainstorming and freewriting to kick-start the process. At times throughout the textbook, you will be given exercises that allow you to use this approach, although we recognize that, at both school and in the workplace, many topics have been thoughtfully planned out for you ahead of time.

You should learn to use both approaches. Sometimes you will discover your subject through writing; at other times, using top-down strategies will help you to express clearly what you already know. If you are familiar with both approaches, you can comfortably choose whichever is more appropriate for a particular writing task.

What Your Readers Expect

Whichever approach you use, your goal is to make your finished writing easy for your audience to read and understand. To achieve this goal, you must meet your readers' expectations.

When your readers begin to read a piece of extended prose, they unconsciously expect to find

- a preview (in the introduction) of the content and organization of the paper
- paragraphs that contain the necessary content
- a sentence (usually the first) in each paragraph that identifies its topic
- unified paragraphs, each of which explores a single topic
- connections (transitions) within and between paragraphs

Keep in mind that readers want to obtain information quickly and easily, without backtracking. They rely on the writer—you—to make efficient reading possible.

Your readers will read more easily and remember more of what they have read if you include a thesis statement to introduce them to the content and organization of the paper and if you begin each paragraph with a topic sentence. If you do not organize and develop your paper and its paragraphs in a clearly identifiable way, readers will impose their own organization on it. The result will be longer reading time, difficulty in understanding and remembering the content, or, worse, the assumption that a paragraph or even the whole paper has a meaning other than the one you intended.

How to Begin

Having a conversation with someone who never seems to get to the point is a tiresome and frustrating experience. Similarly, an essay—or any other form of written communication—that has no point and rambles on will turn readers off. So how can you avoid boring, confusing, or annoying your readers? To begin with, you need to have something to say and a reason for saying it. Very few people can write anything longer than a few sentences from start to finish without taking time to think about and plan what they'll say. Prewriting will help you to plan and develop your writing projects more efficiently. We will explore some prewriting strategies in Chapter 4.

Writing an essay is like building a house: if you have a clear plan or blueprint, you can construct the house without having to double back or even start all over again. A good plan saves time.

Once you've determined what you want to say, the next step is to arrange your main points in the most effective order possible. If you organize your ideas carefully, you won't ramble. As a general rule, the more time you spend on prewriting and planning, the less time you'll need to spend on drafting and revising. Careful planning will enable you to produce papers that your readers will find clear and understandable.

The Parts of an Essay

Most students come to college or university with some familiarity with the five-paragraph theme, the most basic form of essay composition, so we will start with it and then move on to adaptations and variations of this basic format.

An essay, like any document, has a beginning, a middle, and an end.

The beginning, or *introduction,* tells your reader the thesis (i.e., the single main idea you will explain or prove) and the scope of your essay. If your introduction is well crafted, its *thesis statement* will identify the points you will discuss in the paragraphs that follow.

The middle, or *body,* consists of paragraphs that discuss in detail the points that have been identified in the introduction. In a short essay, each paragraph develops a separate main point and each should contain three essential components:

1. a *topic sentence,* which identifies the point of the paragraph
2. development, or *support,* of the topic sentence (*supporting sentences* provide the detailed information the reader needs in order to understand the point)
3. a *concluding sentence* that either brings the discussion of the topic to a close or provides a transition to the next paragraph

The end, or *conclusion,* is a brief final paragraph. Unless your essay is very short, you summarize the main points to reinforce them for readers, and then end with a statement that will give your readers something to think about after they have finished reading your essay.

Think of this tightly structured form of prose not as a straitjacket that stifles your creativity but rather as a pattern to follow while you develop the skills and abilities you need to build other, more complex prose structures. As you seek out and find the links between this type of academic format and workplace structures, you will begin to see all that this deceptively simple form has to offer.

The following essay can serve as a guide, starting point, and reminder of what a five-paragraph essay can do. The introduction contains a clear thesis. Each body paragraph has a topic sentence, is well developed, and has a concluding sentence. The conclusion is brief but leaves the reader with a thoughtful question. Consider this essay as you read through the textbook—it is the kind of work you will want to write before you move on to more complex prose.

Failing Better

Something I have learned over the past thirteen years of schooling is what I call *failing better*. Failing better is a process of learning to grow as a person, to feel better, as a result of failed attempts at a variety of things. From school work to relationships, from D+ essays to fights to lost friendships, failing better is a process I would recommend to anyone. More than a process, failing better is a state of mind. By focusing on seeing failure as a stepping stone, learning to use mistakes to communicate better, and reflecting on how past challenges can become future successes, failing better can work for anyone who feels a need for a new way to look at life.

When you see failure, whether it be a bad grade or a failed customer service interaction at work, always try to use it as a pathway to something better. Give yourself some time to feel disappointed, but try eventually to move past your emotions to consider what led to the failed experience. You will have another paper to write and another customer to please. The last time is in the past. Move forward and try to think of failure as an opportunity not to be missed the next time.

When you feel that you have failed, communication is always a great option. Is a bad grade a chance to talk to your teacher or professor and get some new information? Sometimes that conversation can lead you to grow in ways you might not have imagined. Asking a manager how you could have better made the customer happy and really listening to the reply can set the tone for better interactions later. All in all, you can learn, over time, that there is no such thing as failing.

Really, it is in reflection that failure can be transformed. Talk to anyone about the past experiences that have been most important to them. Sure, some of those things might be successes, but overall, you will most likely find that what most people saw as failures—for example, failed attempts at getting work or failures to make deadlines—ended up being really pivotal and eventually positive moments. Make any experience work for you!

Failing better, in the end, is looking back and seeing any experience as part of who you are and as an opportunity to imagine who you might become.

Part 1

Understanding the Elements of Effective Writing

All effective writing is well thought out, organized, and developed in such a way that the person or people you are writing for understand the message you are trying to send. And most effective writing contains certain writing components, which we will discuss throughout this book. These include skills like developing a clear outline and thesis statement as well as considering the way your **paragraphs** and ideas fit together. Grammar and some stylistic elements are also addressed. When you get good enough, some of these writing components will come naturally to you. In Part 1, we are going to explore the following standard elements of effective writing:

- understanding the role that both you and your *audience* play in the communication process (Chapter 1)
- *reading* about your topic carefully (Chapter 2)
- *thinking* critically about what you have read before you start writing (Chapter 3)

CHAPTER 1

Understanding the Audience, Understanding Yourself

"Begin at the beginning," the King said gravely, "and go till you come to the end; then stop."
—Lewis Carroll, *Alice's Adventures in Wonderland*

Before you start writing—an essay, a report, an email message—you must have something to write about (your **subject**) and someone to write for (your **audience**). In order to produce a clear, effective message for your readers, you must know who they are. A paradox exists in many high school English classrooms as students walk around whispering about their papers: "You know, you must write about what Mr. So-and-So wants in order to get a good grade...."

In other words, many students have learned that writing *for* readers and giving them what they want always offers benefits, be it better grades, a job promotion, or simply a clearer dialogue between two parties. But learning to write for *only* one audience is not enough. You need to develop a flexible writing **style** that will allow you to adapt your writing to the various audiences you will encounter throughout your career. Your boss in the professional world will most likely not care what Professor So-and-So wanted at the beginning of each paragraph.

Addressing Your Readers

Knowing your audience is essential to really writing well. As you plan, draft, and revise your paper with your audience in mind, ask yourself the following questions:

- How old are your readers? Might the readers' generation change their perceptions?
- What is their level of education?
- What do they do for a living?
- Are your readers busy, or will they be able to give your message a great deal of consideration?
- What is their cultural background? Their first language?
- Do they have any other specific traits that might affect their perception of what they are reading?

While you really must be careful to avoid generalizing or stereotyping (for example, assuming that women will be more likely than men to accept your position), the answers to these questions do influence most people's views, and you would be wise to consider them before you begin to write, especially if you don't know your audience personally or they are hard to categorize.

For most college and university assignments, you should assume that your instructor or your classmates are your audience. Some teachers will specify external audiences for short papers (and if they don't, they will be impressed if you ask who your readers are). Learning to write for a variety of audiences will be useful to you in the "real world." If you are given the opportunity, experiment with writing for other readers:

- your high school principal
- a recent immigrant
- a union official
- a member of the Green Party
- a religious or spiritual leader
- the CEO of a local company
- the manager of your school cafeteria

Keeping your reader in mind will help you to plan, develop, and revise your assignment in a tone and style appropriate to your message. Spend some time thinking about your subject in relation to your audience. Consider the following three questions when you are deciding what information your essay should include:

1. What does my reader know about my subject?
2. What are my reader's possible attitudes toward my subject?
3. What are my reader's needs in regard to my subject?

Readers' Knowledge

The first question will help you choose the kind and amount of information that you should include. Are you writing for people who know little about your subject or for people with fairly detailed knowledge? Telling readers things they clearly already know can seem demeaning and offensive.

Do you have to cover all the basics, or can you assume your audience is familiar with them?

While you don't want to offend or bore your readers by providing them with information they already have, if you fail to include facts they need in order to understand your message you'll turn them off or lose them entirely. It's a delicate balance.

Readers' Attitudes

The second question helps you decide how to approach your subject, especially if it is controversial. Will your readers be sympathetic to what you have to say? If so, you will aim to reinforce their agreement and will probably state your opinion up front to show you're on their side. If, however, you think they may be hostile to what you have to say, you might lessen their resistance by providing reasons and support for your ideas before revealing your point of view. If you believe your audience is unsure of your topic, you might need to give them quite a bit of information before you lead them toward your own viewpoint on the topic. The approach you take requires you to know your readers, at least as much as you possibly can, emphasizing the importance of critically reading and analyzing people.

Gentle persuasion is usually more effective than confrontation in writing, as it is in life.

Readers' Needs

The third question helps you to decide whether to persuade or inform, to compare or classify, to describe or analyze.

The needs of your audience will determine whether your remarks should be general or specific. Do you intend to add to or reinforce your audience's general knowledge, or do you want your readers to apply your information only in specific situations? Does your reader need a push or are you just helping someone make a decision? It is only once you have assessed the audience's needs that you can choose the writing style and tone that will best suit the situation.

The Academic Audience

For most of you, your audience for the writing you do as a student will be made up of academics, so it seems important to provide some background on the general expectations of a Canadian academic audience, either in colleges or in universities. The other reason to discuss Canadian academic audiences specifically is that academic expectations may be different across international boundaries.

Instructors across Canada likely have their own guidelines for writing style or level of formality. Some students report stricter guidelines in terms of writing formality, length, or research documentation. Other students have experienced looser or more general writing guidelines. But some general attributes for an academic audience do exist:

- Sharing a commitment to diversity (not addressing the general reader as "he," for example),
- Using clear research documentation to reference quoted, summarized, or paraphrased material, and
- Using a relatively formal level of writing (not using "text" speech or shortened forms of words).

An academic audience expects your work to be as free of typos as possible, especially when it comes to people, places, and technical vocabulary. Work should also be paragraphed properly and not all in one chunk of text, unless that is outlined in the writing requirements.

In short, an academic audience expects the best of you—for you to be thoughtful, considerate, well read on your subject, and well-versed in the organizational and technical requirements of writing. If in doubt, always ask your instructor for feedback or for more detailed requirements. Learning how to do academic writing might sound like a lot of work, but writing is a process that gets easier with practice.

Reflecting Yourself

Choosing and maintaining an appropriate role is essential to successful communication.

Once you are clear about who your readers are, what they know, and what they need to know, you should think about *your role* in the communication process.

We all play a variety of roles. We choose a role, often unconsciously, that we hope will suit the expectations of the people we are communicating with. These roles are not false or hypocritical; they are simply facets of our personality that we try to match to the needs of each situation. For example, even if we love riding motorcycles, when we're in the workplace we can't include references to Harley-Davidson in our correspondence to our accountant unless it is an existing part of the relationship. We must learn to balance our roles in every communication situation we are in.

Any time you speak or write, you present yourself in a particular way to your audience. Each day, for example, you meet a variety of people. Some of them you know well—parents, siblings, friends, classmates, instructors, co-workers, supervisors. Others you know only casually—the server in the restaurant, the police officer at the radar trap, the enumerator for the upcoming election, the cashier in the grocery store. With each of these people, whether the contact is casual or intense, you consciously or unconsciously adjust your language to communicate appropriately.

If you speak to your spouse as you do to your dog, you might find yourself in the proverbial doghouse. If you speak to a salesperson as you would to a love interest, you could be arrested. These are extreme examples, but the point is that most of us already intuitively know to adjust the roles we play in life to the situation. We must do the same in our writing.

When you are deciding what role would be most appropriate in a particular communication situation, consider the following three questions:

1. What is my purpose in writing?
2. What is my attitude toward my subject?
3. What are my readers' expectations of me in this communication?

Your Purpose in Writing

The most common purposes of writing are

- to *inform*
- to *persuade*
- to *entertain*

All essays are to some degree persuasive, in that they attempt to convince the reader of a particular depiction of an event, object, or idea. Most college and university writing assignments fall into one of the first two categories, as does much of the writing done in the workplace. It is important to understand the differences between the two styles, which we cover in Chapters 11 and 12. Unless you are in a creative writing course, you probably will not be assigned a paper that is intended solely to entertain the reader. While some essays might be "entertaining," that shouldn't be your initial concern.

Your purpose will depend largely on the needs and expectations of your readers and will affect your tone—the way your audience hears your unique voice.

How you say something often has more impact on your audience than *what* you say.

Your Attitude toward Your Subject

The second question requires you to understand your attitude toward your chosen subject. This involves more than simply asking, "Am I for or against it?" Whereas a position paper requires you to take a stand on something, most persuasive papers discuss both sides of any situation, even if the purpose is to persuade the reader to choose only one. Of course, before you begin writing, you should consider how strongly you feel about your subject, because your attitude will influence your tone as well as the kinds of evidence you present. If you find you can't quite pin down your attitude toward your subject, doing some reading on the topic, discussing it with others, or doing some free writing (discussed in Chapter 4) can all help you to refine your position.

Consider how closely your attitude toward the subject aligns with your audience's attitude.

Thinking about how personal or how objective you wish (or are able) to be in presenting your ideas is an important step. (Chapter 2 further explores how much your research and writing styles reflect your critical position on your subject.) If your views coincide with those of your readers, then a fairly informal approach may be appropriate; if they differ, then an impersonal, objective approach is preferable.

The match between your writing and your reader's way of understanding your writing will never be perfect, but as long as your audience understands the position you are trying to put forward, it won't matter if you disagree at heart.

Your Readers' Expectations of You

The third question requires you to think about what role your audience is likely to expect you to play. Consider the following three questions when choosing your role:

1. If you write as an authority, will you be credible?
2. If you write as a peer or colleague, will you be effective?
3. What are your readers likely to expect from someone in your position writing to them on this subject?

Taking the time to think about your readers' expectations will help you to make appropriate choices with respect to the point of view you take, the examples and supporting details you provide for your ideas, and the level of language you use. It is especially important to take into account any special rules or requirements you may have been given by your audience.

Levels of Standard English Writing

Written English (except in modes like texting or instant messaging) is usually more formal than spoken English. Because writers have time to consider what they want to say and how best to say it, they can

- choose their words carefully
- arrange them in meaningful sentences
- organize ideas into logical paragraphs

Good writing involves more than knowing what words and sentences mean. It also requires using appropriate language. This means that the actual words you choose will affect readers' understanding of what you are trying to say.

No one would submit a book review written for academic purposes that began, "This is an awesome book with, like, ideas that sort of make you think, you know?" You see instantly that the language is inappropriate for this medium. Similarly, if you were discussing the book casually with friends over coffee and announced, "This book contains provocative and stimulating ideas that engage and challenge the reader," your language would most likely be equally inappropriate.

Another way to think about it is that you have to choose a level that suits both your topic and your reader. There will be times when you need to compromise—for example, when you send one message to several people. In such cases, the safe bet is to aim for the level of writing you believe will reach the most receivers and leave readers options for asking questions (should you be in a position to answer them).

Sometimes it isn't clear what level of English you should be using. At such times, your readers' position, education level, or indicated preference—as well as the writing medium (e.g., email, school essay)—should guide your choice of writing level. When this information is not known, you may have to take your best guess.

An appropriate level of language is an essential part of effective writing.

While there are no fixed divisions of language levels, we have identified three levels, which often overlap: **informal**, **general**, and **formal**. Many colleges and universities expect students to write academic papers in formal English, which requires, among other things, third-person pronouns (*he, she, one, they*). Informal writing, with its first- and second-person pronouns (*I, me, you*) may not be acceptable. (See page 362 for an explanation of "person.")

Ask your instructor about his or her policy and follow it. (*Note:* Not all instructors require the same level of language. Some are sticklers for formality; others are more relaxed. Don't waste time arguing; tailor each assignment to your instructor's requirements, just as you would adhere to an employer's requirements.)

To get a job, you will most likely write a formal cover letter. For a talk you give in your class, an informal, conversational style may be more appropriate. Most of what you read and write will fall somewhere in the middle—a general-level writing style. Business documents, for example, are usually written in general-level Standard English so that they can be read and clearly understood by the majority of readers. Blogs, as another example, are usually written in a general to informal style to appeal to broad audiences. These examples illustrate why learning to be flexible in your writing is important.

Writing in a blog style is not appropriate for the classroom unless your teacher specifically asks for it.

To help you choose the most appropriate level for your message and audience, the table below outlines the basic features of informal, general, and formal written English. Practising with all of them will help you learn to make good guesses when you are unsure of what level to use.

	INFORMAL	GENERAL	FORMAL
Vocabulary and Style	Casual, everyday; usually concrete; some slang, colloquial expressions, contractions. Usually written in 1st or 2nd person.	The language of educated persons; non-specialized; balance of abstract and concrete; readily understood. Can use 1st, 2nd, or 3rd person.	Often abstract, technical, or specialized; no contractions or colloquialisms. Written in 3rd person.
Sentence and Paragraph Structure	Sentences short, simple; some sentence fragments; paragraphs short.	Complete sentences of varying length; paragraphs vary, but are often fairly short.	Complete sentences, often long, complex; paragraphs fully developed, often at length.
Tone	Conversational, casual; sounds like ordinary speech.	Varies to suit writer's message and purpose.	Impersonal, serious, often instructional.
Typical Uses	Personal notes, some fiction, some newspapers, much advertising.	Most of what we read: websites, newspapers, magazines, novels, business correspondence.	Academic writing, some textbooks, scientific reports, journal articles, legal documents.

No one level is "better" than another. Each has its place and uses. Your message, your audience, and your purpose in writing are what should determine the level you choose.

Read the following selections and consider

- the audience for whom the message is intended
- the writer's role
- why the writer's language level is appropriate to the readers, subject, and purpose

Informal

> Love him or hate him, Michael Moore has turned the world of documentary film on its ear. Documentaries are stuffy and boring, aren't they? They certainly aren't supposed to be wildly popular or turn their directors into media stars. But starting with *Roger and Me* back in 1989, Moore has almost single-handedly made the documentary fun, personal, and popular. Like most film students, I began thinking I wanted someday to make blockbuster Hollywood hits like the movies Canadians Norman Jewison and James Cameron are famous for, but now I'm a convert to documentaries and that other Canadian production star: the National Film Board of Canada.

Who is the intended audience? This paragraph is intended for general readers, not people who are looking for a scholarly discussion of film. The writer assumes some interest in and knowledge of Michael Moore and his films.

What is the writer's role? Writers want to inform readers about their point of view. They play the role not of expert or teacher, but rather of a friend or acquaintance supplying the information for discussion in a casual way.

Why is the level of language appropriate? The use of **contractions** and **colloquialisms** ("the world … on its ear," "stuffy and boring") and especially the use of first and second persons in *direct address* (talking right to the reader) clearly mark this as an informal and friendly communication. Short sentences and a conversational style add to the informal tone.

General

> What is a documentary film? The so-called father of documentary film, the late John Grierson, called it "the creative treatment of reality," but that definition is uncomfortably broad. For example, is *Valkyrie* a documentary? What about *Defiance* or *Amadeus* or *Milk* or *Lawrence of Arabia*? All are about real people and contain a version of historical events, but few would classify them as documentaries. The purpose of these films is to entertain (if you discount their real purpose: to make money), and perhaps purpose lies at the heart of the definition. The primary purpose of a documentary film is to inform.

Who is the intended audience? Readers of this paragraph will have to be knowledgeable enough about films to have seen at least one of the five major releases mentioned, and interested enough in film to want to know more about the documentary genre.

What is the writer's role? The writer is providing information from an expert's point of view, but in a friendly way rather than as a lecture or formal instruction. The use of humour and casual language makes the information easy to absorb, and the direct address and use of questions add a friendly tone to the paragraph. Try making a list of specific words or phrases that distinguish this second level from the first.

Why is the level of language appropriate? The vocabulary and writing style of this piece is easily understood by most readers. The use of second person ("if you discount their real purpose") adds to the personal nature of the language, as do the questions directed to the reader. This message is designed to appeal to the widest audience possible.

Formal

> The late John Grierson, best known as "the father of documentary film" and the founder of the National Film Board of Canada, called documentary "the creative treatment of reality." Since its inception in 1939, the NFB has been presenting reality to Canadians and the rest of the world in creative ways. While it has earned recognition in other cinematic fields (notably animation), the NFB has achieved most of its international acclaim from more than 70 years of producing first-class documentary films, many of them Academy Award winners.

Who is the intended audience? The readers of this passage are literate and well read. They are people whose education and experience have enabled them to appreciate that good films can be informative as well as entertaining.

What is the writer's role? The writer's purpose is to highlight the achievements of the NFB to an audience of educated peers who share aesthetic interests. The writer is presented not as an expert addressing non-experts, but rather as an enthusiast who wants to share knowledge with a receptive audience.

Why is the level of language appropriate? The vocabulary is fairly sophisticated, and the sentences are relatively long and complex. There are no contractions or colloquialisms, and no first- or second-person pronouns. The writer addresses the audience as peers—other film enthusiasts—but not as close friends. The objective tone would be suitable for an article in a professional magazine.

Exercise 1.1

This exercise is designed to reinforce your understanding of the importance of knowing your reader. An effective communicator figures out ahead of time not only what his or her readers need to know but also what they do not need to know. Some information is necessary and some is superfluous, with the mix varying widely from audience to audience. With this in mind, write a paragraph describing one of the following topics to three different audiences: choose one from each of the three groups listed below.

Topics:	A favourite musician or group, stand-up comic, or other performer
Group A:	A grandparent, a teacher, an employer
Group B:	A co-worker, a classmate, an old friend you haven't seen in years
Group C:	The president of your college or university, the Student Council Social Committee (persuasive paragraph looking for support of a fundraising event featuring your topic)

Exercise 1.2* Read the excerpts below and discuss the intended audience, the author's role, and the appropriateness of the language. Answers for exercises in this chapter begin on page 460.

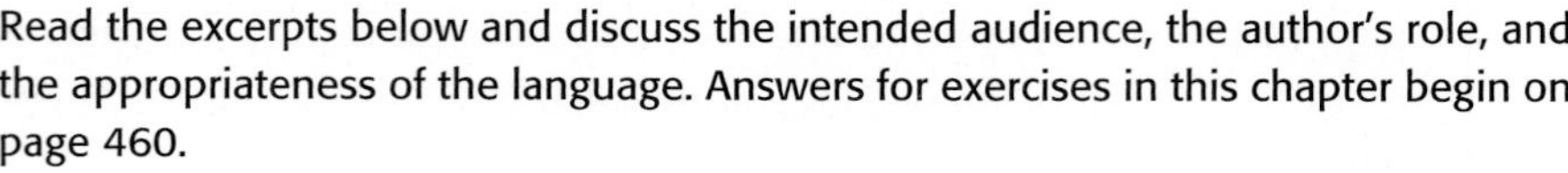

1. One of the most frequent complaints about Walmart, which employs 1.4 million people worldwide, is its failure to pay workers a living wage. Store employees are paid 20–30 percent less than the industry average, making many of them eligible for social assistance. It is estimated that American taxpayers fork out $2.5 billion a year in welfare payments to Walmart employees (Head, 2004). Because the retailer hires hard-to-place workers, like recent immigrants, seniors, and single mothers, its employees are often afraid they will not find work elsewhere. The kind of work Walmart does offer is gruelling: stores are intentionally understaffed—the strategy behind the company's legendary productivity gains—so that existing employees will work harder (Head, 2004). It is alleged that systemic discrimination against women within the corporation has denied the majority of Walmart workers the chance at promotion, a charge that is now the subject of the largest civil-rights suit in U.S. history.

Who is the intended audience? ______________________________

____

____

____

____

What is the writer's role? ______________________________

____

____

____

____

Why is the level of language appropriate? ____________________

____

____

____

____

2. The "inletting" or "butt mortise" plane is designed to cut precise mortises for butt hinges, lock fronts, and strike plates, or to repair jambs, doors, furniture, and millwork, wherever the ability to do inletting is important. The plane has a completely open throat so that you can watch what you are doing. The 3/4" wide cutter is set at a 40-degree pitch for general work. This can be increased to 70 degrees (plus or minus) for difficult grain simply by inserting the blade bevel-up. For inletting, such as hinges, you set the blade extension at the hinge leaf thickness, score the outline, and plane to depth, using overlapping strokes for a smooth bottom. The same technique would be used for a veneer repair on solid wood.

Source: *Lee Valley Catalogue*, Tenth Anniversary Issue, 1987–88:23.

Who is the intended audience? ____________________

____

____

____

____

What is the writer's role? ____________________

____

____

____

____

Why is the level of language appropriate? ____________________

____

____

____

____

3. In Paris there is open season on pedestrians all year round. Find an elderly Parisian pedestrian and you'll have the ultimate in cunning and agility. Watch him cross the street, inciting a bus to charge, then nipping nimbly behind a stalled taxi that has flooded its carburetor in the excitement of trying to nail him. Beautiful footwork. The Paris traffic policeman puts a nice rhythm into the chaos by standing in a concrete pillbox and waving cars in all directions. He is especially useful in the large, busy squares. These squares, which are round, give the motorist a chance to circle and take another crack at a pedestrian. The pedestrian's only defense here is to run with other pedestrians in a pack. Most European cars, being small and light, will not take on more than five people, or two bicycles, at once. The Paris taxi will take on anything except passengers.

Taken from *Still a Nicol: The Best of Eric Nicol*; published by McGraw-Hill Ryerson, 1972.

Who is the intended audience? ________________________________

____

____

____

____

What is the writer's role? ________________________________

____

____

____

____

Why is the level of language appropriate? ________________________

____

____

____

____

4. If only the problem were that simple. For those who like tidy problems with clear solutions, it is disturbing to find that there is another side to the sweatshop debate. To begin with, sweatshops are "the first rung on the ladder out of extreme poverty" (Sachs 11). They allow developing countries to expand their exports and consequently to improve their economies (Arnold and Hartman 2). Workers (usually women) choose to work in sweatshops because they are

often the only means by which women can further their own ends. By working in a sweatshop, women make a small income, learn about business practices, and benefit from the improved social and economic conditions that come with economic growth. Arnold and Hartman explain that as the economy grows, more jobs are created; the labour market tightens, and companies are forced to improve their working conditions in order to attract employees (2-3). Theoretically, this analysis makes sense, but does it apply in practice? Do employees really benefit from working in sweatshops?

Who is the intended audience? ______________________________

____

____

____

____

What is the writer's role? ______________________________

____

____

____

____

Why is the level of language appropriate? ______________________________

____

____

____

____

Exercise 1.3

As a class, select one of the four paragraphs found in Exercise 1.2. Be sure you all agree on the intended audience and the purpose of the paragraph.

Next, in groups of three, choose an audience from the list below for a revision you will write. (Each group must select a different audience.) Then, "translate" the paragraph for this audience. The purpose of your revision will remain the same as that of the original, but the language and tone will be adapted to suit the new audience. Have fun with this, but remember how crucial this step will be for all of your future writing assignments, both in class and in the workplace.

- a supervisor at your part-time job
- your *Instagram* followers

- a parent or guardian
- a high school dropout
- a bored celebrity
- a blind date

Once all groups have completed their "translations," compare the results by reading the revised paragraphs aloud. Try to guess who each group's intended audience is. How do you know? How does the language work to meet the needs of the new audience?

The following exercise will give you practice in communicating effectively by adjusting your level of language to suit your purpose, your message, and your audience.

Exercise 1.4

Imagine, in each of the following situations, that you must deal with three different audiences face to face. Before you begin, analyze each audience in terms of knowledge, attitudes, and needs; then clarify the purpose of your message, your attitude toward your subject, and your audience's expectations of you. Once you have done this, in your small group, try role-playing the situation.

1. You prepared your company's sales presentation in PowerPoint and stored it on the hard drive of your notebook computer. On your way to a meeting with clients in Chicago, Customs inspectors at the airport roughly handled your computer. When you got to the sales meeting, it wouldn't open the PowerPoint. You forgot to make a backup on your USB and don't have it stored on a cloud server.

   You made the sales presentation as well as you could, but the clients were not impressed, and your company did not get the contract. Explain these circumstances to
   - your supervisor in the sales department
   - the U.S. Customs complaint bureau
   - a representative of the computer company, which claims its notebook computers are practically indestructible

2. You applied for a bursary that would allow you to continue your studies abroad and give you enormously valuable experience before you graduate. You receive a letter of congratulations and a large cheque, but, while the cheque is made out to you, the letter is clearly referring to someone else—a mix-up has occurred. Are you the recipient of the bursary, or should the money have gone to the person named in the letter? What letter did that person receive? These are some of the questions that occur to you. Describe your dilemma and your course of action to
   - a professor whom you like and whose opinion you respect
   - the person who sponsored your application
   - the organization granting the bursary

3. To celebrate the World Cup, you invited 15 close friends over to watch the game on your landlord's 70-inch 4K TV. After promising to provide food, you became nervous about your status as a foodie and asked a friend who

works as an apprentice chef to provide a huge vat of chili. She made the chili, along with mounds of garlic bread and homemade nachos. Your friends were so impressed that you couldn't resist taking credit for the food, claiming you had used an old family recipe. Unfortunately, everyone got food poisoning and was sick for three days. How would you explain the situation to

- your very sick friends
- the friend who cooked the food
- your landlord, who had to clean up his recreation room after some people had been sick there

4. Following a round of layoffs and pay cuts, your employer is making an effort to improve flagging morale. She announces that the person who submits the best idea for improving morale will get an extra week of paid vacation. Your idea is to provide 10-minute breaks twice a day, during which lively music will be played in the office and workers will be encouraged to "kick back and chill out." Sell your idea to
   - your employer
   - a co-worker who is a classical music fan
   - the workaholic who never takes a break, not even for lunch

5. You are short of money—so short you can't even get gas for your car. If you can't find gas money, you will be late for work. Your boss is annoyed because you've been late twice this week already. Ask for money from
   - your parents
   - a friend
   - someone who owes you money

6. Turn one of the five role-playing situations above into a written assignment.

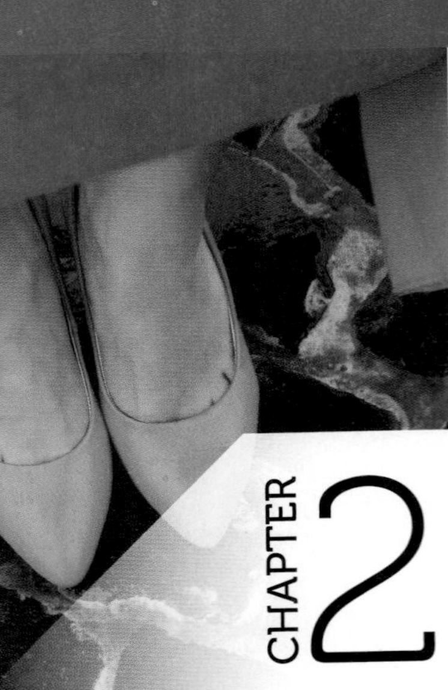

CHAPTER 2

Understanding the Role of Reading as a Writing Component

If you don't consider the role of your audience in your writing, you could end up writing a cookbook for pastry chefs that reads like a children's book.

Without doing thorough research of your topic, how good is your essay going to be?

As we discussed in Chapter 1, different forms of writing are meant for different audiences. This is certainly important to you as a writer, but it is also important to you as a reader. Consider the difference between books you might read for pleasure (a Stephen King novel or the *Harry Potter* series, for example) and books that you might read for school (*The Fundamentals of Economics* or *The Foundations of Philosophy*). These are written for different audiences in different contexts. Not only do these differences affect the content inside the books, but they also tend to affect the way we read them. The roles of reading as a writing component are to help you

- become a good reader of many types of writing styles
- understand how to get the best information out of each source you encounter (in terms of academic writing, the process of becoming a good reader includes becoming a good researcher)
- consider how the intended audience and context impact the way that authors write

Reading for content and comprehension means understanding what the writer intends to say. Later, when you are writing about the piece, you'll be able to think more deeply about the topic than you would have if you had misunderstood it. Comprehension also helps you avoid making content-based errors in your work. Showing that you have understood what you have read can take you a long way toward a more clearly written essay.

Newspaper and magazine articles and many other pieces of writing are written at a level that experts agree a certain majority of people can read. But this majority often comprises a specific readership and context. We might want to think a little more specifically. Exactly who is in your audience? People who are just learning English? People who don't have a post-secondary education? And in the workplace, which audience are you writing for? If you don't know, then you could end up writing for the wrong person.

Imagine a person who is asked simply to prepare a report on drunk driving. She includes graphic images and descriptions to emphasize the dangers. Later the person is berated because the report was sent to thousands of Grade 8 students, who were meant to learn the basics of what drunk driving was. It's always better to know the audience we are writing for before we start the job.

People are busy today, and we all suffer from at least some degree of inattention to detail in our busiest moments. Imagine the young pharmacy technician who is being bullied by her boss. She writes a letter to the general manager but, at the last minute, decides she sounded too mean and so rewrites the first few paragraphs to include how great her boss has been in the past. Someone who isn't paying attention might not even see the most important details hidden below.

Whether it is right or wrong for the reader to ignore the entire message isn't at issue—as writers, it is our duty to ensure that our main messages are up front, and proper planning and organizing can help us do that. In this chapter, we will discuss developing good reading skills, including reading critically, skimming, and scanning, and we will also suggest activities you can do to improve the reading and comprehension skills you already have.

If your writing isn't organized in a way that is logical to most people, your message might be lost!

Start with Good Reading Skills

In Chapter 3 we will discuss critical thinking skills, but before we can start thinking about how we analyze what we read, hear, or think we need to move the basic information into our brains through the act of reading—and reading can include reading people and situations, although, in this text, we focus on text-based reading.

Reading critically and comprehensively means

- identifying the main point of the article, story, chapter, or text
- identifying the supporting details
- determining the author's point of view
- considering how what you already know relates to the author's understanding of the information
- thinking through the author's argument and logical conclusions
- beginning to construct your own opinions (this is critical thinking, which we'll cover in the next chapter)

Reading critically can be quite different from reading for personal purposes, which might include

- reading for pleasure and relaxation
- reading to glean basic ideas but not the details
- reading a chosen part of a work but not the entire thing (e.g., just the opinion section of the newspaper)
- skimming or scanning a text just to have something to speak with others about

Learning how to read critically and comprehensively for academic purposes is the first step of the prewriting process.

Both types of reading are important in life. We don't need to approach our summer beach reading with the same rigour we would approach research materials for an academic essay worth a large percentage of our grade. And that's how it should be.

Let's start with the basics—skimming and scanning texts.

Skimming

While careful reading is very important for academic purposes, **skimming** is also an essential skill. We use skimming to suss out the main point of a work with a conscious view to ignoring any specific information that the text provides.

We identify the points in a text that are most useful to our purposes and then read looking for more about that useful information. Skimming usually involves looking at

- the title of the text
- the table of contents
- the introduction
- the first and last paragraph of each section
- any keywords (places, facts, dates, locations, concepts)
- any bolded, underlined, italicized, or offset information
- the conclusion
- the index or any extra notes

Courses on skimming can teach you to skim up to 1000 words a minute!

Looking at this information can give us a general idea of the content and topics the author discusses, and it usually helps us decide what texts we choose to read in detail. Skimming is definitely a skill that improves over time and with practice.

Scanning

Scanning is useful when we want to look for specific topics or concepts in a work. It isn't as beneficial in more formal academic works, in which we have to follow arguments and identify points of view, but it is a good skill to have in the pursuit of general knowledge or when trying to get a sense of an author's position or purpose.

You most likely have scanned a newspaper for information about a popular topic or scanned the Web for information on the hottest new smartphone—it's a great skill for personal use, but sometimes the more critical perspective is lost.

Scanning is another skill that is widely taught and practised. Scanning can occur even more quickly than skimming because you are looking *only* for specific keywords, phrases, or concepts that you have identified as points of interest beforehand.

A Note on Speedreading and Increasing Your Reading Speed

No doubt there is a large variety of free and paid ways to learn how to read more quickly. And some of them might work, but you also might miss out on valuable content that you need when reading for academic purposes. The tried-and-true best way to learn how to read more quickly is simply to read more. Read things that you love, and read them all the time. It doesn't have to be just books but magazines and online materials, too. There are as many blogs out there as there are ideas. Find something you're interested in, or better yet, start your own!

You will find your reading speed increasing in no time when you are reading things that interest you. Whatever method you choose, remember that reading for academic purposes means not only getting the main points but also understanding the author's point of view and recognizing supporting details. It's much harder to find those things just skimming through material looking for certain words or phrases.

Exercise 2.1

When you apply for a job, you will almost always have to write a cover letter that outlines your past experiences in more detail than a résumé can. But will the human resources representative or manager be reading critically, skimming, or scanning? Make a short list of ways in which you could use what you know about skimming to write a cover letter that will get you noticed quickly. Don't write the letter—just brainstorm some ways you could highlight important information.

___

___

___

So, once we have a good idea about when skimming and scanning are appropriate and, more importantly, when they're not, how do we begin to read for academic purposes, especially as reading relates to writing essays? The following are six steps necessary for critical and comprehensive reading comprehension:

1. Identify the article's main message.
2. Identify supporting details.
3. Determine the author's point of view.
4. Separate the author's experience from your own.
5. Think through the author's arguments and logical conclusions.
6. Begin to construct your own writing.

It makes the most sense to follow these in order, as they proceed logically from reading the article for its content to completing a study of your own perspectives.

1. Identify the Article's Main Message

A good writer, like you will soon be, knows that readers looking for information want to know the main point early so they can decide whether or not the text or article suits their needs. Most of the time, you can quickly find a text's main point by searching the first few paragraphs for keywords. This is an essential part of reading comprehension. Reading comprehension is a skill just like learning how to write more effectively, and you may find you need to do quite a bit of work on steps one and two before you can start to get into the deeper parts of critical reading. You might even want to underline main points and essential information.

Keywords many students highlight include any concepts, ideas, perspectives, or challenges that are unique. You might also include facts about dates, locations, or events.

The main message is often defined as the "argument" of the piece. However, keeping tightly to this definition becomes difficult if you are asked to identify the argument of a document called "The 10 Phases of the Moon" and all it does is list them. It's possible that this article does present an argument (maybe this author thinks there are 10, but others believe there are 12), but finding it is challenging. Similarly, finding the argument of many newspaper articles can be difficult, since newspapers often just present the facts and don't take a stand in a news story. The main point is, in the strictest sense, the summary of the goal or outcome of the piece, whether it is argumentative or fact-based. It's *why* the author has written or compiled the work. It often, but not always, appears in the first few paragraphs of the text (e.g., in the first chapter of a textbook), and it is often expanded upon in the conclusion.

We'll look at two examples. The first is from Navneet Alang's blog post called "Online Freedom Will Depend on Deeper Forms of Web Literacy" (found in Part 8, pp. 304–305):

> 1 Recently, Google ruined my life. I may be exaggerating slightly, given that all they did was redesign and tweak Google Reader, one of their many services that I use daily and for which I pay nothing. But Reader, an admittedly niche product that lets you read articles from many websites in one place, has become my online home. It is the thing that organizes and makes sense of the sprawling, incoherent mass of the Internet and collects it on one familiar light-blue page.

In the first paragraph we have a clear main point: that Google has ruined the author's life by changing one of its products. We also see that this is an argumentative piece. (Argumentative writing is explained in detail in Chapter 13 of this text.) Alang is interested in explaining to us how this particular Google product helps him organize the information he finds on the Internet and how losing it has made things awful for him. The keywords include *redesign, Google, services, organizes,* and *Internet*. These terms help us determine what ideas this author is concerned with.

Now have a look at these first three paragraphs of Sam McNerney's article "Is Creativity Sexy? The Evolutionary Advantages of Artistic Thinking" (found in Part 8, pp. 302–304), and try to find the main point.

> 1 Human evolution is puzzling. Around 45 000 years ago, for no obvious reason, our species took off. Our technology rapidly progressed, populations thrived, and we started painting and crafting instruments. All of this and more culminated in our first civilizations. From there, we started growing food, building cities, reading, and writing. Today, our species is the most dominant on the planet.
>
> 2 What's odd is that natural selection doesn't explain this cultural explosion. Our genetic makeup is identical to our ancestors' who lived 100 000 years ago. As Matt Ridley explains, "all the ingredients of human success—tool making, big brains, culture, fire, even language—seem to have been in place half a million years before and nothing happened." What gives?
>
> 3 The answer might have to do with the relationship between creativity and sex. Consider a study conducted by evolutionary psychologists Douglas Kenrick, Bob Cialdini, and Vlad Griskevicious. In one clever experiment the psychologists asked college students to write a short story about an ambiguous picture. Before the students tested their prose, Kenrick and his partners divided them into two groups. One half was put in a mating mindset by looking at six photos of attractive females, picking which one they most desired as a romantic partner, and imagining an ideal date with her. The other half, the control condition, saw photos of a street and wrote about the most pleasant weather conditions for walking around and looking at the buildings.

What is the first paragraph about? It discusses human evolution and suggests that it is "puzzling" and that, at a certain point, we "took off." This sets up the question asked at the end of the second paragraph: How did this happen? It is not until the third paragraph that the author suggests an answer, a link between creativity and sex. Why not discuss this link in the first paragraph?

Perhaps the reason is that believing the author's main point requires a real stretch of the imagination. Perhaps it is because the author needed to give us background information before setting up his main ideas. The keywords here include *human evolution, technology, species,* and *cultural explosion*. These are the main ideas this author will expand on through the text.

Ultimately, when we look for the author's main point, we are trying to discover the "why" behind the writing of the text. A good way to practise is to scan the newspaper and identify the main point of several articles. Once you have found the main ideas, you can more quickly get into the supporting material.

2. Identify Supporting Details

Many writers will list some supporting details in the first few paragraphs. Another way to think about this writing technique is in terms of the 1:1 paragraph:topic style. A good writer knows that one paragraph should contain one central idea, and that idea should be presented up front. So, again, have a look at the first few paragraphs of your text, and underline or highlight the keywords.

In the examples above, check to see if the keywords identified are actually expanded upon in the body of the work. The supporting details are the facts and the arguments that were hinted at in the main idea. In the selection by Alang, for instance, we would expect each paragraph to tell us another way that the loss of Google Reader has led to more confusion and less organization of the Internet for him. Each paragraph should present a different point.

Exercise 2.2

Find Senator Grant Mitchell's selection on transgender rights in Part 8. Check to see if each paragraph presents a specific supporting detail that links to what you believe is the main idea of the work. For each paragraph, summarize the supporting detail presented.

3. Determine the Author's Point of View

We'll discuss finding out the author's point of view in detail in Chapter 3, but here it is enough to say that all authors have an opinion, even if they are trying to present a balanced view, as most journalists do. How much we should take the author's point of view into account when we analyze a reading is debatable, but beginning critical thinkers should recognize that all authors do have a point of view and that their ideas aren't *dogma*, something we should blindly agree with.

Part of becoming a critical reader is not only finding the author's opinions about given subjects but also challenging the author's assertions should you disagree. It isn't always easy to see what an author's point of view is, though. Here are some ways to help you find it:

- Consider the types of resources authors use to back up their ideas and opinions (journals, blogs, textbooks, movies, music). For example, is there something we can say about a work that cites only the *Calgary Herald* in the discussion of the author's ideas versus that of an author who uses not only articles from the *Herald* but also ones from Edmonton, Halifax, Vancouver, and Toronto newspapers?
- Consider not only what information the author presented but also what he or she left out (when reading, it is important that you also think about what the author hasn't discussed). If you are reading an article on a controversial subject, does the author present both sides of the story or just one? What does this tell you about the way the author thinks?
- Think about the author's use of any personal stories or vignettes to make the point. If an author feels comfortable enough to give personal examples, or works exceptionally hard to make sure a reader understands his or her perspective, what does that say about the author's relationship to the reader?
- Think about whether the author tells you his or her own view outright. Increasingly, it has become important or meaningful if authors tell you about their "social location"—the various perspectives that indicate where they are coming from. Saying something like "As a mother, my views on abortion might differ from others" is an honest way of telling the reader that bias exists in the work. That doesn't devalue the work but it helps readers put the information in context. But does it matter who the author is if he or she makes a good argument? This question is controversial—one you can answer for yourself as you read further in the text and practise writing in the real world.

Knowing the author's point of view allows you to present both the writer's perspective and, eventually, your own. It shows your reader you know how to read and collect information but not be ruled by it. This leads to the next step....

4. Separate the Author's Experience from Your Own

To clarify your own opinions on a given subject matter, find a way to link what you are reading to your own experiences. While it is very important to follow the logic of the argument you are reading (by finding the main point and supporting details), it is also important to think about how *you* would write about the same topic and what differences there would be between the author's opinions and your own.

One of the great things about reading this way is that it allows even the driest material to take on new meaning as you try to apply it to something that has happened or might happen to you. Even if that information never becomes important in a paper or discussion you are having, you will have found the thread that leads from what you are reading to who you are.

At this point, it might seem as though there are a lot of steps to take before writing, but they happen quickly once you've learned the critical skills presented here, starting with learning to be a good academic reader.

5. Think through the Author's Arguments and Logical Conclusions

Once you have looked at the main point and supporting details and have considered the author's point of view and your own, it is time for a last check of the author's argument and conclusions. This means reviewing the conclusion of the reading and analyzing how all the author's previous points link together to reach this conclusion.

In the next chapter, we'll talk more about logical fallacies and ways to critique an author's argument, but at this point, our focus is on identifying the link between argument and conclusion as an essential component of good reading practice.

6. Begin to Construct Your Own Writing

If you are reading for research, even personal research, the last step is preparing to construct your own response. Ideally, the final thoughts you have on the subject come only after you have read deeply and critically through the sources you have chosen.

It isn't enough simply to include articles or quotations in a paper—those articles must be meaningful, logical, and relevant to your own ideas!

Annotating Sources

Have you ever made notes in the margins of your textbooks, such as comments or helpful hints that your teacher gave you, as you read through and highlighted important information? If you have, you have engaged in the practice of annotation.

An annotation is a piece of writing that often is meant to "check" your understanding and interpretation of what you have read; it is your own commentary or your own explanation of a reading. Annotations are often attached to research reports in the form of an *annotated reference*. An annotated reference includes a list of sources (you will learn how to make one in Chapter 17), with one or two paragraphs of commentary for each one.

An annotation, it is important to note, is different from a summary of what you have read. It includes your own ideas, analysis, and understanding of the content. It might also include pertinent quotations or information about the topic for reference. In addition, you might use an annotation to highlight key or essential information.

Annotations can be made on entire books or documents, or just on a piece of information from those books or documents. Annotations can also be done online with shared documents or in collaborative spaces.

As an example, let's say you are asked to find a paragraph to annotate in Gabor Maté's "Embraced by the Needle" on pages 284–286. You choose paragraph 12 because it really jumps out at you:

> Stressed, anxious, or depressed parents have great difficulty initiating enough of those emotionally rewarding, endorphin-liberating interactions with their children. Later in life such children may experience a hit of heroin as the "warm, soft hug" my patient described: what they didn't get enough of before, they can now inject.

To begin your annotation, you might consider the variety of other sources people look to for those "warm, soft hugs," such as alcohol, food, and other addictions. You may even note that at times you have felt the type of loneliness that might drive others to seek out addictive substances to make up for those feelings. You might consider your own parents' lives and whether they, too, felt stressed and anxious at times, and took it out on you. You might talk to others who have experienced those feelings, or look up other articles that discuss addiction as a replacement for love and care. You might also consider this paragraph in light of the article as a whole, noting Maté's use of personal stories of addiction to highlight continuing problems and how his particular use of the "warm, soft hug" was already mentioned in paragraph 3 of the article within a quotation from a 27-year-old sex-trade worker.

To summarize, here are some things to consider if you are asked to write an annotation:

1. An annotation isn't just a summary, it is a commentary that adds something to the reader's understanding of the text.
2. An annotation should highlight certain aspects of the text specifically, and perhaps make mention of a specific quotation or idea.
3. An annotation should clarify your own understanding of the reading and provide you and the reader with important points to continue discussion or research.

Exercise 2.3

In groups, find three short articles, or use ones your instructor has provided for you, to practise reading for information. Underline any main points that you find and try to isolate three important concepts, ideas, or theories the author or authors are writing about. Share these with the rest of the class by first giving an overview of what you read (Chapter 9 can give you more information on writing summaries) and then stating what three things you found to be most important.

Article 1:

What was read: ______________________________

____

____

____

Key point 1: ______________________________

____

____

____

Key point 2: ______________________________

____

____

____

Key point 3: ______________________________

____

____

____

Article 2:

What was read: ______________________________

____

____

____

Key point 1: ______________________________

____

____

____

Key point 2: ______________________________

____

____

____

Key point 3: ______________________________

____

____

____

Article 3:

What was read: ______________________

____

____

____

Key point 1: ______________________

____

____

____

Key point 2: ______________________

____

____

____

Key point 3: ______________________

____

____

____

Exercise 2.4 In groups, identify three ways poor research methods can lead to a disastrous essay. Share them with other groups by listing them on a whiteboard in the classroom.

Reason 1: ______________________

____

Reason 2: ______________________

____

Reason 3: ______________________

____

Summary

The best way to improve your writing skills is to improve your critical and comprehensive reading skills. This involves learning both to skim and to read carefully, looking for main points as well as details. It also involves learning how to find the author's point of view and to link what you are reading to your own experiences before you start writing.

The first steps in writing might come naturally for some of you, depending on your past skill level, your attitude toward reading and writing, and any interest you have in pursuing a career that involves writing. But what you will find as you work through this book is that everyone's skill level in reading and writing essays can increase. You're already on your way to a more thoughtful and persuasive way of presenting your ideas and information.

Exercise 2.5

Individually, create a list of three topics that you are interested in, but don't share your list. Your instructor will take all the topics and randomly give them out to students. Go online and search for an article on one of the random topics you are given. While you are reading, look for the author's viewpoint. Then think of three ways you can link this topic that you didn't choose to your own experiences. Make it as relevant as possible. Once you have finished, bring your information and ideas back and share them with the class or in small groups. You may be surprised to see how people can take random topics and personalize them.

The type of reading that we have just discussed is often termed *careful reading*.

Careful reading: The skill of drilling into the text looking for individual points and trying to get a keen sense of what the work is about.

It is counterpointed by, or compared with, skimming and scanning, which have different uses, as discussed earlier in this chapter.

CHAPTER 3

Understanding the Role of Critical Thinking

You need to be able to identify the point of view and the goal of the article, book, video, etc., so that you can ultimately decide if it is useful to you.

As a writer, thinking about your audience is a critical task—*critical* referring to the idea that you are delving below what is on the surface, not in the sense that you are being negative.

Critical thinking is the means through which we analyze, or do close readings of, people, situations, and writing. There are various strategic methods for thinking critically, but in all, the ultimate purpose is learning how to read and interpret for yourself, from as deep a view as possible, what messages are being sent. Not only will this skill help you understand your research sources when you are writing a paper, but it will also help you understand the message that you are trying to convey. Finding an article on a topic you've been asked to write about, especially if it is on a contentious issue or presents a clear point of view, is only a first step.

Critical thinking requires you to consider a variety of aspects of a piece of writing before you make judgments on your subject matter and decide on your own way of thinking about it.

A quick search online will yield a variety of ways to perform a critical thinking analysis. We will focus on one method here—an integrated interpretive (or hermeneutic) model. Over time, as you try different ways of filtering out and finding good research, you will find that some analytical methods suit you more than others and will consistently give you the best results.

The Interpretive Critical Thinking Model

In this model, which we'll call the *interpretive critical thinking model*, we will look at 10 aspects to analyze in a text and consider how analyzing each of these can help us become better researchers and better writers. These aspects are

- the main point
- the supplementary messages
- the context
- the author's point of view
- the assumptions and bias
- the facts and theories
- the themes and keywords
- the logic and methods
- the relationship to other works
- reflection on your own ideas

All of these elements are useful in finding out just what you are reading. As we explore how critical thinking works, we'll try putting it in action with some readings and exercises. For this discussion, we'll use Deenu Parmar's "Labouring the Walmart Way," found on pages 282–284. From there, we will look at how these steps can inform and become an essential part of the writing task.

1. The Main Point

Finding the message of a paper is really important in your critical thinking skills and needs to be done no matter what type of text you are analyzing. Another word for main point is **thesis** or *main idea*. What is it that the author or movie or even business is trying to convince you of? Wondering why businesses are included here?

Critical thinking can be used on products, too. For example, think of your favourite shampoo or perfume. What message is that shampoo company sending out—that it will help your hair if it is dry, curly, frizzy? That is a thesis—use this and your hair problems will be solved. And perfume argues an even stronger point—use this and people will find you powerful, feminine, sexy, strong. Whatever the medium, the first thing you want to know is the main point.

Deenu Parmar's piece has a clear thesis—that Walmart has rock-bottom prices, but most likely at the expense of its employees and the use of fair labour practices. We can find Parmar's thesis at the end of paragraph 1, where she writes, "Are [Walmart's] offers of jobs, its attitudes toward unionization, and its influence on industry labour practices worth the low price on the shelf?" At the end of the piece, in paragraph 5, Parmar argues "… the ability to buy at rock-bottom prices does not address the systemic causes of poverty—though it may contribute to them."

In general, the main point is contained in either the introduction or the conclusion of the text you are analyzing. It is important to examine all parts of the text, though, to get a true sense of its message, as some writers do bury the main point rather than stating it right up front. For example, in the case of Parmar's essay, you must look at both the introduction and the conclusion—the opening question and the ultimate answer—to find the main message of the piece.

2. The Supplementary Messages

The supplementary, or supporting, messages are the subtopics or the issues that get discussed in the text. To find them, try to break down the argument or piece into sections—in other words, create a mini-outline of the ideas presented in the text.

The table of contents of a book, for example, can often help you to see a mini-outline of what you are reading. Sometimes the author identifies the supporting messages directly in the thesis statement. Parmar's essay contains a few specific messages—that Walmart's practices when it comes to (1) hiring, (2) union-busting, (3) discrimination, and (4) attitudes toward workers and toward other companies are less than desirable. Each paragraph of the article contains a discussion of one of these ideas.

For your own critical analysis, make a list of supplementary messages in order to get a sense of the topics the author discusses. At this point, you might also make a note of what is missing from that list. Is there something you would think should be included but isn't?

3. The Context

As a critical reader, you might want to know some context about what you are reading and who the author is. The context, or the background, of the text you are analyzing gives you that information—whether it is the author's family life while researching the topic or other interests the author holds. This information might be relevant and give you insight into why a writer takes a certain position.

But what if you can't find background on the author? It is unlikely that you will find any information about Deenu Parmar's piece online because it was written by a student. So where to go then? We can look to facts like when the piece was written or at least how recent the sources are. Parmar uses research from 2004—not extremely current, but still within recent memory. Once we know that, we can search out other clues to the context—for example, the geographical location (Canada and the United States) and the concerns of the day in 2004 (a time of financial crisis, so low prices were important; a time when poverty was increasing and businesses were scrambling to find ways to get cheaper labour, in China or elsewhere).

Context is about situating the argument in the geographical, political, and social location of the time, as well as considering any information you have about the author. Parmar's article might be meaningless in 10 years if Walmart is no longer in business and other giants have risen to take the low-price helm. Or it might continue to be important as a historical document describing the shifts in labour laws and hiring practices in Canada and elsewhere over time. All of this information can help us create our own informed opinion about the topics that Parmar discusses.

In critical thinking, we do the thinking; the author only provides us with his or her version of arguments, ideas, and information.

Exercise 3.1 Choose one of the articles in this textbook and see if you can find both the main point and the supplementary messages. If someone in your group has a device with Internet access, look up who the author is and try to find some information about the context of the piece to share with the rest of the class.

Exercise 3.2 Come up with three other topics that Parmar could have covered in her article. Why do you think she didn't discuss them?

Exercise 3.3 In a group, discuss your own views on Walmart and its policies. Can you come up with counterarguments to any of Parmar's points?

4. The Author's Point of View

It is very important to understand that in almost anything you read, a point of view is presented. Even in a listing of facts, some facts will be left out. Which are they? Why were they left out? Why are the ones that are there important? What story do they tell? All of these questions come into play when we consider the author's point of view—that is, his or her position on the topic chosen. Even in a paper that isn't completely argumentative, it is useful to determine the differences between the way that the author feels and the way that you, the reader, think and feel.

Developing your own process for making up your mind and consolidating your ideas is part of critical thinking. But remember to keep an open mind when you are reading—the point of critical thinking is to listen to the author's point of view, to consider the arguments presented, and then, in light of your analysis, to decide on your own opinion, whether it remains what it was before you read the piece or it has changed.

Parmar works hard to keep her paper balanced, to give time to both sides of the story—the story of why Walmart has the policies that it does and the story of why some employees and people don't like that policy. She works to make the paper not about her view on that but about broader concerns about poverty and employees. Even still, do you have some idea about how Parmar thinks? Do you believe she personally thinks Walmart has some dangerous practices? If you answered yes, identify what convinced you of her feelings.

5. The Assumptions and Bias

All authors and readers have a **bias**, a slant toward a certain view, and all people think differently.

Would Parmar have written a different paper if she believed that all people were ultimately individually responsible for their own poverty and that employees didn't have to work at Walmart if they didn't want to? Alternatively, does the piece show that Parmar believes that poverty is a problem that can be fixed by companies using fair hiring practices, perhaps even using a union? Either would show the author's bias, her personal ideas about the world. Bias is more general than, for example, Parmar's specific point of view about Walmart or about its hiring practices. It has to do with the beliefs and values of the author—in this case, perhaps having sympathy toward the poor or understanding the goals of big-box-store corporations.

Whereas bias includes the ideas the author has about the world and how it works, **assumptions** are the decisions the author has made about the reader.

Do you think that Parmar is *biased* about Walmart's practices? Do you think she *assumes* you will agree with her arguments about Walmart? How hard does she think she needs to work to persuade you to her point of view? These assumptions are important to take into account when we look critically at a piece because they can give us information about how the writer developed his or her ideas. For example, if Parmar assumes that you understand the terminology associated with her subject (e.g., what a union is or how minimum wage works), she might not explain it in her writing. If she assumes that you are on her side about the issue she has presented, she may spend more time making suggestions about how to put pro-union measures into place rather than simply trying to convince you of wrongdoing on Walmart's part.

Once you understand the author's assumptions and biases, you can assess whether the author's viewpoints align with your own ideas and beliefs. And even if you disagree with the author's position, you can still comment upon the validity of the argument or the expertise with which the piece was written. Disagreeing with the author's view may also prompt you toward further research on the topic written from a different perspective.

Exercise 3.4

Consider some of your own biases toward the following topics, and discuss with a partner some of the ways you might make those biases clear to others when you are writing a paper:

- being late to class
- driving at the speed limit
- eating healthfully
- using cellphones in public places
- drinking and driving

Exercise 3.5

Can a person write a paper that is unbiased and carries no assumptions about the topic or the reader? Prepare some arguments for or against the idea and, as a class or within a group, discuss the topic.

6. The Facts and Theories

The author of the work you are reading may use **facts** (statistics, percentages, or readily available and accepted data) and **theories** (academic ideas or systems applied to different subjects, such as feminist theory or Freudian theory) to support his or her ideas. Parmar, for example, lists quite a few facts, such as that Walmart's prices are "14 percent lower than its competitors" (p. 282) and that it has 235 stores in Canada (p. 282).

Theories that Parmar uses include ideas about labour (the right of unionization, business competition over cooperation, discriminatory practice, and the causes of poverty) as well as theories of capitalism (should businesses be able to get ahead at any cost to people?) and economic globalization (companies outsourcing labour to other countries).

Looking for theories can be tricky. These are systems and ideas that the writer calls upon and possibly expects you to understand without their being fully discussed.

Understanding the facts and theories the author uses is important since they give you background into the larger issues involved. For example, what is the overall impact Walmart has had by having lower prices than any other company? Thinking about the facts, issues, and theories can even help you come up with essay topics or questions of your own.

7. The Themes and Keywords

The themes and keywords section of your analysis will be a list of words that pop out at you. This list might also include words that you aren't familiar with but that appear to be important to the work. It will also likely include those words that get repeated throughout the work.

Using Parmar's work, our list might look something like the following:

Themes

- Market competition
- Industry labour and wages
- Hiring processes and union activity

Keywords

- Unions/anti-unions
- Low wages/living wages
- Labour
- Fairness
- Benefits
- Consumers
- Competing
- Big-box stores

Exercise 3.6

In small groups, choose three other readings from the text and identify the larger themes and perhaps a few keywords. This is good practice for when you have a longer essay to write and need to quickly see what ideas are being discussed in your topic area.

Reading 1: ____________________

Themes: ____________________

____

____

Keywords: ____________________

____

____

Reading 2: ____________________

Themes: ____________________

____

____

Keywords: ____________________

____

____

Reading 3: ______________________________

Themes: ______________________________

____

____

Keywords: ______________________________

____

____

Alternatively, choose a topic and, as a group, find two articles on the topic and find some themes and keywords.

8. The Logic and Methods

Understanding logic and methods has to do with thinking about the author's way of thinking. Does the writer assume that if *x* is true, then so must be *y*?

For example, Parmar sees a relationship between the low prices that Walmart charges and its decision to pay employees less and to deny unions access. There are two sets of logic here. The first is Walmart's: the company wants the lower pay it gives to employees to be directly proportional to lower prices. The second is Parmar's: she sees the low pay of employees relating to an increase in the poverty of people who are forced to accept the wages. By using her logic, Parmar can criticize Walmart's practices; however, Walmart might defend itself by saying that low costs mean less revenue, which means less pay. If we as consumers want to pay less, we must understand that employees will have to be paid less.

Most logic is about interpretation of facts, statistics, or ideas. And interpretation is an art, rather than a science. One area of logic that is important to understand is the role of fallacies—pseudo-arguments that authors use to try to get you to respond in a certain way but that don't hold up to testing. Although there are many **logical fallacies**, we will present only the seven most widely used here.

1. **The slippery slope.** This is an appeal to our fear of extremism. If we allow something, A, to happen, then certainly something else, B to Z, will also occur. An example might be "If we allow you to have one cookie, you will likely eat the entire bag."

2. **The straw man.** The straw man fallacy is at play when an author has completely misrepresented an argument, perhaps even made up information or "hollowed out" an argument in order to make his or her own claim more valid. An example might be "Well, of course John hates multinational food corporations; he believes we should have a small grocery store on every block and have to pay $100 for a loaf of bread."

3. **Either/or (black or white).** An either/or argument oversimplifies things, suggesting there is no middle ground between two extremes. For example, "You either love television or you hate it."
4. **Red herring.** A red herring is the introduction of a diversionary claim or question that appears linked to the topic or argument at hand but that really isn't. For example, "I know that exercising is healthy, but what can I do to avoid junk food?"
5. **Ad hominem.** The ad hominem fallacy is an attack on the character of the speaker or writer instead of on the argument or claims made. For example, "I would love Toronto's commitment to equity, if it weren't for all the dirty politicians."
6. **Circular argument (begging the question).** In this fallacy, instead of an offer of proof, the initial idea or argument is simply restated. For example, "That show is so awesome because it is so cool and great."
7. **Appeal to emotion.** In this case, people's feelings are used instead of a logical argument. For example, "Everyone will freak out and hate you if you don't accept the fact that Jennifer did not cheat on the test."

Exercise 3.7

In groups, take the statistic that 50 percent of students love school and find two ways to deliver that fact. Then, choose two audiences to whom you will present that information and practise short discussions that refer to this statistic.

Exercise 3.8

Take the following argument: only healthy food should be provided in school eating areas. Try to think of seven logical fallacies (one of each) that could be used (unsuccessfully) to argue the point.

9. The Relationship to Other Works

One of the last elements of critical thinking is not taking anything on its own—that is, we don't want just one opinion on a subject; we want many facts, opinions, and ideas so that we can come up with our own views on the issues presented. One way that writers can help readers reach their own conclusions is by using various sources in their work.

At the end of Parmar's work, you can see that she has cited a variety of media in her paper—sources such as *The Globe and Mail* and *The New York Times*, which tend to be highly esteemed and reputable. Other sources that aren't reviewed by peers or experts, such as blogs or personal sites, are often not regarded as highly. When we read information from a variety of reputable sources and then make up our mind, we can be more confident that our ideas are based on a solid foundation.

When you are writing a paper for a class, often the instructor will ask you to use a minimum number of sources to make your argument. This is so that you will use your critical thinking skills to find out which arguments and ideas hold more sway—so that you won't only be parroting back what someone else said. Be wary of one thing, though: it is better to find articles that present a variety of viewpoints rather than just those that support your view so that readers don't suspect that you have just ignored the "other side." When we talk about constructing arguments in Chapter 13, we will discuss this in more detail.

Exercise 3.9 Find an article on the same topic as the one presented by Parmar on unionization and labour practices. Does the author take a similar position on the topic? What assumptions are different? What facts and theories are used to support the author's position?

10. Reflection on Your Own Ideas

Once you have done your analysis, in whatever order makes the most sense to you, it is time to consider where your thoughts fit in. Of course, to speak plainly, you will consider your own opinions the entire time. What you want, though, is always to come back to your ideas *in light of* what you have read and experienced and to see how those filters change your view (or not).

Did Parmar convince you that Walmart was creating more poverty by paying its employees less? If you could personally afford to shop only at Walmart, would Parmar's idea that it might be causing dangerous precedents seem weaker to you? What is it about your own experience that adds to what you have read?

Your ideas are valid and should be discussed in conjunction with the material that you are analyzing. That said, you should always keep an open mind. Just because you want Walmart to keep offering lower prices doesn't mean you couldn't advocate that it find ways to save money that don't impact wages. It doesn't mean you can't still agree that it might be causing more harm than good. It just means other issues sway your opinion. In other words, you can remain open-minded.

Exercise 3.10 Which of the following topics would you be open to reading alternative viewpoints on? Which ones would take a lot of persuading? Which topics do you have views on that wouldn't ever be changed?

• Eating more fruits and vegetables	OPEN	FAIRLY OPEN	CLOSED
• Sharing homework with students	OPEN	FAIRLY OPEN	CLOSED
• Eliminating the costs of schooling	OPEN	FAIRLY OPEN	CLOSED
• Sharing health records with governments	OPEN	FAIRLY OPEN	CLOSED
• Changing the drinking age to 21	OPEN	FAIRLY OPEN	CLOSED
• Having Canada merge with the United States	OPEN	FAIRLY OPEN	CLOSED

The act of critical thinking is meant to open your mind to alternative viewpoints before you ever start writing your own papers. It can be useful when it comes to writing your thesis, collecting your ideas, and doing research. Being backed by a variety of sources and ideas about what you have read improves your ability to argue and to persuade.

The following short chart will help guide you through the steps of reading and thinking critically as you research essays both academically and professionally.

THE CRITICAL THINKING STEP	WHAT TO DO
1. The main point	Find the author's thesis and conclusion.
2. The supplementary messages	Find the author's main points—either listed in the thesis or in the main paragraphs or in various sections of the work.
3. The context	Research the author, the issues, and the time period in which the work was created.
4. The author's point of view	Look for personal opinions, examples, or anecdotes that make the author's intentions or ideas clear.
5. The assumptions and bias	Look for opinions or ideas that the author holds that might be contentious. Look for evidence of ideas that you or others might disagree with.
6. The facts and theories	Look for any statistics, stated facts, or use of other theories or ideas that form a basis for the author's argument.
7. The themes and keywords	Look for generic ideas or key statements or phrases the author relies on heavily. In a book, look in the index or table of contents.
8. The logic and methods	Look for evidence of "if *x*, then *y*" issues. What is the author's reason for thinking or arguing the way he or she does?
9. The relationship to other works	Read other works on the same topic and look at any listed references that the author used. Do the references look at a variety of views or focus on only one opinion?
10. Reflection on your own ideas	Consider your own opinions and think of what the author didn't discuss. Do you have any lingering questions or doubts, or are you convinced by what the author has said?

Critical Thinking and Analysis Practice

The following is an article from the *Toronto Star* on the topic of child poverty. Read through the article and then read two student responses to the following critical thinking questions (these questions don't address all 10 aspects of analyzing a text, but they represent some of the most important):

1. What is the main point of the article?
2. What are the supplementary messages?
3. What is the context of the article?

4. What are the themes and keywords?
5. What are your own ideas on the topic?

At the end of the two student responses, there is a brief discussion about their work and some commentary on possible improvements and ways to move the discussion further.

Toronto Holds onto Its Shameful Title: Child Poverty Capital of Canada

Laurie Monsebraaten

October 13, 2015

1 Toronto remains the child poverty capital of Canada, with 28.6 per cent of children living in low-income households, according to a new report being released Tuesday as the city prepares to release its final poverty reduction strategy to address the problem.

2 "It is shameful that our leaders have allowed widespread poverty of young people to continue," said Michael Polanyi of the Children's Aid Society of Toronto, one of six community groups that began comparing child poverty rates in cities across the country in 2014.

3 "Until all levels of government make poverty reduction a priority, the success of tens of thousands of young people will remain at risk," he said.

4 Toronto's child poverty rate remains virtually unchanged since last year's report, with more than one in four, or 144,000 children, living in households with incomes below Statistics Canada's After-Tax Low-Income Measure, the report notes.

5 Among Canada's largest cities, Toronto has the highest percentage of impoverished children. Montreal is second with 25 per cent, Winnipeg is third at 24 per cent followed by Hamilton with 22 per cent of children under age 18 growing up in poverty.

6 Of Toronto's 140 neighbourhoods, 18 have child poverty rates above 40 per cent, according to the report, based on the latest available 2013 Revenue Canada tax filer data.

7 (In 2011, the low-income measure for a single person in Toronto was $16,456 and $39,912 for a two-parent family with two children under age 16.)

8 The group's report underscores the need for Toronto to adopt a poverty reduction strategy with significant investment, said Anita Khanna of Family Service Toronto.

9 "The large and persistent neighbourhood and racial gap in children's economic conditions and opportunities is alarming," she said. "Mayor Tory and city council can do something about this disparity—by adopting a comprehensive and bold poverty reduction strategy this fall and making action a priority in the city's 2016 Budget."

10 Eight of the city's neighbourhoods with the highest concentrations of child poverty are in the city's north-west and five are downtown, including Regent Park, which has the highest rate at 63 per cent.

11 Regent Park community engagement worker Sureya Ibrahim created sewing and catering collectives two years ago to help local women use their skills to earn money.

---

12 "It is helping these families get a little extra to help make ends meet," said Ibrahim, who is also an area resident.

13 Single parent Hawo Ali, 53, who has raised 11 children in Regent Park, earned her Toronto Public Health Food Handler Certificate through Ibrahim's program. Her samosas are very popular, Ibrahim said.

14 Ali, who came to Canada from Somalia in 1992 with five children, had six more kids with her husband after she arrived. But in 1999 her husband left and a year later a workplace injury forced her to quit her job as a cleaner.

15 "I see all my neighbours and friends and it's a hard life," she said. But all of her children, including six who are in university and college, are doing well.

16 "I am grateful for these programs," she said.

17 Ibrahim, who arranged for a group of Regent Park youth to give their input to the city's anti-poverty efforts, has participated in numerous city hall meetings on the issue herself.

18 "We need more training for youth to get jobs," she said.

19 "It is hard for our community to access public services and programs when they don't have computers for online registration," she added. "Everything is always full."

20 Child poverty in Toronto

- Poverty rates among Toronto children outpace other age groups. The poverty rate for working-age adults is 24 per cent while just 10 per cent of Toronto seniors live in poverty.
- Child poverty rates in Toronto range from over 50 per cent in Regent Park, Moss Park, Oakridge and Thorncliffe Park to less than 5 per cent in Lawrence Park North and Kingsway South.
- Children with disabilities and those from newcomer, indigenous, single-parent and non-white households, are more likely to experience poverty.
- Of 25 neighbourhoods in Scarborough, 18 had child poverty rates above 30 per cent.
- Child poverty rates in Toronto's 10 most linguistically diverse neighbourhoods are about four times higher than rates in neighbourhoods where most residents speak only English.

Student Response 1

The main point, or the thesis, of the article is that many children living in Toronto, almost 30 percent of them, are living in poverty. This makes Toronto the poverty capital of Canada when it comes to children. The argument is that this situation is shameful and things should be done about it.

The supplementary messages have to do with the fact that the number of one in four kids living in poverty hasn't changed in 2015 from 2014. Another message is that, like Toronto, Montreal, Winnipeg, and Hamilton have levels almost as high. Anita Khanna argues that Toronto needs a reduction strategy to help these children. Finally, certain areas, including those that come from "newcomer, indigenous, single-parent and non-white households, are more likely to experience poverty."

The context of this article is that it was written by a woman, Laurie Monsebraaten, who is a social justice reporter for the *Toronto Star.* It was published in October of 2015, which is quite recent. There is an image in the article of a person of colour who lives in one of the poorest neighbourhoods of Toronto and who takes part in collectives to help others.

The large overall themes are poverty, the common good of all people, and the division between big cities and smaller towns. The key words in the article are child poverty, neighbourhoods, community engagement, and reduction strategy.

My own ideas are that this sort of makes sense. Most people want to live in big cities because they seem to have more jobs and more community, but that isn't always the case. But there is often more diversity there. I come from a small town where there doesn't seem to be much child poverty but maybe I just don't see it. I think this article would be very useful to me as a child and youth worker, though, especially if I do work in a big city, because this information is useful to know and it is good to be part of the solution.

Student Response 2

1. The thesis here is that poverty is high among certain types of children in Toronto and that they mostly live in big cities, with Toronto being the worst.

2. Supplementary messages include statistics about how bad poverty is for kids in Toronto. It is also high in another Ontario city, Hamilton. And in Montreal and Winnipeg. No information is given about other provinces. There are specific neighbourhoods where kids are poor in Toronto and a lot of those are new Canadians and "non-white" households. This shows the racism in Toronto's workplaces even though Toronto is a big city. Most people are ashamed that Toronto has such poverty and want to do something about it.

3. The context is that this information has been collected about Toronto and other cities and sent on to City Hall. It is stated that there has been no reduction in child poverty since last year at this time (the article is written in 2015). There isn't really any information on the author of the story, just that she works for the *Toronto Star*. I found another article she wrote on disability in Ontario. The article really only talks about child poverty in cities as well, not in rural areas.

4. Themes: poverty, children, low-income families, economic conditions. Keywords: impoverished, shameful, bold poverty reduction strategy, community

5. Since the beginning of time there has been inequality. People are always trying to pull one over on others. Kids often have it the worst because they don't have control over how their families work. But they still suffer. It is my goal to go into healthcare and I expect I may see a lot of impoverished children who might not have had enough food or might be the victims of violence due to poverty in their households. I do agree that cities are probably the worst for this. I have never been to Toronto, or Ontario, but where I live there are a lot of people on the street—not usually kids, but there are definitely neighbourhoods where things are much worse.

About the Student Responses

Both of these student responses are fairly good at getting to the heart of the article and both try to get into the particular context of the article quite well. This article is recent; it shows that little has changed in the big city of Toronto and things are bad for the poor children who live there. Using facts and data about children and about Toronto's poorest neighbourhoods, both students picked up on the argument that this is something people should feel ashamed about. This is not good for a big international city and something, a poverty reduction strategy, is needed to make change.

The themes and keywords are highlighted in both student responses, but a good idea in critical thinking practice is to consider why the themes are themes and why the keywords are key to the piece. Both students also begin to grapple with the idea of child poverty in the big city as "shameful," and this is where they both could have pushed farther. Is the fact that the poor are mostly non-white city dwellers especially shameful? What does it mean for these kids and their future that they are living this way? Does it disadvantage them? How can they reflect on that more? One final idea is to bring in the idea of audience in the final reflection question. When you do your own reflection on this article, do you think it was meant for you to read? Is it for the general reader? Is it for the parents whose children are impoverished? For people who can help? What does it mean that this article was in the *Toronto Star*? We know that it was written by a social justice reporter. What is that? There are many questions to consider with this article.

By using your knowledge about your audience when you are writing, and through careful reading and close analysis of arguments, you have the ability to create a logical and persuasive piece of writing that can be clearly understood. But how do you use all of this to craft an effectively written paper? That is what we cover in the next part of this textbook as we look at organizing our material.

Part 2

Beginning the Writing Process

Once you have learned more advanced ways of reading and thinking critically, it is important to start out writing on a firm footing by planning and preparing up front. This section will look at a variety of ways of organizing your work so that it is clear and audience-focused.

Organizing Your Work and Preparing for Writing

CHAPTER 4

Think about Your Subject

> I'm writing. The pages are starting to stack up. My morale is improving the more I feel like a writer.
> —Neil Gaiman

The first chunk of time you invest in your writing project should be spent planning. (The remainder is devoted to drafting and revising.) If you take the time to analyze your audience (Chapter 1), read carefully (Chapter 2), and do some critical thinking (Chapter 3), you will find you are well prepared to start planning. Your next steps are to find a good subject, to identify interesting main points, and to start outlining your material (covered in Chapter 6). You will find that the mechanics of writing and discovering your thesis statement (covered in Chapter 5)—that all important aspect of essay writing—fall into place much more easily than if you try to sweat your way through the paper the night before it's due.

In most academic and business situations, you are given your subject beforehand. This, nevertheless, requires some deep thinking on your part. What angle do you want to take with the subject? What angle might most interest your readers? What if the subject is something that you are uncomfortable with? Some freewriting, brainstorming, or talking with an instructor (in an academic setting) or a supervisor (in a business setting) is usually helpful here. Even talking with your peers about a paper you think you might have trouble with can give you new insight and a sense that you have your own opinions and ideas to give to the subject. Your first task, then, really is to make sure you have a satisfactory subject, one that satisfies the basic principles of the **4-S test:**

> If you are free to choose your own subject, the 4-S test is even more important for making sure you have the right ideas to move forward with.

> A satisfactory subject is *significant*, *single*, *specific*, and *supportable*.

If it passes the 4-S test, your subject is the basis of a good paper. In the workplace, passing the 4-S test means you can write a persuasive, thoughtful, and clear professional communication.

Make Your Subject Significant

Usually when your instructor or boss gives you something to write about, he or she has already decided that the topic is significant—that your readers will want to know what you have to say on the topic. When you have control over the subject, though, you are the one to make sure that it is worthy of the time and attention you expect your readers to give to it. Can you imagine presenting an essay on "How to buy movie tickets" or "Why I hate pants without pockets," for example, as being meaningful to readers who think your expertise is in IT strategy?

Significance is about meshing your ideas, thoughts, and research with a subjective focus that will elicit the response you are hoping for.

Exercise 4.1*

From the list below, choose those subjects that would be significant to a reader interested in being a good first-year student at a college or university. Revise the others to make them significant, if possible. If not, suggest another, related subject that is significant. When you have finished this exercise, see which items need to be revised on page 460–461.

1. Tips for using *Snapchat* and/or *Twitter* wisely
2. How to identify good online sources
3. How to take notes from a textbook
4. The perfect vacation destination
5. How to use an iPhone
6. *Netflix*—a threat to your local cable company
7. Winter weather

Make Your Subject Single

Don't try to crowd too much into one paper. If you attempt to write about two or three related ideas, your readers will get only a superficial and possibly confusing overview instead of the interesting and satisfying detail they expect to find in a well-planned paper. A subject such as "the problem of league expansion in hockey and other sports" is too broad to be dealt with satisfactorily in one three- to five-paragraph essay. More manageable *singular* alternatives are "the problems of league expansion in the NHL" or "why Hamilton can't get an NHL franchise." Ensure the topic fits the space you can give it.

Exercise 4.2*

From the following list, choose the subjects that are singular and could be explored meaningfully in a short essay. Revise the others to make them singular.

1. Causes of unemployment among college and university students and new graduates
2. Pub night at different campuses
3. Why *Twitter* and *Facebook* are so popular

4. The importance of accuracy in blogs and news sites

5. Methods of preventing the spread of sexually transmitted infections

6. Causes of injury in manufacturing careers and pro sports

7. Wildlife management and gerontology: rewarding careers

Make Your Subject Specific

Almost all good writing begins with terrible first efforts. You need to start somewhere. Start by getting something—anything—down on paper.... [T]he first draft is the down draft—you just get it down.
—Anne Lamott

Given a choice between a broad, general topic and a narrow, specific one, always choose the specific one. This may be different from the way you were taught to write essays in high school, but those often weren't reader specific. Most readers, especially in the workplace, find concrete, specific details more interesting than broad generalizations. It would be difficult to say anything very detailed about a huge subject such as "the roles of women in history," for example. But with some research, you could write an interesting paper on "the roles of 19th-century Canadian women" or "famous Canadian women."

You can narrow a broad subject and make it more specific by applying one or more *limiting factors* to it. Try thinking of your subject in terms of a specific *kind, time, place, number,* or *person* associated with it. By applying this technique to the last potential subject above, you might come up with "Viola Davis Desmond's favourite movie."

Make Your Subject Supportable

Supporting information can be gathered from your own experience, from the experience of other people, or from both.

You must know something about your subject (hopefully more than your readers know), or you must be able to find out about it. Remember, your readers want information that is new, interesting, and thought-provoking—not obvious observations familiar to everyone. You must be able to include *specific examples, facts, figures, quotations, anecdotes,* or other *supporting details.*

If you don't know enough about your topic to write anything but the obvious, be prepared to do some research. This is the foundation of any good argument or persuasive writing (which we will cover in Chapters 13 and 12). It's not a bad thing to be given a topic to write about that you have only basic knowledge in. Learning as you go is part of the writing process.

Exercise 4.3*

From the subjects given below, choose those that are clearly supportable in a short essay (perhaps 500 words). Revise the others to make them supportable.

1. Journalism as a career

2. Movie review: *Twilight* or *The Dark Knight* or *The Lord of the Rings*

3. Crisis in the Canadian automotive industry

4. The North Korean, British, and Canadian secret service

5. Time travel and *Doctor Who*

6. Art through the ages

7. The hazards of working in a fast-food franchise

Exercise 4.4*

Together with a partner, discuss the acceptability of the potential subjects listed below. Indicate with check marks (✓) whether each subject passes the 4-S test by being significant, single, specific, and supportable. Revise each unsatisfactory subject (fewer than four check marks) to make it a satisfactory subject for a short essay.

THE 4-S TEST

Subject	*significant*	*single*	*specific*	*supportable*	Revision
1. Tablet computers	☐	☐	☐	☐	______
2. Insomnia, anxiety, or stress-related disorders	☐	☐	☐	☐	______
3. The Arctic 200 years from now	☐	☐	☐	☐	______
4. Healthy lunches for busy people	☐	☐	☐	☐	______
5. Architectural trends	☐	☐	☐	☐	______

Organizing Subject Ideas into Main Points

Main points are the two or three or four most important things you have to say about your subject.

While you were thinking about subjects and testing them against the four principles presented here, perhaps you were thinking, consciously or unconsciously, about what you could say about them. It's difficult to get a subject and not immediately consider ways to talk or write about it. And don't forget, should you get a topic that you are unsure about discussing, research can really help you to find a way to connect that topic to your experience.

Once you have your topic, you will want to begin thinking about the various ways you can write about it. We generally discuss that in terms of considering our main points—those that will support our point of view.

Many standard essay-style responses, including the outline style we discuss in Chapter 6, use three main points preceded by an introduction and followed by a conclusion. Selecting main points carefully is a vital part of the writing process. We're going to go through a variety of ways to come up with your main points once you have been given or have chosen your subject. We'll start with three prewriting approaches, which include talking, freewriting, and brainstorming. In contrast, the questioning approach focuses on asking structured questions about a given topic.

Generating Main Points: Prewriting Techniques

If you are feeling intimidated by your task and unsure about how to present your subject, some prewriting activities can be helpful. Many students think of them as topic life-savers because once the outline is done, the paper is almost ready. The goals of any prewriting activity are to help you find out what you know about your subject and to prepare you for the drafting process. Before we look at some potentially helpful prewriting strategies, we would like you to consider what we covered in Chapter 2, the old truism "The more you read, the better you write." Reading is not just essential to learning about subject matter; it also influences the quality of your writing. Reading broadly will expose you to a wide variety of styles as well as points of view, and as you work consciously at mastering the content of what you read, your brain is working unconsciously to absorb the qualities of different kinds of writing.

Writers use several methods to stimulate thinking. Three are especially effective: talking, freewriting, and brainstorming. All will make your creative juices flow. We recommend that you try all three to see which works best for you in a particular writing situation. Understand that these techniques work only when you already have some ideas in your head. Either you will be writing from personal experience, or you will have done some research. (You'll learn about research in Part 5.)

Talking

In a focused dialogue, you can build on the ideas of others, discover what you yourself think, and evaluate the clarity of your reasoning.

In our experience, many students love to talk and therefore feel frustration in classes because there is no time to "just talk" about the material. The prewriting strategy of talking can work for writing too, as long as you are clearly and tightly focused on a specific subject. *Focused dialogue* works best in groups of three or four students, all of whom are interested in the subject. As long as your peers don't wander off-topic, you might find small-group discussion a non-threatening way of clarifying what you know and don't know about a topic. If your group is disciplined enough to stay focused, you can also learn a lot by hearing what your peers think.

Like any other skill, keeping on-topic during a focused dialogue becomes easier with practice. If you haven't tried this prewriting strategy before, you may want to use the questions on page 60 as a guide to help you stay on-topic or to bring you back if you find yourselves straying. And, like any other skill, it's a good idea to start small and work up. At first, 10 minutes may exhaust your group's thoughts. With practice, 15 to 20 minutes may be necessary to allow everyone a chance to voice an opinion and for everyone to discuss, modify, and build on each person's contribution.

In a focused dialogue, we suggest that every participant take notes. What seems significant to one student may not seem so to another, and since the point of the exercise is to discover ideas in preparation for the paper you will write on your own, only you know what you may need as a written record of the discussion.

Freewriting

Freewriting is talking written down. It does what its name implies—it sets you free to write without worrying about any of the errors you may make that block the flow of your ideas. Forget about grammar, spelling, word choice, and so on, until you get some ideas down on the page. Here's how to go about freewriting:

1. Put your watch and a pad of paper on your desk. If you can type faster than you can write, open a new document on your computer. (Some writers find it helpful to turn off the monitor.) Write your subject at the top of the page or tape it to the top of your computer monitor. Ideally, your subject will have passed the 4-S test, but if you're really stuck, you can begin with just a word or a phrase.

2. Make a note of the time and start writing. Don't stop until you have written for three, five, or even ten minutes straight. Write anything that comes to mind, even if it seems boring or silly. If you get stuck for words, write your subject or even the last phrase you've written over and over until something new comes to mind. (Don't worry, it will!)

3. Write as quickly as you can. Don't pause to analyze or evaluate your ideas, and don't scratch out or delete anything. This technique is designed to get thoughts into words as quickly as possible without self-consciousness.

4. When the time is up, stop and stretch. Then read over what you've written. Highlight anything that is related to your subject. Much of your freewriting will be irrelevant nonsense that you can delete. But what you have highlighted will be useful in the next step: identifying the main points you will use to explain your subject.

5. Turn the highlighted phrases, fragments, and sentences into clear, understandable points. If you don't end up with at least 10 points, continue freewriting for another few minutes and see what new ideas you can discover.

6. On a separate piece of paper, list the points you have identified. Study the possible relationships among these points and cluster them under two or three headings. These are your main points. Now you can move on to the next step: testing each main point to be sure it is satisfactory for your essay.

Here is an example of the freewriting technique. The assigned writing topic for a course in human resource fundamentals was "embracing inclusivity." Shakira Lao was interested in creating a work environment that was inspiring and motivating for all Canadians and she was concerned about prejudices and preconceived notions that people might have, especially from what they have seen on television. After doing some research that she thought would be useful and interviewing and talking with others in her field, she drafted the following on her computer in about 15 minutes.

> When we think about an inclusive and diverse workplace, we need to broaden our ideas from what we may be used to, or from what we

see on television. So many television shows or movies have all-white casts or just have a "token" gay person or black person on them. Shows with black people in them seem to be all black, although that might just be a chance for them to shine and not have second billing. Everyone is tiny on television, or sometimes there is one larger person but they always have to be funny or dress in certain ways. People make judgments about how workplaces should work or who is right for jobs based on what they see. If only male police officers or judges are shown on television, for example, children might believe those jobs are only meant for males.

When we think about embracing inclusivity in the workplace, we need to start by considering hiring practices and how we train recruiters and interviewers. Is their language inclusive? Where do they advertise for new hires? Have they even considered specific outreach for trans people or queer people or even just for those who don't necessarily use newspapers or online venues to find jobs? Do they know if their workplace is up on their requirements with people with disabilities? What have they done to create an equitable space for everyone? When I spoke with two Human Resource managers in the Vancouver area they seemed really proud of their diverse and inclusive workspace. They had created what they called "gentle" but effective guidelines around scent, they had a gender neutral set of washrooms, and their dress code was all-gendered. They agreed that they were in a big city and that things might be very different across Canada but said it shouldn't matter where a person's workplace was, everyone had a right to a dignified workplace and to an equitable chance at a job. They said that everyone who was hired in their workplace was more than able to do their jobs and that everyone worked as hard as they could to get things done. The two employees at the same workplace had fairly similar ideas about the inclusive strategies and noted that they felt very comfortable learning and sharing knowledge with the staff where they worked. They did say that one person who worked there had felt "confused" about hiring policies and worried that if, say, an Indigenous person were applying for the job, whether they would get it just because they were diverse. They did note, though, that person no longer worked for the company. Only watching television and movies, it is probably easy to think that if someone wasn't looking a certain way, that maybe they wouldn't or shouldn't be there.

After completing the exercise in freewriting, Shakira went through her ideas and tried to pick out what would be considered significant, supportable, and related to the subject. Since her specific goal in the assignment was to interview people, those became her supported facts, and she felt good about that data. She did think, however, that she didn't need to mention the angry employee who ended up leaving the workplace anyway. She ended up with a rough outline of an essay with three main compare-and-contrast points:

> Intro: The reality of the Canadian workplace should reflect the reality of the country and not of the media's accounts and representations. When it comes to race, gender, and size we need to reflect truth and not distortion.
>
> 1. Race:
>   - *In the media*—mostly white, only tokens in other cultures
>   - In reality—all different races, cultures, especially in large cities according to interviews
> 2. Gender:
>   - *In the media*—mostly males, especially for certain jobs (police, judges) and females. No trans persons or persons of multiple experience of gender. People are supposed to wear clothes that "suit" their sex.
>   - *In reality*—all different genders, all different jobs. There is no gender requirement for jobs. People should be able to wear clothing that suits them and that is respectable for a workplace but not gender specific.
> 3. Size:
>   - *In the media*—mostly very thin, almost sick looking. A certain height as well.
>   - *In reality*—all different sizes, all different abilities. All different heights.
>
> Conclusion: Those who have power in the media should be working to create a more realistic and equitable space to show others that they aren't "abnormal" or don't fit into the workplace.

Working with this rough outline, Shakira was able to develop a first draft of a persuasive paper. In reading it over, she noted where she needed to add in quotations from those she interviewed and where she should find some actual data from media sources. After a few more edits, Shakira could have a carefully worked compare-and-contrast essay.

Exercise 4.5

Choose a subject, or work with an assigned subject. Follow the six steps outlined on page 55 to see what main points you can come up with. Don't worry if your work is messy. Freewriting is a record of your thoughts, and thinking is messy.

Brainstorming

In **brainstorming**, you write down a list of every idea you can think of about a specific subject. You can brainstorm alone, with a partner, or—best of all—in a group. If you run out of ideas too quickly, then try the age-old journalist's technique:

ask the questions *who, what, why, when, where,* and *how* about your subject. Here's how to proceed. (The first three steps below assume you are working with a partner or in a small group. You can also do them by yourself, but you'll have less fun.)

1. Write your topic at the top of the page. Again, you will save time if you've checked your subject against the 4-S test. Decide how much time you will spend on this exercise: three, five, or more minutes. As in freewriting, working against the clock can bring surprising results.

2. Write down in short form—words or phrases—every idea you can think of that is even vaguely related to your subject. Choose the fastest writer in your group to be the recorder. Work quickly. Don't slow yourselves down by worrying about grammar or repetition.

3. When the time is up, relax for a minute, then go over the list carefully. Highlight the points that seem most clearly related to your subject and cross out any duplicates or any ideas that are vague, trivial, or irrelevant. If you don't end up with at least three or four points that are meaningful to you, brainstorm again for a few minutes, using the six journalist's questions to generate more ideas.

4. Working alone now, take your three or four most significant points and rephrase them in clear sentences on a new sheet of paper. Now you're ready to move on to the next step: testing your main points to ensure that they are suitable for use in your essay.

The following example demonstrates how brainstorming can be used to overcome the most frustrating inertia. The subject is "your college English course." As you might expect, the class groaned when the subject was assigned, but one group's quick brainstorming produced some interesting approaches to the topic. The time limit given for this exercise was four minutes. After brainstorming, at least one student was convinced that her career opportunities would improve if she learned how to communicate better.

Your College English Course

- have to take it
- should like it but I don't
- writing is important
- speaking's easier than writing
- bosses will hire you if you can write
- you can get a job
- letter of application
- have to write on the job
- have to write to the boss, other departments
- have to write to customers
- embarrassed about my writing
- people don't respect a poor writer
- writing helps you think
- writing helps you read better
- have to write reports
- need to know how to write a good report
- have to prepare slides for presentations
- need to write to get promoted

This list contains several significant points along with some irrelevant and trivial ones, which the group deleted. Then they talked about possible relationships among the remaining items on the list.

At this point, each student began working alone. After one student had highlighted the points she felt were most important, she noticed that these points could be divided into two related ideas: what college English teaches and why it is useful. She then combined these ideas into a thesis (a point of view about a subject). Here is her list of revised points.

College English is useful because

- it improves writing and thinking skills
- you will communicate better on the job
- job promotion requires good communication skills

Exercise 4.6

In groups of four or five, brainstorm to identify as many topics as you can in five minutes. Do not censor or cut any ideas. You should end up with at least 20 topics. Then exchange papers with another group and edit that group's topics, crossing out any that are too broad or too narrow. Switch papers again, but with a different group, and choose four topics that pass the 4-S test. Finally, select the best of the four topics and present it to the rest of the class, explaining why it's a good choice for an essay.

Exercise 4.7

Choose one of the three prewriting techniques presented in this chapter: talking, freewriting, or brainstorming. Generate as much information as you can in five minutes about one of the topics presented to the class in Exercise 4.6. Then narrow your information down to an opinion supported by two or three main points. Finally, write a brief outline (about as long as the example given on page 57) for a short essay.

An Alternative Approach: Questioning Your Subject

Another way to find out what you have to say about a subject is to ask specific questions about it. Questioning lets you "walk around" your subject, looking at it from different angles, taking it apart and putting it back together again. Each question is a probe that enables you to dig below the surface and find out what you know. This approach is more structured than the strategies we have discussed so far, but it has the advantage of producing clear main points with few or no off-topic responses. It also identifies for you the kinds of development you can use in your essay.

Questioning your subject works best if you know it well or have done some research but are not sure how to approach it. Any subject can be approached in a number of ways.

Your purpose in writing should determine how you choose to approach your subject.

Here's how to use the questioning technique to generate ideas:

1. Begin by writing your proposed subject at the top of the page, or tape it to your monitor.
2. Now apply the 12 questions listed below, one at a time, to your subject to see which ones "fit" best. That is, find the questions that call up in your

mind answers that could be used as points to develop your subject. As you go down the list, you will probably find more than one question for which you can think up answers. Do not stop with the first question that produces answers. The purpose of this idea-generating technique is to discover the *best* approach for your target audience and writing purpose.

3. Go through the entire list and record your answers to any questions that apply to your subject. Ignore the questions that make no sense in relation to the subject.
4. Finally, study the questions that produced answers and choose the one that generated the ideas that are closest to what your reader needs to know and what you want to say.

The questions listed in the left-hand column below lead to the kinds of essay development listed in the column on the right. Don't worry about these types now. We'll discuss them in detail in Part 4.

The Answers to This Question	Produce This Kind of Paper
1. How is your subject *made* or *done*? 2. How does your subject *work*?	*Process*
3. What are the main *kinds* of your subject? 4. What are the component *parts* of your subject? 5. What are the significant *features, characteristics*, or *functions* of your subject?	*Classification/ Division*
6. What are the *causes* of your subject? 7. What are the *effects* or *consequences* of your subject?	*Cause/Effect*
8. What are the *similarities* and/or *differences* between your subject and *x*?	*Comparison/ Contrast*
9. What are the main *advantages/disadvantages* of your subject? 10. What are the reasons *in favour of/against* your subject?	*Argument/ Persuasion*
11. What does your subject *look, feel, sound, smell*, and/or *taste* like?	*Description*
12. How did your subject *happen*?	*Narration*

Here is an example of how the process works. Maya Tam, a recent college graduate, has decided to write about her first job as a management trainee. Her target audience is general readers, not experts in her field. The subject passes the 4-S test: it is significant, single, specific, and supportable.

1. **How is my job done?**
   The answer to this question is basically a job description, which would be of little interest to anyone other than Maya's close friends, her supervisor, or the person hired to replace her. Let's move on.

2. **How does my first job work?**
   All jobs are different; this question doesn't take us anywhere.
3. **What are the main kinds of first jobs?**
   This question might lead to an acceptable topic for a research paper on the kinds of entry-level jobs that graduates from specific programs can expect to get, but the answers won't produce the sort of personal experience essay Maya wants to write.
4. **What are the component parts (i.e., main requirements) of my job?**
   Our writer might use this question as a starting point for a discussion of her main job functions, but this information would be of interest only to those in her career field, not to a broad, general audience.
5. **What are the significant features of my job?**
   This question has possibilities. Maya could tell her readers about those aspects of her job that apply to all first-time employees, perhaps limiting her focus to the aspects of the working world that she hadn't expected—that, in fact, surprised her.
6. **What were the causes of my first job?**
   Broadly interpreted to mean, "Why did I want my first job," this question probably wouldn't produce useful answers. Most people work because they have to support themselves.
7. **What are the effects of my first job?**
   This question raises some interesting answers. What effect has full-time employment had on Maya's life? She might discuss the self-esteem that replaced her earlier insecurity and fear of the job search; she might discuss her new independence, both financial and social.
8. **What are the similarities (or differences) between my first job and … what? A second or third job?**
   Our writer is still in her first job and so can't answer this question.
9. **What are the main advantages (or disadvantages) of my first job?**
   This question produces answers that are easy to explain—and that's the problem with it. Unless Maya has a very unusual first job, the answers to this question are predictable and therefore unlikely to be of interest to a broad audience.
10. **What are the reasons in favour of (or against) my first job?**
    This question leads to answers that overlap with those produced by question 9. It would lead to an average essay, but not to anything outstanding or memorable.
11. **What does my job feel like?**
    At first glance, this question doesn't make much sense. A job can't feel; the employee does. However, by interpreting the question loosely, Maya could describe her nervousness, her desire to do well, the pressures she felt, and the rewards of the job.
12. **How did my job happen?**
    This question doesn't sound promising. How Maya landed her job would be of interest to her family and friends, but probably would not appeal

to a broader audience unless her experience was highly unusual or could be instructive to others.

After patiently going through the list, our writer found two questions, 5 and 7, that produced answers she felt she could work with. She especially liked the possibilities suggested by question 5.

As Maya focused her thoughts, she realized that what she wanted to write about was the unexpected challenges she confronted when she joined the world of work. So she refined the question to capture what she wanted to write about ("What are the most significant challenges I faced in my first job?") and came up with three solid answers: the expectations of her boss, her co-workers, and herself. The essay that resulted from this process, "On-the-Job Training," appears on pages 134–135.

Generating main points is a time-consuming but worthwhile process. The more time you spend at this stage, the less time it will take you to draft your essay. To sharpen your skills, study the examples given below. Each consists of a 4-S test–approved subject, a question about that subject, and some answers the question produces that would form solid main points to support, explain, or prove the subject of the essay.

Subject	**Selected Question**	**Main Points**
Hockey violence	What are the reasons in favour of violence in hockey?	• releases aggression • keeps players alert • attracts fans
Law enforcement officers	What are the main functions of law enforcement officers?	• preventing crime • apprehending criminals • enforcing the law • acting as role models
Job interviews	How do you make a negative impression in a job interview?	• be late • be inappropriately dressed • be ignorant about the company • complain about former employers
Essay topics	What are the characteristics of a satisfactory essay topic?	• single • significant • specific • supportable

Exercise 4.8 Working with a partner, apply the questions on page 60 to each of the subjects listed below. Select the question that produces the answers you both like best, and list three or four of these answers as main points.

Subject	***Selected Question***	***Main Points***
1. Procrastination		• • • •

Subject	*Selected Question*	*Main Points*
2. Text messaging		•
		•
		•
		•
3. Electric or hybrid vehicles		•
		•
		•
		•
4. Business dress codes		•
		•
		•
		•
5. Your favourite meal		•
		•
		•
		•

Exercise 4.9

In pairs, choose two subjects that you think would be suitable for short essays. Be sure both are significant, single, specific, and supportable. For each subject, list at least three strong main points. Use the questions on page 60 to help you identify main points. When you've finished, exchange your ideas with another team, critique each other's main points, and make suggestions.

Subject: ______________________________

Selected Question: ______________________________

Main Points:
-
-
-

Subject: ______________________________

Selected Question: ______________________________

Main Points:
-
-
-

Testing Your Main Points

Once you've identified main points using talking, freewriting, brainstorming, or the questioning approach, your next step is to examine the points you've come up with to make sure each is going to work as a major component in your essay. Some may be too minor to bother with; some may overlap in meaning; some may even be unrelated to your subject. Here's how to test your main points to be sure they are satisfactory. Whether you've arrived at your main points through talking, freewriting, brainstorming, or questioning, the test is the same.

> Main points must always be significant, distinct, and relevant.

Are Your Main Points Significant?

Each main point should be worth writing and reading about. If you can't write at least one interesting and informative paragraph about a point, it is probably not significant enough to bother with. Don't waste your readers' time with trivial matters. In the following example, one of the main points does not have the same importance as the others; it should be eliminated or replaced. Which one would you discard?

Reasons for attending college

- to learn career skills
- to improve one's general knowledge of the world
- to enjoy the social life
- to participate in student government

Are Your Main Points Distinct?

Each of the main points you choose must be different from all the others; there must be no overlap in meaning. Check to be sure you haven't given two different labels to what is really only one aspect of your subject. Eliminate or replace any main points that duplicate other points or that can easily be covered under another point. Here's an example of a list that contains a redundant main point. Which point would you eliminate?

Advantages of yoga

- improves fitness
- stimulates enjoyment of surroundings
- keeps one in shape
- doesn't damage the environment

Are Your Main Points Relevant?

The main points you choose must be clearly and directly related to your subject. They all must be aspects of that subject and must add to the development of your readers' information on the subject. In this example, the third main point listed should be eliminated because it does not relate to the stated topic.

Why buy all-season tires?

- better control on turns
- increased traction in loose snow
- added expense
- decreased stopping distance

Exercise 4.10*

At least one main point in each item below is unsatisfactory. Identify each faulty point and explain why it should be deleted. When you have finished, compare your answers with those on page 461.

1. Business communication devices
   - telephone
   - email
   - fax
   - mail
   - cellphone
2. Advantages of locating a business outside the city
   - cheaper cost of living
   - calmer pace
   - distance from suppliers and markets
   - government subsidies and tax benefits
3. Kinds of television commercials
   - boring
   - clever
   - misleading
   - puzzling
   - repetitive
4. Causes of college and university failure
   - lack of preparation in high school
   - procrastination
   - poor study habits
   - irregular attendance
5. How to choose a place to live
   - determine your needs
   - determine your budget
   - find a reliable real estate agent
   - seek expert advice
6. Reasons for high staff turnover
   - salary lower than industry standard
   - no chance for advancement
   - uncomfortable work environment
   - competitors offer better pay

CHAPTER 5

Developing the Main Points and Writing the Thesis Statement

Organizing Your Main Points

Some points need to be presented before others; order can be especially important in the workplace or in papers that have a strong argument.

After you've identified the main points for your essay and checked to make sure they are satisfactory, your final task in the planning process is to list them in the order in which you will present them. (This list of points is sometimes called a *plan of development* or a *path statement.*) Main points are like menu items on a website: the more logically they are arranged, the easier it is to navigate your way through them. You may want your reader to understand some things before you present other ideas. Once you have the method down, you can logically plan out your entire paper.

> There are four ways to order your main points: *chronological, climactic, logical,* and *random.*

Chronological Order

You are using **chronological order** when you present your points in order of time from first to last. You will find it most appropriate in process essays (discussed in Chapter 11), but it can be used in other types of essays as well. Here are two examples:

Subject	Main Points
The process of writing a paper	• select an appropriate subject • list and edit the main points • write a thesis statement • write an outline for the paper • write a first draft • revise, edit, and proofread
The evolution of a relationship	• meeting • attraction • discovery • intimacy • disillusionment

Climactic Order

Persuasion most often uses a climactic arrangement, but climactic order is also common in papers based on examples, comparison or contrast, and classification or division. In **climactic order**, you save your strongest or most convincing point for last (the climax of your argument). You lead off your essay with your second-strongest point, and arrange your other points in between, as in this example.

Subject	Main Points
Advantages of a post-secondary education	• development of skills and knowledge • friendships and networking contacts with compatible people • potential for higher income and promotion • discovery of one's own potential

Logical Order

Readers must grasp each point before the next can be explained and understood.

Cause-and-effect essays, or any writing in which one point must be explained before the next point can be understood, are based on **logical order**. Your main points have a logical relationship, and you cannot discuss them out of order without confusing your readers. Consider the following sequence.

Subject	Main Points
Main causes of youth violence and bullying	• lack of opportunity for work • lack of recreational facilities • boredom • craving for excitement

The logical links here are clear: because of unemployment, recreational facilities are needed. Because of both unemployment and inadequate recreational facilities, boredom and the craving for excitement become problems.

Random Order

On the rare occasions when your points can be explained in any order without affecting your readers' understanding, you can use **random order.** A random arrangement is possible only if all your main points are of equal significance and if they are not linked together logically or chronologically. In this example, all three points have equal weight.

Subject	Main Points
The garbage disposal crisis	• disposal sites are hard to find • cartage costs are high • new technologies are not yet fully developed

Exercise 5.1* Choose the type of order—chronological, climactic, logical, or random—you think is most appropriate for each of the following subjects. Arrange the main points in that order by numbering them in the spaces provided.

Subject	*Order*	*Main Points*
1. How to impress a client	____________	___ firm handshake ___ friendly closing ___ well-prepared sales presentation ___ knowledge of client's needs ___ appropriate business attire
2. How to handle tax preparation	____________	___ do your own ___ don't bother to file a return ___ go to a franchise tax-preparation company ___ hire an accountant
3. Reasons for listening to CBC Radio	____________	___ it offers informative programs ___ your taxes are paying for it ___ it encourages a sense of Canadian unity
4. Methods of quitting smoking	____________	___ nicotine patch ___ cold turkey ___ gradual withdrawal
5. Causes of dissatisfaction with employment	____________	___ incompetent or unfriendly supervisor ___ incompatible co-workers ___ inappropriate pay for skills and effort ___ unfulfilling work assignments

Exercise 5.2 Go back to the subjects and main points that you organized in Exercise 5.1. First, reconsider the main points that were listed: are they all significant, distinct, and related to the subject?

When you've finished this task, exchange papers with another student and check each other's work. Does your partner agree with your choice?

Writing the Thesis Statement

Once you have a clear outline, a strong main idea, and relevant points, writing the thesis statement is just a matter of clear wording. It doesn't have to be guesswork or a chore!

The key to showing your readers the clear organization of any paper is through a thesis statement. This statement appears near the beginning of your paper and announces the paper's subject and scope—all the prewriting work you have done and organized into your outline. The thesis statement not only helps a reader to see how you are going to approach the subject but also serves to keep you, the writer, on track.

> A **thesis statement** is one or more sentences that clearly and concisely indicate the main idea of your paper, the points that you will discuss, and the order in which you will discuss them.

In business communication, technical writing, and some academic writing (e.g., research papers and dissertations), it is important to indicate the main idea and scope of your paper at the outset. Readers expect this sort of preview.[1]

The number of sentences in a thesis statement depends on what the subject is, how best to phrase it, how many points there are, and how complex your points turn out to be. A thesis statement in a short paper is usually a single sentence at the end of the first paragraph, but in a lengthy paper on complicated issues, it might be several sentences or even a paragraph long. Only occasionally (in a technical description, for example) will a writer choose a short thesis and omit the main points from the thesis statement.

It is best to write a statement that will guide your readers through your paper and its main points.

To write a basic thesis statement, you combine your main idea and your points. Here is a simple formula for constructing a thesis statement.

These three elements can be combined in various ways. For example:

> The most prolific producers of unnecessary jargon are politicians, sportswriters, advertising copywriters, and educators. **(Main idea and points are linked by *are*.)**
>
> Three powerful factors are responsible for the development of anorexia nervosa in young women: the pressures of adolescence, the expectations of family and peers, and the potent influence of mass media. **(Main idea and points are linked by a colon.)**
>
> Because the United States influences Canada's foreign policy, dominates its culture, and controls its economy, Canada is little more than an American satellite. **(Points precede main idea and are linked to the main idea by *Because*.)**
>
> Fad diets are not the quick fix to weight problems that they may appear to be. On the contrary, they are often costly, ineffective, and even dangerous. **(Main idea is one sentence. Points are in second sentence, linked to the first by *On the contrary*.)**

In these examples, we have used three points to discuss our main idea, although your instructor might suggest a different number based on your paper length, topic, style, etc.

Once you have mastered the basic formula, you can experiment with creative ways of expressing a thesis statement. Just be sure that it is appropriate in form, language, and tone to the kind of paper you are writing. For example, the last two thesis statements above are persuasive thesis statements, meaning their main idea is supported by the three points that are made in the thesis statement. The first two statements are made up of main ideas that are linked to—or understood in

[1] In less formal writing, such as newspaper or magazine articles and informal essays—including some of the essays in this book—a thesis statement is not necessarily required. It is best to assume a thesis statement is required unless your instructor says otherwise.

relation to—the points that follow. Both types of thesis statements are effective and useful for writing academic papers.

The thesis statements in the exercise below range from short to long, formal to informal, and serious to flippant. The first four items are straightforward; you should have no trouble analyzing them. The last three are increasingly complex and challenging. Work with a partner to identify their elements.

Exercise 5.3* In each of the following thesis statements, underline the main idea with a double line and the points with a single line. When you have finished all seven, compare your answers with those on page 462.

1. Students who try to combine a full-time job with a full-time program face problems at school, at work, and at home.
2. To be successful in a broadcasting career, applicants must be talented, motivated, and hard-working.
3. Establishing an online network would promote teamwork and increase efficiency in the office.
4. The business traveller can learn much from the turtle. Carry everything you need with you. Move slowly but with purpose and consistency. Keep your head down until you are sure you know what's going on.
5. Cellphones must be turned off during class because they disrupt everyone's concentration, they prevent the user from learning, and they distract and annoy the teacher, to the detriment of all.
6. Although easily dismissed as merely animated entertainment, *The Simpsons* is effective social commentary, tackling with humour and gusto such issues as the environment, social justice, and race relations.
7. Large energy producers and some provincial governments say we cannot afford to live up to the terms of the Kyoto and Copenhagen agreements, which seek to reduce the production of greenhouse gases. But can we afford not to comply? Can we afford to compromise the health of Canadians by continuing to pollute? Can we afford to risk the effects of climate change on our environment? Can we afford to fall behind the rest of the world in research and development leading to a solution to the problem of greenhouse gases?

Exercise 5.4

Each of the five introductions below contains a thesis statement. Working with a partner or in groups of three or four, identify the thesis statement in each paragraph by underlining it.

1. What does an interviewer look for in a job applicant? Good credentials, good preparation, good grooming, and good communication skills are essential features for anyone who wants a job. No interviewer would seriously consider an applicant who comes to an interview without the required educational background and work experience, without information about the job and the company, without appropriate clothing, and without the ability to present ideas clearly in the interview.

2. The numbers from Statistics Canada tell the story: a record one in seven of us is 65 or older; the median age is up; the average age of seniors is up; the number of centenarians is up; and the baby boomers constitute the largest generation in our population. This situation presents us with many difficult challenges in the years to come, but it also provides significant opportunities for those able and willing to take advantage of the trend. Post-secondary-aged Canadians who want secure and useful employment should be looking to gerontology, medicine, and recreation for their career prospects and their investment opportunities.

3. Suddenly a man steps into the road in front of me. He's wearing a uniform and he's waving his hand for me to pull over to the side. My heart pounds and my skin prickles with anxiety. I feel guilty, but I don't know what I've done wrong—maybe speeding 10 kilometres over the limit, but no more. Anyone who has been caught in a radar trap knows these momentary feelings of panic, guilt, and resentment. We fear that the police officer will be brusque and accusing, but we are often surprised. There are as many kinds of police officers as there are people. Four kinds, however, dominate the profession: the confident veteran, the arrogant authoritarian, the cocky novice, and the friendly professional. As I roll down my window, I wonder which kind of police officer has stopped me.

4. After a hard day's work, do you relax with two or three shots? Do you enjoy a few beers while watching a game on TV? Do you believe alcohol makes a party more fun? Do you cool off with vodka coolers on a hot afternoon? If you answered "yes" to most of these questions, you are probably abusing alcohol. The line between excessive social drinking and a serious addictive habit is a blurry one. Most alcoholics don't know they are hooked until they try to stop drinking. What are the signs that a drinker is no longer drinking for pleasure only? If a person "needs" a drink, or drinks alone, or can fall asleep only after a few drinks, or can find enjoyment only when drinking, that person is probably in trouble.

5. Ours is a transient society. Most of us travel more kilometres in a year than our grandparents travelled in a lifetime. We move from one city to another, one province or territory to another, and one country to another. In the course of moving, we inhabit many homes. The family home of the past may have been inhabited by several generations, consecutively or concurrently. Today's average Canadian will probably have 10 or more addresses during his or her adult life. Our restlessness is particularly hard on the children in our migrating families: they have to leave familiar surroundings and friends, and they must adjust to a new environment, new habits, and sometimes a new language. These children pay a heavy price for the mobility of modern impermanence.

Phrasing Your Main Idea

The first part of a thesis statement is the main idea. It identifies *your idea about* or *your approach* to your subject and states a viewpoint that must be explained or proved. The points provide the explanation or proof.

Your main idea should be as clear and concise as you can make it. It should also grab your reader's attention or provide a provocative idea. If a thesis is too obvious—smoking can harm your health, for example—the reader will lose interest quickly. Try to find a unique position.

Beginning writers often fall into the trap of using the helpful starter: "In this paper, I am going to discuss ... " or "The subject of this report is ... " Your readers *know* it's your paper; you don't have to tell them. Although using such a starter can be helpful when you are drafting your work, it is usually better to leave it out in the final version. Once you are putting together your final version, you might consider punching it up for the reader and making sure your meaning is completely clear.

What you don't want to do in your thesis statement is provide only a description of your subject without stating a clear position.

Here are three examples of beginning main ideas and our suggested revisions.

Poor	Better
In this essay, I am going to discuss violence in hockey. (What about it?)	Violence in hockey is misunderstood by the non-playing public.
This paper is about Canada's multiculturalism policy. (What about it?)	Canada's multiculturalism policy is neither practical nor desirable.
I am going to examine the influence of Walmart in Canada. (What about it?)	With over 200 stores in Canada and plans for expansion, Walmart's effects on labour are worth considering.

Always let your reader know what it is about your subject that your paper will explain or prove.

As soon as you write, "In this essay ... " or "I am going to discuss (write about, explore) ... ," you potentially trap yourself into simply announcing your subject, not stating your idea or your opinion about it. Also, make sure to avoid writing your thesis, or your entire essay, in the second person (using "you" or "your"). A statement such as "You really need to consider adopting new ideas on recycling" sounds more like an advertisement or TV commercial than an academic paper. Avoid these traps in your final version.

In Part 4 we will look at the different ways you can tackle your subject.

Phrasing the Thesis Points

When you combine your main idea with your points to form a thesis statement, be sure that all your points are phrased the same way: in grammatically parallel form. If point 1 is a single word, then points 2, 3, and so on must also be single words. If point 1 is a phrase, then all the points following it must be phrases. If point 1 is a clause or a sentence, then the succeeding points must also be clauses or sentences. Only the most experienced writers can produce a perfect thesis statement in one try—this is one reason to hold off on writing it until you've done the legwork of organizing your ideas. Most of us need to draft the thesis statement, revise it, reconsider, revise it again—and probably do it all yet again—to produce a grammatically parallel thesis statement.

The following sentence is not grammatically parallel:

> **Of the many qualities that combine to make a good nurse, the three most important are strength, intelligence, and she must be compassionate.**

Revised to be grammatically parallel, the sentence might read like this:

> **Of the many qualities that combine to make a good nurse, the three most important are strength, intelligence, and compassion.**

Or like this:

> **Of the many qualities that combine to make a good nurse, the three most important are that he or she be strong, intelligent, and compassionate.**

If you have trouble with grammatical parallelism, turn to Chapter 23 before you try the exercise below.

Exercise 5.5

In each of the following lists, one point is not parallel with the others. Rephrase the incorrect item so that all are in grammatically parallel form.

1. Our employees are
   a. motivated
   b. good training
   c. knowledgeable
2. Our doctor is
   a. full of compassion
   b. competent
   c. hard-working
3. I've noticed that my friends are increasingly
   a. concerned about their diets
   b. interested in fitness
   c. environmental awareness
4. To upgrade our educational system, we need
   a. more effective teacher training
   b. better liaison between levels of education
   c. students must be motivated to learn
5. An investment strategy must be
   a. based on current information
   b. appropriately diversified
   c. the client has to be tolerant of the degree of risk

Now choose one of the above statements and write the thesis statement so that it is grammatically correct:

____

____

Exercise 5.6 Work in pairs to develop two thesis statements for potential essays. Perhaps your instructor can give you a topic, or you can spend five minutes brainstorming. Phrase the two thesis statements so that one has a poor main idea and the other lacks parallelism. Exchange your creations with another team and identify each other's problems. Then correct the sentences. Exchange papers again. Did the other team identify and correct the problems you thought you'd created? If not, revise your own team's faulty sentences.

Exercise 5.7 Working with a partner, combine each of the following subjects with its main points to form a clear thesis statement that is expressed in grammatically parallel form.

1. Causes of stress
   - being laid off
   - financial problems
   - the loss of a family member

   Thesis statement: ____

   ____

   ____

   ____

   ____

2. Steps in finding a job
   - conduct an Internet job search
   - prepare a letter of application
   - perform well in the interview

   Thesis statement: ____

   ____

   ____

   ____

   ____

3. How to save money
   - automatic payroll deductions
   - keep a record of expenditures
   - reduce impulse buying
   - establish and maintain a budget

Thesis statement: ____

____

____

____

____

4. Evolution of a recession
   - unemployment causes general economic slowdown
   - consumer buying decreases, resulting in inflation
   - inflation causes fear and a further decrease in consumer demand

Thesis statement: ____

____

____

____

____

5. Evolution of a revolution
   - those in power oppress those they rule
   - oppression leads to revolution
   - revolutionaries take power
   - those in power oppress those they rule

Thesis statement: ____

____

____

____

____

Exercise 5.8

Working independently, combine each of the following main ideas with its points to form a grammatically parallel thesis statement.

1. Comparison between McDonald's and Wendy's (or any other two fast-food restaurants)
   - food
   - atmosphere
   - service
   - price

Thesis statement: ______________________________________

____

____

____

____

2. Effects of urban overcrowding
   - traffic jams
   - air pollution
   - high rate of homelessness
   - violence on the streets
   - domestic violence

Thesis statement: ______________________________________

____

____

____

____

3. Characteristics of a successful small business
   - adequate capital
   - marketable product
   - personnel that are dedicated
   - workable business plan

Thesis statement: ______________________________________

____

____

____

____

Exercise 5.9* In groups of three or four, share the thesis statements you developed for Exercise 5.8 and discuss your decisions. As a group, revise each statement until everyone is satisfied it meets the criteria for satisfactory thesis statements. Then compare your results with our suggestions on page 462.

You have now covered all the steps leading to the construction of a good thesis statement. The exercises above have given you practice in the skills you need to phrase subjects and main points correctly and effectively.

Exercise 5.10 will walk you through the process of developing a thesis statement for a subject of your own or your instructor's choice. As you fill in the blanks in this exercise, you will be applying the 4-S test and showing mastery of the writing skills it presents.

Exercise 5.10

1. Write down the subject that you or your instructor selected.

____

____

2. Test whether your subject is significant, single, specific, and supportable.
   - Significant
   - Single
   - Specific
   - Supportable

3. Using a prewriting approach to generate ideas, identify three to five main points in support of your subject.

____

____

____

____

____

4. Test whether your main points are all significant, distinct, and clearly related to the subject.
   - Significant
   - Distinct
   - Related to the subject

5. Arrange your main points in the order that is most likely to guarantee your readers' understanding of your subject, and circle your order type: chronological, climactic, logical, or random.

____

____

____

____

6. Rewrite your main points so that they are grammatically parallel: all single words, all phrases, or all clauses.

7. Combine your main idea with your points to produce a thesis statement.

The seven points listed in Exercise 5.10 summarize the steps to follow in planning an essay. Keep this outline handy and refer to it when you start your next paper or research report, or copy the short version in the following box:

Thesis Statement Process

1. Select a subject (or consider the one you were given).
2. Test whether your subject is significant, single, specific, and supportable.
3. Using some form of prewriting approach to generate ideas, identify three to five main points in support of your subject.
4. Test whether your main points are all significant, distinct, and clearly related to your subject.
5. Arrange your main points in the order that is most likely to guarantee your readers' understanding of your subject, and confirm your order type: chronological, climactic, logical, or random.
6. Rewrite your main points so that they are grammatically parallel: all single words, all phrases, or all clauses.
7. Combine your main idea with your points to produce a thesis statement.

Writing a More Advanced Thesis Statement

The thesis statement model presented above is a standard one with many benefits. Many papers for first-year students tend to be around four to six pages, and a thesis statement that includes three points will suit that style of writing. When it comes to longer papers, between 6 and 15 pages, for example, a more advanced type of thesis statement may be required by your instructor. In this case, your thesis likely won't include a list of topics that will be covered. Rather, your main point will be presented in terms of the persuasive argument that you will make in the paper, as clearly and as specifically as possible. Then, in the essay itself, it is assumed that you will cover all of the possible aspects and proofs involved in making your point.

Following are examples that point out the distinction between a thesis for a shorter and a longer paper on the same topic. One group of students was assigned a short paper on the topic of tattooing in the workplace. The other group was assigned a very similar topic, body art in the workplace, but that paper was to be 12 to 15 pages.

Here are two example thesis statements from the first group:

> The dangers of having too many tattoos in the workplace include putting off potential customers, ignoring posted dress rules and requirements, and making statements that might go against company ethics or morals.
>
> Tattoos in the workplace promote freedom of expression, equity, and the diversity of all people.

These thesis statements are extremely specific and they guide the reader toward exactly what to expect in the essay ahead.

For a longer essay, you also need to be extremely specific in the argument you present in the thesis statement, but without going into detail about all the specific points that will be made. Here are two more complex thesis statements that better suit a longer or more complicated paper.

> While economic and political claims about body art in the workplace are pervasive, social and cultural explanations for people who want to express themselves as they go about their lives are much more persuasive and should be taken into consideration by employers.
>
> While body art might be seen as a historical and cultural expression, we must consider the ethical and legal implications of going against company policies that restrict it.

Both of these more complex thesis statements have some indication of where the thesis will lead. The first example makes it clear that both economic and political claims against body art will be discussed alongside social and cultural claims. The thesis statement includes the main idea of the argument: that the author will be on the side of those who want to express themselves. In the second example, the author seems more concerned about the ethical and legal implications of not respecting company policies against body art. One strength of this thesis, and something that makes it more complex, is that it predicts the claims of its opponents—the idea of the historical and cultural significance—and yet still argues that the rights of the companies are important. Both viewpoints will be discussed, but the essay's main idea is in the clash between those two dimensions.

Putting the Thesis Elsewhere in Your Paper

Some advanced and highly experienced writers move their thesis around a bit. It may be found in the middle of their paper or even at the end. But these essays are usually written as part of longer works or form part of a professional writer's portfolio. As a beginning writer, you are best advised to start your paper with your controlling ideas up front. As with music, so it is usually with writing. Learning the basics comes first, and then as you gain experience you can get more abstract.

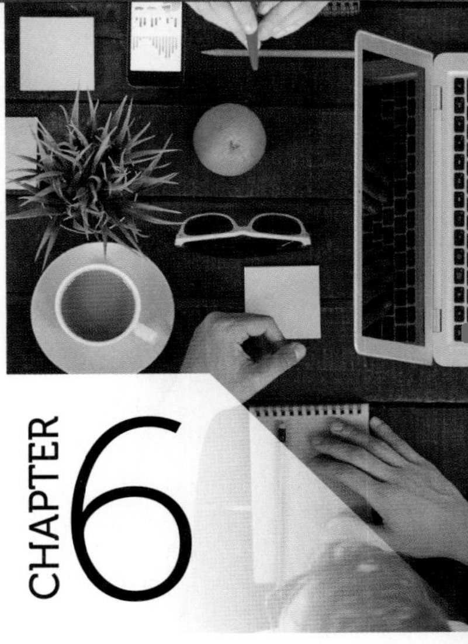

Writing an Outline

Preparing the Outline

For any work longer than about 400 words, writers need a plan or outline to guide them as they begin to build words into sentences, sentences into paragraphs, and paragraphs into the final product—whether it's a term paper, a research report, a business plan, or a market analysis.

Wise writers treat an outline as tentative, not as something chiselled in stone. As you draft your paper, you may discover new ideas or a new structure that better suits your purpose. If so, change your main points and outline to accommodate it. (It's a good idea to make these changes in pencil if working on paper or to use a feature such as Word's Track Changes if working on a computer, because you may decide at the end of the draft that these new ideas weren't so great after all.)

Your word-processing program will likely have an outline feature: try it out. These programs can be a great help to an inexperienced writer with little knowledge of how to plan a writing assignment.

As we have seen, all written messages consist of an introduction, a body, and a conclusion, but each of these may vary from one to several paragraphs in length and from simplified to sophisticated in style. The model format on the next page is an outline for a simple five-paragraph essay.

Once you've mastered this basic structure, you can modify, expand, and develop it to suit any of the kinds of writing you'll be called upon to do.

Writing a paper is like building a house: you save much time and frustration if you start with a plan.

Outline Format

Title ______________________

INTRODUCTION* ______________________

*Attention-getter** ______________________

____

____

*Thesis statement** Main idea consists of points 1, 2, and 3 (this was discussed in Chapter 5).

BODY Topic sentence introducing point 1 goes here.

Support for first point ______________________

____

____

____

____

Concluding sentence goes here.

Topic sentence introducing point 2 goes here.

Support for second point ______________________

____

____

____

____

Concluding sentence goes here.

Topic sentence introducing point 3 goes here.

Support for third point ______________________

____

____

____

____

Concluding sentence goes here.

CONCLUSION ______________________

Summary ______________________

____

*Memorable statement** ______________________

____

*Terms marked with an asterisk are explained and illustrated in Chapter 8.

The outline below follows the format on this page. The final version of "Ready, Willing … and Employable" appears after the outline. At this point, pay special attention to the body paragraphs.

Essay title	**Ready, Willing ... and Employable**
Attention-getter	What are employers looking for today?
Thesis statement	Employers are looking for a new breed of employee: one who has know-ledge, flexibility, and the right attitude.
1. Topic sentence	Knowledge is still first on the list.
Support for first point	• Colleges offer a broad range of programs to meet employers' needs. • Graduates must know current trends as well as theory. • Some employers test for knowledge. • Some rely on school's reputation plus recommendations of professors and recruiters.
2. Topic sentence	Adaptability is essential for a prospective employee.
Support for second point	• Today's jobs require multitasking. • Flexible workers are more cost-effective and better problem solvers. • Flexible workers can adapt to change. • Students need to broaden their education and learn a variety of skills.
3. Topic sentence	Employers complain about graduates' poor attitude.
Support for third point	• Graduates lack the ability to take direction, use team skills, communicate well, and motivate themselves. • Similar problems show up in class: —chronic lateness —lack of cooperation —laziness • Students need to correct these attitude problems on their own.
Summary of points	Students must be ready, able, and willing to work.
Memorable statement	With these skills, a good résumé, and professional contacts, graduates can enter the workforce with confidence.

READY, WILLING ... AND EMPLOYABLE

Attention-getter · *Thesis statement*

What are employers looking for in today's job market? Several recent surveys point to a subtle shift in the requirements of businesses looking to hire college and university graduates. Only a few years ago, knowledge was the prerequisite to employment in most industries. Employers needed workers with the highly specialized skills of an emerging high-tech workplace. Now many of those skills are taken for granted, and other characteristics have become increasingly important. Employers are seeking a new breed of employee:

(continued)

one who has the knowledge required to do the job, the flexibility to adapt, and—most important—the attitude to succeed.

Topic sentence

Support for first point

Concluding statement and transition

Knowledge of how to do the job is, understandably, still first on the shopping list that employers bring to job fairs. Colleges and universities across the country have responded to marketplace requirements with an array of programs designed to prepare students to meet the needs of industries from broadcasting to photonics, from microelectronics to winemaking. Graduates are expected to have up-to-the-minute information on current trends in their fields, as well as solid grounding in the theory and practice of their specialty. Some employers test applicants for this knowledge; others rely on the reputation of the institution, the recommendation of professors with whom they have professional connections, and the insights of recruiters. As valuable as knowledge is to the employer, however, an employee's flexibility is quickly becoming just as important.

Topic sentence

Support for second point

Concluding sentence

Transition to next paragraph

Multitasking is a buzzword often used to describe the ability to move quickly and easily between projects and work environments, bringing a wide range of skills to bear on a variety of situations. Adaptability is an essential characteristic of any prospective employee. Workers who can use their expertise simultaneously on several different tasks within a project are valuable not only because they are more cost-effective than several single-task specialists but also because they tend to see projects holistically and are better problem solvers as a result. In addition, flexible workers are those who most quickly and easily adapt to changes in technology or work practice, and such changes are a way of life in today's work environment. Students must prepare themselves to be flexible workers by broadening their education and by learning as many skills as possible. Unlike their grandparents, workers in the current generation have little hope of finding a job that will require only one skill set over the course of a career. Adaptability is a critical skill, but even when combined with knowledge, it is not enough to ensure employability. Increasingly, attitude is the determining factor in who gets hired—and promoted!

Topic sentence

Support for third point

Employers continually complain to colleges and universities that students on placement and graduates in their first position fail to impress, not from lack of knowledge, skill, or preparation but from a broad range of inadequacies best summed up as "poor attitude." Among the faults cited under this broad heading are inability to take direction, failure to work well with colleagues, inability to communicate effectively, and lack of enthusiasm and initiative. How can such problems be corrected before graduates reach the workplace? Schools do not offer courses in attitude adjustment, but perhaps they should. Most of these problems have surfaced in classes long before graduation. Students who are chronically late, frequently uncooperative, constantly complaining, or visibly lazy are those who, with all the skills and ability in the world, will not succeed in any job worth having. Even highly motivated and ambitious graduates have sometimes had difficulty adjusting to entry-level positions when they find themselves working under the supervision of people they consider to be less talented or skilled. It is up to students themselves to correct their attitudinal deficiencies. They need to pay attention to the criticisms of teachers, classmates, even family members, and make an honest evaluation of consistently noticed faults. Only when such attitude faults have been identified and acknowledged can they be corrected, and only when they have been corrected will the student be an asset to an employer.

Concluding sentence

As graduation draws near, most students view their coming transformation into workers with eagerness liberally mixed with anxiety. Statistics tell us that most college and university graduates find employment in their fields within a year of graduation. Armed with this encouraging information, together with a good résumé, professional contacts, and the knowledge, flexibility, and attitude to succeed, graduates can face employers and the workplace with confidence.

Summary and memorable statement

Exercise 6.1

Read Sam McNerney's "Is Creativity Sexy? The Evolutionary Advantages of Artistic Thinking" (pp. 302–304). Identify the sentences that correspond to the major structural items in the example outline on the next page. This essay uses a slight variation on the basic pattern (be careful identifying the "introduction" as just one paragraph—there may be more than one), so analyze each paragraph carefully. Let meaning be your guide. If you're working through this textbook in order, you may not have studied some of the terms mentioned, but you should be able to make a good guess at identifying the attention-getter, the thesis, and the memorable statement. To make your task easier, the sentences in the essay have been numbered.

After you have completed the task, compare your results with those of a classmate. Discuss any differences you discover and try to resolve them.

Example Outline

INTRODUCTION

Attention-getter	Sentence(s)	____________
Thesis statement	Sentence(s)	____________

BODY PARAGRAPH #1

Topic sentence	Sentence(s)	____________
Support for first point	Sentence(s)	____________
Conclusion	Sentence(s)	____________

BODY PARAGRAPH #2

Topic sentence	Sentence(s)	____________
Support for second point	Sentence(s)	____________
Conclusion	Sentence(s)	____________

BODY PARAGRAPH #3

Topic sentence	Sentence(s)	____________
Support for third point	Sentence(s)	____________
Conclusion	Sentence(s)	____________

CONCLUSION

Summary/Reinforcement	Sentence(s)	____________
Memorable statement	Sentence(s)	____________

So, you've learned how to identify points, how to test them for suitability, and how to arrange them in the most appropriate order. You're ready now to go on to the next step: drafting the actual paper.

Part 3

Drafting Your Work

Part 3 is composed of a fundamental set of chapters—some of the real essay essentials! Drafting your work, instead of just banging out one version and calling it done, is what separates the novices from the experts. An expert, whether it is at playing piano or writing a novel, must practise (or write) the same piece over a few times before it "sounds" right. This means getting to the basics of the essay—understanding its sections from paragraph to individual word—to make sure each part does indeed "sound" right before moving on.

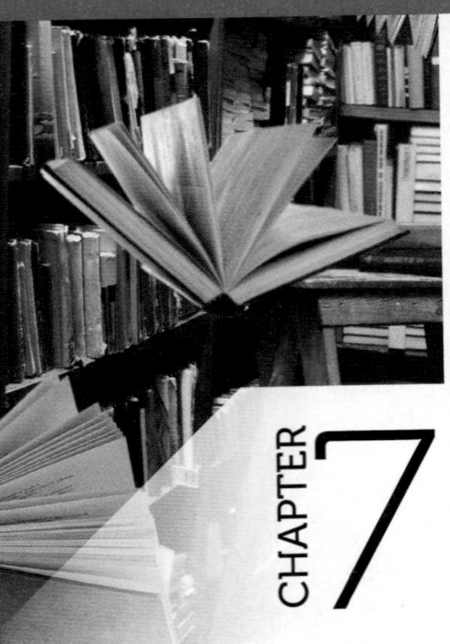

CHAPTER 7

Understanding the Paragraph

What Does a Paragraph Actually Look Like?

Essays are divided into paragraphs that work together to express coherent and unified ideas. **Paragraphs** themselves are sentence groups that are separated from each other in their physical presentation and in their content. They usually have an indentation at the beginning (on a typed page, the first word usually begins 1.25 cm from the left margin) and some white space at the end (the paragraph's last word is followed by what is called a *hard return*). So, between the indentation and the final period is the paragraph itself—a group of sentences that explain a single idea or topic.

If you were to draw a blueprint for a single paragraph, it would look like this:

A sentence that introduces the *topic* (or main idea) of the paragraph goes here.

Three or more sentences that specifically support or explain the topic go in here. { __________ __________ __________ __________ __________ }

A sentence that concludes your explanation of the topic (and may provide a transition to the next paragraph) goes here.

Consider the following sentence group. Is it an acceptable paragraph?

> [1]Scientists have discovered that eating blueberries and having friends are good for the memory and that pregnancy and smoking are bad for it. [2]Nautiluses can remember useful things, but only for a day, whereas cuttlefish, which are much more sophisticated [organisms] observe and form preferences for their future prey when they are still embryos. [3]Swiss biologists determined that stupid flies live longer than smart flies because intelligence wears out flies' brains, and Canadian researchers said that straining to recall information on the tip of the tongue makes us learn our mistaken guesses rather than the correct answers we eventually remember. [4]Strokes were found to generate depolarization waves that spread outward from the affected area and damage other parts of the

brain.... [5]Neuroscientists found that sloths sleep around nine and a half hours a day. [6]Previous research had studied only captive sloths, which sleep on average sixteen hours a day, possibly because they are bored and depressed.

Quotes found at the blog "Harper's Findings" by Jeff Giles, August 6, 2008.

The above passage looks like a paragraph: it is indented, contains six sentences, and leaves blank the space between the last word and the margin. But it is not a paragraph. It does not develop a single idea. There is no topic. True, all of the sentences in this passage are on the topic of the brain: memory, intelligence, and malfunction, but the sentences don't support any one idea. There is no development—they are not linked together in any logical way. In fact, you could rewrite this passage beginning with the last two sentences and working back to the first. It would make just as much (non)sense. Try it!

How Does a Paragraph Function?

A paragraph has three functions. The first one we have started to discuss already. Readers expect a paragraph to present a unit of thought, or a single, developed idea. But paragraphs also do two other things for your readers:

1. Paragraphs provide visual cues that make your writing "reader-friendly." Imagine how intimidating the page you are now reading would be if it were one continuous block of print: no headings, no indentations, no paragraphs. It would be easy to get lost both in the writer's ideas and on the page.

2. Paragraphs also divide your writing into linked but separate sections. Without paragraphs, ideas would blur and blend into one another. Readers would find it difficult to identify them, let alone follow the development of the writer's thinking.

In a typical essay, an introductory paragraph is followed by paragraphs that add details and depth to the ideas set out in the introduction. Your thesis, as we have discussed, often outlines, in order, the points you will be making in the paragraphs that follow. A concluding paragraph brings all the ideas together again and leaves the reader with a complete understanding of your thoughts about the topic.

Readers can tell a great deal about your thinking just by glancing at a page of your paper. A number of short paragraphs indicates a series of ideas, briefly (and perhaps superficially) explained. This might be useful in the workplace, where many ideas may need to be presented succinctly. Long paragraphs—half a page or longer—suggest complex ideas that require explanation and details. They signal serious thought but are more difficult to read because they require close attention.

Longer paragraphs often show up in reports or proposals that require more detailed explanations.

So, to summarize,

1. As a general rule, you explore one major idea or main point in each paragraph.
2. When you have finished exploring one topic and wish to move on to another, you signal this shift to your readers by beginning a new paragraph.

How Long Should a Paragraph Be?

I tend to basically exaggerate in life, and in writing, it's fine to exaggerate. I really enjoy overstating for the purpose of getting a laugh. For another thing, writing is easier than digging ditches. Well, actually, that's an exaggeration. It isn't.
—Theodor Geisel (a.k.a. Dr. Seuss)

The answer to this question depends on the topic, your readers' familiarity with it, and your purpose in writing. If your topic is complex, your readers' knowledge is limited, and your purpose is to persuade readers who do not share your point of view, then you'll probably need a fairly long paragraph to accomplish your goal. On the other hand, if you're writing about a topic your readers are familiar with, and your purpose is simply to share with them your understanding of that topic, you may be able to accomplish your task in a few sentences. In some cases, your instructor might set out parameters for how long a paragraph should be. If you are unsure, just ask. Assuming you have a topic sentence and a concluding sentence to your paragraph, along with three descriptive sentences in the middle, five sentences is an acceptable length. Alternatively, if your paragraph spans more than a page, you should step back and make sure you are covering only one topic in that paragraph. If there is more than one, break it up to avoid confusion.

Exercise 7.1 Individually, write a short paragraph (five to seven sentences) that demonstrates your understanding of paragraph form and function. Choose any topic you like. When you have finished, exchange papers with another student and check each other's paragraph for the following:

- form: Is there a clear introduction and conclusion for the topic in the paragraph?
- function: Does the paragraph develop the main idea or topic? Are all the sentences clearly related to the topic? Is the topic explained in enough detail to satisfy the reader's understanding?

Crafting the Topic Sentence

The **topic sentence** in each paragraph is the sentence that clearly identifies what the paragraph is about—its main idea. The topic sentence focuses the paragraph, helps to unify it, and keeps you and your readers on track. In professional writing, the topic sentence is not always the first sentence of the paragraph. Sometimes it is more effective to announce the topic in the second, third, or even the last sentence. But professional writers, through years of practice, have earned the right to break the rules. We discussed this with regard to thesis statements as well. Beginning writers should remember this: *most readers assume that the first sentence of a paragraph identifies the topic of that paragraph.* If your first sentence doesn't do this, then your readers may go through your paragraph assuming the topic is something other than what you intended. This is especially important to consider when it comes to business writing. Miscommunication frustrates readers and wastes their time.

To be absolutely clear, identify your topic up front.

A good topic sentence does three things:

1. It introduces the topic of the paragraph.
2. It makes a clear point about the topic that links to the thesis statement.
3. It makes a point that is neither too broad nor too narrow.

Readers appreciate writers who get to the point quickly, make the point clearly, and support or explain it adequately. They also appreciate writers who can make their points in an interesting way. Take the time to write topic sentences that are something more than straightforward, flat announcements of your main idea as it relates to your thesis. Compare the following pairs of topic sentences.

Weak	Strong
I am going to explain why I love blogs.	The strength of blogs is that they promote genuine democracy.
This paragraph is about violence.	Violence as a way of achieving racial justice is both impractical and immoral. (Martin Luther King, Jr.)

A good way to introduce the topic so that it is both interesting and effective is to make a point about it—pick a position, and link it to your thesis. You save your readers time and eliminate the risk of confusion if you make clear at the outset your idea about or your attitude toward your topic. Consider these examples:

Weak	Strong
Many people around the world like music.	Nothing bridges gaps between cultures like music.
Canadians are different from Americans.	Canadians should be thankful for their differences from Americans.

Finally, the topic you choose must be the "right size"—neither so broad that you cannot support it adequately in a single paragraph nor so narrow that it doesn't require support. The 4-S test that you used to determine whether a subject was suitable for a paper can also be applied to potential paragraph topics. If your topic is single, significant, specific, and supportable, it should also be the basis for a solid paragraph. Take a look at these topic sentences.

Weak	Strong
The legal system in Canada discriminates against men. (too broad)	Single fathers who seek custody of their children are often treated unfairly in family court.
My children won't eat peas, broccoli, or spinach. (too narrow)	Getting young children to eat a balanced diet is not an easy task.
Cars should be banned from city streets. (too broad)	Cars should be banned from the downtown core from 7:00 a.m. to 7:00 p.m.

Exercise 7.2* Read through each of the following paragraphs, and then underline the topic sentence.

1. The third consideration is perhaps the most important. Canada makes no economic sense. There may be excellent reasons for Canada's existence historically, socially, culturally, and even geographically, but the lines of trade and commerce flow north–south. If a government's chief concern is the economy, that government will naturally draw the country closer and closer to the United States, cinching in those belts of commerce that bind Canada to her southern partner. Only governments whose major goals are cultural or social will loosen the longitudinal ties and seek east–west bonds.

2. Seen by a scanning electron microscope, our taste buds look as huge as volcanoes on Mars, while those of a shark are beautiful mounds of pastel-colored tissue paper—until we remember what they're used for. In reality, taste buds are exceedingly small. Adults have about 10 000, grouped by theme (salt, sour, sweet, bitter), at various sites in the mouth. Inside each one, about fifty taste cells busily relay information to a neuron, which will alert the brain. Not much tasting happens in the center of the tongue, but there are also incidental taste buds on the palate, pharynx, and tonsils, which cling like bats to the damp, slimy walls of a cave. Rabbits have 17 000 taste buds, parrots only about 400, and cows 25 000. What are they tasting? Maybe a cow needs that many to enjoy a relentless diet of grass.

3. "Why do you want it?" This should be the first question a good computer salesperson asks a prospective customer. With the huge variety of computers now on the market, the determining factor in a purchase should be the job the machine will be expected to do. While an HDTV card, a premium audio system, and a 50-inch LCD screen are great for watching movies, a user who wants a basic word processor would be throwing away money to buy them. Home users and small businesses often get carried away with the desire for gigantic memory capacity, lightning speed, and high-resolution capability, but these are advertising gimmicks rather than useful purchases for most infrequent users. On the other hand, it can be a costly error for a buyer to underestimate long-term computer needs and buy a machine that must be upgraded or replaced in a year.

Now compare your answers with ours on page 462.

Exercise 7.3 Each of the following thesis statements contains a main idea and supplementary points. Working with a partner or in a small group, develop the supplementary points of each thesis statement into effective topic sentences that could go into paragraphs.

1. Volunteering is a valuable addition to a college or university education because it provides work experience, develops professional contacts, and enhances self-esteem.
2. Unemployment, poverty, and loneliness are factors that may lead to depression.

3. Canadians immigrate to other countries for three main reasons: a warmer climate, better job opportunities, and new cultural experiences.

Exercise 7.4

For each of the thesis statements below, develop the supplementary points into effective topic sentences. Make sure each topic sentence you write introduces the topic clearly, makes a point about the topic, and is neither too broad nor too narrow.

1. The driver who caused your accident last weekend was probably one of four types: a road hog, a tailgater, a speed demon, or a Sunday driver.
2. There are three types of supervisors in this world: the good, the bad, and mine.
3. The thought of moving to the country is attractive to many city dwellers because of the slower pace, the healthier environment, and the closer-knit communities.

Developing the Topic

Once you've written your topic sentence, the next step is to develop it. An adequately developed paragraph gives enough supporting information to make the topic completely clear to your assumed audience. Unless you are writing from a detailed outline listing all the supporting material you need, it's time to focus once again on that intended audience. Put yourself in your readers' place.

- How much information do your readers already have about your topic?
- Are they inclined to agree or disagree with you?
- What do your readers need to know to understand your point clearly?

There are seven ways to develop a topic. Not all will be appropriate in every case, and some will be more effective than others.

Let your topic, your writing purpose, and your audience guide you in choosing the most appropriate kind(s) of development.

The Seven Ways to Develop a Topic

1. Tell a story. Everyone loves to read a story—if it's relevant and well told. An **anecdote** can be an effective way to help your readers not only understand your idea but also remember it. Below are two examples that illustrate the use of narration to develop a topic.

Example 1:

I first experienced culture shock when I travelled to Egypt. I was walking down the main street on the day of my arrival when it suddenly struck me that the crowds on the street were stepping aside to make way for me. It was 1990, and my height, blond hair, and blue eyes were so unusual to the Egyptians that I was an object of intense curiosity. The staring and pointing followed me everywhere. Finally, unable to cope any longer with being constantly on display, I took refuge in the Canadian Embassy and spent a couple of hours quietly leafing through back issues of *Maclean's* magazine.

Example 2:

Imagine that two accountants do similar jobs for similar companies. One day they make the same discovery: with almost no chance of getting caught, they can embezzle a large sum from their employers. They can both use the money to pay off debts or buy a new car. The first accountant right away says to himself, "It's wrong to steal," and never considers the matter again. But the second accountant is torn. She, too, knows that stealing is wrong, but she's tempted and at first decides to go ahead. Then she decides she won't, and then that she will. Finally, after weeks of agonizing, she decides not to embezzle. Who is the morally better person?

Thomas Hurka. "Should Morality Be a Struggle? Ancient vs. Modern Ideas about Ethics" taken from *Principles: Short Essays about Ethics*. Toronto: Harcourt Brace, 1994, 83.

Exercise 7.5 Using the concept of narration to develop your topic, write a paragraph on one of the following or a topic of your own choosing.

1. A road-rage experience
2. The day I became an adult
3. The customer is not always right
4. How not to treat fellow students
5. Defusing a tense situation

2. Define your topic. The definition paragraph explains and clarifies the meaning of a word or idea. Use a definition paragraph to explain a term that may be unfamiliar to your readers. (Write your own definition please. Quoting from a dictionary is not the most innovative way to start a paragraph.) Below are definitions of two terms that the authors wanted to be sure their readers would understand from the *writers'* point of view.

Term 1:

Culture shock is the inability to understand or cope with experiences one has never encountered before. It commonly affects travellers who journey to lands whose climate, food, language, and customs are alien to the traveller. In addition to confusion and anxiety, culture shock may produce physical symptoms such as chills, fever, trembling, and faintness.

Term 2:

A hybrid is a cross between two established varieties of plant, animal, … or technology. The hybrid bicycle, for example, combines the features of a road bike with those of an off-road bike to produce a comfortable and efficient bicycle for short-distance cycling. For most people today, the word "hybrid" signifies a fuel-efficient, low-emission automobile. Hybrid car technology combines a gasoline or diesel internal combustion engine with a battery-powered electric motor. Its objective is to maximize the best properties of both the gas engine and the electric motor.

"The Gas–Electric Hybrid Demystified." Sara R. Howerth. Reprinted by permission of the author.

You should include a definition, too, if you're using a familiar term in an unusual way. Here Martin Luther King defines what he means by "the length of life":

> Now let us notice first the length of life.... [T]his is the dimension of life in which the individual is concerned with developing his inner powers. It is that dimension of life in which the individual pursues personal ends and ambitions. This is perhaps the selfish dimension of life, and there is such a thing as moral and rational self-interest. If one is not concerned about himself he cannot be totally concerned about other selves.

Martin Luther King, Jr. "The Dimensions of a Complete Life," taken from *The Measure of a Man*, 1959. Philadelphia, Pilgrim Press, 1969.

Using a definition as a hinge point for your topic can either clarify points for readers or get them to consider your topic in a new light, useful outcomes when you are trying to be both informative and persuasive in your writing.

Exercise 7.6

Choose one of the following topics (or select one of your own) and write a paragraph in which you develop the topic by defining it.

1. Stress
2. A good boss (employee, customer, colleague)
3. An extravert (introvert)
4. A great artist (musician, actor, writer, etc.)
5. A bad habit

3. Use examples. Providing examples is probably the most common method of developing an idea and supporting a statement. Readers can become confused or suspicious when they read unsupported statements of "fact," opinion, or ideas. One of the best ways to support your topic is by providing clear, relevant examples that either are personal or are found in other research.

Sometimes, as in the paragraph below, one extended example is enough to allow your readers to see clearly what you mean.

> Culture shock can affect anyone, even a person who never leaves home. My grandfather was perfectly content to be an accountant until he retired and was confident that his company would need his services for the foreseeable future. Computers were "silly toys," and

modern business practices just "jargon" and "a new fad." When he was laid off four years before his scheduled retirement, he went into shock. It wasn't just the layoff; it was the speed of change—the idea that he was stranded in a new and unfamiliar culture for which he was unprepared and in which he had no useful role.

Sometimes a number of examples may be necessary to develop a point, as in this paragraph.

Flynn also credits university—particularly its flexibility—for helping him discover what motivates him to get out of bed in the morning. He started in computer science at Memorial University, but found that it was "just too tedious," so he switched to English. That didn't suit him either. Luckily, his geography 101 elective helped him uncover his passion. "The way everything works together, like land forms and weather systems, just clicked for me," he says, remembering that first class. A college program straight out of high school wouldn't have allowed so much exploration. It was also in that geography seminar that he first seriously considered the balance between humankind and nature. He credits one seminar where the class explored the question, "Should we really kill a bear just because it comes into our community?" for setting him on the path to his career.

Excerpt from Josh Dehaas, "The College Advantage," *Maclean's*, March 3, 2011. Used with permission of Rogers Media Inc.

Exercise 7.7 Using examples to develop your topic, write a paragraph on one of following, or choose a topic of your own.

1. Addiction to *Facebook* (*Tumblr*, smartphones, *Twitter*)
2. Parents and privacy
3. Television: life's biggest time-waster
4. Childless by choice
5. The incompetence (incomprehensibility) of men (women)

4. Use a quotation or paraphrase. Occasionally you will find that someone else—an expert in a particular field, a well-known author, or a respected public figure—has said what you want to say better than you could ever hope to say it. Relevant and authoritative quotations, as long as they are kept short and are not used too frequently, are useful in developing your topic. Two sources of quotations on practically any subject are *John Robert Colombo's Famous Lasting Words: Great Canadian Quotations* (Douglas & McIntyre, 2000) and *Bartlett's Familiar Quotations* (Bartleby.com, 2000).

In the paragraph below, the writer introduces his topic with a thought-provoking quotation.

"Although one can experience real pain from culture shock, it is also an opportunity for redefining one's life objectives. Culture shock can make one develop a better understanding of oneself and stimulate personal creativity." As with any experience that forces us out of our comfort zone and shatters our complacency, culture shock can be an opportunity for growth and development, as this quotation from Dr. V. Patel, dean of the faculty of education at San Diego State University, makes clear. The trick is to recognize this unpleasant experience as a starting point for personal change. Here's an opportunity to re-examine our preconceptions about our place in society, about our interactions with others, even about the path we have chosen to take in life: has it become a rut?

A **paraphrase** is a summary in your own words of someone else's idea. Remember to indicate whose idea you are paraphrasing, the way the author does in the following paragraph.

In society today, various solutions and strategies abound for those who are deemed fat. From the dietary perfection of the ancient Greeks, to the ability of the French to eat fat and remain thin, to the carnivorous habits of the Paleolithic peoples, where there is a history of "thinness," there is a fad diet waiting to be touted as the solution to "fatness." In *Hunger*, by Roxane Gay, she writes that it is each person's individual story that defines their eating, and that being fat shouldn't necessarily be the subject of public shaming. For those who are overweight, in fact, their story often becomes subject matter for all those who aren't, who choose to offer up alternative ways of being (French, Mediterranean, etc.) as though they could rewrite a person's experience of hunger, food, and personal history. Gay offers another way of thinking about hunger that is meant to open up much needed conversations about the role of fatness and its repercussions in our society.

Exercise 7.8

Choose one of the following five topics (or select one of your own) and write a paragraph in which you develop the topic by using quotations, paraphrases, or both.

1. Canada's best author
2. My favourite stand-up comic
3. The best movie of the year
4. The wisdom of children
5. A songwriter whose lyrics move me

---

5. Use a comparison. A comparison shows similarities between things; it shows how two different things are alike in a particular way or ways. If you have a difficult or abstract topic to explain, try comparing it to something that is familiar to your readers, as this writer does.

Being left on your own in a foreign land is a bit like being forced to play a card game when you're the only one who doesn't know the rules. As the stakes get higher and the other players' excitement and enjoyment increase, you get correspondingly more frustrated and miserable. Finally, in desperation, you want to throw your cards on the table, absorb your losses, and go home.

In this next paragraph, the writer uses an **analogy**—an extended comparison—between a date and a car to make her point both clear and interesting.

> The economy-model date features cramped conditions and a lack of power. The econo-date thinks that his personality can make up for the fact that you never go anywhere that costs money and never do anything except go on walks. He tends to be shy, quiet, and about as much fun as an oil leak. It's not that he doesn't have money to spend; it's that he doesn't use any imagination or creativity to compensate for his lack of cash.

Exercise 7.9 Choose one of the following topics (or select one of your own) and write a paragraph in which you develop the topic by using comparison.

1. Being self-employed
2. A horrible class
3. Two consumer products
4. Canadians
5. Engineering (or computer science, arts, or nursing) students

---

6. Explain steps or stages in a process. Sometimes the most effective way to develop the main idea of your paragraph is by explaining how something occurs or is done—that is, by relating the series of steps involved. Make sure you break down the process into its component parts and detail the steps logically and precisely.

> The first sign of culture shock is usually anxiety. The traveller feels uncomfortable and ill at ease; nothing looks, smells, sounds, or tastes familiar. Next, he may become resentful, even angry, and withdraw from his new surroundings, seeking isolation in safe, familiar territory–his room. Unfortunately, solitude reinforces anxiety and makes the situation worse. Over time, the victim of culture shock may begin to perceive the environment not as strange and hostile but as neutral. Friendly interaction with others and positive experiences in the new culture are the cure, but one is not likely to encounter either while cocooned in a small boarding house or hotel room. Fortunately, most travellers find that culture shock diminishes with rest. As anxiety lessens, curiosity grows, and they begin to venture out to participate in the life of the new country. In extreme cases, however, travellers suffering from culture shock can develop flu-like symptoms: fever, chills, sleeplessness, and a debilitating loss of energy. When these symptoms strike, it's time to call home for moral support and

encouragement to get out and enjoy the sights and scenes one has travelled so far to experience.

In writing a process paragraph, you need to pay particular attention to transitions. If you don't, you'll leave your readers gasping in the dust as you gallop through your explanation. The paragraph below illustrates a simple yet effective use of transitions.

In 1983, a Harvard Medical School team led by Dr. Howard Green found a revolutionary way to repair burned skin. Here is how it is done. Doctors cut up a small patch of skin donated by a patient, treat it with enzymes, then spread it thinly onto a culture medium. After only ten days, colonies of skin cells begin linking up into sheets, which can then be chopped up and used to make further sheets. In twenty-four days, enough skin will be produced to cover an entire human body. About ten days later, the gauze is removed, and the skin soon grows into a surface much smoother and more natural-looking than the rough one a normal skin-graft usually leaves.

Exercise 7.10

Choose one of the following topics (or select one of your own) and write a paragraph in which you develop the topic by describing the series of steps or stages involved in the process.

1. Buying a used car
2. Teaching a 16-year-old to drive
3. Learning to live with a roommate
4. Persuading parents to send more money
5. Getting out of debt

7. Provide specific details. Concrete, specific, descriptive details can be an effective way to develop your main idea. In the following paragraph, the writer uses specific details to describe treatment for culture shock.

Culture shock can be alleviated by taking action to reduce the impact of the cause and then treating each of the symptoms separately. Prevention is the best cure: introduce yourself gradually to a new environment. Explore in small stages, while keeping contact with safe and familiar surroundings. Don't plunge into the bazaar within an hour of your arrival in Marrakesh, but begin your exploration in the Western quarter and gradually expose yourself to the sights, sounds, and smells of areas that seem threateningly foreign. If you should come down with symptoms of shock, go to bed, stay warm, drink lots of bottled water, and sleep as much as you can. When you begin to feel better, take things slowly and avoid stressful situations where you have to make decisions or confront the unexpected. A guided bus tour of the city is a good way to begin familiarizing yourself with a new physical and cultural environment and to discover what's available that you want to explore.

Be very sure that your facts are correct and that your statistics are current.

In some paragraphs, numerical facts or statistics can be used to support your point effectively. However, in keeping with Benjamin Disraeli's immortal comment ("There are three kinds of lies: lies, damned lies, and statistics"), critical readers tend to be suspicious of statistics. Always make sure when you are using specific details such as quotations or facts directly from a source that you document them properly. Chapter 17 will start you off on that process.

Canadians are great travellers. Not only do we travel around our own country, exploring every nook and cranny from Beaver Creek in the Yukon territory to Bay Bulls in Newfoundland, but we also can be found touring around every other country on earth. Statistics Canada (2010) reports that we take more than 271 million overnight trips a year within our own borders. Abroad, we favour our next-door neighbour by a wide margin above other destinations, averaging around 16 million overnight trips a year to the United States (Statistics Canada 2008). Mexico is our second-favourite destination, with over 841 000 visits, followed by the United Kingdom (778 000) and France (645 000). Of the Caribbean Islands, Cuba is our favourite winter escape, ranking fifth overall, with about 350 000 visits a year by Canadians. China (including Hong Kong) ranks ninth in popularity with 400 000 visits by Canadians, just behind the Dominican Republic and ahead of Germany and Italy. Canadians' top 15 travel destinations are rounded out by more European nations: the Netherlands, Spain, Switzerland, Ireland, and Austria. We can make a rough estimate from these figures that, on average, Canadians travel five times a year within Canada, and outside of Canada, twice in three years.

Exercise 7.11 Using specific details to develop your topic, write a paragraph on one of following, or choose a topic of your own.

1. A Web page
2. A migraine headache
3. The myth of the shorter workweek
4. The best team in basketball (baseball, football, soccer, lacrosse)
5. Money can't buy happiness

When writing your own paragraphs, you will often need to use more than one method of development to explain your point. The seven methods described in this chapter can be used in any combination you choose. You will choose the most effective combination by keeping in mind the main purpose of your essay (to inform, convince, or entertain), your thesis, and your reader. We will talk more about types of paragraphs in Part 4.

How Do You End a Paragraph?

A good paragraph doesn't just end; like a door, it should close firmly, with a "click." Finish your paragraph with a statement that serves either as a *clincher*—an unmistakable and appropriate conclusion—or a *transition* to the new idea that will be developed in the next paragraph.

Exercise 7.12

Choose one of the readings from Part 8 and find three paragraphs to analyze. How does each paragraph end—with a clincher or with a transition sentence? Be prepared to defend your answer.

Exercise 7.13

To stretch your imagination and improve your mastery of the kinds of support you can choose from to develop a topic, write a paragraph on one of the following topics, using two or more methods of development. Your target audience is your classmates.

1. Getting along with co-workers
2. Performance appraisal
3. Training a new pet
4. Life is like a game of ________________
5. Canadians don't appreciate how lucky they are

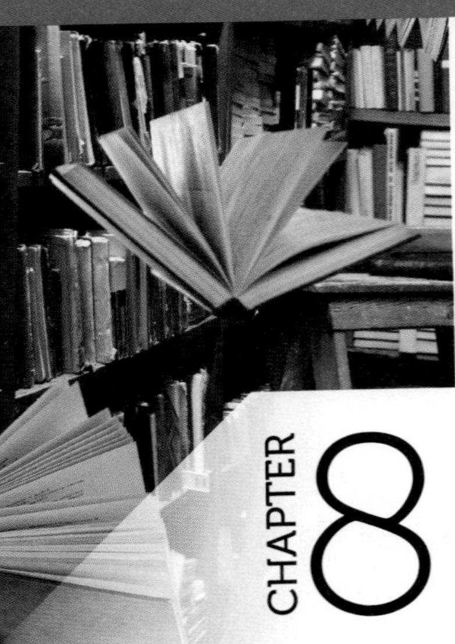

CHAPTER 8

Writing Introductions and Conclusions

It is best to ask your professor or instructor if there are any requirements for introducing or concluding your essay.

Two paragraphs of your paper—the first and the last—serve special functions and deserve special care. Many writers wait until after they have worked through a draft or two of the body of an essay before tackling these two critical paragraphs. There are a few ways to construct introductions and conclusions.

To introduce and conclude your subject effectively, you need to know what main ideas your paper explores and how these ideas are arranged and developed. Only then can you integrate the beginning and the ending of your essay into the whole. That is why this discussion comes after the chapters about development of the main points and how they are presented. If you were to write the paper from start to finish and change your mind about your ideas in the process, you would have to spend more time and effort going back to change the introduction. On the flip side, you don't want to be ruled by an introduction that doesn't make sense if your research presents evidence to the contrary. This is why, during timed in-class writing tests, it is usually better to write the body of your paper and leave room to write your introduction later. Once you have written that, you can finish with a conclusion that ties everything together nicely.

All too often, the introduction and the conclusion of a paper are clumsy and detract from the paper's effectiveness. By *effectiveness*, we mean your readers' ability to understand your purpose and plan for your paper and your ultimate conclusions. In the workplace, writing an effective introduction is especially important. It makes no sense to write four paragraphs about how much work you have done and then only in your conclusion ask for money to go to a conference. Even if the body of your paper would help your boss decide that you should go, while she was reading it, she wouldn't have known that was your argument's purpose! In this chapter, we present how to avoid ineffective introductions and write ones that are clear and audience-focused.

The Introductory Paragraph

The introduction is worth special attention because that's where your readers either sit up and take notice of your paper or sigh and move on to something else. Think about a cover letter for your résumé. You certainly would hope that the reader would move all the way through it—and with a punchy introduction, you have a much better chance that this will happen.

> There are two parts to an introductory paragraph:
> 1. an attention-getter
> 2. a thesis statement

Depending on the needs of your reader, sometimes a third section is needed to provide background to the situation or discussion that you are presenting. Consider this: you are suggesting a budget that would require a major change in your company's operations. You certainly would get your boss's attention by saying big changes are needed, but you might want to first include a line or two that present some background information.

Getting and Holding Your Readers' Attention

Your readers must be engaged with your thesis or there's no point in putting pen to paper or fingers to keyboard. If your paper is just your thoughts expressed and nothing else, you haven't done your job. An **attention-getter**, which is designed to get your reader interested in what you have to say, starts the communication off right, but it must be appropriate to the content of your essay and cater to your intended readers. If your audience is known to take a solemn approach to life and your topic is serious (environmental ethics, for instance, or equal-opportunity policies in the workplace), there is no point in leading off with a pun or joke, no matter how witty. Such an opening would be inappropriate and possibly offensive to your readers. On the other hand, if you are arguing that all employees deserve a vacation, it might be appropriate to set a more casual tone up front. When it comes to writing an effective attention-getter, it is the audience who rules. In an academic paper, the introduction is where you set the tone and where you provide background to your topic. Remember that an academic audience not only is interested in your ideas but also wants to have a sense that you know how to take your topic seriously and with due consideration.

The very definition of *communication* implies that at least two parties take part.

Your attention-getter does not have to be a single sentence; in fact, good ones are often several sentences long. Your readers will be committing varying amounts of their time to reading your writing. Let the parameters of the assignment guide you in determining how much time to spend opening up the dialogue. You owe it to the audience to make your opening sentences clear, interesting, and creative. Achieving this is easier once you have come up with your main points.

An effective attention-getter should be followed by an equally effective thesis statement—one that slides smoothly and easily into place. Following the order suggested in this textbook makes this task easier because, at this point, you already have a sense of the route your paper will take, so "packing your bags" in the form of an introduction isn't much of a challenge. Your readers should be aware only of a unified paragraph, not of two separate parts in your introduction.

Below are eight different kinds of openings you can choose from to get your readers' attention and lead up to your thesis statement. In each of the example paragraphs, note how the attention-getter and the thesis statement are solidly linked to form a unified whole. To demonstrate that you can take many different approaches to a subject, depending on your purpose and your audience, we have used the same subject—opinions on physical fitness—in all of the introductions. The thesis in each is bolded.

1. Spell Out the Significance of Your Subject

If your subject's significance can spark your readers' interest, they will want to know more about it, especially if it is a subject that affects them directly.

More and more young people are dying of heart disease. Despite the statistics that say most people in our society are living longer thanks to advances in medicine and surgery, the figures can be misleading. It is a fact that people in their thirties and forties are dying from coronary problems that once threatened people in their fifties and sixties. What has caused this change? Certainly, the increase in stress, the fatigue of overwork, the rise in obesity, and the decline in physical activity are all contributing factors. To combat the risk of cardiovascular disease, we need physical activity. **Regular exercise can forestall the ravages of heart disease and promote longevity.**

2. Begin with a Well-Phrased Quotation

You might choose a famous statement, a popular slogan, or a common saying. Use a quotation when it sums up your point of view more succinctly and effectively than your own words could. As a rule, you should identify the source of the quotation.

"Who can be bothered?" "I'm much too busy." "I get all the exercise I need at the office." We've all heard excuses like these, excuses for avoiding regular exercise. Modern life, with its distractions and conveniences, tends to make people sedentary and lazy, but the human organism cannot tolerate inactivity and stress indefinitely. Eventually, it begins to break down. Those who want to keep in shape for the challenges of modern life should consider the benefits of working out a few times a week. **Regular exercise can rejuvenate the body, refresh the mind, and improve self-confidence.**

3. Begin with a Generalization Related to Your Subject

Generalizations can be useful for suggesting the context and scope of your subject. Generalizations are often a part of academic introductions because of their ability to summarize background information and give a basic overview of the topic or subject at hand. They must, however, be narrowed down carefully to a focused thesis statement.

Until the 20th century, physical exercise was part of the normal workday. Our ancestors were farmers, pioneers, sailors, and so on. Few of our parents, however, made a living by ploughing the land or chopping down trees. Since the early 1900s, the trend in work has been away from physical exertion and toward automation. Today's generation uses technology to reduce physical activity even further: they pick up the phone, ride the elevator, and take the car to the corner store. Modern inactivity has negative consequences that only physical exercise can counter. **To sustain good health, sharpen your mental edge, and have fun, you should take up aerobics or sports and use your body in the way it was intended—actively.**

4. Ask a Question or Two

Questions are often an effective way to encourage interest because your readers will find themselves thinking of answers. Some questions are rhetorical; that is, they will not have specific answers. Others might be answered in your essay.

> Have you been feeling sluggish and exhausted lately? Has your blood pressure increased along with your waistline in the past few years? Are you stalled in front of the television set every night with potato chips and a beer? If so, you are probably suffering from a common middle-aged ailment called *flabitis*. This malady strikes most people over 30: they put on weight, have trouble concentrating, tire easily, and prefer watching sports to participating in them. Fortunately, there is a cure for flabitis: a three-times-weekly dose of exercise. **With regular exercise, you can rejuvenate your body, refresh your mind, and improve your self-confidence.**

5. Use a Startling Statement

Sometimes a surprising remark (not an insult or a false exaggeration) is effective in getting readers' attention. A little-known or striking fact will have the same effect.

> After the age of 30, the average North American puts on 10 to 20 kilograms of fat. Presumably, the cause for this startling increase in avoirdupois is a combination of metabolic changes, decreased physical activity, and hundreds of kilos of junk food ingested since childhood. It's difficult to stop the spread of middle-aged corpulence, but experts tell us we *can* resist the rise in flab by reducing our caloric intake and increasing our physical activity. **Regular exercise can rejuvenate the body, refresh the mind, and improve self-confidence.**

6. Challenge a Common Opinion

Perhaps your readers have also doubted a popular belief. Your thesis statement can assert that an opinion is false, and the body of your paper can contain evidence to support your opposing view.

> Physical activity is for kids. Adults don't have time to hit a baseball or run around a field chasing after one or to do aerobics and lift weights in a gym. They have to earn a living, raise families, and save money for retirement. They can leave exercise to their children. I firmly believed this until one morning when, late for work, I ran after a bus. My heart pounded, my lungs gasped, my head swam. It had been some years since my last stint of exercise, and I realized I wouldn't be around to do my job, support my family, or enjoy retirement unless I got into the habit of doing something physical to maintain my health. **Regular exercise can rejuvenate the body, refresh the mind, and broaden one's interests.**

7. Begin with a Definition

A definition is a good way to begin if you are introducing a key term that you suspect may be unfamiliar to your readers. It can be useful in an academic essay where you need to develop a complicated topic, or in a report that is meant to educate people on specific concepts they may never have considered. If the subject of your essay depends on a personal meaning of a term that most people understand in a different way, a definition is essential.

> Myocardial infarction—the very term is ambiguous. It occurs when a person's muscles slacken from disuse, the veins clog up with sticky fats, and the heart has to work too hard to sustain even minor exertion such as raking leaves or shovelling snow. The muscles of the heart become strained to exhaustion or balloon outward because the veins cannot pass blood quickly enough. In plain English, a myocardial infarction is a heart attack. **If the victim is lucky enough to survive, physicians prescribe a regimen of less stress, low fat intake, and regular exercise.**

8. Describe an Interesting Incident or Tell an Anecdote Related to Your Subject

Readers like stories. Keep yours short and to the point by narrating only the highlights. The incident or anecdote you select might be a story from the media, an event involving family or friends, or a personal experience.

> Last year, I got a free invitation in the mail to a fitness club. I responded, out of curiosity, but I needed to be convinced. After all, I was 35, had grown a little paunch, and was a bit short of breath on the stairs; 10 years had passed since I had last played sports. My first workout was a nightmare. My joints ached, my muscles throbbed, and my head spun. I was in worse shape than I had thought. After a few weeks, those symptoms disappeared, and I began to enjoy myself. My paunch vanished and my muscles toned up. My capacity for concentration increased. Also, I met some new people who have become friends. **Obviously, 10 years is too long between workouts, given that exercise not only rejuvenates the body and refreshes the mind but also improves one's social life.**

Exercise 8.1 In small groups (four or five people), discuss five movies you have all seen within the past year. How did each of these movies begin so that the audience was "locked in"? How do these movie "grabbers" relate to the kinds of attention-getters you have just read?

Exercise 8.2 Each of the following paragraphs is the introductory paragraph of an essay. Work in pairs and, using the strategy given in parentheses, write an appropriate attention-getter of at least one sentence for each paragraph.

1. (Significance of subject) ____________________

____

TV commercials that portray unrealistic and unattainable lifestyles should be banned. Although I do not support censorship, I believe there is sufficient evidence of the damage done by these advertisements to justify eliminating them in the name of public interest. The objectionable commercials promote sexual stereotyping, set up unrealistic and dangerous expectations, and encourage irresponsible consumerism.

2. (Quotation) ____________________

____

Every sport has its strange expressions, just as every sport has its devoted fans, its famous teams, and its legendary heroes. A sport that gets very little attention in Canada but is very popular in many parts of the world, especially Commonwealth countries, is cricket. Like the sports that millions of Canadians follow enthusiastically, cricket is an exciting and fascinating game once you become familiar with its rules and style. In fact, it compares very favourably with baseball in skill, pace, and strategy.

3. (Generalization) ____________________

____

My first project manager was the sort of person that nightmares are made of. It's been a year since she was finally transferred to another department, but I still shudder when I recall our six months together. Denise was rude, bossy, and, worst of all, thoughtless.

4. (Question) ____________________

____

Arranged marriages are a very important part of my culture. When my family moved to Canada, we left behind many of the traditions and customs that were as natural to us as breathing. However, my parents retained their right to choose a wife for me, even though they are aware that this custom is at odds with the Canadian way of life. Although their decision was at first difficult to accept, I believe there are good reasons that an arranged marriage may be best for me. The decision will be made by mature people in a thoughtful manner, uninfluenced by the enthusiasms of youth; the decision will be made by people who have at heart the best interests of our family, the bride's family, and me; and the decision will be made in accordance with a centuries-old tradition that has proven its success generation after generation.

5. (Startling statement) ____

____

Canadian roads are overrun by drivers who are a danger to themselves, their passengers, and others on the road. Inept drivers demonstrate their inadequacies in so many ways that it would be impossible to list them all in one short paper. Nevertheless, bad drivers can be broadly categorized as texting turtles, careening cowboys, and daydreaming dodos.

6. (Opinion you challenge) ____

____

There's really no reason to retain the Canadian dollar. We are so closely tied to the U.S. economy that independence is an illusion. If the French could give up the franc, the Italians abandon the lira, and the Germans say *auf Wiedersehen* to the mark in favour of the efficiency, convenience, and savings of a common currency, then we ought to follow their lead and adopt the American dollar.

7. (Definition) ____

____

Most people have a hobby of some kind, although not everyone knows it. While traditional hobbies like collecting stamps or building models or arranging flowers are easily identified, other activities may not be thought of as hobbies. Collecting tattoos or watching a game in every major league arena or researching your family tree can all be considered hobbies. As long as you aren't being paid, enjoy the activity, and do it regularly, you are benefiting from a hobby.

8. (Anecdote or incident) ____

____

Blackflies are just one of the pests that make life less than comfortable in Canada during the spring, but they tend to be the most irritating. No method of combating the pests is foolproof, but there are several methods that can be employed, either singly or together, to repel most of them. The campaign against the blackfly begins with protective clothing, follows up with an effective repellent, and goes over the top with the secret weapon: garlic.

Exercise 8.3

With the class divided into four or five teams, consider the following essay topics. Each team will take one of the topics and develop the first sentence of an introductory paragraph for it. The sentence will then be passed in sequence to the next group, who will add a sentence to the paragraph. Continue this exercise until each paragraph contains both an attention-getter and a thesis statement. When each team gets back the paragraph it initiated, it will revise and polish the paragraph, identify the kind of attention-getter that has been developed, and underline the thesis statement. Share the results with the rest of the class. (Keep these paragraphs; you will need them in the next section of the chapter!)

1. Why I want to be a _______________ (fill in your career choice)
2. Why I chose _______________ (fill in your school)
3. How not to treat a co-worker (customer, classmate)
4. My favourite online game or phone app
5. The trouble with roommates (parents, teachers, etc.)

The Concluding Paragraph

Like the introduction, the conclusion of your paper has a special form. Think of your favourite television sitcom. The last section of the show, sometimes only a few minutes long, wraps up the plot, explains any details that might still be unresolved, and leaves you with a satisfying sense that all is well, at least until next week. A concluding paragraph works in a similar way.

Contrary to what some believe, a conclusion doesn't simply restate the main points of the paper. That is only a starting point.

The last paragraph of your paper has two functions:

1. It summarizes or reinforces the main points of your paper.
2. It ends with an appropriate statement, question, or request for action.

Your **summary statement** should be as concise as you can make it and must be phrased in such a way that it does not repeat word for word the portion of your thesis statement that identifies the main points. (Note that a summary statement is not needed in a very short essay.) A summary statement is meant to leave a sense of what the reader has just digested in an easy-to-remember form. If you are trying to convince your reader of something, the summary statement provides the final push toward accepting your opinion.

A memorable statement, question, or request for action is a sentence designed to leave your readers feeling satisfied with your essay and perhaps taking away with them something for further thought. Never end without a "clincher." Don't just quit writing when your main points are covered or you'll leave your readers hanging, wondering what to make of it all. Instead, consider the end of your paper as a valuable opportunity to "have the last word," or, alternatively, to open up further dialogue. This is especially useful in writing courses that have you read and respond to historical or controversial texts. Your opinions matter—update your reader with your own ideas on how things should change.

Six strategies for writing a concluding paragraph are listed below. Each strategy is illustrated by an example paragraph. As with the Introductions section, we have chosen one topic here—plagiarism—to follow through all of the suggestions. As you are reading, try to identify the summary and the memorable statement in each conclusion.

1. End with a Relevant or Thought-Provoking Quotation

You can use this type of ending in two ways:

1. to repeat an earlier quotation but give it a new meaning
2. to place your subject in a larger context by supplying a new quotation from a recognized authority in the field

> The idea that "cheaters never prosper" is certainly true when it comes to plagiarizing. Lost jobs, being found out, and careers coming to an abrupt end—that's just the beginning. The only ones prospering, those who run the essay mills, have a moral and ethical responsibility to stop what they are doing and to force students to learn the hard way: by getting their work done and by doing it fairly and equitably.

2. Offer a Solution to a Problem Discussed in Your Paper

You can plan an organization for your paper that will allow you to resolve a problem or neutralize negative consequences in your conclusion. This allows you to be persuasive or to make a point that you believe is valid.

> Having a full-time job and going to school full time makes the easy solutions offered by essay mills extremely attractive. Undetectable

by plagiarism software, these stellar essays written by credentialled employees seem like a dream, but they are a nightmare. For students who use them, they make school seem like a joke. For students who don't use them but have friends who do, they seem unfair. People, especially students, need to speak up about the dangers of essay mills. Perhaps if they hear it from the person who is sitting beside them trying to do the work on their own it will have the desired impact.

3. End with One or More Relevant or Thought-Provoking Questions

The advantage of clinching your paper with a question is that readers automatically tend to pause and consider it: questions stimulate thought. Before they know it, readers will begin to formulate answers to your question—and that activity will make them remember your points and possibly open up further dialogue. Be sure, though, that your question relates directly to your subject.

My educational career has improved significantly since I stopped considering plagiarizing. I no longer listen jealously as people laugh about the easy A's they receive in difficult courses. Now I know that I am learning and that I am becoming a wiser person. As I inch closer to graduation, I wonder how my next employer will feel about my strong sense of morals and ethics, and my attitude toward education.

4. Point Out the Value or Significance of Your Subject to Your Readers

If you emphasize your subject matter at the end of your paper, you can stamp its importance on your readers' memory.

Writing is power and has the ability to shape and change lives.

Learning exactly what plagiarism is and how essay mills work is important for students and for their families. It is also important for employers to understand and to think about how important good communication skills are for their employees. If everyone valued and shared their appreciation for good writing skills, perhaps people wouldn't be trying to cut corners in the first place.

5. Make a Connection to a Statement Made in Your Introduction

This strategy provides your readers with a sense of closure. They will recall your earlier statement and feel satisfied that the loose ends have been tied up. This is especially useful in a narrative paper where you are telling a story in order to make a point.

Having taken a course in what plagiarism is as well as researching famous Canadian examples of plagiarizers, I can now say I am firmly on the side of making those who cheat accountable for their behaviour. Plagiarism and the use of essay mills to avoid detection are blights on the education system and I for one have become a very vocal opponent.

6. End with a Suggestion for Change or a Prediction about the Future

Make predictions that are possible and plausible.

Your suggestion for change will influence your readers if they have been persuaded by your arguments. In the workplace, this might include a request for further action or for research to continue. Your predictions of events that might occur should not be misleading or exaggerated, or your readers will be skeptical.

> If students don't stand up for academics and for the ethical processes of academia, it seems that incidents of plagiarism will only continue to increase. Education about what plagiarism is, its effects, and the overall impact on what it means to be caught plagiarizing are ways that might help the problem.

Exercise 8.4

Each of the following is the concluding paragraph of an essay. Working in pairs, underline the summary statement and write a memorable conclusion. See if you can use a different kind of concluding style in each paragraph.

1. Both football and soccer are enjoyable for spectators and create real enthusiasm among fans. High schools that have chosen soccer have seen no reduction in school spirit or fan support. For educational institutions to make the switch from football is really a "no-lose" proposition because soccer provides dramatic advantages in reducing player injury, increasing player fitness, and shaving thousands of dollars from school expenses.

____

____

____

____

2. While there are many machines that will help you to get fit, others you can use for commuting to work, and still others that allow you the thrill of competing, nothing but a bicycle will give you all three of these benefits and more.

____

____

____

____

3. Although the causes of dropout among first-year students are as individual as the students themselves, the effects are easier to categorize. Conflict with parents and others whose expectations have not been met comes first, followed by a loss of self-esteem. The determination to succeed despite this unfair setback is common, but statistics show that low-paying, dead-end jobs

are the norm for the college or university dropout. The situation is much worse, of course, for those who don't complete high school.

4. Employers who are looking for skilled young people to replace retiring workers need to understand the major differences between the boomers and the generation that is replacing them. The Internet generation brings to the workplace most of the skills and abilities of their predecessors, along with some new ones, but their attitudes are different. Job satisfaction is not optional; it is required. Work is not as important as family and personal considerations. The Internet generation views the "good life" not as the accumulation of wealth but as the achievement of balance and satisfaction in all aspects of their lives.

5. Drinking and driving must be stopped. To stop it will require substantial commitment from all levels of government, both in terms of money and in terms of political will. The penalties for driving while under the influence of alcohol must be increased, and more money must be spent on education and publicity. But, more than these measures, it will take the individual will of every Canadian to make the promise not to drive after drinking. Nothing will bring my sister back, but there are lots of other sisters out there—and brothers and mothers and fathers—who can be saved.

Exercise 8.5

With the class divided into the same teams as in Exercise 8.3, write concluding paragraphs to complement the introductions you developed. Here's how to proceed:

1. Review the paragraph you developed for Exercise 8.3.
2. Write the first sentence of a concluding paragraph for this same topic.
3. Pass your sentence, together with your introductory paragraph, along to the next team, who will write a second sentence for the conclusion.
4. Continue this process until the conclusion contains both a summary or reinforcement and a memorable statement.
5. Return the paragraph to the team that initiated it for revising and polishing.
6. Share the results with the rest of the class.

CHAPTER 9

Summarizing

When you summarize information, you find ideas in an article, essay, report, or other document and rephrase them—but not just for the sake of putting them in your own words. Rather, when summarizing, you shorten (condense) the most important idea or ideas in the source material and express your understanding of them in your own words. The purpose of summarizing is to give the reader an overview of the source article, report, or chapter. If the reader is interested in the details, he or she can read the original because you will have documented the source just as you would a paraphrase or quotation.

It's hard to overstate how valuable the ability to summarize is. Note-taking in college or university is one form of summarizing that allows your brain to process information in a way that makes sense to you. Abstracts of articles, executive summaries of reports, market surveys, legal decisions, research findings, and records of meetings (called *minutes*), to name only a few kinds of documents, are all summaries. Thesis statements and topic sentences are essentially summaries; so, often, are conclusions. When you work on a committee, group, or team, imagination and creativity are valuable, but the ability to summarize is even more so. There is no communication skill that you will need or use more than summarizing. That said, summarizing is something we all do more often than we think.

As a matter of fact, you summarize for yourself and others in every conversation you have. With friends, you may summarize the plot of a movie you've just seen or what happened in class this morning. When your mother calls, you'll summarize the events of the past week that you want her to know about. But most of us are not very good at summarizing in a really effective and reader-centred way, especially in writing. It is a skill that doesn't come naturally. *You need to practise it.* You'll improve quickly, however, if you think about what you're doing—that is, if you are conscious of the times and circumstances in which you are called on to summarize as well as who it is you are summarizing for. The following exercise will get you started.

Exercise 9.1

1. In groups of three or four, choose a movie you have all seen, a course you have all taken, a party or concert you have all attended, or a book you have all read. Individually, without discussing what you will write about first, spend five minutes writing a one-paragraph summary that is directed at a peer or friend who hasn't yet seen the movie, taken the course, attended the party or concert, or read the book. After you have written your individual summary, read it over and highlight your main points.

2. Read and compare the group's summaries. What similarities and differences do you notice? Can you all agree that one summary is both complete and accurate?

If you can't find one "best" summary, spend another five or ten minutes discussing which are the main ideas and which are secondary to a discussion of your topic to create an ideal summary.

3. Now revise your group's one-paragraph summary to include all the main ideas and no secondary details.
4. Once again, read and compare each other's paragraphs. Which paragraph summarizes the topic best? What features does this paragraph have that the others lack?

How to Write a Summary

The work you summarize can be as short as a paragraph or as long as a book, as short as a list of statistics or as long as a documentary, as the following passage demonstrates:

> One of Edward de Bono's books is called *Six Thinking Hats.* [In it] he proposes that you adopt six different mind sets by mentally putting on six different coloured hats. Each hat stands for a certain way of thinking about a problem. By "putting on the hat" and adopting a certain role, we can think more clearly about the issues at hand. Because we're only "playing a role," there is little ego riding on what we say, so we are more free to say what we really want to say. De Bono likens the process of putting on the six hats one at a time to that of printing on a multicoloured map. Each colour is not a complete picture in itself. The map must go through the printing press six times, each time receiving a new colour, until we have the total picture.

Perrin, Timothy. *"Positive Invention." Better Writing for Lawyers*. Toronto: Law Society of Upper Canada, 1990, 51.

Notice that Perrin is careful to tell his readers the source of the ideas he is summarizing: both the author and the book are identified in the very first sentence. This is a great technique to adopt in the writing process because dealing with the source immediately leaves you freer as a writer to think about what it is you want to summarize. The reader also has the benefit of knowing up front what frames your discussion.

The material you need to summarize is usually an article, essay, or chapter (or some portion of it). Depending on how much of the piece you need, your summary will range from a few sentences to one or two paragraphs.[1] Here's how to proceed:

1. Read through the piece carefully, looking up any words you don't understand. Write their meanings between the lines, above the words they apply to. At this point, don't take any notes. Just read for comprehension.

Before you can summarize anything, you must read and understand it.

[1] This restriction applies only to the kind of research paper we are discussing in this part: one prepared for a college or university course. Other kinds of summaries are longer. A *précis*, for example, is one-third the length of the source document. An *abstract*, which is a summary of a dissertation, academic paper, or public presentation, can be several paragraphs long. Ask your instructor if there are specific types of summary writing that would be helpful for you to learn.

2. Now read the article or essay again. Keep rereading it until you have grasped the main ideas and formed a mental picture of their arrangement. This amount of time will be different for each student, so be accommodating. Highlight the title, subtitle, and headings (if there are any). The title often identifies the subject of the piece, and a subtitle usually indicates its focus. If the article is long, the writer will often divide it into a number of smaller sections, each with its own heading. These headings usually identify the main points. If there are no headings, pay particular attention to the introduction—you should find an overview of the subject and a statement of the thesis—and the conclusion, which often summarizes the information and points to the significance of the topic.

3. In point form, and in your own words, write or type out a bare-bones outline of the piece. Your outline should consist of the controlling idea (thesis) of the article and the main ideas, in the order in which they appear. Do not include any supporting details (statistics, specific facts, examples, etc.).

4. Working from your outline, draft the summary. In the first sentence, identify the article or essay you are summarizing (by title, enclosed in quotation marks) and the author (by name, if known). Complete the sentence by stating the author's controlling idea. Here's an example:

   In his essay "The Canadian Climate," D'Arcy McHayle divides Canadians into two types: warm and cool.

   Then state, in order, the author's main points. After each sentence in which you identify a main point, include any necessary explanation or clarification of that point. (The author, remember, developed each idea in the supporting details.) Try to resist going back to the article for your explanation. If you have truly understood the article, you should be able to explain each point from memory. If the author's conclusion contains any new information (i.e., is more than a summary and memorable statement), briefly state that information in your conclusion.

5. Revise your draft until it is coherent, concise, and makes sense to someone who is unfamiliar with the original work. It's a good idea to get someone to read through your summary to check it for clarity and completeness. Go back to Chapter 6, where we talked about writing an essay outline. In a way, a summary of a piece includes very similar information.

6. Don't forget to acknowledge your source. (Chapter 17 will show you how.)

The paragraph below summarizes the essay found on pages 144–145. Read the essay first and then read the summary that follows.

> In his essay "The Canadian Climate," D'Arcy McHayle divides Canadians into two types: "warm" and "cool." The first category includes people who are enthusiastic about Canada's scenery, climate, and recreational activities, which they encourage newcomers to enjoy. Warm Canadians are also sincerely interested in learning about what life is like in the visitor's country of origin. In contrast, Cool Canadians are negative about their country and find it hard to believe that anyone from a warm climate would choose to endure the cold, bleak Canadian winters. Cool Canadians are not interested in

detailed information about the visitor's country of origin, either; they are comfortable with their stereotypes. Finally, McHayle acknowledges that the two types are mixed: each can at times behave like the other. Canadians, like the weather, are unpredictable, and newcomers are encouraged to accept them as they are and for themselves.

This seven-sentence paragraph (140 words) captures the gist of McHayle's 600-word essay. Admittedly, it isn't very interesting. It lacks the flavour of the original. Summaries are useful for conveying an outline or a brief overview of someone else's ideas, but by themselves they are not very memorable. Details and specifics are what stick in a reader's mind; these are what your own writing should provide.

What you want in a summary is a balance of information that you have researched, presented clearly and concisely in an organized way and in your own writing style.

A summary should be entirely in your own words. Your ability to identify and interpret the author's meaning is evidence of your understanding of the article or essay. To ensure you use your own words, it is usually best not to look directly at the article as you are summarizing it—you'll end up with direct quotes. If you must include a short phrase from the source because there is no other way to word it, enclose the quoted material in quotation marks.

When writing a summary, do not

- introduce any ideas not found in the original
- change the proportion or emphasis of the original
- introduce your own opinion of the material

Exercise 9.2

Following the first five steps of the process outlined above, summarize "Ready, Willing ... and Employable," which appears on pages 83–85. When you have completed your work, exchange papers with a partner. Use the following checklist to critique each other's summary.

	Good	Adequate	Try Again
1. The first sentence gives the title and the author's name.			
2. The essay's thesis is clearly and concisely reworded.			
3. Each supporting point (topic sentence) is restated in a single sentence.			
4. Each supporting point is briefly explained.			
5. The summary includes no secondary details that could be eliminated without diminishing the reader's understanding.			
6. The summary is balanced and objective.			
7. The paragraph flows smoothly; there are no obvious errors in sentence structure, grammar, spelling, or punctuation.			

Exercise 9.3 Select an article from a professional journal in your field. Summarize it by following the six steps given on pages 115–116. Assume your reader is a professional in the field to allow you to get comfortable with writing on an equal level with the reader.

Exercise 9.4 Choose an article that interests you from one of the regular sections (e.g., business, health, sports, arts) of a general newsmagazine such as *Maclean's, The Walrus, Time, Newsweek,* or *The Economist*. Summarize the article for a friend who is not an expert in the field and who has not read it. Do not evaluate the article or give your opinion about it. In a paragraph of approximately 50–75 words, simply inform your friend of its contents. And don't forget to cite your source.

Part 4

Academic and Workplace Writing Styles

Each chapter in this unit begins with a definition of the overall writing strategy, the specific prose patterns of that style, and some suggested practical applications. Next, we offer tips on how to structure your writing to follow the pattern discussed in the chapter. Finally, we provide short essays to illustrate each pattern. We have annotated the first essay in each case, and we ask you to annotate the second in similar fashion.

When you have finished this unit, you should be able to decide which pattern of development to choose for an essay, research paper, or professional document so that your writing provides your readers with a clearly structured presentation of the information they require.

CHAPTER 10

Academic and Workplace Writing

You fail only if you stop writing.
—Ray Bradbury

In school and on the job, you will be required to write nonfiction prose—essays, papers, reports, summaries, and proposals that are based on verifiable, factual evidence. It is important to think about which aspects of the writing process you will need specifically for workplace writing and which are best in academics. There is, however, a lot of overlap.

The most important area of overlap is in the way that writing styles impact organization. For example, traditionally journalists, whose job it is to report events as objectively as possible, have relied on six questions to help them discover what they can say about an incident: *where, when, who, how, what,* and *why*. These are the same questions that we ask when we are writing papers or reports, but we tend to focus on one or two specifically. Each of these questions produces one or more answers that should be structured according to specific patterns of development.

We will explore how answering these specific questions can form the backbone of your document's development, whether it is for school or the workplace.

Four Ideas to Consider as You Develop Your Writing

Once you've discovered which of the six questions your paper or report topic focuses on, you can then choose the types of paragraph or writing style that would best suit that paper.

1. To answer the questions *where, when,* and *who,* you describe, and provide examples (see Chapter 12). These questions do not call for specific structural patterns—we cannot offer you diagrams or blueprints that you could follow to produce answers to them because writing them is personal. Description and example can be used alone or in combination to produce an essay or report, but most often they are used as paragraph-level strategies to provide supporting evidence in papers with broader purposes. They can add colour and emotional punch to your writing.

2. To answer the question *how,* you explain the process by which something is made or happened or works. The answer should follow a pattern called *process analysis* (see Chapter 11). It's almost impossible to explain a process without providing details of where and how it occurs and what equipment or personnel are involved (description) and adding examples of acceptable (and possibly unacceptable) outcomes.

3. Before you can answer the question *what*, you must first choose the angle or viewpoint of the subject you want to explore in your paper. You have three main choices:
   a. If you want to explain the kinds, or parts, or important features of your subject, you should frame your answer in a *classification/division* pattern (see Chapter 11).
   b. If you want to explain the similarities or differences between your subject and something else, your answer should follow the pattern of *comparison* or *contrast* (see Chapter 12).
   c. If you want to explain what caused some event or circumstance, or what the consequences were (or might be), you should organize your paper according to the pattern of *causal analysis* (see Chapter 11).

   As you develop the main points of any of these *what*? structures, you may find it useful to employ the three basic strategies discussed in Chapter 12 (description, example, and comparison and contrast).

4. To answer the question *why*, you need to develop an argument, and there are several ways you can structure your answer. There are two kinds of argumentation: one is intended to convince the reader that your opinion is valid and worthwhile; the other is intended to change the reader's beliefs or behaviour in some way. Fortunately, both kinds rely on the same patterns of development (see Chapter 13). The nature of the evidence you provide differs slightly, but again, description and example are strategies you can use to help build your case.

Be aware of the difference between writing an entire paper using one writing style and using various writing styles for individual paragraphs. Both can be appropriate. For example, in an essay on the harshness of the Canadian winter, you might want to use both persuasion and analysis. You might provide examples of what winters are like but also include a paragraph that discusses the process of what makes a winter harsh. Either way, it is important to understand the differences in writing strategies before you decide what might be best for your current writing project.

Choosing an Overall Writing Strategy

Once you have decided on the angle that develops your topic in the best way, it is time to consider the overall development of your paper: are you persuading, arguing, or analyzing? Comparing and contrasting, describing, and exemplifying are all typically *persuasive*. This means that you are using the information to try to get your reader to believe or think a certain way. *Argumentation*, which is also a type of persuasion, has its own style of development. Finally, *analysis* is used in conjunction with critical thinking skills to discuss a subject when you are organizing a paper using a causal analysis, process analysis, or a classification and division pattern. This is not to say that analytical writing cannot be persuasive or that persuasive writing isn't argumentative. These classifications are tentative—useful for studying, but good to consider as more fluid than fixed!

... And the idea of just wandering off to a cafe with a notebook and writing and seeing where that takes me for a while is just bliss.
—J. K. Rowling

Differences between Workplace and Academic Writing

As you progress through this part of the textbook, you will see that a variety of writing strategies can be used in the workplace. Not all good writing is necessarily compiled into a five-paragraph essay format. What you will find here are some strategies for writing that look at individual paragraph styles and other, shorter styles that can be used in both professional and academic environments.

As you read the chapters, consider the writing situations that are likely to occur throughout your education and working life:

ACADEMIC	WORKPLACE
Essay writing	Report writing
Short responses on exams	Travel requests, conference proposals
Requests for letters of reference	Cover letters
Emails to professors	Emails to co-workers or bosses
Proposals or summaries of information	Information analysis or documentation

Exercise 10.1

As a group, make a list of other types of writing that you might have to do at school, and identify how learning about specific writing styles might help you in your academic endeavours. Then consider the various career interests group members have. What other types of writing might each of you be asked to do in the workplace? Keep this list with you as you read through the chapters and consider how each type of writing will apply to you, or share your lists as a class to see what your classmates are involved in.

Analytical Writing: Process Analysis, Causal Analysis, and Classification and Division

CHAPTER 11

Analytical Writing

Analytical writing has many purposes and can be used across a variety of disciplines both academically and professionally. In this chapter, we look at each style of analysis and show how it can be useful in preparing papers that require more than just a presentation of information, straight opinion, or argument.

Process Analysis

In analysis, you focus on providing steps or stages of a process or event in order to convince your reader that your proposed process should be followed.

Process analysis explains events that follow one another in time, and your job is to direct the reader toward information that involves action (implied or direct). There are two kinds of process analysis: one instructs or directs the reader how to perform a task; the other informs the reader how something is done, is made, or works.

1. *Instructional/directional process:* When you explain how to get from the registrar's office to the resource centre, how to start a wet motor, how to make perfect pastry, or any other how-to topic, your purpose is to enable your readers to perform the process themselves. Giving instructions or directions is often done in point form: think of a recipe, for example, or the instructions that come with a child's toy, a barbecue, or a piece of furniture from Ikea. Instructions are usually written in the second person (*you*) and include commands (e.g., "Allow to dry for 10 minutes," "Leave yourself time to revise").

2. *Informational process:* This type of process analysis describes how something is done, is made, or works. In explaining how a hamburger gets from the farm to McDonald's, how snowflakes form, or how the stock market operates, you do not necessarily expect your readers to be able to reproduce the process. Your purpose is simply to inform them about it and perhaps to get them to make more informed decisions in light of their new knowledge.

The tone of your essay, and the amount and kind of detail you include, will vary depending on your audience and purpose.

Informational process analysis is usually written in the third person (e.g., "Wise writers leave plenty of time for revision") and often includes the passive voice ("When the paper has been proofread, it is ready for submission").

Whether you are writing instructions or providing details about a process, keep your language simple and clear. Remember that your readers probably do not share your expertise on the subject (if they did, they wouldn't be reading your explanation). If you use highly technical language or skip over steps that are obvious only to an expert, you will confuse or mislead your readers.

Consider the following instructions, written for inexperienced anglers who want to learn how to cast a fly:

> To execute the cast, play out about 10 metres of fly line in front of you. Ensure that there is no slack in the line, and begin your back cast. As the rod tip reaches about one o'clock, stop the backward motion and begin a crisp forward motion, loading the rod. On the back cast, the line must straighten behind you, parallel to the ground, before the forward motion begins.
>
> The quick forward thrust, stopping abruptly at about ten o'clock, will result in an aerodynamic loop that will travel the length of the fly line, straightening the line in front of you, and resulting in the perfect cast.

These directions break down the process of fly-casting into chronologically arranged steps, but the writer has forgotten the most basic rule of good writing: remember the reader. Only someone who already knows what the writer is talking about would be able to follow these instructions.

An effective process analysis paper takes into account readers' familiarity—or lack of it—with the process, their experience, and their level of vocabulary. Finally, it communicates the steps of the process in a way that holds the readers' interest.

One of the most challenging aspects of process analysis is making sure that you have included all the necessary steps. Only an expert, someone who knows what the result should look like, can leave out a step or two, or combine steps, or take shortcuts. As you write, try to imagine yourself in the reader's position: someone with little or no experience who is reading the instructions or description for the first time.

Tips for Writing Process Analysis Papers

1. Plan carefully. Prepare an outline listing all the steps of the process.

Include everything that your readers need to know, and use language they can understand. Now put the steps in chronological order (p. 66) or logical order (p. 67). Be prepared to revise your list several times before your steps are arranged correctly. Too much detail can be as confusing as too little, so if there are many small steps, group them into a number of more easily manageable stages.

2. Write the introduction.

State your purpose, and include any background information or theory (for example, identify any necessary equipment).

3. Write a thesis statement that makes it clear what your readers are about to learn.

If it is appropriate, include a preview of the major steps you will describe. The examples of thesis statements below illustrate the three ways you can preview main steps: as nouns, phrases, or clauses.

> The steps involved in becoming a winning tennis player can be summed up in four words: basics, practice, concentration, and attitude. (nouns)
>
> Getting married is a process that involves fulfilling arcane legal requirements, enduring an official ceremony, and surviving the abuse of one's in-laws. (phrases)
>
> According to the Niagara Culinary Institute, creating a signature dish is a process with three key steps: (1) select fresh, local ingredients; (2) prepare them to bring out the best of their flavours in combination; and (3) present the finished product with imagination and flair. (clauses)

4. Develop each step in a paragraph.

Be sure to use transitions both within paragraphs and between paragraphs. Transitions help your reader follow the sequence of the process; they also make your writing easier to read.

5. Avoid shifts in person.

Inexperienced writers often start with the third person and then switch to *you* (second person) and give commands. If you focus on your purpose—either to instruct or to inform—as you write, you will be less likely to use pronouns inconsistently.

6. Write the conclusion.

Sometimes a brief summary is useful, especially if the process is a complex one. Alternatively, you could end your paper with an evaluation of the results, or remind your readers of the importance or usefulness of the process.

7. When revising, put yourself in the position of someone who knows nothing about the process, and see if you can follow the instructions or description with ease.

Have you included all the steps or stages? Have you defined any technical terms? Better yet, ask someone who really is a novice to read your paper and try to follow your directions or understand your description.

The essay that follows illustrates instructional process analysis.

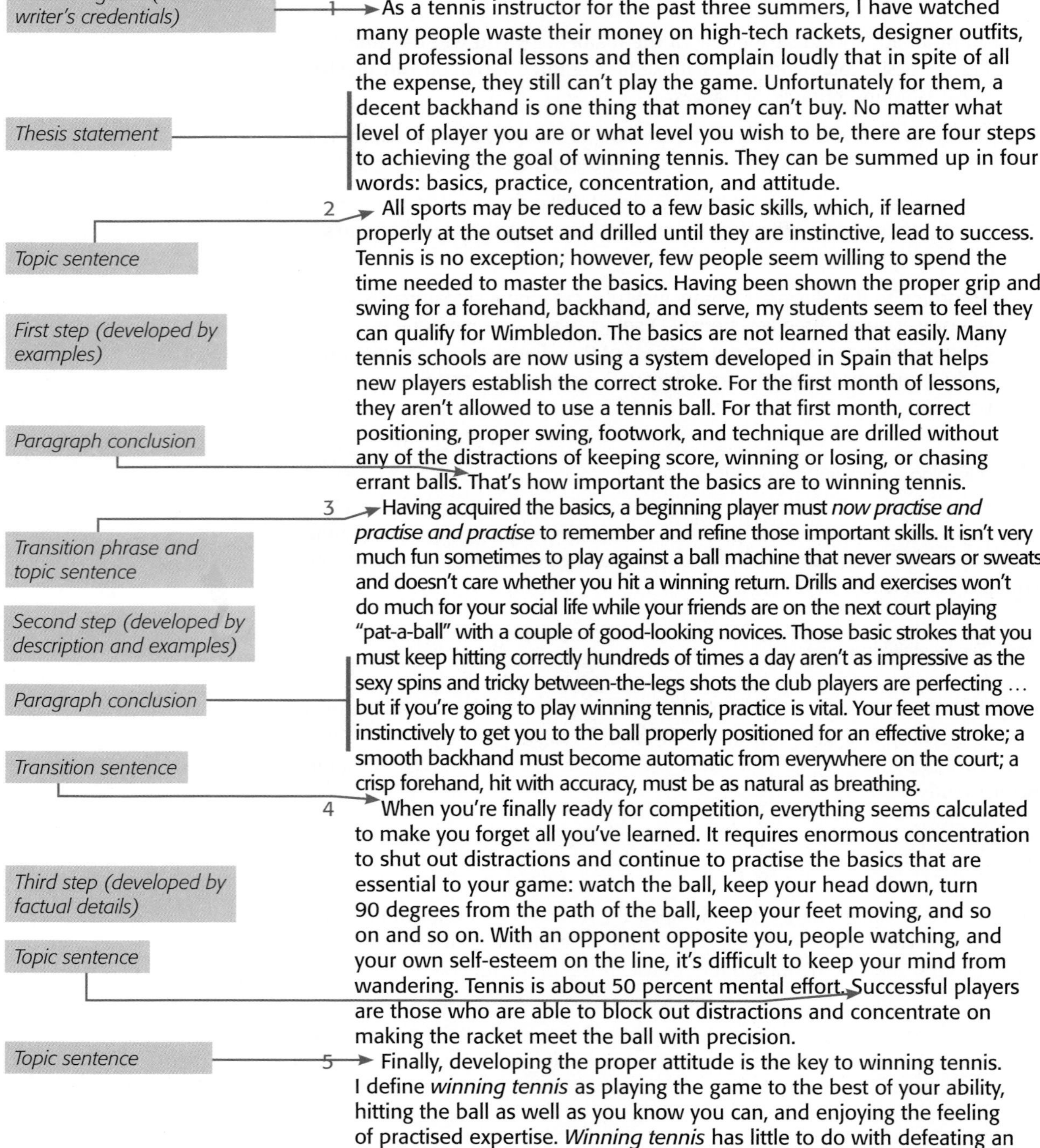

How to Play Winning Tennis

Brian Green

1 As a tennis instructor for the past three summers, I have watched many people waste their money on high-tech rackets, designer outfits, and professional lessons and then complain loudly that in spite of all the expense, they still can't play the game. Unfortunately for them, a decent backhand is one thing that money can't buy. No matter what level of player you are or what level you wish to be, there are four steps to achieving the goal of winning tennis. They can be summed up in four words: basics, practice, concentration, and attitude.

2 All sports may be reduced to a few basic skills, which, if learned properly at the outset and drilled until they are instinctive, lead to success. Tennis is no exception; however, few people seem willing to spend the time needed to master the basics. Having been shown the proper grip and swing for a forehand, backhand, and serve, my students seem to feel they can qualify for Wimbledon. The basics are not learned that easily. Many tennis schools are now using a system developed in Spain that helps new players establish the correct stroke. For the first month of lessons, they aren't allowed to use a tennis ball. For that first month, correct positioning, proper swing, footwork, and technique are drilled without any of the distractions of keeping score, winning or losing, or chasing errant balls. That's how important the basics are to winning tennis.

3 Having acquired the basics, a beginning player must *now practise and practise and practise* to remember and refine those important skills. It isn't very much fun sometimes to play against a ball machine that never swears or sweats and doesn't care whether you hit a winning return. Drills and exercises won't do much for your social life while your friends are on the next court playing "pat-a-ball" with a couple of good-looking novices. Those basic strokes that you must keep hitting correctly hundreds of times a day aren't as impressive as the sexy spins and tricky between-the-legs shots the club players are perfecting … but if you're going to play winning tennis, practice is vital. Your feet must move instinctively to get you to the ball properly positioned for an effective stroke; a smooth backhand must become automatic from everywhere on the court; a crisp forehand, hit with accuracy, must be as natural as breathing.

4 When you're finally ready for competition, everything seems calculated to make you forget all you've learned. It requires enormous concentration to shut out distractions and continue to practise the basics that are essential to your game: watch the ball, keep your head down, turn 90 degrees from the path of the ball, keep your feet moving, and so on and so on. With an opponent opposite you, people watching, and your own self-esteem on the line, it's difficult to keep your mind from wandering. Tennis is about 50 percent mental effort. Successful players are those who are able to block out distractions and concentrate on making the racket meet the ball with precision.

5 Finally, developing the proper attitude is the key to winning tennis. I define *winning tennis* as playing the game to the best of your ability, hitting the ball as well as you know you can, and enjoying the feeling of practised expertise. *Winning tennis* has little to do with defeating an

opponent. Naturally, if you learn the basics, practise sufficiently, and concentrate, you'll win many matches, but that is the reward of playing well, not the reason for playing well. People who swear and throw their rackets when they lose are very useful: they are the most satisfying players to trounce. But I don't understand why they play a game that gives them such pain. Tennis players who enjoy the feel of a well-hit ball and the satisfaction of a long, skillfully played rally are winners, regardless of the score.

Summary of main points

Memorable statement

Questions for Discussion

1. What audience did the author have in mind when he wrote this essay? Consider their interests and goals.
2. The author divides the process into three main steps, each identified and developed in a paragraph. Why does he leave his fourth main point, attitude, for the conclusion?
3. What functions does the introductory paragraph serve in this essay?

Exercise 11.1

The "Dummies" books (e.g., *Poker for Dummies, Computers for Dummies, Office 2012 for Mac for Dummies*) have become bestsellers by explaining how something works or how to do something in simple, easy-to-understand steps. Write a short chapter for the soon-to-be-published book *College for Dummies* entitled "Surviving Your First Day" or "College Clothing" or "How to Eat School Cafeteria Food and Not Gain 5 Kg a Term" (or any other similar topic).

Exercise 11.2

Write a process essay on one of the following topics or on any topic of your choice, as long as it requires an explanation of *how* to do something or *how* something is done, is made, or works. Review the tips on pages 124–126 before you begin.

- How my family came to Canada
- How to build an *iTunes* library
- How to break up with a boyfriend (girlfriend) and still remain friends
- How to find time for everything you have to do in a single day
- How to apologize
- How to get a bargain
- How a biological process works (e.g., how skin heals, how the lungs function)
- How a fuel cell (or any other mechanical, chemical, or electronic device) works

Causal Analysis

In short papers, writers usually concentrate on either causes or effects.

- What are the consequences of dropping out of school?
- What are some of the effects of low interest rates?
- Why is interest in alternative medicine growing so rapidly?

These are the kinds of questions often asked in developing a **causal analysis**. In some instances, cause and effect may be combined in one paper or report, but its length and complexity puts it out of the range of our introductory discussions here.

The most common problem found in causal analysis is oversimplification. Without reasons—solid facts, figures, or evidence—inexperienced writers have a tendency to generalize and to substitute unsupported opinions for reasons. One cause of this problem is choosing a topic that is too large for the prescribed length of the paper. For example, one student decided to analyze the effects of Canada's immigration policy. This is a subject so big and so complicated that the student could do nothing more than give vague and unsupported opinions. The result made the student seem not only ignorant but also racist. You can avoid this pitfall by choosing your subject carefully, focusing it into a limited topic, and supporting each main point with lots of evidence.

Tips for Writing Causal Analysis Papers

1. Your thesis statement should clearly indicate whether you are tackling cause or effect, and it should present your main points in order.

Consider these examples:

The benefits of a long canoe trip include reduced stress and increased fitness.

"Trashy" novels educate, relax, and entertain me in ways that "intellectual" novels do not.

The main complaints of the workers in this office are about pay, safety, and boredom.

2. Avoid three common logical fallacies: oversimplification, faulty causal relation, and leaping to a conclusion.

- An oversimplified analysis is one that ignores the complexities of an issue. If, for example, you claim that "men deliberately keep women down" and base this conclusion on the fact that, on average, the annual salary of women is lower than that of men, you are oversimplifying because the two groups are not identical. To take just one difference, there are more part-time workers among females than among males, and the salaries of part-timers cannot be compared to the earnings of full-time workers. (And even if the two wage groups were identical in all respects except one—annual income—that one difference is not proof of a male conspiracy.)
- Just because one event occurs along with or after another event does not mean that the first *caused* the second. For example, on Tuesday, your little brother swallowed a nickel. On Wednesday, he broke out in a rash. To conclude that the nickel caused the rash is a faulty causal relation. He may be allergic to something; he may have measles. As a writer, you must carefully examine all possible causes before determining that y is the result of x.

- Leaping to a conclusion (sometimes called *hasty generalization*) results when you do not consider enough data before forming a judgment. This is a common error: we commit it every time we form an opinion based on one or two instances. For example, the senate scandal featuring Pamela Wallin that occurred during Stephen Harper's years in office is not proof of the assertion "The Conservative government is full of crooks."

3. Fully support your statements.

You must provide proof of what you say in the form of examples, facts, statistics, quotations, anecdotes, and so on (see Chapter 17). If you begin with the assumption that your reader disagrees with you, you will be more likely to provide adequate support for your points.

The essay that follows demonstrates writing that discusses causes and effects. The writer uses a variety of supporting evidence to develop her points.

The Slender Trap

Trina Piscatelli

> Starvation is not a pleasant way to expire. In advanced stages of famine, as the body begins to consume itself, the victim suffers muscle pain, heart disturbances, loss of hair, dizziness, shortness of breath, extreme sensitivity to cold, physical and mental exhaustion. The skin becomes discoloured. In the absence of key nutrients, a severe chemical imbalance develops in the brain, inducing convulsions and hallucinations. (Krakauer 198)

1 Every day, millions die of hunger. The symptoms of starvation are so horrific that it seems unthinkable anyone would choose this way of death. How is it possible that in the Western world, one in two hundred young women from upper- and middle-class families practises starvation as a method of weight control? How do young women become so obsessed with being thin that they develop anorexia nervosa? To cause such a fearsome and potentially fatal condition, the influencing factors must be powerful indeed. And they are powerful: the psychological pressures of adolescence, the inescapable expectations of family and peers, and the potent influence of the media.

2 A tendency to perfectionism, lack of identity, and feelings of helplessness are three aspects of a young woman's psychology that can contribute to the development of anorexia nervosa. Young women who exhibit perfectionism are particularly susceptible to the disease because they often have unrealistic expectations about their physical appearance. These expectations can lead to feelings of helplessness and powerlessness, and some young women with these feelings see starving themselves as a means to empowerment. Their diet is often the only thing they can control, and they control it with a single-mindedness that astonishes and horrifies their families and friends. As well as the need for control, anorexia in young women can be caused by a weak or

unformed identity. Confused about who they are, many young women define themselves by how closely they approximate our society's notion of the ideal woman. Unfortunately, for the past half-century, Western society's ideal female image has been that of an unrealistically thin young woman. When women focus on this impossible image as the ideal and strive to starve their bodies into submission, they suffer emotional and physical damage.

3 In addition to an unstable psychological state, family and peer pressure can contribute to a fragile young woman's development of anorexia nervosa. By emphasizing physical appearance, by criticizing physical features, and even by restricting junk food, family members can push a young woman over the cliff edge that separates health from illness. A home environment in which physical appearance is overvalued can be destructive for young women. Surrounded by family members and friends who seem to be concerned primarily about appearance, a young woman can begin to feel insecure about how she looks. This uncertainty can produce the desire—and then the need—to look better. And better means thinner. This flawed logic underlies the disease in many young women. A family or peer group that overvalues physical appearance is often also critical of physical flaws. Critical comments about weight and general appearance, even when spoken jokingly, can be instrumental in a young woman's desire to be thin. Ironically, food restrictions imposed by parents can also contribute to anorexia in young women. Restricting the consumption of junk food, for example, has been known to cause bingeing and purging, a condition associated with anorexia.

4 While a young woman's developing psyche and the pressures of those close to her can exert tremendous influence, the root cause of the "thin is beautiful" trap is a media-inspired body image. Television, fashion magazines, and stereotypical Hollywood images of popular stars provide young women with an unrealistic image of the ideal female body. While only 5 percent of North American females are actually underweight, 32 percent of female television and movie personalities are unhealthily thin (ANRED sec. 6). The media's unrealistic portrayal of a woman's ideal body can cause a young woman to develop a sense of inadequacy. To be considered attractive, she feels she must be ultra-thin. Television's unrealistic portrayal of the way young women should look is reinforced on the pages of fashion magazines. Magazine ads feature tall, beautiful, *thin* women. Media images also perpetuate the stereotype that a woman must be thin in order to be successful. Thanks to television and movies, when we think of a successful woman, the image that comes to mind is that of a tall, well-dressed, *thin* woman. This stereotypical image leads impressionable young women to associate success with body weight and image. When internalized by young women, these artificial standards can result in the development of anorexia nervosa.

5 If the media do not begin to provide young women with a positive and healthy image of femininity, we will see no lessening in the numbers of anorexia victims. If our cultural ideal of female beauty does not change to reflect a range of healthy body types, the pressures to realize idealized and unhealthy physical standards will continue, and young women's feelings of helplessness and inadequacy will persist. In order for anorexia to become less prominent among young women, healthier associations must replace the existing connections among beauty, success, and thinness. Young women must realize that self-inflicted starvation is not a means to empowerment, but a process of self-destruction.

Works Cited

ANRED: Anorexia Nervosa and Related Eating Disorders Inc. www.anred.com/causes.html. Accessed 13 June 2004.

Krakauer, Jon. *Into the Wild.* Villard, 1996.

Questions for Discussion

1. Using the outline format on page 82 as your guide, identify the main parts of this essay. Indicate them in the margin, as we have done in the previous essay on pages 126–127.
2. What two supporting points does the author use to develop the main point of paragraph 2? (See sentence 5, which serves as a transition between the two supporting ideas.)
3. What kind of development does Piscatelli use in paragraph 3?
4. Study the concluding paragraph carefully. The author's treatment of her summary and memorable statement is unusual and interesting. Sentence 2 of the conclusion summarizes the three main points that have been developed in the essay but in an original, unpredictable way. Underline the clauses of this sentence, and write above each clause the number of the main point it reinforces.

Exercise 11.3

Develop each of the following thesis statements by adding three good main points.

1. Obesity, a common problem in North America, is the result of three major factors: ______________________________

____

____

____

2. The positive effects of professional daycare upon preschool children are

____

____

____

____

3. The interest in eating locally grown food is a result of______________

____

____

____

____

Exercise 11.4 Begin with the question "What are the causes of ___?" and fill in five career-related topics that you know enough about to identify at least three causes. If possible, work with a partner who shares your career interests.

Examples: What are the causes of the widespread frustration among nurses?

What are the causes of public school teachers' unhappiness with their jobs?

What are the causes of strikes by unionized public workers?

Exercise 11.5 Write a cause essay or an effect essay on one of the following subjects. If you don't know enough to fully support your ideas, be prepared to do some research.

Causes

Adjusting to college (or university) was not as easy as I'd thought it would be.

I doubt I will ever be able to retire.

My first job was a good (or bad) experience.

Self-employment is the best option for many college and university grads.

Many workers have unrealistic expectations of their employers.

Eating a balanced diet is a challenge for many young people.

Homelessness is increasingly widespread in large cities.

Effects

Technology is making us lazy.

A poor manager can have a devastating influence on morale.

Credit cards can be dangerous.

Poor driving skills are a hazard to everyone.

Injuries resulting from overtraining are common among athletes.

Worrying can age you prematurely.

Losing your job can be a positive experience.

Classification and Division

We group like things into categories or classes, and we divide the component parts of something in order to understand them better.

Classification and **division** are structural patterns based on our instinct to arrange and analyze our experiences. For example:

- College and university students can be grouped into undergraduates and graduates, or grouped by year, by political affiliation, or by where they reside during the term (classification).

- An undergraduate class might be divided by programs or majors, such as engineering, nursing, arts, science, and so on (division).
- Items on a restaurant menu are listed in categories such as appetizers, entrées, desserts, and beverages (classification).
- A meal is divided into courses: soup, salad, entrée, dessert (division).
- Plants can be grouped into three categories, based on their effect on humans: edible, inedible, poisonous (classification).

The process of definition involves both classification and division. We define a concept such as a "good student," for example, by identifying the features or characteristics that are shared by all members of the class. That is, having mentally grouped students into three classes (good, poor, and average), we focus on the unique qualities or distinctive features shared by the group (good students) we want to define: a good student is one who is motivated, hard-working, and creative.

Writing a classification paper involves grouping similar things (people, ideas, whatever) to place them into one of several categories. For example, in the first bulleted point above, we classify college and university students according to four different principles: degree status, year of study, political inclination, and place of residence. There are many more ways in which we could classify college students—for example, how they use their leisure time; whether they smoke, drink, or get along with their parents; number of hours they work each week; extracurricular activities; and so on.

There are numerous ways to classify entities into subgroups.

Writing a division paper requires examining a single entity (a person, place, thing, concept) and breaking it down into its constituent parts, features, or characteristics. You are writing a division paper whenever you write about the accomplishments of someone (whether that person is historically real or fictional), the parts of a work of fiction or nonfiction, the qualities of a good leader, the strengths or weaknesses of a particular team, and so on—the possibilities for division are infinite.

The following table gives some examples of classification and division topics, paired according to three subjects: television programming, patients, and parents.

CLASSIFICATION		DIVISION	
Saturday a.m. TV programs	• cartoons • sports shows • interview programs	Saturday a.m. TV programming	• infantile • infuriating • informative
Patients doctors hate to treat	• clingers • deniers • demanders	The ideal patient	• cooperative • knowledgeable • self-disciplined
Types of bad parents	• overprotective • uninterested • disengaged	A good parent	• supportive • firm • consistent

Tips for Writing Classification and Division Essays

1. Make sure that all points are of approximately equal significance and that the points do not overlap.

The key to a good paper is choosing your main points carefully.

> **2.** If you have deliberately left out some aspects of the subject, briefly let your readers know this and why you have limited your discussion.

Some topics are too complex to discuss exhaustively in a short paper. You are better off discussing a few representative points in detail than skimming over all the categories or components.

> **3.** Your thesis statement should set out your subject and its main points, as in the following examples.

Inanimate objects can be classified into three major categories—those that don't work, those that break down, and those that get lost.

An appropriate wardrobe for work consists of outfits that are comfortable, easy to maintain, and, within limits, distinctive.

Our softball team is made up of has-beens, might-have-beens, and never-weres.

The essay that follows illustrates classification and division. Here, the writer explains her subject by dividing it into its main features. Read the essay and then answer the questions that follow.

On-the-Job Training

Alice Tam

Attention-getter

Thesis statement

1 What can you expect from your first job after you leave college? As a recent graduate from a technical program, I entered the workforce fully prepared to do the job I was hired to perform. What I was *not* prepared for were some of the expectations and challenges posed by my employer, my co-workers, and—surprisingly—myself.

1. Topic sentence

Main point developed by examples

Paragraph conclusion

2 During the hiring process, the employer makes sure that you have the knowledge and skills that the position calls for. However, once you are on the job, you will discover that he or she has many other expectations of you as well. Basic job requirements such as being on time should come as no surprise, but volunteering for tasks outside working hours, cheerfully taking on additional responsibilities, and demonstrating work habits that go beyond the basic requirements of the job are all unspoken expectations that employers have of new employees. In my first month on the job, I attended a managers' weekend retreat; joined the company's health and safety committee and United Way campaign; and, on the advice of my supervisor, accepted an offer to serve on my college program's advisory board. My social life suffered, but I felt that I was becoming a valued member of the company's management team.

2. Topic sentence

3 Co-workers present a different challenge. Those who did not attend college may question the value of your diploma or degree; they learned the business the hard way, on the job, and they want you to know that your "book learning" will carry you only so far. You will cope with this hostility more easily if you understand that it is caused by insecurity. Many

---

employees feel intimidated by colleagues who have qualifications they lack; their aggressive stance is their defence. Even those whose college or university days are long behind them may display this attitude. If you show them that you are willing to learn from their experience, you will prove to them that you have the skills and attitude the job requires. One of the unwritten responsibilities of any job is earning the respect of your colleagues. This is not an easy task. It requires time and humility, but, in the long run, it is critical to be an accepted part of the team. Outsiders don't get past the first or second rung on the long ladder to career success.

Main point developed by contrast and examples

Paragraph conclusion

4 Finally, your expectations of yourself may surprise you. In your first job out of college, the stakes are higher than any you have ever experienced. The pressure to succeed can create real stress and even hamper your performance. One of the grads who was hired the same month that I was became so nervous about doing well that he couldn't make decisions in case he was wrong, wouldn't take on extra jobs in case he couldn't handle them, and drove himself (and those around him) crazy by compulsively checking and rechecking everything he did to be sure he hadn't made a mistake. As a new employee, you should expect some performance anxiety. The best way to deal with it is to channel it productively by working extra hours or volunteering for charity work until you develop the confidence to be satisfied with just doing your best at your job.

3. Topic sentence

Main point developed by extended example (illustration)

Paragraph conclusion

5 I celebrated my first year as a full-time employee just a month ago, and when I look back on the past year, I can't believe how fast it has gone or how much I have learned. Because of my college training, I certainly had the ability to do the job, but it has taken me almost the full year to become comfortable with the culture and attitudes of the workplace and to get my own expectations under control. I wish I'd been given this essay to read while I was in school, and I hope it will be helpful to you!

Transition

Summary of main points

Memorable statement

Questions for Discussion

1. Drawing on your own work experience, do you agree that a critical part of on-the-job training is learning how to fit in with your colleagues, even if it means extra time (e.g., volunteering for community or charity work) and extraordinary patience (e.g., holding your tongue when co-workers belittle your education)?

2. The author uses all three "pronoun persons" in this essay. She writes about her own experience in the first person (*I*); addresses the reader in the second person (*you*); and describes the behaviour of a colleague in the third person (*he*). Why do you think Tam has chosen to vary her point of view in this way? Would her essay be more effective if she had told her story as a first-person narrative or as a second-person instructional process or as a third-person division analysis? Support your opinion with evidence from the essay.

Exercise 11.6

This exercise is designed to improve your skill in identifying *unity* within classification and division. In each of the following thesis statements, cross out any irrelevant, insignificant, or overlapping points.

1. A good teacher doesn't bark at the students, give last-minute assignments, study for a test the night before, or grade unfairly.
2. The most important computer interfaces are the keyboard, webcam, voice recognition, mouse, and memory card.

3. A journalist has four major tasks: to report news accurately, to entertain with social information, to collect a big salary, and to resist government control of information.

4. Finding the right career depends on careful planning: getting all the education you can, continually monitoring your enthusiasms and interests, being flexible enough to shift focus as circumstances change, and having luck on your side.

5. The music I enjoy can be divided into six distinct categories: blues, jazz, light rock, pop, hip hop, and rap.

Exercise 11.7 Humans have a strong instinct to classify everything, including themselves. List at least seven classifications (groups or categories) to which you belong.

Exercise 11.8 Write an essay on one of the following subjects.

The main kinds, types, or categories of

- co-workers
- salespeople
- small businesses
- social media
- employers

The characteristics of

- a star player (hockey, football, basketball, soccer)
- a bad movie
- a successful interview
- great art
- a good Web page

The component parts of

- a citizenship hearing
- a love affair
- a golf swing (or slap shot, save, etc.)
- a healthy lifestyle
- a religious service or ceremony

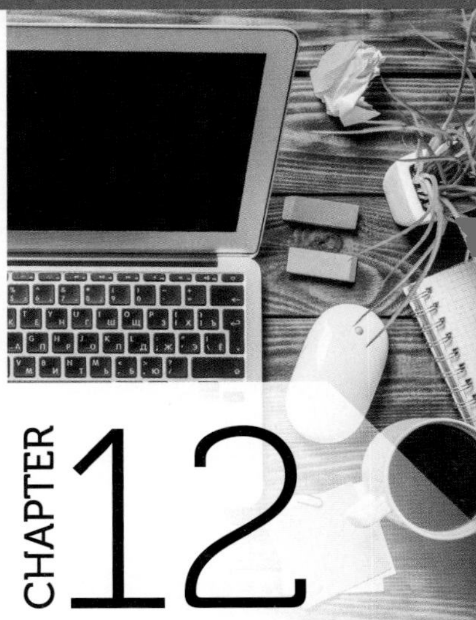

Persuasive Writing: Description, Example, and Comparison and Contrast

The art of **persuasion** is the art of making people change their mind about something, whether it be a world issue or what toothpaste to buy. The way we persuade is often through illustration or another strategy that allows the viewer or reader to see into our thought process and to be convinced that we have the best ideas. (Persuasion is slightly different from argumentation, which will be outlined in Chapter 13.) Description and example are good ways of giving background to persuasive topics. Comparison and contrast essays have long been a staple way for people to decide what they think about ideas, concepts, or even products as well! It would be difficult to write any persuasive essay or report without using at least one of these strategies. In this chapter, we use examples from essays in this book to illustrate what the three strategies are, why we use them, and how to write them. We also talk about types of writing that would be appropriate to use them in.

Description

The goal of descriptive writing is to create a picture in words—to tell readers what something or someone looks or looked like. The more senses your description involves, or the more vivid the details you provide, the better your reader will be able to experience the person, object, or scene you are describing. For example, Rebecca Boyle's "Why Mars Is the Best Planet" (see pages 278–280) gives a variety of striking descriptions of both Earth and Mars. This description of Mars's atmosphere is especially vivid:

Effective description appeals not only to the reader's visual sense but also to the senses of hearing, taste, smell, and touch.

> Mars turned to rust before any skeletons could adorn its deserts, before any creatures could look up and contemplate their place among the other dots in the night sky. While Earth is fecund and bursting with life, Mars is, and may have always been, barren.

We can imagine the green Earth, the sweet air, the life everywhere. The dusty red atmosphere of Mars is also clear, and the idea of it being so devoid of life that not even a skeleton exists is also quite chilling.

Can you imagine or recreate a situation where you live that is just as tense? What would be the purpose of describing it that way?

Tips for Writing Description

1. Decide if your description should be purely factual and objective, or if you want to convey an emotional attitude along with the facts.

This decision might be affected by the parameters of the assignment or the nature of your work (e.g., academic or professional). Select your words according to your purpose. For example, consider the difference between these two sentences:

The woman sat back in her seat.
The woman slumped back into her seat.

The verb sat is objective; the verb *slumped* communicates the writer's attitude toward the woman as well as the way she was sitting. If you were working in legal office administration, for example, making sure to use the objective word sat might be important when transcribing court cases or writing incident reports.

2. Select the most important physical details.

You cannot describe every detail about a topic without losing your focus and that of your reader. If you are uncertain, try reading your description out loud to someone else to see what type of picture they get.

3. Always choose a specific, concrete word in favour of an abstract, general one.

Readers can't "see" an abstraction, so you must choose words that they *can* visualize.

Exercise 12.1

In pairs, select a site or a building or a space that is associated with your career. Then, working individually, write a paragraph describing its physical appearance. When you have finished, exchange papers with your partner and critique each other's descriptions. What similarities do you find in your paragraphs? What differences? What accounts for these similarities and differences?

Finally, highlight three or four descriptive details in each paragraph that you agree would help a reader visualize your topic.

One great way to illustrate that description is highly connotative—meaning that one person can interpret it differently from another—is to try describing a place that everyone knows well, perhaps your own classroom. See how different classmates focus on one detail over another. Think back to Chapter 3, where we discussed critical thinking skills. What we choose to describe or focus on often says something about who we are or what we value. That's why using description can be important.

Example

An example, or a series of examples, is used to give concrete form to abstract ideas. Examples can be taken from research sources, personal experience, or the experience of others. You can choose to use a number of examples to support an idea, as Aliki Tryphonopoulos does in the essay on pages 153–154, "A City for Students":

> Pedestrian-friendly urban planning plays a large part in Montreal's reputation as a festival city that hosts over 40 events annually. In the sultry summer months, streets shut down for the Jazz Festival, the Montreal Grand Prix, and Just for Laughs, while the Fête des Neiges and the Montreal High Lights Festival provide outdoor activities and culinary delights in the winter. Students find plenty of ways to keep active—cycling, jogging, skating, skiing, dancing and drumming at Montreal's sexy Tam-Tams in Mount Royal Park—and gain an appreciation of the city's vibrant arts scene, from the numerous galleries in Old Montreal to fine art cinemas such as Cinéma du Parc and Ex-Centris. Students can argue the merits of the latest Denys Arcand film in one of the many cafés along St. Denis frequented by their compatriots from Concordia, McGill, Université de Montréal, and Université du Québec à Montréal.

Examples in this case make clear the lengths to which people will go to find excitement or to get acclimatized to a new city. Perhaps you have your own favourite way to explore new spaces and places. Instead of giving myriad examples, you can also choose to develop one example in detail (called an *illustration*), as Gabor Maté does in the following paragraph:

> Carl, a 36-year-old native, was banished from one foster home after another, had dishwashing liquid poured down his throat for using foul language at age 5, and was tied to a chair in a dark room to control his hyperactivity. When angry at himself—as he was recently, for using cocaine—he gouges his foot with a knife as punishment. His facial expression was that of a terrorized urchin....

Carl's story serves to humanize Maté's factual account of drug addiction and its causes in "Embraced by the Needle" (see pp. 284–286).

Tips for Using Examples

1. Be sure that any example you use is representative of your topic.

Choose typical examples, not rare or extraordinary ones. If your examples are so wacky that readers cannot relate to them, they will dismiss your argument or discussion. In the workplace, keep examples within the context you are working in. It doesn't often make sense to relate workplace ideas to ideas that are best left in the pub or saved for hockey or baseball night.

2. Remember that examples should *illustrate*, not *be*, the point.

Your job as the writer is to explain the point to your readers in your own words, using credible examples as support. If your example might not convince everyone of your idea, it is best to explain a bit more or use multiple ways of explaining what you mean. When it comes to persuasion, this is key.

3. Include only examples that directly and effectively support your main ideas.

Too many or too-long examples will weaken rather than strengthen your argument. Readers need the highlights, not the whole catalogue.

Exercise 12.2 Using examples as your developmental strategy, write a paragraph of about 150 words on the following topic: "Movies (or TV shows/popular music/fashion) reveal significant insights into ___ culture." (Fill in the blank by applying one of the limiting factors to make the general term *culture* more specific: kind (e.g., *teen*), time (e.g., *1970s*), place (e.g., *Quebec*).)

Putting Description and Example to Use

The two basic strategies of description and example can be used together to convey a thesis. Read the following essay. We have annotated the essay for you; that is, we have indicated in the margin where the writer uses description and example to help develop her ideas.

Looking Both Ways

Amanda van der Heiden

Introduction developed by descriptive details

1 I'm perched on a swing, moving my legs forward and back, forward and back, moving my body forward and back, forward and back. I won't gain any ground. I won't accomplish anything. But I'm swinging and it's relaxing. I love the feeling of jumping off the swing, flinging myself into the air. I look forward to the brief moment of freefall before I land hard on the ground. Sometimes, though, I drag

my feet and kick up stones. I slow down only a little at a time and jump only when I know it is finally safe.

Topic sentence

2 We do a lot of things to ensure safety. We wear seatbelts and drive cars with airbags. We learn to ride our bikes with training wheels and we wear helmets and elbow-pads. We hire health and safety inspectors and spend money to keep everything running properly. We post signs along busy highways, reminding us to make safe choices. We volunteer to wear reflective clothing and carry stop signs so others get home in safety.

Paragraph 2 developed by examples

Topic sentence

3 I'm thinking about crossing guards as I breeze through the air on my swing. I have never really liked them. They come to the street corners, advertising their good works with their orange vests and big, bold stop signs. There are two crosswalks on my way home from school, and both are well equipped with crossing guards and Children Crossing signs. The intersection nearest my house is a four-way stop and it has sixteen of these signs—one double-sided sign on each side of each street. Excessive, I know.

Paragraph 3 developed by descriptive details

4 Each day, as I near the first intersection, a three-way stop, I do my best to avoid eye contact with the crossing guard. I suppose I think that if we don't make eye contact, I can cross the street on my own. Each day this proves to be faulty logic. I wait at the corner for the orange-clad man to walk out into the middle of the street and put the world on hold as I make my way across. I am seventeen years old and I should be able to make it safely on my own.

5 I always dare myself to cross the street on my own before I reach the designated crosswalk. One day I will do it. I will look the crossing guard in the eye and smile. And then I will look both ways and make my way to the other side. I always wonder if he would consider that a failure, a safety breach, a reason to call the police. To be sure, I would survive the incident, but maybe I would feel just a little bit bad inside. He is probably a lonely old man whose only joy is helping children and young people avoid danger.

Topic sentence

6 But I continue my daily walk, all the while making sure I avoid any cracks in the sidewalk. I wouldn't want to fall and break my mother's back or cause her some other harm. The sidewalk ends at the next intersection and again I awkwardly wait for the woman with the sign to signal safety. I could ask her to fulfill her duties one more time, allowing me to walk on the sidewalk, but I would just have to cross the street again. Instead, I crush the hard work of my neighbours as I trample their immaculate lawns.

Paragraph 6 developed by descriptive details

7 Today, though, was a little bit different. Today I watched a little boy race across a busy street to reach his friends who were waiting on the other side. A large green van was barreling down the road and its tires squealed loudly, stopping just in time. I wonder about the boy. Did he realize how horrible that could have been? Or would he laugh it off with his friends? Would he tell his parents? I think about what might have been racing through the mind of the driver. Will he tell his wife? Will he remind his children about the importance of crossing guards and looking both ways? Will he drive more cautiously?

Transition

Climax of the story

End of paragraph 7 reflects on details

Topic sentence

Summary

Memorable statement

8 The streets are full of cars and they can go fast—faster than they can stop. The sidewalks are full of children who are laughing and talking with their friends. Often, neither party pays a lot of attention or realizes the risks. Drivers do not always focus on the road, and neither do children.

9 We value safety, but we easily forget about it too. So today as I swing through the air, I am not going to jump, enjoy the freefall, or land hard. I am going to kick up the stones as I slow to a stop. And I might just wait there for a moment longer. As I walk home, I think I will look the crossing guard in the eye and smile. And then I will wait patiently until he summons me to cross. I will be his best customer and tell him that I appreciate what he is doing, even thank him for being a reminder of safety.

Questions for Discussion

1. What is the meaning of the title? How does it prepare the reader for the essay?
2. In your own words, state the thesis of this essay.
3. How does the first paragraph contribute to the thesis of this essay?
4. How does the conclusion contribute to the unity of the piece?

Suggestions for Writing

1. From the point of view of the little boy, write a paragraph describing the incident that occurs in paragraph 7.
2. From the point of view of the truck driver, write a paragraph narrating the story of the incident that occurs in paragraph 7.
3. From the point of view of the crossing guard, write a paragraph using the incident in paragraph 7 as an illustration of your topic sentence.

Exercise 12.3

Using the first person and the present tense, as the writer of "Looking Both Ways" has done, write a short essay that uses description and example to convey a clear impression of one of the following experiences:

1. the daily trip you take from home to school
2. the time from your arrival at school to the end of your first class
3. an embarrassing (or surprising, joyful, unexpected) incident during your day

When you've completed your essay, exchange papers with a partner and find the descriptive and example passages your partner has used to develop his or her main points. Note them in the margin. Then exchange papers again and see if your partner has correctly identified your methods of development. Discuss any differences between your intentions and your partner's perceptions.

Comparison and Contrast

If you are focusing on the similarities between two things (or ideas or concepts or points of view), you are writing a **comparison**. If you are focusing on the differences, you are writing a **contrast**. Most people, however, use the term "comparison" to cover both (as in "comparison shopping"), and similarities *and* differences are often discussed together in a paper. When we are attempting to persuade others, we are usually asking them to choose one item or concept over another, thus essentially comparing them but focusing on one over the other.

You can choose from two approaches when you are organizing a comparison. In the first option, you discuss one item fully and then turn to the other item. This approach is called the *block method* of organizing. The alternative option is to compare your two items *point by point*. For example, suppose you decided to compare Ryan Gosling and Daniel Craig. You might choose to elaborate on the following three points:

1. physical appearance
2. acting technique
3. on-camera heroics

Using the block method, you would first consider Gosling in terms of these three points; then you would do the same for Craig. You would need to outline only four paragraphs for your essay:

1. Introduction
2. Gosling's physical appearance, acting technique, and on-camera heroics
3. Craig's physical appearance, acting technique, and on-camera heroics
4. Conclusion

The block method works best in short papers, where the points of comparison are easy to understand and remember, and your point of view, the one you are trying to get your reader to believe, is relatively simple. As comparisons get more complex, your readers will be able to understand your points better if you present them point by point. You would then need to write an outline of five paragraphs for your essay:

1. Introduction
2. Physical appearance of Gosling and Craig
3. Acting technique of Gosling and Craig
4. On-camera heroics of Gosling and Craig
5. Conclusion

The introductory paragraph in the comparison essay usually tells readers what two things are to be assessed and what criteria will be used to assess them. If your intent is to persuade, your concluding paragraph will reveal a preference for one over the other.

Tips for Writing a Comparison or Contrast Paper

1. Make sure that the two items you have chosen are appropriately paired; to make a satisfactory comparison, they must have something in common.

Both items might be baseball teams or world leaders, but to compare the Vancouver Canucks and the Hamilton Tiger-Cats or to contrast Barack Obama and your uncle Edgar would likely be futile and meaningless—though perhaps fun in a non-professional and non-academic format.

2. Your main points must apply equally to both items.

Reject main points that apply to one item and have only limited application to the other. For example, in a comparison of digital and analog instruments, a category for dial configuration would be pointless.

3. Your thesis statement should clearly present the two items to be compared and the basis for their comparison.

Consider these examples:

> Email and interoffice memos differ not only in format but also in style and purpose.
>
> The major points of comparison in automobiles are performance, comfort, and economy, so I applied these factors to the two cars in the running for my dollars: the Ford Focus and the Mazda 3.

4. Use transitional words and phrases within and between paragraphs to provide coherence.

The essays that follow demonstrate the two approaches to writing comparisons and contrasts. Read each essay and answer the questions that follow it.

The Canadian Climate

D'Arcy McHayle

Attention-getter

Thesis statement

1 The student who comes to Canada from a tropical country is usually prepared for cold Canadian winters, a sharp contrast to our hot northern summers. What the student may not be prepared for is the fact that Canadian personalities reflect the country's temperature range but are less extreme. Canadian personalities fall into two categories: warm and cool. The two groups share the Canadian traits of restraint and willingness to compromise, but they are dissimilar in their attitudes both to their own country and to the foreign student's country of origin.

Topic sentence

First category (developed by descriptive details and hypothetical quotations)

Paragraph conclusion (sums up first category)

2 Warm Canadians are, first of all, warm about Canada and will, at the first sound of a foreign accent, describe with rapture the magnificence of the country from the Maritimes to the West Coast, praising the beauty of the Prairies, the Rockies, and even the "unique climate of the Far North." Canadian leisure activities are enthusiastically described with a special place reserved for hockey. "So you've never skated? You'll learn. Come with us; you'll have a great time." The Warm Canadian wants the newcomer to share in the pleasures of life in Canada. When she turns her attention to

the foreign student's homeland, she seeks enlightenment, asking questions about its geography, social and economic conditions, and other concerns not usually addressed in travel and tourism brochures. The Warm Canadian understands that the residents of tropical countries are not exotic flower children who sing and dance with natural rhythm but are individuals who, like Canadians, face the problems of earning a living and raising a family.

Transition

3 Compared to the Warm Canadian, who exudes a spring-like optimism, the Cool Canadian is like November. Conditions may not be unbearable for the moment, but they are bound to get much colder before there is any sign of a thaw. The Cool Canadian's first words on hearing that the foreign student is from a warm country are, "How could you leave such a lovely climate to come to a place like this?" Not from him will one hear of Banff, or Niagara Falls, or anything except how cold and dark and dreary it gets in the winter. It sometimes seems that the Cool Canadian's description of his own country is designed to encourage foreign students to pack their bags and return home at once. As for the foreign student's country of origin, the Cool Canadian is not really interested, although he may declare, "I hear it's beautiful. I'd love to go there." Beyond that, however, he has no interest in information that may shake the foundations of his collection of myths, half-truths, and geographic inaccuracies. This type of Canadian, if he does travel to a tropical country, will ensure that he remains at all times within the safe confines of his hotel and that he returns to Canada with all his preconceived ideas intact.

Topic sentence

Second category (developed by examples and descriptive details; two hypothetical quotations balance those in paragraph 2)

Paragraph conclusion (sums up 2nd category)

4 Foreign students should not be upset by the Cool Canadian; they should ignore his chilliness. Besides, like a heat wave in March, an unexpected thaw can occur and create extraordinary warmth. Likewise, a Warm Canadian may become a little frosty sometimes, but, like a cold spell in June, this condition won't last. And when the weather changes, foreign students will find an opportunity to display their own qualities of understanding, tolerance, and acceptance of others as they are.

Concluding paragraph (developed by analogy)

Memorable statement

Questions for Discussion

1. What are the main points of contrast in "The Canadian Climate"?
2. Which method of contrast has the author chosen for the subject: block or point by point?
3. Why did the author choose this approach? Would the essay work as well if it were organized the other way? Outline the main points of contrast as they would look in the other format.
4. What other points of contrast between the two kinds of Canadians can you think of?
5. What audience does the author have in mind? How do you think Canadians would respond to this essay? Foreign students?
6. What is the author trying to persuade you to think or believe?

Shopping Around

Aniko Hencz

1 The word "shopping" inspires visions of crowded, airless malls, aggressive salespeople, whining children, and weary feet. Some consumers embrace the ritual chaos while others recoil in horror. For the mall-weary shopper, help has arrived in the form of the Internet. Online shopping has exploded in recent years and now offers a viable alternative to the bricks-and-mortar experience. However, as my partner and I discovered recently, when it comes to selection, service, pricing, and convenience, there are significant differences between the two options. Which should you choose? It depends on your priorities.

2 Sometimes too much choice leads to confusion, but having a wide selection to choose from is generally considered a good thing. Online shopping makes available millions of products at the click of a mouse. When we explored dozens of sites in our search for a digital video camera, national borders didn't limit us, and we found models with all the latest features and functions. In contrast, when we visited a number of electronics stores—after wasting half an hour looking for a parking space—we found a limited selection of models and options in our price range.

3 While we are not exactly Luddites, we needed the intricacies and features of the latest generation of video cameras explained to us. Most electronics stores are staffed with knowledgeable salespeople who are only too happy to explain technical jargon, demonstrate a product's features, and offer an opinion on its relative merits. On the other hand, if you are willing to spend time on your computer, online information may well serve your needs. You can do all your research and decision-making electronically by visiting manufacturers' and retail outlets' websites, and even by consulting the opinions of other consumers at product comparison and review sites.

4 "Where can I get the best deal?" is something every consumer wants to know. Ask happy customers the reason for their satisfaction, and the answer invariably involves price. Online merchants can often offer lower prices because they can avoid the overhead (rent, inventory, heat and light, wages, etc.) of conventional stores. Not surprisingly, we found that in-store prices for digital video cameras were routinely higher than those posted by online merchants. Electronics stores have responded to the online competition by routinely offering coupons and special discounts.

5 Shopping online is undoubtedly convenient. As long as you have a credit card, you can shop anywhere, anytime. There are no salespeople to pressure you, and you never have to deal with parking or crowds. However, these advantages are countered by the major inconvenience of returning a damaged or unsatisfactory product, especially if you have to repackage the item and ship it across borders. We were disconcerted by the possibility that we

would have to return our video camera, a fragile item that could be easily damaged during shipping. Offsetting the limitations of the bricks-and-mortar experience is the relative speed with which items can be returned or exchanged.

6 So where did we buy our camera? We weighed the pros and cons of the alternative selections, services, prices, and convenience of the two shopping environments, and decided that service—both before and after our purchase—was more important to us than saving money and time by shopping online. While we chose the local electronics store as the supplier that best met our needs, other consumers have different priorities, as the increasing popularity of online shopping demonstrates. Bricks and mortar or mouse and monitor? North Americans should consider themselves fortunate to enjoy the advantages of both—for now.

Questions for Discussion

1. Using the outline format on page 82 as your guide, identify the main parts of this essay. Indicate them in the margins, as we have done with "The Canadian Climate." How is the information organized: in blocks or point by point? Why do you think the author chose this organizational pattern?
2. In your own words, combine the thesis and the main points of this essay in a single sentence. Is it an effective thesis statement? Why?
3. This piece is told from the first-person plural point of view. Consider how the effect on the reader would change if it had been written from either the first-person singular point of view (personal) or from the third-person point of view (impersonal). Did the author choose her point of view wisely? Why?
4. Identify three or four transitional techniques the author has used to enhance her essay's coherence.
5. Early in the essay, the author provides clues as to which shopping option she and her partner eventually chose. Do these hints spoil the conclusion for the reader? Why or why not? Or were the hints intended to lead the reader to a certain way of thinking?
6. Search online to find two or three articles that present evidence of the rapid growth of online shopping and its negative effects on the profitability of bricks-and-mortar stores.
7. Does it matter to you who wins the battle of the shopping options? Why?

Exercise 12.4

List eight to ten characteristics of two people, jobs, or courses. Examine your lists and choose two or three characteristics of each that would make a good basis for a comparison of the two. Then go back over your lists and choose two or three characteristics that would make a good basis for contrasting them. Finally, decide what you would like to convince your reader of. List all the points you could make to persuade your audience to share your perspective.

Exercise 12.5 Write a comparison or contrast essay on one of the following subjects, making sure to indicate your preference for one or the other in either the introduction or the conclusion. Be sure to follow the guidelines for essay development, from selecting a subject, through managing your main points, to outlining your paper and writing your paragraphs.

Two magazines with the same target audience (e.g., *Maclean's* and *Time, People* and *Us, Shift* and *Wired*)

Two bands (or singers or musicians)

A movie and the book it was based on

Two pop stars (music, film, TV, etc.)

Two Canadian writers (or filmmakers)

Your generation and that of your parents (or grandparents)

Two fast-food restaurants

Exercise 12.6

Contrast papers are most often persuasive, but they don't have to be written that way. When you are presenting a contrast, it might be appropriate to discuss why certain comparisons might also be made. You can then use those false comparisons to prove your point. List the arguments on both sides of three of these controversial issues.

Single-sex schools

Cyber policing

The use of animals in medical research

Nuclear power

Physician-assisted suicide

Exercise 12.7 List three professional forms of writing that might require comparison or contrast (those in advertising might find this especially easy). Then list three professional forms that might require description or example. How can you include different types of persuasive writing styles in the workplace? Make a list or practise writing one of them.

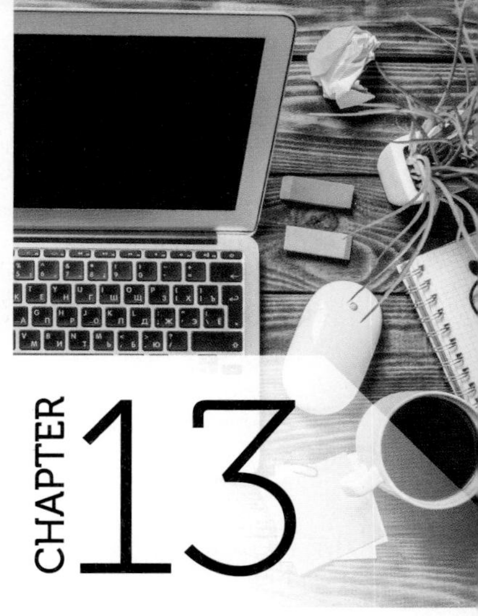

Argumentation

How many times have you won an argument? If you're like most of us, not very often.

Argumentation can be divided into two kinds: *argument* and *persuasion*. In the context of writing, these terms have specific meanings, slightly different from their meanings in general conversation. As discussed in Chapter 12, *persuasion* is intended to change the way readers think or feel about an issue, perhaps even to convince them to act in some way that supports the writer's point of view (e.g., buy a product, donate to a charity, vote for a particular candidate). An **argument** is a piece of writing that is intended to convince readers that the writer's opinion about an issue is reasonable and valid. An *issue* is an opinion or belief, something that not all people agree on; it is *controversial*, a word that literally means "having two sides."

Getting people to understand what you say is hard enough; getting them to agree with you is the most difficult task any writer faces.

Factual reports, memos, and analyses are not likely to be arguments, although some writing intended primarily to inform may also be intended to influence the reader's thinking: "How to Play Winning Tennis" (pp. 126–127) and "The Slender Trap" (pp. 129–130) are just two examples.

Drafting, rewriting, and editing argument and persuasion are much the same as for other kinds of writing. Planning, however, requires a slightly different approach.

Choose Your Issue Carefully

If you have not been assigned a topic, you will need to choose one. Your choice is even more critical for an argumentation essay than it is for a factual analysis that might also be persuasive. You can argue only matters of opinion, not fact. But the thing is that facts can be interpreted in different ways—that's what an argument is: an interpretation of a set of facts. No one can dispute the fact that Canada has ten provinces and three territories. An appropriate subject for your paper is one that can be disputed. Someone has to be able to say, "No. I disagree. That's not what these facts mean." For example, "Canada should be reorganized into five regional provinces and one territory" is an opinion based on the set of facts.

You cannot really argue matters of taste, either. Taste is personal preference: there is no point in arguing that Thai food is better than pizza, or that green is more flattering than blue. Even if you could argue these assertions, you would only be trying to persuade, not to settle an argument. Therefore, choose your subject carefully. It must pass the 4-S test (see page 53), and it should be one you know and care about. Ideally, it should be one your reader cares about, too.

Next, consider the scope of your subject. How much time do you have to prepare? How long is your paper expected to be? Throughout this book, we have recommended that when you choose a subject rather than being given one, you should limit your focus. This recommendation is even more important when you are preparing an argument than when you are proposing to explain something. Even subjects that look narrowly focused can require surprising amounts of development when you are composing an argument for or against them.

It is important to consider this essential difference: facts and beliefs are two related but not equal concepts.

Stay away from large, controversial issues: abortion, for example, or capital punishment or religion. There are two reasons for this caution. First, they are hugely complex issues, and, second, they are issues on which virtually everyone already has an opinion. It is difficult enough to convince readers about an issue on which they have not already formed an opinion. It's practically impossible to get them to change their minds when they hold an entrenched belief.

Consider Your Audience

When you are trying to get readers to agree with you, you must know (or be able to make an educated guess about) what opinions they already hold and how likely they are to disagree with your views. If, for example, you want to convince your readers that television broadcasters should be required to adhere strictly to Canadian content regulations, the approach you take will depend on your readers' level of knowledge, their interest in the subject, even their age. What do they think about the issue? Do they care about it, one way or the other? What beliefs do they hold that would make them inclined to agree or disagree with you? If you know the answers to these questions, you'll know how to approach your subject: what points to argue, which to emphasize, and which to downplay.

Leah Brown, a first-year student, clearly has her audience in mind when she writes about mental health and technology (you can read her paper on pp. 306–310). She assumes her readers have a good level of comfort with technology, but they may struggle with disclosing their mental health issues. Her argument in the paper suggests that technology might help people find some new pathways and methods to cope with mental health issues.

Identify Your Purpose

Do you want your readers simply to understand and respect your opinion on an issue? Or do you want to change their thinking or their behaviour in some way? If your primary purpose is to get them to agree with you, your argument will rely on solid evidence and sound, logical reasoning. If you just want understanding, perhaps a more persuasive approach using description, example, or compare and contrast, as outlined in Chapter 12, would be a better option.

If your primary purpose is to get your readers to change in some way, your argument will need to appeal not only to their sense of what is reasonable but also to their feelings, loyalties, ambitions, or desires.

Organize Your Ideas

Before you begin your first draft, write out your opinion in the form of a *proposition* (opinion statement). You may or may not use this statement in your paper, but you need it in front of you as you (1) identify your reasons for holding the opinion you do, (2) list the evidence you intend to use, and (3) decide on the order of presentation. If you have ever heard a formal debate, you know what a proposition is. It is the statement of opinion that one side argues in favour of and the other side argues against. Here are three examples:

> **Few cities in the world offer the affordable living, student amenities, and cultural dynamism that Montreal does.** (Thesis of "A City for Students," pp. 153–154)
>
> **The objective of the gas–electric hybrid is to maximize the best properties of both the gas engine and the electric motor.** (Thesis of "The Gas–Electric Hybrid Demystified," pp. 276–278)
>
> **Sweatshops are a complicated issue, full of complications that make it a moral grey area.** (Thesis of "No Sweat?" pp. 286–288)

The test of a satisfactory proposition is that it is debatable—that is, someone could defend the contrary point of view. (A statement that includes the word *should* or *must* is likely to be a proposition.) You could argue that fishing is a cruel, unjustifiable sport or that a liberal arts education is a waste of time and money or that to anglophone students, Montreal offers decrepit housing, poor amenities, and few cultural opportunities.

Remember, if you are just giving an opinion rather than making an argument, a persuasive style would be more appropriate.

Identify Your Thesis, Reasons, and Evidence

Once you have a clear statement of a specific opinion, you are ready to identify your reasons for holding it and present evidence to support your reasons. It is possible to support an argument entirely from personal experience, but you are more likely to convince your readers if you provide a variety of kinds of evidence (see Chapters 4 and 15). By thinking about the concepts of grounds (data), claims, and warrants, you become better able to craft a workable thesis.

You will not convince your readers of anything unless they understand your proposition. Whether your purpose is to argue or to persuade, you need to provide reasons for your opinion. Your reasons, which are your main points, must be significant, distinct, and relevant (see Chapter 4). To support each reason, you need to provide accurate evidence: facts, concrete details, statistics, events, or experiences that your readers are familiar with or can relate to, or authorities you can refer to or quote.

When you attempt to persuade through a formal argument, you must engage your readers' hearts as well as their minds, so at least some of your evidence should be emotionally "loaded." That is, it should arouse your readers' compassion, anger, sense of justice, or any other emotion that might tend to bring your reader over to your side.

Decide on an Approach: Direct or Indirect?

If you think your readers are likely to argue with your view or are even slightly inclined to oppose it, it is best to build your case with examples, definitions, and other evidence before stating your own opinion. Readers who are confronted early by a statement they disagree with are often not open to argument or persuasion. Instead, they are inclined to read the rest of the paper while trying to pick holes in the argument and thinking of rebuttals. A potentially hostile audience would respond best to an *indirect*, or inductive, approach:

> **Before we decide how to vote, we should consider the candidates' records, their platforms, and their characters.**

On the other hand, if your readers are sympathetic to your point of view, you can state your opinion up front and then identify your reasons and the evidence that supports those reasons. This is the *direct*, or deductive, approach:

> **Based on her record, her platform, and her character, Julie Kovac is the candidate who deserves your vote.**

Arrange Your Reasons and Evidence

An argument or a persuasive essay can be developed in several ways. It is possible, as you will see in the essays at the end of this chapter, to use a number of different structural patterns to convince your readers. A cause–effect analysis might be an effective way to urge action to lower the carbon monoxide and carbon dioxide emissions that contribute to global warming if it is written in the form of an argument rather than just as an analysis of the situation. You might choose comparison to discuss the efficiency of Canada's regulated airline industry as opposed to the deregulated industry in the United States and to argue in favour of one approach over the other.

Two patterns that are common in argumentation also work with the persuasive style of writing. One is the classic "their side–my side" strategy, which is particularly useful when you are arguing a controversial position that may provoke serious dispute. This pattern involves your presenting the "con" (or "against") points of an argument, then refuting them with the "pro" (or "for") side of the argument. For instance, if a writer were to argue that women in the Canadian Forces should participate in combat, she might choose to present the opposing position and then counter each point with well-reasoned arguments of her own.

Like a comparison, the "their side–my side" strategy can be presented either in block form or in point-by-point form (see Chapter 12), depending on how many points there are to discuss. Be sure to arrange your points in the order in which they will be most effective (see Chapter 7).

If you are a skilled debater, you can often dismiss the opposing side's argument by identifying and exposing flaws in their reasoning or evidence. If you are an inexperienced writer, however, you will probably find it easier to use one or more of the following techniques:

- Identify any irrelevant or trivial points.
- Show that a point covers only part of the issue.
- Show that a point is valid only some of the time.
- Show that a point may have immediate advantages but that its long-term results will be negative.
- Acknowledge the validity of the opposition's point(s), but provide a better alternative.

Usually, writers present their reasons in climactic order, saving their most compelling reason for the end of the paper.

Carefully presented, the "their side–my side" pattern impresses readers with its fairness and tends to neutralize opposition.

The second structural pattern specific to argument and persuasion makes special use of the familiar thesis statement. Add carefully worded reasons to your proposition, and you have a thesis statement that can appear in the introduction of your paper in a direct approach or near the end if you are treating your subject indirectly. Be sure you have arranged your reasons in the most effective order, whether the most persuasive comes at the beginning or is saved for the end.

The keys to good argumentation are to think carefully about your opinion and to present objectively your reasons for believing it—*after* you have analyzed your reader's possible biases or prejudices and degree of commitment to one side or the other.

To argue or persuade successfully, you need to be not only well organized, informative, and thorough but also honest and tactful, especially if your readers are not already inclined to agree with you. This is why, as we discussed in Chapter 1, knowing your audience is important. It is much more difficult to write a convincing argument when you aren't sure what your audience believes.

Tips for Writing Argumentation

1. Choose an issue that you know and care about and can present with enthusiasm.

2. Select your reasons and evidence with your audience in mind.

You are already convinced; now you have to convince your readers.

3. Decide whether your audience can be approached directly or if they should be approached indirectly—gently and with plenty of evidence before receiving your "pitch."

4. Arrange your argument in whatever structural pattern is most appropriate for your issue and your audience.

5. Remember that there is another side to the issue. You can help your own cause by presenting the opposing viewpoint and refuting it.

Present the other side tactfully and fairly. You will only antagonize readers by unfairly stating or belittling the case for the opposition. Opinions are as sensitive as toes: tread carefully to avoid causing pain.

The essays that follow illustrate two approaches to argumentation. Read them carefully so you can answer the questions that follow each one. (Note: The first essay is a research paper with APA-style documentation.)

A City for Students

Aliki Tryphonopoulos

Attention-getter

1 **It is hard to think of a city more exhilarating for a student to live in than Montreal. Where else can you hear a conversation shift between two or even three languages with ease and playfulness at the local coffee shop? Cosmopolitan and cultured, la belle ville is unique**

Definition

in North America for its intersection of two historically established language groups with a large and growing immigrant population. Montrealers have translated this rich cultural diversity into a vibrant civic life with world-renowned festivals, a well-established art scene, lively café culture, and acclaimed international cuisine and fashion. Few cities in the world offer the affordable living, accessible arts scene, and cultural dynamism that Montreal does.

Thesis statement

Topic sentence

First main point (developed by numerical facts)

Paragraph conclusion

2 Long-standing socioeconomic factors make Montreal an affordable city for students—no small consideration given that Canadian undergraduate tuition has risen by 111 percent since 1990 ("Bottom Line," 2004). Naysayers point out that although Quebec has the lowest tuition rates in Canada (frozen since 1994), out-of-province students must pay roughly twice as much as Quebec residents, placing them in the higher bracket of national tuition payers. Some students get around this disadvantage by working and taking part-time classes for a year in order to qualify for the in-province tuition rates. For those who are required to pay the higher rates, however, the financial burden is more than offset by the relatively low cost of rental housing in Montreal (Canada Mortgage, 2004, Table 2). One of the best ways for students to economize is by living close to the university. Montreal is a walking city, so it is possible for students to conduct all of their business within a five-block radius.

Transition and topic sentence

Second main point (developed by examples)

Paragraph conclusion

3 Pedestrian-friendly urban planning plays a large part in Montreal's reputation as a festival city that hosts over 40 events annually. In the sultry summer months, streets shut down for the Jazz Festival, the Montreal Grand Prix, and Just for Laughs, while the Fête des Neiges and the Montreal High Lights Festival provide outdoor activities and culinary delights in the winter. Students find plenty of ways to keep active—cycling, jogging, skating, skiing, dancing and drumming at Montreal's sexy Tam-Tams in Mount Royal Park—and gain an appreciation of the city's vibrant arts scene, from the numerous galleries in Old Montreal to fine art cinemas such as Cinéma du Parc and Ex-Centris. Students can argue the merits of the latest Denys Arcand film in one of the many cafés along St. Denis frequented by their compatriots from Concordia, McGill, Université de Montréal, and Université du Québec à Montréal. As for ambience, the eclectic mix of old European limestone mansions and North American glass towers lends this oldest of Canadian cities a unique architectural allure.

Topic sentence

Acknowledgment of the opposition's point of view

Third main point (developed by examples)

4 Montreal's cultural dynamism, whose historic roots draw comparisons to such international cities as Barcelona and Brussels, is not only the city's most attractive attribute but, sadly, what scares many students away. Bill 101, meant to protect the French language in Quebec, contributed to the exodus of nonfrancophones from Montreal during the 1980s and 1990s. That trend is slowly reversing (DeWolf, 2003). A recent study reveals what Montrealers already know: the unique interaction of francophone, anglophone, and allophone (languages other than French or English) cultures in Montreal is characterized by mutual respect, accommodation, and even a sense of fun (Lamarre, 2002). Students can absorb and appreciate the international flavour of the various bureaus and contribute to the daily cultural exchange. With the city's high rates of bilingualism

and trilingualism, anglophone students do not need to know French in order to function, but their social and cultural life will be far richer if they do. And what better place to learn la langue française than in the second-largest French-speaking city in the world! *Paragraph conclusion*

5 Education is as much about what goes on outside the classroom as in it. Those students who are willing to embrace Montreal's vibrant cultural milieu will find their worldviews challenged and broadened. *Summary* In a global environment fraught with the dangers of intercultural miscommunication and ignorance, that kind of education is vital. *Memorable statement*

References

The bottom line. (2004, November 15). *Maclean's*, 72.

Canada Mortgage and Housing Corporation. (2004, December 1). *Average rents in privately initiated apartment structures of three units and over in metropolitan areas* (Table 2). Retrieved from http://www.cmhc.ca/en/News/nere/2004/2004-12-21-0715.cfm

DeWolf, C. (2003, May 25). The road to Montreal. *The Gazette* [Montreal]. Retrieved from http://maisonneuve.org/about_media.php?press_media_id=21

Lamarre, P. (2002). Multilingual Montreal: Listening in on the language practices of young Montrealers. *Canadian Ethnic Studies, 34*(3), 47–75.

Questions for Discussion

1. This essay's introduction establishes the author's thesis and previews her main points. What other purposes does it serve?
2. In an argument, it is often necessary to address the opposition's point of view. The writer can choose either to turn a negative into a positive or to present the opposition's arguments and then refute them. Find examples of both techniques in this essay. Consider or discuss with a partner how this might have been presented differently in a paper that is meant just to persuade. Use one of the student essays in this book to practise finding more examples of arguments to refute.
3. Do a keyword search of "Montreal." How many hits did you get? Narrow your search to find information that supports the key points of this essay. What keyword gave you the best results?

Of Pain, Predators, and Pleasure

Walter Isaacs

1 The issue of whether fish feel pain when hooked by an angler has recently been a topic of heated debate. Published scientific studies arguing that the fish's mouth does or does not have pain receptors have supported both sides of the argument. It seems to me that this squabble is as irrelevant as the medieval debates about

how many angels can dance on the head of a pin. Of course we cause the fish distress—mortal distress! Like any animal, the fish is programmed to survive and procreate. Any predatory threat to that primal function (from a bear, an osprey, a bigger fish, or an angler) must cause extreme stress. Whether that stress can be called "pain" through anthropomorphism, it's certainly more dire to the fish than the prick of a hook in its jaw (felt as "pain" or not). To argue that we aren't distressing a fish by catching it is to hand opponents of fishing proof that fishers are either ignorant or in denial.

2 I admit that I love tricking fish. I take as much pleasure as anyone in catching them, and my pleasure is increased when I've been especially clever or skillful in fooling one of these cunning creatures into taking my fly. I do everything that I can to minimize the pain and stress on any fish I catch, but I cannot deny that by catching the fish, I am in a sense torturing it for my pleasure. How can I justify my actions?

3 First, I acknowledge that I am a predator and something somewhere in me loves the idea of capturing a wild animal through stealth or guile, even when (as I almost always do) I release it unharmed. Whether this instinct comes from a gene somewhere in my DNA or a gland buried in the folds of my brain, there's no denying that it's there. Just as I enjoy laughter, anchovies on pizza, warm fall days, sex, a Bach concerto, and a good Riesling, I enjoy catching fish on a fly. Some pleasures are instinctive, some are learned, but the fact that they are pleasures cannot be denied. Yes, I could give up these pleasures if the motivation were sufficient, but so far I haven't heard any arguments strong enough to convince me to relinquish any of them.

4 Second, let's acknowledge that, as predators go, anglers are relatively benign. When you compare the millions of fish that are hatched to the number that live long enough to be the prey of anglers, it's clear that other predators are more efficient and more dangerous than fly fishers. I suppose the case could be made that for every salmon killed by an angler, thousands of eels and other sea creatures are saved. If we can anthropomorphize the fish's pain, let's go another step and ask the fish which predator it would rather be caught by: that female osprey gliding over the river, or Walter Isaacs. Both predators will cause it the immediate stress of being caught, but in the first case, the osprey will feed its catch alive to its chicks; in the second, the fish will survive to procreate.

5 Finally, because of my love of fishing, I contribute both time and money to support such activities as the restoration and maintenance of stream habitats, stocking programs, and the development of a cleaner, wilder environment in which fish can thrive. In other words, my conservation efforts help to produce more and healthier fish at the end of each season than there would be if I didn't enjoy fishing so much.

6 If I could fish without harming the creatures in any way, I'd do it in a heartbeat. But since I must hurt the fish somewhat to pursue an activity that gives me such pleasure, these justifications serve to let me do it in good conscience, while recognizing and respecting the stress I cause. I know that what I've said won't convince those who are fundamentally opposed to angling, and I understand their

viewpoint. But such people just don't seem to have that gene or gland that makes fishing such a pleasure for me. Heck, I even know people who don't like sex.

Questions for Discussion

1. In the margin, identify the main parts of this essay (see the outline format on p. 82).
2. The argument that is the basis for this essay is supported by three points. What are they? In what order has the author arranged his supporting evidence?
3. This essay was first published in a fly-fishing magazine. Identify three or four clues that indicate the piece was written for a sympathetic audience.
4. How would the essay differ if it had been written for an audience of animal-rights activists? Draft a rough outline for such an essay.
5. The essay's concluding sentence seems to have been tossed off for the purpose of ending on a light note. What more serious purpose does it serve in supporting the author's argument?
6. This essay is the author's response to contradictory findings about whether or not fish feel pain the way humans do. Use the Internet to find articles on this subject. Be sure to choose articles that reflect both sides of the argument. After reading a few of these articles, decide which side of the debate you support. In a sentence or two, summarize your opinion and identify three or four reasons that support it.

Exercise 13.1

Read through the following list of propositions. With a partner, select one that you are both interested in, but do not discuss it. Working individually, write down two or three points both for and against the issue. Then exchange papers and read each other's work. Which points appear on both lists? Why? Can you tell from the points your partner presented whether he or she is for or against the issue?

Canada should (should not) increase its level of immigration.

The salaries of professional athletes should (should not) be capped.

Professional athletes should (should not) be allowed to use performance-enhancing drugs.

Courses in physical education should (should not) be required throughout high school.

Smartphones should (should not) be allowed in classrooms.

Canadians should (should not) be required by law to vote in national elections (as is done in Australia).

Exercise 13.2

Most people have firm convictions, yet few are willing to take action to uphold them. Everyone agrees, for example, that a cure for cancer should be found, but not everyone participates in fundraising events or supports the Cancer Society. With a partner, choose a charitable cause in which you believe and list all the reasons why people should give money to support it. Then list all the reasons people might give for not donating.

Decide which of you will take the "pro" side and which the "con," and write a short essay arguing your position. You will know from your discussion whether your partner is sympathetic or hostile, so you will know whether you should approach your subject directly or indirectly. Then exchange papers and critique each other's work.

Exercise 13.3 Together with a partner, select a *small*, controversial, local issue (one involving your community, school, or profession, for example). Discuss the two sides and, together, write an argument using the "their side–my side" pattern of organization.

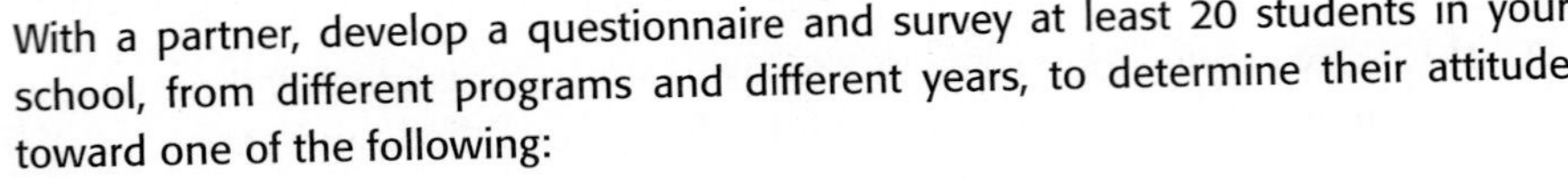

Exercise 13.4 With a partner, develop a questionnaire and survey at least 20 students in your school, from different programs and different years, to determine their attitude toward one of the following:

- food services
- class sizes
- instructors' teaching ability
- required (or general education) courses
- tutorial (or counselling) services

Both of you should take notes during these interviews.

Once you and your partner have gathered enough information, it's time to work independently. Compose an indirect argument that arrives at a conclusion about the issue and makes a recommendation based on the evidence you have gathered. Compare your paper with your partner's. What are the main similarities and differences between your two compositions? What conclusions can you draw from your comparative analysis?

Exercise 13.5 Choose an issue with which you are familiar and about which you feel strongly. If you don't feel strongly about anything, choose a proposition from the list below. Draft a thesis statement and outline your reasons and evidence. Then write a persuasive paper, making sure that your points are well supported and that the paper is clearly structured. Assume that your reader is not hostile, but is not enthusiastically supportive, either.

Grades in college and university courses should (should not) reflect a student's effort as well as achievement.

Our college should (should not) permit the use of computers during exams.

Self-inflicted health problems like smoking and obesity should (should not) be covered by taxpayer-funded healthcare.

Facebook and other social media should (should not) be monitored for unacceptable content such as bullying, racism, and bigotry.

Parents should (should not) be held liable for acts of theft or vandalism committed by their minor children.

Writing in the Workplace: Memos, Letters, and Short Reports

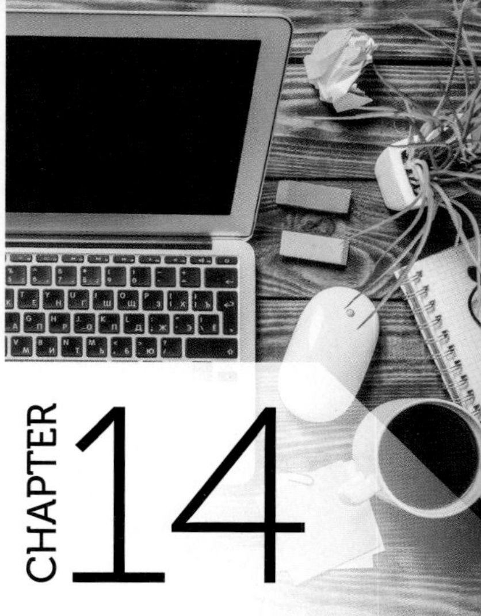

While the majority of our discussion in this textbook has been about essay writing, we have also endeavoured to explain how this basic tool can be used not only in college or university courses but also in the workplace.

Here we will outline the three most common workplace styles of writing: the letter, the memo (more than likely now the electronic memo, or email), and the short report. While we won't get into the specific types of letters, memos, and reports, we will focus on the similarities in style and organization to the basic essay style and give you a very brief review of the most common formats and how to use them.

There is quite a long list of similarities between academic essays and workplace writing. Both

- include an introduction, body, and conclusion
- include the main message (*thesis* in an essay, *main message* in workplace writing) up front
- are written with an audience focus
- contain research as appropriate
- are organized according to writing purpose (persuasive, information-based, etc.)
- are to be carefully edited and proofread
- contain formatting appropriate to their style and function

As you can see, there is little left out of our essay writing toolkit. Basically, all of the elements of essay writing essentials are also workplace writing essentials. The only differences are perhaps the length of paragraphs, the number of paragraphs, and the formatting of pages and information.

The ultimate similarity between essays and workplace writing is one of the reasons that academic writing is a staple in most post-secondary programs: like it or not, the written word is often a stand-in for our spoken thoughts or opinions. As well, writing is a great way to summarize, organize, and inform others of information in a flexible way.

The following is not meant as a definitive guide to workplace writing. Your library likely contains myriad workplace or business writing textbooks. It is even possible to find workplace writing guides meant specifically for your future career. All that we present here is a little road map between the two styles so that you can see ways to adapt the work you have done in your academic career to what you will do in the workplace.

Memos

The memo, or *memorandum* in its fully written form, is the shortest of our workplace documents. Its purpose is to transmit information to a large number of people as quickly as possible. This is why, for the most part, it has been eliminated in many workplaces in favour of emails. The styles of a paper memo and an email are similar. Both begin with whom the message is from, whom it is to, the date, and the subject of the message. The subject line of a memo or email is very important—like the cover page, the title of your essay, or your thesis, it is an indicator of the contents within.

Most memos begin like this:

TO: Kelly Parsons
FROM: Roxane West
DATE: May 1, 2018
SUBJECT: Request for Approval for Conference Travel to Aruba, September 2018

You can see that in these *headers* (as they are usually called in workplace or business writing manuals) all the information is presented clearly and the subject reveals the specific goal of the memo. This helps the reader decide the urgency of the message and determine how much time needs to be given to it.

Emails should be prepared in a similar fashion, keeping the reader in mind as the subject line is prepared:

TO: Roxane West <r.west@bestjobever.com>
FROM: Kelly Parsons <k.parsons@bestjobever.com>
SUBJECT: Approval Granted for September 2018 Conference Request
DATE: May 6, 2018

Without having read the contents of the memo or email, we still have a good idea of what transpired during this communication. Roxane asked for approval for conference travel in September 2018 and Kelly granted the request. The content is important, but the subject lines allow us a good glimpse of the purpose of the correspondence.

Most memos

- are written for a specific audience (we often talk about "internal memos," which are sent out to employees within one business, or "external memos," which are sent from one business to another)
- contain three paragraphs or more (an introduction, a body, and a conclusion)
- offer information or request information
- are written on letterhead and formatted with the appropriate information up front
- do not contain a traditional close or signature line (that information appears at the top)

Memos might be distributed to a lot of people or to just one. As always, it's important to keep the audience in mind when you are organizing your information and writing your memo.

A memo's length can vary but usually doesn't go over two pages. Now let's look at what goes into a memo. A memo is meant to be a short description, a request for information, information itself, or a more general request (for money, approvals, etc.).

The actual memo for the above travel request example might look like this:

TO: Kelly Parsons
FROM: Roxane West
DATE: May 1, 2018
SUBJECT: Request for Approval for Conference Travel to Aruba, September 2018

Kelly,

I have been accepted to present at the annual Best Jobs Ever conference in Aruba in September 2018. While going over some of our policies, I noticed that there is a fund for conference travel, so I would like to request partial funding for the trip and time off (used as holidays).

BJE 2018 will be held at the Aruba Best Hotel Ever Sept. 3–5, 2018. Air Canada flight 649 leaves Victoria for Aruba Sept. 2 at 4:30 in the afternoon. I would be able to work a half day on August 31. I would return Sept. 6, a Thursday, and would be back to work Sept. 7. That totals 3.5 days of holidays.

BJE policy 16a states that employees can receive a maximum of $1200 for conference funding. Here is a general breakdown of the estimated cost of the trip:

Flight:	$648
Hotel (5 nights at $120 per night):	600
Food (5 days at approximately $40 per day):	200
Total:	$1448

If BJE will pay $1200, as the policy states, I would be happy to cover the rest.

Please let me know at your earliest convenience if you accept my conference request, request for holiday time, and allowance for the conference funding. I look forward to representing Best Job Ever in Aruba and will make sure to write a full report upon my return to Victoria.

This memo is four paragraphs and has a clear introduction with a request and a clear conclusion that includes any next steps to be taken. The two body paragraphs provide the information that Kelly needs (and so is audience-focused) to make a decision. This isn't so different from an essay that compares different styles of cars and suggests that readers look at certain brands the next time they are car shopping. The same persuasive style is used, and relevant information is provided. The difference is in the length of the paper and the way that the memo summarizes information into a readable format style with short lists using either bullets or numbering.

Exercise 14.1 Write a memo from a customer service manager of a travel agency to all employees, requesting that they try to make their workplace scent-free. In your paragraphs you could give reasons for the change, suggestions on how to address the issue with someone who is wearing a scent, and methods to contact you if there are any questions. You might also include some information on what other small businesses have done to ensure equity in their environment and request any other suggestions.

Exercise 14.2 Construct an email, including the headers and the subject line, that is sent externally from one coffee franchise to all others introducing a new contest called "Coffee Stories of the World." Include information about the contest, why you developed it, and how others might get involved.

Letters

The letter resembles the essay quite closely in the way that paragraphs are laid out, but, as with memos, the information within can vary widely. For the purposes of this discussion, we'll use an important type of letter that you will likely write many of in your career; that is, we'll look at the cover letter, its various attributes, and how you can use your essay writing skills to craft an excellent version that is likely to get you that all-important interview. You will find this cover letter to be much more comprehensive than a stock version you could find on the Internet.

Like the memo, there are many different ways to write cover letters. For a quick summer job, a short cover letter that outlines your skills and refers to your résumé might be best, but we want to focus on the type of cover letter that you might use to get your dream job or career. These letters are usually longer and more focused. Here we present a five-paragraph cover letter model.

Formatting the Letter

As with memos, it is the formatting that creates the visual difference from the essay.

The overall format of the letter changes in small ways depending on the purpose of the letter. Because most business and academic correspondence is formal, we'll look only at formal styles. Informal styles are usually used for personal correspondence—consider the difference between the memo we outlined and an email you'd send your friends asking what they are doing this weekend.

In formal letter writing, termed the *full block format*, information about both who is sending the letter and who is receiving it is included at the top of the letter. The beginning would look like this:

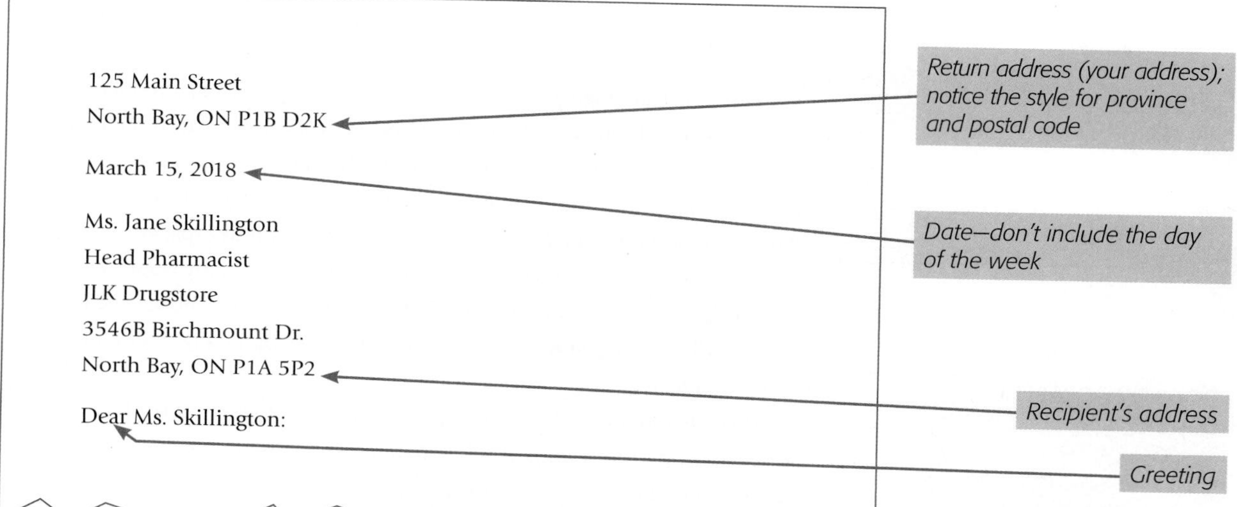
125 Main Street
North Bay, ON P1B D2K

March 15, 2018

Ms. Jane Skillington
Head Pharmacist
JLK Drugstore
3546B Birchmount Dr.
North Bay, ON P1A 5P2

Dear Ms. Skillington:

Usually, this introductory information is single-spaced with two line spaces between each section. Your word-processing program may have a model cover letter or basic letter format that sets the page up for you. If it doesn't, use margins of 2.5 cm on all sides and single-space the body of the letter. It is important to consider the spacing around and within the letter. You don't want the information to appear too cramped, so use a 12-point font.

When writing a cover letter for a full-time professional position, don't worry too much if you go over one page. That said, if you have only one or two lines on the second page, it is better to try to organize or edit the information to fit on one. If you have to go over one page, aim to have at least one paragraph on the second page.

The next section of the letter contains your *body paragraphs*. These paragraphs should not be indented and should be written in a style similar to the essay format discussed throughout this textbook. In the case of a cover letter, which is meant to be persuasive (see Chapter 12), you should outline in the thesis statement the main reasons (three is standard) why company *x* should hire you.

In our example, JLK Drugstore would benefit from having you as a pharmacy technician. Perhaps the advertisement, which you find in the local paper, says the company is looking for someone who has a post-secondary education in your program—that could become one of the main body points of your cover letter essay. It might also want someone who is dedicated—that could be a second point. It is also interested in team players—well, you have lots of volunteer experience with that, so include it as your third point.

The idea is that a cover letter, as a style of persuasive writing, is still meant to be audience-focused and either research- or example-driven. You are sharing your experiences as if they are the data that the company will use to make its decision. Those body paragraphs (there will be five: an introduction, your three points, and a conclusion) should be written in the same format as an essay. You want to ensure clarity, show confidence, and put forward your thesis in an interesting and easy-to-read way. Here is the continuation of our cover letter, using the ideas presented above:

INTRODUCTORY PARAGRAPH

Thesis

JLK Drugstores are highly regarded in North Bay. Having been a resident of the city for fifteen years, I have participated as a volunteer in some of the many community health events your business has hosted. As a new graduate of the pharmacy technology program at Georgian College in Barrie, I took immediate interest in your ad in the local newspaper for a pharmacy technician. My education, stability, and team spirit would be a great fit for your organization, and I hope this letter and the attached résumé will inspire you to have the same confidence in me that I have in your drugstore.

BODY PARAGRAPH 1: EDUCATION
In your topic sentence, reference your education and any specific professional credentials. You can also mention courses you have taken and skills you have—give concrete examples. Each paragraph should be as detailed as possible and should include information that is not on the résumé.

After obtaining my diploma in pharmacy technology in 2016, I followed up with various courses in CPR training, specialized emergency procedures, and a St. John Ambulance training program. I learned how to deal with stressed patients and how to increase my own patience in difficult situations. I think this knowledge can be beneficial when dealing with clients in a pharmacy setting. For example, I once had the opportunity to help a woman with very high blood pressure learn some special breathing techniques that got her through a challenging time. I believe it is not only my educational preparation but also my ability to help people that will make me valuable to JLK.

BODY PARAGRAPH 2: STABILITY
Work this section the same way. After your topic sentence, describe events that show that you are stable and dedicated. Stay audience-focused—keep coming back to JLK, and definitely avoid starting every sentence with I.

In any client-centred career, such as that offered by JLK, it is stability that allows a great employee to make a difference. During my previous work experience, I learned that several factors—my punctuality on the job and my commitment to the company, as well as my temperament and job skills—contribute to my being a stable, reliable employee. At JLK, I know I would display the same behaviours—commitment, dedication, and stability—that kept me at my previous jobs for as long as I was able. It is only because of returning to school in a different town that the time spent at my past jobs was shortened. Now that I have completed my diploma, I look forward to starting a career with JLK.

JLK, as a community member, must reach out to its community—both internally and externally. In my own experience, recognizing that I am a part of a community team has been essential for success. No matter how busy I have been in my past jobs, a simple smile or "I'll be with you in a minute" has helped ensure both customers and co-workers feel important. Making sure to do things correctly is much more important than doing things quickly. I learned that by observing how others have worked in medical settings, and I look forward to meeting the same high standards as part of the JLK team.

After you have looked at my résumé and read this cover letter, I hope my education in pharmacy technology, commitment to a stable and active workplace environment, and positive team spirit will convince you I would make an ideal JLK employee. If you have any questions at all, Ms. Skillington, I would be happy to answer them during an interview for the advertised position. I am available any time through email at jess.marzone@getajob.com. You can also contact me any time after 5 p.m. at (249) 555-7086. If I am not home, please leave a message, and I'll get back to you promptly. I look forward to speaking with you more about how I would be an asset to JLK.

Sincerely,

Jess Marzone

BODY PARAGRAPH 3: TEAM SPIRIT/GOOD TEAM PLAYER
Provide specific information and keep your examples relevant. The more applicable your examples, the better.

CONCLUSION
Your closing is, most importantly, where you ask for an interview. Be specific about how the company can contact you: give a phone number and your availability. Summarize what you believe you can do for the company (not what you want for you!).

COMPLIMENTARY CLOSE
At the left margin, write your close. "Sincerely," or "Thanks," will do. Leave a space for your signature. Then type your name.

Make sure to leave space at the bottom of the page so the letter doesn't look cramped.

To summarize, letters

- include formal elements such as your address, the recipient's full name and address, the date, and a greeting or salutation
- include an introduction, discussion of at least three main points, and a conclusion
- include a complimentary close and your typed name, with space between for your signature
- are audience-focused
- use *I* but not too frequently
- contain relevant information only
- are carefully edited and proofread like any other piece of writing

Your cover letter will be specific to just the one job you are applying for. Creating a generic cover letter that can be sent to multiple companies is a dangerous game. How can your work be audience-focused if you haven't identified the audience? The extra time spent writing individual letters will pay off in more interviews (hopefully) and a better job in the end.

Exercise 14.3 Find an advertisement for a job you might be interested in, either online through a site like www.workpolis.com or www.monster.ca or through the newspaper. The Canadian government also has a general website—http://jobs-emplois.gc.ca/index-eng.htm—that might be useful. Make sure the advertisement you find is linked to a career, not just part-time employment.

Once you have the advertisement, go through it with a highlighter and identify all the main requirements. Now choose what you think are the three most important traits required for the job and, using those three traits, craft a thesis for your cover letter.

Exercise 14.4 Using your thesis from Exercise 14.3, write a cover letter. Since the idea is to create a mock letter that could be useful to you in the future, you can make up "selling points" that you haven't yet achieved (e.g., your education). Remember that each cover letter must be different, but the overall format (e.g., thesis statement and three important skills or traits) should remain the same.

Exercise 14.5 Find a partner or create a group of three. Share your draft cover letters and the advertisement you used. Critique, proofread, and help edit each other's work. Pretend you are a busy human resources worker: could you easily determine your applicant's main skills? Share your letter with as many classmates as you can, and work to get your letter into its best possible state.

Short Reports

There are many types of short reports you might be asked to write in the workplace and many texts designed to outline how to write them. Here we will present the basic structure of the short report and, again, focus on the similarities to essay writing and the transferable skills you can use to prepare excellent short reports.

Short reports, usually one to three pages, present information in such a way that the reader can quickly take action in response to that information. Reports are often persuasive, though sometimes they simply provide information for its own sake. Consider a trip report, which is required in many workplaces to outline details (e.g., people met with, events attended) and discuss what occurred while the employee was off-site.

Formatting the Short Report

Short reports are formatted so that informative bits and pieces are presented together but can be read independently rather than as part of a whole.

Almost all short reports include an introduction, a discussion section, and a conclusion or recommendations section. These sections are identified in the report with titles: "Introduction," "Discussion," and "Conclusions/Recommendations." This formatting is different from that of an essay, in which we tend not to announce such details—after all, writing "Thesis here!" might take the reader out of the essay experience, in which flow, argument, and information come together in one organic whole.

Longer reports, of four pages or more, are often broken down into even more discrete sections and contain a title page, a table of contents, and other formatting elements. One common way to format longer reports is to include the following six sections (sometimes called the SIDCRA method):

- summary
- introduction
- discussion
- conclusion
- recommendations
- appendixes

The short report doesn't usually contain a summary since it is already short, nor does it contain sections at the end in the form of appendixes. It also collapses the conclusion and recommendations into one section.

In essence, a short report is more objective than an essay and is formatted for quick readability. Brevity is essential, and formatting techniques such as numbered lists and bullet points, which provide scannability, are report basics. So, instead of writing paragraphs about the fact that while you were at a conference on mechanisms to promote better handwashing you learned about new technologies, new products on the market, statistics on handwashing and illness, and ways to train employees to have better handwashing techniques, you would present these details either in a bulleted or a numbered list, like this:

Example 1:

While I was in Winnipeg, Manitoba, this past week (April 2–9), I took away four main types of information about handwashing, including

1. new technologies to make handwashing more effective
2. new products on the market for better handwashing
3. statistics on the dangers of not washing hands
4. how to train employees on good handwashing techniques

or

Example 2:

While I was in Winnipeg, Manitoba, this past week (April 2–9), I learned a lot about handwashing, including

- new technologies to make handwashing more effective
- new products on the market for better handwashing
- statistics on the dangers of not washing hands
- how to train employees on good handwashing techniques

Putting the information in a list makes it easy to read and remember.

A fuller description of this information would be included in the Discussion section of your short report, the part that corresponds to the body paragraphs of an essay. The Discussion section of a report, in fact, is often broken up into paragraphs just as the body of an essay is, with one topic per paragraph. If we take the above example of a short report introduction, we can see that the four listed pieces of information that were gathered from the conference would result in four body paragraphs in the report's Discussion section. Each of these paragraphs even might be titled to give the reader a clear sense of what is being discussed:

New Technologies

New Products

Dangers of Poor Handwashing: Some Statistics

Training Employees in Handwashing Techniques

Once you complete the Discussion section, you would write a conclusion or recommendation—in this case, it might be that your organization considers changing some of its present strategies. You might even want to use a compare-and-contrast writing style (see Chapter 12) to convince your employer to adopt new technologies for handwashing. Your conclusions and recommendations should follow naturally from your discussion.

Finally, most reports end with a specific call to action. In our example, as part of your trip report, you might ask your boss to let you know by a certain date whether she or he would be interested in getting the spokesperson for the new handwashing technology to visit your workplace. Or the call to action might simply be a request to discuss your learnings in more detail at a later time. Regardless, most reports have action and change in mind, and your conclusion should reflect that.

Consolidating the information into a report and then providing it to your audience usually also involves attaching a brief letter or memo to introduce the contents. If you are distributing a short report *internally*—that is, within the place you work—a memo would suffice. If you are sending the report out *externally*, a letter might be more appropriate. The following example shows what this short report might look like.

Introduction

TO: Joanna Snow, Vice President, White Lily Nursing Home

FROM: Joel Barthes, Research Assistant, White Lily Nursing Home Safety Unit

DATE: April 11, 2018

SUBJECT: Trip Report from April 2–9 Hygiene Conference, Winnipeg, Manitoba

---

While I was in Winnipeg, Manitoba, this past week (April 2–9), I learned a lot about handwashing techniques and new products that can aid in handwashing improvements. As the Lily White safety coordinator, I know from the research that handwashing is an important aspect of the care we provide. Due to recent problems we have had with increased illness and contamination, we may want to consider making some new and better choices in handwashing. The strategies presented at the conference included the following:

- new technologies to make handwashing more effective
- new products on the market for better handwashing
- statistics on the dangers of not washing hands
- how to train employees on good handwashing techniques

Discussion

New Technologies

Three new technologies were presented at the conference. The first was an all-automatic sanitizer machine. The second was a glove that contained soap. The third was a full washing station with voice commands. The prices for each were as follows:

- Automatic sanitizing machine: $4000 apiece
- Soap glove system: $1000 a set (includes six gloves: one each of small, medium, and large for men and women)
- Full washing station with voice command: $9000 each

All three seemed expensive, and, when asked, all three companies admitted that this was their first year selling the products. That led me to believe that at this point success with the product isn't guaranteed despite the high prices.

New Products

Two new products were demonstrated at the conference. The first one was an allergen-free foaming product called "All Gone." It was supposed to require less time washing the hands and enable quicker hand drying. Many of us tried the product and found that although it seemed to clean and dry well, our hands became really dry even after just one wash. The second product was the Insta-Blue hand-glove washing system; its creator, Harrison Veldt, did a demonstration. The product is a light gel that coats hands and turns them light blue. You know you can stop rinsing when the blue glove it creates is instantly gone. We thought the product had many interesting properties—for one, it left our hands very soft. We tried it multiple times and were still impressed.

Dangers of Poor Handwashing: Some Statistics

These presentations weren't focused on tips for handwashing but just provided information about the increase in illness from poor handwashing techniques. One study that interested us was that of a group that used Insta-Blue in a nursing home. They discovered that of the forty staff members who used the product, more than half reported a decrease in patient illness over six months (as compared to their statistics when they didn't use that particular product).

Training Employees in Handwashing Techniques

These sessions focused on training techniques, which included the use of the new technologies, but nothing new was presented beyond the ministry-supported guidelines for handwashing. In fact, we were told that some of the products don't comply with the guidelines, that we should avoid discussing this fact in training sessions, and that the guidelines were

Conclusions/ recommendations

overly strict at times. Since we are focused on compliance and finding a product that really makes a difference, there were no magic solutions at these sessions, and any training tips offered weren't useful to us.

For most of the conference attendees, Harrison Veldt's presentation on Insta-Blue hand cleaner was a definitive hit. From the information presented above, I hope it is clear that while using good handwashing techniques and keeping track of our illnesses are important, finding good products that will make the task more effective is of primary importance. While the three new technologies were impressive, they are expensive and don't have extensive field-testing yet. For a relatively low fee, Harrison Veldt would be available to make a presentation to our staff and bring along some complimentary products. If you let me know of your possible interest by April 15, I will contact him and set up a visit.

Although there are many types of reports, always keep in mind these two priorities:

1. The reader comes first in almost all writing.
2. Readability is key.

Make sure your work is well edited and proofread and contains a clear request for action.

Exercise 14.6 Go through the report above and see if any more information could be presented using a numbered or bulleted list. Make the changes and determine if the report is more reader friendly.

Exercise 14.7 Pretend you have just gone to a talk on scent-free workplaces. Write a short report to your boss, introduced with a brief memo, that outlines the arguments for and against scent-free workplaces. Try to convince him or her to share your opinion. End with a request for action.

Exercise 14.8 Since you have now come to the end of the main part of the textbook (that is, other than the revising, grammar, and mechanics sections), write a letter or short report to your instructor outlining the three most important writing skills you have learned throughout this course. Consider how improving your skills in writing might help you both in your academic career and later in life. Make sure to edit your work carefully and be audience-focused!

Part 5

Writing Research Papers

These chapters will explain some of the different kinds of source material you can choose from during the research process and tell you the strengths and weaknesses, as well as the functions and organization, of each method. Chapter 15 looks at the preparation process for research. Chapter 16 shows you how to integrate source material into your paper, while Chapter 17 looks at formatting that material.

As with all essays, considering the audience is of critical importance. One of the main reasons to write a report is to share information across boundaries, so it is essential that you consider not only the ideas but also the preparation and formatting of your work so that it can be easily understood.

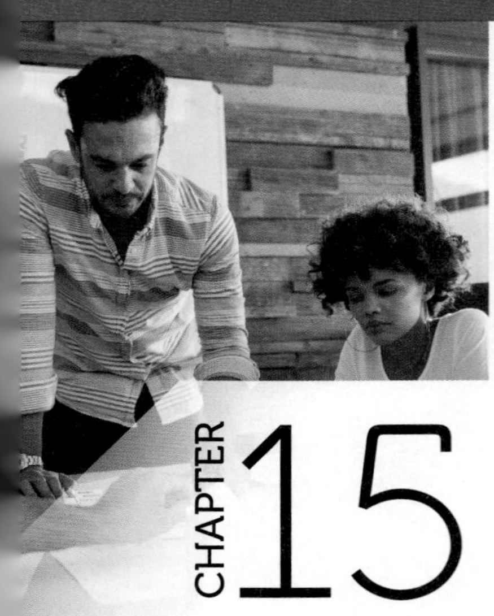

CHAPTER 15 Preparing for Research and Choosing a Research Method

Google is not a synonym for *research*.
—Dan Brown, *The Lost Symbol*

A research paper is an essay that presents the results of a writer's investigation of a topic in print, electronic, or multimedia formats. The skills involved—finding, evaluating, and assimilating the ideas of other writers—are essential in any field of study. They will also be useful to you in your career. Much of the writing you do on the job, especially if you are in management, requires you to express in your own words the facts, opinions, and ideas of others. It is of almost equal importance to know how to understand and interpret the ideas of others, as discussed in Chapter 3, as it is to understand your own mind.

The writing of a research paper follows the same process as other kinds of essay writing, from planning through drafting to revising. The difference is that instead of relying exclusively on what you already know about a topic, you are expected to include additional source material—facts, data, examples, or opinions of other writers—to support your thesis.

A research paper is not simply a collection of what other people have said about a subject. It is your responsibility to set the thesis, determine the focus, and control the discussion. It is *your* paper, *your* subject, *your* main points; ideas from other writers should be included as support for *your* topic sentences. The research paper isn't about how smart others are; it is about how you organize and use others' information to support ideas of your own!

When writing an academic paper, you must be sure from the start that you clearly understand what the instructor will accept as source material to support your thesis—in other words, what types of research you are allowed or expected to do. Some instructors will accept information from popular magazines, *Wikipedia*, blogs, or social networking sites. Others will not. Generally, instructors look for a range of resources, including *primary materials* such as eyewitness accounts, historical documents, literary works, personal interviews, and speeches. Instructors will also be looking for *secondary sources* that contribute supporting ideas or analyses, such as books, government documents, articles in newspapers or journals, and information from reputable websites.

There is nothing like looking, if you want to find something. You certainly usually find something, if you look, but it is not always quite the something you were after.
—J. R. R. Tolkien, *The Hobbit*

One of the challenges of writing a research paper is differentiating between your ideas and those you take from sources. Readers cannot hear the different "speakers," so you have to indicate who said what. To separate your sources from your own ideas, research papers require *documentation*—a system of acknowledging source materials that is covered in Chapter 17. Documentation tells your readers that the ideas they are reading have been borrowed from another writer; it also enables your readers to find the source and read the material for themselves. In academic institutions, two widely used documentation styles are the American Psychological Association (APA) style and the Modern Language Association (MLA) style.

Tips for Writing a Research Paper

1. Don't forget you still need a thesis and well-organized ideas.

Instructors assign research papers so that they can assess not only your research skills but also your writing skills.

2. Choose a subject that interests you.

Define the subject as precisely as you can before beginning your research, but be prepared to modify, adapt, and revise it as you research and write your paper.

3. Once you have a topic in mind, do some preliminary research and talk to a librarian.

Be specific when you discuss your topic and your focus. Every library is unique. In addition to books, journals, and audiovisual sources, there will be library subscriptions to online journals (e-journals) and electronic books (e-books) as well as "best of the Web" or subject guide collections that have been selected by the librarians for your program of study. Working with the library staff early in the research process can save you hours.

4. Even though your instructor may be your only reader, think of your potential audience as your classmates or possibly members of a professional organization.

This way, you can count on a certain amount of common or shared knowledge. Assume that your audience wants to learn more about your topic, what conclusions you have reached, and what evidence you have found to support your thesis.

5. Manage your time carefully.

Divide the work into a number of tasks, develop a schedule that leaves lots of time for revision, and stick to your schedule. Research papers are usually longer than essays, and the planning process is more complex. You will need all the time you've been given to find the sources you need, decide what you want to say, and then draft, revise, and polish your paper.

6. When making research notes, be diligent.

Sources cannot be used unless they are clearly documented. There is nothing worse than having to discard a great quote because you cannot find the original source. Whether it is print, audiovisual, or electronic in format, each resource has specific documentation requirements. For every source you use, record all of the authors' names, the book or document title, publication data, and page numbers. For electronic sources, also record the URL and the date you accessed the website.

7. Document your sources according to whatever style your instructor prefers.

8. Use your source material to support your own ideas, not the other way around.

It is especially important, before you begin to research, to have done some good planning and organizing. Remember that it is your ideas that are central, even in a paper that uses research. Every time you use a summary, a paraphrase, or a quote from something that you have researched, you should explain why it is important to you. Go through some of the 10 critical thinking steps from Chapter 3 (see page 43 for a summary) to help you show just how your research supports your own thesis and ideas.

9. Revise, edit, and proofread carefully.

If you omit this final step, the hours and weeks you have spent on your assignment will be wasted, not rewarded. See Part 6 of this textbook for help.

A little preparation up front will save you a lot of time and possibly much grief later on.

Finally, here are a few final basic reminders. Your first step in writing a research paper is the same as your first step in any writing task: select a suitable subject, preferably one you are curious about. Whether you are assigned a topic or choose your own, don't rush off to the library or log on to the Internet right away. If you're not sure what your instructor expects, clarify what is required of you. Next, even if your subject is tentative, check it with the 4-S test: is it significant, single, specific, and supportable (researchable)? If not, refine it by using the techniques discussed in Chapter 4. Finally, consider what approach you might take in presenting your subject. Does it lend itself to a comparison? Process? Cause or effect? If the topic is assigned, often the wording of the assignment will suggest how your instructor wants you to develop it. Deciding up front what kind of paper you are going to write will save you hours of time, both in the library and at your desk.

In the workplace, people rarely have the opportunity to select a research topic without consultation. In some cases, the subject is assigned or approved by a board of directors; in others, a committee is responsible for ensuring that a research project meets the company's needs. Before you start your own research project, take some time to ensure that your proposed subject is appropriate for the time and space you have been given.

Exercise 15.1

For this exercise, which focuses on workplace research skills, the class should be divided into "committees" of four or five people. Each committee should be assigned a colour and each member given a piece of coloured paper. (For example, everyone in the red group gets a piece of red paper.)

- Identify both a chair and a note-taker for your committee. At the direction of the chair, have each committee member present an idea for a research paper. After each presentation, discuss the subject in terms of its significance to the target audience (the whole class, including the instructor). If your committee feels a subject requires revision to be significant, make these revisions as a group. It is important that the committee come to a consensus regarding any revisions.

- Once each subject is agreed upon as significant, record it on a slip of the coloured paper assigned to your committee.
- Repeat this procedure until your committee has identified at least one significant subject for each of its members.
- Toss your committee's subjects into the company's think tank (a container), along with the subjects submitted by the other committees in the class.
- The chair of each committee draws out of the think tank four or five proposed research subjects, being sure to have a representative sampling of colours from other committees.
- As a committee, discuss each subject that has been drawn from the think tank. Since each has already been approved as significant by another committee, your task is to determine whether each proposed subject is single and specific.
- For each subject, record any revisions that the committee deems necessary and briefly explain why.
- Return the revised subjects to their appropriate committees according to the corresponding coloured paper.
- Once your committee has received its original proposed research subjects, discuss the suggested revisions until everyone understands them.
- Next, as a committee, discuss whether each proposed subject is supportable. What sorts of research materials would you look for to help you explain and defend each subject?
- Record the final version of the proposed research subjects on a flip chart, ready to present to a board of directors. (You should have one subject for each member of the committee.)
- Present your committee's proposed research subjects before the board of directors (i.e., the class). Discuss the revisions and decide whether each proposal now meets the criteria of the 4-S test.

When you're sure your subject is appropriate and you've decided, at least tentatively, on the approach you're going to take, you are ready to focus on the kind of information you need to look for in your research. For example, if you've been asked to apply four theories of conflict to a case study, you won't waste time discussing the major schools of conflict theory or their development over the last few decades. You can restrict your investigation to sources that contain information relevant to your specific subject.

Once you have an idea of the kind of information you need in order to develop your topic, it's time to find the best sources you can. But how will you know if what you've found is "good" information?

Ways of Doing Research

There is a variety of ways to do research, and each method has its own strengths and weaknesses. In this section, we will outline some of the most common methods and help you to start evaluating what will work best for you. We will explain some of the terminology used by library staff, give you tips on how to access electronic information and physical collections, and summarize the strengths and weaknesses of various sources.

The Library Catalogue

Your library catalogue is the first place you should check when beginning a research paper. It is accessible on computer terminals in the library, as well as on computers outside of the library, through the library's website. Search options include title, author, subject, and keyword. How you search the catalogue will depend on what you are looking for and on what you already know.

A title keyword search is often the fastest way of retrieving material. If the library carries a book, journal, government document, audiovisual item, or even a full-text Internet link, chances are a keyword will appear somewhere in the title. Alternatively, ask a librarian to demonstrate an "advanced search" or "power search" feature that will allow you to cross-search several fields at the same time.

The search will result in a list of "brief records." Click on a brief record for more information. The "full record" will include subjects, notes, descriptions, and so on. These descriptions will provide ideas on new subjects to extend your search. The full record may connect you directly to the full text of an online source. In these cases, the linked book, government report, or journal can be reviewed right from the screen, without further searching.

When you find an item that is of interest, be sure to record the author(s)' name(s), book or document title, and the full library call number, location, and status. In many libraries you can use a "shopping cart" feature to create a list of books or other materials that you want to review, and you can email it to yourself.

Your instructor might choose to have a librarian come in to give you more details about using the library's resources; however, it is highly likely that your library's website already supplies a full list of resources and online databases, as well as information about methods of researching. Resource materials vary widely from school to school, so do some digging and find out what is available. The library catalogue connects you to collections of books, government documents, audiovisual materials, and perhaps even maps, archival works, or music scores. The research article from *Qualitative Health Research* called "Negotiating Violence in the Context of Transphobia and Criminalization: The Experiences of Trans Sex Workers in Vancouver, Canada" is an example of the type of in-depth article that you can find in a database. Because the work is from a journal, it contains quite a variety of types of research and interesting discussion.

Your library website, too, is a powerful information portal, with links to specialized online databases and subscriptions to e-book sites, e-journals, and authoritative sites on the Internet that are otherwise inaccessible. It also contains valuable information regarding your library's policies and services. Online resources that don't come from a library need a section of discussion all their own (see Chapter 17).

Strengths	Weaknesses
• Library staff are often on hand to help out. • Libraries efficiently provide directory-type information. • The author may be an authority on the subject. • Books often give an introductory overview of the subject. • Information is usually reliable (if published by a respected publisher). • Several key issues of the subject may be covered in the book.	• Information in print versions may be dated. • Going to the library is not as convenient as using the Internet. • Not all books may be available. • Increasingly, authoritative information is posted on the Web (e.g., government documents, databases of scholarly journals). • Information may not be applicable to a Canadian context.

Internet Resources

If you do not have a subject guide to the "best of the Web" on your library website, there are two important steps to locating current and reliable information on the Internet: develop a good search strategy, and then critically evaluate the results of your search.

Many search engines offer advice on effective searching, including the following four ways in which you can limit and focus the results of an initial query:

We recommend that you use more than one search engine to get the best results.

1. Use one or more of the shortcuts available on most search engines (select the "Canada" option, for example).

2. Use the "advanced search" option that allows you to combine concepts. For example, Google's advanced search option allows you to search for an exact phrase such as "breast cancer" and include the word "treatment" but exclude the word "chemotherapy." You can also limit the type of domain you'd like to search (e.g., "*edu"—indicating a university site), choose the language you'd like for your results, and decide where you'd like the search engine to look for your terms (in the title only, for example). If you decide to use the basic search option, you can do the same search, but it takes a bit more thinking as you won't have all the prompts provided for an advanced search.

3. Put quotation marks around your search term(s). Doing so turns your keyword search into a search for a specific phrase ("breast cancer treatment," for example).

4. Use the tilde sign (~) or plus and minus signs to add or eliminate concepts. Plus and minus signs add or subtract words from your search word or phrase (e.g., "breast cancer" + treatment – chemotherapy). Google interprets the tilde as a signal to search for variations of a word. For example, "~treatment" would include the plural "treatments" in your results list.

Evaluating the reliability of Internet information is not a simple matter, and Canadian sources are not easily identified. An excellent guide for evaluating websites can be found at guides.lib.berkeley.edu/evaluating-resources.

For Canadian sources, look for provincial domain names, such as ab.ca (Alberta) or on.ca (Ontario), or gc.ca for federal government sites. Professional associations normally include the association's name or initials as part of the domain name—for example, the Canadian Medical Association (www.cma.ca).

There is seldom any doubt about who wrote a particular print book or article. In online material, however, often no author or date is identified. For academic research, it's wise to be cautious of no-name sources. If you want to use information from one of these sources, be sure that the organization or institution that originated it is reliable. You wouldn't want to be researching the history of discrimination in Canada, for example, and find yourself quoting from the disguised website of a hate organization.

Cyber sleuthing, part of your critical thinking and writing arsenal, is a useful skill to learn!

Much online work is collaborative: several writers may have contributed to an online document, so it is a good idea to check out the people involved in producing it. Online search engines make checking the author's reliability easier for electronic sources than it is for print sources. Simply key the author's name into a search engine such as Google, and then evaluate the results to see if the author is a credible person in the field. Often you'll be able to check the author's biography, credentials, other publications, and business or academic affiliation. If no author's name is given, you can check on the company, organization, or institution in the same way.

Strengths

- Internet resources are fast and convenient.
- They efficiently provide directory-type information.
- The websites of leading experts are sometimes available.
- Increasingly, authoritative information is posted on the Web (e.g., government documents, databases of scholarly journals).

Weaknesses

- The reliability and authority of Internet resources can be difficult to determine.
- The amount of information provided is staggering (most users will not browse past the first two or three pages of search results, so valuable information may be missed).
- Questionable content may appear to be valid.

Other Sources

The Internet and the library are not the only sources of information you can use. Interviews with people familiar with your subject are excellent primary sources because they provide a personal view, and they ensure that your paper will contain information not found in any other paper the instructor will read. It is perfectly acceptable to email a question or set of questions to an expert in a field of study. (But don't send your email two days before your assignment is due. Allow at least a few weeks between your request and a reply.)

Original research, such as surveys or questionnaires that you design, distribute, and analyze, can also enhance your paper. Doing your own research is time-consuming and requires some knowledge of survey design and interpretation, but it has the desirable advantage of being original and current.

Strengths	Weakness
• Experts in the field and original research provide information not found elsewhere. • Such sources can be specific and current.	• Surveys may be difficult to organize, develop, and administer.

Exercise 15.2

This exercise will quickly familiarize you with your school's library, the variety and extent of its holdings, the different ways you and the library staff can communicate with each other, and basic library policies you should know about.

1. What is the URL for your library's website? What are the library hours?
2. What is the loan period for books? Is there a fine for an overdue book?
3. Does your library have a reserve collection? What does it mean if an item is on reserve?
4. Use a title keyword search in the library catalogue. Does your library have the following books? If so, give the call number and location for each.
   - *MLA Handbook.* 8th ed., MLA, 2016.
   - *Publication Manual of the American Psychological Association.* 6th ed., APA, 2009.
5. Use an advanced search feature in the library catalogue and find a video or DVD that deals with study skills. Note the title, full call number, location, and status.
6. Does your library provide subject guides that provide links to reputable websites?
7. Use one of your library's subscription databases. Search for an article on a topic of your choice. Document the article using the guidelines for either APA or MLA format for electronic articles.
8. Can you access your library's databases from home? If so, what procedure do you follow?
9. Is it possible to contact the library staff by chat, text message, or email?

Exercise 15.3

This exercise will help you to think about how good research can lead you to other good research.

1. Read the article by Grant Mitchell on pp. 273–276. Write out a list of all the main points in the article.
2. To find out the types of themes or ideas linked to the topic of transgender people and marginalization, what could you pull out of the article?
3. Read this paragraph:

   Research projects by the Ontario Trans PULSE Project and by Egale, and the 2015 report *Being Safe, Being Me*, provide stark and startling evidence of what trans people face in Canada today. These studies found that, of those transgender people surveyed with respect to employment barriers and economic marginalization, 13 per cent had been fired for being trans; 18 per cent were turned down for jobs because they are trans; over 70 per cent are earning less than $30,000 per year; and their median income is $15,000 per year. This is despite the fact that they are highly educated: 70 per cent have some form of post-secondary education, and 44 per cent have post-secondary undergraduate and graduate degrees.

Senator Grant Mitchell, "It's Time to Enshrine the Rights and Protections of Transgender Canadians," *LawNow Magazine*, January 4, 2017. Used with permission.

How might this paragraph help you in researching this topic more broadly? Where would you find more information about the sources the author names?

4. Using your own library database or another database you have access to, see if you can find one or more of the sources used in the article.
5. Write short summaries of the articles that you found and comment on how useful they might be if you were writing an essay on transgender people in Canada.

Formatting a Research Paper

CHAPTER 16

Formatting your research paper can be a rewarding process. You take what might be a jumble of raw ideas, quotations, visuals, and so on and turn it all into a reader-friendly piece of evidence and arguments. There are a variety of methods to help get you on your way to a professionally written and edited research paper. They all start with taking good notes from the get-go.

Taking Good Research Notes for Informative Writing

The beginning of formatting the final draft of your research paper starts with the notes you take while you are doing the research.

When taking notes from print and electronic sources, you must apply your critical thinking skills. Is the information reliable, relevant, and current? Is there evidence of any inherent bias? How can you best make use of the findings to support and enhance your own ideas? The answers to these questions are critical to producing a good research paper.

Whether you ultimately decide to summarize, paraphrase, or quote, you will need a record of the publication details of your source.

Once you've found a useful source, record the information you need. You'll save time and money by taking notes directly from your sources rather than photocopying everything. Most often, you will need a summary of the information. Follow the instructions on summarizing given on pages 115–116.

Some word-processing programs, such as Microsoft Word, provide templates to assist in citing sources and formatting information to create a Works Cited or References page. As you key in your draft and make reference to source material, you will be prompted to choose a documentation style (such as MLA or APA) and a source type—book, article, website, broadcast, and so on.

While documentation styles differ in the information they require in a bibliography and in format, the following guidelines provide an overview of the information you are most likely to require in preparing your research paper.

For each published source that you use in your paper, you should record the following information either with an online program or in a notebook.

For books, reports, documents:

1. Full name(s) of author(s) or editor(s)
2. Title of book, report, or document
3. Edition number (if any)
4. City of publication (for printed works)

5. Name of publisher (for printed works)
6. Year of publication
7. Page(s) from which you took notes
8. Library database (for online works)
9. Full electronic address or URL (for online works)
10. Date you accessed the work (for online works)

For articles in journals, magazines, newspapers:

1. Full name(s) of author(s)
2. Title of article
3. Name of the journal, magazine, or newspaper
4. Volume and issue number (if any)
5. Date of publication
6. Inclusive page numbers of the article
7. Page(s) from which you took notes
8. Library database (for online articles)
9. Digital object identifier (if any)
10. Date you accessed the article (for online articles)

For Internet sources:

1. Full names of important contributors (e.g., author, editor, writer, compiler, director)
2. Title of document
3. Name of website
4. Name of institution or organization sponsoring the site (if any)
5. Date of publication, edition, or last update
6. URL for document
7. Date you accessed the source

For audiovisual sources:

1. Full names of important contributors (e.g., director, producer, writer, performer)
2. Title of work
3. Date of work
4. Format of work (e.g., CD, film)

Some researchers record each piece of information on a separate index card or in a separate computer file. Others write their notes on sheets of paper, being careful to keep their own ideas separate from the ideas and words taken from sources. (Using a highlighter or a different colour of ink will help you to tell at a glance which ideas you have taken from a source.) Use the technology available to help you record, sort, and file your notes. You can record and file information by creating a database, and you can use a photocopier to copy relevant pages of sources for later use. Whatever system you use, be sure to keep a separate record for each source and to include the documentation information. If you don't, you'll easily get your sources confused. The result of this confusion could be inaccurate documentation, which could lead your reader to suspect you of plagiarism.

Fortunately, technology is available to help make the task of documenting much less onerous than it once was. As mentioned, many word-processing packages have built-in templates to assist writers in preparing citations and generating bibliographies. As well, some academic libraries have licensed "reference manager" programs for students' use. Programs such as RefWorks, EndNote, and ProCite help you store and organize sources during the research process. These programs also format citations and bibliographies as you write your paper. If your library does not have a site licence, check your bookstore or search online and decide if you are interested in obtaining a personal copy. Some programs offer a 30-day free trial. Zotero is an online program that is completely free, links in with your computer browser, and can automatically detect and create citations for multiple types of documentation. Different programs have different features, but most will help you keep track of the notes you've taken from various sources, and all will format your Works Cited (MLA) or References (APA) list (see Chapter 17) for you.

With so many free online programs that can help you organize your data, there is no excuse for bad documentation or poor organization.

The appearance of your paper makes an important initial impression on your reader. A correctly formatted paper reflects the care and attention to detail that instructors value in students' work. It is certainly just as important in the workplace, where attention to detail can mean the difference between getting a promotion and being back-benched (set aside) when it comes to new projects or exciting new initiatives. The way things look, their appearance, may seem like an artificial criterion; after all, we don't want to "judge books by their covers." But while we don't want to judge documents *only* by their presentation, it is one element we notice because it's the first thing we see and it guides our first impression. So try your best to get it right. No strawberry frappuccino stains on your reports!

Basic Formatting Guidelines

Ask your instructor about any special requirements for the format of your research assignments in your course; these may be quite different from the expectations of a traditional essay. If so, follow them carefully. Otherwise, follow the guidelines in this chapter to prepare your paper for submission.

Paper

Compose your final draft on 22 × 28 cm (8.5- × 11-inch) white paper that is suited to your printer type (e.g., ink jet, laser). Avoid streaky printer marks or last lines that can barely be read because of a dying toner cartridge. Make sure you aren't printing out your report 10 minutes before the deadline—that seems to be the time when machines fail! If you choose to handwrite your assignment and your instructor will accept a handwritten document, make sure it adheres to all of the guidelines that follow, including those regarding ink colour, margins, and spacing. Print out or write your research paper on *one side* of the paper only.

Fasten your paper with a paper clip or a single staple in the upper left-hand corner. Unless your instructor specifically requests it, don't bother with plastic or paper covers; most teachers find it annoying to have to disentangle your essay for marking.

As with wearing makeup, doing too much looks as though you are trying too hard.

Typing and Printing

Choose a standard, easily readable typeface, such as Times New Roman, Arial, or Helvetica (a popular font for Macs), in a 12-point size. Use black ink (or dark blue if you are writing by hand).

Spacing and Margins

Unless you are instructed otherwise, double-space your report, including quotations and the Works Cited or References list. In a handwritten paper, write on every other line of a ruled sheet of white paper.

Adequate white space on your pages makes your paper more attractive and easier to read. It also allows room for instructors' comments. Leave margins of 2.5 cm (or 1 inch) at the top, bottom, and both sides of your paper. If you are using a computer writing program, ensure your paper is formatted to be left-aligned.

Indent the first line of every paragraph 5 spaces or 1.25 cm (0.5 inches); use the tab default setting in your word-processing program. Indent all lines of a block quotation 10 spaces or 2.5 cm (1 inch) from the left margin.

> Always keep a copy of your paper for your files!

Formatting an MLA-Style Research Paper

The "style" of your paper—APA or MLA—will determine the format of your paper. Style rules are important because they set a standard expectation for readers and highlight certain information. We'll begin with the MLA approach, which is more common in English and humanities courses. MLA style for dealing with sources will be discussed in detail in Chapter 17. Here we focus on the general formatting guidelines.

Title Page

Do not prepare a separate title page unless your instructor requires it. Instead, at the top of the left margin of the first page of your essay, on separate lines, type your name, your instructor's name, the course, and the date. Leave a double space and centre the title of your essay. Capitalize main words (see Chapter 26), but do not underline, italicize, or put quotation marks around your title (unless it contains the title of another author's work, which you should treat in the standard way).

Header and Page Numbers

Number your pages consecutively throughout the paper, including the Works Cited list, in the upper right-hand corner, 1.25 cm from the top and 2.5 cm from the right edge of the page. Type your last name before the page number—with no punctuation or *p*.

A sample first page of an MLA-style paper follows. The italicized words in the margin identify the formatting guidelines.

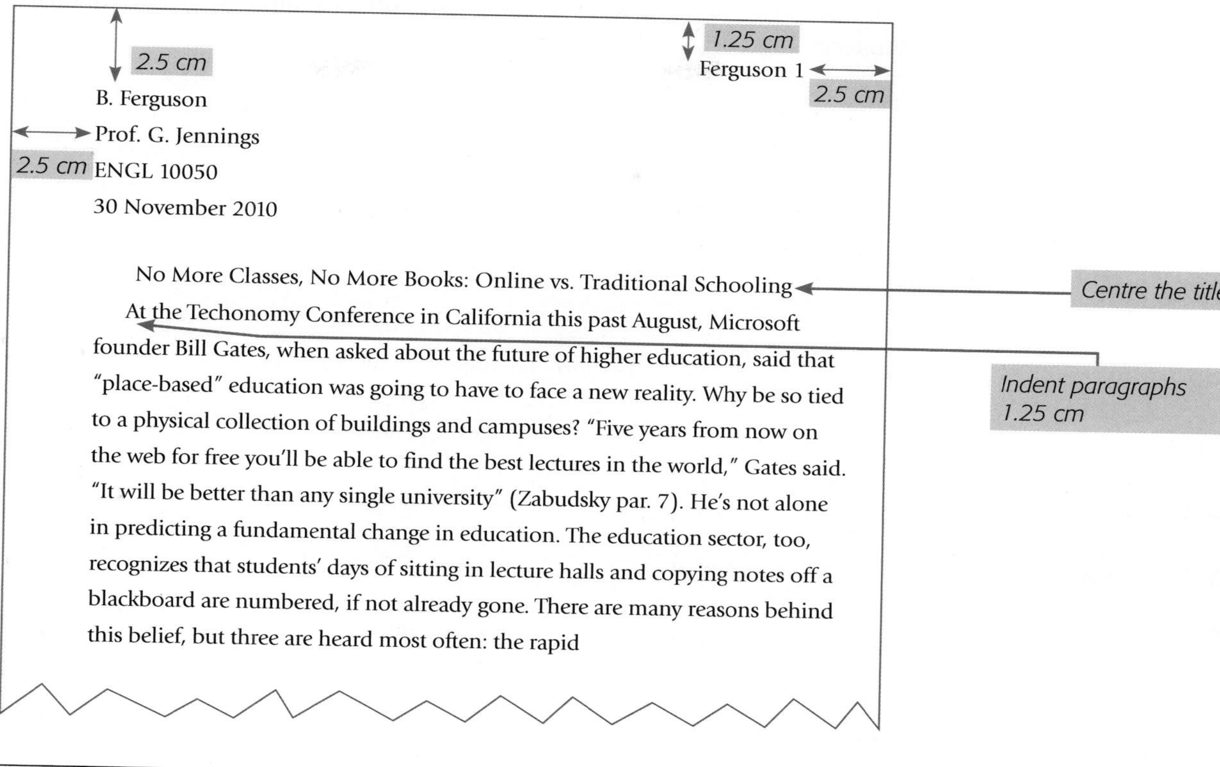

2.5 cm
1.25 cm
Ferguson 1
2.5 cm
B. Ferguson
Prof. G. Jennings
2.5 cm
ENGL 10050
30 November 2010
No More Classes, No More Books: Online vs. Traditional Schooling
Centre the title
At the Techonomy Conference in California this past August, Microsoft founder Bill Gates, when asked about the future of higher education, said that "place-based" education was going to have to face a new reality. Why be so tied to a physical collection of buildings and campuses? "Five years from now on the web for free you'll be able to find the best lectures in the world," Gates said. "It will be better than any single university" (Zabudsky par. 7). He's not alone in predicting a fundamental change in education. The education sector, too, recognizes that students' days of sitting in lecture halls and copying notes off a blackboard are numbered, if not already gone. There are many reasons behind this belief, but three are heard most often: the rapid
Indent paragraphs 1.25 cm

B. Ferguson, "No More Classes, No More Books: Online vs. Traditional Schooling." Used by permission of the author.

Remember, double-space your paper throughout unless instructed otherwise.

Formatting an APA-Style Research Paper

As you read through this section, note the differences and the similarities between MLA style and APA style, the latter of which is used mostly in the social sciences.

Title Page

In APA style, a research paper or essay requires a separate title page. On the title page, include a running head as follows: "Running head: ABBREVIATED NAME OF PAPER" and set it flush left; the page number goes flush right. Choose a concise title that identifies the subject of your paper, and then shorten it (to no more than 50 characters) for the running head, if necessary. Centre the title in the upper half of the page (quadruple-space it from the top of the page). If the title is more than one line, double-space between the lines. Capitalize main words, but don't underline, italicize, or put quotation marks around your title.

After the title, centre your name, the name of the course for which you are preparing the paper, the instructor's name, and the date of submission. Double-space between each of these elements. A sample APA-style title page follows.

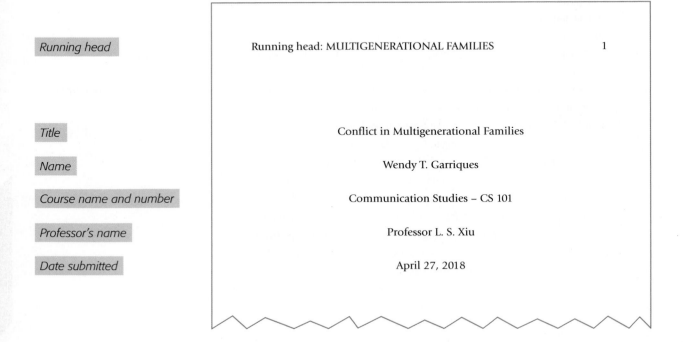

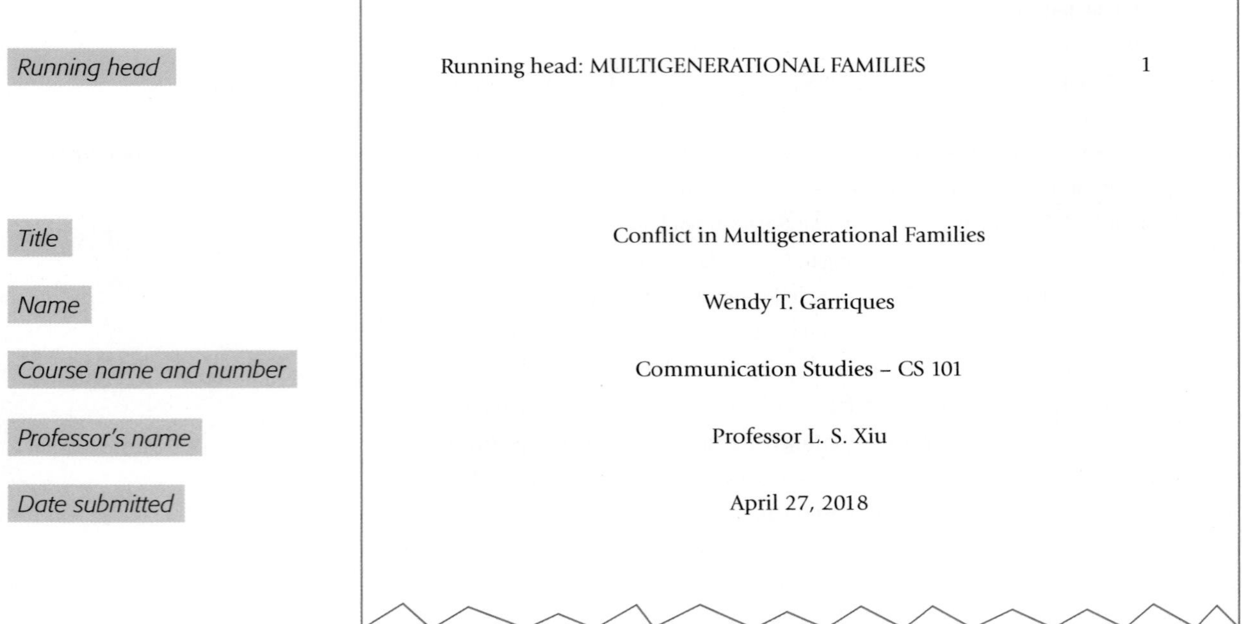

Running head
Title
Name
Course name and number
Professor's name
Date submitted
Running head: MULTIGENERATIONAL FAMILIES
1
Conflict in Multigenerational Families
Wendy T. Garriques
Communication Studies – CS 101
Professor L. S. Xiu
April 27, 2018

Head, Page Numbers, and Spacing

Number your pages consecutively throughout the paper, beginning with the title page and ending with the last page of the References list. If you are using a Microsoft product, from the "Insert" menu, choose "Header," key in the title and then select the option to insert a page number. As on the title page, the title of your paper should appear in upper-case letters, flush left, but this time without the words "Running head," while the page number appears flush right. There is no punctuation or use of *p*.

Double-space between all lines of your paper, including the title page, abstract, headings (if any), pages of the text itself, quotations, and References list. Indent the first line of every paragraph 1.25 cm (0.5 inches).

Abstract

Some assignments require you to provide an abstract—a short summary of the contents of your whole paper. It should give the purpose of your paper and the key ideas; that is, it should give your reader a preview of your paper. An abstract is usually one paragraph long. It must be well organized and carefully written. If you can write a great abstract, you will have an essential skill in your writing arsenal.

Type the abstract on a separate page that includes the running head and the page number (2). Centre the word "Abstract" one double space under the running head. Type the abstract paragraph itself in block format (i.e., without indentation).

First Page of Text

On page 3 (following the title page and abstract), centre the full title of your research paper (in upper- and lower-case letters). Double-space, and begin the text of your essay.

Research Paper Tips: Projecting an Image

As well as presenting your understanding of the topic, a research paper demonstrates your writing skills and your ability to follow the specific requirements of documentation and format. Meeting your instructor's submission requirements is as important as any other aspect of the preparation of your paper. This may be the last stage of your writing task, but it is the first impression your reader will have of your work. Make it a good one!

Exercise 16.1

Open your word-processing program or download one from the Internet (there are many free downloadable versions available that use common document types for saving, such as .doc or .txt). Alternatively, some post-secondary institutions give away free versions of popular writing software programs. In a new file, set up an outline for an MLA-style report, including the title for the documentation section ("Works Cited"). Save that as a template and do the same to create an APA-style document. You can adjust the margins, add your name and other important details, and set up the page numbering. Once you save these as templates, the next time you need to write this type of paper, you can just open the template and save it with a new name, and some of your organizational work is already done.

Exercise 16.2

Go online and read some abstracts for papers that have been posted. Get a feel for that style of summary writing. Then, choose an article or story from this volume and prepare an abstract for it. Exchange abstracts with a classmate and offer one another feedback. It can be easier to learn to write an abstract with someone else's work before trying it with your own writing.

CHAPTER 17

Documenting Your Sources

Documentation is the process of acknowledging source material, something you have read or seen that was created by other people or that you have re-created for another purpose. When you document a source, you provide information that

1. tells your readers that the ideas they are reading have been borrowed from another writer, and
2. enables your readers to find the source and read the material for themselves.

When acknowledging your sources in a research paper, you need to follow a system of documentation that is understandable to your reader. There are many different systems, but two of the most widely used are that of the Modern Language Association (MLA) and that of the American Psychological Association (APA). The instructions and examples provided in this chapter include slightly simplified versions of both styles. For examples not covered in this book, see the source documents:

> *MLA Handbook.* 8th ed., MLA, 2016. An updated guide to MLA electronic style is available at style.mla.org/works-cited-a-quick-guide
>
> *Publication Manual of the American Psychological Association*. 6th ed. Washington: APA, 2009. An updated *APA Style Guide to Electronic References* is available at www.apastyle.org.

Most instructors in English and the humanities require students to use the MLA style. Instructors in the social sciences (e.g., psychology, education, sociology, political science, economics) usually expect papers to conform to the principles of the APA style.

For research papers in the biological sciences, your instructor may require the Council of Science Editors (CSE) style, presented in *Scientific Style and Format: The CSE Manual for Authors, Editors, and Publishers* (www.councilscienceeditors.org).

Be sure to ask your instructor which documentation style he or she prefers.

For research papers in the engineering sciences, your instructor may require the Institute of Electrical and Electronics Engineers (IEEE) style, presented in the *IEEE Standards Style Manual* (www.standards.ieee.org).

Fortunately, technology is available to help make the task of documenting much less onerous than it once was. Some word-processing packages, such as Microsoft Word, have built-in templates to assist writers in preparing citations and generating bibliographies. Some academic libraries have licensed "reference manager" programs for their students. Programs such as RefWorks, EndNote, and ProCite help you store and organize sources during the research process. These programs also format citations and bibliographies as you write your paper. If your library does not have a site licence, check your bookstore or search online and decide if you are interested in obtaining a personal copy. Some programs offer a 30-day free trial. Zotero is an online program that is completely free, links with your browser, and can automatically detect and create citations for multiple types of documentation. Different programs have different features, but most will help you keep track of the notes you've taken from various sources, and all will format your Works Cited (MLA) or References (APA) list for you.

As well, many academic institutions publish their own style guides, which are available in college and university libraries and bookstores.

Introduction: The Two-Part Principle of Documentation

Documentation styles vary in their details, but most styles require authors to

- identify in a parenthetical reference in the text any information taken from a source, and
- list all sources for the paper on a separate page at the end

A **parenthetical citation** tells the reader that the information preceding the parentheses[1] is borrowed from a source and provides a key to the full identification of that source. Footnotes are now rarely used to document source material; instead, they are used to give additional information that cannot be conveniently worked into the body of your paragraph. (Note the example in this paragraph.)

A Works Cited (MLA) or References list (APA) is a list of all the sources from which you have borrowed words, ideas, data, or other material in your paper.[2] Preparing and presenting a Works Cited or References list requires paying close attention to the details of presenting the information required in each entry. The format—including the order of information, capitalization, and punctuation—prescribed by your style guide must be followed *exactly*. This requirement may sound picky, but there is a good reason to abide by it.

Every kind of source you use requires a particular format. If entries are formatted correctly, an experienced reader can tell by glancing at them what kinds of sources you have used: books, journal articles, newspaper articles, Web documents, etc. If you use the wrong style or leave something out or scramble the elements in a citation, you will mislead or confuse your reader.

The MLA Style

Parenthetical References

Every time you include in your paper a quotation, paraphrase, summary, fact, or idea you have borrowed from another writer, you must identify the source in parentheses immediately following the borrowed material. Parenthetical references should be as short and simple as possible while still fulfilling the purposes mentioned earlier: to tell your reader this information is borrowed

---

[1] A punctuation note: *Parentheses* means the pair of curved punctuation marks: ( ). *Brackets* are the pair of square marks that surround altered words or phrases in a quotation: [ ].

[2] Formerly, this list was called a *bibliography*.

and to point your reader to the complete source identified in your Works Cited list for their information or so they can read the source themselves. (For an example of an essay that has been documented in the MLA style, see "No Sweat?" on pp. 286–290.)

The standard practice in MLA style is to provide the surname of the author of the source material and the page number where the material was taken from. Once your reader has the author's name and page number, he or she can find complete bibliographic information about the source in your Works Cited list at the end of your paper. Of course, electronic sources present a challenge to this author-based citation method because they often lack an identifiable author, and they rarely include page numbers. More on this later.

You need to include a piece of source information only once; don't repeat information unnecessarily. For example, if you've already mentioned the author's name in your paragraph, you need to give only the page number in parentheses following subsequent references to the author's work.

On the next page is an excerpt from a research paper. The writer uses summary, paraphrase, and quotation, and gives the necessary source information in parentheses immediately following each borrowing. This excerpt also demonstrates how to omit a word or words from a source, using ellipses, and how to add or change a word or words, using square brackets.

The Works Cited list that follows the excerpt gives the reader full bibliographic information about each source. Note the following word-treatment rules for the entries in a Works Cited list:

1. *Italicize* titles and subtitles of any work that is published as a whole—for example, the names of books, plays, periodicals (newspapers, magazines, and journals), films, radio and television programs, CDs, DVDs (or underline them if you are using a pen).

2. Put quotation marks around the titles of works published within larger works—for example, the names of articles, essays, poems, songs, and individual episodes of television or radio programs. Also put quotation marks around the titles of unpublished works, such as lectures and speeches.

3. Use capital letters for the first, the last, and all main words (i.e., all but coordinating conjunctions, prepositions, and articles—see Chapter 26) in a title and subtitle even if your source capitalizes only the first word in the title.

Smith 3

Until the passage of the Tobacco Act in 2003, cigarette companies were able to exercise the full talents of their advertising and marketing divisions. The attractive young people who were portrayed in tobacco advertising made it easy for viewers to forget the terrible consequences of tobacco addiction. Cigarette advertisements routinely portrayed happy, energetic young people engaging in athletic activities under invariably sunny skies. The implication of these ads was that smoking was not a deterrent to an active lifestyle; in fact, it may even have been a prerequisite (Cunningham 67).

Full parenthetical citation for paraphrase; see the first item in Works Cited

It is difficult to overstate the impact of tobacco advertising on young people. As Cunningham pointed out,

> Few teenagers begin smoking for cigarettes' inherent physical qualities. Instead, teens are attracted to smoking for its image attributes, such as the five Ss: sophistication, slimness, social acceptability, sexual attractiveness, and status. Marketing gives a cigarette a false "personality." (66)

Block quotation

Abbreviated parenthetical citation

Is it any wonder that young people continued to take up the habit?

In an effort to reverse the trend of teenage tobacco addiction, the federal government sponsored awareness campaigns in the 1980s and 1990s to demonstrate how the tobacco industry duped and manipulated young people. This was a progressive campaign that was supported by increasingly restrictive legislation, to which the tobacco companies responded by becoming increasingly creative. In the late 1990s, Robert Sheppard wrote, "the industry plays on teenagers' need [for] something to rebel against ... [which] is exactly how cigarette manufacturers market their wares" (20). To counteract the image of smoking as a symbol of rebellion, government anti-tobacco campaigns presented smoking as a symbol of conformity.

See third item in Works Cited

Short quotation with
- *words left out (ellipses)*
- *words changed or added (square brackets)*

Finally yielding to pressure from the government and the community, the tobacco industry began to sponsor programs aimed at restricting youth access to tobacco products. In a comprehensive review, however, called *More Smoke and Mirrors* (14, 23-24) the Ontario Medical Association concluded that these programs were ineffective and made several recommendations to strengthen youth smoking-reduction initiatives.

Paraphrase; see second item in Works Cited

Reference to paginated Web article; article title and author mentioned in sentence, page reference in parentheses

The OMA (23) recommended that all parties interested in reducing tobacco use endorse a comprehensive tobacco control program and that all tobacco industry–sponsored programs be carefully monitored in the future. These recommendations culminated in 2003 with the passage of the Tobacco Act, which prohibited all advertising and sponsorship aimed at young people.

Summary

Web document with a page number

Smith 6

Works Cited

Cunningham, Rob. *Smoke and Mirrors: The Canadian Tobacco War.* International Development Research Centre, 1996, www.idrc.ca/en/book/smoke-mirrors-canadian-tobacco-war.

More Smoke and Mirrors: Tobacco Industry–Sponsored Youth Prevention Programs in the Context of Comprehensive Tobacco Control Programs in Canada. Ontario Medical Association, Feb. 2002.

Sheppard, Robert. "Ottawa Butts Up against Big Tobacco." *Maclean's,* 6 Dec. 1990, pp. 20-24. *eLibrary Canada.* www.proquest12.com. Accessed 4 Feb. 2013.

Study the way the excerpt on the previous page uses parenthetical references to identify information sources. The introductory paragraph ends with a paraphrase, which is immediately followed by a full parenthetical reference. Because the author's name is not mentioned in the writer's paragraph, it is given in parentheses, together with the number of the page on which the information was found. For more details, the reader would turn to the Works Cited list, reproduced at the top of this page.

The second paragraph includes a block quotation from the same source. The author's name is given in the statement that introduces the quotation, so the parentheses contain only the page number on which the quotation can be found.

The third paragraph includes a short quotation integrated into the writer's own sentence. The introductory phrase gives the author's name, so the parenthetical reference provides only the page number of the article on which this partial quotation is found. Complete bibliographic information for this source appears in the Works Cited list.

In the fourth and fifth paragraphs, the writer includes a paraphrase and a summary of information found in an unsigned article posted on the website of the Ontario Medical Association. Complete information about this source appears in the alphabetical list of Works Cited under the title, "More Smoke and Mirrors," as the Ontario Medical Association is considered the publisher of the source.

EXAMPLES OF PARENTHETICAL REFERENCES: TRADITIONAL PRINT SOURCES

1. If you name the source author in your paragraph, give just the page number in parentheses.

   Isajiw asserts that the twentieth century "has produced more refugees and exiles than any other preceding period since the fall of the Roman Empire" (66).

   The Works Cited entry for this book is on page 203.

2. If you do not name the source author in your paragraph, give the author's surname and the page number.

   The effect of "status drop" on the psychological well-being of immigrants can be substantial: "Especially among those more highly educated, this experience can cause feelings of bitterness or hostility...." (Isajiw 97).

3. If no author is named in the source, give the first few words of the title as it appears in the Works Cited entry.

   Legislation to reduce the amount of pollution generated by large-scale vehicles has been on the federal agenda for some time: "Canada has said it will toughen pollution-emission rules for all new vehicles, ending a loophole that allowed less stringent standards for popular sport-utility vehicles and minivans" ("Canada to Toughen" A6).

   The Works Cited entry for this source is on page 203.

4. If your source was published in more than one volume, give the volume number before the page reference.

   Only once in his two-volume work does Erickson suggest conspiracy (2: 184).

   The Works Cited entry for this source is on page 203.

5. If you are quoting from a literary classic or the Bible, use common abbreviations for the title of the play or book of the Bible, and use Arabic numerals separated by periods to identify act, scene, and lines from a play or a biblical chapter and verse.

   In Shakespeare's play, the duke's threat to give "measure for measure" (*MM* 5.1.414) echoes the familiar passage in the Bible (Matt. 7.1–2).

EXAMPLES OF PARENTHETICAL REFERENCES: ELECTRONIC SOURCES

As you've seen, parenthetical references for print sources in MLA style usually include the author's surname and the page number of the source. This principle is problematic for electronic sources since many of them lack one or both of these elements. Give enough information to guide your reader to the source listed in your Works Cited list.

1. If the electronic source lists an author, give the surname in your parenthetical reference.

   If physics and software engineering were subatomic particles, Silicon Valley has turned into the place where the fields collide (Metz).

   This quotation comes from *Wired*, an online magazine. The Works Cited entry for this quotation is on page 203.

2. If the electronic source does not list an author, give the document title (or a shortened version of the title) in italics or quotation marks as appropriate, instead of the author's name.

New websites are available to help students navigate their way through the challenging works of William Shakespeare:

> There are some people who don't even attempt to learn Shakespeare because they think that Shakespeare is ... only for English scholars. But that's not true! Shakespeare can be FUN. That's right—Shakespeare can actually be something you want to learn about. ("Shakespeare: Chill")

This quotation comes from a website called *ThinkQuest.* The Works Cited entry for this quotation is on page 203.

3. You do not usually find page numbers or other navigation devices in an electronic source. If there are page, paragraph, or section numbers that could guide your reader to the specific material being quoted, include them. If the author's name is included in the parenthetical reference, put a comma after it and include the section or paragraph numbers. Use the abbreviations *sec.* and *par.*

Even Margaret Atwood must endure the editing process before her books are published:

> Being edited is like falling face down into a threshing machine. Every page gets fought over, back and forth, like WWI. Unless the editor and the writer both have in mind the greater glory of the work, ... blood will flow and the work will suffer. Every comma, every page break, may be a ground for slaughter. (sec. 6)

Taken from Atwood, Margaret. "The Rocky Road to Paper Heaven."

This quotation comes from an article posted on a personal website. The Works Cited entry is found on page 203.

If there are no page, paragraph, or section numbers to identify the quotation, simply give the author's name or the title in parentheses. If your reader wants to locate the information, an online keyword search can often yield results.

The MLA Works Cited List

A Works Cited list is required on a separate page at the end of your essay. It includes detailed bibliographic information for all the sources you have summarized, paraphrased, or quoted in your paper. The information in the Works Cited list enables your reader to assess the extent of your research and to find and check every source you used. The sample Works Cited list on page 203 illustrates the information given in the following bulleted list.

- Begin the list on a new page, and number each page, continuing the page numbers of your paper. Your last name and the page number appear in the upper right-hand corner, 1.25 cm from the top and lined up with the right margin. (Note: Use the automatic "Header" function of your word-processing program to create the running head.)
- Centre the heading, "Works Cited," 2.50 cm from the top of the page.

- Double-space the entire list, including the title and the first entry.
- Begin each entry at the left margin. If an entry runs more than one line (and most do), indent the subsequent line or lines one tab space, or 1.25 cm. This format is called a "hanging indent"[3] and can be found in the "Paragraph" menu of most word-processing packages.
- Arrange the entries alphabetically, beginning with the first word of the entry, which is often the author's surname. Do not number your entries.
- If there are several works by the same author, put the author's name in the first entry only. In the subsequent entries, type three hyphens and a period to represent the author's name.
- If no author is identified in your source, alphabetize by the first word in the title, ignoring *A, An,* and *The*. For example, *The Canadian Encyclopedia* would be listed under C, for *Canadian*.

Below you will find examples for Works Cited entries commonly found in research papers, including print, broadcast, and electronic sources.

BOOKS, ENCYCLOPEDIAS, REPORTS, GOVERNMENT PUBLICATIONS

Here is the basic model for a book entry in a Works Cited list. Note the spacing, capitalization, punctuation, and order of the information.

> Last name of author, First name and/or initials. *Title of Book: Subtitle of Book.* Publisher, Year of publication.

- Leave only one space between the comma that follows the author's surname and the author's first name and/or initials, as well as after other commas, colons, semicolons, and periods that separate parts of the citation.
- Capitalize all proper names and significant words (i.e., all words but coordinating conjunctions, prepositions, and articles—see Chapter 26) in the title and subtitle. *Italicize* the title and subtitle.
- In the publication data:
  - Shorten the publisher's name. For example, McGraw-Hill, Inc. is abbreviated to McGraw. If the publisher is a well-known university press, use the abbreviation *UP* (e.g., Oxford UP, U of Toronto P). Write out the names of associations and corporations.
  - The year the book was published is usually found on the back of the title page (the copyright page); if it is not given, use the latest copyright date.

Book with One or More Authors

> Deraniyagala, Sonali. *Wave.* McClelland, 2013.
>
> McCall, Bruce, and David Letterman. *This Land Was Made for You and Me (But Mostly Me): Billionaires in the Wild.* Random House, 2013.

If there are more than two authors, you may give the first author's name only, followed by a comma and the abbreviation *et al.* (meaning "and others").

[3] Hanging indents help readers locate authors' names in the alphabetical listing. If you have only one source to acknowledge, you do not need to indent the second line.

Morgan, Sarah E., et al. *Cosmetic Nanotechnology: Polymers and Colloids in Cosmetics*. American Chemical Society, 2007.

Book with More Than One Edition

Peak, Kenneth J., and Ronald W. Glesnor. *Community Policing and Problem Solving: Strategies and Practices.* 5th ed., Prentice, 2008.

Book with No Author

Webster's New College Dictionary. 3rd ed., Houghton, 2008.

Book with One or More Editors

Guran, Paula, editor. *Once Upon a Time: New Fairy Tales*. Prime, 2013.

If there are more than two editors, you may give the first editor's name only, followed by a comma and the abbreviation *et al.*

Massat, Carol R., et al., editors. *School Social Work: Practice, Policy and Research*. 7th ed., Lyceum, 2009.

Recent Edition of a Classic Work

Shakespeare, William. *The Tempest.* Edited by Stephen Orgel, Oxford UP, 1994.

Multivolume Work

Yates, Arthur. *The Trooper: Memoirs of Arthur Yates*. Trafford, 2001. 2 vols.

Book with Introduction, Preface, Foreword, or Afterword (to which you refer in your paper)

Willmott, Glenn. Introduction. *Think of the Earth*, by Bertrand Brooker. 1936. Brown Bear Press, 2000, pp. 1-6.

Article, Essay, Story, or Poem in a Collection

Mistry, Rohinton. "Journey to Dharmsala." *The Reader: Contemporary Essays and Writing Strategies,* edited by Carolyn Meyer and Bruce Meyer, Prentice, 2001, pp. 38-51.

Encyclopedia Reference

Driedger, Leo. "Ethnic Identity." *Canadian Encyclopedia*. 2000 ed.

Book Published by a Corporation (Company, Commission, Agency)

Protection of the Waters of the Great Lakes: Final Report to the Governments of Canada and the United States. International Joint Commission, 2000.

Resource Efficiency: Economics and Outlook for China. United Nations Environment Programme, 2013.

When an organization is both author and publisher, begin the entry with the title and put the name of the organization as publisher.

Government Publication

If the author is not named, identify the government first, then the agency, then the title, publisher, and date.

> Alberta. Environmental Protection Commission. *A Review of Alberta's Environmental and Emergency Response Capacity: Learning the Lessons and Building Change.* Alberta Environment, 2005.

> Canada. Canadian Heritage. *Canadian Content in the 21st Century: A Discussion Paper about Canadian Content in Film and Television Productions.* Minister of Public Works and Government Services Canada, 2002.

Brochure or Pamphlet

> Barlow, Maude. *Water for Sale: How Free Trade and Investment Agreements Threaten Environmental Protection of Water and Promote the Commodification of the World's Water*. Council of Canadians, 2017.

ARTICLES IN MAGAZINES, NEWSPAPERS, AND JOURNALS

The MLA provides different sets of guidelines for articles published in magazines and for those published in what it calls "scholarly journals." Both sets of guidelines are given below. If you are not sure whether a source should be treated as a magazine or as a scholarly journal, consult your instructor.

Article in a Magazine or Newspaper

Note the spacing, capitalization, punctuation, and order of the information required in a Works Cited entry for a magazine or newspaper.

> Last name of author, First name and/or initials. "Title of Article." *Title of Periodical*, Day Month Year, pages.

- If the writer's name does not appear with the newspaper article, simply give the article's full title (your in-text parenthetical reference would be an abbreviated title; for the article identified below, it would appear as "What You Should Know"):

> Tchir, Jason. "What You Should Know about Online Used Car Scams." *Globe and Mail*, 13 July 2017, p. D7.

Use the same format for a magazine article, although sometimes the date consists of only a month (or two months) and the year, or a season and the year:

> Carter, Sue. "A Level Playing Field." *Quill & Quire*, July-Aug. 2017, pp. 13–15.

- The date of publication is formatted as follows: day [if applicable] month year (e.g., 13 Mar. 2018)

Give the magazine's or newspaper's name as it appears on the masthead (at the top of the front page of the magazine or newspaper) but omit *the* (e.g., the *Vancouver Sun*) even if *The* is part of the official name (e.g., *The Province*). If the name of the city is not included in a locally published newspaper, add it in square brackets after the name of the paper so that readers will know where it was published—for instance, *Comox Valley Record* [Campbell River].

For a magazine or newspaper that is published weekly or every two weeks, provide the day, month, and year, in that order. Abbreviate all months except May, June, and July (Jan., Feb., Mar., Apr., Aug., Sept., Oct., Nov., Dec.). If the periodical is published monthly, provide month and year.

Give the complete page span for each article in your Works Cited list. For example, if an article begins on page 14 and concludes on page 16, put a colon and the page numbers after the date: 5 June 2018, pp. 14–16. If the article begins on page 36, then skips to page 40 and concludes on page 41, give only the first page number and a plus sign: 36+. In a newspaper, the sections are usually numbered separately, so include the section identifier as well as the page number.

> Shufelt, Tim, and James Bradshaw. "Banks Boost Prime Rates after BoC Hike." *Globe and Mail*, 13 July 2017, p. B1+.

Article in a Scholarly Journal

The major differences between a magazine article and one in a scholarly journal are that a volume number and an issue number are often included in the publication information, and the year of publication is enclosed in parentheses. In the following entry, only a volume number ("27") is given because this journal does not use issue numbers:

> Kan, Yinan, et al. "Mechanisms of Precise Genome Editing Using Oligonucleotide Donors." *Genome Research*, vol. 27, July 2017, pp. 1112–25.

The journal cited below publishes in issues within (annual) volumes, so both volume (43) and issue number (7) are required.

> Andresen, Felicia J., and Jeffrey A. Buchanon. "Bullying in Senior Living Facilities: Perspectives of Long-Term Care Staff." *Journal of Gerontological Nursing*, vol. 43, no. 7, 2017, pp. 34–41.

Published Review—Books, Plays, Films, Etc.

> Sinaee, Bardia. Review of Baloney, by Maxime Raymond Bock. *Canadian Notes and Queries*, Winter 2017, pp. 60–61.

> Dixon, Guy. "Mash-Up Doc Argues That Creativity Begins Where Copyright Ends." Review of *RiP: A Remix Manifesto*, directed by Brett Gaylor. *Globe and Mail,* 14 Mar. 2009, p. R11.

OTHER SOURCES

Published Interview

> Tennant, Jamie. "In Our Worst Moments, We Are All Dennis: Krista Foss in Conversation with Jamie Tennant." *Hamilton Review of Books*, hamiltonreviewofbooks.com/krista-foss-interviews-jamie-tennant. Accessed 13 July 2017.

Unpublished Personal Interview

> Brogly, Angela. Personal interview. 22 Jan. 2018.

Personal Communication

Green, Brian. "Re: The Musical Brain." Message to the author. 16 Mar. 2017.

AUDIOVISUAL SOURCES

Television/Radio Broadcast

"Dragonstone." *The Game of Thrones*, directed by Jeremy Podeswa, season 7, episode 1, HBO, 2017.

Struzik, Ed. "Canada Not Prepared for 'Inevitable' Wildfires, Says Environmental Expert." *The Current*, CBC Radio One, 17 July 2017.

Film, Video, CD, DVD

Frozen. Directed by Chris Lee and Jennifer Buck, Disney, 2013.

Delmar's Community Health Nursing: A Case Study. Delmar, 2003.

Tagaq, Tanya. *Retribution*. Six Shooter Records, 2016.

Ward, Al. *Photoshop for Right-Brainers: The Art of Photo Manipulation*. Sybex, 2009.

If you want to acknowledge a specific individual's contribution to a film or recording, begin with that person's name. (This format is useful when you are writing about the work of a particular artist—in this case, Alfred Hitchcock.)

Hitchcock, Alfred, director. *Rear Window.* Performances by Jimmy Stewart, Grace Kelly, and Raymond Burr. 1954. Universal, 2001.

ELECTRONIC SOURCES

The rules for citing electronic sources are essentially the same as for print or broadcast sources. The reference should provide enough information to enable a reader to locate the source quickly—author, title, date, and publishing information. In the case of electronic sources, publishing information includes the name of the container, such as a book, television series, website, or library subscription database. The date you accessed the material is not required but is highly encouraged for online content that can be frequently changed; the date indicates which version you are citing. We recommend that you download and print online material so that you can verify it if, at a later date, it is revised, unavailable, or inaccessible.

Include a location to show where you found a source. Many academic journals and databases use a DOI (digital object identifier). Use a DOI if one is available; otherwise, use a URL.

Capitalization, punctuation, and the order in which the information is provided are very important when citing electronic sources. Here are the elements to look for:

- full name of author (or compiler, director, editor, narrator, performer, translator)

- title of the document (in italics if it is independent; in quotation marks if it is part of a larger work)
- title of the overall website, project, or book in italics
- version or edition statement, if available
- publisher or sponsor of the site
- library database, if applicable
- date of the publication
- the URL or DOI
- the date you accessed the material

Online Book from a Library Subscription Database

Climate Change Secretariat. Yukon Government Climate Change Action Plan Progress Report, Environment Yukon, 2015. *ProQuest*, site.ebrary.com.myaccess.library.utoronto.ca/lib/utoronto/detail.action?docID=11188893&p00=climate+change.

Online Book from a Public Internet Site

Wilton, Geoff, and Lynn Stewart. *The Additive Effects of Women Offenders' Participation in Multiple Correctional Interventions*. Correctional Service of Canada, 2015, publications.gc.ca/site/eng/9.837830/publication.html.

Wollstonecraft, Mary. *A Vindication of the Rights of Women*. Boston, 1792. *Bartleby.com,* www.bartleby.com/144.

Chapter, Essay, Story, or Poem in an Online Book

de Maupassant, Guy. "The Necklace." *The Short Story: Specimens Illustrating Its Development.* Edited by Brander Matthews, American Book Company, 1907. *Bartleby.com*, www.bartleby.com/195/20.html.

Gruen, David, and Duncan Spender. "The Need to Wellbeing Measurement in Context." *Measuring and Promoting Wellbeing: How Important Is Economic Growth*?, edited by Andrew Podger and Dennis Trewin, ANU Press, 2014, pp. 209–222. JSTOR, www.jstor.org/stable/j.ctt6wp80q.12.

Online Encyclopedia, Dictionary

Hayne, David M., et al. "Canadian Literature." *Encyclopaedia Brittanica*, 2012, www.britannica.com/art/Canadian-literature. Accessed 17 July 2017.

"Capricious." *Merriam-Webster Dictionary*. Merriam-Webster, 2009, www.merriam-webster.com/dictionary/capricious.

Falco, Charles. M. "Use of Optics by Renaissance Artists." *AccessScience,* McGraw, 1 Jan. 1970, DOI: 10.1036/1097-8542.YB084340.

Web Document

"Michael Ondaatje." *Canadian Writers*, Athabasca University, 2015, canadian-writers.athabascau.ca/english/writers/mondaatje/mondaatje.php. Accessed 17 July 2017.

Journal Article from a Library Subscription Database

Campolieti, Michelle. "Forecasting Applications to Disability Insurance Programs: Evidence for the Quebec Pension Plan Disability Program." *Canadian Public Policy/Analyse de Politiques*, vol. 41, no. 3, 2015, pp. 223–240. *JSTOR*, www.jstor.org/stable/43699156.

Journal Article from Public Internet Journal

Snider, Tristan, et al. "A National Survey of Canadian Emergency Medicine Residents' Comfort with Geriatric Emergency Medicine." *Canadian Journal of Emergency Medicine*, vol. 19, no. 1, 2017, DOI: 10.1017/cem.2016.344.

Kristensen, Niels Norgaard, and Trond Solhaug. "Students as First-Time Voters: The Role of Voter Advice Applications in Self-Reflection on Party Choice and Political Identity." *Journal of Social Science Education*, no. 1, 2017, DOI: 10.4119/UNIBI/jsse-v16-i1-1503.

Newspaper Article from a Public Internet Site

Hoekstra, Gordon. "Entire City and Area of Williams Lake Ordered Evacuated as Fire Threatens Last Highway Out." *Vancouver Sun*, 15 July 2017, vancouversun.com/news/local-news/xatsull-first-nation-members-fleeing-as-winds-kick-up-huge-fires. Accessed 17 July 2017.

Online News Service Article

"Canada Musters Military to Fight Wildfires, 39,000 Evacuated." Reuters Canada, 17 July 2017, ca.reuters.com/article/domesticNews/idCAKBN1A21YQ-OCADN. Accessed 17 July 2017.

Online Image

Carr, Emily. A Rushing Sea of Undergrowth. 1935. Vancouver Art Gallery, www.museevirtuel.ca/sgc-cms/expositions-exhibitions/emily_carr/en/popups/pop_large_en_VAG-42.3.17.html. Accessed 17 July 2017.

Online Course Materials

"Aanii (Greetings)!" UBCx: IndEdu200x *Reconciliation Through Indigenous Education*, EdX. 28 Feb. 2017. Accessed 19 July 2017.

Wurfel, Marlene. "Canadian Writers: Alice Munro." *Canadian Writers,* Athabasca University, 2015, canadian-writers .athabascau.ca/english/writers/amunro/amunro.php. Accessed 17 July 2017.

Personal Website

Atwood, Margaret. "The Rocky Road to Paper Heaven." *Alcorn. Blogspot.com,* 2 April 2004, http://alcorn.blogspot .ca/2004/02/writing-rocky-road-to-paper-heaven.html. Accessed 17 July 2017.

Audio Podcast

Kheraj, Sean. "Nature's Past Episode 55: Asbestos Mining and Environmental Health." *Niche*, 30 Nov. 2016, niche-canada .org/2016/11/30/natures-past-episode-55-asbestos-mining -and-environmental-health. Accessed 17 July 2017.

The MLA style is intended to be a simple, flexible system of documentation that lends itself to several options for citing a source. Since consistency of presentation is important, we suggest the following formats. (Note: Some instructors may not accept the following formats or, indeed, the following sources, as reputable or reliable. Check with your instructor before including them in your work.)

Full name of author/presenter. "Title of Item." *Website name,* Website sponsor, Date of item, URL. Access date.

Video Web Post

Bostrom, Nick. "What Happens When Our Computers Get Smarter Than We Are?," *TED Talks*, 27 Apr. 2015. *YouTube*, www.youtube.com/watch?v=MnT1xgZgkpk&index=4&list =PLPKaZQAWre5bWqn0Fmm8v7XjIOcPyXeEz.

Blog, Social Network Post

Fullick, Melanie. "Tweeting Out Loud: Ethics, Knowledge, and Social Media in Academe." *Speculative Diction*, 4 Oct. 2012, www.universityaffairs.ca/speculative-diction/tweeting-out -loud-ethics-knowledge-and-social-media-in-academe.

Tweet

@JustinTrudeau. "Lots to celebrate at Pride events in 2017. #BillC16 passed, making it illegal to discriminate based on gender identity/expression." *Twitter*, 6 Aug. 2017, 11:48 a.m., twitter.com/JustinTrudeau/ status/894223678262710272.

Sample MLA Works Cited List

Below, you will find a sample MLA Works Cited list to show you what the final page of your paper should look like. A description of the type of source used appears to the left of each entry.

Author Name 15

Works Cited

Atwood, Margaret. "The Rocky Road to Paper Heaven." *Alcorn.Blogspot.com*, 2 April 2004, http://alcorn.blogspot.ca/2004/02/writing-rocky-road-to-paper-heaven.html. Accessed 17 July 2017.

"Canada to Toughen Auto-Emissions Rules." *Wall Street Journal*, 5 Apr. 2002, p. A6.

"Capricious." *Merriam-Webster Dictionary*. Merriam-Webster, www.merriam-webster.com/dictionary/capricious.

Erickson, Edward W., and Leonard Waverman, editors. *The Energy Question: An International Failure of Policy*. U of Toronto P, 1974. 2 vols.

Frozen. Directed by Chris Lee and Jennifer Buck, Disney, 2013.

Isajiw, Wsevolod W. *Understanding Diversity: Ethnicity and Race in the Canadian Context*. Thompson, 1999.

Metz, Cade. "Move Over Coders—Physicists Will Soon Rule Silicon Valley." *Wired*, 16 Jan. 2017, www.wired.com/2017/01/move-coders-physicists-will-soon-rule-silicon-valley/.

"Shakespeare: Chill with Will." *ThinkQuest*. Oracle Education Foundation, 1 May 2009.

Tchir, Jason. "What You Should Know about Online Used Car Scams." *Globe and Mail*, 13 July 2017, p. D7.

Exercise 17.1

For each of the following quotations, write a short paragraph in which you use all or a portion of the quotation and credit it in a parenthetical citation.

1. From a book entitled Getting it done: the transforming power of self-discipline by Andrew J. Dubrin, published by Pacesetter Books in Princeton in 1995. This sentence appears on page 182: "Stress usually stems from your interpretation and perception of an event, not from the event itself."
2. From a journal article by Linda A. White that appeared on pages 385 to 405 of Canadian Public Policy, a journal with continuous paging: "If a clear connection exists between the presence of child care and high levels of women's labour market participation, that would provide good reasons for governments and employers to regard child care as part of an active labour market policy." White's article is entitled Child Care, Women's Labour Market Participation, and Labour Market Policy Effectiveness in Canada. The quotation appears on page 389 of the fourth issue of the 27th volume, published in 2001.
3. From a newspaper article written by Nancy Cleeland that appeared on page A2 in the March 30, 2005, issue of the Vancouver Sun. You found it on the

eLibrary Canada database on November 26, 2013, at your college library. The article is entitled As jobs heat up, workers' hearts take a beating: "For years, occupational health researchers have struggled to come up with formulas for measuring job stress and determining its effect on health."

4. During the February 3, 2009, CBC broadcast of the Mercer Report, Rick Mercer says, "According to a recent Dominion Institute poll, a majority of Canadians have no idea how Parliament works." You watched the broadcast on *YouTube* on December 6, 2013. The segment is entitled Everything you wanted to know about Canada but were afraid to ask. It was located at the following URL: http://www.youtube.com/ watch?v=yi1yhp-_x7A.

5. From an email message on the subject of time management from your friend, Janet Ford, on June 5, 2013: "Using a daily planner and checking email only once a day are two ways I've found to manage my stress during the school year."

The APA Style

If you have to write a report that falls under the social science, economics, or educational umbrella, then APA style is most commonly used.

Parenthetical References

Remember that a parenthetical reference in the text of your paper serves two functions: (1) it tells your reader that the information comes from somewhere else, and (2) it points the reader to full details about the source in the References list at the end of your paper. (For an example of an essay that has been prepared in the APA style, see "A City for Students" on pp. 153–155.)

One way to acknowledge another author's work is to name the author of the source in your own sentence and include the date of publication in parentheses immediately after the author's name: e.g., Smith (2009) reported.... If you do not name the author in your sentence, put the author's surname followed by a comma and then the date in parentheses—(Smith, 2009)—right after your quotation, summary, or paraphrase. (See the examples on page 206.)

We strongly encourage you to provide page references for all source citations.

If you are quoting from a source, you must include in your parenthetical reference the page number(s) on which the quotation appears, using the abbreviation *p.* (page) or *pp.* (pages)—(e.g., Smith & Dolittle, 2010, p. 32). APA style encourages but does not require page references in citations for paraphrases or summaries.

If no author name is provided in the source information, the in-text reference should include the first few words of the title of the publication or article. The title of a publication is italicized in the in-text reference (e.g., *Essay Essentials,* 2018), while quotation marks are used for the shortened title of an article and capital letters are used for the major words (e.g., "Canada to Toughen," 2002). Note that in the sample References list on page 217, the full title of the article cited in the preceding example is not enclosed in quotation marks, and a capital letter is used for only the first word: Canada to toughen auto-emissions rules.

Electronic sources (discussed below) do not always follow the author–date in-text reference method because they often do not have an identifiable author, rarely include page numbers, and often are not dated. Usually, an abbreviated version of the website name or of the title of the document is used for an in-text reference. For example: "Purdue OWL," the abbreviated version of the Purdue Online Writing Lab (OWL) website name, or "Literary Theory," the abbreviated version of the article "Literary Theory and Schools of Criticism" that appears on the Purdue OWL website.

ITALICS OR QUOTATION MARKS?

Italicize the titles and subtitles of any work that is published as a whole—e.g., names of books, plays, periodicals (newspapers, magazines, and journals), films, radio and television programs, and DVDs. Also italicize the titles of published and unpublished doctoral dissertations and master's theses (unless they are part of a larger work) and the titles of speeches and lectures. (If you are using a pen, underline these titles.)

In all in-text references, whether parenthetical or not, put quotation marks around the titles of works published within larger works—e.g., the names of articles, essays, poems, songs, and individual episodes of television and radio programs. Use capital letters for the first, the last, and all main words (i.e., all but coordinating conjunctions, prepositions, and articles—see Chapter 26) in a title and subtitle. (Note: These rules are different for the References list; see p. 217.)

On the next page is an excerpt from a research paper. The writer uses summary, paraphrase, and quotation, and gives the necessary source citations in parentheses.

Full parenthetical citation for paraphrase; see the first item in References

Block quotation

Abbreviated parenthetical citation

See third item in References

Short quotation with
- words changed (square brackets)
- words left out (ellipses)

Paraphrase; see second item in References

Parenthetical citation; Web document with page number

Parenthetical citation; Web document with page number

Until the passage of the Tobacco Act in 2003, cigarette companies were able to exercise the full talents of their advertising and marketing divisions. The attractive young people who were portrayed in tobacco advertising made it easy for viewers to forget the terrible consequences of tobacco addiction. Cigarette advertisements routinely portrayed happy, energetic young people engaging in athletic activities under invariably sunny skies. The implication of these ads was that smoking was not a deterrent to an active lifestyle; in fact, it may even have been a prerequisite (Cunningham, 1996, p. 67).

It is difficult to overstate the impact of tobacco advertising on young people. As Cunningham pointed out,

> Few teenagers begin smoking for cigarettes' inherent physical qualities. Instead, teens are attracted to smoking for its image attributes, such as the five Ss: sophistication, slimness, social acceptability, sexual attractiveness, and status. Marketing gives a cigarette a false "personality." (p. 66)

Is it any wonder that young people continued to take up the habit?

In an effort to reverse the trend of teenage tobacco addiction, the federal government sponsored awareness campaigns in the 1980s and 1990s to demonstrate how the tobacco industry duped and manipulated young people. This was a progressive campaign that was supported by increasingly restrictive legislation, to which the tobacco companies responded by becoming increasingly creative. As Robert Sheppard (1990) observed, "the industry plays on teenagers' need [for] something to rebel against … [which] is exactly how cigarette manufacturers market their wares" (p. 20). To counteract the image of smoking as a symbol of rebellion, government anti-tobacco campaigns presented smoking as a symbol of conformity.

Finally yielding to pressure from the government and the community, the tobacco industry began to sponsor programs aimed at restricting youth access to tobacco products. In a comprehensive review, however, the Ontario Medical Association (2002, pp. 14, 23–24) concluded that these programs were ineffective and made several recommendations to strengthen youth smoking-reduction initiatives.

The OMA (2002, p. 23) recommended that all parties interested in reducing tobacco use endorse a comprehensive tobacco control program and that all tbacco industry–sponsored programs be carefully monitored in the future. These recommendations culminated in 2003 with the passage of the Tobacco Act, which prohibited all advertising and sponsorship aimed at young people.

UP IN SMOKE 7

References

Cunningham, R. (1996). *Smoke and mirrors: The Canadian tobacco war.* Ottawa, Canada: IDRC.

Ontario Medical Association. (2002, February). More smoke and mirrors: Tobacco industry–sponsored youth prevention programs in the context of comprehensive tobacco control programs in Canada. Retrieved from https://www.oma.org/Resources/Documents/a2002MoreSmokeAndMirrors.pdf

Sheppard, R. (1990, December 6). "Ottawa butts up against Big Tobacco." *Maclean's,* 20–24. Retrieved from http://www.proquestk12.com

EXAMPLES OF PARENTHETICAL REFERENCES: TRADITIONAL PRINT SOURCES

Author's Name Given in Your Text

> Kevin Patterson (2000) wrote about his sailing journey from British Columbia to the South Pacific and back: "Suffused with optimism and rum, I told Peter I wanted to sail to Tahiti" (p. 6).

For the format of a References entry for this type of source, see the sample References list on page 217.

Author's Name Not Given in Your Text

> Long voyages by sea, especially in small boats, present obvious dangers depending on the ocean and the season of crossing: "The North Pacific is cold and volatile in the autumn and anyone who knew enough about the sea to consider sailing to Canada knew that much" (Patterson, 2000, p. 249).

No Author Named in Source

When no author is named, give the first two or three words of the title of the publication or article in which the quotation appeared. For the References entry for this source, see the sample References list on page 217.

> Legislation to reduce the amount of pollution generated by large-scale vehicles has been on the federal agenda for some time: "Canada has said it will toughen pollution-emission rules for all new vehicles, ending a loophole that allowed less stringent standards for popular sport-utility vehicles and minivans" ("Canada to Toughen," 2002, p. A6).

Source with Two Authors

Name both authors in the order in which their names appear on the work.

> Norton and Green (2005) observe that inexperienced writers achieved superior results when they spent half the allotted time on planning and drafting, and the other half on revising.

If you do not name the authors in your own sentence, use an ampersand (&) instead of *and* in the parenthetical reference.

> One approach to writing recommends that students spend half the allotted time on planning and drafting, and the other half on revising (Norton & Green, 2005).

Further information on APA parenthetical citations (e.g., two or more books by the same author, a work in an edited anthology, a work cited in a secondary source) can be found on the APA website (www.apastyle.org).

EXAMPLES OF PARENTHETICAL REFERENCES: ELECTRONIC SOURCES

If the electronic source includes the author's name, give the surname and the publication date (if provided) in your parenthetical reference. If no date is provided and your References list includes another author with the same surname, include the author's initial(s) in your in-text reference. This is all the information your reader needs in order to find the full bibliographical data in your References list. Example:

> Science is about immersing ourselves in piercing uncertainty while struggling with the deepest of mysteries. It is the ultimate adventure.... Einstein captured it best when he wrote, "the years of anxious searching in the dark for a truth that one feels but cannot express." That's what science is about. (Greene, 2009)

The quotation in the example above comes from *Wired*, an online magazine. (The sample References list on page 217 shows you how to format this kind of source.)

If the electronic source does not list an author, use the document title (or a shortened version of the title) instead of the author's name.

> When a victim of abuse won't leave the abuser because of fear for a pet's safety, if approached, local animal rescues will often step up to temporarily care for the animal ("New Foster Program," 2013).

(See the sample References list on page 217 for the bibliographic format for this source.)

Electronic sources don't usually include page numbers or other navigation devices, but if there are page, paragraph, or section numbers that could guide your reader to the specific material being quoted, include them. Use the abbreviation *par.* or *pars.* for paragraph numbers, as shown in the following example from an online edition of a Guy de Maupassant story:

> In the short story "The Necklace" (de Maupassant, 1907), Mme. Loisel undergoes a dramatic change after she loses her friend's jewels:
>
> > The frightful debt must be paid. She would pay it. They dismissed the servant; they changed their rooms; they took an attic under the roof.

> She learned the rough work of the household, the odious labors of the kitchen. She washed the dishes, wearing out her pink nails on the greasy pots and the bottoms of the pans. (pars. 98–99)

(The sample References list on page 217 illustrates the correct bibliographic format for this source.)

More information on the treatment of electronic sources can be found on the APA website (www.apastyle.org).

The APA References List

The References list at the end of your essay must include detailed documentation of all the sources you have summarized, paraphrased, quoted, or referred to in any way in your paper. This information enables your reader to assess the extent of your research and to find every source you used. As you read through the bulleted list below, check each item against the sample References list on page 217.

- Begin the References list on a new page.
- Centre the word "References" on the page, two spaces below your running head (the title of your paper in all upper-case letters, abbreviated if necessary). (Note: Use the automatic "Header" function of your word-processing program to create the running head.)
- Leave a double space between the title "References" and the first entry, and double-space all of the entries.
- Begin each entry at the left margin. If the entry runs more than a single line—and most do—indent the second and subsequent lines 1.25 cm. This format is called a "hanging indent" and can be set automatically in the "Paragraph" menu of most word-processing packages.
- Arrange the entries alphabetically, beginning with the first word of the entry, which is often the author's surname. Do not number your entries.
- If there are several works by the same author, arrange by year of publication, earliest first.
- If no author is identified in your source, alphabetize by the first word in the title, ignoring *A, An,* and *The.* For example, *The Canadian Encyclopedia* would be listed under *C,* for *Canadian* (but would still retain *The* in the title).

Below you will find examples of References entries for the types of sources commonly used in research papers, including print, broadcast, and electronic sources.

BOOKS, ENCYCLOPEDIAS, REPORTS, GOVERNMENT PUBLICATIONS

Here is the basic model for a book entry in a References list.

> Last name of author or editor, Initials. (Year of publication). *Title of book: Subtitle of book.* Place of publication: Publisher.

Note the capitalization, punctuation, and order of the information. Leave one space between the initials in authors' names as well as after commas, colons, semicolons, and periods that separate the parts of the reference citation.

- Give each author's or editor's surname, a comma, and initials.
- In parentheses, give the year the book was published. This is usually found on the back of the title page (the copyright page); if it is not, use the latest copyright date.
- Capitalize only proper nouns and the first word of the title and first word of the subtitle, if any. Italicize the title and subtitle.
- For the place of publication, if several locations are listed, use the first one. Add the two-letter postal abbreviation of the state if the city is not well known and, for cities outside the United States, add the country name in place of the state abbreviation.
- Insert the publisher's name, deleting business identifiers such as *Co.* or *Inc.* but retaining words such as *Press* and *Books.* For example: Prentice Hall (not Prentice Hall, Inc.) and University of Toronto Press.

Book with One or More Authors

Deraniyagala, S. (2013). *Wave*. Toronto, Canada: McClelland.

McCall, B., & Letterman, D. (2013). *This land was made for you and me (but mostly me): Billionaires in the wild.* Toronto, Canada: Random House.

(Note: List up to seven authors or editors. If there are more than seven authors, list the first six, followed by three spaced ellipsis points (. . .) and the name of the last author of the work.)

Book with More Than One Edition

Peak, K. J., & Glesnor, R. W. (2008). *Community policing and problem solving: Strategies and practices* (5th ed.). Upper Saddle River, NJ: Prentice Hall.

A Book with No Author

Webster's new college dictionary (3rd ed.). (2008). Boston: Houghton.

Book with One or More Editors

Baum, J. R., Frese, M., & Baron, R. A. (Eds.). (2007). *The psychology of entrepreneurship*. Mahwah, NJ: Erlbaum.

Bhushan, B. (Ed.). (2007). *Springer handbook of nanotechnology* (2nd ed.). New York: Springer.

See authors' note above for information on citing a book with more than seven editors.

Chapter, Article, Essay, Story, or Poem in an Edited Book or Collection

Mistry, R. (2001). Journey to Dharmsala. In C. Meyer & B. Meyer (Eds.), *The reader: Contemporary essays and writing strategies* (pp. 38–51). Toronto, Canada: Prentice Hall.

Presentation at a Conference

Long, R. J. (2005, September). *Group-based pay, participatory practices, and workplace performance.* Paper presented at the Conference on the Evolving Workplace, Ottawa, Canada.

If the conference proceedings are numbered or published regularly, use the following format:

Toorman, E. A. (2002). Modelling of turbulent flow with suspended cohesive sediment. In J. C. Winterwerp & C. Kranenburg (Eds.), *Fine sediment dynamics in the marine environment: Proceedings in Marine Science 5*, 155–169.

Reference Book

Newland, T. E. (2004). Intelligence tests. In *Compton's encyclopedia & fact index* (Vol. 11, pp. 245–249). Chicago: Britannica.

Book Published by a Corporation (Company, Commission, Agency)

International Joint Commission. (2000). Protection of the waters of the Great Lakes: Final report to the governments of Canada and the United States. Ottawa, Canada: Author.

Government Document

If the author is not named, identify the agency, then the date, title, city of publication, and publisher. Include specific information such as report or catalogue number after the title.

Environmental Protection Commission. (2005). A review of Alberta's environmental and emergency response capacity: Learning the lessons and building change. Edmonton, Canada: Alberta Environment.

Statistics Canada. (2006). *How to cite Statistics Canada products* (Catalogue No. 12-591-XWE). Ottawa, Canada: Statistics Canada.

Brochure or Pamphlet

Barlow, M. (2017). Water for sale: How free trade and investment agreements threaten environmental protection of water and promote the commodification of the world's water [Brochure]. Ottawa, Canada: Council of Canadians.

Further information on APA References can be found on the APA website (www.apastyle.org).

ARTICLES IN MAGAZINES, NEWSPAPERS, AND JOURNALS

Note the spacing, capitalization, punctuation, and order of the information required in a References entry for a magazine, newspaper, or journal:

- each author's last name and initials
- date of publication in parentheses and in year–month–day order; do not abbreviate the names of months: (2009, September 30) or (2010, January–February)

- title of the article with no quotation marks and with an initial capital letter only; a capital letter is also required after the colon that introduces an article's subtitle
- name of the magazine, newspaper, or journal as it appears on the front page, in italics, with capital letters for all major words; include *A*, *An*, or *The* if it is part of the official name of the publication: *The Globe and Mail*
- volume number and issue number (if any); these are rare in magazines and newspapers, but often appear in journal entries and are expressed as, for example: *13*(6), which means Volume 13, Issue 6 (note that the volume number is italicized)
- inclusive page numbers of the article

Give the complete page span for each magazine and newspaper article in your References list. For magazines, if an article begins on page 14 and concludes on page 16, put a comma after the magazine's name (or after the volume and issue numbers, if these are included) and show this span: *Maclean's*, 14–16. (Note: Do not use "p." or "pp." when citing magazines or journals.) If the article begins, for example, on page 36, then skips to page 40 and concludes on page 41, give all three numbers: 36, 40, 41.

In a newspaper, the sections are usually numbered separately, so include the section identifier as well as the page number, which in this case is preceded by "p." or "pp.": *Vancouver Sun*, pp. B1–B2. As in the case of magazines, if the article begins on one page and is continued on another page or pages, give all of the page numbers: pp. C1, C3, C6, C9–C11.

Article in a Monthly/Seasonal Magazine

Carter, S. (2017, July/August). A level playing field. *Quill & Quire*, 13–15.

Article in a Weekly Magazine

Gatehouse, J. (2013, September 23). The real nuclear meltdown. *Maclean's*, 18–20.

Article in a Daily Newspaper

Shufelt, T., & Bradshaw, J. (2017, July 13). Banks boost prime rates after BoC hike. *The Globe and Mail*, p. B1.

Article in a Scholarly Journal

Baier, M., & Buechsel, R. (2012). A model to help bereaved individuals understand the grief process. *Mental Health Practice*, *16*(1), 28–32.

Kan, Y., Ruis, B., Taksugi, T., & Hendrickson, E. A. (2017, July). Mechanisms of precise genome editing using oligonucleotide donors. *Genome Research*, 23, 1112–25.

List up to seven authors. Place an ampersand before the last author's name, as shown in the second entry directly above. If there are eight or more authors, give the names of the first six authors, insert three spaced ellipsis points (. . .), and add the last author's name.

If each issue of a journal begins with page 1, include the issue number. If the journal is paged continuously throughout the year, do not include the issue number.

No Author Named in Source

Carbon credit transfer. (2009). *Alternatives Journal, 35*(2), 5.

Clear as glass; warm as toast. (2009, Summer). *Yukon, North of Ordinary*, 38.

Ottawa recalls sensitive data. (2009, February 16). *Toronto Star*, p. A2.

Published Review: Books, Plays, Films, Etc.

Bland, J. (2008, October/November). [Review of the book The $12 million stuffed shark: The curious economics of contemporary art, by D. Thompson]. *The Walrus*, 94.

Dixon, G. (2009, March 14). Mash-up doc argues that creativity begins where copyright ends [Review of the film *RiP: A remix manifesto*]. *The Globe and Mail*, p. R11.

Published Interview

Radwanski, A. (2009, March 21). Where angels fear to tread [Interview with Patrick Monahan]. *The Globe and Mail*, p. M3.

Unpublished Personal Interview

Personal interviews are not included in the References list. Instead, use a parenthetical citation in the body of your essay:

(A. Brogly, personal interview, September 12, 2018)

Personal Communications

As in the case of personal interviews, memos, letters, telephone conversations, and email messages from non-archived sources are not included in the References list. Instead, use a parenthetical citation in the body of your essay. Never provide your source's email address or telephone number.

(A. Dynes, personal communication, January 22, 2018)

AUDIOVISUAL SOURCES

Television/Radio Broadcast

Anniko, T. (Executive producer). (2008). *Monsoon house* [Radio series]. Toronto, Canada: CBC.

Costello, E. (Writer/host). (2009). Elton John [Television series episode]. In J. Jacobs (Executive producer), *Spectacle: Elvis Costello with* … Toronto, Canada: CTV.

Motion Picture, Music Recording, Video

Delmar's community health nursing: A case study [CD]. (2003). Clifton Park, NJ: Delmar.

Jaiko, C. (Producer), & Barczewska, A. (Writer/director). (2005). *A child unlike any other* [Motion picture]. Montreal, Canada: National Film Board.

Nickelback. (2009). *Dark horse* [CD]. New York: Road Runner Records.

Ward, Al. (2009). Photoshop for right-brainers: The art of photo manipulation [DVD]. San Francisco: Sybex.

ELECTRONIC SOURCES

The rules for citing APA electronic sources are essentially the same as for print and broadcast sources. The reference should provide enough information to enable a reader to locate the source quickly—author, date, title, publisher or sponsor of the site, and the URL (uniform resource locator) or a DOI (digital object identifier).

The URL is an addressing system that links you to a host server and identifies the path to a specific file location. The DOI is an added, unique code. If a DOI listed in a publication is not working, you will be directed to a "DOI resolver" to access the material. This practice ensures that the document is always available, even if there are changes to a host server or file location. If a document has a DOI, it is the only address that you need to use. For items accessed through library subscription databases, you use the database name instead of the URL.

Retrieval dates are not necessary for electronic sources.

Consistency in capitalization, punctuation, and the order of the information are important when you cite electronic sources. Here are a few guidelines:

- Do not use a hyphen to divide a URL over two lines; if you do, you will make the URL invalid.
- URL and DOI address strings can be long and prone to mistakes if retyped. Copy and paste for best results.
- Download and print online material so that you can verify it if, at a later date, it is revised, unavailable, or inaccessible.

Online Book from a Library Subscription Database

Kay, M. (2008). *Practical hydraulics* (2nd ed.). Retrieved from NetLibrary database.

Online Book from a Public Internet Site

Health Canada. (2005). *Regulation and beyond: Progress on Health Canada's therapeutics access strategy*. Retrieved from http://publications.gc.ca/collections/Collection/H42-2-99-2005E.pdf

Wollstonecraft, M. (1792). *A vindication of the rights of women*. Retrieved from http://www.bartleby.com/144

Chapter, Essay, Story, or Poem in an Online Book

de Maupassant, G. (1907). The necklace. In B. Matthews (Ed.), *The short-story: Specimens illustrating its development.* Retrieved from http://www.bartleby.com/195

Mallett, D. (2006). Sampling and weighting. In R. Grover & M. Vriens (Eds.), *The handbook of marketing research: Uses, misuses and future advances* (pp. 159–177). Retrieved from http://books.google.ca/books ?id=RymGgxN3zD4C&printsec=frontcover&source =gbs_summary_r&cad=0#PPA177,M1

Online Encyclopedia, Dictionary

Canadian literature. (2009). In *Encyclopaedia Britannica*. Retrieved from http://www.britannica.com

Capricious. (2009). In *Merriam-Webster's online dictionary*. Retrieved from http://www.merriam-webster.com/dictionary

Falco, C. M. (2009). Use of optics by Renaissance artists. In *AccessScience@McGraw-Hill Online*. doi:10.1036/ 1097-8542.YB084340

Journal Article from a Library Subscription Database

Engardio, P., Hall, K., Rowley, I., Welch, D., & Balfour, F. (2009, February 23). The electric car battery war. *BusinessWeek*, 52. Retrieved from http://www.ebscohost.com/academic/ academic-search-complete

Journal Article from a Public Internet Journal

Herman, D. (2009, Spring/Summer). Wonderland. *Rhythm*. Retrieved from http://rhythmpoetrymagazine.english.dal .ca/i2v2/poet10.html

Chen, G. K., Marjoram, P., & Wall, J. D. (2009). Fast and flexible simulation of DNA sequence data. *Genome Research, 19*, 136–142. doi:10.1101/gr.083634.108

Newspaper Article from a Public Internet Site

Brooymans, H. (2009, March 31). Duck death toll triples at Alberta oilsands pond. *Edmonton Journal*. Retrieved from http://www.edmontonjournal.com

Online News Service Article

CTV News Services. (2009, May 6). *Ontario set to allow medication vending machines*. Retrieved from http:// news.sympatico.msn.ctv.ca

Online Image

Carr, E. (1935). *A rushing sea of undergrowth*. Retrieved from www.virtualmuseum.ca/Exhibitions/EmilyCarr

Online Course Materials

Jenkins, D. (2012). *Teamwork!* [Prezi slides]. Mohawk College. Retrieved from http://prezi.com/bwkg1bmb2wu6/teamwork

Wurfel, Marlene. (n.d.). *Canadian writers: Alice Munro* [Course materials]. Athabasca University. Retrieved from http://canadian-writers.athabascau.ca/english/writers/amunro/amunro.php

Personal Website

Atwood, M. (n.d.). *The rocky road to paper heaven.* Retrieved from http://www.owtoad.com

Television Show (Episode of a Continuing Series)

Thompson, J. (Writer/director). (2008). Shock wave [Television series episode]. In B. Hamilton (Executive producer), *Doc zone* [Television podcast]. Retrieved from http://www.cbc.ca/documentaries/doczone

Audio Podcast

Rule, B. (2009, April 5). *Barbara Ferguson on Vampires, Art Waves #25* [Audio podcast]. Retrieved from https://archive.org/details/BarbaraFergusonOnVampiresArtWaves25

Blog, Social Network Post

Blog, video, or message posts on social network sites include the date of the posting, and titles are not italicized. Some instructors do not accept these sources as valid or reliable, so be sure to check with your instructor before including them in your work.

Fullick, Melanie. (2012, October 4). Tweeting out loud: Ethics, knowledge, and social media in academe [Web log]. Retrieved from http://www.universityaffairs.ca/speculative-diction/tweeting-out-loud-ethics-knowledge-and-social-media-in-academe

Utko, J. (2009, February). Can design save the newspaper? [Video file]. Retrieved from http://www.youtube.com/watch?v=zHuH8P_Vqc0

Young drivers against new Ontario laws. (n.d.). [Discussion group]. Retrieved from http://www.facebook.com/group.php?gid=35271482979

Sample APA References List

Entries in a References list are arranged alphabetically according to the first word in the entry and are not numbered. On the next page you will find a sample References list made up of different kinds of sources.

TITLE OF PAPER 29

References

Canada to toughen auto-emissions rules. (2002, April 5). *The Wall Street Journal*, p. A6.

de Maupassant, G. (1907). The necklace. In B. Matthews (Ed.). *The short-story: Specimens illustrating its development.* Retrieved from http://www.bartleby.com/195/20/html

France, H., Rodriguez, M., & Hett, G. (2004). *Diversity, culture and counselling: A Canadian perspective.* Calgary, Canada: Detselig.

Greene, B. (2009, April 20). Questions, not answers, make science the ultimate adventure. *Wired Magazine.* Retrieved from http://www.wired.com/culture/culturereviews/magazine/17-05/st_essay

Helson, R., & Pals, J. (2000). Creative potential, creative achievement, and personal growth. *Journal of Personality, 68*(2), 39–44.

Mistry, R. (2001). Journey to Dharmsala. In C. Meyer & B. Meyer (Eds.), *The reader: Contemporary essays and writing strategies* (pp. 38–51). Toronto, Canada: Prentice Hall.

Moore, M. (Writer, producer, director). (2002). *Bowling for Columbine* [Motion picture]. United States: United Artists, Alliance Atlantis, and Dog Eat Dog Films.

New foster program coming soon. (2013, October 7). The Animal Guardian Society [Web log]. Retrieved from http://tagstails.blogspot.ca/2013/10/new-foster-program-coming-soon.html

Patterson, K. (2000). *The water in between: A journey at sea.* Toronto, Canada: Vintage Canada.

Sreenivasan, A. (2002, February). Keeping up with the cones. *Natural History*, 40–46.

Statistics Canada. (2013, September 25). *Infant mortality rates, by province and territory.* Retrieved from http://www.statcan.gc.ca/tables-tableaux/sum-som/l01/cst01/health21a-eng.htm

Wahl, A. (2005, February 28). Emission impossible. *Canadian Business*, 24. Retrieved from http://elibrary.bigchalk.com

Article in a newspaper

Selection from an online anthology

Book by three authors

Article in an online periodical

Article in a scholarly journal

Selection from a print anthology

Movie

Electronic source with no author

Book by one author

Article in a monthly magazine

Online government publication

Magazine article from an online library subscription database

Exercise 17.2 For each of the following quotations, write a short paragraph in which you use all or a portion of the quotation and credit it in an APA-style parenthetical reference. Be sure to use capital letters as required and to punctuate titles correctly.

1. From a book entitled Getting it done: the transforming power of self-discipline by Andrew J. Dubrin, published by Pacesetter Books in Princeton in 1995. This sentence appears on page 182: "Stress usually stems from your interpretation and perception of an event, not from the event itself."

2. From a journal article by Linda A. White that appeared on pages 385 to 405 of Canadian Public Policy, a journal with continuous paging: "If a clear connection exists between the presence of child care and high levels of women's labour market participation, that would provide good reasons for governments and employers to regard child care as part of an active labour market policy." White's article is entitled Child Care, Women's Labour Market Participation and Labour Market Policy Effectiveness in Canada. The quotation appears on page 389 of the fourth issue of the 27th volume, published in 2001.

3. From a newspaper article that appeared on page A2 in the March 30, 2005, issue of the Vancouver Sun, written by Nancy Cleeland, found on the eLibrary Canada database at your school library. The article is entitled As jobs heat up, workers' hearts take a beating: "For years, occupational health researchers have struggled to come up with formulas for measuring job stress and determining its effect on health."

4. During the February 3, 2009, CBC broadcast of the Mercer Report, Rick Mercer says, "According to a recent Dominion Institute poll, a majority of Canadians have no idea how Parliament works." The segment was entitled Everything you wanted to know about Canada but were afraid to ask. You watched the broadcast on *YouTube* at http://www.youtube.com/watch?v=yi1yhp-_x7A.

5. From an email message on the subject of time management from your friend, Janet Ford, on June 5, 2009: "Using a daily planner and checking email only once a day are two ways I've found to manage my stress during the school year."

Part 6

Understanding the Revision Process

Planning and drafting should take no more than half the time you devote to writing a paper. That said, these tasks are an essential part of the writing process and should be given a great deal of care. The rest of your time should be devoted to revision: rewriting, editing, and proofreading. It is during this process that ideas that may be unpolished or rough become reader-friendly and easy to understand. This part of the textbook will go into detail about the important and interconnected tasks of making sure you have the right words, rewriting, editing, and proofreading.

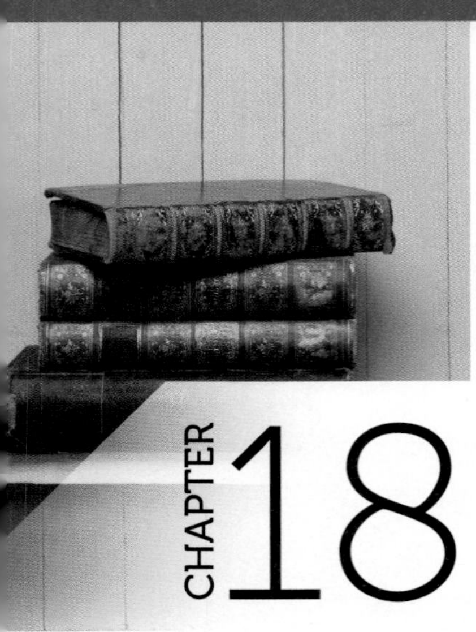

CHAPTER 18

Choosing the Right Words

The difference between the right word and the almost right word is the difference between lightning and a lightning bug.
—Mark Twain

In this chapter, we provide a brief introduction to language that is concise and appropriate. In other words, we are looking at language that says what you mean and is appropriate for your message and for your audience. Our goal is to help you convey a clear message in a way that will leave your readers with a positive impression of you and your ideas, whether you are handing in an essay to your instructor or a research report to your new boss.

For editing your paper, you need to equip yourself with a few essential resources and some basic knowledge of what kinds of language are appropriate and inappropriate when you write.

The Writer's Toolkit

In addition to basic skills, all workers need tools. As a general rule, the better their tools, the better their work. If you are a concert pianist, a toy piano just won't cut it. Every writer comes equipped with a set of language skills acquired from birth. In most cases, however, these skills are used more for talking than for writing. Most everyday writing situations are not sufficiently sophisticated to handle the complex task of producing clear, error-free prose in a professional style. Fortunately, tools are available to assist writers in bringing their language skills up to the standards required by professional environments. Collectively, we call these indispensable aids the Writer's Toolkit.

No one expects a writer to write without assistance. In fact, our first recommendation to beginning writers is to GET HELP! Every writer needs three basic tools and to know how to use them.

1. Use a good dictionary.

A dictionary is a writer's best friend. You will need to use it every time you write, so if you don't already own a good dictionary, you need to buy one or find a good one online. For Canadian writers, a good dictionary is one that is Canadian, current, comprehensive (contains at least 75 000 entries), and reliable (published by an established, well-known firm).

A convenient paperback reference is the *Collins Gage Canadian Dictionary,* available in an inexpensive edition. It is the dictionary on which we have based the examples and exercises in this chapter. Also recommended are the *Nelson Canadian Dictionary of the English Language*, the *Canadian Oxford Dictionary* (2nd ed., 2004), and, for those whose native language is not English, the *Oxford Advanced Learner's Dictionary*. For online options, check out your college or university library; most have subscriptions to the *Oxford English Dictionary,* which includes the Canadian version, or to other dictionaries.

Whichever dictionary you choose, begin by reading the information in the front on how to use the dictionary. This information may not be very entertaining, but it is essential if you want to understand how to use your dictionary efficiently. No two dictionaries are alike. You need to be familiar with your dictionary's symbols, abbreviations, and the format of its entries.

Knowing how the dictionary entries are set up will also save you time. Entries include irregular forms of verbs, **adjectives**, and **adverbs**. And, if you've forgotten how regular plurals, verbs, adjectives, and adverbs are made, you'll find that information on the inside cover and in the first set of pages, as well.

2. Use spelling and grammar checkers responsibly.

Good spell-check programs can find typing errors and common spelling mistakes that distract your readers and make you look careless. They do have limitations, however. As we'll see, they can't tell if you meant to write *your* or *you're* and will not flag either word, even if it's used incorrectly. (You'll learn more about such words, called *homonyms*, in Chapter 26.)

Also, since we use Canadian English, our spelling is frequently different from American spelling, which is the standard on which most word-processing spell-check programs are based. Set your program to Canadian spelling. If it does not have this option, be aware that words such as *colour, traveller, grey, doughnut,* and *metre*—all correct Canadian spellings—will be flagged as errors.

Another useful tool if you are struggling with spelling is your cellphone. Smartphone dictionary apps contain a large bank of words and can provide the correct spelling if the "guess" you key in is not too far off. Some checkers even pronounce the word for you. While useful in class, cellphones are often not allowed in testing situations, so ask before you pull out your phone and start typing away! Again, these programs may offer only American spelling, so be cautious in their use.

The best advice we can give you about grammar checkers (they announce their presence by producing wavy green lines under words or sentences as you write on your word processor) is to use them with caution. So far, no grammar check has been able to account for even most, let alone all, of the subtleties of English grammar. A grammar program is as likely to flag a perfectly good sentence, even to suggest a "fix" that is incorrect, as it is to ignore a sentence full of errors. "I done real good on my grammar test," for example, escapes the dreaded wavy green line.

3. Use a good thesaurus.

If you repeat yourself, using the same words again and again, you won't communicate your thoughts interestingly, let alone memorably. Worse, you will bore your reader. A thesaurus is a dictionary of *synonyms*—words with similar meanings. For any word you need to use repeatedly in a document, a good thesaurus will provide a list of alternatives. (Again, there are both print and online versions of many popular thesauruses.)

Synonyms are *not* identical in meaning. Your dictionary will help you decide which of the words listed in your thesaurus are suitable for your message and which are not. We do not recommend that you rely on the thesaurus in your word-processing program. For any given word, a word-processing thesaurus provides a list, in alphabetical order, of more-or-less synonyms, with no **usage** labels or examples. "More-or-less" is not good enough. At the very least, you need to know whether the synonyms offered are nouns or verbs and whether they are in general use or are informal, technical, derogatory, or even obsolete. For this information, have a good book-form or online thesaurus and use it in conjunction with your dictionary. Two thesauruses are available in inexpensive paperback editions: the *Oxford Thesaurus of Current English* (2nd ed., 2006) and *Roget's 21st Century Thesaurus in Dictionary Form* (3rd ed., 2005).

Have a look at the synonyms for creativity in this excerpt from Scott Barry Kaufman's "The Creative Gifts of ADHD." Did he do a good job of using words that all worked together to create the image he was looking for?

> **The ability to control your attention is most certainly a valuable asset; difficulty inhibiting your inner mind can get in the way of paying attention to a boring classroom lecture or concentrating on a challenging problem. But the ability to keep your inner stream of fantasies, imagination, and daydreams on call can be immensely conducive to creativity. By automatically treating ADHD characteristics as a disability—as we so often do in an educational context—we are unnecessarily letting too many competent and creative kids fall through the cracks.**

Scott Barry Kaufman, "The Creative Gifts of ADHD," *Scientific American*, October 21, 2014. Used with permission.

Use the information you find in a thesaurus with caution. Inexperienced writers sometimes assume that long, obscure words will impress their readers. In fact, most readers are irritated by unnecessarily "fancy" language. For more information on this topic, see the Pretentious Language section on pages 227–228.

Never use a word whose meaning you do not know. When you find a potential but unfamiliar synonym, look it up in your dictionary to be sure it's the word you need.

So far, we've introduced you to the tools you'll need as a writer and to the levels of language you can choose from when writing a message for a particular audience. Let's turn now to the writing errors you must not commit, no matter what message you're sending or the audience to which you're sending it: wordiness, slang and jargon, pretentious language, clichés, sexist language, offensive language, and the misused words and phrases that we call "abusages."

The Seven Deadly Errors of Writing

1. Wordiness

Wordiness—words and phrases that are not essential to the communication of your message—is annoying to readers, no matter what topic you are writing about. Good writing communicates a message as concisely as possible. Wordy messages take up your readers' time and try their patience. Many students remember packing essays with extra words in high school to meet length requirements. The idea now at this level and in the business world is to organize ideas and present them concisely.

If you want to please your audience, be brief.

Sometimes wordiness results from a failure to revise carefully. In the editing stage of writing, you should be looking for the best words to express your meaning. (We'll talk more about editing in Chapters 19 and 20.) Wordy expressions and awkward phrasing often pop into your mind when you are struggling to express an idea, and they may make their way into a first draft. There is no excuse for them to survive a careful edit and end up in the second draft, however.

Here's an example of what can happen when a writer fails to prune his or her prose:

> In my personal opinion, the government of this country of ours needs an additional amount of meaningful input from the people of Canada right now.

This wordy sentence could be nicely condensed into "In my opinion, our government needs to hear more from the people." The writer has chosen impressive-sounding phrases (*meaningful input, this country of ours*) and has slipped in unnecessary and meaningless words that should have been caught during editing (*personal opinion, an additional amount*). The result is a sentence that is so hard to read that it isn't worth the effort to decipher. The issue isn't whether the sentence is interesting or packs a punch. (The only punch is one that leads to a long sleep.) Rather, the sentence's wordiness actually lessens the interest a reader might have in the topic.

As you can see from the above example, one of the symptoms of wordiness is *redundancy*, or saying the same thing twice. Another is using several words where one or two would do.

The following list contains some of the worst offenders we've collected from student writing, corporate memoranda, form letters, and advertisements.

Wordy	**Concise**
a large number of	many
absolutely nothing (everything/ complete/perfect)	nothing (everything/ complete/perfect)
actual (*or* true) fact	fact
almost always	usually
at that point in time	then
at the present time	now
consensus of opinion	consensus
continue on	continue
could possibly (*or* may possibly, might possibly)	could (*or* may, might)
crisis (*or* emergency) situation	crisis (*or* emergency)

Wordy	**Concise**
due to the fact that	because
end result	result
equally as good	as good
few and far between	rare
final conclusion	conclusion
for the reason that	because
free gift	gift
I myself (or you yourself, *etc.*)	I (*or* you, *etc.*)
I personally think/feel	I think/feel
in actual fact	in fact
in every instance	always
in my opinion, I think	I think
in the near future	soon
in today's society/in this day and age	now (*or* today)
is able to	can
many different kinds	many kinds
mutual agreement/cooperation	agreement/cooperation
my personal opinion	my opinion
no other alternative	no alternative
personal friend	friend
real, genuine leather (*or* real antique, *etc.*)	leather (*or* antique, *etc.*)
red in colour (*or* large in size, *etc.*)	red (*or* large, *etc.*)
repeat again	repeat
return back	return (or go back)
really, very	*These words add nothing to your meaning. Leave them out.*
8:00 a.m. in the morning	8:00 a.m.
such as, for example	such as
take active steps	take steps
totally destroyed	destroyed
truly remarkable	remarkable
very (most, quite, almost, rather) unique	unique

Working with a partner, revise these sentences to make them as concise and clear as possible. Then compare your answers with our suggestions on pages 462–463.

Exercise 18.1*

1. I wondered why the baseball seemed to keep getting bigger and bigger and bigger. Then, at that point in time, it hit me.
2. Would you repeat again one more time the instructions about wordiness? In actual fact, I didn't hear them because I was busy texting at the very same time you were speaking.
3. It has come to my attention that our competitor's products, although not equally as good as ours, are, nevertheless, at this point in time, selling better than our products.
4. In my opinion, I believe that my writing is equally as good as Ashley's and deserves equally as good a mark, especially considering that I use a larger number of words to say exactly the same thing.
5. Basically, I myself prefer the Marvel franchise to the DC comics movie franchise because the DC characters aren't as interesting and the movies aren't as funny as the ones from the Marvel universe.
6. I doubt that this particular new innovation will succeed in winning much in the way of market share.
7. In my view, I feel that a really firm understanding of the basic fundamentals of English is an essential prerequisite to a person's success in college or university, the business world, and the community at large.
8. "As a new beginning teacher," we told our English instructor, "you need to understand the fact that the grammar, spelling, and punctuation conventions and rules you insist on are totally stifling our creativity."
9. There are many different kinds of social media we use in today's society, but I think that in the not too distant future, we'll see a convergence with the end result that the electronic world will in actual fact resemble the "real" world so closely that the boundaries between the two will blur and begin to disappear.
10. Due to the fact that the law, not to mention our company's policy, rules, and regulations, absolutely prohibits any mention of race, age, gender, religion, and marital status in official documents such as human resources documents, we have made sure that all such descriptors have been entirely eliminated from our files. Now, as a result, all our HR documents are now almost practically identical.

2. Slang and Jargon

The point of slang is its exclusivity.

Slang is "street talk": nonstandard words and phrases used by members of a group—people who share a culture, interest, or lifestyle. The group may be as large as a generation or as small as a high-school clique. Do you know what *amped, badload, busting,* and *hodger* mean? Perhaps not. It's a private language and thus not appropriate for a message aimed at a general reader.

Another characteristic of slang is that it changes quickly. Terms that were "in" last month are "out" today. Except for a few expressions that manage to sneak across the line that separates private language from mainstream English, most slang expressions are quickly outdated and sound silly. And finally, slang is an oral language. It is *colloquial*—that is, characteristic of casual speech—and not appropriate for use in professional or academic writing.

When you aren't sure if a word is appropriate for a written message, consult your print dictionary. The notation *sl.* or *slang* appears after words that are slang or have a slang meaning. (Some words, such as *house, cool,* and *bombed,* have both a general and a slang meaning.) If the word you're looking for isn't listed, chances are it's a recent slang term, and you should avoid using it in writing. You can also consult one of the many online dictionaries of slang, which list the variety of meanings that words can take. Taking the time to choose words that are appropriate to written English increases your chances both of communicating clearly and of winning your readers' respect. It also helps you avoid having a reader misunderstand what you are trying to say, almost always to your detriment.

Exercise 18.2

1. Working in groups of three or four, identify five current slang expressions.
2. Now list five slang expressions that are no longer in use among your peers.
3. Finally, define each current slang term in language appropriate to a general reader. (If you don't have a clear picture of a "general reader," write each definition in words your parents or teachers would understand.)

Although jargon is useful, even necessary, in the context of some jobs, it is inappropriate in most writing because it does not communicate to a general reader.

Jargon is similar to slang because it, too, is the private language of a subgroup; however, whereas the subgroups for slang are formed by culture or lifestyle, the subgroups who speak jargon are formed by profession or trade. The jargon of some professions is so highly technical and specialized it amounts almost to a private language.

Our vocabulary and even the content of our writing are influenced by the contexts within which we work and live. In the following paragraph, D. Miller explains the extent to which our individual perceptions are influenced by our life experience.

> A group of people witness a car accident. What each person sees, and how he or she describes it, is determined to a large extent by the language each one normally uses. A doctor or nurse would see and describe contusions, lacerations, and hemorrhages. A lawyer would think in terms of civil liabilities and criminal negligence. A mechanic would see crushed fenders, bent axles, and damaged chassis. A psychologist would be concerned about stress reactions, trauma, and guilt. You or I might see and describe the pain and injury caused by a driver's error in judgement or lapse of skill.

D. Miller, *The Book of Jargon*. New York: Collier, 1981, p. 26.

Jargon restricts your audience to those who share your specialized vocabulary and limits or destroys your ability to reach a wider audience. The cure for jargon is simple: unless your readers share your technical background, use non-specialized language. Even jargon that has crept into our consciousness through such media as television shows—the medical shows have made *stat* an everyday term—should be avoided when you are writing for a general reader since this is mainly a North American phenomenon.

Exercise 18.3

Working in small groups, list as many examples of technical jargon as you can for each of the following occupations (some are provided to give you a start).

1. chef (e.g., sauté, braise, *sous vide*)
2. computer technician (e.g., TWAIN, burn)
3. music (e.g., sample, bridge, axe)
4. financial analyst (e.g., fallen angel, dead cat bounce)
5. filmmaker (e.g., take, MOS)

Choose five technical terms from your own career field and write a general-level equivalent for each one. If your class is made up of students from a variety of programs, share your terms for everyone's benefit.

3. Pretentious Language

Many beginning writers try so hard to impress their readers that they forget that the purpose of writing is to *communicate*.

One of the challenges writers face when trying to adapt their style from the familiar (what you would write every day—e.g., a grocery list or an email to a friend) to the formal level (e.g., essays, professional work) is a tendency to overcompensate. Writing filled with abstract nouns, multi-syllable words, and long, complicated sentences contains **pretentious language**. Most readers hate pretentious writing because they have to take the time to "translate" it into language they can understand. (Most instructors and supervisors won't bother. They'll just return the piece to the student or employee for revision.)

Unless you're a career civil servant or a long-time bureaucrat, writing pretentious language is a time-consuming and tiring task. You have to look up practically every word in a thesaurus to find a polysyllabic equivalent. Sometimes called *gobbledygook*, pretentious language has sound but no meaning:

> Our aspirational consumer strategy must position the brand's appeal to women shoppers who are seeking emblematic brands that are positively identified with health-oriented and fitness-centred lifestyles so they can align their personal images with those lifestyle indicators.

This sentence, part of a marketing presentation to senior management, was written by a middle manager for a major yogurt company. What the struggling writer is trying to say is that the company's customers want to be seen as people interested in fitness and health, so the company should advertise its yogurt accordingly.[1]

[1] This anecdote is paraphrased from Saunders, Doug. "Aspiration Nation: Life Is but a Brand-name Dream." *Globe and Mail*, 3 July 2004, p. F3.

Does making our words longer make us look smarter?

One symptom of pretentious writing is the use of "buzzwords." These are words and phrases that become popular because they reflect the latest academic or psychological fad. They are often nouns with *ize* added to them to make them into verbs: *utilize, verbalize, conceptualize, operationalize*. What's wrong with *use, say, think,* and *implement*?

Every instructor knows this annoying trick, and so do most managers. Instead of impressing readers, pretentious writing makes readers impatient and causes them to lose respect for the writer. If you really want to get your message across, write plainly and clearly in language your readers can understand.

Exercise 18.4* **Rewrite the following sentences, expressing the ideas in a way that allows the reader to grasp your meaning clearly and quickly. Then compare your answers to our suggestions on page 463.**

1. We were forced to utilize the moisture-removing apparatus in our motorized personal conveyance when precipitate liquid impacted our windshield.
2. The chronologically less-advanced generation sometimes achieves a communication deficit with authority figures and parental units.
3. The witness was ethically disoriented truth-wise when she claimed that her interface with the accused resulted in his verbalization of an admission of guilt.
4. The parameters of our study vis-à-vis the totality of research in the field demonstrate that survey-wise our validity is on a par with that of other instruments.
5. The cancellation of IMF funds to the Pacific Rim countries could lead to negative distortion of mutual interrelationships between developed and developing nations.

4. Clichés

A **cliché** is a culturally specific phrase that has been used so often it has lost its ability to communicate a meaningful idea to a reader.

> In this day and age, it seems that anything goes in our private lives. But in our professional lives, the name of the game is what it has always been: the bottom line.

Clichés are easy to produce: they represent language without thought.

In this day and age, anything goes, the name of the game, and *the bottom line* are clichés. Readers know what these phrases are supposed to mean, but they have been used so often they no longer communicate effectively. Cliché-filled writing will not only bore readers, but also affect their reaction to your message: "There's nothing new here. It's all been said before."

Spoken English is full of clichés. In the rush to express an idea, we often take the easy way and use ready-made expressions to put our thoughts into words. There is less excuse to use clichés in writing. Usually, writers have time to think through what they want to say. They also have the opportunity to revise and edit.

Writers are expected to communicate with more care, more precision, and more originality than speakers.

Clichés are easy to recognize if you are a native speaker but not as easy when English isn't your first language. When you can read the first few words of an expression and automatically fill in the rest, the phrase is a cliché: free as a ___; a pain in the ___; last but not ___; it goes without ___; it's raining ___________. It is difficult to get rid of *all* clichés in your writing, but you can be aware of them and use them as seldom as possible.

Finding a solution to a cliché problem requires time and thought. Think carefully about what you want to say; then say it in your own words, not everyone else's.

As you read through Exercise 18.5, notice how hard it is to form a mental picture of what the sentences mean and how hard it is to remember what you've read—even when you've just read it!

Exercise 18.5

Working with a partner, rewrite these sentences, expressing the ideas in your own words. When you're finished, exchange papers with another team and compare your results.

1. The classroom was so quiet you could hear a pin drop.
2. At midnight, I didn't think I had a hope, but I managed to finish the assignment at the crack of dawn.
3. All our good intentions fell by the wayside when we passed a fast-food joint and caught the mouth-watering smell of French fries and grilled burgers.
4. When you are playing poker, you must keep your cool; otherwise, you could lose your shirt.
5. The CEO could not find a way to keep her company afloat, so she threw in the towel.
6. In these difficult times, we must all tighten our belts and hope for a silver lining.
7. Their offer is a far cry from what we had hoped for, but let's make the best of it and show them what we're made of!
8. Until he got the sack, he was a legend in his own mind, but once the axe fell, even he had to face the truth: he was only a flash in the pan.
9. Your proposal is as good as they get; however, until the deal is signed, sealed, and delivered, we had better not count our chickens.
10. I hate to eat and run and stick you with the bill, but I'm between a rock and a hard place, so I have to lie low until my ship comes in.

5. Sexist Language

Any writing that distracts your readers from your meaning is weak writing. Whether the distraction is caused by grammatical errors, spelling mistakes, slang, or the use of sexist language, your readers' concentration on your message is

It is easy to dismiss non-sexist writing as overly "politically correct," but the language we use is a powerful force that influences the way we (and others) think.

broken, and communication fails. **Sexist** (or **gender-biased**) **language** includes the use of words that signify gender (e.g., *waitress, sculptress, actress*) and the use of the pronouns *he, his, him* (or *she, hers, her*) to refer to singular antecedents such as *everybody, anyone, no one*. Some readers object to terms that draw attention to gender differences, such as *man and wife* or *host and hostess*, preferring instead gender-neutral, inclusive terms such as *married couple* and *hosts*.

If we consistently refer to a *chairman* or *businessman*, we are perpetuating the idea that only men qualify for these positions. Far from being a politically correct fad, the use of inclusive or neutral words is both accurate and even-handed.

Here are three tips to help you steer clear of sexist writing:

- Avoid using the word *woman* as an adjective. There is an implied condescension in phrases such as *woman athlete* and *woman writer* and *woman engineer*. We would never consider saying *man lawyer*.
- Be conscious of the dangers of stereotyping. Physical descriptions of women are appropriate only where you would offer a similar description if the subject were a man. Just as some men can be excellent cooks, some women can be ruthless, power-hungry executives. It is possible for men to be scatterbrained and gossipy, while women can be decisive, tough, even violent.
- When writing and making pronouns agree with singular antecedents, be careful that your pronouns do not imply bias. For example, "A teacher who discovers plagiarism must report it to *his* supervisor." Either use masculine and feminine pronouns interchangeably, or switch to a plural noun and avoid the problem: "Teachers who discover plagiarism must report it to their supervisors."

Exercise 18.6*

Correct the use of sexist or gender-biased language in the following sentences. Exchange papers with a partner and compare revisions. Then turn to page 463 and compare your answers with our suggestions.

1. The well-known female writer and director Nora Ephron regrets that she cannot go out in public without attracting the attention of fans and photographers.
2. Amy King, an attractive, blonde mother of two, first joined the company as a saleswoman; only 10 years later, she was promoted to president.
3. A businessman sitting in the first-class cabin rang for the stewardess, a friendly gal who quickly arrived to assist him.
4. The list of ingredients on food packages contains information that may be important to the housewife, especially if she is the mother of young children.
5. The typical working man with a wife and two children is often hard-pressed to find time for recreation with his bride and the kids.

---

6. Offensive, Racist, or Non-Equitable Language

The last thing you want to do when you write is to offend your reader, even if you are writing a complaint. After all, you want the person to read what you have written. As we've seen above, some words occasionally used in speech are always inappropriate in writing. Swear words, for example, are unacceptable in a written message. So are obscene words, even "mild" ones. Offensive language appears much stronger in print than in speech and can provoke, shock, or even outrage a reader. Racist language and blasphemy (the use of names or objects that are sacred to any religion) are deeply offensive and always unacceptable.

Many writers have experienced the acute embarrassment of having a message read by people for whom it was not intended. What might have seemed at the time of composition to be an innocent joke may prove hateful to the unintended audience and mortifying to the writer.

It is wise to avoid all questionable, let alone unacceptable, expressions in your writing. Language has power: as many linguists have observed, our language actually shapes as well as reflects our attitudes and values. Those who use racist, blasphemous, sexist, or profane terms not only reinforce the attitudes contained in those terms but also project a profoundly negative image of themselves to their readers. Once ideas like this are in print, they are subject to legal proceedings. This is especially important to consider when we are writing or, in many cases, emailing in the workplace. Always show the utmost respect for both yourself and your readers when you are writing.

You never know where your words will find you.

7. Abusages

Some words and phrases, even ones we hear in everyday speech, are *always* incorrect in written English. Technically, they are also incorrect in speech, but most people tolerate them in informal conversation. If these expressions appear in your writing, your reader will assume you are uneducated, ignorant, or worse. Even in some conversations, particularly in academic and professional environments, these expressions make a poor impression on your listeners.

Carefully read through the following list and highlight any words or phrases that sound all right to you. These are the ones you need to find and fix when you revise.

allready	A common misspelling of *already*.
alot	There is no such word. Use *much* or *many*. (*A lot* is acceptable in informal usage.)
alright	A common misspelling of *all right*.
anyways (anywheres)	There is no *s* in these words.
between you and I	The correct expression is *between you and me*.

can't hardly couldn't hardly	Use *can hardly* or *could hardly*.
could of (would of, should of)	The helping verb needed is *have*, not *of*. Write *could have*, *would have*, *should have*.
didn't do nothing	All double negatives ("couldn't see nothing," "couldn't get nowhere," "wouldn't talk to nobody") are wrong. Write *didn't do anything, couldn't see anything, couldn't get anywhere, wouldn't talk to anyone*.
for free	Use *free* or *at no cost*. (Also note: "free gift"—is there any other kind of gift?)
in regards to	Use *in* (or *with*) *regard to*.
irregardless	There is no such word. Use *regardless*.
media used as singular	The word *media* is plural. The singular is *medium*. Newspapers and television are mass *media*. Radio is an electronic *medium*.
most all	Use *most* or *almost all*.
off of	Use *off* alone: "I fell *off* the wagon."
prejudice used as an adjective	It is wrong to write "She is *prejudice* against blondes." Use *prejudiced*.
prejudism	There is no such word. Use *prejudice*. "A judge should show no *prejudice* to either side."
real used as an adverb	"Real good," "real bad," and "real nice" are wrong. You could use *really* or *very*, but such filler words add nothing to your meaning.
reason is because	Use *the reason is that*: "The reason is that my printer blew up."
seen used as a complete verb	Used as a complete verb, as in "I seen him yesterday," *seen* is nonstandard. It is a past participle and requires a helping verb such as *to be* or *to have*.
suppose to	This expression, like *use to*, is nonstandard. Use *supposed to* and *used to*.
themself	Also "theirself," "ourselfs," "yourselfs," and"themselfs." These are all nonstandard words. The plural of *self* is *selves*: *themselves*, *ourselves*, and so on. Don't use "theirselves"; it's another nonstandard word.
try and	Use *try to*.
youse	There is no such word. *You* is both the singular and plural form of the pronoun.

Exercise 18.7*

Correct the following sentences where necessary. Suggested answers are on pages 463–464.

1. Irregardless of what you think, the problem between her and I has nothing to do with you.
2. If you want to be in the office pool, I need $5.00 off of you today because there will be no spots left by tomorrow.
3. If I hadn't of texted you this morning to remind you that you were suppose to write your chemistry exam, you would of missed it.
4. I didn't feel like seeing nobody, so I went home, turned on the TV, and didn't do nothing for the rest of the night.
5. This use to be a real good place to work, but now we are suppose to work a full shift every day, or a penalty is deducted off of our pay.
6. When Barack Obama was elected president for the second time, most all U.S. liberals hoped that alot of the prejudism in that country had finally been put to rest.
7. Irregardless of media hype, Dr. Who as played by David Tennant is not the best; that distinction had allready been won by Tom Baker in the 1970s.
8. It's unresponsible of us to blame television or any other media for causing violence.
9. Television is partly responsible, however, for the fact that alot of ungrammatical expressions sound alright to us.
10. Between you and I, the reason I didn't speak to no one about Elmo's cheating is because he would of broke my arm.

The Seven Deadly Errors of Writing

1. Wordiness: Make every sentence as clear and concise as possible.
2. Slang and jargon: When you are writing for a general audience, avoid expressions that may be understood only by specific social or professional groups.
3. Pretentious language: Avoid gobbledygook in all of your writing.
4. Clichés: As you revise, reword any clichés that have slipped into your prose. (Guarantee: There will be some.)
5. Sexist language: Refer to the three tips on page 230 to ensure that your paper is free of gender-biased language.
6. Offensive, racist, or non-equitable language: Do not use swear words, obscene words, racist expressions, or blasphemy (unless you are quoting from a source).
7. Abusages: Check every paper you write to be sure you have excluded all nonstandard words and phrases (see pages 231–232).

Exercise 18.8 Find an online blog entry on a popular topic such as movies, books, or video games. Go through the post and identify as many of the "seven deadly errors of writing" that you can. Look for slang (especially outdated slang), clichés, pretentious language, jargon, and wordiness. Be prepared to explain your "deadly" selections.

Exercise 18.9 Read through Josh Dehaas's piece in Part 8 called "The College Advantage" and evaluate it based on the seven deadly errors of writing. Does Dehaas make the cut, or does he fall into sin one or two times?

Rewriting Your Work

CHAPTER 19

> *Revision* means "re-seeing." It does not mean "re-copying."

No one can produce in a first draft a document that is effectively organized and developed, let alone one that is free of errors. The purpose of both the outline and the first draft is to get down on paper something you can work with until it meets your readers' needs and expectations.

I'm sorry this letter is so long; I didn't have time to make it short.
—George Bernard Shaw

The purpose of **rewriting** is to clarify the message of your essay. The purpose of **editing** is to polish the style. **Proofreading** confirms that you have corrected all errors in your earlier drafts and not introduced any new ones. Why bother? Read on, and we will show you how and why revision is essential to a message that communicates clearly and makes a positive impression on your readers. Just as a pianist doesn't perform a piece for the first time while on stage, a writer should never hand in his or her "first performance."

The three phases of revision are not separate and distinct: you don't march lock-step from one to the other. While you are working on rewriting, you'll find the sorts of errors we discuss in the section on editing. While you are editing, you'll undoubtedly come across the kinds of errors we discuss in the proofreading section. The revision process is not fixed but fluid, and it is essential to good communication. You'll find helpful tips in these chapters, and the information here is worth referring to again once your course has ended. The exercises—and there are many—are meant to aid you in editing your own work as well as in becoming an efficient and helpful peer editor and proofreader.

Good communication requires that you learn to revise from your readers' point of view.

Because a first draft reflects the contents of the writer's mind, it often seems all right to the writer. But in order to transfer an idea clearly from the mind of the writer to the mind of the reader, revision is usually necessary. It is not easy to put down your paper and come back to it as another person, but it can be done, and with practice, it definitely gets easier. If you can master the revising, editing, and proofreading processes, you will feel much more confident and in control of your communication success.

Getting someone to read your work is the smartest thing you can do as a writer.

It is often difficult to identify muddled thinking and stylistic errors in your own writing—this is why we recommend another way of thinking about the revision process. Most students can recognize problems in another's writing more easily than they can identify problems in their own. You may not be able to put a name to the problem, but you know when the writing goes off-track, is unconvincing, needs more (or less) detail, or somehow confuses you. Working with a peer reviewer is not easy on the ego: you must be prepared for any criticism you receive and avoid becoming defensive. If you appear sensitive to criticism, your peer reviewer will soften his or her critique, and you won't get the information you need in order to revise effectively. Of course, you don't have to follow every suggestion your reader makes, but the comments you get will provoke a rethinking of your paper that you will profit from in the end. And all you're required to do is return the favour.

The second-smartest thing you can do as a writer is be a reader for someone else.

In fact, there's no better way to learn how to revise a paper than to help someone else revise hers or his. Because you come to someone else's document without the tangle of ideas that influence your own writing, you can be objective. You can see where holes in the argument exist, where the author has given too little information to develop a point convincingly, or where too much information is provided—to the point of boredom. You are also in an ideal position to critique your partner's introduction and conclusion—two critical parts of every essay. Once you do this enough, you can start to look at your own papers, with adequate time between writing the paper and reading the draft, as if someone else wrote them.

A partnered revision takes time: each of you will need to read the other's essay multiple times.

Partnered revisions are the best way of getting objective feedback at each stage of the process. We don't mean to discourage you, but it would be irresponsible of us not to warn you that partners must take into account each other's schedules when they consent to work together. Treat the agreement as a contract. Determine up front the dates by which you will exchange your essays for at least two readings. And stick to these dates. Another advantage to a partnered revision is that you probably won't want to let your partner down, so you'll be less likely to procrastinate and more likely to get each stage of the project finished on time.

The Three Steps of Revision

Let's look at the entire process of revision before we get into talking about each of the steps.

Rewriting, editing, and proofreading: by working carefully through these steps, you can produce a paper that is organized, accurate, and error-free. Each stage of the process requires you to read your essay from start to finish—sometimes more than once.

Here are the steps to follow in revising a paper:

1. **Rewriting.** Improve the whole paper or large portions of it by modifying its content, organization, paragraph development, usage, or tone (or a combination of several of these elements).
2. **Editing.** Refine sentence structure and correct any errors in grammar.
3. **Proofreading.** Correct typos and any remaining errors in spelling and punctuation.

Inexperienced writers often skip the first two stages and concentrate on the third, thinking they will save time. In fact, they waste time—both theirs and their readers'—because the result is often writing that doesn't communicate clearly and won't make a positive impression.

Let as much time as possible pass between completing your first draft and rereading it.

Before you begin the revision process, take some time away from your paper. Ten minutes or even half a day is not enough. The danger in rereading too soon is that you're likely to "read" what you *think* you've written—what exists in your head, not on the paper. Too often students ask for meetings to discuss their paper and persist in "explaining" what they meant when they were writing. This explaining, or the desire to be clear about what you have written, should take place during the rewriting stage.

There are two other things you can do to help you get some distance from your draft. First, if it is handwritten, type it into your computer. Reading your essay in a different form helps you to "re-see" its content. If you have arranged to revise with a partner, this is the point at which you should exchange papers. (You won't get a useful critique if you expect your partner to struggle to read your handwriting while attempting to follow your reasoning.) Most people find it easier to revise on paper than on a computer screen, so print your draft double- or triple-spaced. Read it through carefully, making notes for changes in the margins or in the spaces between the lines, and then go back to the computer to make the changes.

Second, if you don't have a revision partner, or even if you do, read your paper aloud and try to hear it from the viewpoint of your readers. Listen to the way your explanation unfolds, and mark everything you think your readers might find unclear, irrelevant, inadequately developed, or out of order. This step can help you find two types of errors: grammatical and logical. Try it with an old paper you have written and see if you can find any sentences or phrases that make you pause, that you have to read a few times, or that just don't make sense.

Step 1: Rewriting

The goal of rewriting is to adjust the logical organization of your message and the quality of your language for readability. There are four kinds of changes you can make at this stage.

1. You can rearrange information. This is the kind of rewriting that is most often needed but least often done. Consider the order in which you've arranged your paragraphs. From your readers' point of view, is this the most effective order in which to present your ideas? Try going back to your outline and moving the main ideas around. Certain types of order work best with certain types of arguments and information (see Chapter 6). Might there be a better way to get your message across?

2. You can add information. Adding new main ideas or more development is often necessary to make your message interesting and convincing as well as clear. Here is where your revision partner can be especially helpful, by identifying what needs to be expanded or clarified. Just be wary of adding too much information—always consider what the reader already knows, needs to know, and will want to know.

3. You can delete information. Now is the time to cut out anything that is repetitious, insignificant, or irrelevant to your subject, your purpose, or your readers. Again, your partner can be invaluable in this evaluation process. Many writers working with word count requirements don't want to remove information, even if it is repetitive. But repetition only does more harm, as your reader will get bored with too much of the same.

4. You can adjust your level of language and tone. Even a well-organized, logical argument with adequately developed paragraphs will fail to convince a reader if the tone or level of language is inappropriate. See Chapter 18 for errors that can trip you up and cause your reader to sigh, stop reading, and toss your paper aside. Make sure you are writing for your reader and adjust accordingly.

Keep your outline beside you and change it as you rearrange, add, and subtract ideas. When you think you've completed the rewriting stage, check your revised outline one last time to be sure your changes have improved the organization and persuasiveness of your essay.

Have a look at paragraph 2 from the student paper "Dancing with Language: Don Quijote's Words and Consensual Reality" by Emily Silbert on pages 320–324:

> As he attempts to convince the Cathedral priest of the inherent value in reading chivalric romances, Don Quijote describes the plot of a chivalric tale in an extremely detailed and convincing manner. A mighty castle Don Quijote describes has "solid gold walls, parapets of diamond, and gates of topaz," and is built out of "diamonds, garnets, rubies, pearls, gold and emeralds." Don Quijote's choice of words, the references in particular to pearls, diamond and gold, recall Zoraida, who is described as she appeared to the captive: "more pearls hung from her lovely neck, her ears and her hair than she had hairs on her head; on her ankles . . . she wore two *carcajes* . . . of the purest gold, set with so many diamonds."

In this paragraph, Silbert makes her topic sentence claim and an argument about the details given to describe a chivalric tale. She then includes a couple of quotations to back up that point. Could these points be rearranged to make the link between her claim of value in reading romances and the opulence of storytelling more clear? Is more detail needed to make the claim? Remember, this is a student paper—but what would you edit?

When you find a mismatch between the thesis statement and the paper, change one or the other—or both—until the two agree.

Your thesis statement is your contract with your reader, so it should be the guiding principle of your paper. It should contain nothing that is not developed in the body of the essay, and there should be nothing in the essay that is not directly related to your thesis statement.

If you are thinking that this process will probably take two, three, or more passes (reads) to complete, you're right. But if the message is important to you (e.g., your grade is at stake, your promotion is on the line), you will take the time.

If you are not already using a word-processing program, now is the time to begin. Using a word processor to move blocks of text around is as easy as shuffling a deck of cards. Before you start to revise, change the computer's settings to meet the format requirements of your paper: set the spacing, margins, font style and size, running head, and so on. (See Chapter 16 for instructions and examples.)

Remember to save your work frequently. It takes only a split second to click Save, but that split second could save you hours—even days—in the event of a computer disaster. (Most programs have an auto-save function; if so, use it and let the computer be the one to remember to save your work every two or three minutes.) Save your work in a systematic and easy-to-find filing system. Give each file a distinctive name (e.g., Your Name English essay 3), and save each draft separately (e.g., English essay 3-rev 2) in case you want to go back and use material from a previous version of your document. Don't get stuck rewriting something and then deciding you liked the old version better only to find you have completely deleted it. Using a "track changes" function in your word-processing program can also be useful.

Use the following checklist to guide you as you review your paper's form and content.

Rewriting Checklist

Accuracy

- Is your information consistent with your own experience and observations and/or with what you have discovered through research?
- Are all of your facts and evidence up-to-date and clearly referenced?

Completeness

- Have you included enough main ideas and development to explain your subject and convince your reader? (Remember that *enough* means from the reader's point of view, not the writer's.)

Subject

- Is your subject
  - significant? Does it avoid the trivial and the obvious?
  - single? Does it avoid double and combined subjects?
  - specific? Is it focused and precise?
  - supportable? Have you provided enough evidence to make your meaning clear?

Main Points

- Are your main points
  - significant? Have you deleted any unimportant ones?
  - distinct? Are they all different from one another, or is there an overlap in content?
  - relevant? Do all points relate directly to your subject?
  - arranged in the most appropriate order? (Again, *appropriate* means from the reader's perspective. Choose chronological, climactic, logical, or random order, whichever is most likely to help the reader make sense of your information. See Part 3 for more information on paragraph types.)

Paragraphs

- Does each paragraph
  - begin with a clear, identifiable topic sentence?
  - develop one—and only one—main idea?
  - use one or more kinds of development appropriate to the main idea?
  - contain clear and effective transitions to signal the relationship between sentences? Between paragraphs?

Usage

- Have you used words to convey meaning rather than to impress?
- Have you eliminated any pretentious language, slang, or offensive language?
- Have you cut out any unnecessary words?
- Have you corrected any "abusages"?

Tone

- Is your tone consistent, reasonable, courteous, and confident throughout your essay?
- Does your tone match what your audience expects and will look for?

Introduction

- Does your introduction
  - catch the reader's attention and make him or her want to read on?
  - contain a clearly identifiable thesis statement?
  - identify the main points that your paper will explain?

Conclusion

- Does your conclusion
  - contain a summary or reinforcement of your main points, rephrased to avoid word-for-word repetition?
  - contain a statement that effectively clinches your argument and leaves the reader with something to think about?

Exercise 19.1 Read this excerpt from Trevor Jang's "How Reporting on Indigenous Issues as an Indigenous Journalist Can Get Complicated." Which three aspects of the rewriting checklist do you think were the most important in writing this section of the article?

> I didn't find pride in my Wet'suwet'en identity until I learned about my great-grandfather and the impact he had on First Nations land rights in Canada. But this pride in my lineage also complicated my involvement in this story on the Gitxsan.
>
> Johnny David, who held the hereditary chief name Mikhlikhlekh, was the first Wet'suwet'en chief to give evidence in the historic Delgamuukw land claims court case.
>
> Launched by the Gitxsan and Wet'suwet'en chiefs in 1984, their eventual legal victory was significant because it was the first time the courts confirmed Aboriginal title, or ownership of traditional land, had never been extinguished in British Columbia, where treaties hadn't been signed.

Exercise 19.2* Starting below is the first draft of an essay on the "3 Rs" of environmental responsibility. This draft needs to be rewritten. Using the Rewriting Checklist as your guide, rewrite the draft to ensure the content is accurate (to the best of your knowledge) and well organized. Improve the introduction and conclusion. Improve the topic sentences and examine the development of the body paragraphs. If you think more support is needed to develop a main point, add some supporting details. Delete any inappropriate, irrelevant, or repetitious material. Ignore the spelling and grammar errors for now. We'll come back to these when we are editing in Chapter 20.

When you have finished your rewrite, exchange papers with another student and compare results. Go through the essay one paragraph at a time and discuss any significant differences you find: Whose version is clearer? More logical? More concise?

1 We are having a garbage crisis. There is so much waste being produced in North America, we no longer have any idea of were to put it. Toronto's garbage problem is so great that they are trucking thousands of tonnes of it to Michigan every year. A short-term solution that is just plain stupid and how long can it last? We must act now, and we must act as individuals. We

cannot wait for the Government to save us from this crisis. We produce the garbage; we must solve the problem, that much is perfectly obvious to anyone. In very practical, down to earth, concrete terms, here are some things we can do to reduce, recycle, and reuse.

2 First, we must reduce the amount of garbage we produce. We can do this be refusing to buy products that are over packaged, like fast food that comes in styrafoam containers and chocolates that have a paper wrapping, a box, lining paper, a plastic tray for the candies, and foil wrap around each chocolate. By not purchasing such wasteful items, we say to the manufacturer, either reduce the packaging of your product or lose business to your competition. We can also be less wastful in our own habits by carpooling, for example.

3 We must recycle everything we can instead of sending it to the dump. Old cloths can be sent to the Salvation Army, Goodwill, or other charitable organizations. As can furniture, appliances, books, and most other household items. There are dozens of ways to make useful items from things that would otherwise be thrown away, such as quilts from old clothes; bird feeders from plastic jugs, and fire logs from newspapers. We don't need to consume as much as we do, and it won't hurt us to use things longer instead of buying new items before the old ones are completely worn out. Many companies now manufacture products from recycled goods. We should be on the lookout for their products to support their efforts and to reduce the waste that is dumped into landfills. And whatever we can't use ourselves can be sent to organizations that help others where they will have a life away from a landfill.

4 We can reuse most things. Composting vegetable garbage is a good way to put waste to valuable use. Things we no longer need or want can be offered to others through lawn sales and flea markets.

5 This is an absolute necessity. If we do not stop producing so much waste, we will inevitibly destroy our own enviornment. Unlike most efforts to improve things, the move to recycle, reuse, and reduce has one other advantage, it doesn't cost any money. In fact, it can save every household that practises it hundreds of dollars a year.

Exercise 19.3 Bring in an assignment you have written (in paragraph form) for another class. Go through the paper with a partner and have him or her explain how the work might be rewritten. Then switch. This is a valuable exercise for seeing through another's eyes.

Exercise 19.4 Rewrite each of the following sentences without changing the meaning:

1. You have to understand that 50% of the students didn't want to be there. Right?

   Rewrite: ____________________

2. All the people agree with me about climate change.

   Rewrite: ____________________

3. You must never practise drunk driving.

   Rewrite: ____________________

4. They weren't friendly: the baboons ended up throwing their food in our faces.

   Rewrite: ____________________

5. Having been accepted into the program, I started searching out some jobs right away to think about for the future.

   Rewrite: ____________________

Editing and Proofreading Your Work

CHAPTER 20

Step 2: Editing

Editing is the fine-tuning of sentences, grammar, spelling, and punctuation to ensure clarity and correctness. By now you're probably so tired of refining your paper that you may be tempted to skip this step. Don't. Careful editing is essential if you want your paper to make a positive impression. Just as with revising, leave the paper awhile before you check it for errors.

Have a dictionary handy during the editing process.

Most word-processing programs include a spelling and grammar checker. These programs have some useful features. For example, they will question (but not correct) your use of apostrophes, they will sometimes catch errors in subject–verb agreement, and they will catch obvious misspellings and typos. But don't make the mistake of assuming these programs will do all your editing for you. Many errors slip past them. Only you or a knowledgeable and patient friend can find and correct all errors. While most word-processer spell checkers offer a Canadian dictionary, the default is most likely American spelling, so check your dictionary's language before obeying what your spell checker tells you to do.

Again, you should allow time—at least a couple of days—between rewriting and editing. If your deadline is tight, see if your revision partner can take time to review your paper right away. (Your partner may be feeling deadline pressure, too, and might be happy to check your edits in exchange for your checking his or hers.) If your partner is unavailable, read your draft aloud and use the checklist on page 245 to help you identify and correct errors in sentences, grammar, and mechanics (spelling and punctuation). Use this chapter in conjunction with Part 9 of this book, which provides an overview of grammar and mechanics. Having a good foundation in at least the most common types of errors in essays—run-on sentences (Chapter 23) and subject-verb agreement problems (Chapter 24)—will help you edit your work or a colleague's.

The following table shows some commonly used editing symbols to indicate errors. These are a form of shorthand that you and your partner can use to alert each other to possible grammatical or structural errors. Teachers often use them, too, so it is important to understand what they mean.

Editing Symbols

CORRECTION MARK	MEANING
agr	Agreement error: subject–verb or pronoun–antecedent
apos	Insert (') or delete (') apostrophe
awk	Awkward sentence
cap/≡	use capital letter
colloq	Colloquial language
^,	Insert comma
cs	Comma splice
DM	Dangling modifier
frag	Sentence fragment
FS	Fused sentence
Ital/no ital	Use italics/*do not use italics*
lc or /	Use lower case (small) letters, not capitals
MM	Misplaced modifier
¶	Start a new paragraph
no ¶	Do not start new paragraph here
para or llism	Use parallel structure
pass	Incorrect use of passive voice
pro	Pronoun error
" "	Insert quotation marks
ref	Vague pronoun reference
sl	Slang
sp	Spelling error
trans	Transition needed
tr	Transpose lettre words or
vb	Verb form error
wordy	Omit unnecessary words
W (or WW)	Wrong word (check your dictionary)
?	Word/phrase is illegible or makes no sense
ℓ	Delete the marked letter, word ~~word~~, or punctuation mark
^	Add missing leter or word
⊙;/⊙: ⊙/=	Insert missing punctuation: semicolon; colon: period⊙ or hyphen=
✓	Good idea, detail, phrasing

As you read through your own or your partner's work, try to find sentences or paragraphs that require editing. When you are editing another's work, the idea is that the author of the paper will make the changes. Don't rewrite the paper yourself. The following checklist gives some more complete information about what you should look for when editing.

Editing Checklist

Sentences

- Is each sentence clear and complete?
  - Are there any fragments or run-ons?
  - Are there any misplaced or dangling modifiers?
  - Are all lists (whether words, phrases, or clauses) expressed in parallel form?
- Are your sentences varied in length? Could some be combined to improve the clarity and impact of your message?

Grammar

- Have you used verbs correctly?
  - Are all verbs in the correct form?
  - Do all verbs agree with their subjects?
  - Are all verbs in the correct tense?
  - Are there any confusing shifts in verb tense within a paragraph?
  - Are all verbs in active voice unless there is a reason to use the passive?
- Have you used pronouns correctly?
  - Are all pronouns in the correct form?
  - Do all pronouns agree with their antecedents?
  - Have any vague pronoun references been eliminated?

Spelling

- Are all words spelled correctly?
- Have you double-checked any homonyms?
- Have you used capital letters where they are needed?
- Have you used apostrophes correctly—for contractions and possessive nouns but not for plurals?

Punctuation

- Within sentences:
  - Have you eliminated any unnecessary commas and included commas where needed? (Refer to the comma rules on pages 399–404 as you consider this question.)
  - Have you used colons and semicolons where appropriate?
  - Are all quotations appropriately marked?
- Sentences' beginnings and endings:
  - Does each sentence begin with a capital letter?
  - Do all questions—and only questions—end with a question mark?
  - Are all quotation marks correctly placed?

When you're sure you've answered these questions satisfactorily, it's time to go to the third and last stage of the revision process.

Exercise 20.1*

Read the following sentences and consider each one against the Editing Checklist. Correct any errors in sentence structure, grammar, spelling, and punctuation. Then compare your edited sentences with ours on page 466. (Our thanks to *Fortune* magazine [July 21, 1997] for collecting these howlers from real résumés and cover letters.)

1. I demand a salary commiserate with my qualifications, and extensive experience.
2. I have lurnt Microsoft Word and Excell computor and spreasheet progroms
3. In 2007, I recieved a plague for being salesperson of the year.
4. Reason for leaving last job; maturity leave.
5. You will want me to be Head Honcho in no time!
6. I am a perfectionist and rarely if if ever forget details.
7. Marital status: single. Unmarried. Unengaged. Uninvolved. No comitments.
8. In my previous job I became completely paranoid trusting completely no one and absolutely nothing.
9. As indicted, I have over five years of analyzing investments.
10. I was responsible for ruining the entire operation for a western chain store.

Exercise 20.2* Turn to the draft of the essay you rewrote for Exercise 19.2. With the Editing Checklist beside you, go through your essay and correct the errors in sentence structure, grammar, spelling, and punctuation. (You may have corrected some of these errors as you were rewriting, but there will be others.)

Exercise 20.3 Read the following paragraph, and insert some editing symbols to help the writer make his or her work better. Then, pretending you are the author, rewrite the work.

There are two ideas I have no how to make the college bedder. The first one is that there really is no need to have class on Friday the other one is that all our classes should or could be online. In the first place, most of us working so we need time to do that. Get real! We have lives, too, an dFridays are often times when we are tired. Online classes could be funner than in class and I would take them. As for practical experience, I get that with my job. In summary I think that no classes on Friday and in fact all classes online would make me happier with the college experience becuz I could go out with friends, having my job, and get a degree.

Revised paragraph (or paragraphs if you think there should be more than one):

____

____

____

____

____

____

____

____

Exercise 20.4

Share your version of the above revised paragraph with a partner. Did you use many of the same symbols and rewrite it in a similar way? Discuss any differences.

Exercise 20.5

How was the tone of the piece? Did you have to change the tone in your editing process? If so, identify some reasons you changed the tone.

Step 3: Proofreading

Careful proofreading will ensure that the appearance of your paper reflects the care you have put into writing it.

Why proofread? To confirm that you have corrected all errors and that your paper is ready to be submitted. Misspellings, faulty punctuation, and messiness don't always create misunderstandings, but they do cause the reader to form a poor opinion of you and your work. You would never hand in a résumé or cover letter with coffee stains all over it (or you won't now!), so treat your papers as though they are professional documents—which they are!

By the time you get to this stage, you will have gone over your paper so many times you may have practically memorized it. When you are very familiar with a piece of writing, it's hard to spot the small mistakes that tend to creep in as you produce your final copy. Once again, a dedicated revision partner can be helpful, possibly saving you embarrassment and lost marks. Here are some tips to help you find those tiny, elusive errors both in your paper and in your partner's:

1. Read through the essay line by line, using a ruler to guide you.
2. Read the essay one more time, really considering the wording and flow of the paper one last time.
3. If you have been keeping a list of your most frequent errors in this course (as recommended in the introduction), check your essay for the mistakes you're most likely to make. Also use the list of correction marks on page 244 to check for errors your instructor has identified in your writing.

Your "last" draft may need one more revision after your proofreading review. If so, take the time to reprint or rewrite (by hand) the paper so that the version you submit is clean and easy to read. Computers make editing and proofreading almost painless since they make errors so easy to correct.

Finally, here are a few more steps to take before the paper is hand-in ready:

- Make sure to reread your assignment sheet and assignment guidelines.
- If there are formatting rules, font information, sizing, or other requirements, now is the time to double- and triple-check that you have conformed to these guidelines.
- If there are content requirements, make sure you have followed those, as well.
- Make sure your bibliography does not contain grammatical or formatting mistakes. See Chapter 17 for more information on preparing References or Works Cited lists.
- Always make sure to spell your instructor's name correctly, as well as your own!
- Print your work if required and make sure that it is easy to read. Staple the pages if no other requirements are given.
- If you are using online software, upload the document with a title that includes your last name and identifies what the assignment is. Following this tip ensures that your work isn't lost and is graded correctly.

Working with Rubrics

Although we've outlined in this textbook a clear and detailed guide to essay writing, that in itself doesn't trump your individual instructor's decisions about how to mark papers. Always pay attention to any marking guidelines (called *rubrics*) your instructor provides. It is those documents that will help you ultimately make sure that your thesis and main points are at the level they should be at. A simple rubric might look something like this:

Thesis and introduction—5 marks
3 body paragraphs with good detail—8 marks
A clear conclusion ending with some questions—2 marks
/Total 15 marks

Some might be more complex, giving you possible grades for each level of performance:

A clear thesis—5 marks
An acceptable but not clear thesis—3 marks
The beginning of a thesis—2 marks
No thesis—0 marks

Always aim for the best grade and don't settle for "acceptable" when you see a rubric. Push yourself to improve your work with revision, editing, and proofreading.

That's it! At long last, you're ready to submit your paper. If you've conscientiously followed the revising, editing, and proofreading steps we've presented in this part of the textbook, you can submit your paper with confidence that the content says what you want it to say and that its appearance reflects the time and care you put into writing it. One last word of advice:

> Don't forget to keep a copy for your files!

It doesn't need to be printed out, but you should have a copy safely backed up in case something happens and the work is lost.

Exercise 20.6*

Is the following essay ready for submission? Go over it carefully, correcting all errors (there are 20), looking to revise, edit, and proofread. Then get together with another student and compare your results.

According to a recent survey in Maclean's magazine, only 43 percent of Canadians are satisfied with their jobs. What can you do to ensure that you will not be one of the 57 percent who are unhappy with the work they do. There are three questions to consider when seeking employment that will provide satisfaction as well as a paycheque.

First are you suited to the kind of work you are applying for. If you enjoy the outdoors, for example, and like to be active, your not going to be happy with a nine to five office job, no matter how much it pays.

Second is the job based in a location compatible with your prefered lifestyle. No matter how much you like your work, if you go home every night to to an environment you are miserable in, it will not be long before you start transfering your disatisfaction to your job. If you like the amenities and conviences of the city, you probably will not enjoy working in a small town. If, on the other hand, you prefer the quiet and security of small-town life, you may find the city a stressful place in which to live.

Finally, is it one that you want to work for. Do you need the security of generous benefits, a good pension plan, and incentives to stay and grow with one company? Or are you an ambitous person who is looking for variety, quick advancement, and a high salary. If so, you may have to forego security in favour of commissions or cash incentives and be willing to move as quickly and as often as opportunities occur. Some carful self-analysis now, before you start out on your career path, will help you chose a direction that will put you in the 43 percent minority of satisfied Canadian workers.

Exercise 20.7 Ask your instructor if he or she uses rubrics and, if so, how. Can the rubric be explained in class or does it show up after you have submitted your paper? Does it change for each assignment? What is the marking structure? Can you as a student have input into the marking guidelines? You'd be surprised how many instructors do welcome input into their marking.

Exercise 20.8 Planning the process of revising, editing, and proofreading takes time. Choosing one of your assignment due dates, work backward, factoring in at least one or two days between each stage of revision, perhaps even more if you are working with a revision partner or a peer tutor. Figure out what day you need your final draft done by. Try to work so that you are giving yourself enough time for the editing process. Once you have completed that for one assignment, work on the timing for another.

Part 7

Presenting Your Work

The two chapters in Part 7 discuss using your writing in a new way, as the basis for oral and visual work. Chapter 21, Academic Presentations, focuses on creating, developing, and editing presentations, and provides some helpful dos and don'ts for digital formats. Chapter 22 covers academic and workplace posters and portfolios. Originally used in the healthcare field, posters have been adopted by students in education and business as a great way to share their new and innovative ideas. Portfolios are another great way to showcase work—they are a type of developed résumé that can also tell a story about research and ideas within themes or topics of interest. As with the chapter on presentations, the focus in Chapter 22 is on the creation, development, and editing of posters and portfolios for use both in and out of the classroom.

The basis of a great oral presentation is a great written presentation, but that is just the foundation. Issues of organization, methods, and delivery are also important when it comes to presenting material. In these two chapters, we provide information on the types and best practices for presenting work, along with practical exercises to help make your presentations sing.

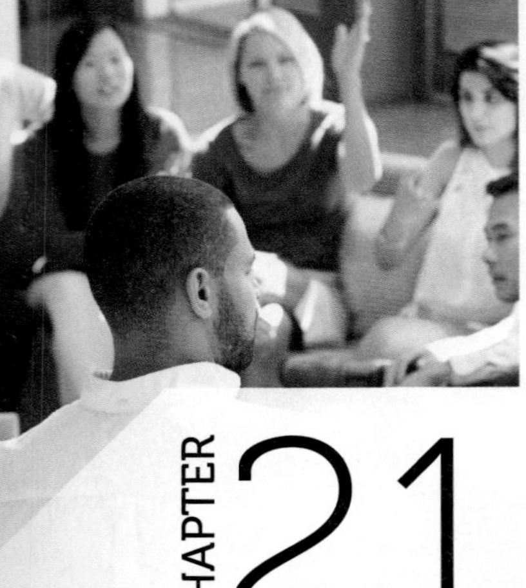

CHAPTER 21

Academic Presentations

It is quite likely that you will be asked to give a presentation in your essay writing classroom, and learning more about how to give a good presentation using some of the same methods you would use for polishing up a final essay may help you on that journey.

In this chapter we cover the basics of creating, developing, and editing presentations. We look at what types are available, how to plan and organize them, how to write and edit them, tips for the actual presentation process, and some dos and don'ts. These general comments should be integrated with the expertise your instructor has in these areas, and the exercises in this chapter will help integrate your learning and increase your comfort level.

Academic Presentations

The purpose of an **academic presentation** in a classroom is usually to summarize, describe, or outline work you have done. If you are asked to present an academic paper to a conference the purpose is usually to represent the majority of your work, either by reading your actual essay or by putting together a detailed version in a presentation-friendly form such as a slide show. As you will see, for many types of presentations the same rules apply as they would to any essay writing format: there is a thesis, an outline of the work to be presented, the work itself, and a conclusion. For the purposes of this chapter we will talk only about individual academic presentations, although it is to be noted that a variety of collaborative presentations may be assigned to you that will follow a similar format. Check the notes at the end of this section on collaborative writing and presentations for a good starting point.

In each case, when it comes to presentations your instructor will, as with essays, decide up front if there is research attached to the topic you will present on, or if you will be presenting on a topic using your own descriptions, narration, or critical thoughts. Your instructor will also decide if your presentation will be followed by questions or a group discussion; these are sometimes called seminars. Will you present your material to the entire class or to a small group of classmates or just to the instructor? Knowing the answers to these questions will give you a good head start on your work and help you to define your audience.

Types of Presentations

There are endless varieties of presentations that your instructor might assign in a college or university setting. The main types are the following:

1. An individual oral presentation of approximately 5–15 minutes on a topic you have been assigned/chosen.
2. An individual digital presentation of approximately 8–20 slides on a topic you have been assigned/chosen.
3. A blend of both an oral and a digital presentation.

When the ideas you present are mainly your own thoughts or ideas or experiences, a simple oral presentation might suffice. If you were discussing an experience many of your classmates would not have shared, however—say, helping build schools in Africa—a digital element such as images or short videos from your trip might be a great addition. If you were discussing your own views on a book the entire class read, simply standing up and talking about those views may be all that you need.

When you add formal research to a topic a Works Cited or References list may automatically require you to bring some form of digital element to your work, unless your requirement is to hand in those sources on a sheet of paper. If you need to explain charts or graphs, however, and the entire group you are presenting to should see them, it makes sense to work with an online digital presentation viewer or software such as PowerPoint. (See Chapter 17 for how to format APA or MLA documentation.)

Exercise 21.1

Read the following list and decide what type of presentation might best fit each topic: an oral presentation with or without research, a digital presentation with or without research, or a blend of the two. After you choose, write a sentence or two explaining why you think that option is best suited to the topic.

1. A talk on how you spent your last vacation.
2. A discussion of the role of educational assistants in the classroom.
3. A summary of your experiences as an Olympic athlete.
4. A talk on the cycles of domestic abuse.
5. An outline of how to deal with a measles outbreak in a hospital.
6. A talk on your experience in higher education so far.
7. A summary of the last three books you've read.
8. A discussion of how you manage money.
9. A talk on the process of booking a vacation.
10. A seminar on starting your own blog.

Planning and Organizing Presentations

When you are organizing presentations it is best to start with a basic outline. Using the one for writing essays provided on page 82 is a good place to start.

Whether your presentation is spoken, submitted digitally, or presented as a blend of both, each presentation should have:

1. **An attention getter.** The attention getter in an oral presentation is extremely important. You want to grab your audience's attention right away and get them into the topic at hand. Don't forget to also introduce yourself and share a bit about your background. This is easy to do in a slide if you are using a computer slide show as part of your presentation, but give your audience a chance to learn a bit about who you are before you launch into your actual topic. Chapter 8 provides more information about crafting an attention getter.

2. **A thesis.** A thesis is no less important in a presentation than in an essay. You should have a good reason for presenting on a topic, and a clear position of subject and outline of main points helps you get there. It is rare you would be given a topic in college or university that wouldn't lend itself to a clear statement of position or an argument. Even a summary of points should include an explanation of how those points work together to cause a desired outcome.

3. **An outline.** Whether spoken or on a slide, an outline lets your audience (and you) know where it is this presentation is going. Don't be afraid to share your path with your audience beforehand in an academic presentation.

4. **A main discussion of your points as they link to your thesis.** Each point in your presentation should clearly link back to your thesis. Charts or graphs, even images—all should be explained in relation to your overall topic. If you are simply speaking, it is even more important to keep coming back to your main point.

5. **A summary of your points.** At the end of your points, a brief summary will keep the most salient points in your audience's mind. This snapshot allows people to think back on what you've said and take it all into consideration.

6. **A conclusion.** As with an essay's conclusion, the main idea here isn't just to restate your points. Instead, consider the variety of ways you can enhance your audience's experience and get them even more into your topic. Conclude with a desired action the audience should take, research they should have a look at, conversations they might start with others on the topic.

7. **A memorable statement.** It is a great idea to end your presentation with one final bit of information—perhaps a story or personal anecdote—to bring things to a close. These last statements are intended to stick in the audience's mind and leave them feeling they've understood your main point. Chapter 8 contains more information on how to write memorable statements.

When presenting information orally to people, it is important to repeat and to organize information constantly so your audience can remain on topic, especially those who might be visual learners. Having an outline or table of contents on screen and then sticking to it also helps people know where you've been, where you're going, and what you are hoping to achieve with your presentation.

Choose one of the following topics for an oral presentation (no research required!) and create an outline you could use for a five-minute talk on the topic.

Exercise 21.2

1. The best food you've ever eaten
2. The one book everyone should read
3. How to survive a long plane ride
4. The difference between equality and equity
5. Being a _____ collector
6. The three most important things to do if you get lost in a forest
7. The moment you became an adult
8. Why learning a second (or third or fourth) language is amazing
9. A life-changing moment
10. Something that makes you really happy to be Canadian

Writing Presentations

If you are delivering your presentation orally, you'll want to write out a few versions to try. Practise with each one and note which sentences aren't quite as conversational as you might like them to be. Good presenters sound like they are having a conversation with an audience rather than just reading through a document that is meant to be read. A great way to learn about good presentation skills is by watching TED Talks (TED stands for Technology, Entertainment and Design; videos of the talks can be found at www.ted.com). A useful exercise is to find a TED Talk and consider how the speaker uses presentation skills to draw in the audience and keep them interested. Consider the speaker's tone of speech, volume, body language, and use of visuals/charts. In the past there were few ways to see examples of effective presentations, but now the opportunities are endless and a variety of good models are out there.

If you are delivering your presentation in only a digital format you will need to consider the "body language" of your slide show. PowerPoint, Prezi, and other slide-sharing tools all have various themes and model presentations that can help you with designing your show. In a sense these designs stand in for you as you prepare and insert your own ideas into their templates. If you can, the addition of a voiceover to slide-only presentations can be a nice way to add a personal touch. Regardless, a focus on design, editing, and proofreading is essential.

If you are delivering your presentation both orally and with a digital slide show as a prop, remember that the slide show should be just that—a prop. That is, it stands with you, not for you. Don't simply read your slide show as if you need not be present. Use your slides to add visual pop or to show charts or graphs that aren't easily explained. Don't include all your facts or interesting information, either; give the audience something to listen to. And definitely don't be swayed by the promise that these tools will time your presentation for you. Many a presentation has gone completely awry because the timer in the presentation tool was far too fast for the presenter to get through the material.

Don't give in to overly bright colours, transitions, or flashing words! They are a distraction and better meant for a kids' show than an academic presentation.

Images or small cartoons might be fine, but multi-coloured lines of text or bright neon backgrounds are over the top and frankly difficult to read. Remember too that some students may also have visual or image-related challenges that would make your work harder to see. Go for high-contrast light backgrounds with dark text, or vice versa. And make text large enough that it can be seen on any screen. What looks readable on a laptop is completely different on a large classroom screen. Practice can help with this, or ask your instructor for detailed guidelines on what might be the best options. In general, the rules are not to use font sizes smaller than 24 point, though 28 or 32 might be preferable. Titles on slides are usually even larger, between 36 and 44 points in size. And don't fill slides with text: three or four lines is likely enough for each slide. Again, the idea is that if you are presenting with a slide show, the show is a prop and you are meant to be the focus.

Good:

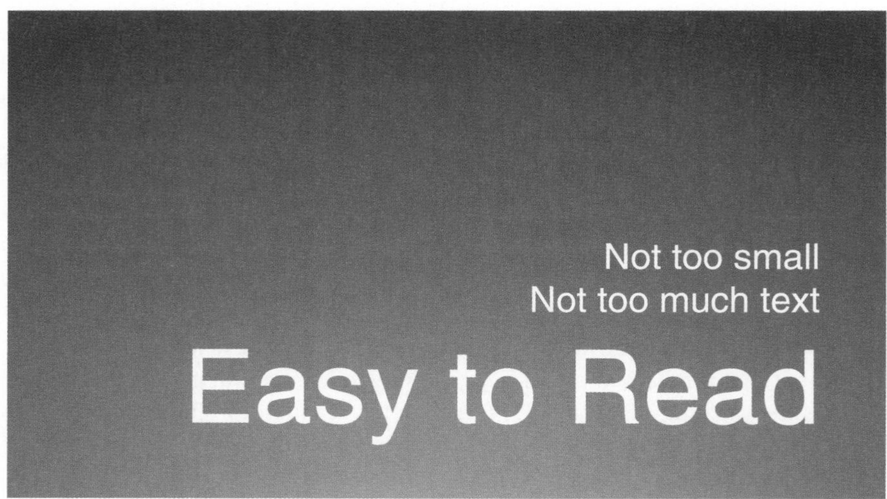

Needs work:

Not really large enough and hard to read

Way too much text and quite hard to read

Way too much text and quite hard to read

Way too much text and quite hard to read

Way too much text and quite hard to read

Way too much text and quite hard to read

Way too much text and quite hard to read

Way too much text and quite hard to read

Way too much text and quite hard to read

Way too much text and quite hard to read

A few more tips for creating a delivery-ready presentation include the following:

- Make sure to go back and look at your assignment sheet and assignment guidelines, or, if you are presenting at a conference, at the time and other requirements.
- If you have been given formatting rules for online presentations, check font information, sizing, or other requirements. Make sure your work will be easy to read on whatever screen you might be presenting on. Now is the time to double check and triple check.
- If there are content requirements, make sure you have followed those as well. Your References or Works Cited pages should not contain style or formatting mistakes. (See Chapter 17 for more information on preparing these elements.)
- Always make sure to spell your instructor's or moderator's name correctly, as well as your own!
- Print your work if required and make sure that it and any notes you will have with you are easy to read. If you are presenting your work digitally, make sure you have multiple backups, perhaps on a USB thumb drive plus a copy you've sent to yourself via email.

Don't forget to practise! Then practise again!

Delivering Presentations

The first and most important rule before delivering your presentation is to make sure you are comfortable with all aspects of it. Practise your timing, and practise saying words if you are using research that includes vocabulary you aren't used to. The following considerations during delivery can make things go even more smoothly in the face of jitters or nerves:

1. Remember to make eye contact and be aware of your body language while presenting. Eye contact keeps your audience focused on you and what you are saying. Smile! People like to mirror those they are watching in front of a room. If you smile, it's very likely many of those in your audience will smile right back.

2. If you are using PowerPoint or another tool to digitally project part of your presentation, make sure to have notes or information readily available to you without having to arch your neck toward the screen. Don't partake in PBB—"presentation by bum"—which is what happens if you spend the entire time turned toward the screen and away from the audience.

3. Wear clothing that is fairly basic. Avoiding logos or writing is best—you don't want to draw people's eyes toward the writing and away from you.

4. If your hands shake, consider wearing something that allows you to keep your hands in your pockets for a few moments until they—or you—calm down.

5. Keep breathing. One reason why people lose their place when they are speaking is that they forget to breathe. It really is the most important thing!

6. When you are finished presenting, say "Thanks" instead of just "Well, that's it. I'm done." Reach out to your audience and let them know you appreciate their attention and interest.

Presentations Dos and Don'ts

There are some things to keep in mind as you choose your presentation topic and prepare it for delivery.

- **Do—keep** your vocabulary in your presentation clear and concise. Always consider your audience when you choose your words.
- **Do—make** sure to edit any slides that you use carefully; your words are a stand-in for you.
- **Do—make** sure to include research and proper MLA or APA citations as required.
- **Do—remember** to present the best view of yourself that you can while also providing your information in a clear and correct manner.
- **Don't—include** too many slides of the same type of thing. Don't overdo it on visuals or words. Consider white space if you are using slides.
- **Don't—worry** if you make a mistake. People do laugh when presenters make a mistake, but it's usually because they feel sorry for you, not because they think you are incompetent. Smiling and continuing on shows clarity and confidence in your subject matter.
- **Don't—include** irrelevant information. Stick to your thesis or main point and try not to stray off topic.
- **Don't—forget** to include any presentation requirements an instructor or conference team has given you. Time limits should be strictly adhered to. Good planning will help you stay on track.

Exercise 21.3

Practise introducing yourself in a small group setting. Work on creating an introductory statement that includes your name, program area, and maybe one other important thing you'd like your audience to know about you. Then practise your standard thank you as you might say it at the end of a presentation. Getting these common elements down can help you keep calm during the worst moments of a presentation.

CHAPTER 22

Academic and Workplace Posters and Portfolios

Posters and portfolios are great ways to showcase your work, and each format has its own styles and uses. If you are in the social sciences or health-related fields you will find that posters are rapidly becoming the preferred way for idea presentation both in the workplace and during conferences at school. Portfolios are useful when applying to jobs or programs that require samples of your past work.

In this chapter we cover the basics of creating, developing, and editing posters and portfolios. We look at what types are available, how to plan and organize them, how to write and edit them, some tips for the actual presentation process, and some dos and don'ts. As mentioned in Chapter 21, these general comments should be integrated with the expertise your instructor has in these areas, and the exercises in this chapter will help integrate your learning and increase your comfort level.

Posters

Posters are meant to give an overview into a topic and to provide viewers with an argument based on a topic. They are very similar to an essay in that way, and you could consider them to be a poster-sized version of an essay or report that you have written. Most posters comprise a blend of visuals and writing. They usually include perhaps two or three main charts, graphs, or a variety of images appropriate to the topic discussed.

Planning and Organizing Posters

Planning and organizing posters can be time consuming because of the visual size requirements. Making sure all the required information is viewable, understandable, and flows for the reader can take some time and quite a bit of editing. If you have a poster to create, make sure to give yourself enough time to play with how it looks before you finalize it to print.

If you are given a poster to prepare in class, it is likely that your instructor will have prepared or have available some form of poster template. Sometimes these templates are blocked into physical zones so you know just how much space or how many sections you have to fill in on the poster. A standard layout may look something like the figure below, which is a template built into the PowerPoint program.

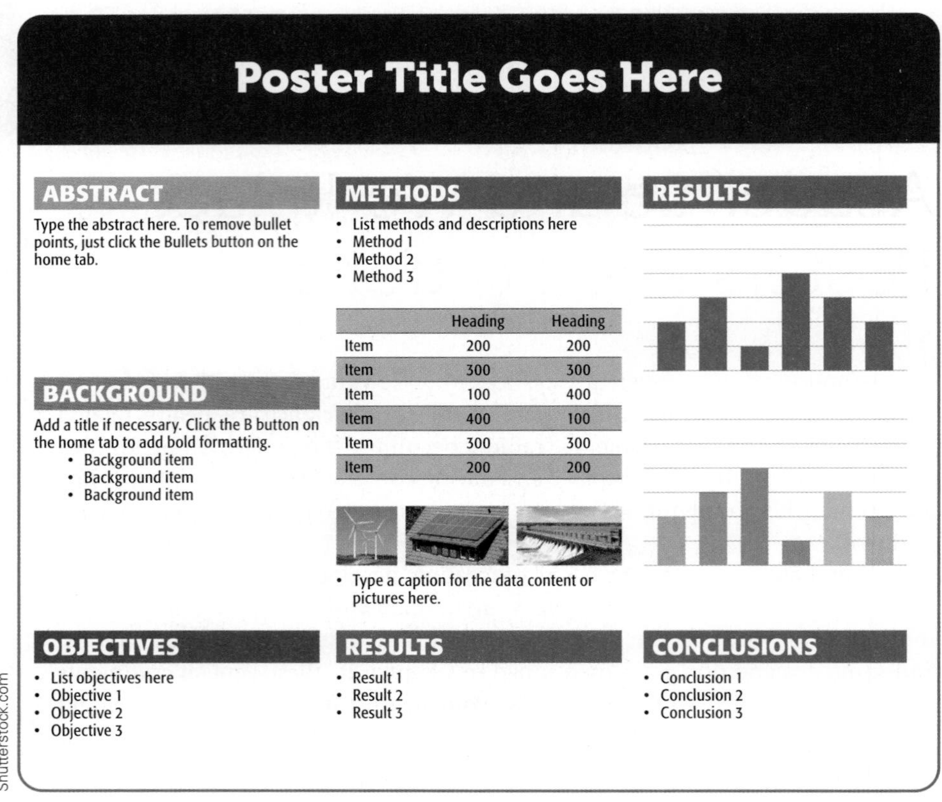

Shutterstock.com

Writing Posters

As with most types of writing and academic work, planning ahead is key. Since posters tend to be used in the social sciences and health fields, APA formatting is the standard for references and often shapes the visual sections on the poster. An abstract, findings, and conclusion are all fairly standard on posters, and all images should be referenced according to APA guidelines.

As you fill in the information, perhaps from a previously written report, remember that clarity and conciseness are key to making everything fit on the poster. Don't forget to proofread, as spelling and grammar mistakes show up front and centre to the reader who is looking at your work printed onto one page. Use your skills in summarizing and paraphrasing to highlight the essential information, because it is unlikely you will fit every piece of relevant material on your poster.

Delivering Posters

Make sure to follow whatever guidelines or process for printing your poster are required by your instructor or by the organization you are sending your poster to.

Sometimes poster presentations include only the posters themselves. Some poster sessions at conferences are simply made up of a variety of boards with posters pinned to them. Other times poster creators are on hand to explain their posters to interested viewers. If you are asked to discuss your poster you will want to prepare a short presentation, perhaps two or three minutes, that summarizes the main sections of the work. Spend the majority of the time outlining what interested you about the project and the project's main thesis. Then the viewer can take a look at the poster; if you have especially relevant charts or graphs, point viewers toward them for more information.

Poster Dos and Don'ts

Keep the following tips in mind as you create and deliver a poster presentation.

- **Do**—keep each section fairly brief. A one- or two-paragraph description and summary is fine. The poster shouldn't be so full that there is no white space left. It also shouldn't be so empty that it could have been printed on a smaller sheet than you are asked to provide.
- **Do**—make sure to edit the paragraphs, titles, and references carefully, as they are a stand-in for you.
- **Do**—make sure to include relevant images, graphs, and tables that are readable and easily viewable by your audience.
- **Do**—remember to present the best view of yourself that you can while also providing the information requested by viewers if you are asked to stand with your poster.
- **Don't**—include too much of the same type of thing. A couple of images is likely enough; balance out images and text.
- **Don't**—include more than a summary of your work in each section. If you have written a fairly comprehensive report, you won't be able to get it all in. Keep the highlights in the poster, and if you are presenting with the poster perhaps have a few copies of the full report handy for those interested.
- **Don't**—be shy about pre-presenting your work to peers or colleagues. It can be very useful to share drafts of your posters with others to see if they can quickly and easily read the work and see all the relevant information.
- **Don't**—forget to include any requirements given by your instructor.

You can find many well-made posters that are viewable online, which can provide you with good examples of what to do.

Exercise 22.1

Search online with a partner or group to find both a well-done poster and a not-so-well-done poster. Where are the differences? The use of white space? The editing? The font choice and sizing? Have your instructor put some posters up in your classroom, perhaps on a screen, so you can discuss the differences.

Academic Portfolios

Academic portfolios, compilations of work related to a theme, career, or discipline, can be useful for a variety of reasons. They may be used as a documentation addition to a résumé, or they may be required in a classroom as a summative project that contains work completed through the semester. Like presentations, they can be physical or digital. Digital portfolios are sometimes called electronic portfolios and can stand in for detailed résumés or CVs (*curriculum vitae*, Latin for your life's work). Regardless of whether you create a physical portfolio or one that is viewable online, the purpose of the portfolio is to provide a detailed sample of your best work. You may be accustomed to hearing "portfolio" used for an artistic collection of images or photos, but many careers now require their use, including those related to teaching, the computer sciences, writing/journalism, and, of course, anything involving graphics or visual art.

Careful proofreading will ensure that the appearance of your portfolio reflects the care you have put into writing it.

The quality of writing for all of these portfolios is important, especially the art of summarizing and descriptive paragraph writing. Critical thinking is also a key skill that can be exercised in a portfolio as you include representative works related to your future career and provide a critical discussion of how the work has shaped you (as an engineer, chef, nurse, educational assistant, etc.). In the case of a portfolio, both your best work and your best writing to describe that work are essential ingredients.

As with essay writing, your final portfolio product must be carefully edited and organized to ensure that what it represents—you and your best work—are highlighted in the most positive way possible.

Exercise 22.2 If you were to put together a portfolio of work that defined you as a student, what would you choose? Test results? A CPR certificate? An essay? Brainstorm a list of all the things you might include in a portfolio of who you are as a student right now.

Planning and Organizing Portfolios

Your portfolio should be organized to present a specific picture. Although a portfolio doesn't necessarily have a thesis, in a way it still has a unifying idea or purpose, especially if you are using it to apply for a job. Academic portfolios should include some type of covering letter that summarizes the contents and provides a thematic or organizational overview. Understanding and having a purpose for each item in that portfolio provides integration and unity to your work.

Could you organize your portfolio like a résumé or cover letter, highlighting education, experience, or skills? You definitely could. You could also highlight volunteer work or paid work experiences by putting them in a strategic order. You could put work done chronologically as well, to show growth. You could organize work thematically to show, for example, nursing skills across a variety of areas.

A portfolio should have a table of contents. If you are creating a digital portfolio, the table of contents becomes a clickable link that users can use to navigate through your materials. In a physical portfolio, consider using a table of contents and then a set of page flags to separate out each section, making them easy to access or retrieve information from.

Here is an example of an online portfolio's table of contents.

Julia Ng's Academic Portfolio
Educational Support Worker

About Me
Academic Background
Experience—Day Care
Experience—Kindergarten
Experience—K–12
Volunteer Work
Co-op Placements
Certifications
Medical and Legal Checks
Additional Information

Depending on the job or the purpose of your portfolio you may have more or less in terms of what to include. It is probably a good idea to aim for 9 or 10 great samples of your work or 9 or 10 documents overall, one of which might be a more detailed résumé.

Exercise 22.3

Plan a table of contents for a portfolio you could use to apply for a job when you finish your program. Should it be electronic or would a paper version be better? Explain your choice.

Writing Portfolios

A job-related portfolio should include samples of completed work, certificates, and notices (scanned or online versions should be easily obtainable), alongside written summaries or reflections of how each piece relates to your growth. In the above example, Julia might consider including a scan of a thank you picture a student drew for her in the Experience—Kindergarten section. She should then write a paragraph or two describing when the student gave her the picture and her experience of working in a kindergarten setting. A portfolio due for class might include documents, essays, reflections, or summaries alongside critical comments or edits that were made. It might include peer feedback or comments that others made to help the work improve.

Here are a few tips to consider before the portfolio is hand-in or submission ready:

- Make sure to go back and have a look at your table of contents and the job or submission guidelines.
- Double check and triple check that you have followed any formatting rules, font guidelines, sizing, or other requirements.
- Make sure you have followed any content requirements.
- Always make sure to spell correctly the name of any person or organization the portfolio may be sent to (as well as your own).
- Make sure all of your work is easy to read.
- If you are using online software, upload the document using a title that summarizes your work well.

Delivering Portfolios

Follow the requirements for delivering or handing in your portfolio. Check to make sure you are getting it in before the due date and according to any specific rules you may have been given. Some organizations require a certain number of submissions, or have a maximum size for the portfolio submitted. If you are handing in a physical portfolio, have you made a backup copy? If you are handing in certificates, does copy of the certificate suffice or must you submit the original? Check beforehand to see what is acceptable and make sure you have backups in case something is lost. If you have to send items in the mail, be aware of options to get a signature on delivery or make sure to check in with the organization to make sure they have received your portfolio. If you are handing in a digital portfolio, find out who you can email to ensure they have received your link or set of documents.

Portfolio Dos and Don'ts

Keep the following tips in mind as you choose your portfolio documents and summaries or reflections.

- **Do**—keep your summaries or reflections fairly brief. A one- or two-paragraph description or summary is fine.
- **Do**—make sure to edit those paragraphs carefully, as they are a stand-in for you.
- **Do**—make sure to include papers you did well on and that include positive comments from professors or instructors.
- **Do**—remember to present the best view of yourself that you can while also providing the information required by a prospective group or employer.
- **Don't**—include too much of the same type of thing. A couple of thank you notes will suffice. Twenty of them is just overkill.
- **Don't**—include negative information, comments from others, or other items that will present a bad picture of you if you can't contextualize them.

- **Don't**—include elements just because you are trying to hit a certain number of things to include. This should be your best work and the work that best relates to the job or program you are applying to.
- **Don't**—forget to consider the standard job application documents as well. A nicely done up résumé should still be included if you are applying for a job, either on paper or digitally as required. Don't expect people to infer information; guide them through it.

Exercise 22.4

Choose two items you have written for your writing class or another class. Write a one- to two-paragraph reflection on why that piece of writing is important. What did you learn? What was your process to create the document? How did it help you in some way? If it was an essay, what did the writing process teach you about editing, proofreading, or critical thinking—all transferable skills good for many jobs?

Part 8

Readings

Sam McNerney	"Is Creativity Sexy? The Evolutionary Advantages of Artistic Thinking"
Navneet Alang	"Online Freedom Will Depend on Deeper Forms of Web Literacy"
Leah Brown	"Using Technology to Fight Depression"
B. Ferguson	"No More Classes, No More Books: Online vs. Traditional Schooling"
Syneba Mitchell	"Mislabelled by Society"
Emily Silbert	"Dancing with Language: Don Quijote's Words and Consensual Reality"

The College Advantage

Josh Dehaas

1 University graduates are tossing their mortarboards in the air, sliding their degrees into the filing cabinet—and then heading straight to college. In Ontario, applications for postgraduate diploma programs (which accept only university grads) have jumped 21 per cent since 2007. In Atlantic Canada and Western Canada, college programs that recruited high school grads a decade ago have become de facto postgrads with most applicants already holding degrees. Dianne Twombly, the manager of York University's career centre, has noticed the trend on her campus, too, and she thinks she understands why. "As more and more students get bachelor's degrees, postgrads are a way to distinguish yourself—a way to get an edge." York has seen so much interest, it's offering at least one postgrad workshop each month.

2 Aisling Nolan, a 27-year-old philosophy graduate of McMaster University in Hamilton, Ont., attended university and then college, rather than a master's program. Her university degree helped her understand what she wants to do with her life—help people overseas. Once she knew that, she was ready for the one-year college certificate in international development from Humber College, because it promised practical skills and connections to put her plan into action.

3 Humber certainly delivered action. On the first day of her school-facilitated internship with GlobalMedic, a charity that parachutes medical workers into disaster zones, her boss asked her to write a proposal to acquire funding for 15,000 rainwater purification units for Haiti. "I know exactly how to do that," she told him. Humber had forced her to practise grant writing from week one. Haiti got the units and her boss was impressed. Weeks later he sent her to Pakistan to help deliver aid to flood victims. A master's student might have been sitting with a stack of books working on a paper about Pakistan, while she was being helicoptered in.

4 Reg Flynn, a 30-year-old from Forteau, Nfld., is glad he chose the fast track to action, too. He enrolled in the geographic information systems (GIS) applications specialist program at the College of the North Atlantic in Corner Brook, Nfld., after graduating with an arts degree from Memorial University. His major project at college was to produce a multi-layered computer map to help solve the riddle of why caribou stocks are declining in the province. He included information like topography and vegetation along with data showing how far bears were venturing from their dens after hibernation for food. Was it the bears that were depleting the caribou? It's not clear yet, but the project gave him something tangible he could show to potential employers.

5 Nolan and Flynn are big boosters of their postgrad experiences at college, but they don't knock university, either: they needed both university and college to reach the start of their careers.

6 After all, it was Nolan's political science courses in her undergrad that made her curious about travel and geopolitics in the first place—and illuminated her desire to help impoverished people full-time. It happened like this: after teaching for two years in South Korea (a job she got because of her university credential), she travelled across the developing world. On a beach in Thailand one night, her calling became clear as the night sky. "Everybody was drinking and dancing under the moon, but I couldn't help

---

Josh Dehaas, "The College Advantage," *Maclean's*, March 3, 2011. Used with permission of Rogers Media Inc.

but notice little girls out on the beach picking up beer cans to make money, until three, four and then five the morning," she says. "I realized that I was a part of the problem for these people. I wanted to help." By the end of her trip, she was living with a Masai family in Ilnarooj, Kenya, and volunteering at a school. As soon as she got back, she enrolled in the international development program at Humber. She had found her calling.

7 Flynn also credits university—particularly its flexibility—for helping him discover what motivates him to get out of bed in the morning. He started in computer science at Memorial University, but found that it was "just too tedious," so he switched to English. That didn't suit him either. Luckily, his geography 101 elective helped him uncover his passion. "The way everything works together, like land forms and weather systems, just clicked for me," he says, remembering that first class. A college program straight out of high school wouldn't have allowed so much exploration. It was also in that geography seminar that he first seriously considered the balance between humankind and nature. He credits one seminar where the class explored the question, "Should we really kill a bear just because it comes into our community?" for setting him on the path to his career.

8 University helped Flynn and Nolan to find themselves, but they learned transferable skills, too. Nolan says it was McMaster that taught her how to structure an argument and express her thoughts in writing—a skill that international development workers use all the time to plead for money. Flynn says university taught him how to write clearly, a key requirement for his new job.

9 That job involves making a GIS map for a researcher who's tracking how forests in Newfoundland are changing over time. While a master's student might be studying the competing theories behind environmental stewardship, Flynn is already helping to protect forests and getting paid to do it.

10 Nolan is busy implementing her plan to help the Masai families she met in Ilnarooj on her trek around the world. She's using the financial skills and industry connections that she picked up at Humber to create her new social enterprise, My Masai. She's ordering beaded leather bags from the women in Ilnarooj by the dozens and selling them to Canadian women who want to know their accessories weren't made in a sweatshop. If the business takes off, women in Ilnarooj will have more cash in their pockets and their children will be able to focus on school instead of working (unlike those children on the beaches of Thailand). For Nolan, it feels better to be acting on her values, rather than sitting in a library. She did enough of that in university.

Questions for Discussion

1. This article is more than a few years old; does its argument still apply? What do you see as the main advantages of going to college or university?
2. Would you say the thesis of this article is that college is better than university, or the reverse? Or is it something else? Find the thesis in this article—it may not be in the usual place.
3. To make his point, Dehaas relies mainly on the voices of those in college and university: Reg Flynn and Aisling Nolan. Choose one viewpoint and summarize the point you think the person is trying to make.
4. What has your own experience of college or university taught you about your future plans? What is your opinion of the article's thesis?

The Creative Gifts of ADHD

Scott Barry Kaufman

1 In his 2004 book "Creativity is Forever," Gary Davis reviewed the creativity literature from 1961 to 2003 and identified 22 reoccurring personality traits of creative people. This included 16 "positive" traits (e.g., independent, risk-taking, high energy, curiosity, humor, artistic, emotional) and 6 "negative" traits (e.g., impulsive, hyperactive, argumentative). In her own review of the creativity literature, Bonnie Cramond found that many of these same traits overlap to a substantial degree with behavioral descriptions of Attention Deficit Hyperactive Disorder (ADHD)—including higher levels of spontaneous idea generation, mind wandering, daydreaming, sensation seeking, energy, and impulsivity.

2 Research since then has supported the notion that people with ADHD characteristics are *more likely* to reach higher levels of creative thought and achievement than people without these characteristics. Recent research by Darya Zabelina and colleagues have found that real-life creative achievement is associated with the ability to *broaden* attention and have a "leaky" mental filter—something in which people with ADHD excel.

3 Recent work in cognitive neuroscience also suggests a connection between ADHD and creativity. Both creative thinkers and people with ADHD show difficulty suppressing brain activity coming from the "Imagination Network."

4 Of course, whether this is a positive thing or a negative thing depends on the context. The ability to control your attention is most certainly a valuable asset; difficulty inhibiting your inner mind can get in the way of paying attention to a boring classroom lecture or concentrating on a challenging problem. But the ability to keep your inner stream of fantasies, imagination, and daydreams on call can be immensely conducive to creativity. By automatically treating ADHD characteristics as a disability—as we so often do in an educational context—we are unnecessarily letting too many competent and creative kids fall through the cracks.

5 Nine percent of children aged 5–17 years old are labeled ADHD on average per year, and placed in special education programs. However, new data from The National Center for Learning Disabilities shows that only 1% of students who receive IDEA (Individuals With Disabilities Act) services are in gifted and talented programs, and only 2% are enrolled in an AP course. The report concludes that "students with learning and attention issues are shut out of gifted and AP programs, held back in grade level and suspended from school at higher rates than other students."

6 Why does this matter? Consider a new study conducted by C. Matthew Fugate and colleagues. They selected a population of students with ADHD characteristics who were part of a summer residential camp for gifted, creative, and talented students. The large majority of the students were selected for the program because they either scored in the 90th percentile or above on a standardized test, or had a GPA of 3.5 or greater in specific areas (e.g., mathematics, chemistry).

7 The researchers then compared this ADHD group of students with a non-ADHD group of students who were participating in the same gifted program. They gave all the students tests of fluid reasoning, working memory, and creative cognition. Fluid reasoning involves the ability to infer relations and spot novel and complex patterns that draw on minimal prior knowledge

---

and expertise. *Working memory* involves the ability to control attention and hold multiple streams of information in mind at once. They measured *creative cognition* by having the students come up with novel drawings that included one of the following elements: an oval shape, incomplete figures, and two straight lines.

8 The researchers found that students with ADHD characteristics (especially those who scored high in "inattention") had lower working memory scores than the non-ADHD students, *even though they did not differ in their fluid reasoning ability*. This is consistent with past research showing that people with ADHD tend to score lower on tests of working memory, but these findings also suggest that people with ADHD can still be quite smart despite their reduced ability to hold multiple pieces of information in memory. Also, despite their reduced working memory, 53% of the academically advanced students with ADHD characteristics scored at or above the 70th percentile on the creativity index. In fact, for both the ADHD and the non-ADHD group of students, the poorer the working memory, the *higher* the creativity!

9 This obviously has some important educational implications. To be sure, ADHD can make it difficult for students to pay attention in class and organize their lives. The importance of learning key attentional control skills should not be undervalued. But let's not throw out the baby with the bathwater. As the researchers note, "in the school setting, the challenge becomes how to create an environment in which creativity is emphasized as a *pathway* to learning as well as an outcome of learning."

10 One issue involves the identification of "twice exceptional" students and their appropriate educational programming. Assessments of creativity are notably absent from most gifted and talented programs in this country. Instead of automatically putting children with ADHD characteristics in special education, a broader assessment should be conducted. For one, IQ tests could be administered that focus less on working memory and memorization, and allows for a fairer assessment of fluid reasoning and non-sequential thought among this population of students.

11 A broader assessment could also allow students with ADHD characteristics to display their creative strengths, including divergent thinking, imagination, and hyperfocus (when interested). People with ADHD often are able to focus *better* than others when they are deeply engaged in an activity that is personally meaningful to them. Recent research suggests that the brain network that people with ADHD have difficulty suppressing (the "Imagination Network") is the same brain network that is conducive to flow and engagement among musicians, including jazz musicians and rappers!

12 In terms of programming, problem-based learning (PBL) approaches may enable ADHD students to engage more with the material, and become active learners, rather than passive observers. Additionally, learning can be assessed through project-based learning (PBL), in which students demonstrate their knowledge of the course material through the creation of different products (e.g., cartoons, role-playing, blogs, videos, newspaper articles), and the constant revision of these products.

13 Of course, these same possibilities should extent to all students in the classroom, academically advanced or not. Because we never really know whether an ADHD characteristic is a learning impediment or a creative gift.

14 Consider the case of John, who in 1949 attended Eton College and dreamed of becoming a scientist. However, last in his class, he received the following comment on his report card:

> His work has been far from satisfactory... he will not listen, but will insist on doing his work in his own way... I believe he has

> ideas about becoming a Scientist; on his present showing this is quite ridiculous, if he can't learn simple Biological facts he would have no chance of doing the work of a Specialist, and it would be a sheer waste of time on his part, and of those who have to teach him.

15 This was Sir John B. Gurdon, winner of the 2012 Nobel Prize in Physiology or Medicine for his revolutionary research on stem cells. Like so many other highly creative, competent individuals, he might have been referred for testing and given the label "attention deficit hyperactive disorder."

16 It's time to stop letting this happen.

Questions for Discussion

1. What is Kaufman's thesis? Would you say it is controversial? How does Kaufman set up the introduction to this piece to make a compelling argument?
2. What are the main ways that Kaufman tries to prove his argument? What themes are used to make his argument more clear?
3. For whom do you think this article is written? Find examples to back up your point. Do you think there is only one audience this might be intended for, or can you think of more than one?
4. Find the memorable statement that Kaufman uses at the end of his piece. What is he trying to say here? How did his point affect you when you first read it?

It's Time to Enshrine the Rights and Protections of Transgender Canadians

Senator Grant Mitchell

1 Diversity, inclusion, acceptance and understanding are core Canadian values. We believe that they define who we are, and we are very proud that they do. And yet, in what we all hold to be a remarkably open and inclusive society, transgender people face an extreme level of exclusion, discrimination, prejudice and violence.

2 Research projects by the Ontario Trans PULSE Project and by Egale, and the 2015 report *Being Safe, Being Me,* provide stark and startling evidence of what trans people face in Canada today. These studies found that, of those transgender people surveyed with respect to employment barriers and economic marginalization, 13 per cent had been fired for being trans; 18 per cent were turned down for jobs because they are trans; over 70 per cent are earning less than $30,000 per year; and their median income is $15,000 per year. This is despite the fact that they are highly educated: 70 per cent have some form of post-secondary education, and 44 per cent have post-secondary undergraduate and graduate degrees.

- With respect to discrimination in medical care: of those people surveyed, 10 per cent who had accessed an emergency room were refused care because they were trans; 21 per cent avoided emergency at one time or another specifically due to being trans; and 40 per cent experienced discriminatory behaviour from a family doctor.

Senator Grant Mitchell, "It's Time to Enshrine the Rights and Protections of Transgender Canadians," *LawNow Magazine,* January 4, 2017. Used with permission.

- With respect to bullying and violence: of those studied, 20 per cent had been physically or sexually assaulted; 34 per cent had been verbally threatened or harassed; and 24 per cent reported being harassed by police.
- With respect to mental health and suicide: of those studied, more than 50 per cent presented symptoms consistent with clinical depression; 77 per cent reported that they had considered suicide; 43 per cent had actually attempted suicide and—this is striking and startling—of those, 70 per cent had done so at 19 years of age or younger.
- With respect to youth, of those studied: 90 per cent reported being subjected to transphobic comments frequently, often daily; 23 per cent of students reported that teachers directed transphobic comments at them; 25 per cent of students reported physical harassment; 36 per cent had been physically threatened or injured in the past year; 9 per cent had been threatened or injured with a weapon; 33 per cent said they had been bullied through the Internet in the past year; and trans youth are more than twice as likely as their non-trans counterparts to consider suicide.

3 Among the many frustrations experienced by transgender people, their families and their supporters are the seemingly endless delays in getting their rights and protections enshrined in legislation. It has not been for lack of trying.

4 MP Bill Siksay introduced a bill dealing with trans rights in the House of Commons in 2005 and then again in 2009. His Bill C-389 was passed by the House of Commons in February 2011. It then arrived in the Senate, where it died on the Order Paper without coming to a vote.

5 In September 2011, over five years ago, MP Randall Garrison developed and presented Bill C-279 in the House of Commons. In 2013 this Bill was passed in the House of Commons with Liberal, New Democrat and some Conservative MP support. Over the subsequent two years, it advanced to third reading twice in the Senate. Both times it died there, without even being allowed to come to a vote.

6 This past November, the House of Commons passed Bill C-16 *An Act to amend the Canadian Human Rights Act and the Criminal Code*. This Bill is designed to support and facilitate the inclusion of transgender and other gender-diverse people in Canadian society and to provide them with enhanced protection against criminal aggression. It passed third reading with Liberal and New Democrat support, and support from a very significant cadre of Conservative MPs.

7 Now Bill C-16 is before the Senate of Canada. I am pleased to be the sponsor of this legislation in the Senate and will be working to advance it through the legislative process.

8 Why is Bill C-16 so important? The Ontario Human Rights Commission notes that there are arguably few groups in society today who are as disadvantaged and disenfranchised as the transgender community. Transgender people suffer profound alienation and discrimination in their daily lives. They live in fear of frequent, often brutally violent, physical and verbal bullying. They live in fear of sexual assault. They suffer significant economic discrimination and discrimination in housing and medical care. Their circumstances have led to extreme levels of suicide and suicide attempts. They need our help.

9 For most people, the sense of self as being a man or woman aligns with their anatomical and biological characteristics. For others, it does not. These people are referred to as transgender or trans people.

10 "Gender expression" refers to how people publicly present their gender, through behaviour and outward appearance such as clothing, hair, body language and chosen name.

11 A transgender person simply knows they are of a gender different from the one assigned to them at birth, the one indicated by the physical and physiological features of their body. They cannot live honestly or comfortably in their birth-assigned gender, where they are literally and profoundly uncomfortable in their own skins. If they can overcome their fear, they transition to their true gender identity. To do otherwise is to live in a continuous, often agonizing, confounding and alienating condition. In some sense, it is to live a lie. No one should ever have to do that.

12 What does this bill do? Bill C-16 will make a number of changes to the *Canadian Human Rights Act* and the *Criminal Code* designed to protect transgender people.

13 To begin, the *Canadian Human Rights Act* applies to the federal government in its role as employer and service provider to Crown corporations, the postal service and the federally regulated private sector, including telecommunications companies and charter banks. Bill C-16 will amend the *Canadian Human Rights Act* to add two prohibited grounds of discrimination: gender identity and gender expression. As a result, it will be explicitly discriminatory to disadvantage people because of their gender identity or expression in any workplace, in hiring and promoting, and in the provision of goods, services, facilities and accommodation by or in entities under federal jurisdiction.

14 If the grounds "gender identity or expression" were added, this would mean that a trans person working for the federal government, or one of the federally-regulated employers, could not be passed over for a job or promotion simply because they are trans. It would also be unacceptable to harass a trans person because of their gender identity or expression, turning their workplace into a hostile and poisoned environment for reasons that have nothing to do with their skills or ability to do their job.

15 Similarly, if a trans person applies for a bank account or a passport, they should receive the same level of respectful service as any other Canadian.

16 The bill will also amend the *Criminal Code* in three ways. It will expand the list of identifiable groups that are protected from hate propaganda by adding "gender identity" and "gender expression" to the list.

17 Second, there are three crimes of hate propaganda in the *Criminal Code.* Their purpose is to eliminate extreme and dangerous speech that could incite others to violence against groups listed in the *Code.* The amendment proposed by Bill C-16 would add gender identity and gender expression to this list.

18 The third amendment to the *Criminal Code* will establish that hatred on the basis of gender identity or gender expression is an aggravating factor in sentencing for a criminal offence, along with other listed categories like race, colour and religion. The aggravated sentencing provision in the *Criminal Code* will therefore allow judges to:

- recognize and denounce crimes against trans people motivated by bias, prejudice or hate;
- condemn these hate crimes as being against a group of people who are more vulnerable to crime simply because they are identifiable as trans;
- send a special message of deterrence for these crimes; and
- encourage prosecutors and law enforcement offers to be aware of the particular vulnerability of trans people.

19 Passing this bill will send an important, powerful and hopeful message of inclusion and acceptance to a group of Canadians who experience alienation and discrimination that most of us cannot even imagine. It will elevate awareness of the plight of transgender people and inspire Canadians' compassion.

Questions for Discussion

1. What is the main argument of this piece? What do you see as the core values of Canadians? Do "we" have core values?
2. Would you say that this article has been well researched? What types of pieces does the author use? How does Mitchell use the research to back up his point?
3. Evaluate Mitchell's conclusion. Who do you think is the audience of this piece? Are Mitchell's concluding points successful and persuasive?
4. What has your own experience learning about human rights or the *Human Rights Act* in Canada led you to think about its importance? If you have never had to read about or consider a human rights issue, how can reading a text such as Canada's *Human Rights Act* support your understanding? Do you think Mitchell would see this as required critical reading?

The Gas–Electric Hybrid Demystified

Sara R. Howerth

1 A hybrid is a cross between two established varieties of plant, animal, ... or technology. The hybrid bicycle, for example, combines the features of a road bike with those of an off-road bike to produce a comfortable and efficient bicycle for short-distance cycling. For most people today, the word "hybrid" signifies a fuel-efficient, low-emission automobile. Hybrid car technology combines a gasoline or diesel internal combustion engine with a battery-powered electric motor. Its objective is to maximize the best properties of both the gas engine and the electric motor.

2 A gasoline engine is powerful enough for the pickup, torque, and speed any driver requires. Because of the petroleum infrastructure that has developed over the past 100 years, gas-powered vehicles are also easy to refuel and can travel 400 km to 800 km between fill-ups. On the other hand, they are expensive to operate and will become even more so as fuel prices rise. More importantly, they are a major cause of the pollution that contributes to smog, environmental degradation, and global warming.

3 Battery-powered electric motors are quiet, efficient, and relatively clean—depending, of course, on how the electricity that charges them is produced. However, they cannot yet travel very far on a charge (some can go 200 km), and most need to be recharged 12 hours or overnight. The technology is evolving rapidly, however, and these limitations of distance and time will probably be significantly reduced in the coming years.

4 The hybrid vehicle uses both types of motors and exploits the advantages of each. A gasoline engine provides the power and torque, while an electric engine adds power and thus reduces the amount of gasoline required. There are two types of hybrid vehicle; the difference between them consists of their approach to the twinning of the two engines.

---

5 The "mild hybrid" uses a small electric motor that boosts the capability of the gas engine, thus enabling a smaller gas engine to get the same performance as a larger power plant. Small engines consume less gas and produce fewer emissions, so the smaller the gas engine, the more cost and environmental benefit, as long as the electric motor can deliver the performance equivalent of a more powerful engine. Another way the mild hybrid saves fuel is by allowing the gas engine to shut down when the vehicle is stopped, even for a few seconds at a stoplight. The electric engine starts instantly when the accelerator is touched, and it acts as a starter for the gas motor.

6 The "full hybrid" uses the two motors quite differently. Like the mild hybrid, the full hybrid allows the gas engine to shut down when the vehicle is stopped, but it stays off at low speeds (under about 40 km/h), since the vehicle is powered only by the electric motor until more power is required. As speed increases, the gas or diesel motor kicks in automatically and the two work in tandem to provide the power needed for highway driving, acceleration, and climbing. This arrangement means that cars equipped with full-hybrid engines get better mileage in stop-and-start city driving than they do in long-distance highway conditions.

7 Both hybrid models use the power produced by the gas engine to recharge the onboard batteries, so they never need to be recharged by plugging the vehicle into an outlet. In addition, both models use the electric motor as a generator during deceleration; therefore, power that is normally lost as heat when a conventional car brakes is recaptured and sent to the batteries, keeping them charged. This process is called "regenerative braking."

8 Each year, the marketplace offers more hybrid technology models to cost-conscious and environmentally aware consumers. This trend will continue as long as gas prices rise (which they must do as oil resources decline), and as long as people and governments are concerned about the pollution caused by petroleum-powered vehicles. The hybrid will no doubt be a stepping stone to even more efficient, less polluting technologies, such as fully electric or hydrogen fuel-cell powered cars. But for now and in the immediate future, the hybrid automobile is a technology whose time has arrived.

Questions for Discussion

1. The structure of this essay is more complex than that of the essays we used to illustrate comparison and contrast in Chapter 12. To understand how this piece is put together, write an outline for it.
2. What audience did the author have in mind when she wrote this essay? Car enthusiasts? Auto mechanics? The general reader? Identify at least three examples from the essay to support your answer.
3. What methods of paragraph development does Howerth use to help her readers understand her explanation of her subject? Support your answer with specific examples in the essay.
4. Search online to find another article that discusses the differences between the "full hybrid" and the "mild hybrid." Compare that article to Howerth's essay. Consider the target audience, level of language, and purpose of the two pieces. Which was easier for you to understand? Why?

Why Mars Is the Best Planet

Rebecca Boyle

1 Our tale of two planets begins four billion years ago. One planet was Earth, and the other planet was Mars, and the two had much in common in their infancy. Rivers and lakes etched their surfaces, craters pockmarked their faces, and volcanoes rose from their plains. But something seems to have changed on one and not the other.

2 In Earth's burbling warm water, fate and chemistry combined amino acids into complex molecules, and in a process we still don't understand, these gave rise to single cells that figured out how to make copies of themselves. Tiny mistakes in those copies eventually turned them into oxygen-exhaling organisms we call algae. Endless forms flowed from these humble ancestors, and after eons, there we were: All of human culture and hope and possibility arising within a tiny slice of time.

3 Mars was not so lucky. Mars dried up. Mars is small, about half Earth's diameter, so it cooled off faster than Earth did after their birth in the cloud of dust left over from the sun's creation. Compared to its overall volume, more of Mars' mass is exposed to the icy blackness of space. As it cooled, its iron-nickel core solidified. When this happened, we think, the Martian magnetic field shut down, robbing Mars of its protective shield, of the sort that still safeguards Earth from solar and cosmic rays. Time and the brightening sun stripped away the Martian atmosphere before the planet's algae, if it existed, had a chance to make the air thick and warm. Mars turned to rust before any skeletons could adorn its deserts, before any creatures could look up and contemplate their place among the other dots in the night sky. While Earth is fecund and bursting with life, Mars is, and may have always been, barren.

4 To me, this is why Mars is the best planet. A few simple changes turn its history into our history, and vice versa. That's the key thing; that could have been us.

5 Ashwin Vasavada has a similar view. He is the project scientist for the Mars Science Laboratory, the six-wheeled robot car we know and love as Curiosity. He can quote the easy answer for why we go to Mars, the assumption most scientists and science writers make: Mars is close. It's practically right next door, and you can fling a robot there in half a year.

6 "That's the NASA answer. It's the most accessible place for life other than on Earth. But I have my own answer," he says. "It's a place that you can go today that's like going to early Earth. You remove that dusty exterior of Mars, and you have this planet that is just so reminiscent of Earth. It's like finding a dusty Earth in your attic. Shake off the dust a little bit, and it's this amazing place that you can recognize. That's why I like it."

7 Mars would seem familiar to anyone who has seen the national parks of the American West, especially the ones full of wind-whipped rock formations and surprising color. The terrain at Gale Crater's Mount Sharp, where Curiosity has been trundling along since 2012, might as well be Utah or Colorado. The rocks are reddish brown, sun-baked, and partly blanketed in sand dunes. Their carved-away hillsides are jagged, however—no rivers or softening rains have given them Earth's gentle countenance.

8 Of course, Mars was familiar to us long before we sent robots there. With Mercury, Venus, Jupiter, and Saturn, Mars is one of the night sky's unblinking wanderers, visible with eyes alone. The planets have accompanied human

culture since we started writing stories. The next planet over has been a fixture in myths dating to the Babylonians, who called it Nergal, after the god of destruction. In Roman mythology, Mars was the god of war and destabilization. This figure also appears in various forms in Greek, Norse, and Hindu mythologies. To ancient Chinese, it was Ying-huo, the Shimmering Planet.

9 Even now, we acknowledge Mars on the third day of every week. In romance languages, the name comes from the Latin day of Mars, or "Dies Martis"—that became martes in Spanish, mardi in French. In Norse mythology, Mars is associated with the god Tyr, so our Tuesday comes from the Old English word Tiwesdæg. We also honor Mars on the third month of every year. Bellicose Mars was also a protector of the Roman people and a patron of agriculture, so the month named for this god marked the beginning of the growing season.

10 Mars has always stood out from the other wanderers, in part because it is so obviously red, a ruddy, unblinking dot hanging with an air of menace. Its hue—which comes from oxidized iron, in the same chemical reaction that turns blood red—linked Mars to war, and to death, long before we knew it was dead in a literal sense. What's more, it moves backward, or seems to. The sun, moon and stars rise in the east and fall in the west because of Earth's rotation. But the planets orbit the sun at different rates, and so sometimes, Earth will lap one of them, like a runner on an inside track lane. From our perspective on Earth, the other planet seems to be moving west to east. This aberrant behavior has long been associated with omens or astrological predictions.

11 Its omnipresence in our sky made Mars a prime target as soon as we figured out how to use glass to make the night sky's features appear larger. By the 17th century, astronomers resolved its polar ice caps through telescopes—perhaps one of the earliest discoveries that the fourth planet shared something in common with ours. And the more we looked, the more we found these similarities. Mars is the best planet because Mars and Earth have more in common than any other worlds in the solar system. It cowers next to humongous Jupiter, but unlike that gas giant, its hard surface beckons visitors. Mars lacks our dewy, oxygen-rich atmosphere, but neither is it shrouded in a poisonous, bone-crushingly dense one like Venus. Its day (called a sol) is just 40 minutes longer than our own. Its axis is tilted slightly more than ours, at 25 degrees, unlike weirdly slanted Uranus. And anyone who argues it is ugly, especially compared to the art deco elegance of Saturn, is simply mistaken. Mars is lovely to behold. Mars has snow. It has mountains, and lake beds, and recognizable *landscapes*. Earth and Mars are the same in so many ways. And yet. The biggest difference is the only one that really matters. The only life on Mars is the kind we imagine.

12 Martian fantasies grew in complexity alongside Martian observations. Astronomers frequently turned to the red planet when Mars was opposed to the sun and close to Earth, making it appear larger and brighter. The most famous of these was the opposition of 1877, in which the Italian astronomer Giovanni Schiaparelli observed networks of lines on Mars, which later turned out to be optical illusions (though Mars does have streaks of water lining its slopes today). He called them *canali*, which was translated into English as "canals."

13 This momentous finding brought Mars closer to Earth than ever. It became even easier to imagine Mars as a place just like Earth, positively crawling with life. "The present inhabitation of Mars by a race superior to ours is very probable," the French astronomer Camille Flammarion wrote in 1892. Around the same time, the American astronomer Percival Lowell

scrutinized Mars extensively. He believed he saw "non-natural features," including canals, which he imagined were devised to transport water from the drying planet's ice caps. Mars soon loomed even larger in science fiction and pop culture. By 1897, H.G. Wells' "War of the Worlds" imagined Mars as a slowly drying planet full of desperate beings who launch rockets to Earth, where they feast on human blood.

14 If Mars was arguably the first place storytellers imagined we would find aliens, it was indeed the first place we went looking for them. Project Ozma, in which astronomer Frank Drake pointed a radio telescope at the stars Tau Ceti and Epsilon Eridani, is the traditional SETI origin story. But we listened to Mars first. In Aug. 22, 1924, the head of the U.S. Navy, Edward Eberle, instructed all naval stations to turn their receivers toward Mars. The red planet was at its closest approach to Earth in 120 years, and some astronomers thought Martians might use the opportunity to make contact over the airwaves. Onshore stations were advised to listen to as many frequencies as possible, and to "report any electrical phenomenon [of] unusual character," according to a telegram from Eberle. If someone wanted to talk, the Navy was ready to listen.

15 No Martians made contact that day, because there are no Martians, as far as any of our satellites and robots can tell. But this has not stopped our storytellers, and it certainly has not stopped our scientists. We have been attempting to land spacecraft on Mars for nearly 50 years, and almost all of them have been looking for life, in one way or another.

16 The history of Mars landings has shown that the planet is anything but hospitable now, however. And that goes for machines just as much as microbes. More than half of the robots sent to Mars have been destroyed in the process, most recently last fall. The European Space Agency's Schiaparelli lander plummeted through the atmosphere Oct. 19, but crashed after it cut its parachute too soon and its hovercraft-like retrorockets didn't fire long enough.

17 Still, those lucky few that have made it, most notably Curiosity, have shown us Mars was habitable in its past. The fleet of orbiters looping around the planet have sent back data that suggests there is some water there today, mostly at the poles. But we are still not sure if Mars had lasting oceans, or just big lakes and rivers, says Ray Arvidson, a renowned planetary scientist who has directed or taken part in every NASA Mars mission since Viking. And we certainly don't know whether it had life.

18 "It's not a given. It's not a shoo-in, by any means, that Mars developed life, and if it did, that the evidence is still there," Arvidson says. "Whether or not you get organic molecules that move to prebiotic compounds, that then move to replicating systems, that's a big leap."

19 Even assuming that leap happened, Vasavada and others say we are more likely to find evidence of ancient life than modern life. Extant or extinct Martians would probably be bacteria or some other simple cells, definitely not limbed beings that communicate using light or language. In this way, Mars may seem disappointing to some. But it is the best planet precisely because a null result, as scientists would call it, would raise an even bigger question: Why here? Why us?

20 "I think it just becomes a real scientific mystery if we don't find life. That tells us we don't quite understand how unique life is on Earth," Vasavada says. "If you don't find it, that almost becomes more interesting, and makes you get more existential about life on Earth. That's where I am now."

21 For those who take an even longer existential view, Mars is important—vital, even. When Elon Musk unveiled his plans for giant rockets and

spaceships to transport human settlers to Mars, he invoked not only exploration, but our shared future. Mars is an opportunity for humans to carry forward the light of consciousness, letting it propagate alongside us, and to survive after we are gone, much like the first cells on Earth found a way to send copies of themselves into the future. If Musk and other dreamers have their way, the first life forms on Mars might be us.

22 But make no mistake: It will be a horrible, destructive journey. Unlike the territories of colonial history—the West Indies, the American West and other frontiers—Mars does not tickle the mind with dreams of untold riches. Mars is no El Dorado. Its atmosphere does not hold any heat. It has no pressure to prevent your blood from vaporizing. Without a spacesuit, you would literally boil and freeze to death, simultaneously. Mars travelers would be consigned forever to pressurized domes or, more likely, radiation-shielding caves. They would never again see waves lapping at a shoreline. They would never again hear the wind singing through pine trees. They would never again be surprised by the sight of a silvery crescent moon.

23 Why go, then?

24 I was at JPL when Curiosity landed in August 2012, and I couldn't help clapping along with the NASA engineers and scientists who whooped and hollered at the news. The dust had barely settled after Curiosity's audacious sky crane landing when the rover sent back its first postcard, the grainy image you see here [www.jpl.nasa.gov/news/news.php?feature=3459].

25 "It's the wheel! It's the wheel!" someone in the control room shouted. Squinting at the black-and-white image of a wheel on a rocky plain, I felt a rush of emotion. The rover's belly cast a shadow in the afternoon sun. The scene looked so *familiar*, but felt so wrong. It could have been the mountain West where I grew up, only it was empty, lifeless but for the robot now perched on the sand.

26 If Saturn is a spur to the scientific imagination, letting us glimpse how far our minds must go to meet what the cosmos has in store, Mars does the opposite. It is a sign of how unlikely we are. It makes us confront how fragile the Earth is. It's a reminder of how lonely we remain on our pale blue dot, the only home we have ever known. Mars is the best planet because Mars is a mirror. We look to it and we see ourselves—our past and possibility, and, with some imagination, our future.

Questions for Discussion

1. This essay is filled with facts and information but it still has a clear thesis. What is Boyle's main point in this article?

2. What level of language does Boyle use in this essay? (Go back to pages 13–14 for help.) Support your answer with examples of words and phrases taken from the piece.

3. Review the ways that Boyle tries to describe how Mars mimics some of Earth's landscape and terrain. How does Boyle make comparisons? What is similar between Earth and Mars? What is different? Is this a comparison and contrast essay?

4. Rebecca Boyle argues that "Mars is the best planet because Mars is a mirror. We look to it and we see ourselves—our past and possibility, and, with some imagination, our future." What does Boyle mean by this? Can you find examples from the text that back up this point?

Note: The following research paper has been documented in APA style.

Labouring the Walmart Way

Deenu Parmar

1 *Always low prices. Always.* This is the slogan of the world's largest corporation, a U.S.-based retailer whose big-box stores offer a one-stop shop, from groceries to garments to garden hoses. The secret of Walmart's success is to give consumers the lowest prices—14 percent lower than its competitors (Greenhouse, 2003)—by increasing the efficiency of the supply chain, the productivity of the labour force, and the use of labour-saving technology. Competitors must adopt a similar business plan, offer something Walmart does not, or go out of business—as Woolco, Eaton's, Simpsons, and Woodwards have in Canada (Moore & Pareek, 2004). The influence of the Walmart model is not likely to wane in the near future. With over 235 stores in Canada and plans for rapid expansion, Walmart and its effects on labour are worth considering. Are its offers of jobs, its attitude toward unionization, and its influence on industry labour practices worth the low price on the shelf?

2 One of the most frequent complaints about Walmart, which employs 1.4 million people worldwide, is its failure to pay workers a living wage. Store employees are paid 20–30 percent less than the industry average, making many of them eligible for social assistance. It is estimated that American taxpayers fork out $2.5 billion a year in welfare payments to Walmart employees (Head, 2004). Because the retailer hires hard-to-place workers, like recent immigrants, seniors, and single mothers, its employees are often afraid they will not find work elsewhere. The kind of work Walmart does offer is gruelling: stores are intentionally understaffed—the strategy behind the company's legendary productivity gains—so that existing employees will work harder (Head, 2004). It is alleged that systemic discrimination against women within the corporation has denied the majority of Walmart workers the chance at promotion, a charge that is now the subject of the largest civil-rights suit in U.S. history.

3 The corporation's staunch anti-unionism is its main defence in keeping workers' wages down and profits up. Without a union to give them collective clout, the store's employees suffer not only lower wages and benefits but abuses like being forced to work overtime without pay. The hiring process is designed to weed out union sympathizers; however, if organizing activity is reported in the store, an anti-union team is flown out from the headquarters in Bentonville, Arkansas, to break it up (Featherstone, 2004). The unionizing of the first Walmart store in Canada (Jonquière, Quebec) exposed the company's strategy in the event that its anti-union efforts fail: condemn the store as unprofitable and announce a closing date. Although Walmart's methods of keeping its workforce union-free have been ruled illegal in the United States, the company often finds it cheaper to pay labour violations than abide by labour rules (Featherstone, 2004). As a result, litigation is a common but costly form of redress for Walmart workers whose rights have been violated.

4 One of the main reasons retail workers at other stores want to see Walmart unionized is to preserve the gains their own unions have made. The necessity of competing with Walmart has already been used as an

---

excuse for supermarkets all over the United States to lower the wages and benefits of their employees (Featherstone, 2004). In early 2004, unionized grocery workers in southern California were forced to accept cuts to their benefits so their employers could compete with a soon-to-open Walmart Supercenter. Walmart's reputation for putting local stores out of business also means that employees of the competition may find themselves working at Walmart for less.

5 Although Walmart's record of paying low wages, crushing unionizing efforts, and lowering industry employment standards bodes ill for Canadian labour, it is unlikely that Canadians will refrain from shopping there. The lure of good prices is hard to resist, and the company's widely admired business model would continue to thrive, even if Walmart were to vanish tomorrow. In the interest of justice and fairness—and in avoiding pitting the customer's savings against the worker's ability to make a living—it falls on the government to pass laws that balance the interests of big business with the protection of labour, environmental, and community rights (Golden, 2004). This kind of legislation will require pressure from organized citizens acting not as consumers but as workers and concerned members of a community. The price on the shelf might rise as a result, causing Walmart supporters to point out that the poor can no longer afford to shop there. However, the ability to buy at rock-bottom prices does not address the systemic causes of poverty—though it may contribute to them.

References

Featherstone, L. (2004, June 28). Will labor take the Wal-Mart challenge? *The Nation.* Retrieved from http://www.thenation.com/doc.mhtml?i=20040628&s=featherstone

Golden, A. (2004, October 7). Productivity, but not at any price [Comment section]. *The Globe and Mail,* p. A23.

Greenhouse, S. (2003, October 19). Wal-Mart, driving workers and supermarkets crazy. *The New York Times,* p. D3.

Head, S. (2004, December 16). Inside the leviathan. *The New York Review of Books, 51*(20). Retrieved from http://www.nybooks.com/articles/17647

Moore, K., & Pareek, N. (2004, August 19). A whole new take on shock and AWE: There's BWE (before Wal-Mart entered), and there's AWE (after Wal-Mart entered). *The Globe and Mail,* p. A17.

Questions for Discussion

1. In this essay, is the author addressing general readers, Walmart's customers, or Walmart itself? What effect does she hope the essay will have on her target audience?
2. Consider the essay's attention-getter and memorable statement. Given the author's purpose and target audience, are they effective? Why?
3. What are the main kinds of evidence the author uses to support her causal analysis?
4. Why do you think the author uses documented sources to support her thesis? How would the effect of the essay change if the sources were omitted?
5. The author says that even if Canadians are aware of the effects of Walmart's policies and practices, they will continue to shop there. Has this essay reduced your desire to shop at Walmart?

6. Do a keyword search online of "Walmart." Limit your search to three business journals. Note the kind of article that appears in these journals. Now do the search again, looking for articles from general-interest magazines such as *Maclean's, Time, The New York Times*, and *The Walrus*. What are the main differences between the articles taken from the two categories of print sources?

Embraced by the Needle

Gabor Maté

1 Addictions always originate in unhappiness, even if hidden. They are emotional anesthetics; they numb pain. The first question—always—is not "Why the addiction?" but "Why the pain?" The answer, ever the same, is scrawled with crude eloquence on the wall of my patient Anna's room at the Portland Hotel in the heart of Vancouver's Downtown Eastside: "Any place I went to, I wasn't wanted. And that bites large."

2 The Downtown Eastside is considered to be Canada's drug capital, with an addict population of 3000 to 5000 individuals. I am a staff physician at the Portland, a non-profit harm-reduction facility where most of the clients are addicted to cocaine, to alcohol, to opiates like heroin, or to tranquilizers—or to any combination of these things. Many also suffer from mental illness. Like Anna, a 32-year-old poet, many are HIV positive or have full-blown AIDS. The methadone I prescribe for their opiate dependence does little for the emotional anguish compressed in every heartbeat of these driven souls.

3 Methadone staves off the torment of opiate withdrawal, but, unlike heroin, it does not create a "high" for regular users. The essence of that high was best expressed by a 27-year-old sex-trade worker. "The first time I did heroin," she said, "it felt like a warm, soft hug." In a phrase, she summed up the psychological and chemical cravings that make some people vulnerable to substance dependence.

4 No drug is, in itself, addictive. Only about 8 per cent to 15 per cent of people who try, say alcohol or marijuana, go on to addictive use. What makes them vulnerable? Neither physiological predispositions nor individual moral failures explain drug addictions. Chemical and emotional vulnerability are the products of life experience, according to current brain research and developmental psychology.

5 Most human brain growth occurs [immediately] following birth; physical and emotional interactions determine much of our brain development. Each brain's circuitry and chemistry reflects individual life experiences as much as inherited tendencies.

6 For any drug to work in the brain, the nerve cells have to have receptors—sites where the drug can bind. We have opiate receptors because our brain has natural opiate-like substances, called endorphins, chemicals that participate in many functions, including the regulation of pain and mood. Similarly, tranquilizers of the benzodiazepine class, such as Valium, exert their effect at the brain's natural benzodiazepine receptors.

7 Infant rats who get less grooming from their mothers have fewer natural benzo receptors in the part of the brain that controls anxiety. Brains of infant monkeys separated from their mothers for only a few days are measurably deficient in the key neuro-chemical, dopamine.

---

8 It is the same with human beings. Endorphins are released in the infant's brain when there are warm, non-stressed, calm interactions with the parenting figures. Endorphins, in turn, promote the growth of receptors and nerve cells, and the discharge of other important brain chemicals. The fewer endorphin-enhancing experiences in infancy and early childhood, the greater the need for external sources. Hence, the greater vulnerability to addictions.

9 Distinguishing skid row addicts is the extreme degree of stress they had to endure early in life. Almost all women now inhabiting Canada's addiction capital suffered sexual assaults in childhood, as did many of the males. Childhood memories of serial abandonment or severe physical and psychological abuse are common. The histories of my Portland patients tell of pain upon pain.

10 Carl, a 36-year-old native, was banished from one foster home after another, had dishwashing liquid poured down his throat for using foul language at age 5, and was tied to a chair in a dark room to control his hyperactivity. When angry at himself—as he was recently, for using cocaine—he gouges his foot with a knife as punishment. His facial expression was that of a terrorized urchin who had just broken some family law and feared Draconian retribution. I reassured him I wasn't his foster parent, and that he didn't owe it to me not to screw up.

11 But what of families where there was not abuse, but love, where parents did their best to provide their children with a secure nurturing home? One also sees addictions arising in such families. The unseen factor here is the stress the parents themselves lived under even if they did not recognize it. That stress could come from relationship problems, or from outside circumstances such as economic pressure or political disruption. The most frequent source of hidden stress is the parents' own childhood histories that saddled them with emotional baggage they had never become conscious of. What we are not aware of in ourselves, we pass on to our children.

12 Stressed, anxious, or depressed parents have great difficulty initiating enough of those emotionally rewarding, endorphin-liberating interactions with their children. Later in life such children may experience a hit of heroin as the "warm, soft hug" my patient described: what they didn't get enough of before, they can now inject.

13 Feeling alone, feeling there has never been anyone with whom to share their deepest emotions, is universal among drug addicts. That is what Anna had lamented on her wall. No matter how much love a parent has, the child does not experience being wanted unless he or she is made absolutely safe to express exactly how unhappy or angry or hate-filled he or she may feel at times. The sense of unconditional love, of being fully accepted even when most ornery, is what no addict ever experienced in childhood—often not because the parents did not have it to give, simply because they did not know how to transmit it to the child.

14 Addicts rarely make the connection between troubled childhood experiences and self-harming habits. They blame themselves—and that is the greatest wound of all, being cut off from their natural self-compassion. "I was hit a lot," 40-year-old Wayne says, "but I asked for it. Then I made some stupid decisions." And would he hit a child, no matter how much that child "asked for it"? Would he blame that child for "stupid decisions"?

15 Wayne looks away. "I don't want to talk about that crap," says this tough man, who has worked on oil rigs and construction sites and served 15 years in jail for robbery. He looks away and wipes tears from his eyes.

Questions for Discussion

Maté wrote "Embraced by the Needle" for *The Globe and Mail*, a newspaper distributed across Canada. Keeping his audience in mind, answer the following questions.

1. The author's introduction (paragraph 1) and conclusion (paragraphs 14 and 15) are structured the same way: he makes a general statement and then supports it with a specific example or illustration. Identify the generalization and the example/illustration the author has used in each case. Why do you think the author chose this structure rather than the introduction and conclusion patterns we recommended in Chapter 8?
2. Why does the author insert himself into his writing? Identify the four times he uses first-person pronouns. Would the piece be as effective if he did not mention his personal involvement with the issue? Why?
3. In point form, summarize the causes that Maté thinks lead to addiction.
4. What is the author's attitude toward drug addicts? Highlight words, phrases, and examples that reveal how he feels about them.

Note: The following essay is a research paper documented in MLA style.

No Sweat?

Rubi Garyfalakis

1 When I began investigating the use of sweatshops in the garment industry, I thought there would be a simple answer: sweatshops were morally wrong, and their products should be boycotted by conscientious North American consumers. As I looked more deeply into the issue, however, I found surprising and perplexing information that left me more aware and educated but less convinced than before. My research revealed that sweatshops are a complex issue, full of complications that make it a grey moral area. Through my journey, I ultimately found that there is no "right or wrong," "yes or no," "do or do not do" solution to this dilemma, and that our duty as moral, ethical consumers is difficult to determine. Although this realization can lead consumers to feel frustrated, helpless, and eventually indifferent, there are effective actions we can take.

2 I began my research believing that sweatshops were unethical. The definition of a sweatshop confirmed my conviction. According to ethics teachers and researchers Denis Arnold and Laura Hartman, a sweatshop is

> ... any working environment in which the workers are subject to two or more of the following conditions: systematic health and safety risks caused by employer negligence; systematic forced overtime, coercion, or underpayment; or income for a 48-hour work week that is less than the amount needed to satisfy basic survival needs. (2)

Stories of such conditions are common in the media. For example, in Uzbekistan, thousands of children must pick 10 to 40 kg of cotton per day, earning a wage of 38 cents for their efforts. The children carry pesticides in

---

plastic water bottles, a practice that results in skin burns as the pesticides splash onto the children's arms and hands.

3 Ethics professor C. D. Meyers claims that sweatshops contradict "the commonsense moral presumption against economic exploitation, which is supported by the dominant moral theories of today" (1). The exploitation of sweatshop workers is wrong because it is unfair: the exploiters gain at the expense of the exploited, who are not fairly compensated (Mayer 2-4). Sweatshop employers could afford to pay their workers more, but they do not because it benefits them to pay as little as possible. Essentially, sweatshops violate globally recognized basic labour rights, including the right to freedom from forced labour, the right to a limited number of hours in a workday, and the right to just and favourable working conditions (Arnold and Hartman 6). The evidence of blatant exploitation and violation of workers' human rights would probably lead any ethical consumer to conclude that sweatshops are morally wrong.

4 If only the problem were that simple. For those who like tidy problems with clear solutions, it is disturbing to find that there is another side to the sweatshop debate. To begin with, sweatshops are "the first rung on the ladder out of extreme poverty" (Sachs 11). They allow developing countries to expand their exports and consequently to improve their economies (Arnold and Hartman 2). Workers (usually women) choose to work in sweatshops because they are often the only means by which women can further their own ends. By working in sweatshops, women make a small income, learn about business practices, and benefit from the improved social and economic conditions that come with economic growth. Arnold and Hartman explain that as the economy grows, more jobs are created; the labour market tightens, and companies are forced to improve their working conditions in order to attract employees (2-3). Theoretically, this analysis makes sense, but does it apply in practice? Do employees really benefit from working in sweatshops?

5 As I dug deeper into the research, I was surprised to learn that in some cases, sweatshops *can* have positive effects. A clear example is Bangladesh's garment industry. Thousands of women, mostly between the ages of eighteen and twenty-five, work in sweatshops to cut, stitch, and package clothing for common brands, such as GAP and Walmart, that are sold in Europe and North America (Sachs 11). Economic advisor Jeffrey Sachs reports that his interviews with Bangladeshi women working in sweatshops revealed an unexpected reality. Although all of the women admitted that they worked long hours, were subject to harassment, and were denied labour rights, they also affirmed that the job provided an opportunity greater than they could otherwise have hoped for, and that it had improved the quality of their lives (Sachs 12). With their small income, the women experienced some independence. Earning a salary gave them the opportunity to manage their own finances, have their own rooms, choose when and whom they wanted to marry, and choose when they wanted to have children. They could save to improve their living conditions or to return to school to improve their literacy or job-market skills.

6 Sweatshops provide work that is difficult and underpaid, but any job in an economically depressed region offers women an opportunity that had previously been unavailable, even unthinkable. Without the option of sweatshop work, women have no choice but to submit to arranged marriages in their early teens and to begin bearing children. The evidence suggests that in the highly patriarchal society of Bangladesh, sweatshops are helping to change attitudes toward women. Encouragingly, because of the garment industry, Bangladesh's economy has grown by 5% per year in the

last decade (Sachs 13). If Arnold and Hartman's theory holds, improvements in working conditions will follow.

7 Well-meaning protestors in the first world have suggested that Bangladesh's sweatshops should pay higher wages or be shut down, but closing factories would take jobs away from women (Sachs 12). Thus the consumer faces a dilemma: the issue is not one of choosing between right and wrong, but of choosing the best possible (or least wrong) option.

8 What can concerned consumers do? Boycotting companies that contract their production to sweatshops may seem like a viable anti-sweatshop action; however, boycotts themselves raise complex issues. First, they normally result in job losses for workers ("Labour behind the Label"), thus only adding to the injustice because it is not the workers but the employers whom consumers want to punish. Second, most sweatshop workers choose the job because it is better than the available alternative; without their jobs, women have no choice but to settle for marriage—assuming they are still young enough to attract a husband. On the other hand, some studies show that boycotting can have an impact on companies because they become known as "ethical offenders" (Shaw et al. 5). Nike and GAP are two examples of companies that were forced by negative publicity to modify their labour practices to maintain their place in the competitive market. Unfortunately, most large companies that advertise their "positive action" on the labour front simply go through a public relations exercise: they develop and publicize new codes of conduct (5). Codes of conduct may look impressive on paper, but they do not guarantee action or change. Unless top-level management endorses and enforces a firm's code of conduct, little or nothing changes at the level of the sweatshops, which cling precariously to the bottom rung of the company hierarchy.

9 Nevertheless, a code of conduct is a start, and a start is better than nothing. But even the most determined consumers confront problems in deciding which companies or products to boycott. Identifying consumer goods produced wholly or in part by workers in sweatshops is nearly impossible. Over the last 30 years, North American and European multinational corporations have greatly increased the amount of production that they contract to the developing world (Arnold and Hartman 2). This massive relocation of work in the garment industry is part of an economic system called "triangular manufacturing": transnational companies based in Europe or North America receive orders for consumer goods, contract the production orders to lower-wage (usually third-world) economies, and ship the finished goods back to the buyers (Hale 3). As a result of triangular manufacturing, developing countries, where goods are produced and assembled, are forced to compete in a "race to the bottom." The winner is the country that can produce the most goods at the fastest pace and at the lowest cost. The race to the bottom requires suspending workplace and environmental regulations, resulting in below-par wages and dismal working conditions ("Labour behind the Label").

10 Another effect of triangular manufacturing is that it is virtually impossible to know where a product came from or where it was made. For example, a large amount of Uzbekistan's cotton, picked by child labourers, is sent to China, the world's largest exporter of garments and textiles (Belli 2). Uzbek cotton ends up in T-shirts that are made in China and sold in the USA. Because the label on the "made in China" T-shirt does not say where the cotton is from, it is impossible to know whether children were exploited in the process of producing the garment (Belli 2). Similarly, a

label claiming that a product is "organic" refers to how the cotton was produced. An "organic" product sounds good to the conscientious consumer, but the organically grown cotton may have been picked, packed, shipped, woven, cut, and sewn into completed garments by children in sweatshops (Belli 2). This confusion (and sometimes deception) is possible because there are no regulations for clothing labels. Unlike the fair trade food labels, there are no internationally recognized labels for clothing to ensure that fair trade standards were maintained throughout the chain of production (Shaw et al. 4). Consequently, consumers turn to clues such as the country of origin stated on the label, and try to avoid products made in countries notorious for exploitation, such as China. Stigmatizing certain countries is unfair, however, because it is based on prejudice, not proof, and it could potentially harm ethical companies in those countries who need to attract business in order to survive.

11 If boycotting has both pros and cons, "targeted" boycotting is virtually impossible, and product information is unreliable, how are consumers to shop ethically? One alternative is to shop from the limited niche market for ethical clothing. The options in Canada are basically limited to garments produced by two firms: American Apparel and No Sweat. American Apparel designs, knits, dyes, sews, markets, and distributes its products in Los Angeles ("American Apparel Investor Relations"), but it does not claim that the raw material it uses was grown in the United States. The cost of producing cotton in the United States forces this fair trade–conscious company to buy it from overseas (Belli 2). No Sweat is an online store that sells clothing and footwear produced by independent trade union members in Canada, the United States, and the developing world. Established in 2000, this company guarantees that its products are fairly traded and that all workers receive a living wage ("No Sweat"). While these two outlets sound good, they offer a limited selection at relatively high prices. As a student, I am tempted to resist the increased price level, but then I am reminded that, as Meyers points out, "whatever extra we have to pay for a new pair of sneakers is not comparable to the suffering that could be prevented by giving sweatshop workers a living wage" (2).

12 The lack of ethical alternatives and the confusion about product information in the garment industry make supporting sweatshops almost unavoidable for consumers. It would be easy to become discouraged and to conclude that there is nothing we can do about sweatshop injustices. Such a conclusion would be a mistake, however, because each option has the potential to make a partial positive change. Boycotts help to raise awareness; they also send the message to large companies that labour policies matter. Buying from alternative stores shows support for companies who do uphold fair trade practices. Shopping at thrift stores may help to decrease the enormous demand for new clothing that fuels triangular manufacturing (Hale 2). Above all, each of these actions represents a rejection of complacency, sending the message that our current consumer culture is substantially flawed.

13 Sweatshops and the solution to the problem they represent are extremely complex. There is no clear moral answer to the issue, and there is no clear course of action for the ethical consumer in the developed world. It is our duty, however, to try our best to make moral choices when we shop for clothing. Although change must ultimately come from the top, our conscientious actions will help the change to begin from the bottom and to work its way up.

Works Cited

"American Apparel Investor Relations." *American Apparel.* Web. 27 Nov. 2008.

Arnold, Denis G., and Laura P. Hartman. "Beyond Sweatshops: Positive Deviancy and Global Labour Practices." *Business Ethics: A European Review*, vol. 14, no. 3, July 2005, pp. 206-22.

Belli, Brita. "Fashion Victims." *E Magazine*, vol. 18, no. 5, Sept. 2007, pp. 32-33. *Academic Search Premier*. 28 Nov. 2008.

Hale, Angela. "What Hope for 'Ethical' Trade in the Globalised Garment Industry?" *Antipode*, vol. 32, no. 4, Oct. 2000, p. 349. *Academic Search Premier.* 1 Dec. 2008.

"Labour behind the Label." *UK Clean Clothes Campaign.* 1 Dec. 2008.

Mayer, Robert. "Sweatshops, Exploitation, and Moral Responsibility." *Journal of Social Philosophy*, vol. 38, no. 4, Winter 2007, pp. 605-19.

Meyers, C. D. "Moral Duty, Individual Responsibility, and Sweatshop Exploitation." *Journal of Social Philosophy*, vol. 38, no. 4, Winter 2007, pp. 620-26. *Academic Search Premier.* 28 Nov. 2008.

"No Sweat." *No Sweat Apparel.* 27 Nov. 2008.

Sachs, Jeffrey D. *The End of Poverty*. Penguin Books, 2005.

Shaw, Deirdre, et al. "Fashion Victim: The Impact of Fair Trade Concerns on Clothing Choice." *Journal of Strategic Marketing*, vol. 14, no. 4, Dec. 2006, pp. 427-40.

Questions for Discussion

1. Most research papers are written in the third person (*one, he, she, they*), and the author's voice is silent (no use of first person *I*). Yet this essay begins in the author's voice (paragraphs 1 and 2), and then changes to third person, which is the dominant point of view of the rest of the essay (exceptions are paragraphs 5 and 13). Why do you think the author begins and ends the account of her research findings by inserting herself into the essay?

2. Identify the thesis statement of this essay and the topic sentences in paragraphs 2, 4, 8, and 11. Now identify the kind(s) of support the author has used to develop her topic in these paragraphs.

3. The author supports her argument that working in a sweatshop can be a positive experience for women in developing countries by focusing primarily on one country. What country does she choose to illustrate her point? How could she have strengthened her support for her argument?

How Reporting on Indigenous Issues as an Indigenous Journalist Can Get Complicated

Trevor Jang

1 Indigenous issues are a complicated topic for any journalist, but for Indigenous reporters, covering them can also get personal.

2 I experienced this complexity while investigating the internal governance challenges of the Gitxsan Nation in northwestern British Columbia. The Gitxsan are territorial neighbours to my own nation, the Wet'suwet'en.

Trevor Jang, "How Reporting on Indigenous Issues as an Indigenous Journalist Can Get Complicated," *CBC News*, March 7, 2017. Used by permission of CBC Licensing.

3 The investigation was sparked by a pair of confidential documents that had been leaked into the community last fall. They revealed a group of Gitxsan hereditary chiefs had accepted millions of dollars in exchange for their support of a natural gas pipeline proposed to cross their territory.

4 When I visited the community, Gitxsan members expressed concern that these chiefs did this without consulting the membership.

5 But when I began investigating, I was scolded for challenging the authority of the Gitxsan chiefs to make decisions for their people.

6 One Gitxsan leader told me that as a Wet'suwet'en person, I have no right to question the business of their territory. This is based on traditional Gitxsan law. The Wet'suwet'en have similar laws.

7 This leader was right. Our neighbour's business is not our business.

8 But as a journalist writing for an organization that wants to serve northern B.C., Gitxsan business became my business.

Gitxsan and Wet'suwet'en Legacy

9 I didn't find pride in my Wet'suwet'en identity until I learned about my great-grandfather and the impact he had on First Nations land rights in Canada. But this pride in my lineage also complicated my involvement in this story on the Gitxsan.

10 Johnny David, who held the hereditary chief name Mikhlikhlekh, was the first Wet'suwet'en chief to give evidence in the historic Delgamuukw land claims court case.

11 Launched by the Gitxsan and Wet'suwet'en chiefs in 1984, their eventual legal victory was significant because it was the first time the courts confirmed Aboriginal title, or ownership of traditional land, had never been extinguished in British Columbia, where treaties hadn't been signed.

12 Johnny David, Mikhlikhlekh, was the first Wet'suwet'en chief to give evidence in the historic Delgamuukw land claims court case that set several precedents. (Jennifer David)

13 Thanks in part to Mikhlikhlekh and the other chiefs and elders who gave testimony, almost all subsequent land rights cases in Canada have favoured Indigenous plaintiffs.

14 The impact of their words helped to shape the government's legal obligation to consult First Nations when proposing resource development projects on traditional lands.

15 The case concluded at the Supreme Court of Canada on Dec. 11, 1997. As a journalist who writes about Indigenous issues, I felt compelled to return to Delgamuukw 20 years after the historic court case.

16 This fuelled my investigation into First Nations land rights and self-governance in a post-Delgamuukw legal environment, particularly where those rights and issues clash with or influence resource development projects in northern B.C., such as pipelines.

17 The situation involving the confidential documents leaked in fall magnified broad internal divisions over how decisions are made and who can speak for the Gitxsan.

18 The Wet'suwet'en struggle with similar governance challenges, but I decided to focus my attention on the Gitxsan, because I felt uncomfortable writing about my own nation's internal politics. I feel it would be a conflict of interest for me to investigate my own people.

19 But it turns out I'm close to the Gitxsan, too.

20 And so I stuck my nose in my neighbour's business to complete my investigation, thus breaking the traditional law of the land—the same law my great-grandfather described in the historic court case.

Walking in Both Worlds

21 In the end, the Gitxsan leader who scolded me was pleased with my investigation. They found it fair and respectful. They also apologized for being harder on me than they would be on another journalist, simply because I'm Wet'suwet'en.

22 The experience made me realize that as I move forward with my career, sometimes my role as a journalist and my cultural identity will contradict each other and lead to conflict.

23 But my cultural identity and the legacy of my great-grandfather are also what drive my curiosity to explore and explain complex Indigenous issues through journalism.

24 Finding that ever fluid balance is the challenge of walking in both the Western world and the Indigenous world, while attempting to bridge the two.

25 Mikhlikhlekh's evidence in Delgamuukw was epic, filling more than eight volumes.

26 His testimony has been transcribed and analyzed in a book by anthropologist Antonia Mills called *Hang Onto These Words*. In its opening, Mills wrote that she used my great-grandfather's evidence "as a primer on the problems of unmasking colonization and of creating cross-cultural communication."

27 I didn't realize until after my stories were published that I was attempting to do the same thing in my investigation.

Questions for Discussion

1. Trevor Jang is both from the Wet'suwet'en Nation and of Chinese descent. This article deals very personally with Jang's experience. What is the conflict that Jang experienced and how was it eventually, or tentatively, solved?

2. How does Jang make this piece about more than just personal experience? Who do you think Jang's audience is? Give examples from the article.

3. Describe Jang's writing journey in a sentence or two. That is, what, where, when, how, and why does Jang write?

4. Indigenous issues are really important to Canadian culture. What issues exist in your own province? Find an article from a newspaper in your own regional area on an Indigenous issue and summarize it in a paragraph or two.

Farming It Out

Maria Amuchastegui

1 It was the Thursday before Easter that Henk Sikking Jr. got the doctor's call. The 28-year-old tulip farmer was getting ready to take his crew of Mexican migrant workers grocery shopping. The workers live on his property and get around with bicycles, but rely on their boss to take them on major shopping trips. He had arranged for a bus to take the workers into town.

2 Sikking's best worker, Hermelindo Gutiérrez, had gone to see the doctor earlier in the week, complaining of swollen feet and ankles. Sikking assumed that Gutiérrez had injured himself while driving one of the carts used to

---

"Farming It Out." Maria Amuchastegui. Originally published in *This Magazine*. May–June 2006.

navigate the sprawling complex of greenhouses. The doctor was blunt. The bloodwork revealed that both of Gutiérrez's kidneys had failed. If Gutiérrez did not go to the hospital, he was going to die.

3 The family business, Pioneer Flower Farms, was started by Henk Sr., who immigrated to Canada from Holland in 1972. Henk Jr. is in charge of potted plants, his brother Peter runs the cut flowers division, while Henk Sr. oversees the entire operation. The farm is the main supplier of buds for Ottawa's annual tulip festival. Until he fell ill, the 32-year-old Mexican had been working at the St. Catharines, Ontario, greenhouse for six years, working his way up to become foreman. "He was my right-hand guy," said Sikking. "He pretty much ran the crew. He could speak English. He was really interested in the job."

4 Gutiérrez was diagnosed with kidney failure and admitted to the Hotel Dieu Hospital in St. Catharines. His co-workers suggested he call the Mexican consulate in Toronto to let them know he was sick. Before long, the consulate began to call Gutiérrez, demanding that he return to Mexico. Sikking knew that for Gutiérrez this was a death sentence. Unless he received a kidney transplant, he would require dialysis for the rest of his life. The rural village that he comes from does not have dialysis facilities. And Gutiérrez hadn't bothered to buy health insurance in Mexico because he spends most of the year working in Canada. Sikking said to Gutiérrez, "You're not going back. You got sick in Canada. It's Canada's responsibility to take care of you."

* * *

5 Gutiérrez came to Canada through the Seasonal Agricultural Workers Program (SAW), a federal guest-worker program that has been in existence since 1966. The original participants in the program were from Jamaica, Trinidad-Tobago and Barbados; Mexico followed suit in 1974; other Caribbean nations joined in 1976. According to statistics provided by Human Resources and Skills Development Canada (HRSDC), in 2004, 18 887 migrant workers came to Canada under the SAW program, 10 777 of whom were from Mexico.

6 Compared to the undocumented masses who make the dangerous trek to the US, migrant workers in Canada—theoretically at least—receive more social benefits and have more legal rights. According to Juan José Martínez de la Rosa, coordinator of the agricultural program at the Mexican consulate in Toronto, Mexico considers Canada's SAW program to be a "best practices" model for managed migration, especially compared to the US, where the vast majority of migrant workers are illegal immigrants. "It's a tangible, positive example of what can happen when two parties agree to administer migration, given the need of one party for labour, and the need of the other party to provide jobs. It's a way to manage the phenomenon of migration without the risk associated with border crossing by *indocumentados*."

7 For Mexico, and other countries that participate in the SAW program, the money sent home by migrant workers is an important source of hard currency. According to the World Bank, Mexico received $18.1 billion US in foreign remittances in 2004—about 2.5 percent of its GDP—making it the third-greatest recipient of remittances in absolute terms, after India and China. In 2003, remittances were Mexico's second-largest source of foreign exchange after oil, eclipsing foreign investment and tourism. The Canadian Department of Foreign Affairs estimated that in 2002, Mexico received about $80 million in remittances from participants in the SAW program. Mexican participation in the SAW program had more than doubled from 1994 to 2004.

8 Canada benefits, according to the HRSDC website, because the program provides farmers with a "reliable" source of labour. From the farmers'

perspective, the chief attraction of guest workers is that they can't easily quit their jobs. "If you want 100 Canadians, you have to hire 300," said Sikking. The temporary work permits given to migrant workers are for specific farms; workers need the farmer's permission to transfer elsewhere. If workers complain about their work conditions, farmers have the power to have them repatriated to Mexico. If workers return to Mexico before completing half their work term, they have to reimburse the farmer for their airfare, a powerful disincentive to quit.

9 The farmers benefit, too, from securing workers who are comparatively cheap. The agreement between Canada and Mexico stipulates that migrants must be paid the "prevailing wage" that Canadians are paid for the same work. According to a United Food and Commercial Workers' (UFCW) draft 2005 report on the SAW program, the rate paid to migrant workers in 2006 will be $8.30 an hour. HRSDC's own stats, however, show the average for Canadian agricultural workers is closer to $10.50 an hour. Assuming a 40-hour work week, migrant workers gross about $332 per week before taxes. The actual hours worked are much longer: Gutiérrez initially assumed that his feet had swollen from working 16- and 17-hour days. Farmers don't always pay the required rate: in 2005, Mexican workers who were picking berries in Pitt Meadows, British Columbia, returned to Mexico of their own accord, complaining of being paid $24 for 10-hour days.

10 Still, $332 per week is a lot of money in Mexico. From the workers' perspective, the SAW program gives them a well-paying job and raises their family's standard of living. According to a report prepared for the North-South Institute by Mexican researchers Gustavo Verduzco and María Isabel Lozano, the same workers make an average of $55 US per week in Mexico. Verduzco and Lozano also found that the program may be helping to keep the workers' kids in school: the longer a worker participated in the SAW program, the higher the level of schooling reached by his children.

11 The Canadian government takes a big cut from the workers' paycheques. According to Verduzco and Lozano, about 20 percent of workers' paycheques is deducted in taxes, including EI, CPP and income tax; 77 percent of the workers have their income tax deductions refunded because they make less than $14 000 per year. The cost of housing and airfare to and from Canada is borne by the farmer.

12 In exchange, the workers receive some social benefits. Retired workers can collect CPP, even if they retire in Mexico. Health coverage varies by province, but in Ontario the workers get provincial health cards that are valid for the calendar year. In addition, the workers receive Worker's Comp for work-related injuries, and are required to purchase private health insurance for expenses not covered by their provincial health cards. The Mexican workers have a group policy with RBC Insurance.

13 The workers' relative prosperity comes at a price. Although the workers are helping to subsidize Canadian social programs with their taxes, they don't receive all the benefits that Canadians receive. Many social benefits require Canadian residency. Because the workers have to leave Canada when their work permits expire, they are not eligible to receive those benefits. For example, migrant workers are not eligible for most EI benefits, despite paying EI premiums. In the case of medicare, workers who have returned to Mexico do not have coverage for conditions developed in Canada.

14 The exclusion of migrant workers from EI is currently the subject of a Supreme Court challenge. The federal government tried to have the case dismissed, arguing that the UFCW does not have standing in the case. The judge ruled in January [2006] that the UFCW does have the right to represent

migrant workers, the first time a union has ever won the right to represent unorganized workers. It is illegal in Ontario for agricultural workers, both migrant and Canadian, to join trade unions and to strike. (They can join "associations," but the associations can't bargain on their behalf.) The rationale given by farmers and by the government is that crops are time-sensitive. If agricultural workers take collective action, farmers could lose their crops.

* * *

15 In the spring-bulb world, crops are planted in the fall and harvested in the spring. Sikking summons Mexican workers to his farm in two stages: in spring to coincide with the harvest, and again in fall to coincide with the planting. In the barn, workers are stationed along an assembly line, planting tulips. Some workers feed bulbs onto a conveyor belt. Others sort bulbs onto trays, 100 bulbs to a tray. The bulbs are watered, covered in dirt and sand, and placed in cold storage for four months, until they sprout roots. The bulbs then are taken to the greenhouse for three weeks, where they will form buds. Tulips are classified as hardy bulbs because they can withstand low temperatures. They must be "forced" to bloom by being placed in cold storage.

16 Sikking is a tall man, with Elvis sideburns and a kindly face. He picks up a tulip bulb and holds it before him. "These are the best bulbs," he says proudly. Pioneer Flower Farms imports all its tulip bulbs from Holland. It is one of the largest flower-bulb forcing farms in North America, producing over 40 million blooms per year, 20 million tulips and 20 million other varieties. The farm includes 300 000 square feet of greenhouse and nearly two acres of cold storage. Eighty percent of the farm's business is with the United States; its customers include [Metro], Costco and the National Capital Commission.

17 When Gutiérrez fell ill, he had just arrived at the farm for the spring harvest. He spent one week in the Hotel Dieu hospital. The consulate said they would send someone to see him, but no one ever came. Gutiérrez was discharged from the hospital and went back to the farm. He continued to receive dialysis treatment as an outpatient. During this time, the cost of his dialysis was covered by OHIP, Ontario's medicare.

18 One day, the phone rang at the farm, and it was the consulate. The consulate told Gutiérrez that he would have to go back to Mexico because he had a pre-existing condition that was not covered by his insurance, and because his treatment was too expensive. He offered Gutiérrez a payment of $3500 from RBC Insurance on the condition that he return.

19 The Mexican Ministry of Labour is supposed to ensure that workers have received yearly medical checkups before sending them to Canada. When Gutiérrez was first admitted to the SAW program, he got a clean bill of health. When he was diagnosed with kidney failure, he had not had a medical checkup in several years.

20 "Do you have any idea what your treatment costs?" said the consulate.

21 Gutiérrez is modest and soft-spoken in the way of the Mexican campesino, but now he raised his voice. "I don't care what it costs," said Gutiérrez. "I've been working here seven years. I don't have health insurance in Mexico. I've brought everything to Canada, just like you. I want to be treated here."

22 "That doesn't matter," said the consulate. "You're going back to Mexico."

23 The consulate contacted Gutiérrez's wife in Mexico, and asked her to sign a power of attorney authorizing the consulate to forcibly return her husband to Mexico. She refused. When Gutiérrez found out about the conversation, he was furious. The consulate told Gutiérrez he was starting to become difficult, *sangrón*.

24 The consulate says it contacted Gutiérrez's family so that it could arrange for Gutiérrez to receive medical treatment in Mexico. Gutiérrez initially went along with the plan, and then backed out. According to Lourdes Borofsky, a Mexican community activist who does outreach with workers and advocated on Gutiérrez's behalf with the consulate, Gutiérrez didn't believe the consulate's promises. "He didn't believe it because he had heard of other cases in which workers are returned to Mexico and once they are there, the government totally forgets about them," said Borofsky. "They promise things and don't deliver. That's what he heard."

25 Gutiérrez did what migrant workers are supposed to do. Workers are told to contact their consulate if they have a health issue or a problem with their employer. But because the consulates have an interest in attracting farms and in ensuring the smooth functioning of the program, they often sacrifice individual workers.

26 In Gutiérrez's case, his work permit gave him the legal right to remain in Canada for eight months, until December 15, and his medicare was valid until December 31. According to Marina Wilson, a spokesperson for Citizenship and Immigration Canada, temporary workers aren't forced to leave Canada immediately if they become sick or injured. "They can stay for the duration of their permit. They still have status for as long as their work permit is valid. They are not deported if they break their leg on the job or if they develop a condition." Under Canadian law, migrant workers who fall ill in Canada can legally remain here until their work permits expire. Under the terms of their employment contract, farmers can send them back to Mexico for any "sufficient reason," including illness. According to a report prepared for the North-South Institute by human rights lawyer Veena Verma, "workers are not provided equal treatment with Canadian workers when the effect of the repatriation provisions make it difficult to enforce their rights." In theory, migrant workers are protected by the same laws that protect Canadians. In practice, because they can be repatriated at any time, they can't enforce their rights.

27 Jorge Aceytuno, a spokesperson for HRSDC, said that sick workers are generally returned to Mexico only if they have a long-term illness, and that Mexico makes arrangements for treatment to continue there. "If it's a short-term illness, it's in nobody's interest for the worker to go back," he said. He acknowledged that Mexico is not obligated by the Canada–Mexico agreement to provide health care for sick workers after they return. According to a report published in 2004 by the UFCW, the Canadian government washes its hands of its responsibility toward the workers. "The government believes its responsibility with regard to migrant workers begins and ends with the issuance of work visas," said the report. "The government has indicated that the consulates of the sending countries and their staffs are responsible for supporting and advocating on behalf of workers."

28 The small Mexican community in St. Catharines rallied around its beleaguered countryman. When Gutiérrez's co-workers realized he was having difficulty getting to his dialysis treatments (Sikking would sometimes lend Gutiérrez his van, but he couldn't always spare it), they chipped in $1600 to buy him a used car.

29 The consulate then began to call Sikking, pressuring him to send his worker back to Mexico. RBC Insurance called Sikking too, offering Gutiérrez a $3000 payment. Sikking asked Gutiérrez if he had health insurance in Mexico; Gutiérrez said no. Sikking was afraid of what the government would think if it found out he helped his worker. "We depend on these guys

for our livelihood," he said. Sikking's friends advised him to send Gutiérrez back. "People were saying, 'Don't take it personal, just send the guy back,'" said Sikking.

30 Gutiérrez recalled Sikking's reaction to the consulate's pressure. "When they insisted on removing me, my boss said, 'Hermelindo'—he always calls me Hermelindo—'You have worked for me. You have been a good worker. I am going to help you. I don't know how we're going to do it, but you're going to stay here.'" Someone at the office happened to know a human rights lawyer, Ryan Persad. Sikking paid the $2000 retainer fee, and the lawyer filed a claim for refugee status. They are currently awaiting a court date.

31 Gutiérrez's case is not exceptional. Workers are routinely sent back to Mexico when they are gravely ill. There was a case in Hamilton of a worker who fractured his skull in a bicycle accident. The doctors had to remove a seven-centimetre piece of his skull to accommodate the swelling of his brain. "They took him out of the Hamilton hospital with his skull in a bag and a nurse to escort him back to Mexico," said Stan Raper, agricultural coordinator at the UFCW.

32 Workers can also be repatriated if they complain about their working or housing conditions. In 2003, a Caribbean worker was sent home after he complained that pesticides were seeping into his living quarters. In 2001, in an incident that caused the Canadian labour movement to take notice of migrant workers, Mexican workers at a greenhouse in Leamington, Ontario, organized a wildcat strike. The farmer had the ringleaders repatriated.

33 What makes Gutiérrez's case different is that his employer wants him to stay in Canada, against the wishes of the consulate. What is also different is the involvement of a private insurance company. RBC Insurance applied pressure to Sikking and to the consulate to persuade Gutiérrez to return to Mexico, offering him a financial incentive to go home. "They wanted him out of the country," said Sikking.

* * *

34 One day in September, Borofsky called Gutiérrez to see how he was doing. He had moved into a refugee settlement house in St. Catharines. "He didn't say he was depressed, but I could tell he was depressed," said Borofsky. "He was sad and afraid he wouldn't have anyone to talk to. And he said, 'I would like to spend Christmas with my family. I don't know if you could help me out.'"

35 Borofsky contacted Wayne Manne, a priest at Ste. Marguerite d'Youville parish in Brampton. He arranged for one of the members of the congregation, who wishes to remain anonymous, to purchase plane tickets for Gutiérrez's wife, María del Rosario Romero, his 11-year-old daughter Sayuri and his eight-year-old son Sergio. The family arrived in Canada on a tourist visa, and planned to stay until April.

36 According to Kerry Preibisch, a sociology professor at the University of Guelph, the preference given by Mexico to hiring married men is one of the mechanisms used to ensure that workers go home. "This program works through cooperation between Canada and the labour-sending countries. They're not wanted as citizens by Canada, they're wanted as labourers. Allowing workers to stay in the country when they're not working jeopardizes the smooth functioning of the program," said Preibisch. "If you think about it, it's remarkable that every year, nearly 20 000 workers come up to Canada to fill labour shortages in agriculture, and then go back to their country."

37 Meanwhile, Gutiérrez continues to live at the settlement house and to receive dialysis, while awaiting a court date for his refugee hearing. The irony

is that, although he has medicare and a willing organ donor, he can't afford a kidney transplant. Gutiérrez is not eligible to be on Canada's waiting list for donated organs since he is not a permanent resident, but he is sure that one of his brothers and sisters will be willing to donate a kidney. The cost of transplanting a kidney into Gutiérrez is covered by OHIP, but the cost of removing a kidney from his sibling is not.

* * *

38 Back on the farm, Mexican *cumbia* music pulsates from a boombox. Migrant workers carefully stack tulip buds into crates: red, pink and white. Using forklifts, the workers transport the crates from the assembly line area in the barn to the loading dock at the other end of the greenhouse complex. They load the crates into trucks and dispatch them to the National Capital Commission in Ottawa. At the tulip festival, the buds will bloom, a symbol of the safe refuge that the Dutch royal family found in Canada during the Second World War.

39 "What happened to Hermelindo happens to almost everyone," says Sikking. "If they're not getting medical treatment in Mexico, then I think they should get something here. Some of these guys have been working here 40 years."

Questions for Discussion

1. The narrative that threads through this essay is not told in a straight line. Why did the author choose to develop her argument by alternating narrative incident with general/background information?
2. Would it have been more effective to tell the story of Hermelindo Gutiérrez first, and then provide the background/context? Why?
3. Where in the essay does the author first clearly state her opinion that migrant workers are discriminated against in Canada?
4. In addition to narration, the author frequently uses direct quotations to develop her argument. Why?
5. The author acknowledges that both the workers (paragraphs 7, 10, and 12) and the employers—including the government—(paragraphs 8, 9, and 11) benefit from the Seasonal Agricultural Workers Program. She also acknowledges that there are risks on both sides. Nevertheless, one side benefits more than the other. Which one? Support your answer with specific reference to the essay.
6. The author quotes a University of Guelph sociology professor: "This program works through cooperation between Canada and the labour-sending countries. [The migrant workers] are not wanted as citizens by Canada, they're wanted as labourers.... If you think about it, it's remarkable that every year, nearly 20 000 workers come up to Canada to fill labour shortages in agriculture, and then go back to their country." Why do you think Canada does not want agricultural workers as citizens? Do you agree with the government's position?
7. How did you react to this essay? Would your response have been the same if the author had stated her opinion up front and then listed and developed her reasons?

A Deafening Silence on Aboriginal Issues

Nancy Macdonald

1 News of Jamie Prefontaine's death, apparently by suicide, shattered Winnipeg's Indigenous community last week. There, the 30-year-old Metis father of four was better known as Brooklyn, the stage name he adopted five years ago, before rocketing to fame with the award-winning hip-hop trio Winnipeg's Most.

2 They were assailed for glorifying the criminal lifestyle. But Winnipeg's Most also used their star power to help draw attention to the issue of missing and murdered Indigenous women and girls, buying headstones for Carolyn Sinclair, a 25-year-old from the Mathias Colomb Cree Nation, whose body was found in a city Dumpster, and Divas Boulanger, a transgender Berens River woman, whose body was found at a highway truck stop. Prefontaine, who'd lost an aunt to murder growing up, said the issue hit "close to home."

3 In much the same way, his death is affecting young men around him. Karmen Omeasoo, considered the "grandfather of Native hip-hop," penned a moving tribute to the fallen rapper, opening up about a suicide attempt that's left him unable to close his left hand: "I feel for all the lives we have lost to this demon—it's time to start speaking about it daily. We can't lose any more."

4 Prefontaine's death came days after the start of a coroner's inquest into Nunavut's horrific suicide rate—40 times the national average for boys aged 15 to 19. But in that 450-word Facebook post, Omeasoo—better known by his stage name, Hellnback—said more about the suicide epidemic tearing apart Indigenous communities than all the federal party leaders combined have at a major public forum in this election cycle.

5 Indeed, in the past seven weeks—during which there have been four leaders debates covering wide-ranging topics—the leaders have been effectively silent on the critical issues facing Indigenous people. In a typical eight-week period in Canada, more than 33,000 Indigenous people are violently victimized and 11 are murdered, more than 17 times the national average. Yet in the *Maclean's* National Leaders Debate on Aug. 6, Indigenous issues earned only passing mentions. In the *Globe and Mail* debate on the economy, they got a mention when Liberal Leader Justin Trudeau plugged his plan to boost spending on First Nations education. At this week's Munk Debate in Toronto, they got no mention. Liberal candidate Michèle Audette, an Innu and Liberal candidate in Quebec, notes the leaders were not solely to blame: they weren't asked the urgent questions.

6 On the campaign trail, in a country that has lost more than 800 Indigenous women to violence since 1995, compared to two men lost to domestic terrorism, the discourse has been dominated by fears of Islamic State and a new anti-terror law—a wedge issue that's split progressive votes.

7 "I don't want to play oppression Olympics," says Indigenous scholar Hayden King, contrasting the parties' silence to the massive debate on the Syrian refugee crisis sparked by the death of three-year-old Alan Kurdi last month. "But we have Native children being taken from families, kids dying of preventable causes in northern communities, and we haven't talked about any of it. You really have to ask: What will it take to compel Canadians to make these electoral issues?"

Nancy Macdonald, "A Deafening Silence on Aboriginal Issues," *Maclean's*, September 30, 2012.

8 It's all the more galling given the election was called just weeks after the release of the findings on Canada's Truth and Reconciliation Commission (TRC) on June 2. Canada, it seemed then, was finally at a turning point, ready to acknowledge its dark past and formative role in creating a situation whereby an Indigenous child born tomorrow is expected to live seven fewer years than any other Canadian. He has a 50 per cent chance of growing up in poverty and better odds of being jailed than of graduating high school. If born on Saskatchewan's Ahtahkakoop Cree Nation, he has a better chance of being infected with HIV than in some African countries.

9 "Canadians should be appalled," says B.C. consultant Michelle Corfield, former vice-president of the Nuu-Chah-Nulth Tribal Council, where she oversaw economic development. "Every citizen of Canada deserves to live in a country that recognizes them as equals. If we continue to do nothing, Indigenous people will fall from Third to Fourth World living conditions." The TRC provided a once-in-a-lifetime opportunity to meaningfully address these issues, she adds. Unless something changes in the next three weeks, she fears we'll have wasted it entirely.

10 Over the weekend, author and university administrator Wab Kinew, Rwandan genocide survivor Eloge Butera, Broadbent Institute director Jonathan Sas and 19 honorary witnesses to the TRC issued a call to action, urging Canadians to "make reconciliation an election issue." Kinew told *Maclean's* he remembers NDP Leader Tom Mulcair and Liberal Leader Justin Trudeau "immediately in front of news cameras" after the tabling of the TRC report. "When it was politically expedient to jump on the stories of my father, of our ancestors, I remember them being there."

11 "At this late stage, it will certainly be difficult to insert reconciliation into the conversation," says Justice Murray Sinclair, chair of the Truth and Reconciliation Commission. "Time's a-wasting; and the opportunity has almost passed."

12 "The reality is the federal government has been largely responsible for causing this harm, and the chaos that results lies in their lap. And to a certain extent, they are a bit confused—looking for direction, continuing to dither while they try to gauge the public appetite."

13 Sinclair says he always knew the federal government would be the slowest agent of change; he notes strides made by educators—who are changing school curricula in several provinces—by churches and private industry. But federal players are approaching this from a political perspective: Are there votes in it or not? "I think that's what's at play here. But at some point we're going to have to have a serious conversation: The federal government can't continue to ignore this. They're going to have to show some leadership."

14 In the meantime, Sinclair says, the public needs to recognize where it can effect change. This, he adds, "is going to be the most effective way to combat racism, which is still quite prevalent in our society." Sinclair believes reconciliation will take hold neighbourhood by neighbourhood, street by street, family by family. "The reality is, it took us 150 years to get to this situation so it's going to take us a while to get out of it. Let's not get frustrated by lack of action in the immediate future." Frustration, however, is what many people feel right now.

15 There were hopeful signs, after all, that things would be different this time around. Soon after the campaign launched, the leaders of the Liberal, NDP and Green parties addressed the Assembly of First Nations (AFN). They made significant promises: The Liberals and Greens have agreed to adopt each of the TRC's 94 recommendations and the NDP have pledged to act on adopting them. Neither the Liberals nor the NDP have costed their

reconciliation planks. The Conservatives have said they will wait for the commission's full report, due next year, before making any commitments. The Liberals, NDP and Greens have said they would adopt the United Nations Declaration on the Rights of Indigenous Peoples; all three are calling for an inquiry into the issue of missing and murdered Indigenous girls and women.

16 One of the Liberals' first campaign promises in August was to invest $2.6 billion for on-reserve education and $500 million over three years for school infrastructure, notes Michèle Audette, a Liberal candidate and former president of the Native Women's Association of Canada; over the past 18 months, Audette, who is challenging NDP incumbent Charmaine Borg in the Montreal-area riding of Terrebonne, was part of the team that drafted the party's Indigenous platform with Paul Martin.

17 The Conservatives have not released an Indigenous platform, but in the 2015 budget, they pledged to direct $200 million over five years to Indigenous education and re-announced plans to direct $500 million over six years to on-reserve schools.

18 The NDP, meanwhile, is planning to release more details on its Indigenous platform later in the campaign; sources suggest it will include investments to First Nations education and infrastructure.

19 The Idle No More movement initiated a massive push for change; and a huge number of activists have been channelling their energy to get-out-the-vote initiatives like Indigenous Rock the Vote.

20 Sara Mainville, chief of the Couchiching First Nation, near Rainy Lake, Ont., is among them: "If it's the only arrow in your bonnet, use it, because voting is the only way this is going to change," the 46-year-old lawyer tells potential voters. "The status quo is so dangerous. I don't want my 10-year-old daughter to grow up feeling unsafe on city streets the way I did. This has to change."

21 In nearby Kenora, Tania Cameron, the riding's former NDP candidate and a key Idle No More organizer, has devoted her every free minute to helping Indigenous voters navigate the new restrictions brought in with the government's Fair Elections Act. Cameron considers the new rules a "voter suppression tactic," akin to "what used to be done in Mississippi."

22 Indeed, many fear the new identification requirements, which insist on addresses, will disproportionately disqualify people on crowded reserves. The new rules also end the practice of vouching, which allowed chiefs and council to affirm the identify of someone lacking complete ID, which many on-reserve voters do.

23 "The relationship between the current government and Indigenous people is unnecessarily adversarial," says AFN Chief Perry Bellegarde in an interview. "They spent [$110] million this year fighting court battles over Aboriginal rights and title. If we continue this approach, we'll continue to lose generations of people; we'll continue to lose languages and potential and opportunity.

24 "Party leaders need to pay attention to our issues and priorities; they are Canada's issues and priorities," Bellegarde tells *Maclean's*. "If we win, Canada as a country will win."

25 In Nunavut this week, the coroner agreed with the inquest jury that suicide should be declared a public health emergency. The inquest had heard from families of the 45 people who killed themselves in the territory in 2013, a torrent of tragedy that sparked the inquest. Rex Uttak, who turned 11 just weeks before he hanged himself on Aug. 10, 2013, was the youngest.

26 He was a happy boy who loved to laugh; before he died, his family had been living with as many as 24 relatives in his grandmother Bernadette's four-bedroom home. They'd been waitlisted for social housing.

27 Rex was not the first in his family to succumb to suicide: his older brother Bernie had killed himself, as had an aunt. And he was grieving the murder of his older sister. "I'm lifeless," his grandmother Bernadette testified in Inuktitut. "You think: 'What did I do wrong?'"

28 It's hard to imagine a topic more urgent in Canada than this one. Twenty-seven Nunavummiut have already died by suicide this year. Will this be a topic the leaders grapple with and debate in detail in the final leaders debate in Montreal this week? Given their interests and talking points so far, it seems very unlikely.

Questions for Discussion

1. This essay is developed around a variety of complex issues. Where is the thesis in this piece? What is the article attempting to explore? How does the author develop the issue?

2. This article is from *Maclean's* magazine. What level of language does Macdonald use in this essay? (Go back to pages 13–14 for help.) Support your answer with examples of words and phrases taken from the piece.

3. This article uses a variety of research, including the results of the TRC—the Truth and Reconciliation Commission—which can be found online at www.trc.ca. Have a look at some of the findings and write one or two paragraphs outlining what you learned.

4. Macdonald quotes a variety of well-known Indigenous writers such as Wab Kinew, Hayden King, and Karmen Omeasoo. Who are these people, and how do the voices of experts enhance arguments in a persuasive paper? Write one or two paragraphs giving reasons and details.

Is Creativity Sexy? The Evolutionary Advantages of Artistic Thinking

Sam McNerney

1 Human evolution is puzzling. Around 45 000 years ago, for no obvious reason, our species took off. Our technology rapidly progressed, populations thrived, and we started painting and crafting instruments. All of this and more culminated in our first civilizations. From there, we started growing food, building cities, reading, and writing. Today, our species is the most dominant on the planet.

2 What's odd is that natural selection doesn't explain this cultural explosion. Our genetic makeup is identical to our ancestors' who lived 100 000 years ago. As Matt Ridley explains, "all the ingredients of human success—tool making, big brains, culture, fire, even language—seem to have been in place half a million years before and nothing happened." What gives?

3 The answer might have to do with the relationship between creativity and sex. Consider a study conducted by evolutionary psychologists Douglas Kenrick, Bob Cialdini, and Vlad Griskevicious. In one clever experiment, the psychologists asked college students to write a short story about an ambiguous picture. Before the students tested their prose, Kenrick and his partners divided them into two groups. One half was put in a mating mindset

---

Sam McNerney, "Is Creativity Sexy? The Evolutionary Advantages of Artistic Thinking," *Big Think*, June 17, 2012. Used by permission of the author.

by looking at six photos of attractive females, picking which one they most desired as a romantic partner, and imagining an ideal date with her. The other half, the control condition, saw photos of a street and wrote about the most pleasant weather conditions for walking around and looking at the buildings.

4 Kenrick and his team found that students in the mating mindset were more creative with their stories of the ambiguous pictures than the control group. Did the reproductive motivations trigger their creativity? Because the effect showed itself only for the men, the researchers concluded that "these studies establish that temporary activation of a mating motive can have the same effect on humans as the mating season has on peafowl; in both cases, mating opportunities inspire males to strut their stuff."

5 Kenrick was also interested in the relationship between creativity, non-conformity and sexual selection. He wondered if sexual motivations cause males to stand out from the crowd artistically. To find out, Kenrick teamed with Chad Mortensen and Noah Goldstein and asked subjects to judge how interesting they found an artistic image. However, before the subjects gave their two cents, they listened to the judgments of several other members of the group who tended to agree with each other. Did the subjects conform to the group?

6 It depended on gender and motivational state. Kenrick and his team created two groups. One was primed with a fearful mindset by recalling tragic murder stories. Subjects in the other group imagined themselves spending a romantic day with the person of their dreams. The different motivational states mattered. Those in the mating mindset tended to go against the group opinion compared to their more fearful peers. Women did not show the same effect, suggesting that when it comes to artistic taste, men are motivated to show off by strutting their creativity.

7 This helps explains why muses are predominantly women who inspired men. Consider, as Kenrick did, examples throughout history:

> Pablo Picasso [is] the most prolific artist in history with an astounding 147 800 works of art.... [A] closer look at Picasso's generative periods reveals an intriguing constant: each new epoch blossoms with paintings of a new woman—not a sitter or a model, but a mistress—each of whom is touted to have served Picasso as an incandescent, albeit temporary, muse. Picasso's artistic history, however, is not unique: creative juggernauts such as Salvador Dalí, Friedrich Nietzsche, and Dante were also acutely inspired by their own muses. The enigmatic notion of a muse is rooted in Greek mythology, in which nine godly muses traversed the land, stirring the creative spirits of mortal artists and scientists. And according to historian Francine Prose (2002), all muses share one striking and inextricable feature: muses—both in history and in mythology—are universally female. Yet if "there is no biological reason why a man can't provide the elements of inspiration" (p. 9, Prose, 2002), how could it be that the elixir of inspiration seems to be primarily concocted by women and predominantly imbibed by men?

8 It appears that the answer has to do with sexual selection. Does this explain how our species went from hunting and gathering to mass-producing iPhones and airplanes? There are many pieces to that puzzle. The relationship between sex and creativity might be one of them.

Questions for Discussion

1. Is McNerney persuasive in his argument? What is his evidence?
2. What type of essay is this?
3. McNerney's work comes from a blog. Do you believe that online writing should be held to the same standards as print works? Are blogs a valid form of writing?
4. What is McNerney's attention-getter in this piece? It is effective? Who do you think his audience is?

Online Freedom Will Depend on Deeper Forms of Web Literacy

Navneet Alang

1 Recently, Google ruined my life. I may be exaggerating slightly, given that all they did was redesign and tweak Google Reader, one of their many services that I use daily and for which I pay nothing. But Reader, an admittedly niche product that lets you read articles from many websites in one place, has become my online home. It is the thing that organizes and makes sense of the sprawling, incoherent mass of the Internet and collects it on one familiar light-blue page.

2 So when Google swooped in and changed things, I felt as if someone had rearranged all my furniture like in some undergraduate prank. Making matters worse, the ability to share things with other Reader users was now gone—sacrificed to the company's need to push their new social network, Google+. Not only had they redecorated the place; they had gone and redone all the wiring, too—and I was stranded in this newly alien environment that used to seem like home.

3 There were, however, those who had the tools and wherewithal to respond. People—people far more tech-savvy than me—used a browser plug-in called Greasemonkey to write pieces of code that magically restored the old Google Reader to me. Greasemonkey, as its auto mechanic–derived name suggests, lets you pop open the hood of your web browser and mess around, and there's almost no end to what you can do with it.

4 It isn't something just anyone can pick up, however. In order to create your own personalized experience of the web, you need to know how to code or, at the very least, wait for someone else to do it for you. And that requirement highlights a simple fact about the online world: if you aren't literate in the languages of digital technology, your capacity to control your own experience is constrained. From the latest outrageous Facebook redesign that millions of people freak out over, to subtle tweaks to the ways in which Twitter operates, many of us—even those like me who really care about this stuff—find ourselves powerless to suit the web to our own needs.

5 It's a problem that will require immensely complex solutions, primarily in how we conceive of education. If today we teach kids language and rhetoric so that one day they might pick apart politicians' speeches or learn to recognize a scam (and let's face it, we're not even doing that very well), we may soon have to do something analogous for programming skills. Much

---

Navneet Alang, "Online Freedom Will Depend on Deeper Forms of Literacy," found in *This Magazine*, February 13, 2012. Used by permission of the author, Navneet Alang.

as "freedom of the press" was only ever true for those who owned [a press], protecting our freedoms online is going to require millions more people to better understand just how [the Internet] works. Even those "digital natives" you hear about—the terrifying Tweeting, texting tweens—seldom have even the foggiest idea of how their favourite websites work. They can update their Facebook status without breaking stride, but could they code even a rudimentary equivalent? Vanishingly few could.

6 Thankfully, in the meantime there are intermediate bits of software that simplify and automate some aspects of coding so that those of us who can't tell JavaScript from HTML can still control our digital lives in novel, unexpected ways. Take new service ifttt.com, for example. An acronym for "if this, then that," ifttt allows you to cobble together dozens of commonly used web services to suit your own needs. Perhaps you want to know when a friend has posted a new picture on Flickr. Hook it up to ifttt, and it can send you an email, a text message, even a phone call alerting you that your friend has uploaded their latest cat photo.

7 It isn't quite idiot-proof. Yet it's also a far cry from Greasemonkey and other programming-based tools because it asks you to think in terms you already know, rather than in sophisticated new ones you must learn. And in a sense, this is the strange paradox of access and control on the web. On one hand, you are subject to the companies who become the default ways of connecting online, making you subject to their interests. On the other, the freer, less corporate versions of the web offer you tools to tweak how you use those services and to what end. It is—until coding literacy becomes the norm—almost akin to the economics of the 1920s or the 2000s: with the tools of power centralized among a tiny few, the public is left at the mercy of those in control.

8 To get a sense of what is at stake, though, one need only turn to the ambivalent story of Diaspora*. In 2010, a four-person team of young programmers from New York University's Courant Institute of Mathematical Sciences set out to build an alternative to Facebook that would address privacy worries and protect user data. Their announcement hit, however, amidst heightened concerns over Facebook's record on privacy, and the team was thrown into a harsh spotlight, especially after a fundraising campaign suddenly netted them $200 000. Their plan was to create a Facebook with none of the drawbacks of Facebook, a task even Google can't manage to do. Tragically, in late 2011 one of the four founders, 22 year-old Ilya Zhitomirskiy, was found dead, apparently after committing suicide.

9 No one knows, of course, if the pressure of trying to build an alternative to an all-powerful website contributed to Zhitomirskiy's decision to take his life. But it's an unsettling symbol of something—of how difficult it is for even young, brilliant programmers to take control of their and our online experience from multibillion-dollar entities. And, if truth be told, a redesign of a website is but a minor inconvenience. But the capacity of web firms to "rewire" whole swaths of our day-to-day lives is nonetheless ominous. It's also a sign that, in future, freeing oneself from their grasp will come from seizing their tools and methods as our own, and learning how to code.

Questions for Discussion

1. What is the thesis of this piece? Is it convincing?
2. Does the introduction effectively gain the reader's attention? Why or why not?
3. Is this piece argumentative or merely persuasive? Discuss with a partner.

Running head: USING TECHNOLOGY 1

Using Technology to Fight Depression

Leah Brown

Mohawk College

Using Technology to Fight Depression

Depression is a common yet severe mental illness that affects everyone, either directly or indirectly though family, friends, or coworkers. Major depressive disorder, more commonly referred to as just "depression," is more than just feeling sad or having a bad day. The Canadian Mental Health Association describes depression by saying that "Someone experiencing depression is grappling with feelings of severe despair over an extended period of time. [...] For people with depression, it does not feel like there is a "light at the end of the tunnel"—there is just a long, dark tunnel" (2016, para. 1). Despite the fact that there are effective treatments for depression, people are not always able to seek help for it. Factors such as lack of resources and social stigma against mental illness can keep people from accessing the appropriate treatment. Because of this, many people just suffer in silence, assuming there is no help out there for them. This situation may seem dire, but there are other options. Technology is available that can help us learn more about the disease, develop new resources to assist people who are dealing with depression, and give people easy access to support through the internet.

Technology is capable of helping us learn about depression as a disease, and how it physically affects the body. This kind of information is invaluable when it comes to learning how to treat depression more effectively and to discover ways of preventing it. As Black states, "Brain imaging may help pick out people more likely to experience recurring depression and help design preventive treatment" (2003, para. 9). Doctors are also using technology to learn about the biology of the disease by looking at hormones, genes and neurochemicals. This knowledge will lead to the development of more effective treatments, like new forms of antidepressants that "work in different pathways and affect different hormones and chemicals in the brain than today's medication" (Black, 2003, para. 23). Depression is a complex disease, and doctors are still fighting to understand it. However, these glimpses into how depression affects people will pave the way to find more efficient ways to treat and prevent it. In addition to assisting doctors and researchers in obtaining this kind of new information, technology also allows for the spread of information. Using the internet, information can easily be shared with people all over the world, bringing together the brightest minds to help develop new treatments. Knowledge is power, and having access to scientific findings from all over the world can only be a positive in the fight against depression. Not only is technology helping us learn more about the physical realities of depression, it is also leading to the development of apps that aid in diagnosing the disease and in symptom management.

Researchers are leading the way in developing apps and other resources which can be used by people experiencing depression in a variety of ways, such as helping diagnose the disease, and helping people manage their symptoms. For people who have trouble accessing effective medical treatment for depression, technology can offer another way to get support. According to Ziv, "Technological tools to flag mental health problems could have a huge impact on [people who lack access to mental health care, who] could use an easily downloadable app for early screening instead of jumping through hoops to find a qualified clinician just to start the process" (2014, para. 5). Apps can be used to self-diagnose, which helps people understand what they are experiencing and know what sort of professional help to seek. This kind of free and accessible help could save lives. While resources like apps would never replace trained professionals, they could help streamline the process or manage symptoms while waiting to receive professional care. Carol Epsy-Wilson, a professor of computer and electrical engineering at the University of Maryland, hopes one day to develop a single streamlined app that will be "a tool, a Siri on steroids, that can track mental health outside of formal treatment or between therapy sessions" (Ziv, 2014, para. 15). There are already many apps that track people's thoughts and moods and offer advice on things like mindfulness and, as we learn more about how to use the technology available to us, we can create even more effective tools based on thorough research into this developing field. In addition to revealing more about the nature of depression and developing new apps to help people in the future, technology as it exists right now is an amazing tool that can provide people with easy access to much needed support via online resources.

The internet is full of websites that offer support for people dealing with depression, as well as information for concerned friends and family on how to better help their loved ones. For example, one quick Google search will bring up the website for a local Crisis Outreach and Support Team in Hamilton, Ontario, which offers a 24 hour a day crisis line and a "mobile team, consisting of a mental health worker, and a police officer, will respond to crisis calls between the hours of 8 a.m. and 1 a.m. daily" (COAST, 2016). This is only one of the many professional resources available to people with depression and their families. People can also post about their experiences online and find others who have gone through the same thing. People suffering from depression can connect with peers as well as professionals, and find encouragement and validation when they need it most, or anonymously access advice or resources. Thanks to modern technology, all of this is easily accessible to anyone with an internet connection. This kind of support is vital, not only because of the staggering number of people suffering from depression, but because "at its worst, depression can lead to suicide. Over 800 000 people die due to suicide every year" (WHO, 2016, para. 1). The internet can give people the unique opportunity to find a safe community with others who understand them and what they are going through. This connection, this kinship, can not only help destroy the stigma surrounding depression, it can even save lives.

We live in a world oversaturated with technology. The argument can be made that modern technology, like the internet and social media, makes things worse for people dealing with mental illnesses like depression. However, there are undeniable positive effects of this technological revolution as well. Technology allows us to learn how diseases like depression affect the body and facilitates the spread of medical knowledge. Researchers are using this information to develop and improve apps that can help detect depression and help people manage their symptoms. The internet is already being used every day to connect people: to each other, to mental health professionals, and to supportive communities that only exist online. These developments and resources are completely fundamental to society's wellbeing as, according to the World Health Organization, "globally, an estimated 350 million people of all ages suffer from depression" (2016, para. 1). If you think someone in your life is struggling with depression, take advantage of the vast amount of knowledge available to you online and learn about what you can do to support them. Being able to easily access this information makes a world of difference to someone experiencing a severe depressive episode who is feeling scared or alone. For me, the internet has been a place of solace, and being able to connect with other people online has saved me more than once. Technology, like any complex issue, can be difficult to understand and can seem daunting. However, I believe that technology is a powerful tool in the fight against depression and, if harnessed correctly, can provide crucial support for those suffering from depression.

USING TECHNOLOGY 5

References

Black, D. (2003, June 7). Using cutting-edge technologies, researchers are getting closer to revolutionary new treatments 'There are going to be huge breakthroughs over the next 10 years,' says one doctor. *Toronto Star*, p. A23

Canadian Mental Health Association—CMHA. (2016). *Depression*. Retrieved from http://www.cmha.ca/mental-health/understanding-mental-illness/depression

Crisis Outreach and Support Team Hamilton—COAST. (2016). *Depression*. Retrieved from https://coasthamilton.ca/?page_id=93

World Health Organization—WHO. (2016). *Depression: Fact sheet*. Retrieved from http://www.who.int/mediacentre/factsheets/fs369/en

Ziv, S. (2014, November 21). Technology's latest quest: Tracking mental health. *Newsweek, 163*(20).

Questions for Discussion

1. Define what type of essay the author is writing and outline the thesis as well as the introductory attention-getter.
2. What level of language does the author use? Is the author clearly writing to a specific audience? If yes, who is that audience?
3. Review the concluding paragraph. Is it effective in bringing together the main points of the paper? Why or why not?
4. How does the author use research? What type of documentation is used? Is the research used effectively? Accurately? Are there improvements that could be made?
5. Can you see spots in the paper that need editing? Do you have any advice for the author on how to improve the paper?

B. Ferguson
Prof. G. Jennings
ENGL 10050
30 November, 2010

No More Classes, No More Books: Online vs. Traditional Schooling

At the Techonomy Conference in California this past August, Microsoft founder Bill Gates, when asked about the future of higher education, said that "place-based" education was going to have to face a new reality. Why be so tied to a physical collection of buildings and campuses? "Five years from now on the web for free you'll be able to find the best lectures in the world," Gates said. "It will be better than any single university" (Zabudsky par. 7). He's not alone in predicting a fundamental change in education. The education sector, too, recognizes that students' days of sitting in lecture halls and copying notes off a blackboard are numbered, if not already gone. There are many reasons behind this belief, but three are heard most often: the rapid advances in informational technology, the growing demand from a generation of students who have grown up with instant knowledge at their fingertips, and the changing economic realities facing students and administrators alike. As Jeff Zabudsky, CEO of Sheridan Institute of Technology and Advanced Learning, points out, "Institutions of all kinds are reinventing themselves to cope with changing times" (par. 2).

The first two concerns, advancement and demand, are closely related. Educators now face rooms full of students who are not only savvy enough to find information on the internet, but turn it to as their first, free, fast source of information. Asking those same students to pay tuition fees to learn book-based material seems almost ridiculous. Educators realize that they may have to justify their methods, as well as keep current with information and innovation in their field. They're investing serious money and effort in exploring alternative learning methods such as blended or online delivery. As Zabudsky writes, "The laptop is today's pencil and we must find more ways to get the learning out of our institutions and onto students' screens" (par. 8).

The economic challenges in education had been making administrators nervous even before the current global downturn. The government has pledged to raise the proportion of university- and college-educated Canadians to 70% in the coming years (Zabudsky par. 8), but has not pledged any additional funds to the schools themselves. Thus tuition fees will likely continue to rise, and so will the common public perception of post-secondary education as available only to the wealthy. Then, if enrolment declines, tuition fees will rise again to cover the cost of operating and maintaining the "place-based" environment of a school campus. Put this spiral alongside the students' preference for technologically-based learning, and there is "an intensifying realization on the part of students, educators and government that bricks and mortar no longer constitute the only way to experience education" (Zabudsky par. 6).

So what will the future of education look like? No one knows for sure, but most seem to agree that the current model will see fundamental changes. Jeff Zabudsky suggests at least four major changes, including integrating more technology into the classroom delivery; operating campuses more efficiently (such as offering full course options throughout the year, rather than scaling back during the summer); improving access to higher education to all sectors of society, and, finally, encouraging all educators to customize course material to the needs of the field (2010). Apprenticeships and hands-on training programs are already on the rise, as more employers demand skilled graduates. That on-the-job learning is seen as key to a student's later career, and coincidentally saves the classroom time and cost to the college. Online courses, too, save the operating costs of a classroom, offer access to those in distant locations, and have limitless multimedia resources available at the click of a mouse button. Want to quickly double your school's enrollment capacity? Have an instructor teach a course to a classroom full of students while simultaneously being video-streamed online to another hundred students scattered across the country. For those who can't fit that class into today's schedule, the lecture is stored electronically for later access.

However, that virtual classroom, and other possibilities of tech-savvy learning, will only be possible if the school has invested heavily in the infrastructure of technology: computers for all students, easy internet access including wireless networking, and of course server, storage and bandwith capability enough to handle thousands of simultaneous users.

Not all schools have the budget or the capacity to do that anytime soon—or not soon enough to satisfy the growing clamour from their students.

At the same time, educators are concerned about those students who learn best through real-life, face-to-face interaction with a teacher and fellow students. Will they still have classrooms available to learn in? Will the classic image of a vibrant, tree-lined campus fade into history? For that matter, some ask, how problematic is it to ask online students to complete assignments or tests, without any real guarantee that the student enrolled is the one doing the work? Will a respected institution find itself awarding a degree to a student who paid a friend to do the work? How would the school even find out? Would it fall to an employer to discover the student doesn't know the work after all?

Some suggest that perhaps technology will solve that thorny problem, too. Others, like McMaster University's Dr Nick Bontis, assert that "Ivy-covered buildings, theatre-style classrooms, residence life, cafeteria food and beer drinking can never be duplicated through a network connection" (Bontis par. 4). It seems clear that colleges and universities across Canada are facing some major decisions. The possibilities stretch beyond the horizon, but educators and administrators will need to do some careful looking to see a clear path.

Ferguson 4

Works Cited

Bontis, N. "Traditional university education to be supplemented by options." *Hamilton Spectator*, 20 November 2010, p. T6. *TheSpec* online. Accessed 25 Nov. 2010.

Zabudsky, J. "Post-secondary educators need to go back to school." *Toronto Star*, 5 September 2010, p. A19. *TheStar* online. Accessed 23 Nov. 2010.

**Note:* Ideally the URL would be included in these online citations. However, these were not noted when collecting data for the original 2010 version of this article, and thus cannot be reproduced here. ~BF

Questions for Discussion

1. Define what type of essay the author is writing and outline the thesis as well as the introductory attention-getter.
2. What level of language does the author use? Is the author clearly writing to a specific audience? If yes, who is that audience?
3. Review the concluding paragraph. Is it effective in bringing together the main points of the paper? Why or why not?
4. How does the author use research? What type of documentation is used? Is the research used effectively? Accurately? Are there improvements that could be made?
5. Can you see spots in the paper that need editing? Do you have any advice for the author on how to improve the paper?

Mislabelled by Society

Syneba Mitchell

Sunday April 10, 2016

Every child has the right to learn in a safe learning environment, and feel included amongst their peers. The idea of segregating special needs students from a regular classroom only fuels the stigma about mental illness. It is hard enough for children and teenagers to find their place while at school, as that is the place they spend most of their time during the week. When special needs students are segregated it only puts emphasis on their disability. Throughout this essay we will be looking at why segregating special needs students is ineffective, why educators need the necessary training for working with special needs students and lastly the importance of erasing mental health stigmas amongst young people.

Students with special needs are often looked at differently from their peers who don't have any disabilities. And though in some sense students with special needs have to be treated differently, it is not effective to segregate them. As Liza Long, writer of the article "Don't Segregate My Special Needs Child" pointed out,

> But by not integrating children with mental illness, which admittedly sometimes manifests through challenging behavioral symptoms like unpredictable rage, into the general school population, we are contributing to the ongoing stigma of mental illness. Worse, more often than not we are condemning these children to prison. (Long, 2014)

Continuing with her idea of condemning children with special needs to prison, a lot of that is connected to societal norms. Most of their major social interactions are done while at school, everything they do is applicable to society. The way they are taught, their actions and so on. Their environments also influence their behavior, which makes them a product of their society. A school setting parallels many aspects of a prison such as set times for lunch and leisure activity, and punishments for those who don't follow the rules. School in general molds children to be sheep within society. Made to follow rules that may not necessarily benefit them in the long run, to act and behave in certain ways and when there are those who do not fit societal norms, they are treated differently.

Regarding the basis of this paper, the way society looks at those with a mental illness is not a positive outlook. They are looked down upon, treated differently which also effects the way they interact within a social setting. Neurotypicals have taken it upon themselves to be the judges in society which in turn places children with disabilities in a prison that has already been created for them. They aren't given the chance to treated like their classmates and they spend their entire school career being seen as just their disability. Some would argue that it is not fair that their child's learning environment should be disrupted by the child with a learning disability (Long, 2014), but what needs to be remembered is that children need to be taught that they are all equal. By having that outlook on how their child should be educated it takes away from the idea that all children have the right to an education.

Furthermore, looking at the idea that there can be ways for children with or without a disability to be taught in an inclusive learning environment. In order to create the steps necessary, it starts with the educators. Educators have to be taught on how to effectively work with a special needs child. Teachers are not always aware of what could trigger their students, and that is certainly something they should be taught. Language is very complex, and with special needs children it could simply be the word or how it is said that could trigger aggressive or dissociative behavior. For example, the special needs child and the teacher could agree on a safe space where the child could go if they are not feeling comfortable or if they are having an episode. What this does is it allows the child to still be apart of the classroom while also allowing them to pace themselves and not feel singled out. This also eliminates the disruption it may have on their classmates. Too often, teachers, are presented with students for whom they are unprepared to teach (Pratt, 1997). That sentences rings true, as there are special needs classes for children that completes takes them out of the classroom setting. The curriculum for future teachers does not offer the tools to work with special needs children. As Cathy Pratt stated,

> At a very basic level, teachers will need to know the primary characteristics associated with autism spectrum disorders. While it is important to ensure that information is not stigmatizing to the student, teachers need to know about any areas of difficulty, special talents, and other important information. (Pratt, 1997)

If the teacher is given the necessary tools to work with a special needs child, they will be able to create lesson plans that can accommodate their entire class. Ensuring that it is inclusive also helps with the child's social interactions, allowing them to have that confidence amongst their peers. Creating alternative spaces for the child also helps in creating an overall positive learning environment. It is the little things that count, such as the lightning of the room or the placement of their desk which can also contribute their behavior within the classroom. If the demands of the school day become too intense, it may be necessary to provide the student with a safe area in which to escape (Pratt, 1997). Allowing the child to want to be apart of the class is important, especially when they are not seen differently by their peers, in the sense that they should not be seen as their disability but as their classmate who has a disability.

Lastly, by not defining the child as their disability it helps to erase the stigma that surrounds mental illness. One way to look at it is, there would not be a need for awareness organizations like *Bell Talks* or books like *Price of Silence* by Liza Long. The reasons for organizations or books as such, is because there is an evident cloud of negativity connected to those who have a mental illness that society has created. One of the biggest factors of that would be the media painting people with mental illness to be 'crazy' or 'violent'. Society is a selfish place where everyone has to better that the other person. If everyone saw each other as equals, then parents with special needs children would not be feeling the backlash for putting their children in exclusive academic programs. Because children with special needs are looked down upon and certainly treated differently from their neurotypical classmates, a riff is created. In movies, characters dealing with a mental illness hardly ever get seen in a positive light, and if they do it is seen a comedic relief, like in the movie *The Hangover*. By creating that sort of outlook on people experiencing mental illness, neurotypicals create a certain stereotype they associate with neuroatypicals. These stereotypes hinder those with special needs from creating more connections with their neurotypical peers, and in way puts them in a box from everyone else. Along with these stereotypes come blame, and a lot of the time the parents and the children are blamed for the child's special needs. It is not the child or the parent's fault for their condition, and a lot of people fail to put themselves in their shoes. Stigma can be shown in little ways too, like a father not taking his kid to the park because he knows the other parents do not feel comfortable around his kid. The stigma of mental illness does not only affect the child but it also affects the parents. These stigmas condemn children to inferior education at best (Long, 2014), and because of that their chances are taken away from them before they can begin. By talking about mental illness and educating their classmates it allows these children to be seen as who they are and not their disability.

To conclude, segregation of children with special needs robs them of the opportunities to create connections with their neurotypical classmates, hinders them from building social skills and also to feel apart of the class. Also providing teachers with the right tools to effectively work with special needs children will also create an overall positive learning environment for children with or without special needs. By taking those steps it also teaches the generations to come about how to end the stigma of mental illness by seeing those children as more than just their disability. It gives them the tools to look at everyone on an equal playing field and to also put themselves in their positions and see that society needs to make changes in what they deem as 'normal'. Society fears what they do no understand, and because of that children with special needs are treated poorly. By working towards ending those stigmas, those children have a chance to be accepted into society for who they are.

References

Long, L. (2014). Children with Special Needs Are Often Condemned to Inferior Education and Even Incarceration. Retrieved from http://www.alternet.org/books/children-special-needs-are-often-condemned-inferior-education-and-even-incarceration

Long, L. (2014). Don't Segregate My Special Needs Child. Retrieved from http://time.com/3257982/special-needs-children-education

Pratt, C. (1997). There is No Place Called Inclusion. Retrieved from http://www.iidc.indiana.edu/pages/There-is-No-Place-Called-Inclusion

Questions for Discussion

1. Define what type of essay the author is writing and outline the thesis as well as the introductory attention-getter.
2. What level of language does the author use? Are the author clearly writing to a specific audience? If yes, who is that audience?
3. Review the concluding paragraph. Is it effective in bringing together the main points of the paper? Why or why not?
4. How does the author use research? What type of documentation is used? Is the research used effectively? Accurately? Are there improvements that could be made?
5. Can you see spots in the paper that need editing? Do you have any advice for the author on how to improve the paper?

SILBERT PAGE 1

Dancing with Language: Don Quijote's Words and Consensual Reality

By: Emily Silbert

October 31, 2000

For: Prof. Mary Nyquist

Literary Studies II - VIC210Y

SILBERT PAGE 2

Throughout Miguel de Cervantes' *Don Quijote*, readers watch the protagonist perform a dance with language. If *Don Quijote* the novel is about the tension between the textual reality of chivalric romance that Don Quijote devours and the experiential world of the concrete, it is impalpable language that like a dance, transports, binds and finally separates Don Quijote from the world around him. This experiential reality is one shared by the characters in the novel interacting with Don Quijote and readers alike, one that is repeatedly affirmed verbally not only by the individuals Don Quijote meets but also repeatedly affirmed silently by the reader. This reality can be called consensual, recalling the discussion in class on this topic. One has only to take a closer look at the first half of the fiftieth chapter in Volume One of Don Quijote, from the beginning of the chapter to "except that I fear he hasn't the ability to take charge of such an estate"[1] as a perfect example of a passage that illuminates how Don Quijote's choice of language transports the reader, attempts to persuade, but finally repels the reader and consequently those who believe in the consensual reality.

As he attempts to convince the Cathedral priest of the inherent value in reading chivalric romances, Don Quijote describes the plot of a chivalric tale in an extremely detailed and convincing manner. A mighty castle Don Quijote describes has "solid gold walls, parapets of diamond, and gates of topaz,"[2] and is built out of "diamonds, garnets, rubies, pearls, gold and emeralds."[3] Don Quijote's choice of words, the references in particular to pearls, diamond and gold, recall Zoraida, who is described as she appeared to the captive: "more pearls hung from her lovely neck, her ears and her hair than she had hairs on her head; on her ankles…she wore two *carcajes*…of the purest gold, set with so many diamonds."[4]

By recalling Zoraida, a character who figures prominently in an in-set narrative, readers are reminded of the nature of in-set narratives to transport readers and cause them to forget about Don Quijote. Similarly, Don Quijote, in his use of descriptive, jewelled language,

---

[1] Cervantes, P.340
[2] Cervantes, P.339
[3] Cervantes, P.339
[4] Cervantes, P.280

carries the reader off and causes him or her to forget about our hero. Then suddenly, the long-winded Don Quijote decides to drive his point home and cuts off his speech, saying, "I've no wish to draw this out any further."[5] Caught in the act of being enthralled, the reader becomes sheepishly aware of the power of language to transport them into an imaginary, textually based reality. The dangerous nature of being transported by language and books recalls Prospero in Shakespeare's The Tempest, who, "being transported and rapt in secret studies"[6] lost the Dukedom of Milan to his usurping brother. This same danger has already been revealed throughout the text as we watch our hero attempting to live out a textual reality and being constantly physically and verbally assaulted.

Don Quijote's language in the passage we are examining is obviously concerned with persuasion. Don Quijote blatantly says to the cathedral priest, "Just believe me, your grace, as I've already told you, and read these books."[7] Trying to persuade him to read chivalric romance, another incident is recalled. Later in the text another priest assaults Don Quijote verbally for his belief in the value of chivalric romances and Don Quijote says it isn't sensible, "without full knowledge of the sin being censured, to simply label the sinner an out and out dolt and a fool."[8] However, both times Don Quijote is verbally assaulted by the priests, he responds with pleas to read the books but doesn't fully substantiate why. The most effective way of persuading is to be specific and give examples. Where he should be persuading, with specific examples, the reason these books should be read, Don Quijote instead concludes with an oath to God and a declaration of virtuous desire that Fortune will allow him to give Sancho Panza a count's title. We later read that the cathedral priest, who represents consensual reality, was "astonished by what beautifully organized nonsense Don Quijote had spoken."[9]

Language can be used to persuade but it can also obfuscate. Obviously, from the priest's statement, he is not convinced by Don Quijote's reasoning. Why is that? When language is general, it can end up as something that hides instead of illuminates. Because the reader has been reminded of the ease with which he/she can be transported by language and the dangers inherent in that, careful inspection of

---

[5] Cervantes, P.339

[6] Shakespeare, William. *The Tempest*, ed. Stephen Orgel. New York: Oxford University Press, p.105

[7] Cervantes, P.339

[8] Cervantes, P.527

[9] Cervantes, P.341

Don Quijote's language seems to be a good idea. Don Quijote's appeal to God and virtuous desire to give his squire a count's title appeal to the emotions but serve no other purpose. Don Quijote attempts to reason why one should read chivalric romance when he states that, "a reader—any reader whatever—will be delighted and astonish at what he finds."[10] His choice of language here is interesting. He does not state what inherent value the reader will find, just that they will be astonished. His use of the word 'astonish,' while it is an effective word for piquing interest, is general and does not serve to explain the value of the books.

Don Quijote does attempt to explain the influence of the books on the reader in a more specific manner saying that since he has been a knight errant—something which resulted from his reading these books—Don Quijote has been "brave, courteous, open-handed."[11] Most of his adventures however, have gone poorly and the reader quickly recalls this when Don Quijote acknowledges to having just been shut up like a madman in a crate—though he would attribute this to enchantment.

Don Quijote states that, "Here we have books printed by royal license, after careful inspection…and how can they be mere lies, how can they only seem to be true"?[12] Don Quijote's choice of words show that he believes at least some of the inherent factual value of these virtuous and valorous books lies in the fact that royalty licenses them. The reader recalls however, that in *Don Quijote* royal licence also sanctioned the slavery of the galley slaves. As well, another earlier text we have studied is recalled, one relevant to Cervantes' time that was also authorized by royal license. This was the Requerimiento of 1513, where the King and Queen of Spain demand obedience from the conquered world or "shall do you all the mischief and damage that we can...and we protest that the deaths and losses which shall accrue from this are your fault, and not that of their Highnesses, or ours, nor of these cavaliers who come with us."[13] Don Quijote's imagination or madness somehow allows his reality to be one where royalty is as valorous as he is. For readers, the factual nature of chivalric romance is somewhat more hidden behind simple sentences.

---

[10] Cervantes, P.339
[11] Cervantes, P.340
[12] Cervantes, P.338
[13] Greenblatt, Stephen J. "Learning to Curse: Aspects of Linguistic Colonialism in the Sixteenth Century." *First Images of America*. Ed. Freddie Chiapelli. 2 vols. Berkeley: U of California Press, 1976 Vol 2, P. 573

SILBERT PAGE 5

Don Quijote's reasoning, because of his choice of language, examples general in nature, and belief in the factual history of chivalric romance simply do not persuade the Cathedral priest or the readers of the value in reading chivalric romance. Because of his deviation from consensual reality, we find ourselves held to our hero only by a thin thread. It is Don Quijote's choice of language that both ties and separates the reader from Don Quijote, our hero. And paradoxically, it is intangible language that acts as a rope tying Don Quijote to the corporeal, consensual world, just as he has been tied to a rope attached to a doorknob, earlier in the text, stuck dangling by his arm in the straw hole of the inn. Language ties him to the world, but his imagination, his belief and attempts to live out a reality that exists only in texts, leaves him dangling like the feet that were "constantly deceiving themselves with the hope that, with just a little more effort, they really can and will reach the ground."[14]

---

[14] Cervantes, P.303

Questions for Discussion

1. Define what type of essay the author is writing and outline the thesis as well as the introductory attention-getter.
2. What level of language does the author use? Is the author clearly writing to a specific audience? If yes, who is that audience?
3. Review the concluding paragraph. Is it effective in bringing together the main points of the paper? Why or why not?
4. How does the author use research? What type of documentation is used? Is the research used effectively? Accurately? Are there improvements that could be made?
5. Can you see spots in the paper that need editing? Do you have any advice for the author on how to improve the paper?

Part 9

Workbook

This part of *Essay Essentials* is a workbook designed to improve the accuracy of your writing. In Chapters 23 through 26, we look at the errors that give many writers trouble, whether they are writing student papers, professional reports, PowerPoint presentations, or office correspondence. This workbook will provide you with all the tools you need in editing and formalizing your work. Even though most of us feel we know the basic skills in writing, we often have gaps or inconsistent learning in the more formal elements. Finding a good set of standard practices, such as you will get here, is essential for good essay writing.

CHAPTER 23

A Review of the Basics

How to Use This Workbook

The material presented here is prepared in an easy-to-access format and is organized into four areas:

- A Review of the Basics
- Grammar
- Punctuation
- Spelling

This material might be used by your instructor throughout your course or simply referenced as something you can work through on your own time. Regardless, you will find not only a lot of information presented here but also many exercises to help you improve and expand the skills you already have.

In each section, we do three things: explain a point, illustrate it with examples, and provide exercises in the text and on the website to help you master the point. The exercises are arranged in sets that become more difficult as you go along. By the end of the last set in each chapter, you should have a good grasp of the skill. You will lose that grasp, however, if you do not practise. To maintain and reinforce mastery of the skills you are learning, make a conscious effort to apply them every time you write.

The basics in Chapter 23 cover the larger aspects of writing—sentences, sentence-structure issues such as run-ons and fragments, and modifier problems. It also covers parallelism, important to any research report or workplace writing, and sentence combining. Chapter 24 is the grammar section, covering subjects, verbs, and pronouns. Punctuation is the topic of Chapter 25, featuring essential information on commas, semicolons, colons, quotation marks, dashes, parentheses, and question and exclamation marks. The final workbook chapter, Chapter 26, focuses on spelling challenges such as homonyms, apostrophes, hyphens, capital letters, and numbers.

Here's how to proceed in each section:

1. Read the explanation. Do this even if you think you understand the point being discussed.

2. Study the highlighted rules and the examples that follow them.

3. Turn to the exercises. Try at least one set even if you are confident that you understand the principle.

4. **Always check your answers to each set of exercises before going on to the next.** Only if you check your answers after every set can you avoid repeating your mistakes or—worse—reinforcing your errors. For those exercises marked with an asterisk (*), you will find the answers in the back of the

book. For exercises on the website, the answers are marked automatically, so you will know instantly whether you have understood the material.

5. When you make a mistake, go back to the explanation and examples and study them again. Try making up some examples of your own to illustrate the rule. If you are truly stuck, check with your instructor. You can reinforce your understanding by doing the exercises on the website.
6. At the end of each section, there is a mastery test marked with the icon shown in the right margin. Your instructor can provide you with the answers for these tests. Use these tests to help track your progress as you master basic writing skills.

On the inside front cover, you will find a "Quick Revision Guide." Use it to ensure that you have covered all the essentials before handing in your paper.

On the inside back cover, you will find a list of correction marks commonly used by instructors to draw your attention to specific errors. Use this list to be sure you've eliminated all errors your instructor has previously identified in your writing. (Teachers are paid, in part, to pay attention to student errors. So, even if you choose not to track your errors from one assignment to the next, you can be assured your teacher will.)

Cracking the Sentence Code

There is nothing really mysterious or difficult about sentences; you've been speaking them since you were two. The difficulty arises when you try to write not sentences, oddly enough, but paragraphs. Most college or university students, if asked to write 10 sentences on 10 different topics, could do so without error. However, when those same students write paragraphs, then fragments, run-ons, and other sentence faults appear.

The solution to sentence-structure problems has two parts.

> Be sure every sentence you write
> 1. has both a subject and a verb
> 2. expresses a complete thought

If English is your first language, your ear may be the best instrument with which to test your sentences. If you read a sentence aloud, you may be able to tell by the sound whether it is complete and clear. Sometimes, however, your ear may mislead you, so this section will show you, step by step, how to decode your sentences to find their subjects and verbs. When you know how to decode sentences, you can make sure that every sentence you write is complete.

Read these sentences aloud.

> **Every lab assistant should wear protective gloves.**
> **Although every lab assistant should wear protective gloves.**

The second "sentence" doesn't sound right, does it? It does not make sense on its own and is, in fact, a sentence fragment.

Testing your sentences by reading them aloud won't work if you read your paragraphs straight through from beginning to end. The trick is to read from the end to the beginning. That is, read your last sentence aloud and *listen* to it. If it sounds all right, then read aloud the next-to-last sentence, and so on, until you have worked your way back to the first sentence you wrote.

Now, what do you do with the ones that don't sound correct? Before you can fix them, you need to decode each sentence to find out if it has both a subject and a verb. The subject and the verb are the bare essentials of a sentence. Every sentence you write must contain both. There is one exception:
Consider these examples.

> In a **command**, the subject is suggested or implied rather than stated.

Sign here. = [You] sign here. (The subject you is implied or understood.)
Charge it. = [You] charge it.
Play ball! = [You] play ball!

Finding Subjects and Verbs

A sentence is about *someone* or *something*. That someone or something is the **subject**. The word (or words) that tells what the subject *is* or *does* is the **verb**. In the following sentences, the subject is underlined once and the verb twice.

Snow falls.
Kim dislikes winter.
We love snowboarding.
Mt. Whistler offers excellent opportunities for winter sports.
In Canada, winter is six months long.
Some people feel the cold severely.

The subject of a sentence is always a **noun** (the name of a person, place, thing, or concept) or a **pronoun** (a word such as *I, you, he, she, it, we,* or *they* used in place of a noun). In the examples above, the subjects include persons (*Kim, we, people*); a place (*Mt. Whistler*); a thing (*snow*); and a concept (*winter*). In one sentence, a pronoun (*we*) is the subject.

> Find the verb first.

One way to find the verb in a sentence is to ask what the sentence says about the subject. There are two kinds of verbs:

- **Action verbs** tell you what the subject is doing. In the examples above, *falls, dislikes, love,* and *offers* are action verbs.
- **Linking verbs** link or connect a subject to a noun or adjective describing that subject. In the examples above, *is* and *feel* are linking verbs.

  Linking verbs tell you the subject's condition or state of being (e.g., "Tadpoles *become* frogs," "Frogs *feel* slimy"). The most common linking verbs are forms of *to be* (*am, is, are, was, were, have been,* etc.) and verbs such as *look, taste, feel, sound, appear, remain, seem,* and *become*.

Another way to find the verb in a sentence is to put a pronoun *I, you, he, she, it,* or *they*) in front of the word you think is the verb. If the result makes sense, it is a verb. For example, you could put *it* in front of *falls* in the first sentence listed above: "it falls" makes sense, so you know *falls* is the verb in this sentence. Try this test with the other five example sentences.

Keep this guideline in mind as you work through the exercises below.

> To find the subject, ask who or what the sentence is about.
> To find the verb, ask what the subject is or is doing.

Exercise 23.1*

In each of the following sentences, underline the subject with one line and the verb with two. Answers for exercises in this section begin on page 467. If you make even one mistake, go to the website and do the exercise listed beside the Web icon that follows this exercise. Be sure you understand this material thoroughly before you go on.

1. Canadians love doughnuts.
2. We eat more doughnuts than any other nation.
3. Doughnuts taste sweet.
4. Glazed doughnuts are my favourite.
5. Most malls contain at least one doughnut shop.
6. Hot chocolate is good with doughnuts.
7. Try a bran doughnut for breakfast.
8. Bran is good for your health.
9. Doughnut jokes are common on television.
10. Dentists like doughnuts too, but for different reasons.

> Usually, but not always, the subject comes before the verb in a sentence.

Occasionally, we find the subject after the verb:

- In sentences beginning with *Here* + a form of *to be* or with *There* + a form of *to be*
  Here and *there* are never the subject of a sentence.

  Here are the test results. (Who or what are? Results.)
  There is a fly in my soup. (Who or what is? A fly.)

- In sentences that are deliberately inverted for emphasis

  Finally, at the end of the long, boring joke came the pathetic punch line.
  Out of the stadium and into the pouring rain marched the parade.

- In questions

  Are we there yet?
  Is she the one?

  But notice that in questions beginning with *who, whose, what, where,* or *which,* the subject and verb are in normal order: subject followed by verb.

  Who took my car?
  What caused the accident?
  Whose car came first?
  Which car runs best?

Exercise 23.2* Underline the subject with one line and the verb with two. Watch out for inverted sentences.

1. There are many errors here.
2. She likes the Rolling Stones.
3. Chew quickly.
4. Here, under the bench, we found the ring.
5. The dancing girl got a lot of attention.
6. After summer, things really started to heat up.
7. Here is my essay.
8. In 2001, I started using a cellphone every day.
9. After buying my cellphone, I bought a computer.
10. Here is my famous spaghetti.

More about Verbs

The verb in a sentence may be a single word, as in the exercises you've just done, or it may be a group of words. When you are considering whether or not a word group is a verb, there are two points you should remember:

1. No verb preceded by *to* is ever the verb of a sentence.[1]
2. **Helping verbs**[2] are often added to **main verbs**.

The list below contains the most common helping verbs.

be (all forms of *to be* can act as helping verbs: e.g., *am, are, is, was, were, will be, have/had been,* etc.)	can could/could have do/did have/had may/may have might/might have	must/must have ought shall/shall have should/should have will/will have would/would have

The complete verb in a sentence consists of the main verb together with any helping verbs.

Here are a few of the forms of the verb *write*. Notice that in questions the subject may come between the helping verb and the main verb.

You may write now.
He certainly can write!
We should write home more often.
I shall write tomorrow.
He could have written yesterday.
She is writing her memoirs.
Did he write to you?
You ought to write to him.
We will have written by then.
He had written his apology.
I will write to the teacher.
The proposal has been written.
Orders should have been written.
Could you have written it in French?

One verb form *always* takes a helping verb. Here is the rule:

A verb ending in *-ing* MUST have a helping verb (or verbs) before it.

Here are a few of the forms an *-ing* verb can take:

I am writing the report.
Is she writing the paper for him?
You are writing illegibly.
I was writing neatly.
You will be writing a report.
They must have been writing all night.
Have you been writing on the wall?

Beware of certain words that are often confused with helping verbs.

Words such as *not, only, always, often, sometimes, never, ever*, and *just* are NOT part of the verb.

---

[1] The form *to* + verb—for example, *to speak, to write, to help*—is an infinitive. Infinitives can act as subjects, **objects**, or modifiers, but they are never verbs.

[2] If you are familiar with technical grammatical terms, you will know these verbs as **auxiliary verbs.**

These words sometimes appear in the middle of a complete verb, but they are modifiers, not verbs. Do not underline them.

> I have just won a one-way ticket to Victoria.
> She is always chosen first.
> Most people do not welcome unasked-for advice.

Exercise 23.3* **Underline the subject once and the complete verb twice.**

1. I am making a healthy breakfast.
2. It does not include Coca-Cola.
3. You can add fresh fruit to the cereal.
4. The toast should be almost ready now.
5. My doctor has often recommended yogurt for breakfast.
6. I could never eat yogurt without fruit.
7. With breakfast, I will drink at least two cups of coffee.
8. I don't like tea.
9. I simply cannot begin my day without coffee.
10. I should probably switch to decaf.

More about Subjects

Often groups of words called **prepositional phrases** come before the subject in a sentence or between the subject and the verb. When you're looking for the subject in a sentence, prepositional phrases can trip you up unless you know the following rule:

> The subject of a sentence is never in a prepositional phrase.

You must be able to identify prepositional phrases so that you will know where *not* to look for the subject.

> A prepositional phrase is a group of words that begins with a **preposition** and ends with a noun or a pronoun.

The noun or pronoun is called the *object of the preposition*. It is this word that, if you're not careful, you might think is the subject of the sentence.

Below is a list of prepositional phrases. The words in red print are prepositions; the words in black are objects of the prepositions.

about the book
above the desk
according to the book
across the street
after the meeting
against the wall
along the hall
among the books
around the office
before lunch
behind the desk
below the window
beside the book
between the desks
by the book
concerning the memo
despite the policy
down the hall
during the speech
except the staff
for the manager
from the office
in an hour
inside the office
into the elevator
like the book
near the wall
of the typist
on the desk
onto the floor
over a door
through the window
to the staff
under the book
until the meeting
up the hall
with a book
within a day
without them

Before you look for the subject in a sentence, cross out all prepositional phrases.

The keyboard ~~of your computer~~ should be cleaned occasionally.

What should be cleaned? The keyboard (not the computer).

Regardless ~~of the expense~~, one ~~of us~~ should go ~~to the IT conference in Las Vegas~~.

Who should go? One (not the group).

Exercise 23.4*

In the following sentences, first cross out the prepositional phrase(s), then underline the subject once and the verb twice.

1. In Canada, poutine is considered a national treasure.

2. I felt lost among the books in the large library.

3. Over dinner, we discussed our upcoming wedding.

4. You shouldn't stand under the new construction.

5. Joel's laughter at the clowns in the park made me smile.

6. During the fall, I ate apples every day.

7. Despite my workload, I still completed the essay on time.

8. Through the school year, I don't let texting rule my life.

9. In high heels and a long skirt, I still was able to run from the werewolf at the prom.

10. The house beside Sylvia's is for sale.

Multiple Subjects and Verbs

So far, you have been decoding sentences containing a single subject and a single verb, even though the verb may have consisted of more than one word. Sentences can, however, have more than one subject and one verb, called **compounds**. Multiple subjects are called *compound subjects*; multiple verbs are *compound verbs*.

Here is a sentence with a compound subject:

> Esquimalt and Oak Bay border the city of Victoria.

This sentence has a compound verb:

> She groped and stumbled her way down the aisle of the darkened movie theatre.

And this sentence has a compound subject and a compound verb:

> The detective and the police sergeant leaped from their car and seized the suspect.

The parts of a compound subject or verb are usually joined by *and* (sometimes by *or*). Compound subjects and verbs may contain more than two elements, as in the following sentences:

> Thoughtful planning, careful organization, and conscientious revision are the keys to good essay writing.
>
> I finished my paper, put the cat outside, shut off my cellphone, and crawled into bed.

Exercise 23.5* In the following sentences, cross out all prepositional phrases, then underline the subjects once and the verbs twice. Be sure to underline all the elements in a compound subject or verb. Check your answers before continuing.

1. Management and union met for a two-hour bargaining session.
2. They debated and drafted a tentative agreement for a new contract.
3. The anesthetist and the surgeon scrubbed for surgery and hurried to the operating room.
4. Frederick Banting and Norman Bethune are considered medical heroes around the world.

5. Kevin and Sandor hiked and cycled across most of Newfoundland.

6. My son or my daughter will meet me and drive me home.

7. Knock three times and ask for Stanislaw.

8. In the 17th and 18th centuries, the French and the English fought for control of Canada.

9. Buy the base model and don't waste your money on luxury options.

10. Ragweed, goldenrod, and twitch grass formed the essential elements in the bouquet for his English teacher.

Here's a summary of what you've learned in this section. Keep it in front of you as you write the mastery test.

Sentence Code Summary

- The subject is *who* or *what* the sentence is about.
- The verb tells what the subject *is* or *does*.
- The subject normally comes before the verb (exceptions are questions and sentences beginning with *there* or *here*).
- The complete verb = a main verb + any helping verbs.
- By itself, a word ending in *-ing* is not a verb.
- An infinitive (a phrase consisting of *to* + a verb) is never the verb of a sentence.
- The subject of a sentence is never in a prepositional phrase.
- A sentence can have more than one subject and/or verb.

Exercise 23.6

This challenging exercise will test your ability to find the main subjects and verbs in sentences. In each sentence below, first cross out any prepositional phrases, and then underline each subject with one line and each verb with two lines. Be sure to underline all elements in a multiple subject or verb.

1. The politicians of all parties try in vain to change the world, but they seldom try to change themselves.

2. In the past, men and women had clearly defined roles and seldom broke away from them.

3. Police, firefighters, and paramedics comforted, rescued, and treated my aunt and uncle after their car accident.

4. Among the many kinds of cheese made in Canada are Camembert, Fontina, and Quark.

5. French fries, gravy, and cheese curds are the ingredients in traditional Quebec poutine.

6. Increasingly, in high-end restaurants, chefs are experimenting with Canadian foods like elk meat, fiddlehead greens, and Saskatoon berries.

7. On the Lovers' Tour of Lake Louise were two elderly women with walkers, a couple of elderly gentlemen with very young wives, half a dozen middle-aged divorcées, and my younger sister Margaret.

8. Negotiate in English, swear in German, argue in Spanish, and speak of love in French.

9. After the rain, the sun came out, the birds sang, and the tourists returned to their chairs by the pool.

10. According to its campaign literature, the incoming government will provide jobs for all Canadians, eliminate the national debt, find a cure for cancer, land a Canadian on Mars, and reduce income tax by 50 percent, all in its first year in office!

Solving Sentence-Fragment Problems

Every complete sentence has two characteristics. It contains a subject and a verb, and it expresses a complete thought. Any group of words that is punctuated as a sentence but lacks one of these characteristics is a **sentence fragment**. Fragments are appropriate in conversation and in some kinds of writing, but normally they are unacceptable in school, technical, and business writing.

There are two kinds of fragments you should watch out for: the "missing-piece" fragments and the dependent-clause fragments.

"Missing-Piece" Fragments

Sometimes a group of words is punctuated as a sentence but is missing one or more of the essential parts of a sentence: a subject and a verb. Consider these examples.

1. **Found it under the pile of clothes on your floor.**

   Who or what found it? The sentence doesn't tell you. The subject is missing.

2. **Their arguments about housework.**

   The sentence doesn't tell you what the arguments were or did. The verb is missing.

3. **During my favourite TV show.**

   Who or what was or did something? Both subject and verb are missing.

4. **The programmers working around the clock to trace the hacker.**

   Part of the verb is missing. Remember that a verb ending in *-ing* needs a helping verb to be complete.

Finding fragments like these in your work when you are revising is the hard part. Fixing them is easy. There are two ways to correct sentence fragments. Here's the first one.

To change a "missing-piece" fragment into a complete sentence, add whatever is missing: a subject, a verb, or both.

1. You may need to add a subject:

   Your sister found it under the pile of clothes on your floor.

2. You may need to add a verb:

   Their arguments were about housework. (linking verb)
   Their arguments about housework eventually destroyed their relationship. (action verb)

3. You may need to add both a subject and a verb:

   My mother always calls during my favourite TV show.

4. Or you may need to add a helping verb:

   The programmers have been working around the clock to trace the hacker.

Don't let the length of a fragment fool you. Students sometimes think that if a string of words is long, it must be a sentence. Not so. No matter how long the string of words, if it doesn't contain both a subject and a verb, it is not a sentence. For example, here's a description of a student overwhelmed by frustrating circumstances:

With his assignment overdue and penalty marks eating into the grade he had hoped to achieve, and his computer behaving

A Review of the Basics

erratically thanks to a virus that his roommate had downloaded while playing Texas Hold 'Em against a gamer somewhere in Arkansas, the same roommate who was now in the next room with four of his friends loudly cheering on their favourite team—the Calgary Flames—during the Western Conference semifinals against his own beloved Canucks.

At 75 words, this "sentence" is long—but it is a fragment. It lacks both a subject and a verb. If you add to the end of the fragment, "Dennis broke down and sobbed," you would have a complete sentence.

In the following exercises, decide whether each group of words is a complete sentence or a "missing-piece" fragment. Put *S* before each complete sentence and *F* before each fragment. In Exercise 23.8, make each fragment into a complete sentence by adding whatever is missing: the subject, the verb, or both. Then compare your answers with our suggestions.

Exercise 23.7*

___ Social media is not unlike a party. ___ Fun, but can also get out of hand very quickly. ___ *Facebook* should be blocked in schools. ___ Because my friends are bullied. ___ Also, I have seen many students on *Facebook* instead of doing their homework. ___ In fact, parents should have to sign on to social media for their children. ___ And should get emails of all *Facebook* posts. ___ Making social media safe should be a priority. ___ The people who bully on *Facebook* must think they can get away with it. ___ Often because they can.

Exercise 23.8*

1. ___ We laughed.
2. ___ Calling during the TV show.
3. ___ She checked it out.
4. ___ To create my own espresso.
5. ___ Trying to gather up my courage, I handed him the résumé.
6. ___ Changing into a bad person.
7. ___ About this party.
8. ___ After changing my cellphone plan.
9. ___ Want to get the most out of the course.
10. ___ Wanting to catch up, she ran faster.

Dependent-Clause Fragments

Any group of words containing a subject and a verb is a **clause**. There are two kinds of clauses. An **independent clause** is one that makes complete sense on its own. It can stand alone, as a sentence. A **dependent clause**, as its name suggests, cannot stand alone as a sentence; it depends on another clause to make complete sense.

Dependent clauses (also known as *subordinate clauses*) begin with dependent-clause cues (**subordinating conjunctions** or relative pronouns). Here is a partial list of common dependent-clause cues:

Dependent-Clause Cues

after	if	until
although	in order that	what, whatever
as, as if	provided that	when, whenever
as long as	since	where, wherever, whereas
as soon as	so that	whether
because	that	which, whichever
before	though	while
even if, even though	unless	who, whom, whose

Whenever a clause begins with one of these words or phrases, it is dependent.

> A dependent clause must be attached to an independent clause. If it stands alone, it is a sentence fragment.

Here is an independent clause:

I am a terrible speller.

If we put one of the dependent-clause cues in front of it, it can no longer stand alone:

Because I am a terrible speller.

We can correct this kind of fragment by attaching it to an independent clause:

Because I am a terrible speller, I carry a smartphone with a dictionary.

Exercise 23.9*

Put an *S* before each item that contains an independent clause and is therefore a sentence. Put an *F* before each clause that is dependent and therefore a sentence fragment. Circle the dependent-clause cue in each sentence fragment.

1. ___ Before we watched the zombie movie.
2. ___ Because we wanted the shoes.
3. ___ That was nice to hear.
4. ___ Unless the homework is complete.
5. ___ While we were at the mall.

Exercise 23.10* **Identify the sentence fragments in the paragraph below by highlighting the dependent-clause cue in each fragment you find.**

[1]Although many companies are now experiencing difficulty because of tough economic times. [2]Middle managers seldom breathe easily even during times of expansion and high profits. [3]In difficult times, middle managers are vulnerable to the cost-cutting axe. [4]As companies seek to reduce overhead. [5]In times of fast growth, the executive branch of many companies expands rapidly. [6]Which leads to a surplus of managerial talent, especially among junior executives. [7]And it is these younger, well-educated, ambitious young hires who can threaten middle managers. [8]Who have reached, or overreached, their potential. [9]Whether it is through termination, early retirement, or buyout. [10]Such mid-level executives are the first to feel the effects of a company's desire to streamline the hierarchy in good times or eliminate paycheques in bad times.

Most sentence fragments are dependent clauses punctuated as sentences. Fortunately, this is the easiest kind of fragment to recognize and fix. All you need to do is join the dependent clause either to the sentence that comes before it or to the one that comes after it—whichever linkage makes better sense.

Read the following example to yourself; then read it aloud (remember the proofreading hint to read the last sentence first).

> Montreal is a sequence of ghettos. Although I was born and brought up there. My experience of French was a pathetically limited and distorted one.

The second "sentence" sounds incomplete, and the dependent-clause cue at the beginning of it is the clue you need to identify it as a sentence fragment. You could join the fragment to the sentence before it, but then you would get "Montreal is a sequence of ghettos, although I was born and brought up there," which doesn't make sense. The fragment should be linked to the sentence that follows it, like this:

> Montreal is a sequence of ghettos. Although I was born and brought up there, my experience of French was a pathetically limited and distorted one. (Mordecai Richler)

If, as in the example above, your revised sentence *begins* with the dependent clause, you need to put a comma after it. If, however, your revised sentence *ends* with the dependent clause, you don't need a comma between it and the independent clause that precedes it.

My experience of French was limited although I was born and brought up in Montreal.

See The Comma, Rule 3 (pages 400–401).

Exercise 23.11*

Return to Exercise 23.10 and revise it by joining each dependent clause fragment to an independent clause that precedes or follows it, whichever makes better sense.

Exercise 23.12*

The items in these exercises each contain three clauses, one of which is dependent and therefore a fragment. Highlight the dependent clause fragment in each item.

1. Walking is probably the best form of exercise there is. Unless you're in the water. Then swimming is preferable.

2. Rain doesn't bother me. I like to stay inside and read. When the weather is miserable.

3. Please try this soup. After you've tasted it. I am sure you'll be able to tell me what's missing.

4. Whenever Ashley gets the opportunity. She loves to dance. But her boyfriend hates dancing, so she seldom gets the chance to show off her moves.

5. The report identifies a serious problem that we need to consider. Whenever our website is revised or updated. It is vulnerable to hackers.

Exercise 23.13

As a final test of your skill in finding and correcting sentence fragments, try this exercise. Make each fragment into a complete sentence.

1. I had never eaten curry. But the first time I tasted it. I decided I liked it.

2. In France, they say that an explosion in the kitchen could have disastrous results. Such as linoleum blown apart.

3. Our family thinks my sister is too young to get married. Since she and her boyfriend want to be registered at Toys "R" Us.

4. It may surprise you to know that Canadians have made significant contributions to world cuisine. Two of the best known being baby pabulum and frozen peas.

5. Bathing the family cat. It's an activity that carries the same risks as tap dancing in a minefield. Or juggling with razor blades.

6. After working for three nights in a row trying to make my essay perfect so that I would get a high grade in my course. I lost my entire project when my brother crashed the computer while playing *Candy Crush Saga*.

7. I decided to take swimming lessons for two reasons. The first is fitness. Second, water safety.

8. There is good news. The man who was caught in an upholstery machine has fully recovered.

9. All of us are more aware of the effects of pollution now than we were 10 years ago. Because we are continually bombarded with information about the environment and our impact on it. In school, on television, and in newspapers.

10. My second favourite household chore is ironing. The first being hitting my head on the top bunk bed until I faint. (Erma Bombeck)

Solving Run-On Problems

Some sentences lack certain elements and thus are fragments. Other sentences contain two or more independent clauses that are incorrectly linked together. A sentence with inadequate punctuation between clauses is a **run-on**. Run-ons tend to occur when you write in a hurry, without first organizing your thoughts. If you think about what you want to say and punctuate carefully, you shouldn't have any problems with them.

There are two kinds of run-on sentences to watch out for: comma splices and fused sentences.

Comma Splices and Fused Sentences

As its name suggests, the **comma splice** occurs when two complete sentences (independent clauses) are joined together with only a comma between them. Here's an example:

> I am deeply in debt, I cut up my credit cards.
> The tunes are good, the lyrics are not.

A **fused sentence** occurs when two complete sentences are joined together with no punctuation at all:

> I am deeply in debt I cut up my credit cards.
> The tunes are good the lyrics are not.

There are four ways to fix run-on sentences.

1. Make the independent clauses into separate sentences.

> I am deeply in debt. I cut up my credit cards.
> The tunes are good. The lyrics are not.

2. Separate the independent clauses with a comma followed by one of these words: *for, and, nor, but, or, yet,* or so (remembered by the acronym **FANBOYS**).[3]

> I am deeply in debt, so I cut up my credit cards.
> The tunes are good, but the lyrics are not.

3. Make one clause dependent on the other by adding one of the dependent-clause cues listed on page 339.

> Because I am deeply in debt, I cut up my credit cards.
> I cut up my credit cards because I am deeply in debt.
> Although the tunes are good, the lyrics are not.

Your turn:

> The tunes are good ______________________________.

4. Use a semicolon, either by itself or with a transitional word or phrase, to separate independent clauses. (See page 407.)

> I am deeply in debt; I cut up my credit cards.
> The tunes are good; however, the lyrics are not.

Note: All four solutions to comma splices and fused sentences require you to use a word or punctuation mark strong enough to come between two independent clauses. A comma by itself is too weak, and so is a dash.

The sentences in the following exercises will give you practice in fixing comma splices and fused sentences. Correct the sentences where necessary and then check your answers, beginning on page 470. Since there are four ways to fix each sentence, your answers may differ from our suggestions. If you find that you're confused about when to use a semicolon and when to use a period, be sure to read page 407 before going on.

Exercise 23.14*

1. The doctor is busy right now you will have to wait.

2. Press on the wound that will stop the bleeding.

---

[3] These words are called **coordinating conjunctions** because they are used to join equal (or coordinating) clauses, phrases, or words. If you are not sure how to punctuate sentences with coordinating conjunctions, see The Comma, Rule 2 (page 400).

3. Don't let your worries kill you, let the church help. (Sign outside a church)

4. I can't read it the print is too small.

5. Here is my number, give me a call.

6. Consider hiring an event planner, you cannot arrange this function by yourself.

7. Eat sensibly exercise regularly die anyway.

8. That was a great dive, you get a perfect 10.

9. Listen to this man play, he's a jazz–blues musician who calls himself Dr. John.

10. No one in the department supports the chair because he's arrogant and lazy.

Exercise 23.15*

1. Computers do not prevent mistakes they just make them faster.

2. I'm trying to stop playing computer games, they take up too much of my time.

3. I'm innocent, this is a case of mistaken identity.

4. Time is the best teacher, unfortunately, it kills all its students.

5. Place your hands on the table, and do not open your eyes.

6. The microwave oven is the most important appliance in my home, without it, I'd starve.

7. Money may not be everything, it is far ahead of whatever is in second place.

8. Allow enough time to complete the project, a rush job is not acceptable.

9. Teachers are finding more and more students who went from printing straight to using a keyboard, they have never learned cursive script.

10. These students are at a huge disadvantage during exams, it takes far longer to print block capitals than it does to write cursive script.

Exercise 23.16

As a final test of your ability to identify and correct run-on sentences, find and correct the 10 errors in the following paragraphs.

After the last time we went into the haunted house, I decided I won't be doing it again. I think it really is haunted. My friends and I did it the first time on a dare. We took my friend Monica's car and drove up to the old mansion, it was almost midnight last Halloween. My parents had gone on a business trip. There were three of us there, and we were all afraid, we went into the house anyway since we had flashlights. It was easy to get in because there were so many broken windows. I almost tripped getting in but made it through. My heart was racing, it was so dark. Once we were inside, things really started to get creepy we heard noises everywhere and creaking floors. I tried to laugh them off, saying it was just the house settling. I called out to my friends in the dark, but they didn't answer me, I couldn't see them, so I started moving quickly, calling their names. I was freaking out! Then, after a few minutes, I felt a hand on my shoulder, pushing me toward a staircase going up. I thought it was Monica, it was so pitch-dark I couldn't tell. I went up.

When I got to the top, I really freaked out, there was Monica and my other friend. I looked behind me to see who had been pushing me up the stairs, but no one was there. I thought I saw a strange glow but blinked it away. I told them what had happened, they didn't believe me, we were still freaked out though, so we decided to leave, sprinting back to the car. This Halloween we're just going out for candy, being old enough to drive is great, but I won't be going to any more haunted houses.

Solving Modifier Problems

Oscar was complimented on a great game and a fine job of goaltending *by his mother.*

Snarling furiously and baring his teeth, Maurice crawled through a basement window only to confront an angry watchdog.

When she was a first-year student, the English professor told Sofya she would *almost* write all her assignments in class.

These sentences show what can happen to your writing if you aren't sure how to use modifiers. A **modifier** is a word or phrase that adds information about another word in a sentence. In the examples above, the italicized words are modifiers. Used correctly, modifiers describe, explain, or limit another word, making its meaning more precise. Used carelessly, however, modifiers can cause confusion or, even worse, amusement.

You need to be able to recognize and solve two kinds of modifier problems: **misplaced modifiers** and **dangling modifiers**.

Misplaced Modifiers

Modifiers must be as close as possible to the words they apply to. Usually, readers will assume that a modifier modifies whatever it's next to. It's important to remember this because, as the following examples show, changing the position of a modifier can change the meaning of your sentence.

Jason walked only as far as the corner store. (He didn't walk any farther.)

Jason only walked as far as the corner store. (He didn't jog or run.)

Only Jason walked as far as the corner store. (No one else went.)

Jason walked as far as the only corner store. (There were no other corner stores.)

> To make sure a modifier is in the right place, ask yourself "What does it apply to?" and put it beside that word or word group.

When a modifier is not close enough to the word it refers to, it is said to be *misplaced*. A misplaced modifier can be a single word in the wrong place:

The supervisor told me she needed someone who could use both Word and Excel badly.

Is some compawny really hiring people to do poor work? Or does the company urgently need someone familiar with word- and data-processing programs? Obviously, the modifier *badly* belongs next to *needed*.

The supervisor told me she badly needed someone who could use both Word and Excel.

Be especially careful with these words: *almost, nearly, just, only, even, hardly, merely, scarcely*. Put them right before the words they modify.

Misplaced: Caro nearly answered every question.

Correctly placed: Caro answered nearly every question.

Misplaced: After driving all night, we almost arrived at 7:00 a.m.

Correctly placed: After driving all night, we arrived at almost 7:00 a.m.

A misplaced modifier can also be a group of words in the wrong place:

She died in the home in which she had been born at the age of 89.

The modifier *at the age of 89* is too far away from the verb it is supposed to modify, *died*. In fact, it seems to modify *had been born,* making the sentence ridiculous. We need to rewrite the sentence:

She died at the age of 89 in the home in which she had been born.

Look at this one:

I drove my mother to Saskatoon, where my aunt lives in her old car.

In her old car applies to *drove* and should be closer to it.

I drove my mother in her old car to Saskatoon, where my aunt lives.

Notice that a modifier does not always need to go right next to what it modifies; it should, however, be as close as possible to it.

Occasionally, as in the examples above, the modifier is obviously out of place. The writer's intention is clear, and the sentences are easy to correct. But sometimes modifiers are misplaced in such a way that the meaning is not clear, as in the following example:

David said after the game he wanted to talk to the press.

Did David *say* it after the game? Or does *he want to talk to the press* after the game? To avoid confusion, we must move the modifier and, depending on which meaning we want, write either

After the game, David said he wanted to talk to the press.

or

David said he wanted to talk to the press after the game.

In Exercises 23.17 and 23.18, rewrite the sentences that contain misplaced modifiers, positioning them as closely as possible to the words they modify. Check your answers to the first set before continuing. Answers for this section begin on page 471.

Exercise 23.17*

1. The Argos only lost by six points.
2. They just closed before five.
3. I applied for every job that was posted almost.
4. The French nearly drink wine with every meal, including lunch.
5. On the first day of Sarah's new exercise program, she was only able to walk 500 metres.
6. I had scarcely answered 12 of the 25 questions when time was up.
7. We went camping in a national park with lots of wildlife in August.
8. I have been fired nearly every week that I have worked here.
9. The attack submarine approached the tanker, nearly 20 metres under the water.
10. Steven Spielberg predicted an "inevitable implosion" in the film industry this week.

Exercise 23.18*

1. *Essay Essentials* is designed to help college and university students learn to write good prose with clear explanations and lots of exercises.
2. Each year, half a million Canadian men almost have a vasectomy.
3. Juan caught sight of a doe and her two fawns with his new binoculars.
4. Vancouver is a wonderful city for anyone who likes rain and fog to live in.
5. Some games are less demanding in terms of fitness and strength, such as Scrabble and Settlers of Catan.

6. Thanks to my new camera, I can take professional-quality pictures with digital functions.

7. We looked for a suitable retirement gift for our boss online.

8. The Canadian Human Rights Act prohibits discrimination against anyone who is applying for a job on the basis of race, religion, sex, or age.

9. One finds the best Chinese food in restaurants where the Chinese eat usually.

10. Tonight, Liam Neeson will talk about his wife, Natasha Richardson, who died after falling on a ski slope at Mont Tremblant with George Stroumboulopoulos.

Dangling Modifiers

A dangling modifier occurs when the sentence does not contain a specific word or idea to which the modifier could sensibly refer. With no appropriate word to modify, the modifier seems to apply to whatever it's next to, often with ridiculous results.

> **After a good night's sleep, my teachers were impressed with my unusual alertness.**

This sentence seems to say that the teachers had a good night's sleep.

> **Trying desperately to finish an essay, my roommate's CD player made it impossible to concentrate.**

The *CD player* was writing an essay?

Dangling modifiers are harder to correct than misplaced ones; you can't simply move danglers to another spot in the sentence. There are, however, two ways in which you can fix them. One way requires that you remember the following rule:

> When a modifier comes at the beginning of a sentence, it almost always modifies the subject of the sentence.

This rule means that you can avoid dangling modifiers by choosing the subjects of your sentences carefully.

> 1. Ensure the subject is an appropriate one for the modifier to apply to.

Using this method, we can rewrite our two examples by changing the subjects.

After a good night's sleep, I impressed my teachers with my unusual alertness.

Trying desperately to finish an essay, I found it impossible to concentrate because of my roommate's CD player.

2. Change the dangling modifier into a dependent clause.

Using this rule, the dangling modifiers have been revised as dependent clauses (in blue print).

After I had had a good night's sleep, my teachers were impressed with my unusual alertness.

When I was trying desperately to finish an essay, my roommate's CD player made it impossible to concentrate.

Sometimes a dangling modifier comes at the end of a sentence:

A Smart car is the one to buy when looking for efficiency and affordability.

Can you correct this sentence? Try it; then look at the suggestions at the foot of the page.

Below is a summary of the steps to follow in solving modifier problems.

Modifier Summary

1. Ask "What does the modifier apply to?"
2. Be sure there is a word or group of words *in the sentence* for the modifier to apply to.
3. Put the modifier as close as possible to the word or word group it applies to.

Exercise 23.19* Most of the following sentences contain dangling modifiers. Correct each sentence by using whichever solution given on pages 471–472 best suits your purpose. There is no one right way to correct these sentences; our answers are only suggestions.

1. Having heard the end of the murder trial, a decision had to be made.

2. Knowing about the upcoming restructuring, her résumé was always kept up to date.

Here are two suggestions:

1. Add a subject: Looking for efficiency and affordability, I decided a Smart car was the one to buy.
2. Change the dangler to a dependent clause: A Smart car is the one to buy since I am looking for efficiency and affordability.

3. He showers before getting into bed.

4. Having tested the speed and RAM, MacBook Pros are great.

5. After finishing the roof, the decaying mansion still flooded.

6. To be eligible for the reward, the cat must be returned.

7. At the age of 21, graduation was only days away.

8. After working all day, movies are a good way to relax.

9. Walking down the street, rain started pouring down.

10. While texting my friends, the food was delivered.

Exercise 23.20*

In the following sentences, correct the misplaced and dangling modifiers in any way you choose. Our answers on page 472 are only suggestions.

1. Only she was the baker's daughter, but she could loaf all day.

2. Being horribly hungover, the problem with a free bar is knowing when to quit.

3. Rearing and kicking, Samson finally got the terrified horse under control.

4. In a hurry to get to the interview on time, my résumé was left lying on my desk at home.

5. As a college student constantly faced with new assignments, the pressure is sometimes intolerable.

6. Listening to the rumours, the newlyweds are already on the road to separation.

7. As a non-drinker, the liquor in the duty-free outlet is of no interest.

8. The bride was given in marriage by her father, wearing a strapless gown with a short lace jacket.

9. Rolling on her back, eager to have her tummy scratched, Queen Elizabeth couldn't resist the little Corgi puppy.

10. Wearing a small Canadian flag on your backpack or lapel, people abroad will be less likely to assume you're American.

Exercise 23.21 **As a final test of your ability to use modifiers, correct the misplaced and dangling modifiers in the sentences below, using any solution you choose.**

1. Obviously having drunk too much, I drove poor Taniya to her apartment, made her a pot of coffee, and called her mother.
2. When trying for your Red Cross bronze medal, your examiner will evaluate your speed, endurance, and resuscitation techniques.
3. The Riel Rebellion this month will be featured in *Canadian History* magazine.
4. Sinking like a ball of fire below the horizon, our sailboat was the perfect vantage point from which to watch the setting sun.
5. Not being reliable about arriving on time, I can't hire her to supervise others who are expected to be punctual.
6. While they were in my pocket, my children managed to break my glasses by leaping on me from behind.
7. Combining comfortable accommodation and economical travel, my wife and I find a camper van ideal for travelling both here and abroad.
8. The only used motorcycles we could find were in overpriced dealerships that were in good condition.
9. After submitting the lowest bid that met all the developer's criteria, not being awarded the contract was bitterly disappointing.
10. This bus has a seating capacity of 56 passengers with a maximum height of four metres. (Sign on a double-decker bus in Charlottetown)

The Parallelism Principle

Brevity, clarity, and force: these are three characteristics of good style. **Parallelism** will reinforce these characteristics in everything you write.

When your sentence contains a series of two or more items, they must be grammatically parallel. That is, they must be written in the same grammatical form. Consider this example:

> Sophie likes *swimming*, *surfing*, and *to sail*.

The three items in this series are not parallel. Two are nouns ending in *-ing*, but the third, *to sail*, is the infinitive form of the verb. To correct the sentence, you must put all the items in the same grammatical form. You have two choices. You can write

> Sophie likes *swimming*, *surfing*, and *sailing*. (all nouns)

Or you can write

> Sophie likes *to swim*, *to surf*, and *to sail*. (all infinitives)

Now look at this example with two non-parallel elements:

> Most people seek happiness in long-term relationships and work that provides them with satisfaction.

Again, you could correct this sentence in two ways. You could write "Most people seek happiness *in relationships that are long-term* and *in work that provides them with satisfaction*," but that solution produces a long and clumsy sentence. The shorter version works better: "Most people seek happiness in *long-term relationships* and *satisfying work*." This version is concise, clear, and forceful.

> Correct faulty parallelism by writing all items in a series in the same grammatical form: all words, all phrases, or all clauses.

One way to tell whether the items in a series are parallel is to write them out in list form, one below the other. That way, you can see at a glance if all the elements are in the same grammatical form.

Not Parallel	Parallel
My brother is messy, rude, and an obnoxious person.	My brother is *messy, rude,* and *obnoxious*.
(This list has two adjectives and a noun phrase.)	(This list has three adjectives.)
I support myself by delivering pizza, poker, and shooting pool.	I support myself by delivering pizza, playing poker, and shooting pool.
(This list has two phrases and one single word as objects of the preposition *by*.)	(This list has three phrases as objects of the preposition *by*.)
Jules wants a job that will interest him, that will challenge him, and that pays well.	Jules wants a job that will interest him, that will challenge him, and that will pay him well.
(This series of clauses contains two future tense verbs and one present tense verb.)	(All three subordinate clauses contain future tense verbs.)

A Review of the Basics

As you can see, achieving parallelism is partly a matter of developing an ear for the sound of a correct list. A parallel sentence has a smooth, unbroken rhythm. Practice and the exercises in this chapter will help. Once you have mastered parallelism in your sentences, you will be ready to develop ideas in parallel sequence—in thesis statements, for example—and thus to write clear, concise prose. Far from being a frill, parallelism is a fundamental characteristic of good writing.

Correct the sentences where necessary in the following exercises. As you work through these sentences, try to spot parallelism errors from the change in rhythm that the faulty element produces. Then revise the sentence to bring the faulty element into line with the other elements in the series. Check your answers to each set of 10 before going on.

Exercise 23.22*

1. This program is easy to understand, and using it is not difficult, either.
2. We were told to leave and that we should take everything with us.
3. We organized our findings, wrote the report, and finally our PowerPoint presentation was prepared.
4. Both applicants were unskilled, not prepared, and lacked motivation.
5. Elmer's doctor advised that he should be careful with his back and not to strain his mind.
6. The company is looking for an employee who has a car, and knowledge of the city would be a help.
7. If consumers really cared, they could influence the fast-food industry to produce healthy, delicious food that doesn't cost very much.
8. When I want to get away from it all, there are three solitary pleasures I enjoy: a walk in the country, reading a book, and music.
9. A recent survey of female executives claims that family responsibilities, being excluded from informal networks, and lacking management experience are the major factors keeping them from advancement.

10. If it is to be useful, your report must be organized clearly, written well, and your research should be thorough.

Exercise 23.23*

1. For my birthday, I requested either a Roots bag or a scarf from Dior.

2. In my community, two related crimes are rapidly increasing: drug abuse and stealing things.

3. Bodybuilding has made me what I am today: physically perfect, very prosperous financially, and practically friendless.

4. After reading all the explanations and all the exercises have been completed, you'll be a better writer.

5. Bruce claimed that, through repetition and giving rewards, he had trained his centipede to be loyal and demonstrate obedience.

6. During their vacation in New Brunswick, Trevor and Jamal visited many beautiful locations and wonderful seafood.

7. I'm an average tennis player; I have a good forehand, my backhand is average, but a weak serve.

8. The problem with being immortalized as a statue is that you will be a target for pigeon droppings and artists who write graffiti.

9. Never disturb a sleeping dog, a baby that is happy, or a silent politician.

10. I'd like to help, but I'm too tired, and my time is already taken up with other things.

Exercise 23.24*

Make the following lists parallel. In each case, you can make your items parallel with any item in the list, so your answers may differ from ours.

Example:	Incorrect:	report writing	program a computer
	Correct:	report writing	computer programming
	Also correct:	write a report	program a computer

1. Incorrect: Correct:	laughter	trusting	dancing
2. Incorrect: Correct:	giving a speech	talk loudly	
3. Incorrect: Correct:	ideals	foundations	discussing
4. Incorrect: Correct:	paper	lots of staples	
5. Incorrect: Correct:	slowly	fast	
6. Incorrect: Correct:	democracy	fascist	anarchy
7. Incorrect: Correct:	cram	learning	teaching
8. Incorrect: Correct:	punctual	friendliness	honest
9. Incorrect: Correct:	French	English	Germanic
10. Incorrect: Correct:	dancing all night	to go out during the day	

Exercise 23.25* Correct the faulty parallelism in these sentences.

1. Trying your best and success are not always the same thing.

2. Maya's symptoms included a high fever, severe headaches, and joints that ached painfully.

3. I hold a baseball bat right-handed but play hockey left-handed.

4. A good student attends all classes and projects are always finished on time.

5. Small businesses must be creative and show flexibility if they are to succeed in this economy.

6. Rain that pours down in buckets, driving snow, and freezing temperatures are only a few of the conditions that make road construction in Alberta a challenge.

7. Licking one's fingers and to pick one's teeth in a restaurant are one way to get attention.

8. A good teacher motivates with enthusiasm, informs with sensitivity, and is a compassionate counsellor.

9. In the simplest terms, health is defined by four factors: age, current level of physical fitness, nutritional health, and genetics.

10. Henry Lieberman, a computer scientist with MIT, found that cyberbullying attacks fall into one or more of five categories: the way you look, intelligence, racial identification, ethnicity, and sexual preference.

Exercise 23.26

As a test of your mastery of parallel structure, correct the errors in the following paragraph.

Working at a pharmacy is a challenging and rewarding endeavour. Not only must you work long hours, not many breaks, and talk to many people, but you also have to be calm and have patience. Dispensing drugs can be dangerous, it can require time, and results in legal issues when mistakes are made. With perseverance, being dedicated, and practice, however, being a pharmacy assistant can be very rewarding. Further education and being reliable can lead to raises or promotions. I suggest if you want a career that focuses on helping others, working with medicine and to interact with the public, working at a pharmacy is for you!

Refining by Combining

To reinforce what you've learned about sentence structure, try your hand at **sentence combining**, a technique that enables you to avoid a choppy, monotonous, or repetitious style while at the same time producing correct sentences. Sentence combining accomplishes three things: it reinforces your understanding of sentence structure; it helps you to refine and polish your writing; and it results in a style that will keep your reader alert and interested in what you have to say.

Let's look at two short, technically correct sentences that could be combined:

I prefer champagne.
My budget allows only beer.

There are several ways of combining these two statements into a single sentence.

1. You can connect them with a comma and an appropriate linking word, such as *for, and, nor, but, or, yet,* or so (the FANBOYS words).

I prefer champagne, *but* my budget allows only beer.

2. You can change one of the sentences into a subordinate clause.

***Although I prefer champagne,* my budget allows only beer.**
My budget allows only beer *even though I prefer champagne.*

3. You can change one of the sentences into a modifying phrase.

Living on a beer budget, I still prefer champagne.

4. You can sometimes reduce a clause to a single-word modifier.

I have champagne tastes and a beer budget.

In sentence combining, you are free to move parts of the sentence around, change words, add or delete words, or make whatever other changes you find necessary. Anything goes, as long as you don't drastically alter the meaning of the base sentences. Remember that your aim in combining sentences is to create effective sentences, not long ones. Clarity is essential, and brevity has force.

Exercise 23.27* **Read through the sentences below and decide whether each one is correct or incorrect. In the incorrect sentences, cross out the unnecessary conjunction. Be sure your revised sentences are correctly capitalized and punctuated. Check your answers on page 474.**

1. When you find a mistake, so you should correct it.

2. Since my test is tomorrow morning, so I must stay up late tonight.

3. Although the test was difficult, but I passed it.

4. When December is over, winter continues for another two or three months.

5. Even though the photographer was good, yet I hate the pictures of myself.

6. After doing a couple of hours' research in the library, then we went back to work on our project.

7. Before the party, she cooked food for 12 people.

8. If this book will help me, so I will buy it.

9. Though having a car would be convenient, but I need the money for other things.

10. Although that program frequently crashes, but this program is stable.

Exercise 23.28*

Using dependent-clause cues (see page 339), combine the following sentences into longer, more interesting units.

Hint: Read each set of statements through to the end before you begin to combine them, and try out several variations aloud or in your head before writing down your preferred solution.

1. Leonardo da Vinci was a great artist and inventor.
   He invented scissors, among other things.

2. Cats can produce over 100 vocal sounds.
   Dogs can make only 10 vocal sounds.

3. It is said that men don't cry.
   They do cry while assembling furniture.

4. The name Wendy was made up for a book.
   The book was called *Peter Pan*.

5. Ten percent of Canadians are heavy drinkers.
   Thirty-five percent of Canadians abstain from alcohol.

6. Travel broadens the mind.
   Travel flattens the bank account.

7. We are seeking an experienced and innovative director.
   The candidate should be fluent in French.

8. One hundred thousand Vietnam veterans have taken their own lives.

   This is twice the number who were killed in action.

9. My cooking class went on a field trip to gather greens for a salad.

   We discovered that what we had thought was watercress was not watercress. It was poison ivy.

10. Ten of my classmates ate the salad.

    Eight were hospitalized.

    No one was critically ill.

Exercise 23.29 Combine the following sentences using the connecting words *for, and, nor, but, or, yet,* or *so* and the dependent-clause cues listed on page 339.

1. Melissa bakes a cake.

   She has a party.

2. Silence can be wonderful.

   There is nothing else so restful after a long day.

3. We didn't pass the first test.

   We have another one tomorrow.

4. Television shows have become boring.

   I still like to watch TV.

5. It's way too hot in here.

   Let's open a window.

6. Tensions are high.

   Money is tight.

   We should talk about making some changes.

7. I hate talking on the phone.

   I love texting.

   I need a smartphone.

8. I forgot to wear socks.

   I snuck in with my shoes on.

   The custom is to take shoes off.

9. Education can be a confusing concept.

   It is meant to help you think for yourself.

   Many people just want to learn facts.

10. Many people want to visit Toronto.

    They dislike how crowded it is.

    They travel to other places.

After you have combined a number of sentences, you can evaluate your work. Read your sentences out loud. How they *sound* is important. Test your work against the following six characteristics of successful sentences.

Sentence Combining Summary

1. Meaning: Have you said what you mean?
2. Clarity: Is your sentence clear? Can it be understood on the first reading?
3. Coherence: Do the parts of your sentence fit together logically and smoothly?
4. Emphasis: Are the most important ideas either at the end or at the beginning of the sentence?
5. Conciseness: Is the sentence direct and to the point? Have you cut out all redundant or repetitious words?
6. Rhythm: Does the sentence flow smoothly? Are there any interruptions in the development of the key idea(s)? Do the interruptions help to emphasize important points, or do they distract the reader?

If your sentences pass all six tests of successful sentence style, you may be confident that they are both technically correct and pleasing to the ear. No reader could ask for more.

CHAPTER 24

Grammar

This chapter builds on what you learned in Chapter 23 and helps you master the correct use of subjects, verbs, and pronouns. Although much of this may be familiar to you, work through it and try to identify any challenging issues for you. Using effective verbs, for example, might be the difference between getting a job interview and being left behind. Pronoun problems often stymie students trying to write persuasive arguments in essays and reports. A solid grounding in the **grammar** of standard English can help make your work more reader-friendly.

Mastering Subject–Verb Agreement

Singular and Plural

One of the most common writing errors is lack of **agreement** between subject and verb. Both must be singular, or both must be plural. If one is **singular** and the other **plural**, you have an agreement problem. You have another kind of agreement problem if your subject and verb are not both in the same "person" (see page 393).

Let's clarify some terms. First, it's important to distinguish between *singular* and *plural.*

- *Singular* means one person or thing.
- *Plural* means two or more persons or things.

Second, it's important to know what we mean when we refer to the concept of **person:**

- *First person* is the person(s) speaking or writing: *I, me; we,* or *us.*
- *Second person* is the person(s) being addressed: *you.*
- *Third person* is the person(s) being spoken or written about: *he, she, it; they,* or *them.*

Here's an example of the singular and plural forms of a regular verb in the present tense.

	SINGULAR	PLURAL
First person	I walk	we walk
Second person	you walk	you walk
Third person	she walks (or he, it, the horse walks)	they walk (or the horses walk)

The form that most often causes trouble is the third person because the verb endings do not match the subject endings. Third-person singular present tense verbs end in -*s*, but their singular subjects do not. Third-person plural verbs never end in -*s*, while their subjects normally do. Look at these examples.

> A fire burns.
> The car skids.
> The father cares for the children.

The three singular verbs, all of which end in -*s* (*burns, skids, cares*), agree with their singular subjects (*fire, car, father*), none of which ends in -*s*. When the subjects become plural, the verbs change form, too.

> Four fires burn.
> The cars skid.
> The fathers care for the children.

Now all of the subjects end in -*s*, and none of the verbs do.

To ensure *subject–verb agreement*, follow this basic rule:

> Subjects and verbs must both be either singular or plural.

This rule causes difficulty only when the writer doesn't know which word in the sentence is the subject and so makes the verb agree with the wrong word. As long as you decode the sentence correctly (see Chapter 23), you'll have no problem making every subject agree with its verb.

If you have not already done so, now is the time to memorize this next rule:

> The subject of a sentence is never in a prepositional phrase.

Here's an example of how errors occur.

> Only one of the 2000 ticket buyers are going to win.

What is the subject of this sentence? It's not *buyers*, but *one*. The verb must agree with *one*, which is clearly singular. The verb *are* does not agree with *one*, so the sentence is incorrect. It should read

> Only one ~~of the 2000 ticket buyers~~ is going to win.

Pay special attention to words that end in *-one, -thing,* or *-body*. They cause problems for nearly every writer.

> Words ending in *-one*, *-thing*, or *-body* are always singular.

When used as subjects, these pronouns require singular verbs.

anyone	anything	anybody
everyone	everything	everybody
no one	nothing	nobody
someone	something	somebody

The last part of the pronoun subject is the tip-off here: every*one*, any*thing*, no*body*. If you focus on this last part, you'll remember to use a singular verb with these subjects. Usually, these words cause trouble only when modifiers crop up between them and their verbs. For example, you would never write "Everyone are here." The trouble starts when you insert a group of words in between the subject and the verb. You might, if you weren't careful, write this: "Everyone involved in implementing the company's new policies and procedures are here." The meaning is plural: several people are present. But the subject (*everyone*) is singular, so the verb must be *is*.

More subject–verb agreement errors are caused by violations of this rule than any other. Be sure you understand it. Memorize it, and then test your understanding by doing the following exercise before you go any further.

Exercise 24.1* Rewrite each of the following sentences, using the alternative beginning shown. Answers for this section begin on page 474.

Example:

> She wants to make a short documentary.
> They want to make a short documentary.

1. She wants to go to Halifax.

   They

2. That cellphone has horrible ring tones.

   Those

3. Everyone who waited in line got free tickets to the concert.

   All those

4. The man thinks he ran over a skunk.

   The men

5. That man's dog sure is adorable.

   Those men's dogs

So far, so good. You can match up singular subjects with singular verbs and plural subjects with plural verbs. Now let's take a look at a few of the complications that make subject–verb agreement such a disagreeable problem.

Five Special Cases

Some subjects are tricky. They look singular but are actually plural, or they look plural when they're really singular. There are six kinds of these slippery subjects, all of them common and all of them likely to trip up the unwary writer.

1. Compound subjects joined by *or, either . . . or, neither . . . nor,* or *not . . . but*

Most of the compound subjects we've dealt with so far have been joined by *and* and have required plural verbs, so agreement hasn't been a problem. But watch out when the two or more elements of a compound subject are joined by *or, either ... or, neither ... nor,* or *not ... but.* In these cases, the verb agrees in number with the nearest subject. That is, if the subject closest to the verb is singular, the verb will be singular; if the subject closest to the verb is plural, the verb must be plural, too.

> Neither the coach nor the players are ready to give up.
>
> Neither the players nor the coach is ready to give up.

Exercise 24.2*

Circle the correct verb in each of the following sentences.

1. Not your physical charms but your honesty (is are) what I find attractive.
2. Either your job performance or your school assignments (is are) going to suffer if you continue your frantic lifestyle.
3. The college has decided that neither final marks nor a diploma (is are) to be issued to students who owe library fines.
4. Not the rising costs of health care but unemployment (is are) Canadians' chief concern.
5. Neither the compensation nor the benefits you offer (tempt tempts) me to work for your firm.

2. Subjects that look like compound subjects but really aren't

Don't be fooled by phrases beginning with words such as *with, like, together with, in addition to,* or *including.* These prepositional phrases are NOT part of the subject of the sentence. Since they do not affect the verb, you can mentally cross them out.

> Mario's brother, ~~together with three of his buddies~~, is going to the Yukon to look for work.

Obviously four people are looking for work. Nevertheless, the subject (brother) is singular, and so the verb must be singular (is going).

> All my courses, ~~except economics~~, are easier this term.

If you mentally cross out the phrase *except economics,* you can easily see that the verb (are) must be plural to agree with the plural subject (courses).

Exercise 24.3* Circle the correct verb in each of the following sentences.

1. *The Hunger Games*, in addition to other books written by Suzanne Collins, (is are) famous.
2. The man, together with three assistants, (register registers) all the complaints.
3. The baseball coach, as well as the players, (is are) unhappy with the team's place in the league.
4. Do zoo animals, including the panda and the elephant, ever (wonder wonders) why their trainers scoop their poop?
5. Every parent, in addition to teachers, (need needs) to put more pressure on kids not to drink and drive.

3. *Each* (of), *either* (of), *neither* (of)

Used as subjects, these words (or phrases) take singular verbs.

Either is acceptable to me.
Each wants desperately to win.
Neither of the stores is open after six o'clock. (Remember, the subject is never in a prepositional phrase.)

Exercise 24.4* Circle the correct verb in each of the following sentences.

1. Unless we hear from the coach, neither of us (is are) playing tonight.
2. Each of these courses (involve involves) a field placement.
3. When my girlfriend asks if she looks fat in a dress she is trying on, I know that either of my answers (is are) bound to be wrong.
4. Each of the women (want wants) desperately to win the Ms. Comox Valley bodybuilding competition.
5. Strict discipline is what each of our teachers (believe believes) in.

4. Collective nouns

A **collective noun** is a word that names a group. Some examples are: *company, class, committee, team, crowd, band, family, audience, public,* and *jury*. When you are referring to the group acting as a *unit*, use a *singular* verb. When you are referring to the *members* of the group acting *individually*, use a *plural* verb.

> **The team is sure to win tomorrow's game.** (Here *team* refers to the group acting as a whole.)
>
> **The team are getting into their uniforms now.** (The members of the team are acting individually.)

Exercise 24.5*

Circle the correct verb in each of the following sentences.

1. The student body (is are) going to vote in the next election.
2. The group (has have) a great dance routine.
3. The staff (gets get) staggered breaks throughout the day.
4. The marching band (was were) late this morning because of traffic.
5. The late shift (is are) slowly trickling in.

5. Units of money, time, mass, length, and distance

When used as subjects, they all require singular verbs.

> **Four kilometres is too far to walk in this weather.**
> **Remember that 2.2 pounds equals a kilogram.**
> **Three weeks is a long time to wait to get your paper back.**

Exercise 24.6*

Circle the correct verb for each of the following sentences. Check your answers against ours on page 475.

1. Anyone with two cars (has have) huge insurance payments.
2. Nothing (succeed succeeds) like success.
3. Nobody on the team (show shows) much respect for the coach.
4. Why is it that everybody we meet (talk talks) to you instead of me?
5. No one in Canada (admit admits) to hating hockey; the Leafs, yes, but hockey, no.

In Exercises 24.7 and 24.8, correct the errors in subject–verb agreement. (Some rephrasing may be required.) Check your answers to each exercise before going on.

Exercise 24.7*

1. Neither of the following sentences are correct.
2. The faculty, with the full support of the college administration, treats plagiarism as a serious offence.
3. Either good looks or intelligence run in our family, but never at the same time.
4. None of the computer experts have been able to untangle our billing problems.
5. The enjoyment of puns and jokes involving plays on words are the result of having too little else on your mind.
6. Anyone who jumps from one of Paris's many bridges are in Seine.
7. It is amazing how much better the orchestra play now that the conductor is sober.
8. The number of layoffs in the last quarter are truly alarming.
9. Her colleagues, along with her supervisor, agrees that Emily needs further training.
10. Canada's First Nations population are thought to have come to this continent from Asia thousands of years before the Europeans arrived in North America.

Exercise 24.8*

Quebec City, along with Montreal, Toronto, and Vancouver, are among Canada's great gourmet centres. Whereas Toronto and Vancouver are relative latecomers to this list, neither Quebec City nor Montreal are strangers to those who seeks fine dining. Indeed, travel and food magazines have long affirmed that including these two cities in a Quebec vacation are a "must." Montreal is perhaps more international in its offerings, but Quebec City provides exquisite proof that French Canadian cuisine and hospitality is second to none in the world. Amid the Old World charm of the lower city is to be found some of the quaintest and most enjoyable traditional restaurants, and the newer sections of town boasts equally fine dining in more contemporary surroundings. The combination of the wonderful food and the charm of the city are sure to entice any visitor to return. Either summer, when the city blooms and outdoor cafés abound, or winter, when Carnaval turns the streets into hundreds of connecting parties, are wonderful times to visit one of Canada's oldest and most interesting cities.

Subject–Verb Agreement Summary

- Subjects and verbs must agree: both must be singular, or both must be plural.
- The subject of a sentence is never in a prepositional phrase.
- Pronouns ending in *-one*, *-thing*, or *-body* are singular and require singular verbs.
- Subjects joined by *and* are always plural.
- When subjects are joined by *or*, *either ... or*, *neither ... nor*, or *not ... but*, the verb agrees with the subject that is closest to it.
- When looking for the subject in a sentence, ignore phrases beginning with *as well as*, *including*, *in addition to*, *like*, *together with*, and so on. They are prepositional phrases.
- When *each*, *either*, and *neither* are used as subjects, they require singular verbs.
- Collective nouns are usually singular.
- Units of money, time, mass, length, and distance are always singular.

Grammar

Exercise 24.9

As a final check of your mastery of subject–verb agreement, correct the following sentences as necessary.

1. Each of the options you outlined in your concluding remarks are worth examining further.
2. My opinion of the college's accounting programs are that neither of them are what I need.
3. Every one of the dozen people we interviewed qualify for the position.
4. My whole family, with the exception of the cat, dislike anchovies on pizza.

5. The applause from a thousand enthusiastic fans were like music to the skaters' ears.

6. Neither of your decisions are likely to improve sales, let alone morale.

7. Three thousand dollars per term, the students agree, are too much to pay for their education.

8. Neither age nor illness prevents Uncle Alf from leering at the nurses.

9. The birth of triplets, after six other children in eight years, were too much for the parents to cope with.

10. Everything you have accomplished in the past three years are wasted if you fail this assignment.

Using Verbs Effectively

Good writers pay especially careful attention to verbs. A verb is to a sentence what an engine is to a car: it's the source of power—but it can also be a source of trouble. Now that you've conquered subject–verb agreement, it's time to turn to the three remaining essentials of correct verb use: *form*, *consistency*, and *voice*.

Choosing the Correct Verb Form

Every verb has four forms, called its **principal parts:**

1. The **infinitive** form: used with *to* and with *can, may, might, shall, will, could, should, would, must*
2. The **simple past** (also called the *past tense*)
3. The **present participle** (the *-ing*) form
4. The **past participle** form: used with *has* or *have*

Here are some examples:

Infinitive	Simple Past	Present Participle	Past Participle
dance	danced	dancing	danced
learn	learned	learning	learned
play	played	playing	played
seem	seemed	seeming	seemed

To use verbs correctly, you must be familiar with their principal parts. Knowing three facts will help you:

1. The present participle, the *-ing* form, is always made up of the base form of the verb + *ing*.

2. Your dictionary gives you the principal parts of all **irregular verbs**. Look up the base form, and you'll find the simple past and the present and past participles beside it, usually in parentheses. For example, if you look up *sing* in your dictionary, you will find *sang* (simple past), *sung* (past participle), and *singing* (present participle) listed immediately after the verb itself. If the past tense and past participle are not given, the verb is a **regular verb**.

3. To form the simple past and the past participle of regular verbs: add *-ed* to the base form. The examples listed above—*dance, learn, play, seem*—are all regular verbs.

Unfortunately, many of the most common English verbs are irregular. Their past tenses and past participles are formed in unpredictable ways. The verbs in the list that follows are used so often that it is worth your time to memorize their principal parts. (We have not included the *-ing* form because, as we have noted above, it never causes any difficulty.)

THE PRINCIPAL PARTS OF IRREGULAR VERBS

Infinitive (Use with *to* and with helping/auxiliary verbs)	Simple Past	Past Participle (Use with *have, has, had*)
awake	awoke/awaked	awaked/awoken
be (am, is)	was/were	been
bear	bore	borne
beat	beat	beaten
become	became	become
begin	began	begun
bid (offer to pay)	bid	bid
bid (say, command)	bid/bade	bid/bidden
bite	bit	bitten
bleed	bled	bled
blow	blew	blown
break	broke	broken
bring	brought (*not* brang)	brought (*not* brung)
broadcast	broadcast	broadcast
build	built	built
burst	burst	burst
buy	bought	bought
catch	caught	caught
choose	chose	chosen
come	came	come
(Use with *to* and with helping/auxiliary verbs)		(Use with *have, has, had*)
cost	cost	cost
cut	cut	cut
deal	dealt	dealt

Grammar

Infinitive	Simple Past	Past Participle
dig	dug	dug
dive	dived/dove	dived
do	did (*not* done)	done
draw	drew	drawn
dream	dreamed/dreamt	dreamed/dreamt
drink	drank (*not* drunk)	drunk
drive	drove	driven
eat	ate	eaten
fall	fell	fallen
feed	fed	fed
feel	felt	felt
fight	fought	fought
find	found	found
fling	flung	flung
fly	flew	flown
forget	forgot	forgotten/forgot
forgive	forgave	forgiven
freeze	froze	frozen
get	got	got/gotten
give	gave	given
go	went	gone (*not* went)
grow	grew	grown
hang (suspend)	hung	hung
hang (put to death)	hanged	hanged
have	had	had
hear	heard	heard
hide	hid	hidden
hit	hit	hit
hold	held	held
hurt	hurt	hurt
keep	kept	kept
know	knew	known
lay (put or place)	laid	laid
lead	led	led
leave	left	left
lend	lent (*not* loaned)	lent (*not* loaned)
(Use with *to* and with helping/ auxiliary verbs)		(Use with *have*, *has*, *had*)
lie (recline)	lay	lain (*not* layed)
light	lit/lighted	lit/lighted
lose	lost	lost

Infinitive	Simple Past	Past Participle
mean	meant	meant
meet	met	met
pay	paid	paid
raise (lift up, increase, bring up)	raised	raised
ride	rode	ridden
ring	rang	rung
rise	rose	risen
run	ran	run
say	said	said
see	saw (*not* seen)	seen
sell	sold	sold
set (put or place)	set	set
shake	shook	shaken (*not* shook)
shine	shone	shone
sing	sang	sung
sink	sank	sunk
sit	sat	sat
sleep	slept	slept
slide	slid	slid
speak	spoke	spoken
speed	sped	sped
steal	stole	stolen
stick	stuck	stuck
strike (hit)	struck	struck
strike (affect)	struck	stricken
swear	swore	sworn
swim	swam	swum
swing	swung (*not* swang)	swung
take	took	taken
teach	taught	taught
tear	tore	torn
tell	told	told
think	thought	thought
throw	threw	thrown
wake	woke/waked	woken/waked
wear	wore	worn
(Use with *to* and with helping/ auxiliary verbs)		(Use with *have*, *has*, *had*)
weave	wove	woven
win	won	won
wind	wound	wound

Grammar

Infinitive	Simple Past	Past Participle
wring	wrung	wrung
write	wrote	written

Exercise 24.10* **The sentences below require both the simple past and the past participle of the verb shown at the left. Write the required form in each blank. Do not add or remove helping verbs. Check your answers on page 476.**

1. ride Having __________ a cow once, I wouldn't mind if I never __________ one again.
2. eat Alison had never __________ lobster until she had a lobster supper on Prince Edward Island, where she __________ three lobsters at one sitting.
3. grow Tara __________ the plant in a pot on her balcony, where she had __________ similar plants successfully in the past.
4. hide John, who hated bologna sandwiches, __________ his lunch in the bottom drawer of his dresser, on top of the other sandwiches that he had __________ there during the week.
5. write I __________ a novel when I was in college, but I have not __________ anything since.

Exercise 24.11 **As a final test of your mastery of verb forms, correct the errors in the following sentences.**

1. She lighted the fire and tried not to burn herself.
2. She wanted to teach because she loved the ways she had been teached.
3. Marya choosed where to go to school based on the college's reputation.
4. The cats bleeded all over the floor, and I was really worried.
5. I wasn't quite sure what I writed on the paper.
6. Jim quitted because he didn't like the way his boss speaked to him.
7. I liked the way he rided his Harley.
8. I appreciated the way he swinged the bat in the game.
9. I thinked I saw a poltergeist last Halloween.
10. I speeded away after I failed that test.

Keeping Your Tenses Consistent

Verbs are time markers. Changes in **tense** express changes in time: past, present, or future.

I was hired yesterday; I hope this job will last longer than my last one.

past ***present*** ***future***

Sometimes, as in the example above, it is necessary to use several different tenses in a single sentence to get the meaning across. But most of the time, whether you're writing a sentence or a paragraph, you use one tense throughout. Normally, you choose either the past or the present tense, depending on the nature of your topic. (Few paragraphs are written completely in the future tense.) Here is the rule to follow:

> Don't change tense unless meaning requires it.

Readers like and expect **consistency**. If you begin a sentence with "I worried and fretted and delayed," your readers will tune in to the past-tense verbs and expect any other verbs in the sentence to be in the past tense, too. Therefore, if you finish the sentence with "... and then I decide to give it a try," your readers will be jolted abruptly out of one time frame and into another. This sort of jolting is uncomfortable, and readers don't like it.

Shifting tenses is like shifting gears: it should be done smoothly and only when necessary. Avoid causing verbal whiplash: keep your tenses consistent.

Wrong:	Monika starts the car and revved the engine.
Right:	Monika started the car and revved the engine.
Also right:	Monika starts the car and revs the engine.
Wrong:	Carrie flounces into the room and sat down. Everyone stares.
Right:	Carrie flounced into the room and sat down. Everyone stared.
Also right:	Carrie flounces into the room and sits down. Everyone stares.

Exercise 24.12*

Most—but not all—of the following sentences contain unnecessary tense shifts. Use the first verb in each sentence as your time marker and change the tense(s) of the other verb(s) to agree with it. Answers are on page 476.

1. The umpire stands there, unable to believe what he was seeing.
2. Some people believe that in the future humans will live for 200 years.
3. The class had just ended when in walks Jason.
4. The rebellion failed because the people do not support it.
5. The party was just getting started when Eva decides it's time to leave.

6. I enjoy my work, but I was not going to let it take over my life.

7. Prejudice is learned and will be hard to outgrow.

8. A Canadian is someone who thinks that an income tax refund was a gift from the government.

9. Robert went to Laval for his vacation every summer and stays with his aunt and uncle on a farm.

10. Shahn likes to play cricket with his Canadian friends even though most of them didn't understand the rules.

Exercise 24.13* Correct the 15 faulty tense shifts in this passage.

For some reason, when mistakes or accidents happen in radio or television, they were often hilariously funny. If, in the course of a conversation, someone said, "Here come the Duck and Doochess of Kent," listeners would probably be mildly amused. But many years ago, when an announcer makes that slip on a live radio broadcast, it becomes one of the most famous blunders in radio history. Tapes of the slip will be filed in "bloopers" libraries all over the world. This heightened sense of hilarity is the reason that so many people who work in radio dedicated their creativity to making the on-air announcer laugh while reading the news. To take one example, Lorne Greene's is the deeply serious voice that is heard on the CBC news during World War II. He is the victim of all kinds of pranks aimed at getting him to break up while reading the dark, often tragic, news of the combat overseas. The pages of his news script are set on fire while he reads. He is even stripped naked as he reads, calmly, and apparently without strain. Lorne Greene will be a true professional. Many other newscasters, however, will have been highly susceptible to falling apart on air at the slightest provocation. And there were always people around a radio station who cannot resist giving them that little push.

Exercise 24.14

To test and reinforce your mastery of correct verb forms and tense consistency, correct the 10 errors in the following paragraph. Use the italicized verb in the first sentence as your time marker.

Critical thinking *is* a lost art, in my opinion. People did research but only in a minimal way, using Google or other online search engines, when they should have read books. When I had used the word *critical*, many friends are thinking I meant putting something down. When I tried to teach them about what it really will mean to be *critical*, they seemed surprised. Being critical will require thinking deeply about our topic and doing research so that we speak and wrote about it in an informed and persuasive way.

Choosing between Active and Passive Verbs

Verbs have another quality besides tense (or time). Verbs also have what is called *voice*, which means the quality of being either active or passive. In sentences with **active voice** verbs, the "doer" of the action is the grammatical subject of the sentence.

Active voice: Good parents support their children.
A car hit the raccoon.
Someone will show a movie in class on Friday.

In sentences with **passive voice** verbs, the grammatical subject of the sentence is the "receiver" of the action (that is, the subject is passively acted upon), and the "doer" becomes an object of the preposition *by* or is absent from the sentence entirely, as in the third example below.

Passive voice: Children are supported by good parents.
The raccoon was hit by a car.
A movie will be shown in class on Friday.

> Always use an active verb unless you have a specific reason to choose a passive one.

You probably use the passive voice more often than you think you do. To be a better writer, you need to know the distinction between active and passive, to understand their different effects on the reader, and to use the passive voice only when it is appropriate to your meaning.

There are three good reasons for choosing a passive verb rather than an active one.

1. The person or agent that performed the action is unknown (or the writer does not wish to disclose the identity).

My books were stolen from my locker.

Giovanna's father was killed in Bosnia.

Unlike the streets of a typical prairie city, which are laid out on a grid, Vancouver's streets are laid out to follow the curves and bends of the harbour and the Fraser River.

2. You want to place the emphasis on the person, place, or object that was acted upon rather than on the subject that performed the action.

Early this morning, the Bank of Montreal at 16th and Granville was robbed by four men wearing balaclavas and carrying shotguns.

This sentence focuses the reader's attention on the bank rather than on the robbers. A quite different effect is produced when the sentence is reconstructed in the active voice:

Four men wearing balaclavas and carrying shotguns robbed the Bank of Montreal at 16th and Granville early this morning.

3. You are writing a technical or scientific report or a legal document.

Passive verbs are the appropriate choice when the focus is on the facts, methods, or procedures involved rather than on who discovered or performed them. Passive verbs also tend to establish an impersonal tone that is appropriate in these kinds of writing. Contrast the emphasis and tone of the following sentence pairs.

Passive: **The heat was increased to 200°C and was maintained at that temperature.**

Active: **My lab partners and I increased the heat to 200°C and maintained it at that temperature.**

Passive: **Having been found guilty, the accused was sentenced to two years.**

Active: **The jury found the accused guilty, and the judge sentenced him to two years.**

In general, because active verbs are more concise and forceful than passive verbs, they add vigour and impact to your writing. The distinction between active and passive is not something you should worry about during the drafting stage, however. The time to focus on verbs and decide whether active or passive would best serve your purpose is during revision. When you find a passive verb in your draft, think about *who is doing what*. Ask yourself why the "doer" is not the subject of the sentence. If there's a good reason, then use the passive verb. Otherwise, choose an active verb.

Exercise 24.15*

Rewrite the sentences below, changing their verbs from passive to active. Note that you may have to add a word or word group to identify the "doer" of the action of the verb.

Example: Matt's two front teeth were knocked out by Clark's shot.
Clark's shot knocked out Matt's two front teeth.

1. A meeting was called by the department head.
2. Your espresso will be made by the barista in a few minutes.
3. When it gets cold, the block heater is plugged in overnight.
4. For many years, steroids have been used by professional athletes to improve speed and endurance.
5. No photos may be taken during the performance.
6. These letters were written by my great-grandfather, who served in the army overseas.
7. This film was made for less than $100 000 by a crew of students.
8. While our neighbours were vacationing in Cuba, their house was broken into by thieves.
9. An error was made in the code you wrote for this program.
10. Teamwork is a valuable concept, especially when someone is needed to take the blame for the boss's mistakes.

Exercise 24.16*

Rewrite each of the sentences below, changing the verbs from active to passive or vice versa, and then decide which sentence is more effective.

1. Feist won another Juno.
2. Jian spiked the ball after scoring the go-ahead touchdown.
3. City Council passed a bylaw forbidding backyard bird feeders.
4. Later that night, a shadowy figure was seen entering the lab.

5. After standing in line all night, Courtenay managed to get four tickets to the Michael Bublé concert.
6. The 10 p.m. news revealed the truth behind the fake diploma scandal.
7. Passive voice is often used by people who want to shift responsibility from themselves to others.
8. After a long debate, the student council finally agreed to endorse Yasmin's idea of a class *Facebook* page.
9. A computer program that analyzes speech patterns has been developed by language psychologists.
10. After years of research among college students, it has been concluded by language psychologists that people who frequently use passive voice tend to be maladjusted.

Exercise 24.17 **Rewrite the following paragraphs, changing the 15 misused passive verbs to active verbs. (Remember, passive-voice verbs are sometimes appropriate.)**

The last time Glenn had his hair cut by the barber at the local mall was the day of the big high-school graduation dance. One of the prettiest girls in the school had been invited to the prom by Glenn, and to make a good impression was what was wanted. The barber was thought to be talented, if a little unconventional: he had long hair and a vaguely dreamy smile. It was well known by everybody that he had been a hippie back in the 1970s; it was thought by some that his youthful excesses might be responsible for his soft voice and mumbling speech.

Glenn settled into the chair, and a few inaudible words were muttered by the barber. Glenn made a guess at what had been said and replied that the weather was fine. Another mumble from the barber. This time, Glenn thought he'd been asked which college he planned to attend in the fall, and he answered politely. At this point, the conversation was stopped, and the barber got on with his work.

Half an hour later, the sheet was swept away, and the chair was spun so that Glenn could see his image in the mirror. To his horror, it was discovered that he was practically bald, except for an 8-cm high strip of hair running from his forehead to the nape of his neck. Glenn's scream was heard through the entire mall. After the excitement died down, it was learned by the crowds of curious shoppers that when Glenn had been asked what kind of haircut he wanted, Glenn had replied, "Mohawk."

So the prom was attended by Glenn in a tux, sporting a startling haircut and accompanying a very unsympathetic date. The following week, Glenn left for Hamilton and Mohawk College. His high-school sweetheart was never seen by him again.

Solving Pronoun Problems

Look at the following sentences. Can you tell what's wrong with them?

"Dev must choose between you and I," Miranda said.

When you are on a diet, it is a good idea for one to avoid Bagel World.

We had invited everybody to come with their partner, so we were a little surprised when Marcel showed up with his Doberman.

Everyone is expected to do their duty.

Gary's nose was badly sunburned, but it has now completely disappeared.

Most of the students that were protesting tuition increases were ones which had been elected to council.

These sentences all contain pronoun errors. After verbs, pronouns are the class of words most likely to cause problems for writers. In this section, we will look at the three aspects of pronoun usage that can trip you up if you're not careful: pronoun form, agreement, and consistency. We'll also look at the special problems of usage that can lead to sexist language.

Choosing the Correct Pronoun Form

First you need to be sure you are using the "right" pronouns—that is, the correct **pronoun forms**—in your sentences. Some examples of incorrect pronoun usage follow.

Her and me cannot agree on anything.
The reason for the quarrel is a personal matter between he and I.

How do you know which form of a pronoun to use? The answer depends on the pronoun's place and function in your sentence.

Subject and object pronouns. There are two forms of personal pronouns: one is used for subjects, and the other is used for objects. Pronoun errors occur when you confuse the two. In Chapter 23, you learned to identify the subject of a sentence. Keep that information in mind as you learn the following basic rule.

> When a subject or a **complement** is a pronoun, the pronoun must be in *subject form*. Otherwise, use the *object form*.

SUBJECT PRONOUNS

Singular	Plural
I	we
you	you
he, she, it, one	they

She and I tied for first place. (The pronouns are the subject of the sentence.)

The lucky winners of the all-expenses-paid weekend in Paris are they. (The pronoun is the complement and refers to the subject of the sentence, *winners*.)

The student who regularly asks for extra help is he. (The pronoun is the complement and refers to the subject of the sentence, *student*.)

OBJECT PRONOUNS

Singular	Plural
me	us
you	you
him, her, it, one	them

Between you and me, I think he's cute. (*Me* is not the subject of the sentence; it is one of the objects of the preposition *between*.)

Omar asked him and me for help. (*Him* and *me* are not the subject of the verb asked; *Omar* is, so the pronouns need to be in object form.)

Be especially careful when using pronouns in compound subjects or after prepositions. If you can remember the following two rules, you'll be able to eliminate most potential errors.

> 1. A pronoun that is part of a compound subject is *always* in subject form.
> 2. A pronoun that follows a preposition is *always* in object form.

Examples:

***She* and *I* had tickets to U2.** (The pronouns are used as a compound subject.)

It is up to *you* and *her* to pay for the damage. (The pronouns follow the preposition *to*.)

When you're dealing with a pair of pronouns and can't decide which form to use, try this test.[1] Mentally cross out one pronoun at a time, then read aloud the sentence you've created. Applying this technique to the first example above, you get "*She* had tickets" and "*I* had tickets." Both sound right and are correct. In the second sentence, if you try the pronouns separately, you get "It is up to *you*" and "It is up to *her*." Again, you know by the sound that these are the correct forms. (You would never say "*Her* had tickets," or "*Me* had tickets," or "It is up to *she*.") If you deal with paired pronouns one at a time, you are unlikely to choose the wrong form.

Note, too, that when a pair of pronouns includes *I* or *me*, that pronoun comes last. For example, we write "between *you* and *me*" (not "between *me* and *you*"); we write "*she* and *I*" (not "*I* and *she*"). There is no grammatical reason for this rule. It's based on courtesy. Good manners require that you speak of others first and yourself last.

Exercise 24.18*

Choose the correct pronouns from the words given in parentheses. Answers are on page 478.

1. Katie and (I me) stayed up most of the night to complete our assignment.
2. There wasn't much (us we) could do to rescue it, however.
3. Peng and Yvon were supposed to be in our group, but neither of (they them) showed up.
4. When (us we) poor, sleep-deprived students submitted the assignment, our professor glared at (us we).
5. Between (us we), (us we) had managed to produce barely four pages.
6. After all, what do Katie and (I, me) know about the topic assigned to (us we)?
7. Both of (us we) thought "relative deprivation" had something to do with families.
8. (Her She) and (I me) spent hours writing about being grounded by our parents, forgetting Mother's Day, and suffering our older siblings' bullying.
9. It never occurred to (she her) or (I me) that the term was a definition of poverty.
10. Katie and (I me) have often been late and sometimes absent from class this term, so when the prof adds our class participation mark to the grade we get

[1] This test is reliable only for those who are fluent in English. English language learners must rely on memorizing the rules.

on our major paper, whose topic we misinterpreted, it's unlikely that (her she) and (I me) can count on an A in sociology.

Using Pronouns in Contrast Constructions

Choosing the correct pronoun form is more than just a matter of not wanting to appear ignorant or careless. Sometimes the form you use determines the meaning of your sentence. Consider these two sentences:

> Adam is more interested in his new car than *I*.
> Adam is more interested in his new car than *me*.

There's a world of difference between the meaning of the subject form ("Adam is more interested in his new car than *I* [am]") and the object form ("Adam is more interested in his new car than [in] *me*").

> When using a pronoun after *than, as well as,* or *as,* decide whether you mean to contrast the pronoun with the subject of the sentence. If you do, use the subject form of the pronoun. If not, use the object form.

> Sylvie is more likely to ask Dan to the party than I. (*I* is contrasted with the subject, *Sylvie*.)
>
> Sylvie is more likely to ask Dan to the party than me. (*Me* is contrasted with the object, *Dan*.)

Here's a quick way to check that you've used the correct pronoun form. If you've used a subject form, mentally insert a verb after it. If you've used an object form, mentally insert a verb before it. If your sentence makes sense, you've chosen correctly. For example,

> Sylvie is more likely to ask Dan to the party than I [am].
>
> Sylvie is more likely to ask Dan to the party than [to ask] me.

Some writers prefer to leave the added verb in place, a practice that eliminates any possibility of confusion.

Exercise 24.19* Correct the following sentences where necessary.

1. She knows she can't score less than I.
2. Jennifer is more into Disney than me.
3. No one in the class except Lida did as well as me on the assignment.
4. Although Sarah, too, likes music, Franco spends more time listening to the radio than her.

5. The subject of Harry Potter is more exciting to my students than to I.

6. The team wants to play as well as we.

7. Serge likes to play video games through the night more than me.

Revise the following paragraph to correct the errors in pronoun form. **Exercise 24.20***

(1) My boyfriend and me have different opinions when it comes to food. (2) I like fast food better than him. (3) He likes vegetables better than me. (4) In fact, between you and I, he is a vegetarian, though he would deny it. (5) When we go out with friends, it is difficult for they to know where to take him and I because our tastes are so different. (6) The only type of restaurant where us and them can all have what we like is Italian. (7) There, him and his friends can sample pasta primavera and eggplant parmigiana while my friends and I tuck into spaghetti and meatballs and pepperoni pizza. (8) We are probably not as healthy as they, but they don't seem to enjoy their food as much as us.

Grammar

Now that you know how to choose the correct form of pronouns within a sentence, let's turn to the problems of using pronouns consistently throughout a sentence and a paragraph.

Pronoun–Antecedent Agreement

The name of this pronoun problem may sound difficult, but the idea is simple. Pronouns are words that substitute for or refer to the name of a person, place, or thing mentioned elsewhere in your sentence or your paragraph. The word(s) that a pronoun substitutes for or refers to is called the **antecedent**.

> **Dracula had his own way of wooing women.** (The pronoun *his* refers to the antecedent *Dracula*.)
>
> **Soula respects her parents.** (The pronoun *her* refers to the antecedent *Soula*.)
>
> **The computer is processing as fast as it can.** (The pronoun *it* substitutes for the antecedent *computer*.)

Usually, as in these three examples, the antecedent comes before the pronoun that refers to it. Here is the rule to remember.

A pronoun must agree with its antecedent in

- **number** (singular or plural)
- **person** (first, second, or third)
- **gender** (masculine, feminine, or neuter)

Most of the time, you follow this rule without even realizing that you know it. For example, you would never write

Dracula had *your* own way of wooing women.

Soula respects *its* parents.

The computer is processing as fast as *she* can.

You know these sentences are incorrect even if you may not know precisely why.

There are three kinds of pronoun–antecedent agreement that you do need to learn about. They lead to errors that, unlike the examples above, are not obvious, and you need to know them so you can watch out for them. The rules you need to learn involve indefinite pronouns ending in *-one*, *-body*, or *-thing*; vague reference; and relative pronouns.

1. Indefinite pronouns: pronouns ending in *-one*, *-body*, or *-thing*. The most common pronoun–antecedent agreement problem involves **indefinite pronouns:**

anyone	anybody	anything
everyone	everybody	everything
no one	nobody	nothing
someone	somebody	something
each (one)		

At the beginning of this chapter, you learned that when these words are used as subjects they are singular and take singular verbs. So it makes sense that the pronouns that stand for or refer to them must also be singular.

Antecedents ending in *-one, -body,* or *-thing* are singular and must be referred to by singular pronouns: *he, she, it; his, her, its*.

Please put everything back in *its* place.

Anybody can retire comfortably if *he* or *she* begins planning now.

Everyone is expected to do *his* share.

No one in *his* right mind would claim *he* enjoys living in this climate.

Now take another look at the last two sentences. Until about 30 years ago, the pronouns *he, him,* and *his* were used with singular antecedents to refer to both men and women. In order to appeal to the broadest possible audience, most writers today are careful to avoid this usage and other examples of what may be seen as sexist language.

In informal speech, it has become acceptable to use plural pronouns with *-one*, *-body*, or *-thing* antecedents. Although these antecedents are grammatically singular and take singular verbs, they are often plural in meaning, and in conversation we find ourselves saying,

Everyone is expected to do *their* share.
No one has to stay if *they* don't want to.

This usage is acceptable in speech, but it is not acceptable in academic or professional writing.

Writers sometimes make errors in pronoun–antecedent agreement because they are trying to write without indicating whether the person referred to is male or female. A sentence such as "Everyone is required to do *their* oral presentation" is incorrect, as we have seen, but it does avoid making "everyone" male. It also avoids the awkwardness of "Everyone is required to do *his* or *her* oral presentation." There are two better ways to solve this problem:

1. Revise the sentence to leave the pronoun out.

Everyone is required to deliver an oral presentation in the last week of class.

or

An oral presentation is required of everyone in the last week of class.

Such creative avoidance of gender-specific or incorrect constructions can be an interesting challenge. The results often sound a little artificial, however. The second method is easier to accomplish.

2. Revise the sentence to make both the antecedent and the pronoun plural.

You are all required to deliver an oral presentation in the last week of class.

or

All students are required to deliver an oral presentation in the last week of class.

Here are two more examples for you to study.

Problem:	Everybody has been given his or her assignment.
Revision 1:	Everybody has been given an assignment.
Revision 2:	All of the students have been given their assignments.
Problem:	No one wants his copy edited.
Revision 1:	No one wants copy editing.
Revision 2:	Most writers object to having their work copy edited.

Exercise 24.21*

Circle the most appropriate word(s) from the choices given in parentheses. Check your answers carefully before continuing. The answers for this exercise begin on page 478.

1. A bird left (his her a) message on the windshield of my new car.

2. Everyone is a product of (his her their) environment as well as heredity.

3. Behind every great woman is (their a) baffled husband.

4. Each of the mothers had a good excuse for (their her) son's behaviour.

5. Everyone who has a smartphone seems to spend a great deal of time typing with (their his) thumbs.

6. Is someone going to provide (his her an) opinion on the question?

7. Anyone from overseas will have to show (their his her a) passport at Border Services.

8. All Canadian citizens must present photo identification and (their his her a) customs declaration.

9. Anyone who is going across the border must have (his her their the) car inspected.

10. Border Services will match to (its their) owners anything confiscated at the checkpoint.

Exercise 24.22* **Correct the following sentences where necessary. Avoid sexist language.**

1. Everyone I know has his own cellphone.

2. Someone has their eye on you.

3. Anyone who writes a generic cover letter can expect that their work won't be taken seriously.

4. No one wants their ideas rejected.

5. If you're lost, ask someone if they can give you directions.

2. Vague reference. Avoiding the second potential difficulty with pronoun–antecedent agreement requires common sense and the ability to think like your readers. If you look at your writing from your readers' point of view, it is unlikely that you will break the following rule:

> Every pronoun must have a clearly identifiable antecedent.

The mistake that occurs when you fail to follow this rule is called **vague reference.**

Chris told his brother that he was losing his hair.

Who is going bald? Chris or his brother?

Here's another example:

The faculty are demanding higher salaries and fewer teaching hours, but the administration does not support them.

What does the administration not support: higher salaries, fewer classes, or the faculty themselves?

In sentences like these, you can only guess the meaning because you don't know who or what is being referred to by the pronouns. You can make such sentences less confusing by using either more names or other nouns and by using fewer pronouns. For example:

Chris told his brother Sam that Sam was losing his hair.

The faculty are demanding higher salaries and fewer teaching hours, but the administration does not support their demands.

Another type of vague reference occurs when there is no appropriate antecedent in the sentence for the pronoun to refer to.

I sold my skis last year and can't even remember how to do it anymore. (Do what?)

Reading is Sophia's passion, but she says she doesn't have a favourite. (A favourite what?)

Now that I have a well-paying job, my friends borrow money from me, which puts a strain on our friendship. (There is no noun or pronoun for *which* to refer to.)

I hate homework; this is my downfall. (*This* refers to homework, but homework is not my downfall. My hatred of doing it is.)

How would you revise these sentences? Try it, and then see our suggestions in the footnote below.[2]

Be sure that every pronoun has a clear antecedent with which it agrees in number, person, and gender. Once you have mastered this principle, you'll have no further trouble with pronoun–antecedent agreement.

---

[2] I sold my skis last year and can't even remember how to *slalom* anymore.

Reading is Sophie's passion, but she says she doesn't have a favourite *writer*.

Now that I have a well-paying job, I have given friends loans, *which* put a strain on our friendship.

I have a hatred of homework; *this* is my downfall.

Grammar

Exercise 24.23* Correct the following sentences where necessary. There are several ways to fix these sentences. In some cases, the antecedent is missing, and you need to supply one. In other cases, the antecedent is so vague that the meaning of the sentence can be interpreted in more than one way. You need to rewrite these sentences to make the meaning clear.

1. I know that smoking is bad for me and everyone else, but I can't give them up.
2. If your pet rat won't eat its food, feed it to the kitty.
3. Our cat is a picky eater, which is inconvenient and expensive.
4. Whenever Stan and Matt played poker, he stacked the deck.
5. The gorilla was mean and hungry because he had finished it all in the morning.
6. Madonna has transformed herself at least five times in her career, which makes her unique.
7. Dani backed her car into a garbage truck and dented it.
8. Rocco was suspicious of handgun control because he thought everyone should have one for late-night subway rides.
9. Get your ears pierced during this week's special and take home an extra pair free.
10. Our car is in the shop, but this won't keep us from going to the party.

3. Relative pronouns. The third potential difficulty with pronoun–antecedent agreement is how to use relative pronouns—*who/whoever*, *whom/whomever*, *which*, and *that*—correctly. Relative pronouns refer to someone or something already mentioned in the sentence or paragraph. Here is the guideline to follow.

> Use *who/whom* and *whoever/whomever* to refer to people.
> Use *that* and *which* to refer to everything else.

The student *who* won the Governor General's Academic Medal decided to go to Dalhousie.

For *whom* are you voting: the Liberals or the New Democrats?

The moose *that* I met looked hostile.

Her car, *which* is imported, is smaller than cars *that* are built here.

Tips for Using Relative Pronouns Correctly:

1. Whether you need *who* or *whom*, *whoever* or *whomever*, depends on the pronoun's place and function in your sentence. Apply the basic rule of pronoun usage: if the pronoun is acting as, or refers to, the subject or the complement, use *who/whoever*. Otherwise, use *whom/whomever*.

It was Madison *who* drew the winning ticket for a week's holiday in Moose Factory. (The pronoun refers to the subject of the sentence, *Madison*.)

The trip's promoters were willing to settle for *whomever* they could get. (The pronoun does not refer to the sentence's subject, *promoters*; it is the object of the preposition *for*.)

An even simpler solution to this problem is to rewrite the sentence so you don't need either *who* or *whom*.

Madison drew the winning ticket for a week's holiday in Moose Factory.

The trip's promoters were willing to settle for anyone they could get.

2. *That* is required more often than *which*. You should use *which* only in a clause that is separated from the rest of the sentence by commas. (See Comma Rule 4 on page 401.)

The moose *that* I met looked hostile.

The moose, *which* was standing right in front of my car, looked hostile.

Grammar

Exercise 24.24*

Correct the following sentences where necessary.

1. The teacher that I had last year liked me so much he made sure I had to take his class again.
2. Broccoli is a vegetable which I just don't like.
3. I think movie stars that speak up against animal cruelty are cool.
4. I'm someone which isn't good to cross.
5. People that take long naps are said to live longer lives.
6. Maple Leaf Interiors, who redecorated my office, just won an award.
7. Mr. Morales is the teacher which I respect the most.
8. Chefs that don't use real butter usually suffer from harsh criticism.

9. The problems which we're having at work could drive anyone to quit.

10. We walked across Dead Man's Bluff, that he told us would take us to the store, as quickly as possible.

Exercise 24.25

To test your understanding of the pronoun problems we have covered so far, try this exercise, which contains all three kinds of pronoun–antecedent agreement errors. Correct the following sentences where necessary.

1. Each of her suitors had their faults, but Denise decided to overlook the shortcomings of the one that had the most money.

2. Embezzling is what he does best, but he hasn't been able to pull one off lately.

3. Everyone may pick up their exams in my office on Tuesday after 9:00 a.m.

4. None of the candidates brought their résumé, so we had to reject them all.

5. Every applicant must submit their portfolio of work, their essay on why they want to enter the program, and a neatly folded $50 bill.

6. When I go fishing, I expect to catch at least a few.

7. Every administrative assistant knows that their boss is someone that could not survive for 15 minutes without competent secretarial assistance.

8. All the women in this beauty pageant are treated like a sister even though the competition is fierce.

9. Everybody that joins the tour will receive their own souvenir hat.

10. Before a Canadian votes, it is their responsibility to make themselves familiar with the candidates and the issues.

Person Agreement

So far, we have focused on using pronouns correctly and clearly within a sentence. Now let's turn to the problem of **person agreement**, which means using pronouns consistently throughout a sentence or a paragraph. There are three categories of person that we use when we write or speak:

	Singular	Plural
First person	I; me	we; us
Second person	you	you
Third person	she, he, it, one; her, him *and all pronouns ending in* -one, -thing, -body	they; them

Here is the rule for person agreement:

> Do not mix "persons" unless meaning requires it.

In other words, be consistent. If you begin a sentence using a second-person pronoun, you must use second person all the way through. Look at this sentence:

If *you* wish to succeed, *one* must work hard.

This is the most common error—mixing second-person *you* with third-person *one*. Here's another example:

***One* can live happily in Vancouver if *you* have a sturdy umbrella.**

1. We can correct this error by using the second person throughout:

   ***You* can live happily in Vancouver if *you* have a sturdy umbrella.**

2. We can also correct it by using the third person throughout:

   ***One* can live happily in Vancouver if *one* has a sturdy umbrella.**

or

***One* can live happily in Vancouver if *he* or *she* has a sturdy umbrella.**

These examples raise two points of style that you should consider.

> 1. Don't overuse *one*.

All three revised sentences are grammatically correct, but they make different impressions on the reader, and impressions are an important part of communication.

- The first sentence, in the second person, sounds the most informal—like something you would say. It's a bit casual for general writing purposes.
- The second sentence, which uses *one* twice, sounds the most formal—even a little pretentious.
- The third sentence falls between the other two in formality. It is the one you'd be most likely to use in writing for school or business.

Although it is grammatically correct and non-sexist, the third sentence raises another problem: frequent use of *he or she* in a continuous prose passage, whether that passage is as short as a paragraph or as long as a paper, is guaranteed to irritate your reader.

> 2. Don't overuse *he or she*.

He or she is inclusive, but it is a wordy construction. If used too frequently, the reader cannot help shifting focus from what you're saying to how you're saying it. The best writing is transparent—that is, it doesn't call attention to itself. If your reader becomes distracted by your style, your meaning gets lost. Consider this sentence:

> A student can easily pass this course if he or she applies himself or herself to his or her studies.

Readers deserve better. A paper—or even a single paragraph—filled with this clumsy construction will annoy even the most patient reader. There are two better solutions to the problem of sexist language, and they are already familiar to you because they are the same as those for making pronouns ending in *-one*, *-body*, or *-thing* agree with their antecedents.

1. You can change the whole sentence to the plural.

   Students can easily pass this course if they apply themselves to their studies.

2. You can rewrite the sentence without using pronouns.

   A student can easily pass this course by applying good study habits.

Exercise 24.26* In each of the following sentences, select the correct word from the choices given in parentheses. Check your answers before continuing.

1. If you're going to San Francisco, I urge (them her you) to visit the museums there.
2. Everyone in the office understood that (they she) needed to stay late tonight.
3. Someone who wants a new job should have (their your his her an) up-to-date résumé ready.
4. If you make your famous chili, will (one he you) tell (one's his your) family?
5. When visiting the Queen, (you we he one) should always bow or curtsy.

Exercise 24.27* Work with a partner to correct the errors in pronoun consistency in the following sentences.

1. Most people enjoy eating when you are with good friends in a pleasant environment.
2. One is never too old to learn, but you are never too young to know everything.

3. One should always remove your shoes when entering a mosque.

4. Students who don't learn from history are doomed to find yourself back in Grade 9 for a second try.

5. When one visits Beijing, you must see the Great Wall, the Forbidden City, and the Temple of Heaven.

6. Experience is that marvellous thing that enables us to recognize a mistake when you make it again. (F.P. Jones)

7. Middle age is that time of life when you've met so many people that everyone one meets reminds one of somebody else.

8. The penalties for plagiarism are severe, but most of us don't think about them until after you've been caught.

9. Always read through the entire test before one begins to answer the questions.

10. Anyone can learn another language if they have enough motivation; the most effective method is to fall in love with someone who speaks the language you are trying to learn.

Exercise 24.28*

Revise the following passage to make the nouns and pronouns agree in person (first, second, or third) and number (singular or plural). Use the italicized word in the first sentence of each paragraph as your marker. Ten corrections are necessary in this exercise.

When *people* see a dreadful occurrence on television, such as a bombing, an earthquake, or a mass slaughter, it does not always affect one. It is one thing for people to see the ravages of war oneself and another thing to see a three-minute newscast of the same battle, neatly edited by the CBC. Even the horrible effects of natural catastrophes that wipe out whole populations are somehow minimized or trivialized when I see them on TV. And

Grammar

although viewers may be horrified by the gaunt faces of starving children on the screen, you can easily escape into your familiar world of Egg McMuffins, Shake'n Bake, and Labatt Blue that is portrayed in commercial messages.

Thus, the impact of television on *us* is a mixed one. It is true that one is shown terrible, sometimes shocking, events that you could not possibly have seen before television. In this way, one's world is drawn together more closely. However, the risk in creating this immediacy is that one may become desensitized and cease to feel or care about other human beings.

Exercise 24.29 Revise the following paragraphs, which contain 15 errors representing the three different kinds of pronoun–antecedent agreement errors. If you change a subject from singular to plural, don't forget to change the verb to agree. Some of your answers may differ from our suggestions and still be correct. Check with your instructor.

Everyone that has been to Newfoundland and Labrador knows that an outport is a small fishing community along the coast of that vast island province. Ladle Cove, for example, is a tiny outport with fewer than 200 residents that live there all year. Despite its small population, Ladle Cove is a village which enjoyed a nationwide moment of fame when a man that lives there met the Queen. Fred had left Ladle Cove, as just about every man does when they need to find work, and gone to St. John's. Fred wanted to work, but he had few marketable skills to help him get one. Fortunately, he had relatives in St. John's that helped him find a place to stay and eventually found him a job at Purity Foods, a company famous for their baked goods—and for Newfoundland's favourite treat, Jam Jam cookies.

During Queen Elizabeth's visit to St. John's, the officials that organized her tour decided it would be a good idea for her to visit a local industry which had a national reputation. Purity Foods was the logical choice. While touring the plant, the Queen stopped to talk to a few of the men and women that were on the production line. Near the end of the tour, that was being filmed by the national media, the Queen stopped by one of the workers that were making the famous Jam Jams: Fred. As the television lights glared and each reporter held their pencil poised over their notebook, the Queen leaned toward Fred and asked, "And what are we making here?" With a courteous bow in Her Majesty's direction, Fred replied, "Ten-fifty an hour, Ma'am. Ten-fifty an hour."

Punctuation

Punctuation problems can certainly be pesky when it comes to writing research papers. The material presented here will help you use a standard format for your ideas to help make them clear to your readers. Using punctuation with ease makes writing easier, and using it properly makes *reading* your writing easier.

The Comma

Many writers-in-training tend to sprinkle punctuation marks like pepper over their pages. Do not use punctuation to spice up your writing. Punctuation marks have a function: they indicate to the reader how the various parts of a sentence relate to one another. By changing the punctuation, you can change the meaning of a sentence. If you don't believe that, ask Rogers Communication about its two-million-dollar legal dispute with Aliant Inc. over the wording of a contract—the disagreement hinged on the placement of a comma!

Here are two examples that demonstrate how commas can influence meaning:

1. An instructor wrote the following sentence on the board and asked the class to punctuate it: "Woman without her man is nothing."

   The men wrote, "Woman, without her man, is nothing."

   The women wrote, "Woman! Without her, man is nothing."

2. Now it's your turn. Punctuate this sentence: "I think there is only one person to blame myself."

   If you wrote, "I think there is only one person to blame, myself," the reader will understand that you believe only one person—who may or may not be known to you—is to blame.

   If you wrote, "I think there is only one person to blame: myself," the reader will understand that you are personally accepting responsibility for the blame.

The comma is the most frequently used—and misused—punctuation mark in English. One sure sign of a competent writer is the correct use of commas, so it is important that you master them. This section presents five comma rules that cover most instances in which you need to use commas. If you apply these five rules faithfully, your reader will never be confused by missing or misplaced commas in your writing. And if, as occasionally happens, the sentence you are writing is not covered by one of our five rules, remember the default commandment of comma usage: when in doubt, leave it out.

Five Comma Rules

> 1. Use commas to separate three or more items in a series. The items may be expressed as words, phrases, or clauses.

Words	The required subjects in this program are *math*, *physics*, and *English*.
Phrases	Punctuation marks are the traffic signals of prose. They tell us to *slow down, notice this, take a detour,* and *stop*. (Lynne Truss)
Clauses	*Karin went to the movies, Jan and Danuta went to play pool,* and *I went to bed*.

The comma before the *and* at the end of the list is optional, but we advise you to use it. Misunderstandings can occur if it is left out.

Exercise 25.1*

Insert commas where necessary in the following sentences. Answers for exercises in this chapter begin on page 480.

1. My favourite comedians are Curly Larry and Moe.
2. If you ignore my terrible accent poor grammar and limited vocabulary, my French is excellent.
3. A panda is a bear-like marsupial that eats shoots and leaves. (Lynne Truss)
4. Cambodian food is spicy colourful nourishing and delicious.
5. In Canada, the seasons are spring summer fall winter winter and winter.
6. We'll have a hamburger and French fries to begin with.
7. Regan cannot decide if her bridesmaids should wear black green or camouflage dresses.
8. The successful applicant will have computer skills, of course, as well as excellent communication skills a friendly disposition a willingness to work hard and a sense of humour.
9. Both my doctor and my wife agree that I should eat better exercise more and stop smoking.
10. Much of the world sees Canada as a land where French is spoken ice and snow are year-round hazards and violent hockey is a favourite pastime.

2. Put a comma between independent clauses when they are joined by these connecting words:

for	but	so
and	or	
nor	yet	

(You can remember these words easily if you notice that their first letters spell **FANBOYS**.)

I hope I do well in the interview, for I really want this job.
I like Norah Jones, but I prefer Diana Krall.
We shape our tools, and our tools shape us. (Marshall McLuhan)
I knew I was going to be late, so I went back to sleep.

Be sure that the sentence you are punctuating contains two independent clauses rather than a single clause with one subject and a multiple verb. For example,

We loved the book but hated the movie.

(We is the subject, and there are two verbs: loved and hated. Do not put a comma between two or more verbs that share a single subject.)

We both loved the book, but Kim hated the movie.

(This sentence contains two independent clauses—We loved and Kim hated—joined by *but*. The comma is required here.)

Exercise 25.2* **Insert commas where they are needed in the following sentences, then check your answers on page 481.**

1. I didn't get an A+ in that course but at least I passed.
2. She looked beautiful yet she also looked quite sad.
3. Omar would have gone to Toronto but he didn't want to leave Saskatoon.
4. Give me the apple for I know it's good for me.
5. The cats are acting up but I still love them dearly.
6. I like only rap music but I am going to a ballet with my girlfriend anyway.
7. We haven't bought our winter boots nor have we unpacked our mitts and scarves.
8. Either Magda gets the last piece of pie or I won't bake one again.
9. I really want to mow the lawn but I need to go job hunting.
10. I came down with the flu so I can't make it to work.

3. Put a comma after an introductory word, phrase, or dependent clause that comes before an independent clause.

Lucas, you aren't paying attention. (word)
After staying up all night, I staggered into class 15 minutes late. (phrase)
If that's their idea of a large pizza, we'd better order two. (clause)
Until she got her promotion, she was quite friendly. (clause)

Exercise 25.3*

Insert commas where they are needed in the following sentences. Check your answers on page 481 before you move on to Rule 4.

1. Remember a clear conscience is often just a sign of a poor memory.
2. If you think nobody cares try missing a few payments.
3. When the cannibals ate a missionary they got a taste of religion.
4. No matter how much I practise my singing never gets any better.
5. First cook the noodles in a large pot of boiling water.
6. If Barbie is so popular why do you have to buy friends for her?
7. Until I had my performance review I thought my manager had no appreciation of my efforts.
8. No matter how much you push the envelope it will still be stationery.
9. Ladies and gentlemen please put away all cellphones iPads and any other electronic devices you may have concealed on your person before entering the examination room.
10. In democracy it is your vote that counts; in feudalism it is your count that votes.

> **4.** Use commas to set off any word, phrase, or dependent clause that is NOT ESSENTIAL to the main idea of the sentence.

Following this rule can make the difference between whether your readers understand or misunderstand your meaning. For example, the following two sentences are identical, except for a pair of commas. But notice what a difference those two tiny marks make to meaning:

The children who were dressed in Halloween costumes got little. bags of candy. (Only the children wearing Halloween costumes got candy.)

The children, who were dressed in Halloween costumes, got little bags of candy. (All the children wore costumes and were given candy.)

To test whether a word, phrase, or clause is essential to the meaning of your sentence, mentally put parentheses around it. If the sentence still makes complete sense (i.e., the main idea is unchanged; the sentence just delivers less information), the material in parentheses is *not essential* and should be set off from the rest of the sentence by a comma or commas.

Non-essential information can appear at the beginning of a sentence,[1] in the middle of a sentence, or at the end of a sentence. Study the following examples.

> Alice Munro {one of Canada's best-known storytellers} spends summers in Clinton and winters in Comox.

Many readers would be puzzled the first time they read this sentence. Because all the information is presented without punctuation, the reader assumes it is all equally important. In fact, the material in broken parentheses is extra information, a supplementary detail. It can be deleted without changing the sentence's meaning, and so it should be separated from the rest of the sentence by commas:

> Alice Munro, one of Canada's best-known storytellers, spends summers in Clinton and winters in Comox.

Here's another example:

> The Queen {who has twice as many birthdays as anyone else} officially celebrates her birthday on May 24.

Again, the sentence is hard to read. You can't count on your readers to go back and reread every sentence they don't understand at first glance. As a writer, your responsibility is to give readers the clues they need as to what is crucial information and what isn't. In the example above, the information in broken parentheses is not essential to the meaning of the sentence, so it should be set off by commas:

> The Queen, who has twice as many birthdays as anyone else, officially celebrates her birthday on May 24.

In this next sentence, the non-essential information comes at the end.

> Writing a good cover letter isn't difficult (if you're careful).

The phrase "if you're careful" is not essential to the main idea, so it should be separated from the rest of the sentence by a comma:

> Writing a good cover letter isn't difficult, if you're careful.

And finally, consider this sentence:

> Writing a cover letter {that is clear, complete, and concise} is a challenge.

If you take out "that is clear, complete, and concise," you change the meaning of the sentence. Not all letters of application are a challenge to write. Writing vague and wordy letters is easy. Anyone can do it. The words "that is clear, complete, and concise" are essential to the meaning of the sentence, and so they are not set off by commas.

> Writing a cover letter that is clear, complete, and concise is a challenge.

---

[1] Comma Rule 3 covers non-essential information at the beginning of a sentence.

Insert commas where they are missing in the following sentences, then check your answers on page 481.

Exercise 25.4*

1. A good day in my opinion always starts with a few cuts of high-volume heavy metal.
2. This photograph which was taken when I was eight months old embarrasses me whenever my parents display it.
3. Mira's boyfriend who looks like an ape is living proof that love is blind.
4. Isn't it strange that the poor who are often bitterly critical of the rich buy lottery tickets?
5. A nagging headache the result of last night's party made me miserable all morning.
6. Our ancient car made it all the way to Saskatoon without breaking down a piece of good luck that astonished us all.
7. Professor Repke a popular mathematics teacher won the Distinguished Teaching Award this year.
8. We're going to spend the afternoon at the mall a weekly event that has become a ritual.
9. No one who watched Patrick Roy play could doubt that he was a superstar.
10. Classical music which I call Prozac for the ears can be very soothing in times of stress.

Insert commas where they are needed in the following sentences. Check your answers on page 482 before continuing.

Exercise 25.5*

1. Unfortunately we'll have to begin all over again.
2. Lord Black your wife would like a word with you.
3. In college the quality of your work is more important than the effort you put into it.
4. Hopelessly lost my father refused to stop and ask for directions.
5. Finally understanding what she was trying to say I apologized for being so slow.
6. After an evening of watching television I have accomplished as much as if I had been unconscious.
7. Since the doctor ordered me to walk to work every morning I have seen three accidents involving people walking to work.
8. That same year Stephen Leacock bought his summer home in Orillia, Ontario.
9. When an optimist is pulled over by a police officer the optimist assumes it's to ask for directions.
10. Having munched our way through a large bag of peanuts while watching the game we weren't interested in supper.

> **5.** Use commas between coordinate adjectives but not between cumulative adjectives.

Coordinate adjectives are adjectives that pass two tests: (1) they can be reordered without changing the meaning of the sentence, and (2) the word *and* can be inserted between them without changing the meaning of the sentence. For example,

Our company is looking for energetic, courteous salespeople.

The adjectives *energetic* and *courteous* could appear in reverse order, and you could put *and* between them: "Our company is looking for courteous and energetic salespeople."

In a series of **cumulative adjectives**, however, each adjective modifies the word that follows it. You cannot change their order, nor can you insert *and* between them.

The bride wore a pale pink silk dress, and the groom wore a dark blue wool suit.

You cannot say "The bride wore a silk pink pale dress" or "The groom wore a dark and blue and wool suit," so no commas are used with these adjectives.

One final note about commas before you try the review exercises: never place a SINGLE comma between a subject and its verb.

Wrong:	Those who intend to register for hockey, must be at the arena by 8:00 a.m.
Right:	Those who intend to register for hockey must be at the arena by 8:00 a.m.

Two commas, however, between a subject and its verb are correct if the commas set off non-essential material.

Saied and Mohamed, who intend to register for hockey, have never played before.

Exercise 25.6* Insert commas where they are needed in the following sentences. Check your answers before continuing.

1. Dietitians recommend that we eat at least two servings daily of green leafy vegetables.
2. Do you want your portrait in a glossy finish or a matte finish?
3. Bright yellow fabric that repels stains is ideal for rain gear.
4. Toronto in the summer is hot smoggy and humid.
5. St. John's, on the other hand, is cool sunny and windy.
6. The dining room table was made of richly stained ornately carved walnut.
7. This ergonomic efficient full-function keyboard comes in a variety of pastel shades.

8. We ordered a large nutritious salad for lunch and then smothered it in calorie-laden creamy ranch dressing.
9. For my sister's birthday, her boyfriend gave her a cute cuddly seven-week-old puppy.
10. Today's paper has an article about a new car made of lightweight durable carbon fibre.

The rest of the exercises in this section require you to apply all five comma rules. Before you start, write out the five rules and keep them in front of you as you work through the exercises. At the end of each sentence, write the number(s) of the rule(s) you applied to correct it. After you've finished each exercise, check your answers and make sure you understand any mistakes you've made.

Exercise 25.7*

1. If it doesn't stop raining soon we will begin to think we are in Vancouver.
2. The gates are down and the lights are flashing but the train is nowhere in sight.
3. No words in the English language rhyme with *month orange silver* or *purple*.
4. At our retirement banquet instead of the traditional gold watch we were presented with an Inuit soapstone sculpture.
5. Dorothy got lost in the Land of Oz for she had three men giving her directions.
6. No meal is complete in my opinion without a sweet preferably chocolate dessert.
7. My first acting role was as the husband in a school play but sadly it was not a speaking role.
8. According to my professor the difference between mechanical and civil engineers is that mechanical engineers build weapons and civil engineers build targets.
9. Canadian football unlike the American version is full of exciting plays risky strategy and frequent upsets.
10. The optimist sees a glass that is half full while a pessimist sees a glass that is half empty but an engineer sees a glass that is twice as big as it needs to be.

Exercise 25.8*

1. Whereas the Super Bowl tradition goes back about four decades the Grey Cup has a history that stretches back to the 19th century.
2. Otherwise Mrs. Lincoln said she very much enjoyed the play.
3. Our guard dog a Rottweiler caught an intruder and maimed him for life.
4. Unfortunately my Uncle Ladislaw was the intruder and he intends to sue us for every penny we have.
5. The year 1945 marked the end of World War II and the beginning of assistance to war-torn nations.
6. We bought a lovely old oak dining table at auction for $300.
7. If there were more people like Gladys global warming would be the least of our worries.
8. We are pleased with your résumé and are offering you an interview this week.

9. Deciding on the midnight blue velvet pants was easy but paying for them was not.
10. Igor asked "May I show you to your quarters or would you prefer to spend the night in the dungeon?"

Exercise 25.9 To test your mastery of commas, provide the necessary punctuation for the following paragraph. There are 15 errors.

When my brother and I were growing up my mother used to summon us home from playing by ringing a solid brass bell that could be heard for miles. All of the other kids to our great embarrassment, knew when our mother was calling us and they would tease us by making ringing noises. We begged her to yell like all the other moms but she knew she had a foolproof system and wouldn't change. One day while we were playing with our friends in the fields behind our homes the bell rang in the middle of an important game. The other kids began their usual taunts that our mother was calling but this time we bravely ignored the bell. When it rang the second time we ignored it again. By the third ring, however we knew that we were in big trouble so we dashed for home. We agreed on the way that we would tell our mother that we just didn't hear the bell. We arrived hot sweaty and panting from our run. Before Mom could say a word my brother blurted out, "We didn't hear the bell until the third ring!" Fortunately for us our mother couldn't stop laughing and we escaped the punishment we deserved.

The Five Comma Rules

1. Use commas to separate items in a series of three or more. The items may be expressed as words, phrases, or clauses.
2. Put a comma between independent clauses when they are joined by *for, and, nor, but, or, yet,* or *so*.
3. Put a comma after an introductory word, phrase, or dependent clause that comes before an independent clause.
4. Use commas to set off a word, phrase, or dependent clause that is NOT ESSENTIAL to the main idea of the sentence.
5. Use commas between coordinate adjectives but not between cumulative adjectives.

The Semicolon

The semicolon and the colon are often confused and used as if they were interchangeable. They have distinct purposes, however, and their correct use can dramatically improve a reader's understanding of your writing. The semicolon has three functions.

> **1.** A semicolon can replace a period; in other words, it can appear between two independent clauses.

You should use a semicolon when the two clauses (sentences) you are joining are closely connected in meaning, or when there is a cause-and-effect relationship between them.

> I have used up all my sick days; now I call in dead.
> Montreal is not the city's original name; it was once called Ville-Marie.

A period could have been used instead of a semicolon in either of these sentences, but the close connection between the clauses makes a semicolon more effective in communicating the writer's meaning.

> **2.** Certain transitional words or phrases can be put between independent clauses to show a cause-and-effect relationship or the continuation of an idea.

Words or phrases used in this way are usually preceded by a semicolon and followed by a comma:

; also,	; furthermore,	; nevertheless,
; as a result,	; however,	; on the other hand,
; besides,	; in addition,	; otherwise,
; consequently,	; in fact,	; then,
; finally,	; instead,	; therefore,
; for example,	; moreover,	; thus,

> The forecast called for sun; instead, we got snow.
>
> My monitor went blank; nevertheless, I kept on typing.
>
> "I'm not offended by dumb blonde jokes because I know I'm not dumb; besides, I also know I'm not blonde." (Dolly Parton)

In other words, ***a semicolon*** + ***a transitional word/phrase*** + ***a comma*** = a link strong enough to come between two related independent clauses.

Note, however, that, when these transitional words and phrases are used as non-essential expressions rather than as connecting words, they are separated from the rest of the sentence by commas (The Comma, Rule 4, page 401).

> I just can't seem to master particle physics, however hard I try.
>
> The emissions test, moreover, will ensure that your car is running well.

> **3.** To make a *complex list* easier to read and understand, put semicolons between the items instead of commas.

A complex list is one in which at least one component part already contains commas. Here are two examples:

> I grew up in a series of small towns, including Cumberland, British Columbia; Red Deer, Alberta; and Timmins, Ontario.
>
> When we opened the refrigerator, we found a limp, brown head of lettuce; two small containers of yogurt, whose "best before" dates had long since passed; and a hard, dried-up piece of something that might once have been cheddar cheese.

Exercise 25.10* Put a check mark next to the sentences that are correctly punctuated. Check your answers before continuing.

1. ___ It is difficult to tell what does bring happiness; for both wealth and poverty have failed. (Kim Hubbard)
2. ___ It has been raining steadily for almost a month; if it doesn't stop soon, I'm building an ark.
3. ___ If a tree falls in the forest where no one can hear it; does it make a sound?
4. ___ Here is a book you should read; it's about overcoming challenges to achieve success.
5. ___ My brother and I have not spoken face to face in almost three years; which is how long we have had phones with text messaging.
6. ___ I don't remember if my childhood was happy or not; I was only a kid at the time.
7. ___ My sister just had a baby; I can't wait to find out if I'm an aunt or an uncle. (Gracie Allen)
8. ___ Cooking is one of my favourite hobbies; because I can eat the result.
9. ___ My neighbour works for a high-tech company; but he can't change the ring tone on his phone.
10. ___ I think; therefore, I'm single. (Lizz Winstead)

Exercise 25.11 Correct the faulty punctuation in Exercise 25.10.

Exercise 25.12*

Insert semicolons where necessary in these sentences. Then check your answers.

1. Juanita was wondering when that book would arrive after all, she had already waited a month.
2. It really isn't an inconvenience nevertheless, I will take the compensation.
3. Jamal wasn't the only one who deserved punishment his brother did, too.
4. Playing video games isn't detrimental to kids' health they are constantly moving their hands.
5. We were planning to leave on Thursday however, I am open to leaving earlier if it is possible.
6. You have to stop smiling otherwise, I think you might get a face cramp.
7. Writing a great résumé isn't easy I appreciate all your hard work.
8. You should consider applying for jobs in Red Deer, Alberta Victoria, British Columbia or Charlottetown, Prince Edward Island.
9. Kathe is the top of our class everyone wishes for grades like hers.
10. We have important work to do this week, for example, we need to write an email congratulating the boss on his new yacht.

Exercise 25.13

Test your mastery of semicolons and commas by correcting the punctuation in these sentences.

1. It's important to go with the flow when it comes to group work, on the other hand, you have to make sure things get done.
2. Next time you should try harder you beat only three world records.
3. Shares are up this quarter however the company had to pay out a great many dividends.
4. My family watches nothing but sit-coms, therefore almost daily, I have been forced to endure the slapstick I hate so much.
5. Canadians really are polite for example I ran into a door yesterday and apologized to it.
6. Don't ever give up on your dreams if you do you'll never sleep at night.
7. I was given a huge list of administrative tasks to finish, including counting and putting together all the bills folding and packaging all the contracts, which need to be sent out next week, and throwing out any documents that are older than seven years.
8. Sometimes people know that things aren't great but believe they will get better.
9. Kumar tried to convince me to jump out of an airplane, I steadfastly refused.
10. To use or not to use the semicolon is sometimes a matter of the writer's choice, a few syntactical constructions however require a semicolon—no other punctuation mark will do.

The Colon

The colon functions as an introducer. When a statement is followed by a list, one or more examples, or a quotation, the colon alerts the reader that some sort of explanatory detail is coming up.

> When I travel, I am never without three things: sturdy shoes, a money belt, and my journal.
>
> There is only one enemy we cannot defeat: time.
>
> We have two choices: to study or to fail.
>
> Early in his career, Robert Fulford did not think very highly of intellectual life in Canada: "My generation of Canadians grew up believing that, if we were very good or very smart, or both, we would someday *graduate* from Canada."

> The statement that precedes the colon must be a complete sentence (independent clause).

A colon should never come immediately after *is* or *are*. Here's an example of what *not* to write.

> The only things I am violently allergic to are: cats, ragweed, and country music.

This is incorrect because the statement before the colon is not a complete sentence.

> 1. Use a colon between an independent clause and a list or one or more examples that define, explain, or illustrate the independent clause.

The information after the colon often answers the question "what?" or "who?"

> I am violently allergic to three things: (what?) cats, ragweed, and country music.
>
> Business and industry face a new challenge: (what?) rebuilding their pension funds.
>
> The president has found the ideal candidate for the position: (who?) her brother.

> 2. Use a colon after a complete sentence introducing a quotation.

> Lucille Ball observed that there were three secrets to staying young: "Live honestly, eat slowly, and lie about your age."

> 3. Finally, use a colon to separate the title of a book, film, or TV show from a subtitle.

> *Word Play: What Happens When People Talk*
>
> *The Chronicles of Narnia: Prince Caspian*
>
> *Trading Spouses: Meet Your New Mommy*

If you remember the following summary, you'll have no more trouble with colons:

> The colon follows an independent clause and introduces an example, a list, or a quotation that amplifies the meaning of that clause.

Exercise 25.14*

Put a check mark next to the sentences that are correctly punctuated. Check your answers before going on.

1. ___ J. K. Rowling wrote some of the world's most famous books: the *Harry Potter* series.
2. ___ The best thing to have for breakfast is: cereal and a banana.
3. ___ It's an undeniable fact, Canada's trees are truly beautiful.
4. ___ It has always been about only one thing love conquers all.
5. ___ The most important clothes to have for winter include: mittens, boots, and a toque.
6. ___ When I am really stressed, only one thing helps *Star Wars, Episode 2: Attack of the Clones.*
7. ___ What it takes is this perseverance.
8. ___ Paula often repeats her mantra to get through the day: "Never despair."
9. ___ It isn't nice to critique her she is just starting out in the business.
10. ___ Whether or not you believe it, there are three types of workers: fast, slow, and slower.

Exercise 25.15*

Insert colons in the following sentences where necessary and then check your answers. If you've made any mistakes, review the explanations on the previous page and this one, study the examples, and be sure you understand why your answers were wrong before going on.

1. Right after we moved in, we discovered we had a problem termites.
2. I have set myself three goals this year to achieve an 80 percent average, to get a good summer job, and to buy a car.
3. After our bankruptcy, our credit card consultant asked us an interesting question "Why don't you cut up your credit cards?"
4. Many Canadian writers are better known abroad than they are at home Carol Shields, Neil Bissoondath, and Michael Ondaatje are three examples.
5. There are a number of inexpensive activities that will improve physical fitness; swimming, tennis, jogging, even brisk walking.
6. Jocelyn is trying to achieve two contradictory goals a significant weight loss and success as a restaurant critic.

7. Several of the animals on the international list of endangered species are native to Canada; the wood bison, the northern kit fox, and the whooping crane.
8. We'll finish the assignment by tomorrow only if we stay up all night and consume vast quantities of pizza and black coffee.
9. Canada's population is worn out and exhausted at the end of a long, hard winter, but most people are able to console themselves with one comforting thought, spring will arrive sometime in May or June.
10. There are several troublesome implications of biological engineering, but one in particular disturbs most people the cloning of human beings.

Exercise 25.16* Correct the incorrectly punctuated sentences in Exercise 25.14.

Exercise 25.17 The following paragraph contains 15 punctuation errors. Replace the incorrect punctuation marks—including the dashes—with commas, colons, and semicolons, as needed. (No other punctuation marks are required.)

After a long day at work Greta couldn't wait to get home, however she could not find: her car keys. She looked in her purse in her desk drawer even in the filing cabinet. Knowing that she had a bad habit of leaving the keys in the ignition she decided to check the car in the parking lot. When she saw that her car was missing she panicked and called the police to tell them her car had been stolen because: she had stupidly left the keys in the ignition. Then she called the one person she didn't want to talk to at a time like this; her husband. When she explained what had happened there was a long pause, eventually he patiently reminded her that he had dropped her off at the office that morning. Embarrassed but relieved Greta sheepishly asked her husband to come and pick her up. There was an even longer pause. "I will: just as soon as I convince this police officer that I have not stolen your car."

Quotation Marks

Quotation marks are used to mark the beginning and end of direct speech (dialogue), quoted material, and some titles. For information on how to punctuate and insert quoted material into your papers, see Chapter 17. To review when to use quotation marks for titles, see pages 190 and 204.

A **direct quotation** is someone's exact words, whether they are spoken or written. A quotation is usually introduced by a reporting expression such as *she said*, *he replied*, or *they commented*. Put quotation marks before and after the person's exact words.

Tim asked angrily, "Did you delete my address book?"

"No, a virus attacked the computer and ate your files," I replied.

Nearly 50 years ago, Marshall McLuhan observed, "The medium is the message."

Do not use quotation marks with **indirect quotations** (reported speech):

Tim asked angrily if I had deleted his address book. (These are not Tim's exact words, so no quotation marks are necessary.)

I replied that a virus had attacked his computer and destroyed his files. (Note that indirect quotations are often introduced by *that*.)

A half-century ago, Marshall McLuhan observed that the meaning of a message was determined by the medium through which it was delivered.

Use single quotation marks to enclose a quotation within a quotation:

"I don't understand what you mean by the term 'creative memory,'" said Lauren.

The final thing you need to know about direct quotations is how to punctuate them. Here are the rules to follow.

1. Use a comma to separate a reporting expression from a quotation.

Professor Lam announced, "You will write the midterm test on Tuesday."

"You will write the midterm test on Tuesday," announced Professor Lam.

2. If there is no reporting verb, use a colon after an independent clause to introduce a quotation.

Too late, I remembered Professor Lam's advice at the beginning of term: "Keep up with your work each week, and the tests will cause you no trouble."

3. Begin each quoted sentence with a capital letter. If a quoted sentence is divided into two parts, begin the second part with a small letter.

"Our national anthem," Justin informed us, "was written by Calixa Lavallée. First composed in French, it was later translated into English."

4. Always put commas and periods inside the quotation marks.

"I love you." Jessica waited for Fernandez to reply. "Well, let's just forget I said it," she continued, after waiting for his response for what felt like an hour.

5. If a question mark or exclamation mark is part of the direct quotation, put it *inside* the second quotation mark of a pair.

"Could you help me?" the woman asked. "I'm trying to find Melrose Avenue." Almost in tears, she went on, "I'm already late for my job interview!"

6. If the question mark or exclamation mark is *not* part of the direct quotation, put it *outside* the second quotation mark. (It's part of your sentence, not the speaker's.)

Did you hear her say, "I'm late for my job interview"?

7. Put colons and semicolons *outside* the second quotation mark (unless they are part of the direct quotation).

Near tears, the woman begged, "Please help me"; we could hardly leave her standing there alone.

The woman cried, "Please help me"; she was near tears.

"Please help me; I'm late for my job interview," pleaded the woman.

Exercise 25.18*

Together with a partner, work through the following items carefully. Insert any necessary punctuation, including quotation marks. As you go through these sentences, notice how difficult it is to tell which words are not the writer's—until you insert the necessary punctuation. Answers for exercises in this chapter begin on page 480.

1. Pioneer hockey broadcaster Foster Hewitt made famous the words He shoots! He scores!
2. Another broadcasting legend Danny Gallavan once described a move by Montreal defenceman Serge Savard as a Savardian spinorama.
3. All hockey players are bilingual. They know English and profanity according to the great Detroit Red Wings player Gordie Howe.
4. Wayne Gretzky was arguably the best hockey player ever; he said that his secret was to skate not to where the puck had been, but to where it was going.
5. It was Paul Gallico who summed up ice hockey as a fast body-contact game played by men with clubs in their hands and knives laced to their feet.

The Question Mark

Everyone knows that a question mark follows an interrogative (or asking) sentence, but everyone sometimes forgets to include it! Let this section serve as a reminder not to forget.

The question mark is the end punctuation for all interrogative sentences.

The question mark gives your readers an important clue to the meaning of your sentence. "There's more?" is vastly different in meaning from "There's more!" and that difference is communicated to readers by punctuation.

The only time you don't end a question with a question mark is when the question is part of a statement.

Is anyone there? (question)

I asked if anyone was there. (statement)

Do you understand? (question)

I wonder whether you understand. (statement)

What costume have you decided on for the Halloween party? (question)

I'm curious to know what costume you've chosen for the Halloween party. (statement)

Exercise 25.19*

Supply the correct end punctuation for the following sentences. Then check your answers. Answers for this section begin on page 485.

1. Do you ever wonder why we park in a driveway and drive on a parkway
2. I cannot understand how you can listen to that music
3. I find it hard to believe that you would question my integrity
4. I wonder if my apartment will ever be the same after their visit
5. What's another word for *thesaurus*
6. If we can't finish the project on time, will we lose the contract
7. I question the results you got on your survey
8. Did you know there are only 18 000 elephants in all of India
9. Human Resources wants to know why we hired an unqualified, inexperienced person for such a sensitive position
10. If corn oil comes from corn, where does baby oil come from

The Exclamation Mark

In informal or personal writings, the exclamation mark is a useful piece of punctuation for conveying **tone** to your readers. Consider the difference between these two sentences:

There's a man behind you.
There's a man behind you!

In the first sentence, information is being supplied, perhaps about the lineup at a grocery store checkout counter. The second sentence might be a shouted warning about a mugger.

Use an exclamation mark as end punctuation in sentences requiring extreme emphasis or dramatic effect.

Exclamation marks have "punch" or dramatic effect only if you use them sparingly. If you use an exclamation mark after every third sentence, how will your readers know when you really mean to indicate excitement? Note also that exclamation marks are seldom used in academic or professional writing.

Practically any sentence could end with an exclamation mark, but remember that the punctuation changes the meaning of the sentence. Read each of the following sentences with and without an exclamation mark and picture the situation that would call for each reading.

He's gone

The room was empty

Don't touch that button

There she goes again

Exercise 25.20* Supply the correct end punctuation for each of the following sentences. In many cases, the punctuation you use will depend on how you want the sentence to be read.

1. You must be kidding
2. Turn left Now
3. I can't believe I actually passed
4. Oh, great We're moving to Backwater, Alberta
5. Run It's right behind you
6. I'm freezing Turn up the heat
7. "Workers of the world, unite" (Karl Marx)
8. At last Someone is finally coming to take our order
9. For the last time, leave me alone
10. What a great game I've never seen a better one

Exercise 25.21 Supply appropriate end punctuation to the questions below. Note that some items include more than one sentence.

1. I passed
2. Stop, thief
3. This salsa is scorching
4. He's on the stairway, right behind you
5. We won I can't believe it
6. The crowd chanted triumphantly, "Go, Habs, go "
7. Customer: "Waiter, what's this fly doing in my soup" Waiter: "Looks like the backstroke to me, sir "
8. Take the money and run

9. Go Leave immediately and don't look back
10. If we are chased by a bear, I don't have to outrun the bear; I just have to outrun you

Dashes and Parentheses

When you are talking with someone, you use your voice to punctuate: you pause for a short time (commas) or for a longer time (semicolons and periods), you shout (exclamation marks), or you query (question marks). In writing, punctuation substitutes for these vocal markers: it helps you ensure that your writing will make sense to your readers.

One way you can add variety and flexibility to your sentences is by inserting words or phrases that add to but are not essential to the sentence's meaning. That is, the word or words could be omitted and the sentence would still be complete and make sense. It might, however, lack grace or interest.

You can use three punctuation marks to add non-essential material to your sentences: commas, dashes, and parentheses. You are already familiar with the first one. Here is your opportunity to master the last two: the dash—which looks like this—and parentheses (round brackets). (If you are typing, the dash is two hyphens with no space between them or on either side.)

Punctuation

Dashes

Dashes are used to mark a break in thought or an abrupt shift in emphasis.

1. Use a dash or a pair of dashes to set off a series of items separated by commas.

I still love dried apricots, raisins, and pickled beets—foods my mother gave me as treats when I was a child.

Three qualities—perseverance, spirit, and skill—ensure a good game.

Atwood, Ondaatje, Laurence, Davies, Clarke, and Richler—for a country with a relatively small population, Canada has produced an extraordinary number of internationally acclaimed novelists.

2. Use a dash or a pair of dashes to set off from the rest of the sentence a climactic or emphatic moment.

Please welcome our new managers—Muhsin and Lisa.

Because they were afraid of the police, my so-called friends—Cory, Shane, and Mark—all betrayed me.

The apartment she showed me would have been fine, had it not been for the tenants—moths, cockroaches, and silverfish—already making it their home.

3. Use a dash to introduce a word, phrase, or clause that summarizes or restates what has just been said. (The dash in this context is interchangeable with a colon.)

The car sold quickly despite the damages—a dent in the fender, scratches on the hood, and a malfunctioning key fob.

My best friends and I all agreed—that movie was awful.

The Wright brothers invented the first flying machine—the airplane.

Note that dashes set off material that is not grammatically part of the sentence. If you were to omit the words between the dashes, the sentence would still make sense.

Dashes can be misused if you use them too frequently. Unless you are writing informally—in a personal message, for instance—save dashes for the very occasional phrase to which you want to draw emphatic attention.

Exercise 25.22* Add dashes where they are appropriate.

1. Your very angry parents they are still awake are waiting for you in the house.
2. If we get to the movie and we really want to get to the movie I know you'll enjoy it.
3. Other people have expressed concern over the state of your paper which really is quite messy.
4. I am really craving eggs, butter, and toast foods that are good when I feel sick.
5. What everyone needs to remember recalling it when appropriate is that there is usually time to correct past mistakes.
6. Conner has given us a lot to think about it's almost time for our yearly evaluation.
7. Books like that and movies too are so thought-provoking.
8. Applying to relevant jobs can result in only one thing eventual success.
9. The most we can afford and it isn't much is $1000 a month.
10. Science fiction and fantasy if you like these genres, you'll love watching *Battlestar Galactica.*

Parentheses

Like dashes, parentheses are used to enclose an interruption in a sentence. The difference between them is a matter of tone: dashes SHOUT—they serve to draw the reader's attention to the material they enclose—but parentheses (which should be used sparingly) "whisper." Parentheses are similar to theatrical asides; they are subordinate to the main action but are not to be missed.

1. Use parentheses around additional information that you wish to include but not emphasize.

Marita's teaching schedule (she is in class seven hours a day) gives her little time to meet with students individually.

They brought me to their village and presented me to their chief (a woman) and to the tribal councillors.

Note the difference in tone your choice of punctuation makes. Compare the examples above with the following versions:

Marita's teaching schedule—she is in class seven hours a day—gives her little time to meet with students individually.

They brought me to their village and presented me to their chief—a woman—and to the tribal councillors.

2. Use parentheses to enclose explanatory material that is not part of the main sentence.

"Mislabelled by Society" (an essay in Part 8) was written by a college student.

The Malagasy (people of Madagascar) like to eat a *kapoaka* of rice (enough to fill a condensed-milk can) three times a day.

3. Use parentheses to enclose reference data in a research paper. (See pp. 189–194.)

Exercise 25.23*

Add parentheses where they are appropriate.

1. Five of the students I was asked not to name them have volunteered to be peer tutors.
2. The apostrophe is explained in Chapter 26 pages 432–438.
3. Jason complained that being a manager he became one in March was like being a cop.
4. I have enclosed a cheque for one hundred and fifty dollars $150.
5. More members of the Canadian Forces died in World War I 1914–18 than in any war before or since.
6. Although Mozart lived a relatively short time he died when he was 36, he composed hundreds of musical masterpieces.
7. As news of her "miracle cures" spread patients began to come to her from all over the province, the doctor had to move her clinic to a more central location.
8. The new contract provided improved working conditions, a raise in salary 3 percent, and a new dental plan.

9. Ontario and British Columbia now produce award-winning, world-class wines from small estate wineries Inniskillin, Hillebrand, and Quails' Gate are three examples.
10. "One of the most important tools for making paper speak in your own voice is punctuation; it helps readers hear you the way you want to be heard" Baker 48-49.

Exercise 25.24 **Insert dashes and parentheses where appropriate in the following sentences.**

1. Jasper needs to stop eating he is always so hungry.
2. I met with Atom Egoyan a Canadian director as part of the film festival package.
3. It is not the time to ask for a raise the boss is on a rampage.
4. Jessica and George both students won the prize for best screenplay.
5. We all decided we wanted the same thing for dinner pizza.
6. Read that book I can't recommend it enough and get back to me.
7. After I checked out that last customer he really was slow, my boss came up to me he was very angry and fired me.
8. I like all kinds of dancing tango, ballet, and jazz.
9. She had been kind to me as kind as she could be given the circumstances but it wasn't enough.
10. If you interrupt the author again I'm pretty sure you will, we will probably get kicked out.

Exercise 25.25 **Correct the following paragraph, which contains 20 errors (each set of dashes, parentheses, and quotation marks counts as one error).**

As a final review of punctuation here's a paragraph that should contain all the punctuation marks we have discussed in this section of the book however 20 pieces of punctuation are missing. Your job is to provide the missing punctuation. Let's quickly deal with punctuation marks one by one. The comma probably the hardest-working of them all is used to separate items in a series to set off non-essential material to join with a conjunction two separate independent clauses to set off material that comes before a main clause and to separate coordinate adjectives. Whew. The semicolon can replace a period it often separates two independent clauses that are closely connected in meaning. The colon has a different function it follows an independent clause and introduces a list a clarification or a quotation. Did you remember that a colon should never follow "is" or are. A question mark must be used at the end of all interrogative sentences. We all know this but sometimes we forget. Exclamation marks are used at the end of sentences for one purpose only to supply dramatic effect. But remember that they are seldom used in academic writing. Finally dashes and parentheses allow a writer to interrupt a train of thought and insert an "aside" into a sentence. That's it. If you have correctly inserted all the punctuation in this paragraph then you are ready to tackle spelling problems.

CHAPTER 26

Spelling

Poor spelling plagues even the best writers at times. Relying too much on computer spell-checking functions can make our own practices lax. This section will help introduce you to the most common spelling errors and give you exercises and tasks to help improve your overall confidence when it comes to spelling.

Hazardous Homonyms

This section focuses on **homonyms**—words that sound alike or look alike and are easily confused: *accept* and *except*; *weather* and *whether*; *whose* and *who's*; *affect* and *effect*. A spell checker will not help you find spelling mistakes in these words because the "correct" spelling depends on the sentence in which you use the word. For example, if you write, "Meat me hear inn halve an our," no spell checker will find fault with your sentence—and no reader will be able to overlook your poor spelling.

Careful pronunciation can sometimes help you tell the difference between words that are often confused. For example, if you pronounce the words *accept* and *except* differently, you'll be less likely to use the wrong one when you write. You can also make up memory aids to help you remember the difference in meaning between words that sound or look alike.

Below is a list of the most common homonym hazards together with some word pairs that, while technically not homonyms, are often confused. Only some of the words on this list will cause you trouble. Make your own list of problem pairs and tape it on the inside cover of your dictionary or post it close to your computer. Get into the habit of checking your document against your list every time you write.

accept
except
Accept means "**take**" or "receive." It is always a verb. ***Except*** means "**ex**cluding."

I *accepted* the spelling award, and no one *except* my mother knew I cheated.

advice
advise
The difference in pronunciation makes the difference in meaning clear. *Advise* (rhymes with *wise*) is a verb. *Advice* (rhymes with *nice*) is a noun.

I *advise* you not to listen to free *advice*.

affect
effect
Affect as a verb means "ch**a**nge." Try substituting *change* for the word you've chosen in your sentence. If it makes sense, then *afFECT* is the word you want. As a noun, *AFfect* means "a strong feeling." *Effect* is a noun meaning "r**e**sult." If you can substitute *result*, then *effect* is the word you need. Occasionally, *effect* is used as a verb meaning "to bring about."

Learning about the *effects* (results) of caffeine *affected* (changed) my coffee-drinking habits.

Depressed people often display inappropriate *affect* (feelings).

Antidepressant medications can *effect* (bring about) profound changes in mood.

a lot
allot

A lot (often misspelled *alot*) should be avoided in formal writing. Use *many* or *much* instead. *Allot* means "distribute" or "assign."

He still has **many** ~~a lot of~~ problems, but he is coping *much* ~~a lot~~ better.
The teacher will *allot* the marks according to the difficulty of the questions.

aloud
allowed

Aloud means out loud, not a whisper. *Allowed* means permitted.

We were not *allowed* to speak *aloud* during the performance.

amount
number

Amount is used with uncountable things; *number* is used with countable things.

You may have a large *number* of jelly beans in a jar but a small *amount* of candy floss.
(Jelly beans are countable; candy floss is not.)

are
our

Are is a verb. *Our* shows ownership.

Marie-Claire Blais and Margaret Atwood *are* two of Canada's best-known writers.

Canada is *our* home and native land.

assure
ensure
insure

Assure means "state with confidence; pledge or promise."

She *assured* him she would keep his letters always.
The prime minister *assured* the Inuit their concerns would be addressed in the next budget.

Ensure means "make certain of something."

The extra $20 will *ensure* that you get a good seat.

No number of promises can *ensure* that love will last.

Insure means "guarantee against financial loss." We *insure* lives and property.

Kevin *insured* the parcel before he sent it.

We have *insured* both our home and our car against fire and theft.

choose
chose

Pronunciation is the clue here. *Choose* rhymes with *booze* and means "select." *Chose* rhymes with *rose* and means "selected." (Some people would *choose* booze before flowers.)

> Please *choose* a topic.
>
> I *chose* filmmaking when I went to college.

cite
sight
site

To *cite* is to quote or mention. A lawyer *cites* precedents. Writers *cite* their sources in research papers. You might *cite* a comedian for her wit or a politician for his honesty. A *site* is a place (where something is *situated*).

> You have included only Internet sources in your Works *Cited* list.
>
> Tiananmen Square is the *site* of the massacre.
>
> Pape and Mortimer is the *site* of our new industrial design centre.

A *sight* is something you see.

> The view over the Plains of Abraham is an unforgettable *sight*.
>
> With his tattooed forehead and three nose rings, he was a *sight* to behold.

coarse
course

Coarse means "rough, unrefined." (Remember: The word ***arse*** is co***arse***.) For all other meanings, use *course.*

> That sandpaper is too *coarse*.
>
> You'll enjoy the photography *course*.
>
> Of *course* you'll do well.

complement
compliment

A *complement* completes something. A *compliment* is a gift of praise.

> A glass of wine would be the perfect *complement* to the meal.
>
> Some people are embarrassed by *compliments*.

conscience
conscious

Your *conscience* is your sense of right and wrong. *Conscious* means "aware" or "awake"—able to feel and think.

> After Katy cheated on the test, her *conscience* bothered her.
>
> Katy was *conscious* of having done wrong.
>
> The injured man was *unconscious* for an hour.

consul
council
counsel

A *consul* is a government official stationed in another country. A *council* is an assembly or official group. (Members of a council are *councillors.*) *Counsel* can be used to mean both "advice" and "to advise." (Those who give advice are *counsellors.*)

The Canadian *consul* in Mexico was very helpful.

The Women's Advisory *Council* meets next month.

Maria gave me good *counsel*.

She *counselled* me to hire a lawyer.

continual
continuous *Continual* refers to an action that goes on regularly but with interruptions. *Continuous* refers to an action that goes on without interruption.

The student *continually* tried to interrupt the lecturer, who droned on *continuously*.

There is a *continuous* flow of traffic during rush hour.

credible
credulous
creditable *Credible* means "believable." A person who believes an incredible story is *credulous*.

Nell was fortunate that the police officer found her story *credible*.

My brother is so *credulous* that we call him Gullible Gus.

Creditable means "worthy of reward or praise."

After two wasted semesters, Ellen is finally doing *creditable* work.

desert
dessert A *DEsert* is a dry, barren place. As a verb, *deSERT* means "leave behind." *DesSERT* is the part of the meal you'd probably like a double serving of, so give it a double *s*.

The tundra is Canada's only *desert* region.

While technically the night watchman did not *desert* his post, he did sleep on the job.

Dessert is my favourite part of the meal.

dining
dinning You'll spell *dining* correctly if you remember the phrase "wining and dining." You'll probably never use *dinning*. It means "making a loud noise."

The children are in the *dining* room.

We are *dining* out tonight.

The noise from the bar was *dinning* in our ears.

disburse
disperse *Dis**bur**se* means "to pay out money," which is what ***bur**sars* do. *Disperse* means "to break up"; crowds are sometimes *dispersed* by the police.

The college's financial-aid officer will *disburse* the students' loans at the end of this week.

The protesters were *dispersed* by the police.

Spelling

does
dose

Pronunciation provides the clue. *Does* rhymes with *buzz* and is a verb. *Dose* rhymes with *gross* and refers to a quantity of medicine.

> John *does* drive quickly, doesn't he?
>
> My grandmother gave me a *dose* of cod liver oil.

farther
further

You'll have no trouble distinguishing between these two if you associate ***far**ther* with *distance* (think "far") and *further* with *time.*

> Ralph wanted me to walk a little *farther* so we could discuss our relationship *further*.

faze
phase

Fazed usually has a *not* before it; to be *not fazed* means to be not disturbed, concerned, or taken aback. *Phase* means "stage of development or process."

> Unfortunately, Theo was not *fazed* by his disastrous grade report.
>
> Since Mei Ling works full-time, she has decided to complete her degree in *phases*.

fewer
less

Fewer is used with countable things. *Less* is used with uncountable things.

> In May, there are *fewer* students in the college, so there is *less* work for the faculty to do.
>
> The *fewer* attempts you make, the *less* your chance of success.

With units of money or measurement, however, use *less*:

> I have *less* than $20 in my wallet.
>
> Our house is on a lot that is *less* than four metres wide.

forth
fourth

For**th* means "**for**ward" or "onward." ***Four**th* contains the number ***four, which gives it its meaning.

> Please stop pacing back and *forth*.
>
> The BC Lions lost their *fourth* game in a row.

hear
here

*H**ear*** is what you do with your **ear**s. *Here* is used for all other meanings.

> Now *hear* this!
>
> Ray isn't *here*.
>
> *Here* is your assignment.

imply
infer

A speaker or writer *implies*; a listener or reader *infers*. To *imply* is to hint or say something indirectly. To *infer* is to draw a conclusion from what is stated or hinted at.

In her introduction of the speaker, Carol *implied* that she greatly admired the mayor.

I *inferred* from the mayor's remarks that he was very fond of Carol.

it's
its
It's is a shortened form of *it is* or *it has*. (The apostrophe takes the place of the *i* in *is* or *ha* in *has*.) If you can substitute *it is* or *it has*, then *it's* is the form you need. If you can't, then *its* is the correct word.

It's really not difficult. (*It is* really not difficult.)

It's been a good year. (*It has* been a good year.)

The book has lost *its* cover. (Neither "The book has lost *it is* cover" nor "The book has lost *it has* cover" makes sense, so you need *its*.)

later
latter
Late**r* refers to time and has the word ***late in it. *Latter* means "the second of two" and has two *ts*. It is the opposite of *former.*

It is *later* than you think.

You take the former, and I'll take the *latter*.

loose
lose
Pronunciation is the key to these words. *Loose* rhymes with *goose* and means "not tight." *Lose* rhymes with *booze* and means "misplace" or "be defeated."

A *loose* electrical connection is dangerous.

Some are born to win; some to *lose*.

martial
marshal
Martial refers to warfare or military affairs. *Marshal* has two meanings. As a noun, it refers to a person of high office, either in the military or (especially in the United States) the police. As a verb, it means to arrange or assemble in order.

She is a *martial* arts enthusiast.

When the troops were *marshalled* on the parade grounds, they were reviewed by the army *marshal*.

miner
minor
A ***mine**r* works in a **mine**. *Minor* means "lesser" or "not important" or refers to a person of less than legal age.

Liquor can be served to *miners*, but not if they are *minors*.

For me, spelling is a *minor* problem.

moral
morale
Again, pronunciation provides the clue you need. *MORal* refers to the understanding of what is right and wrong. *MorALE* refers to the spirit or mental condition of a person or group.

People often have to make *moral* decisions.

The low *morale* of the workers prompted the strike.

peace
piece

Peace is what we want on **Earth**. ***Piece*** means "a part or portion of something," as in "a ***pie****ce* of ***pie***."

> Everyone hopes for *peace* in the Middle East.
>
> A *piece* of the puzzle is missing.

personal
personnel

Personal means "private." *Personnel* refers to the group of people working for a particular employer or to the office responsible for maintaining employees' records.

> The file was marked "*Personal* and Confidential."
>
> We are fortunate in having qualified *personnel*.
>
> Fatima works in the *personnel* office.

principal
principle

Principal means "main." A *principle* is a rule.

> A *principal* is the main administrator of a school.
>
> Oil is Alberta's *principal* industry.
>
> I make it a *principle* to submit my essays on time.

quiet
quite

If you pronounce these words carefully, you won't confuse them. *Quiet* has two syllables; *quite* has only one.

> The librarian asked us to be *quiet*.
>
> We had not *quite* finished our homework.

roll
role

Turning over and over like a wheel is to *roll*; a bun is also a *roll*. An actor in a play has a *role*.

> His *role* called for him to fall to the ground and *roll* into a ditch, all the while munching on a bread *roll*.

simple
simplistic

Simple means uncomplicated, easily understood. Something described as *simplistic* is too simple to be acceptable: essential details or complexities have been overlooked.

> This problem is far from *simple*. Your solution to it is *simplistic*.

stationary
stationery

Stationary means "fixed in place." *Stationery* is writing paper.

> Sarah Ferguson works out on a *stationary* bicycle.
>
> No matter how far you push the envelope, it is still *stationery*.

than
then

Than is used in comparisons. Pronounce it to rhyme with *can*. *Then* refers to time and rhymes with *when*.

> Rudi is a better speller *than* I.
>
> He made his decision *then*.
>
> Eva withdrew from the competition; *then* she realized the consequences.

their
there
they're

Their indicates ownership. *T**here*** points out something or indicates place; it includes the word ***here***, which also indicates place. *They're* is a shortened form of *they are*. (The apostrophe replaces the *a* in *are*.)

> It was *their* fault.
>
> *There* are two weeks left in the term.
>
> You should look over *there*.
>
> *They're* late, as usual.

too
two
to

The *too* with an extra *o* in it means "more than enough" or "also." *Two* is the number after one. For all other meanings, use *to*.

> He thinks he's been working *too* hard. She thinks so, *too*.
>
> There are *two* sides *to* every argument.
>
> The *two* women knew *too* much about each other ever *to* be friends.

weather
whether
wether

Whether means "which of the two" and is used in all cases when you aren't referring to climatic conditions (*weather*). A *wether* is a castrated ram, so that word's uses are limited.

> *Whether* you're ready or not, it's time to go.
>
> No one immigrates to Canada for its *weather*.

were
where
we're

If you pronounce these three carefully, you won't confuse them. *Were* rhymes with *purr* and is a verb. *W**here*** is pronounced "hwear," includes the word **here**, and indicates place. *We're* is a shortened form of *we are* and is pronounced "weer."

> You *were* joking, *weren't* you?
>
> *Where* did you want to meet?
>
> *We're* on our way.

who's
whose

Who's is a shortened form of *who is* or *who has*. If you can substitute *who is* or *who has* for the *who's* in your sentence, then you are using the right spelling. Otherwise, use *whose*.

> *Who's* coming to dinner? (*Who is* coming to dinner?)
>
> *Who's* been sleeping in my bed? (*Who has* been sleeping in my bed?)
>
> *Whose* calculator is this? ("*Who is* calculator" makes no sense, so you need *whose*.)

woman
women

Confusing these two is guaranteed to irritate your female readers. *Wo**man*** is the singular form; compare ***man***. *Wo**men*** is the plural form; compare ***men***.

A *woman's* place is wherever she chooses to be.

The *women's* movement promotes equality between *women* and men.

you're
your

You're is a shortened form of *you are.* If you can substitute *you are* for the *you're* in your sentence, then you're using the correct form. If you can't substitute *you are,* use *your.*

You're welcome. (*You are* welcome.)

Unfortunately, *your* hamburger got burned. ("*You are* hamburger" makes no sense, so *your* is the word you want.)

Exercise 26.1* **Choose the correct word from those in parentheses. If you don't know an answer, go back and reread the explanation. Answers for this chapter begin on page 487.**

1. The limited (coarse course) selection will (affect effect) our academic development and subsequent job opportunities.
2. (Are Our) you going to (accept except) the offer?
3. Eat your vegetables; (than then) you can have your (desert dessert).
4. If (your you're) overweight by 20 kg, (loosing losing) the excess will be a long-term proposition.
5. It's (quiet quite) true that they did not get (hear here) until the party was over.
6. It is usually the saint, not the sinner, (who's whose) (conscience conscious) is troubled.
7. He (assured ensured insured) me he would keep the (amount number) of changes to a minimum.
8. (Its It's) hard to tell the dog from (its it's) owner.
9. To (choose chose) a (coarse course) of action against your lawyer's (advice advise) would be foolish.
10. (Continual Continuous) (dining dinning) out becomes boring after a while.

Exercise 26.2* **Find and correct the 15 errors in the following sentences.**

1. Our decorator choose a stunning fabric for our dinning room chairs, in colours that perfectly complimented our carpet.
2. My wife is a women who heres everything and forgets nothing.
3. She's quiet hopeful that the committee will except her résumé, even though its late and printed on coloured stationary.
4. Other then hope and pray that voters will chose our candidate, their is not much we can do.
5. Blindfolded, my wrists and ankles bound with duct tape, I was lead to the car and driven out into the dessert, were I was left by the side of the road.

Exercise 26.3*

Each of the items below is followed by two statements. Identify the one that makes sense as a follow-up to the introductory sentence.

1. All former students will be welcomed back to class.
   a. We will except all former students.
   b. We will accept all former students.
2. The lawn mower next door has been running nonstop for over an hour.
   a. The continual noise is driving me crazy.
   b. The continuous noise is driving me crazy.
3. This author only hints at how the story ends.
   a. She implies that they live happily ever after.
   b. She infers that they live happily ever after.
4. Your proposal is not worth our consideration
   a. It's simple.
   b. It's simplistic.
5. We're looking for a female role model.
   a. The women must lead by example.
   b. The woman must lead by example.
6. How many assistants will be required?
   a. The amount of helpers we will need is hard to estimate.
   b. The number of helpers we will need is hard to estimate.
7. While their skill sets are very different, together, the two make a good team.
   a. She compliments his weaknesses.
   b. She complements his weaknesses.
8. Are you permitted to talk during the lectures?
   a. It is not allowed.
   b. It is not aloud.
9. Where did she wake up?
   a. She regained her conscience in the hospital.
   b. She regained her consciousness in the hospital.
10. How close are we to the cottage?
    a. We have only a little farther to go.
    b. We have only a little further to go.

Exercise 26.4

Now test your mastery of homonyms by correcting the 15 errors in the following paragraph.

The Slow Food Movement rejects everything that are fast-food culture stands for: unhealthy food from unknown sources, prepared on assembly lines, served in plastic environments, and gobbled quickly. The affects of are fast-food culture are all around us: the well-publicized obesity epidemic and huge increases in diabetes, heart disease, and gastrointestinal disorders. Based in Italy, Slow Food is an organization of more then 100 000 members who's principals include chosing food from local providers, honouring the farmers and producers of they're food, preparing it with care and creativity, and consuming it in convivial surroundings. A lot of farmers, chefs, and restaurateurs are members of the movement. They enthusiastically except the idea that they must make a conscience effort to deliver dinning experiences that promote healthier, more sustainable eating. And while the Slow Food Movement supports local farmers and producers, their are many benefits for consumers, including loosing weight, enjoying better health, and experiencing tastier food. It is an allusion that fast food is cheaper then well-prepared good food; we pay the cost of fat-, salt-, and sugar-laden food not at the cash register, but with our health.

The Apostrophe

Most punctuation marks indicate the relationship among parts of a sentence. Apostrophes and hyphens, on the other hand, indicate the relationship between the elements of a word. That's why we've chosen to discuss them in this section, along with other spelling issues.

Misused apostrophes display a writer's ignorance or carelessness. They can also confuse, amuse, and sometimes annoy readers.

- Sometimes you need an apostrophe so that your reader can understand what you mean. For example, there's a world of difference between these two sentences:

The instructor began class by calling the students' names.
The instructor began class by calling the students names.

- In most cases, however, misused apostrophes just amuse or irritate an alert reader:

  The movie had it's moments.
  He does a days work for every weeks salary.
  The Lion's thank you for your contribution.

It isn't difficult to avoid such mistakes. Correctly used, the apostrophe indicates either contraction or possession. It never makes a singular word plural. Learn the simple rules that govern these uses and you'll have no further trouble with apostrophes.

Contraction

Contraction is the combining of two words into one, as in *they're* or *can't*. Contractions are common in conversation and in informal written English. Unless you are quoting someone else's words, however, you should avoid them in the writing you do for school or work.

The rule about where to put an apostrophe in a contraction is one of those rare rules that has no exception. It *always* holds.

> When two words are combined into one, and one or more letters are left out, the apostrophe goes in the place of the missing letter(s).

Here are some examples.

I am	→	I'm	they are	→	they're
we will	→	we'll	it is	→	it's
she is	→	she's	it has	→	it's
do not	→	don't	who is	→	who's

Exercise 26.5*

Place apostrophes correctly in these words, which are intended to be contractions. Notice that when the apostrophe is missing, the word often has a different meaning. The answers for this exercise begin on page 487.

1. cant __________
2. shed __________
3. hell __________
4. wed __________
5. whos __________
6. shell __________
7. wont __________

8. well __________

9. lets __________

10. your __________

Exercise 26.6* In some formal kinds of writing—academic, legal, and technical, for example—contractions are not acceptable. A good writer is able not only to contract two words into one, but also to expand contractions into their original forms. In the following paragraph, find and expand the contractions into two-word phrases (e.g., he'll = he will).

> I'm writing to apply for the position of webmaster for BrilloVision.com that you've advertised in the *Daily News*. I've got the talent and background you're looking for. Currently, I work as a Web designer for an online publication, Vexed.com, where they're very pleased with my work. If you click on their website, I think you'll like what you see. There's little in the way of Web design and application that I haven't been involved in during the past two years. But it's time for me to move on to a new challenge, and BrilloVision.com promises the kind of opportunity I'm looking for. I guarantee you won't be disappointed if I join your team!

Possession

The apostrophe is also used to show ownership or **possession**. Here is the rule that applies in most cases.

> If the owner word is singular, add *'s* to indicate possession.
> If the owner word is plural and ends in *s*, add only an apostrophe.

Here are some examples that illustrate the rule.

woman + 's = woman's voice	women + 's = women's voices
student + 's = student's transcript	students + '~~s~~ = students' transcripts
player + 's = player's uniform	players + '~~s~~ = players' uniforms
boss + 's = boss's office	bosses + '~~s~~ = bosses' offices

To form a possessive correctly, you must first identify the word in the sentence that indicates possession and determine whether it is singular or plural. For example, "the managers duties" can have two meanings, depending on where you put the apostrophe:

the manager's duties (the duties belong to one manager)
the managers' duties (the duties belong to two or more managers)

To solve an apostrophe problem, follow this two-step process:
1. Find the owner word.
2. Apply the possession rule.

Problem: Carmens hair is a mess.

Solution: 1. The word that indicates possession is *Carmen* (singular).
2. Add *'s* to *Carmen*.

Carmen's hair is a mess.

Problem: The technicians strike halted the production.

Solution: 1. The word that indicates possession is *technicians* (plural).
2. Add *'* to *technicians.*

The *technicians'* strike halted the production.

Sometimes the meaning of your sentence is determined by where you put the apostrophe.

Problem: I was delighted by the critics response to my book.

Now you have two possibilities to choose from, depending on your meaning.

Solution A: 1. The owner word is *critic* (singular).
2. Add *'s* to *critic*.

I was delighted by the *critic's* response to my book.

Solution B: 1. The owner word is *critics* (plural).
2. Add *'* to *critics.*

I was delighted by the *critics'* response to my book.

Both solutions are correct, depending on whether the book was reviewed by one critic (A) or by more than one critic (B).

Possession does not have to be literal. It can be used to express the notion of "belonging to" or "associated with." That is, the owner word need not refer to a person or group of people. Ideas or concepts (abstract nouns) can be "owners" too.

a month's vacation = a vacation of one month
a year's salary = the salary of one year
"A Hard Day's Night" = the night that follows a hard day

Note that a few words, called **possessive pronouns**, are already possessive in form, so they don't have apostrophes.[1]

Yours	ours	whose
hers, his, its	theirs	

1. If you add an apostrophe to any of these words, you create an error. There are no such words as *your's*, *her's*, *their's*, or *our's*.

His music is not like *yours*.

Whose lyrics do you prefer, *theirs* or ours?

The dog lost *its* bone.

Four of these possessive pronouns are often confused with the contractions that sound like them. It's worth taking a moment to learn how to avoid this confusion. When you are trying to decide which spelling to use, follow these steps:

1. Expand the contraction into its original two words.
2. Substitute those words for the contraction in your sentence.
3. If the sentence still makes sense, use the contraction. If it doesn't, use the possessive spelling.

		Possessive	Contraction		
Its	=	*It owns* something	it's	=	it is/it has
Their	=	*They* own something	they're	=	they are
Whose	=	*Who* owns something	who's	=	who is
Your	=	*You* own something	you're	=	you are

Error: They're (they are) going to sing they're (they are) latest song.

Revision: They're going to sing their latest song.

Error: You're (you are) parents were thrilled by you're (you are) achievement.

Revision: Your parents were thrilled by your achievement.

Exercises 26.7 and 26.8 will test and reinforce your understanding of both contraction and possession.

Exercise 26.7* In each of the following phrases, make the owner word possessive.

1. a woman role ________________
2. witness testimony ________________
3. families budgets ________________
4. children school ________________
5. the soldiers uniforms ________________
6. the book title ________________
7. everyone choice ________________
8. the Simpsons cottage ________________
9. the oldest child responsibility ________________
10. our country flag ________________

In each of the sentences below, choose the correct word from those in parentheses. Check your answers before going on. **Exercise 26.8***

1. Where (your you're) going, (your you're) biggest problem will be maintaining (your you're) tan.
2. (Someones Someone's) got to take responsibility for the cats and dogs (whose who's) owners have abandoned them.
3. The (ships ship's ships') captain agreed to donate a (weeks week's weeks') salary to the Scott Mission.
4. Contrary to some (people's peoples) opinions, postal (workers worker's workers') contracts are most often settled by both (sides side's sides') willingness to bend long before a strike is necessary.
5. My (turtles turtle's) legs are shorter than your (turtles turtle's), but I bet (its it's) going to run (its it's) laps faster than (yours your's).

Plurals

The third apostrophe rule is very simple. Memorize it, apply it, and you will instantly correct many of your apostrophe errors.

> Never use an apostrophe to make a word plural.

The plural of most English words is formed by adding *s* to the root word (not *'s*). The *s* alone tells the reader that the word is plural—for example, *memos, letters, files, broadcasts, newspapers, journalists.* If you add an apostrophe + *s,* you are telling your reader that the word is either a contraction or a possessive.

Wrong: Never use apostrophe's to make word's plural.
Right: Never use apostrophes to make words plural.

Correct the misused and missing apostrophes in the following sentences. There are 10 errors in this exercise. **Exercise 26.9***

1. Two silkworm's had a race; they ended up in a tie.
2. When you feel like a snack, you can choose between apples and Timbit's.
3. Teds career took off when he discovered how easy it was to sell childrens toy's to grandparents.
4. A beginning golfer needs three different kinds of clubs: wood's for long shots, iron's for short ones, and a putter for the last four or five shots.
5. Good writing skill's wont guarantee success in you're career, but poor writing skill's are guaranteed to hold you back.

Exercise 26.10 Before you try the final exercise in this section, carefully review the information in the Summary box at the bottom of this page. Then test your mastery of apostrophes by correcting the 15 errors in the passage below.

In the next five years, it will be a challenge to see whos going to win the war in online learning. There are many company's who will fight to have their online learning product's win out over each other and who will try to find plenty of research that suggests that student's in the 21st century require the use of multiple technology's. What we cant really predict is what students will think of online learning tools as they evolve. Its really up in the air at the moment, but there are some way's that you might be able to determine whether an online course is right for you.

For example, have you had to listen to you're teacher read long slide show presentation's that you couldve read at home? Have you done writing in class that would have been more polished if youd written it on a computer? Finally, were there sometimes so many questions that the teacher had to stop the lesson just to answer them all? An online course could eliminate these issue's by having a discussion area just for question's, a function to hand in papers from your computer, and the ability to read slide shows on your own time.

By taking in both the research that online course companies provide and your own experiences, you can decide for yourself whether online course's might be right for you.

Apostrophe Summary

- When contracting two words into one, put an apostrophe in the place of the missing letter(s).
- Watch for owner words: they need apostrophes.
- To indicate possession, add *'s* to the owner word if it's singular, and *'* if it is plural.
- Possessive pronouns (e.g., *yours, its, ours*) do not take apostrophes.
- Never use an apostrophe to form the plural of a word.

The Hyphen

The hyphen (-) has three different functions:

1. It may be part of the correct spelling of a word (e.g., *mother-in-law, self-esteem*).
2. It may be used to divide a word at the end of a line.
3. It may be used to separate or join two or more words or parts of words (e.g., *re-created, picture-perfect setting*).

There are five rules to follow.

> 1. Use a hyphen to divide a word at the end of a written or typed line.

Your dictionary tells you where words can be divided. Most dictionaries mark the syllables of a word with a dot: syl•la•bles. So *syllables* could break as *syl-lables* or *sylla-bles*. If the word is already hyphenated (e.g., *self-reliance, ex-president*), break it only after the hyphen. If the word begins with a **prefix**, break it after the prefix (e.g., *anti-virus*, not *antivi-rus*). And never break a proper noun.

Spelling

> 2. Use a hyphen to separate a prefix from the main word when two of the same vowels occur together.

Examples:

re-elected, co-operate, anti-imperialism

When the two vowels are different, however, no hyphen is required: *realign, semiautomatic, preamble*.

> 3. Use a hyphen with compound numbers from *twenty-one* to *ninety-nine*, with fractions, and with dimensions.

Examples:

forty-six, one-eighth, ninety-eight, six- by eight-metre room

> 4. Use a hyphen to join two or more words that serve as an adjective *before* a noun.

Examples:

The first-born child is often the best loved.

The best-loved child is often the first born.

Word-of-mouth advertising is very effective.

A good writer has a well-thumbed, up-to-date dictionary.

> 5. Use a hyphen to avoid ambiguity.

Consider the differences in meaning between the following pairs of statements:

Examples:

I resent everything you asked for. (I'm angry.)

I re-sent everything you asked for. (I sent it all again.)

The contractor re-covered the roof with asphalt shingles. (He repaired the roof.)

The contractor recovered his money. (He got his money back.)

The government's plan provided for nursing-home care. (care in a nursing home)

The government's plan provided for nursing home-care. (care at home by nurses)

The prime minister will address small business owners. (Do you really want to say he will talk only to short people?)

The prime minister will address small-business owners. (These people are owners of small businesses.)

Exercise 26.11* Most of the following sentences require one or more hyphens. Review the rules on this page and the previous page then try correcting these sentences.

1. I really can't explain why I coopted your look.
2. I really can't stand big business owners.
3. I had a dream I would live to be ninety eight.
4. Short term loans are my bank's specialty.
5. I had to walk up to the seventh floor washroom because ours was broken.

Exercise 26.12* In the following sentences, some hyphens are missing, and some are included where they don't belong. Correct the errors in these sentences.

1. A rubber band pistol was confiscated during algebra-class because it was considered a weapon of math disruption.
2. Please re-lay this message to Mr. Chan: the masons want to relay the bricks tomorrow.
3. Our next door neighbour teaches high-school, but she doesn't like being introduced as a high school teacher.
4. We had a presentation by Atheists-Anonymous, a non prophet organization.
5. Because Angela was an attorney at law and had once been an all Canadian athlete, no one was surprised when she became Minister-of-Recreation.

Exercise 26.13

This last exercise is a mastery test. Insert hyphens where they are needed and delete them where they are not.

1. At 20 years-of-age, Trudy began to reorganize her life.
2. Because she is the instructor who is the most up to date on trends in the industry, Alysha is the coordinator of our program.
3. Only one third of the team seemed to be reenergized by the 20 minute break.
4. Vernon wore his hand tailored three piece suit to his former-girlfriend's wedding.
5. In spite of its country garden atmosphere, the hotel's up to the minute décor and facilities could not be faulted.
6. The space shuttle will reenter the atmosphere in exactly eighty five seconds.
7. Tim began to recover from his career threatening injury after taking an antiinflammatory.
8. Some very successful businesses are coowned by the employees; these cooperative ventures ensure that workers' hard earned dollars are put to work on their-own behalf.
9. Computer generated graphics are ninety nine percent of our over the counter business.
10. Trevor was treated for post traumatic stress after his no hope, last minute attempt to pass chemistry.

Spelling

Capital Letters

Capital letters belong in a few specific places and nowhere else. Some writers suffer from "capitalitis." They put capital letters on words without thinking about their position or function in a sentence.

Capitalize the first letter of a word that fits into one of the six categories listed below:

1. The first word of a sentence or a direct quotation

Are you illiterate? Write to us today for free help.
The supermodel cooed, "Makeup gives me so much confidence."

Exercise 26.14*

Correct the missing or misused capital letters in the following sentences.

1. The man chuckled and said, "don't quote me on that."
2. Love your sweater! hate the shoes!
3. "when in B.C., make sure to try the halibut," Mary told Jeff.

4. Interested in seeing a movie? definitely check out the one I told you about yesterday.

5. Gibson argued, "testosterone may not accurately predict aggression in the sexes."

2. The names of specific people, places, and things

Names of people (and their titles):

> **Shania Twain, Governor General David Johnston, the Rev. Jeremiah Wright, the Hon. Eugene Forsey, Senator Mike Duffy**

Names of places, regions, and astronomical bodies (but not general geographic directions):

> **Stanley Park, Lake Superior, Cape Breton Island; Nunavut, the Prairie Provinces, the Badlands; Saturn, Earth, the Asteroid Belt; south, north**

Names of buildings, institutions, organizations, companies, departments, products, etc.:

> **the Empress Hotel; McGill University, Red Deer College; the Liberal Party, the Kiwanis Club; Petro-Canada, Future Shop; the Department of English, the Human Resources Department; Kleenex, Nissan, Labatt's**

Exercise 26.15* Add capital letters where necessary in the following sentences. There are two errors in each sentence.

1. I don't know, jim. I hear canada is a great place to live!

2. The conservatives let me know that the liberal candidate wasn't a good choice.

3. Planets such as jupiter can be seen from McMaster university's observatory.

4. I really don't like shreddies or cheerios.

5. If you are going to victoria, travel up to nanaimo, too.

3. Names of major historical events, historical periods, religions, religious texts, and religious holidays

> **World War II, the Depression; the Renaissance; Islam, Judaism, Christianity, Buddhism, Hinduism; the Torah, the Koran, the Bible, the Upanishads; Ramadan, Yom Kippur, Easter**

Correct the 15 improper uses of capital letters in the following sentences.

Exercise 26.16*

1. Don't you think that the authors of this book could have come up with a more imaginative title for this section? Why not "conquering capitals," for example?
2. C. S. Lewis's books *the chronicles of narnia* are being made into a series of films.
3. The producers are hoping these films will be as successful as Tolkien's *lord of the rings* movies.
4. Vermeer's most famous painting, *girl with a pearl earring*, became first a novel and then a movie.
5. In his Eighties, Leonard Cohen created a juno award–nominated album, *popular problems*.

Spelling

4. The days of the week, months of the year, and specific holidays, but not the seasons

Wednesday; January; Remembrance Day, Canada Day; spring, autumn

The following sentences contain both missing and unnecessary capitals. Find and correct the 15 errors.

Exercise 26.17*

1. Next monday is valentine's day, when messages of love are exchanged.
2. By thursday, I'll have finished my st. patrick's day costume.
3. My favourite months are january and february because I love all Winter sports.
4. In the summer, big meals seem to be too much trouble; however, after thanksgiving, we need lots of food to survive the winter cold.
5. A National Holiday named flag day was once proposed, but it was never officially approved.

> **5.** The main words in titles of published works (books, magazines, websites, films; essays, poems, songs; works of art; etc.)

Do not capitalize minor words, such as articles (*a, an, the*), prepositions, and coordinating conjunctions (FANBOYS), in titles unless the word is the first word in the title.

The Colony of Unrequited Dreams	*The Thinker*
Of Mice and Men	"An Immigrant's Split Personality"
Maclean's	"In Flanders Fields"
Facebook	"O Canada"

Exercise 26.18* Add the 30 capital letters that are missing from the following sentences.

1. The review of my book, *the life and times of a hog rider*, published in *the globe and mail*, was not favourable.
2. Clint eastwood fans will be delighted that the two early movies that made him internationally famous, *a fistful of dollars* and *for a few dollars more*, are now available on DVD.
3. Joseph Conrad's short novel *heart of darkness* became the blockbuster movie *Apocalypse now*.
4. My essay, "a bright and silent place," was published in the april issue of *landscapes* magazine.
5. Botticelli's famous painting "birth of venus" inspired my poem "woman on the half shell."

Pay special attention to this next category. It is one that often causes trouble.

> **6.** The names of specific school courses

Marketing 101, Psychology 100, Mathematics 220, English 110,

but

> a) not the names of general school subjects

marketing, sociology, mathematics

> b) *unless* the subjects are languages or pertain to specific geographical areas whose names are capitalized

English, Greek, the study of Chinese history, modern Caribbean literature, Latin American poetry

(Names of languages, countries, and geographical regions are *always* capitalized.)

Exercise 26.19*

Add capital letters where necessary in the following sentences. There are 10 errors in this exercise.

1. We began our study of sociology with the concept of relationships.
2. After passing Professor Bacchus's course, introduction to wine, I registered for oenology 200.
3. After studying geography for two years, I began taking courses in ancient greek and modern history.
4. While math is her strong subject, Louisa has trouble with accounting, english, and conversational french.
5. The prerequisite for theology 210 is introduction to world religions, taught by Professor O'Connor.

Exercise 26.20

The following exercise is the mastery test and contains 25 errors. Before you begin, it would be a good idea to review the six capitalization rules presented in this section.

Once, long ago, both the montreal canadiens and the toronto maple leafs failed to make it into the NHL playoffs, so all the players were home for the late Winter weeks. The Teams' managers were worried about their players' morale, so they consulted a Professor of Psychology at McGill university who taught a course called motivational sports psychology. The professor told them that a friendly competition between their teams in a sport other than Hockey would be beneficial.

And so, on the victoria day weekend in may, the two teams were bused to a remote Northern lake near the border between Ontario and Quebec, called trout lake. There, they were to engage in a friendly ice-fishing competition. After the first day, the Canadiens had caught 100 fish, the Leafs none. At the end of the second day, the score was 200 to 0, and the Leafs players were becoming very discouraged. Their Coach called them together and said, "those guys must be cheating. I want one of you to

Spelling

dress up as a canadien and spend tomorrow with them to find out what they're up to."

The following night, with the score now 320 to 0, the Leafs coach called his players together and asked his spy if the Montreal players were cheating. "they sure are!" was the reply. "they're cutting holes in the ice!"

Numbers

Numbers may be expressed as words (*one, four, nine*) or as figures (*1, 4, 9*), depending on the kind of document you are writing and what the numbers refer to. In a few circumstances, a combination of words and figures is required. In scientific and technical papers, numbers are normally given in figures; in humanities papers, numbers that can be expressed in one or two words are spelled out. For your assignments, ask your instructor which style he or she prefers. For general purposes, including most business writing, follow the guidelines given below.

When to Use Words

1. Use words to express whole numbers *one* through *nine* and simple fractions. Use figures for numbers *10* and above.

The novel's three parts chronicle the nine-week journey of the five Acadian teenagers.

China and India together account for more than one-third of the Earth's population.

Approximately 45 years ago, Paul Henderson scored the most famous goal in the history of Canadian hockey.

There are two exceptions to this general rule.

a) Spell out any number that begins a sentence, or rewrite the sentence so that the number does not come first.

Wrong: 157 students submitted essays to the awards committee.

Right: One hundred and fifty-seven students submitted essays to the awards committee.

Also right: The awards committee received essays from 157 students.

b) Use *either* figures *or* words to express numbers that modify the same or similar items in one sentence. (That is, be consistent within a sentence.)

We are looking for three accountants, fifteen salespeople, and two customer service representatives. (not "three, 15, and two")

Only 9 of the 55 applicants had both the qualifications and the experience we required. (not "nine of the 55 applicants")

2. Treat ordinal numbers (*first, second,* etc.) as you would cardinal numbers (*one, two,* etc.).

Up to its sixth or seventh month, an infant can breathe and swallow at the same time.

In a 1904 speech, Sir Wilfrid Laurier predicted that the 20th century would belong to Canada. Maybe our luck will improve in the 21st century.

Exercise 26.21*

Applying the first two highlighted rules in this section, correct any errors in the following sentences.

1. It was so cold for the 1st ½ of winter that hardly anyone was out on the street.
2. He was down 2 strikes in the 8th inning, and tensions were running high for the 1st time.
3. We have been waiting twelve months to hear if we are going to get the contract.
4. When I turned thirteen, my parents bought me my first computer.
5. 365 days seems a long time, but 1 year seems so short.
6. I wonder if, by the year two thousand and thirty everyone will be able to go to space.
7. Second place is all right, but I would have preferred 1st.
8. 80 people came to my talk even though I had already given it twelve times.
9. Of the 10 players, nine couldn't catch the ball.
10. ¾ of a teaspoon is what the recipe called for.

When to Use Figures

As a general rule, you should use figures when you are presenting precise or technical numerical information or when your sentence or paragraph contains several numbers.

3. Use figures to express dates, specific times, addresses, and percentages; with abbreviations or symbols; and with units of currency.

Dates	April 1, 2014, or 1 April 2014
Times	8:45 a.m. or 08:45, 7:10 p.m. or 19:10 (Use words with *o'clock*—e.g., *nine o'clock, four o'clock sharp.*)
Addresses	24 Sussex Drive, 2175 West 8th Street
Percentages	19 percent, a 6.5 percent interest rate (Use the % symbol only with figures in tables or illustrations.)
With abbreviations or symbols	7 mm, 293 km, 60 km/h, 40 g, 54 kg, 18°C, 0.005 cm, 1.5 L, 8½", p. 3
Amounts of money	79 cents or $0.79, $2, $100, $30 000, $20 million, $65 billion (Use words if the unit of currency follows whole numbers *one* through *nine*—e.g., *two dollars, seven euros*—unless the number includes a decimal—e.g., *1.5 trillion pesos.*)

Exercise 26.22* With Rule 3 in mind, correct the errors in the following sentences.

1. Researchers at Cornell University conducted a study that showed that sixty-six percent of all businessmen wear their ties too tight.
2. More than ten percent of those studied wore their ties so tight that blood flow to the brain was diminished.
3. 99 percent of the people who read the report wondered why Cornell had conducted such a study.
4. 1 plan is to retire on December seventeenth, 2055, when I will be 80.
5. At precisely eight-ten p.m. on June third, your flight will leave for Whitehorse.
6. You will arrive at approximately 10 o'clock on June fourth if you make all your connections.
7. I won 5 dollars from Ted by proving that February eighteen sixty-five was the only month in recorded history not to have a full moon.
8. You must be present at one thirty-three West Eighteenth Street by exactly 7:00 o'clock to claim your prize.
9. So far this year, I have spent thirty-eight thousand dollars, or twenty percent more than my anticipated income for the entire year, and it's only May fifteenth!

10. At the Indianapolis Speedway, the race cars burn approximately four L of fuel for each lap, while the ship *Queen Mary 2* moves just fifteen cm for every 4 L of fuel it burns.

When to Use Both Words and Figures

4. When one number immediately follows another, spell out the one that makes the shorter word.

The Grey Cup is contested by *two 12-man teams* of heavily padded and helmeted warriors.

Our local car dealers sold more than *200 four-wheel*-drive vehicles the day after our first big storm.

5. For numbers over a million, express introductory whole numbers 10 and above in figures, and the quantity in words (*million, billion, trillion,* etc.). (If the numbers involve decimals, use figures.)

The human stomach contains more than *35 million* digestive glands.

The Earth's population was estimated to be *6.79 billion* as of July 1, 2009.

The following exercises will test your ability to apply all of the rules and exceptions presented in this chapter.

Exercise 26.23*

Correct any errors in the expression of numbers in the following sentences.

1. The speedboat is powered by 2 80-horsepower outboard motors.
2. 1 8-cylinder SUV emits more pollution than two four-cylinder Volkswagens or 3 Toyota gas–electric hybrids.
3. Because she sold seven $2 000 000 homes last year, she topped the agency's earnings list.
4. Eighty-two percent of people whose net worth is over three million dollars say they got rich by hard work.
5. 200 people were invited to celebrate my parents' twenty-fifth wedding anniversary on August Thirty-first, 2013.
6. A total of 10 fifteen-year-old girls and 4 fifteen-year-old boys applied for the commercial acting position we advertised.

7. Our lawyer told us that thirty-eight % of people who die between the ages of 45 and 54 have not prepared a will.

8. Canada's population of about 33 000 000 puts us in thirty-sixth place on the list of most populous countries.

9. 10 years ago, the average speed on urban freeways was fifty kph, but it has been steadily declining and is expected to be thirty kph within the next 5 years.

10. 7000 ecstatic fans celebrated their team's unexpected two–one win in the Memorial Cup final, partying in the streets until four-thirty a.m.

Exercise 26.24 **Before you tackle this final exercise, review the five highlighted rules given in this section. It's a good idea to copy them onto a single sheet of paper and keep them handy. There are 15 errors in this paragraph.**

Roughly ninety-nine % of a human's body mass is composed of just 6 elements: oxygen (sixty-five %), carbon (eighteen percent), hydrogen (10 percent), nitrogen (three percent), calcium (1-1/2 percent), and phosphorus (one percent). The remaining one percent of the recipe consists of tiny amounts of potassium, sulphur, sodium, chlorine, and magnesium, plus even smaller traces of iron, copper, molybdenum, zinc, and iodine. According to science reporter Scott LaFee of *The San Diego Tribune,* "The average human body contains enough sulphur to kill all the fleas on an average-sized dog, enough carbon to make nine hundred pencils, enough potassium to fire a toy cannon … enough phosphorous to make two thousand, two hundred match heads, enough water to fill a ten-gallon [thirty-eight L] container, and enough iron to make a three inch [eight cm] nail."

Appendix A

List of Terms: A Vocabulary of Writing

The following list contains definitions of some common terms referring to writing formats, syntax, and style. For some of the terms, you will find further information in the book or on the *Essay Essentials* website. If a term you are looking for is not listed, check the index or consult your dictionary. For punctuation marks, see Chapter 25.

academic portfolio   A compilation of work related to a theme, career, or discipline. (p. 262)

academic presentation   A classroom presentation intended to summarize, describe, or outline work that has been done. (p. 252)

action verb   See **verb**.

active voice   See **voice**.

adjective   A word that modifies (i.e., describes, restricts, makes more precise) a noun or pronoun. Adjectives answer the questions *What kind? How many?* and *Which?* For example, the *competent* student, *five* home runs, my *last* class. When two or more adjectives modify a noun, they may require commas between them. **Coordinate adjectives** can be arranged in any order and can have *and* inserted between them. When there is no *and*, a comma is required (e.g., a spoiled, selfish child). **Cumulative adjectives** build upon one another and are not separated by a comma (e.g., an unopened cardboard box). (p. 221)

adverb   A word that modifies a verb, adjective, or other adverb. Adverbs answer the questions *When? How? Where? Why?* and *How much?* For example, Matt talks loudly (*loudly* modifies the verb *talks*); he is a *very* loud talker (*very* modifies the adjective *loud*); he talks *really* loudly (*really* modifies the adverb *loudly*). Adverbs often—but not always—end in *ly*. (p. 221)

agreement   Grammatical correspondence in person and number between a verb and its subject, or in person, number, and gender between a pronoun and its antecedent. (p. 362)

analogy   A comparison between two dissimilar things that share at least one element or characteristic in common (e.g., Time is like a river. Just as the river flows from higher to lower ground, so time flows from the past into the future). Analogies are often used for stylistic or dramatic effect as well as to explain or illustrate a point. (p. 98)

anecdote   A short account of an event or incident, used to illustrate a point and sometimes intended to entertain. (p. 93)

antecedent   The word that a pronoun refers to or stands for. Literally, it means "coming before, preceding." The antecedent usually comes before the pronoun that refers to it: My sister thinks she is always right (*sister* is the antecedent of the pronoun *she*). (p. 385)

argument   A piece of writing that is intended to convince readers that the writer's opinion about an issue is reasonable and valid. (p. 149)

assumptions   The decisions the author has made about the reader. Contrast **bias**. (p. 37)

attention-getter A sentence or more that comes before the thesis statement and that is designed to get the reader interested in what the writer has to say. (p. 103)

auxiliary verb A verb form that adds further meaning to the main verb. Some auxiliary verbs, also called *helping verbs*, show when an action took place (e.g., forms of *be, do/did, have/had, will*), and some suggest possibility or probability (e.g., *can, could, may, might, must, should, would*). (p. 331)

bias A slant toward topics or ideas. All authors and readers have a bias, and all people think differently. (p. 37)

brainstorming A prewriting technique in which the writer makes a list of every idea that comes to mind about a specific subject. Brainstorming can be done alone, with a partner, or—best of all—in a group. (p. 57)

causal analysis A writing style that tries to answer the question of why events happen. It also can look at the effects of events once they have happened. (p. 127)

chronological order Events or ideas that are arranged in order of time sequence. (p. 66)

classification A structural pattern based on our instinct to arrange and analyze our experiences. (Compare to **division**, which looks at the differences between experiences, classification focuses on similarities.) (p. 132)

clause A group of words containing a subject and a verb. If the group of words can stand by itself as a simple sentence, it is an **independent** (or *main*) **clause**: Great minds think alike. A **dependent** (or *subordinate*) **clause** cannot stand alone as a sentence; it must be linked to an independent clause: *Because great minds think alike,* I am sure you will agree with me. (p. 339)

cliché A phrase that has become meaningless through overuse. (p. 228)

climactic order The arrangement of key ideas in order of importance. The most important or strongest idea comes last. Thus, the paper builds to a climax. (p. 67)

collective noun A noun that names a group—for example, *class, faculty, jury, choir*. Collective nouns are singular when the group is considered as a unit, plural when the focus is on individual members: The class wants a midterm break. The class have not yet handed in *their* papers. See **agreement**. (p. 367)

colloquialism A word or group of words that is appropriate in casual conversation and informal—but not formal—writing. Some common examples are *guy, kid,* and *flunk*. (p. 13)

command A sentence that tells the listener or reader to do something. In this type of sentence, no subject appears, but *you* is understood. (p. 328)

Examples:
Look up unfamiliar words in the dictionary.
Be all that you can be.
Sit!

comma splice Two independent clauses joined with a comma: The comma splice is a type of run-on sentence, it is a serious error. (p. 342)

comparison Writing that points out similarities, showing how two different objects, people, or ideas are alike. (p. 143)

complement A word or phrase that completes the meaning of a verb. Also called a *subjective completion*, a complement can be a noun, a pronoun, or an adjective that follows a linking verb. (p. 382)

Examples:
Ramani is the *manager.* (noun complement)
The winner was *she.* (pronoun complement)
The president's speech was *encouraging.* (adjective complement)

compound Two or more grammatical elements (words, phrases, clauses) joined so that they function as a unit: ***Hans, Peter, and Walter* are brothers** (*compound subject*); **Hans *works and studies*** (*compound verb*); **Peter expects an *A or a B+*** (*compound object*). Also called *multiple* subjects, verbs, objects, or complements. (p. 334)

consistency In pronoun use, the maintenance of number, person, and gender. For example, a sentence that begins in the first person but shifts to the second person is incorrect: ***We* chose not to drive to Calgary because, these days, *you* just can't afford the gas.** (p. 375)

contraction The combining of two words into one, spelled with an apostrophe to mark the missing letter or letters: *isn't* (is not), *here's* (here is), *should've* (should have). Contractions are common in conversation and in informal written English. (p. 433)

contrast Writing that points out dissimilarities between things, showing how two objects, people, or ideas differ. (p. 143)

coordinate adjectives Adjectives that can be arranged in any order and can be separated by the word *and* without changing the meaning of the sentence. Commas come between coordinate adjectives not joined by *and*. (p. 404)

coordinating conjunction A linking word used to join two or more words, phrases, or clauses of equal importance: *for, and, nor, but, or, yet,* and *so* (remembered by the acronym FANBOYS). (p. 343)

critical thinking The means through which we analyze, or do close readings of, people, situations, and writing. (p. 34)

cumulative adjectives Adjectives that modify the word that follows. Unlike **coordinate adjectives,** these adjectives cannot be reordered, nor can they have *and* inserted between them. (p. 404)

dangling modifier See **modifier**.

dependent clause A group of words containing a subject and a verb but not expressing a complete idea. It depends on an independent clause for its meaning. Also called *subordinate clause*. (p. 339)

dependent-clause cue A word or phrase that introduces a dependent clause—for example, *when, because, in order that, as soon as*. May be a subordinating conjunction or a relative pronoun. (p. 339)

direct quotation The exact words of a speaker or writer reported by another person. (p. 413)

division A structural pattern based on our instinct to arrange and analyze our experiences according to what is different about them. (Whereas **classification** looks for similarities in experiences, division focuses on differences.) (p. 132)

editing The correction of errors in grammar, word choice, spelling, punctuation, and formatting. See Chapter 20. (p. 243)

facts Statistics, percentages, and other readily available and accepted data. (p. 38)

FANBOYS See **coordinating conjunction**.

formal level The level of language often used (and expected) in university and college papers. Formal English avoids the use of contractions and of the first and second person. It uses no colloquial expressions or slang. (p. 13)

4-S test A satisfactory subject is SIGNIFICANT, SINGLE, SPECIFIC, and SUPPORTABLE. (p. 50)

fragment See **sentence fragment**.

freewriting Talking written down. This prewriting technique sets the writer free to write without worrying about errors, a concern that often blocks the flow of ideas. (p. 55)

fused sentence Two independent clauses with no punctuation between them: ***The fused sentence is a type of run-on it is a serious error.*** (p. 343)

gender Nouns and pronouns may be masculine (*father, boy, stallion; he, his, him*), feminine (*mother, girl, mare; she, hers, her*), or neuter (*laughter, book; it*). (p. 386)

gender-biased language See **sexist language**.

general level The level of language of educated persons. General-level English is used in college and professional writing. It is non-technical and readily understood by most readers. It uses few if any colloquial expressions, no slang, and few contractions. (p. 13)

grammar The description and study of how the elements of language function, by themselves and in relation to one another. (p. 362)

helping verb See **auxiliary verb**.

homonyms Two or more words that are identical in sound (e.g., *meet, meat, mete*) or spelling (e.g., *bank*—a place to deposit money; *bank*—a slope) but different in meaning. (p. 422)

indefinite pronoun See **pronoun**.

independent clause A group of words containing a subject and a verb and expressing a complete idea. Also called *main clause*. (p. 339)

indirect quotation Reported spoken or written content not using the original source's exact words. (p. 413)

infinitive A verb form usually consisting of *to* + the base form of the verb: *to be, to walk, to read, to procrastinate*. An infinitive or infinitive phrase can function as a noun, adjective, or adverb, but never as the main verb in a clause—for example, I offered *to help* (*to help* functions as a noun, direct object of the verb *offered*). (p. 370)

informal level One of the three levels of writing (informal, general, and formal). Many colleges and universities expect students to write academic papers in formal English, which requires, among other things, third-person pronouns (*he, she, one, they*). Informal writing, with its first- and second-person pronouns (*I, me, you*), may not be acceptable. Informal writing involves short sentences and paragraphs, has a conversational tone, and is more appropriate for casual writing. It is usually used in personal notes, some fiction, some newspapers, and much advertising. (p. 13)

irregular verb A verb that does not form its past tense and past participle by adding *ed* or *d*—for example, *write, wrote, written; sing, sang, sung*. (p. 371)

jargon Strictly, the specialized technical vocabulary of a particular profession. More broadly, **pretentious language**: wordy, confusing language that is intended to impress the reader. (p. 226)

linking verb See **verb**.

logical fallacies Pseudo-arguments that authors use to try to get you to respond in a certain way but that don't hold up to testing. (p. 40)

logical order A pattern of organization that depends on causal connections among the main points. One point must be explained before the next can be understood. (p. 67)

main verb The verb that follows the auxiliary or helping verb and tells the action in the sentence. (p. 331)

misplaced modifier A modifier that is next to a word or phrase that it is not meant to modify. A misplaced modifier can change the meaning of your sentence. (p. 346)

modifier A word or group of words that describes, qualifies, or restricts another word, phrase, or clause in a sentence. A modifier can act as an adjective or as an adverb. If there is no word in the sentence to which the modifier can logically refer, it is a **dangling modifier**: *Standing on the dock,* many fish could be seen. A **misplaced modifier** is not placed close enough to the word it is intended to modify: Our team has *nearly* lost half its regular players. (p. 346)

noun A word that names a person, place, thing, or concept and that has the grammatical capability of being possessive. Nouns are most often used as subjects and objects. There are two classes of nouns: concrete and abstract. (p. 328)

Concrete nouns name things we perceive through our senses; we can see, hear, touch, taste, or smell what they stand for. Some concrete nouns are proper: they name people, places, or things and are capitalized—for example, *Justin Trudeau, Beijing, Canada's Wonderland*. Other concrete nouns are common (*woman, city, car, coffee*); still others are collective (*group, audience, crowd, committee*).

Abstract nouns name concepts, ideas, characteristics—things we know or experience through our intellect rather than through our senses (e.g., *truth, pride, prejudice, self-esteem*).

number The form of a verb, a noun, or a pronoun may be singular or plural. (p. 386)

object The "receiving" part of a sentence. The *direct object* is a noun or noun substitute (pronoun, phrase, or clause) that is the target or receiver of the action expressed by the verb. It answers the question *What?* or *Whom?* (p. 331)

Examples:

Jai threw *the ball.* (Jai threw what?)
He wondered *where the money went.* (He wondered what?)
Munira loves *Abdul.* (Munira loves whom?)

The *indirect object* is a noun or pronoun that is the indirect target or receiver of the action expressed by the verb in a sentence. It is always placed in front of the direct object. It answers the question *To whom?* or *To what?*

Dani threw *me* the ball. (Dani threw to whom?)
Ian forgot to give *his essay* a title. (Give to what?)

The *object of a preposition* is a noun or noun substitute (pronoun, phrase, or clause) that follows a preposition—for example, *after the storm* ("storm" is a noun, object of the preposition "after"); *before signing the lease* (*signing the lease* is a phrase, object of the preposition *before*); he thought *about what he wanted to do* (*what he wanted to do* is a clause, object of the preposition *about*). Notice that what follows a preposition is always its object; that is why the subject of a sentence or clause is never in a prepositional phrase.

paragraphs Sentence groups that are separated from each other in their physical presentation and in their content. Each paragraph should contain one idea, identified in a topic sentence. (p. 88)

parallelism Consistent grammatical structure. In a sentence, for example, all items in a series would be written in the same grammatical form: words, phrases, or clauses. Julius Caesar's famous pronouncement, "I came, I saw, I conquered," is a classic example of parallel structure. The symmetry of parallelism appeals to readers and makes a sentence read smoothly and rhythmically. Lack of parallelism, on the other hand, is jarring: My favourite sports are water skiing, swimming, and I particularly love to sail. (p. 353)

paraphrase The rephrasing of another writer's idea in your own words. A good paraphrase reflects both the meaning and the tone of the original; it is usually about the same length as or shorter than the original. Whenever you borrow another writer's ideas, you must acknowledge your source. If you don't, you are plagiarizing. See Chapter 9. (p. 97)

parenthetical citation Brief information presented in parentheses at the end of a quotation or paraphrase to identify the source of the original information. (p. 189)

participle The form of a verb that can be used as an adjective (e.g., the *starving* artist, the *completed* work) or as part of a verb phrase (e.g., am *working*, have *purchased*).

The present participle of a verb ends in *ing*.
The past participle of a regular verb ends in *d* or in *ed*.
For a list of past participles of irregular verbs, see Chapter 24. (p. 370)

passive voice See **voice**.

past participle See **participle**.

person A category of pronouns and verbs. *First person* refers to the person who is speaking (*I, we*). *Second person* refers to the person being spoken to (*you*). *Third person* is the person or thing being spoken about (*he, she, it, they*). Regular verb forms remain constant except in the present tense third-person singular, which ends in *s*: I run; you run; he/she/it runs; we run; they run. (p. 362)

person agreement The consistent use of the first-, second-, or third-person pronoun throughout a sentence or a paragraph. (p. 392)

persuasion The art of making people change their mind about something, whether it be a world issue or what toothpaste to buy. (p. 137)

plural More than one person or thing. (p. 362)

possession Ownership, as denoted in writing by the addition of *s* to a singular noun or just an apostrophe (') to a plural noun ending in *s*. (p. 434)

The *writer's* goal was to tell as many fallen *soldiers'* stories as she could in one book.

possessive pronoun A group of words that are already in the possessive form and do not require *s*. The possessive pronouns are *my, mine, your, yours, his, her, hers, its, our, ours, their, theirs,* and *whose*. (p. 435)

poster A presentation tool used to give an overview into a topic and to provide viewers with an argument based on a topic. (p. 259)

prefix One or more letters that can be added to the beginning of a word (1) to make a new word or (2) to change its part of speech. (p. 439)

1. *a* + sexual = asexual
   contra + diction = contradiction
   mis + spell = misspell
   un + thinkable = unthinkable
2. *a* + board (verb) = aboard (adverb, preposition)
   in + put (verb) = input (noun)
   con + temporary (adjective) = contemporary (noun, adjective)

Some prefixes require a hyphen: e.g., *anti*-reform, *all*-Canadian, *mid*-season, *self*-control.

preposition A word that connects a noun, pronoun, or phrase to some other word(s) in a sentence. The noun, pronoun, or phrase is the object of the preposition. (p. 332)

Examples:
I prepared the minutes *of* the meeting. (*of* relates *meeting* to *minutes*)
One *of* the parents checks the children every half hour. (*of* relates *parents* to *One*)

prepositional phrase A group of grammatically related words beginning with a preposition and having the function of an adjective or adverb. (p. 332)

Examples:

Mine is the second office *on the right.* (adjective modifying noun *office*)
Please go *into my office*. (adverb modifying verb *go*)

present participle See **participle**.

pretentious language Wordy, roundabout, or unintelligible language. Also called *gobbledygook* or *bafflegab*. Pretentious writing is a kind of jargon characterized by wordiness, long words, vague abstract nouns, and frequent use of the passive voice. (p. 227)

principal parts The verb elements we use to construct the various tenses. The principal parts are the infinitive form (*to* + the base verb), the simple past, the present participle (*ing*), and the past participle. (p. 370)

process analysis A type of writing style that explains events that follow one another in time. The writer must direct the reader toward information that involves action (implied or direct). There are two kinds of process analysis: one instructs or directs the reader how to perform a task; the other informs the reader how something is done, is made, or works. (p. 123)

pronoun A word that functions like a noun in a sentence (e.g., as a subject or as an object of a verb or a preposition). Pronouns usually substitute for nouns, but sometimes they substitute for other pronouns. (p. 328) There are several kinds of pronouns:

personal: I, we; you; he, she, it, they; me, us; him, her, them
possessive: mine, ours; yours; his, hers, its, theirs
demonstrative: this, these; that, those
relative: who, whom, whose; which, that
interrogative: who? whose? whom? which? what?
indefinite: all one, thing, body pronouns, such as everyone, something, and anybody; each; neither; either; few; none; several
Note: Possessive pronouns also have adjective forms: *my, our; your; his, her, their*. Possessive adjectives follow the same rules for agreement that govern pronouns. They must agree with their antecedents in person, number, and gender.

Example:

Every young boy wants to be the goalie on *his* team. (not *their team*)

pronoun form Pronoun form is determined by the pronoun's function in a sentence: **subject** or **object**. (p. 381)

Subject Pronouns		Object Pronouns	
Singular	Plural	Singular	Plural
I	we	me	us
you	you	you	you
he, she, it, one	they	him, her, it, one	them

proofreading The correction of errors in typing or writing that appear in the final draft. See Chapter 20. (p. 235)

proper noun See **noun**.

random order A shopping-list kind of arrangement of main points in a paper. The points could be explained in any order. Random order is appropriate only when all points are equal in significance and are not chronologically or causally connected to one another. See Chapter 5. (p. 67)

regular verb A verb whose simple past and past participle forms are formed by adding *ed*, or just *d* when the verb ends in *e*. (p. 371)

relative pronoun A pronoun that refers to someone or something already mentioned in the sentence. The relative pronouns are *who/whoever, whom/whomever, which,* and *that.* (p. 390)

rewriting The act of entirely changing a sentence or group of sentences to increase clarity and effectiveness. (p. 235)

run-on A sentence with inadequate punctuation between independent clauses. The two kinds of run-on sentences are **comma splices** and **fused sentences**. (p. 342)

scanning A reading strategy that requires looking only for specific keywords, phrases, or concepts. (p. 24)

sentence combining A technique that enables you to produce correct and pleasing sentences. Sentence combining accomplishes three things: it reinforces your meaning; it refines and polishes your writing; and it results in a style that will keep your reader alert and interested in what you have to say. (p. 357)

sentence fragment A group of words that is punctuated like a sentence but either does not have both a subject and a verb or does not express a complete thought. (p. 336)

sexist language Exclusive language that includes the use of a word or words that signify gender (e.g., *waitress, sculptress, actress*) and the use of the pronouns *he, his, him* (or *she, her, hers*) to refer to singular antecedents such as *everybody, anyone, no one*. (p. 230)

simple past Also called *past tense*. This verb tense expresses the idea that something has happened and been completed in the past. (p. 370)

singular One person or thing. (p. 362)

skimming A reading strategy that requires searching out the most useful points in a text. (pp. 23–24)

slang A highly colloquial word or phrase, used by speakers belonging to a particular group—for example, high-school students, music lovers, or sports fans. Slang is not appropriate in academic or professional writing. (p. 225)

style A characteristic of written language; good style, whether formal or informal, is concise, clear, and pleasing. (p. 8)

subject In a sentence, the person, place, thing, or concept that the sentence is about (see Chapter 23). In a paper, what the essay is about—the topic (see Chapter 1). (p. 328)

subordinate clause See **dependent clause**.

subordinating conjunction A word or phrase that introduces a dependent clause—for example, *when, because, in order that, as soon as*. See Chapter 23 for a list of subordinating conjunctions. (p. 339)

summary statement Part of the conclusion; a brief review of the main points of an essay. (p. 110)

tense The form of the verb that indicates past, present, or future time. The verb ending (e.g., *plays, played*) and any helping verbs associated with the main verb (*is playing, will play, has played, had played, will have played*) indicate the tense of the verb. (p. 375)

There are simple tenses:	present: ask, asks
	past: asked
	future: will ask
and perfect tenses:	present: has (have) asked
	past: had asked
	future: will (shall) have asked

The simple and perfect tenses can also be **progressive**: *am asking, have been asking, had been asking, will be asking.*

theories Any collective points of view or thinking systems (e.g., a feminist theory or a Freudian theory) that might be discussed in one's own writing or research. (p. 38)

thesis The idea or point about a subject that the writer wants to explain or prove to the reader. (p. 35)

thesis statement A statement near the beginning of a paper that announces the paper's subject and scope. (p. 68)

tone A reflection of the writer's attitude toward his or her topic. For instance, a writer who is looking back with longing to the past might use a nostalgic tone. An angry writer might use an indignant tone or an understated, ironic tone, depending on the subject and purpose of the paper. (p. 415)

topic sentence A sentence that identifies the main point or key idea developed in a paragraph. The topic sentence is usually found at or near the beginning of the paragraph. (p. 90)

usage The customary or conventional way of using words and combinations of words in a language. The incorrect use of words and expressions (called *abusages* in this book) is a sign of nonstandard English. (p. 222)

vague reference A pronoun without a clearly identifiable antecedent. (p. 389)

verb A word or phrase that says something about a person, place, or thing and whose form may be changed to indicate tense (or time). Verbs may express action (physical or mental), occurrence, or condition (state of being). (p. 328)

action:	Ravi *stopped* the ball. (physical action) Nina *believed* the team would win. (mental action)
occurrence:	Father's Day *falls* on the third Sunday in June.
condition:	Minnie *felt* ill.

Action verbs can be divided into two types:

Transitive verbs require a direct object: I *hate* chemistry; Minnie *lifts* weights.

Intransitive verbs do not require an object: Please *listen* and *learn*.

Linking verbs help to make a statement by linking the subject to a word or phrase that describes it or renames it: Phil is the *manager* of our department (noun); Phil is *ambitious* (adjective).

The most common linking verb is *be* (*am, is, are, was, were,* etc.) Other linking verbs are *appear, become, feel, grow, look, taste, remain, seem, smell,* and *sound*.

See also **auxiliary verb**. (p. 449)

voice Verbs may be active or passive, depending on whether the subject of the verb is acting (active voice) or being acted upon (passive voice). (p. 377)

In 2013, the government *introduced* a new set of tax reforms. (active)

A new set of tax reforms *was introduced* in 2013. (passive)

wordiness The use of more words than necessary. Wordiness results when information is repeated or when a clause is used when a phrase will suffice or a phrase is used when a single word will suffice. (p. 222)

Appendix B

Answers for Selected Exercises

Answers for Chapter 1: Understanding the Audience, Understanding Yourself (pp. 7–21)

Exercise 1.2

1. Audience: Literate readers who are interested in exploring a serious analysis of what is often treated as a trivial topic—the living wage.
   Writer's role: To provide information.
   Language: Formal. Sentences vary in length; some are quite long and complex. While there are no technical terms, the writer assumes the reader has a broad general vocabulary and good reading ability. Use of third-person point of view contributes to the impersonal tone.
2. Audience: Experts in woodworking.
   Writer's role: To provide information in an accessible way. The writer is not instructing the reader but outlining the function of the tool and some of its possible applications.
   Language: General level, combining technical vocabulary with an informal tone. Sentences vary in length. Writer addresses reader as "you."
3. Audience: General readers. (The author wrote a popular newspaper column for many years.)
   Writer's role: Primarily to entertain. Readers who have been to Paris will smile with recognition; those who haven't will smile at Nicol's imagery and will learn something about Parisian traffic.
   Language: Mostly general level, with some informal constructions (e.g., contractions, sentence fragments). Writer addresses readers as "you," as if speaking directly to them.
4. Audience: Business owners and concerned citizens
   Writer's role: To demonstrate that research on sweatshops is showing that their negative status should be questioned.
   Language: Formal. No contractions or colloquialisms. Writer uses the third-person approach, which contributes to the impersonal, objective tone. Sentences vary in length.

Answers for Chapter 4: Organizing Your Work and Preparing for Writing (pp. 49–65)

Exercise 4.1

1. significant

2. significant

3. significant

4. Travel destinations for students on a budget
5. Tips for using an iPhone for educational purposes
6. *Netflix*—the best choice for students' downtime
7. Getting to school in winter weather

Exercise 4.2

1. revise (focus on one cause)
2. revise (choose one campus)
3. revise (choose *Twitter* or *Facebook*)
4. single (the subject is the *importance of accuracy*, not the two media)
5. revise (one way of preventing sexually transmitted infections)
6. revise (main cause of injury or one cause of injury)
7. revise (wildlife management or gerontology as a career)

Exercise 4.3

1. supportable
2. revise (choose only one movie)
3. supportable
4. revise (choose only one secret service)
5. revise (don't add in other science-fiction shows)
6. revise (through one age, not all ages)
7. supportable

Exercise 4.4

1. supportable
2. supportable
3. supportable
4. revise (not single)
5. revise (not single or specific)

Exercise 4.10

1. cellphone (not distinct, overlaps with *telephone*)
2. distance from suppliers and markets (not related)
3. repetitive (not related: repetition is a programming problem, not a characteristic of commercials)
4. procrastination (not distinct, overlaps with *poor study habits*)
5. *find a reliable real estate agent* overlaps with *seek expert advice*; also not necessarily relevant—not all people need an agent
6. *competitors offer better pay* overlaps with *salary lower than industry standard*

Answers for Chapter 5: Developing the Main Points and Writing the Thesis Statement (pp. 66–80)

Exercise 5.1

1. chronological (4, 5, 2, 1, 3)
2. climactic (2, 1, 3, 4)
3. random

4. climactic (3, 1, 2. This order reflects the amount of time it takes for a smoker to quit using each method and also the amount of agony the smoker will suffer in the process.)
5. random

Exercise 5.3

1. Students who try to combine a full-time job with a full-time program face problems at school, at work, and at home.
2. To be successful in a broadcasting career, you must be talented, motivated, and hard-working.
3. Establishing an online network would promote teamwork and increase efficiency in the office.
4. The business traveller can learn much from the turtle. Carry everything you need with you. Move slowly but with purpose and consistency. Keep your head down until you are sure you know what's going on.
5. Cellphones must be turned off during class because they disrupt everyone's concentration, they prevent the user from learning, and they distract and annoy the teacher, to the detriment of all.
6. Although easily dismissed as merely animated entertainment, *The Simpsons* is effective social commentary, tackling with humour and gusto such issues as the environment, social justice, and race relations.
7. Large energy producers and some provincial governments say we cannot afford to live up to the terms of the Kyoto and Copenhagen agreements, which seek to reduce the production of greenhouse gases. But can we afford not to comply? Can we afford to compromise the health of Canadians by continuing to pollute? Can we afford to risk the effects of climate change on our environment? Can we afford to fall behind the rest of the world in research and development leading to a solution to the problem of greenhouse gases?

Exercise 5.9 (suggested answer)

1. When choosing between two fast-food restaurants, consider food, atmosphere, service, and price.
2. Urban overcrowding results in traffic jams, air pollution, homelessness, and both street and domestic violence.
3. Successful small businesses are usually those with adequate capital, a marketable product, dedicated personnel, and a workable business plan.

Answers for Chapter 7: Understanding the Paragraph (pp. 87–101)

Exercise 7.2

1. Canada makes no economic sense.
2. In reality, taste buds are exceedingly small.
3. With the huge variety of computers now on the market, the determining factor in a purchase should be the job the machine will be expected to do.

Answers for Chapter 18: Choosing the Right Words (pp. 220–234)

Exercise 18.1 (suggested answer)

1. I wondered why the baseball kept getting bigger. Then it hit me.
2. Would you repeat the instructions about wordiness? I didn't hear them because I was texting while you were speaking.

3. Our competitor's products, although inferior to ours, are now selling better than ours.

4. My writing is as good as Ashley's and deserves an equivalent (*or* as good a) mark, especially since I use more words to say the same thing.

5. I prefer Marvel movies to DC, because DC movies aren't funny to me.

6. I doubt that this innovation will succeed.

7. A firm understanding of English fundamentals is a prerequisite to success in college or university, business, and the community.

8. "As a new teacher," we told our English instructor, "you need to understand that grammar, spelling, and punctuation rules stifle our creativity."

9. I think that the [many] social media we use today will soon converge, and the electronic world will resemble the "real" world so closely that the boundaries between the two will blur.

10. We have eliminated any unlawful descriptors, such as race, age, gender, religion, and marital status, from our personnel documents. Now they are all practically identical.

Exercise 18.4 (suggested answer)

1. When the rain began, we turned on the windshield wipers.
2. Young people often have difficulty communicating with parents and others in authority.
3. The witness lied when she claimed that the accused had confessed in a meeting with her.
4. The results of our study demonstrate that our survey instrument is as valid as any other.
5. Cancelling IMF loans to Pacific Rim countries could affect the relationship between developed and developing nations.

Exercise 18.6 (suggested answer)

1. The well-known writer and director Nora Ephron regrets that she cannot go out in public without attracting the attention of fans and photographers.
2. Amy King first joined the company as a salesperson; only 10 years later, she was promoted to president.
3. An executive sitting in the first-class cabin rang for the flight attendant, a friendly woman who quickly arrived to assist him.
4. The list of ingredients on food packages contains information that may be important to consumers, especially if they are the parents of young children.
5. The typical family is often hard-pressed to find time for family recreation.

Exercise 18.7 (suggested answer)

1. **Regardless** of what you think, the problem between her and **me** has nothing to do with you.
2. If you want to be in the office pool, I need $5.00 **from** you today because there will be no spots left by tomorrow.
3. If I **hadn't texted** you this morning to remind you that you were **supposed** to write your chemistry exam, you would **have** missed it.
4. I didn't feel like seeing **anybody**, so I went home, turned on the TV, and **did nothing** for the rest of the night.

5. This **used** to be a good place to work, but now we're **supposed** to work a full shift every day, or a penalty is deducted **from** our pay.
6. When Barack Obama was elected president for the second time, **most** U.S. liberals hoped that **much** of the prejudice in that country had finally been put to rest.
7. **Regardless** of media hype, Dr. Who as played by David Tennant is not the best; that distinction had already been won by Tom Baker in the 1970s.
8. It's **irresponsible** of us to blame television or any other **medium** for causing violence.
9. Television is partly responsible, however, for the fact that **many** ungrammatical expressions sound **all right** to us.
10. Between you and **me**, the reason I didn't speak to **anyone** about Elmo's cheating is **that** he would **have broken** my arm.

Answers for Chapter 19: Rewriting Your Work (pp. 235–242)

Exercise 19.2 (suggested answer)

In this suggested answer, we have reorganized the main points to conform to the usual way of presenting them (reduce, reuse, recycle); added supporting evidence and transitions (in colour); deleted repetitious, irrelevant, or insignificant material (~~by drawing a line through it~~); and revised inappropriate words and tone (changes appear **in bold**; *** indicates the removal of a word or punctuation mark). We've also added some explanatory comments in the margin. The first-stage revision below still contains errors, but we will address them when we come to the editing and proofreading phases.

Since our rewrite will not match yours (rewording, transitions, and supporting details can be supplied only by an individual writer), how can you tell if your revision makes the changes that need to be made at this stage? If you have rearranged the main points, added transitions and supporting details, and reworded at least some of the inappropriate passages, you're on the right track.

Weak opening

Lapse in tone

Redundant

Lapse in tone

Wordy

Reorder points

Transition added

Wordy

1 ~~We are having a garbage crisis~~. Canadians are experiencing a huge cultural shift, one that has been caused not by politics or films or music, but by garbage. We are drowning in garbage. ~~There is~~ So much waste ~~being~~ **is produced** in North America **that** we no longer ~~have any idea of~~ **know** were to put it. Take Toronto, for instance. ~~Toronto's garbage problem is so great that they are trucking~~ The city produces so much garbage **that it trucks** thousands of tonnes of it to Michigan every year. A short-term solution that is **unsustainable**. ~~just plain stupid, and how long can it last? We must act now, and we must act as individuals.~~ We cannot wait for the Government to save us from this crisis. We produce the garbage; we must solve the problem. ~~that much is perfectly obvious to anyone. In very practical, down to earth, concrete terms, here are some things we can do to~~ We cannot afford to delay: we must act now to reduce, reuse, and recycle. Yes, the "3 *R*s" of environmental ~~responsibility~~, the same rules we've paid so little attention to ~~for years~~.

2 First, ~~we~~ must reduce the amount of garbage we produce. We can do this be refusing to buy products that are ~~over packaged~~ **overpackaged**, like fast food ~~that comes~~ in styrafoam containers tucked into plastic bags for carrying, and **foil-wrapped** chocolates ~~that have a paper wrapping, a box, lining paper,~~ **in** a plastic tray ~~for the candies, and foil wrap around each chocolate~~ **inside a fancy, paper-lined, nonrecyclable cardboard**

box. By not purchasing such wasteful items, we say to the manufacturer, either reduce the packaging of your product or lose business to your competition. We can also ~~be less wastful in our own habits~~ **reduce waste** by carpooling, for example, and by turning up the temperature in our homes a few degrees in summer and down a few degrees in winter. David Suzuki gives sound advice in his TV commercials: switch to low-energy light bulbs, wear a sweater indoors when it's cold, and supplement fossil fuel heating systems with a wood-burning stove or fireplace. How could anyone sitting in front of a warm, cozy wood fire complain about "having to cut back"?

Wordy

The point is not adequately supported in this paragraph. We've added some detail and new examples.

[The paragraph that follows was originally the fourth paragraph in our first draft, but most of the information in it more logically belongs in the discussion of *reducing* waste.]

Transition added

3 ~~We can reuse most things~~. Another way to reduce the amount of garbage we produce is to reuse goods whenever possible. ~~Composting vegetable garbage is a good way to put waste to valuable use. Or~~ We can carry our groceries home in washable cloth or reusable plastic containers rather than disposable plastic bags. Instead of paper towels, we can use frayed towels and tattered cotton T-shirts as cleaning rags around the house. We can build and renovate with reclaimed lumber instead of new wood. **Items** we no longer need or want can be offered to others through lawn sales and flea markets. We can even advertise lawn sale leftovers on Craigslist or Kijiji. You'll be surprised how many people are interested in free "stuff"!

The first draft provided little support for this point. We've added details and examples to develop the paragraph adequately.

Composting is a recycling activity. See paragraph 4.

Transition sentence added

4 Once we have reduced our consumption and trained ourselves to reuse rather than replace, the last step is to ~~We must~~ recycle everything we can ~~instead of sending it to the dump~~. ~~Old cloths can be sent to the Salvation Army.~~ Composting vegetable garbage is a good way to put waste to valuable use. **Unwanted or outgrown items of clothing** can be **donated** to the Salvation Army, Goodwill, or other charitable organizations that support everyone from refugees to radical environmentalists. As can furniture, appliances, books, and most other household items. There are dozens of ways to make useful items from things that would otherwise ~~be thrown away~~ **become landfill**, such as quilts from old clothes; bird feeders from plastic jugs; and fire logs from newspapers. ~~We don't need to consume as much as we do, and it won't hurt us to use things longer instead of buying new items before the old ones are completely worn out~~. Many companies now manufacture products from recycled goods, some of which are quite surprising, would you believe high-fashion, waterproof jackets made from recycled plastic bottles? We should ~~be on the lookout for their~~ **learn about these** products, to support **these companies'** efforts and to **thus further** reduce the waste that is dumped into landfills. ~~And whatever we can't use ourselves can be sent to organizations that help others where they will have a life away from a landfill.~~

The examples in this paragraph have been rearranged to reflect our production of recyclable waste, from daily to infrequently to rarely.

Redundant—point has already been made

Too colloquial

Redundant

Poor sentence: What does "This" refer to?

5 ~~This is an absolute necessity~~. This cultural shift is one that all of us who care about our families, our country, and our planet should wholeheartedly support. If we do not stop producing so much waste, we will inevitibly destroy our *** enviornment. Unlike most efforts to improve ~~things~~ **our lives**, the move to **reduce, reuse, and recycle** ~~has one other advantage, it doesn't cost any money~~ **costs us nothing**. In fact, it can save ~~every~~ households ~~that practises it~~ hundreds of dollars a year. Everyone wins when we commit to the "3 Rs."

Vague

Wordy

Reordered

Memorable statement added

Exercise 20.1 (suggested answer)

Note: The removal of words or punctuation marks is indicated by ***.

1. I **expect** a salary **commensurate** with my qualifications *** and *** experience.
2. I have **learned** Microsoft Word and **Excel** *** **spreadsheet programs.**
3. In 2007, I **received** a **plaque** for being salesperson of the year.
4. Reason for leaving last job: **maternity** leave.
5. You will want me to be a **manager** in no time.
6. I am a perfectionist and rarely, **if ever**, forget details.
7. Marital status: single. ***
8. In my previous job, **I learned to trust no one**. (Not an admission you should make in a job application.)
9. As **indicated**, I have over five **years' experience in** analyzing investments.
10. I was responsible for **running** *** a **Western** chain store. (*Better*: I was responsible for managing a Western chain store.)

Exercise 20.2 (suggested answer)

We developed this suggested answer by checking each sentence and paragraph of our answer to Exercise 19.2 against the Rewriting Checklist on pages 239–240. Changes we have made to sentence structure, grammar, spelling, and punctuation appear in **bold type.**

Note: The removal of words or punctuation marks is indicated by ***.

1 Canadians are experiencing a huge cultural shift, one that has been caused not by politics or films or music, but by garbage. We are drowning in garbage. So much waste is produced in North America that we no longer know **where** to put it. Take Toronto, for instance. The city produces so much garbage that it trucks thousands of tonnes of it to Michigan every year, **a** short-term solution that is unsustainable. We cannot wait for the **government** to save us from this crisis. We produce the garbage; we must solve the problem. We cannot afford to delay: we must act now to reduce, reuse, and recycle. Yes, **we're talking about** the "3 *R*s" of environmental responsibility, the same rules we've paid so little attention to for years.

2 First, we must reduce the amount of garbage we produce. We can do this **by** refusing to buy products that are overpackaged, like fast food in **Styrofoam** containers tucked into plastic bags for carrying, and foil-wrapped chocolates in a plastic tray inside a fancy, paper-lined, nonrecyclable cardboard box. By not purchasing such wasteful items, we say to the manufacturer, "**Either** reduce the packaging of your product or lose business to your competition." We can also reduce waste by carpooling, for example, and by turning up the temperature in our homes a few degrees in summer and down a few degrees in winter. David Suzuki gives sound advice in his TV commercials: switch to low-energy light bulbs, wear a sweater indoors when it's cold, and supplement fossil fuel heating systems with a wood-burning stove or fireplace. How could anyone sitting in front of a warm, cozy wood fire complain about "having to cut back"?

[Paragraph 3 contains no editing errors.]

4 Once we have reduced our consumption and trained ourselves to reuse rather than replace, the last step is to recycle everything we can. Composting vegetable garbage is a good way to put waste to valuable use. Unwanted or

outgrown items of clothing can be donated to the Salvation Army, Goodwill, or other charitable organizations that support everyone from refugees to radical environmentalists, **as** can furniture, appliances, books, and most other household items. There are dozens of ways to make useful items from things that would otherwise become landfill, such as quilts from old clothes, bird feeders from plastic jugs, and fire logs from newspapers. Many companies now manufacture products from recycled goods, some of which are quite surprising: Would you believe high-fashion, waterproof jackets made from recycled plastic bottles? We should learn about these products *** to support these companies' efforts and to thus further reduce the waste that is dumped into landfills.

5 This cultural shift is one that all of us who care about our families, our country, and our planet should wholeheartedly support. If we do not stop producing so much waste, we will **inevitably** destroy our **environment**. Unlike most efforts to improve our lives, the move to reduce, reuse, and recycle costs us nothing. In fact, it can save households hundreds of dollars a year. Everyone wins when we commit to the "3 *R*s."

Exercise 20.6

According to a recent survey in ***Maclean's*** magazine, only 43 percent of Canadians are satisfied with their jobs. What can you do to ensure that you will not be one of the 57 percent who are unhappy with the work they do? There are three questions to consider when seeking employment that will provide satisfaction as well as a paycheque.

First, are you suited to the kind of work you are applying for? If you enjoy the outdoors, for example, and like to be active, **you are** not going to be happy with a **nine-to-five** office job, no matter how much it pays.

Second, is the job based in a location compatible with your **preferred** lifestyle? No matter how much you like your work, if you go home every night to *** an environment you are miserable in, it will not be long before you start **transferring** your **dissatisfaction** to your job. If you like the amenities and **conveniences** of the city, you probably will not enjoy working in a small town. If, on the other hand, you prefer the quiet and security of small-town life, you may find the city a stressful place in which to live.

Finally, is **the company you are applying to** one that you want to work for? Do you need the security of generous benefits, a good pension plan, and incentives to stay and grow with one company? Or are you an **ambitious** person who is looking for variety, quick advancement, and a high salary? If so, you may have to **forgo** security in favour of commissions or cash incentives and be willing to move as quickly and as often as opportunities occur. Some **careful** self-analysis now, before you start out on your career path, will help you **choose** a direction that will put you in the 43 percent minority of satisfied Canadian workers.

Answers for Chapter 23: A Review of the Basics (pp. 326–361)

Exercise 23.1

1. Canadians love doughnuts.
2. We eat more doughnuts than any other nation.
3. Doughnuts taste sweet.
4. Glazed doughnuts are my favourite.
5. Most malls contain at least one doughnut shop.
6. Hot chocolate is good with doughnuts.

7. [You] Try a bran doughnut for breakfast.
8. Bran is good for your health.
9. Doughnut jokes are common on television.
10. Dentists like doughnuts too, but for different reasons.

Exercise 23.2

1. There are many errors here.
2. She likes the Rolling Stones.
3. [You] Chew quickly.
4. Here, under the bench, we found the ring.
5. The dancing girl got a lot of attention.
6. After summer, things really started to heat up.
7. Here is my essay.
8. In 2001, I started using a cellphone every day.
9. After buying my cellphone, I bought a computer.
10. Here is my famous spaghetti.

Exercise 23.3

1. I am making a healthy breakfast.
2. It does not include Coca-Cola.
3. You can add fresh fruit to the cereal.
4. The toast should be almost ready now.
5. My doctor has often recommended yogurt for breakfast.
6. I could never eat yogurt without fruit.
7. With breakfast, I will drink at least two cups of coffee.
8. I don't like tea.
9. I simply cannot begin my day without coffee.
10. I should probably switch to decaf.

Exercise 23.4

1. ~~In Canada~~, poutine is considered a national treasure.
2. I felt lost ~~among the books in the large library~~.
3. ~~Over dinner~~, we discussed our upcoming wedding.
4. You shouldn't stand ~~under the new construction~~.
5. Joel's laughter ~~at the clowns in the park~~ made me smile.
6. ~~During the fall~~, I ate apples every day.
7. ~~Despite my workload~~, I still completed the essay ~~on time~~.
8. ~~Through the school year~~, I don't let texting rule my life.
9. ~~In high heels and a long skirt~~, I still was able to run ~~from the werewolf at the prom~~.
10. The house ~~beside Sylvia's~~ is ~~for sale~~.

Exercise 23.5

1. Management and union met ~~for a two-hour bargaining session~~.
2. They debated and drafted a tentative agreement ~~for a new contract~~.
3. The anesthetist and the surgeon scrubbed ~~for surgery~~ and hurried ~~to the operating room~~.

4. Frederick Banting and Norman Bethune are considered medical heroes ~~around the world~~.

5. Kevin and Sandor hiked and cycled ~~across most of Newfoundland~~.

6. My son or my daughter will meet me and drive me home.

7. [You] Knock three times and ask ~~for Stanislaw~~.

8. ~~In the 17th and 18th centuries~~, the French and the English fought ~~for control of Canada~~.

9. [You] Buy the base model and don't waste your money ~~on luxury options~~.

10. Ragweed, goldenrod, and twitch grass formed the essential elements ~~in the bouquet for his English teacher~~.

Exercise 23.7

_S_ Social media is not unlike a party. _F_ Fun, but can also get out of hand very quickly. _S_ *Facebook* should be blocked in schools. _F_ Because my friends are bullied. _S_ Also, I have seen many students on *Facebook* instead of doing their homework. _S_ In fact, parents should have to sign on to social media for their children. _F_ And should get emails of all *Facebook* posts. _S_ Making social media safe should be a priority. _S_ The people who bully on *Facebook* must think they can get away with it. _F_ Often because they can.

Exercise 23.8 (suggested answers)

We have made the sentence fragments into complete sentences to give you an idea of how the sentences might be formed. Different sentences can be made out of the fragments in this exercise; just be sure each sentence has a subject and a verb.

1. _S_ We laughed.
2. _F_ They kept calling during the TV show.
3. _S_ She checked it out.
4. _F_ I want to create my own espresso.
5. _S_ Trying to gather up my courage, I handed him the résumé.
6. _F_ I am changing into a bad person.
7. _F_ I want to talk about this party.
8. _F_ I am much happier after changing my cellphone plan.
9. _F_ I want to get the most out of the course.
10. _S_ Wanting to catch up, she ran faster.

Exercise 23.9

1. Before we watched the zombie movie. (Before)
2. Because we wanted the shoes. (Because)
3. That was nice to hear.
4. Unless the homework is complete. (Unless)
5. While we were at the mall. (While)

Exercise 23.10

1. Although many companies …

4. As companies seek …

6. Which leads to a surplus …

8. Who have reached …
9. Whether it is through termination …

Exercise 23.11

Although many companies are now experiencing difficulty because of tough economic times, middle managers seldom breathe easily even during times of expansion and high profits. In difficult times, middle managers are vulnerable to the cost-cutting axe as companies seek to reduce overhead. In times of fast growth, the executive branch of many companies expands rapidly, which leads to a surplus of managerial talent, especially among junior executives. And it is these younger, well-educated, ambitious young hires who can threaten middle managers who have reached, or overreached, their potential. Whether it is through termination, early retirement, or buyout, such mid-level executives are the first to feel the effects of a company's desire to streamline the hierarchy in good times or eliminate paycheques in bad times.

Exercise 23.12

1. Walking is probably the best form of exercise there is. Unless you're in the water. Then swimming is preferable.
2. Rain doesn't bother me. I like to stay inside and read. When the weather is miserable.
3. Please try this soup. After you've tasted it. I am sure you'll be able to tell me what's missing.
4. Whenever Ashley gets the opportunity. She loves to dance. But her boyfriend hates dancing, so she seldom gets the chance to show off her moves.
5. The report identifies a serious problem that we need to consider. Whenever our website is revised or updated. It is vulnerable to hackers.

Exercise 23.14 (suggested answer)

1. The doctor is busy right now. You will have to wait.
2. Press on the wound; that will stop the bleeding.
3. Don't let your worries kill you. Let the church help.
4. I can't read it **because** the print is too small.
5. Here is my number. Give me a call.
6. Consider hiring an event planner. You cannot arrange this function by yourself.
7. Eat sensibly; exercise regularly; die anyway.
8. That was a great dive, **so** you get a perfect 10.
9. Listen to this man play. He's a jazz–blues musician who calls himself Dr. John.
10. Correct.

Exercise 23.15 (suggested answer)

1. Computers do not prevent mistakes; they just make them faster.
2. I'm trying to stop playing computer games, **for** they take up too much of my time.
3. I'm innocent. This is a case of mistaken identity.
4. Time is the best teacher; unfortunately, it kills all its students.
5. Correct.
6. The microwave oven is the most important appliance in my home; without it, I'd starve.

7. Money may not be everything, **but** it is far ahead of whatever is in second place.
8. Allow enough time to complete the project. **A** rush job is not acceptable.
9. Teachers are finding more and more students who went from printing straight to using a keyboard. They have never learned cursive script.
10. These students are at a huge disadvantage during exams, **for** it takes far longer to print block capitals than it does to write cursive script.

Exercise 23.17

1. The Argos lost by **only** six points.
2. They closed **just** before five.
3. I applied for **almost** every job that was posted.
4. The French drink wine with **nearly** every meal, including lunch.
5. On the first day of Sarah's new exercise program, she was able to walk **only** 500 metres.
6. I had answered **scarcely** 12 of the 25 questions when time was up.
7. **In August,** we went camping in a national park with lots of wildlife.
8. I have been **nearly** fired every week that I have worked here.
9. **Nearly 20 metres under the water,** the attack submarine approached the tanker.
10. **This week,** Steven Spielberg predicted an "inevitable implosion" in the film industry.

Exercise 23.18

1. With clear explanations and lots of exercises, *Essay Essentials* is designed to help college and university students learn to write good prose.
2. Each year, almost half a million Canadian men have a vasectomy.
3. With his new binoculars, Juan caught sight of a doe and her two fawns.
4. Vancouver is a wonderful city to live in for anyone who likes rain and fog.
5. Some games, such as Scrabble and Settlers of Catan, are less demanding in terms of fitness and strength.
6. Thanks to my new camera with digital functions, I can take professional-quality pictures.
7. We looked online for a suitable retirement gift for our boss.
8. The Canadian Human Rights Act prohibits discrimination on the basis of race, religion, sex, or age against anyone who is applying for a job.
9. One usually finds the best Chinese food in restaurants where the Chinese eat.
10. Tonight, Liam Neeson will talk with George Stroumboulopoulos about his wife, Natasha Richardson, who died after falling on a ski slope at Mont Tremblant.

Exercise 23.19

1. Having heard the end of the murder trial, we had to make a decision.
2. Knowing about the upcoming restructuring, she always kept her résumé up to date.
3. Correct
4. Having testing the speed and RAM, I think that MacBook Pros are great.
5. After the builders finished the roof, the decaying mansion still flooded.
6. To be eligible for the reward, the person who finds the cat must return it.
7. At the age of 21, I would graduate in only days.

8. After working all day, I find movies a good way to relax.
9. As I walked down the street, rain started pouring down.
10. While I was texting my friends, the food was delivered.

Exercise 23.20

1. She was the baker's only daughter, but she could loaf all day. (*Or* She was only the baker's daughter, but she could loaf all day.)
2. Being horribly hungover, I realized that the problem with a free bar is knowing when to quit.
3. Sam finally got the terrified horse, which was rearing and kicking, under control.
4. In a hurry to get to the interview on time, I left my résumé lying on my desk at home.
5. As a college student constantly faced with new assignments, I find the pressure is sometimes intolerable.
6. Listening to the rumours, I'll bet the newlyweds are already on the road to separation.
7. As a non-drinker, I find the liquor in the duty-free outlet of no interest.
8. The bride, who was wearing a strapless gown with a short lace jacket, was given in marriage by her father.
9. Queen Elizabeth couldn't resist the little Corgi puppy, which was rolling on her back, eager to have her tummy scratched.
10. If you wear a small Canadian flag on your backpack or lapel, people abroad will be less likely to assume you're American.

Exercise 23.22

1. This program is easy to understand and to use.
2. We were told to leave and take everything with us.
3. We organized our findings, wrote the report, and finally prepared our PowerPoint presentation.
4. Both applicants were unskilled, unprepared, and unmotivated.
5. Elmer's doctor advised him not to strain his back or his mind.
6. The company is looking for an employee who has a car and who knows the city.
7. If consumers really cared, they could influence the fast-food industry to produce healthy, delicious, inexpensive food.
8. When I want to get away from it all, there are three solitary pleasures that I enjoy: walking in the country, reading a book, and listening to music.
9. A recent survey of female executives claims that family responsibilities, exclusion from informal networks, and lack of management experience are the major factors keeping them from advancement.
10. If it is to be useful, your report must be clearly organized, well written, and thoroughly researched.

Exercise 23.23

1. For my birthday, I requested either a Roots bag or a Dior scarf.
2. In my community, two related crimes are rapidly increasing: drug abuse and theft.
3. Bodybuilding has made me what I am today: physically perfect, financially prosperous, and practically friendless.

4. After reading all the explanations and completing all the exercises, you'll be a better writer.
5. Bruce claimed that, through repetition and reward, he had trained his centipede to be loyal and obedient.
6. During their vacation in New Brunswick, Trevor and Jamal visited many beautiful locations and ate wonderful seafood.
7. I'm an average tennis player; I have a good forehand, an average backhand, but a weak serve.
8. The problem with being immortalized as a statue is that you will be a target for pigeon droppings and graffiti.
9. Never disturb a sleeping dog, a happy baby, or a silent politician.
10. I'd like to help, but I'm too tired and too busy.

Exercise 23.24

1. Incorrect:	laughter	trusting	dancing
Correct:	laughing	trusting	dancing
2. Incorrect:	giving a speech	talk loudly	
Correct:	giving a speech	talking loudly	
3. Incorrect:	ideals	foundations	discussing
Correct:	ideals	foundations	discussion
4. Incorrect:	paper	lots of staples	
Correct:	paper	staples	
5. Incorrect:	slowly	fast	
Correct:	slowly	quickly	
6. Incorrect:	democracy	fascist	anarchy
Correct:	democracy	fascism	anarchy
7. Incorrect:	cram	learning	teaching
Correct:	cramming	learning	teaching
8. Incorrect:	punctual	friendliness	honest
Correct:	punctual	friendly	honest
9. Incorrect:	French	English	Germanic
Correct:	French	English	German
10. Incorrect:	dancing all night	to go out during the day	
Correct:	dancing all night	going out during the day	

Exercise 23.25

1. Trying your best and **succeeding** are not always the same thing.
2. Maya's symptoms included a high fever, severe headaches, and **painful joints.**
3. I hold a baseball bat right-handed but **hold a hockey stick** left-handed. (*Or* I **play baseball** right-handed but hockey left-handed.)
4. A good student attends all classes and **finishes all projects** on time.
5. Small businesses must be creative and **flexible** if they are to succeed in this economy.
6. **Pouring rain**, driving snow, and freezing temperatures are only a few of the conditions that make road construction in Alberta a challenge.
7. Licking one's fingers and **picking one's teeth** in a restaurant are one way to get attention.
8. A good teacher motivates with enthusiasm, informs with sensitivity, and **counsels with compassion**.

9. In the simplest terms, health is defined by four factors: age, current level of physical fitness, nutritional health, and genetics.

10. Henry Lieberman, a computer scientist with MIT, found that cyberbullying attacks fall into one or more of five categories: **appearance**, intelligence, **race**, ethnicity, and sexual preference.

Exercise 23.27

1. When you find a mistake, you should correct it.
2. Since my test is tomorrow morning, I must stay up late tonight. (*Or* My test is tomorrow morning, so I must stay up late tonight.)
3. Although the test was difficult, I passed it. (*Or* The test was difficult, but I passed it.)
4. Correct.
5. Even though the photographer was good, I hate the pictures of myself. (*Or* The photographer was good, yet I hate the pictures of myself.)
6. After doing a couple of hours' research in the library, we went back to work on our project.
7. Correct.
8. If this book will help me, I will buy it. (*Or* This book will help me, so I will buy it.)
9. Though having a car would be convenient, I need the money for other things. (*Or* Having a car would be convenient, but I need the money for other things.)
10. Although that program frequently crashes, this program is stable. (*Or* That program frequently crashes, but this program is stable.)

Exercise 23.28 (suggested answers)

1. Leonardo da Vinci was a great artist and inventor **who** invented scissors, among other things.
2. Cats can produce over 100 vocal sounds, **whereas** dogs can make only 10.
3. **Although** it is said that men don't cry, they do while assembling furniture.
4. The name Wendy was made up for a book **that** was called *Peter Pan*.
5. **Although** 10 percent of Canadians are heavy drinkers, 35 percent abstain from alcohol.
6. Travel broadens the mind **even though** it flattens the bank account.
7. We are seeking an experienced and innovative director **who** is fluent in French.
8. One hundred thousand Vietnam veterans have taken their own lives, **which** is twice the number who were killed in action.
9. **After** my cooking class went on a field trip to gather greens for a salad, we discovered that what we had thought was watercress was poison ivy.
10. Eight of my ten classmates **who** ate the salad were hospitalized, **although** no one was critically ill.

Answers for Chapter 24: Grammar (pp. 362–397)

Exercise 24.1

1. They want to go to Halifax.
2. Those cellphones have horrible ring tones.
3. All those who waited in line got free tickets to the concert.

4. The men think they ran over a skunk.
5. Those men's dogs sure are adorable.

Exercise 24.2

1. is
2. are
3. is
4. is
5. tempt

Exercise 24.3

1. is
2. registers
3. is
4. wonder
5. needs

Exercise 24.4

1. is
2. involves
3. is
4. wants
5. believes

Exercise 24.5

1. are
2. has
3. get
4. were
5. are

Exercise 24.6

1. has
2. succeeds
3. shows
4. talks
5. admits

Exercise 24.7

1. Neither of the following sentences **is** correct.
2. The faculty, with the full support of the college administration, **treat** plagiarism as a serious offence.
3. Either good looks or intelligence **runs** in our family, but never at the same time.
4. None of the computer experts **has** been able to untangle our billing problems.
5. The enjoyment of puns and jokes involving plays on words **is** the result of having too little else on your mind.
6. Anyone who jumps from one of Paris's many bridges **is** in Seine.

7. It is amazing how much better the orchestra **plays** now that the conductor is sober.
8. The number of layoffs in the last quarter **is** truly alarming.
9. Her colleagues, along with her supervisor, **agree** that Emily needs further training.
10. Canada's First Nations population **is** thought to have come to this continent from Asia thousands of years before the Europeans arrived in North America.

Exercise 24.8

Quebec City, along with Montreal, Toronto, and Vancouver, **is** among Canada's great gourmet centres. Whereas Toronto and Vancouver are relative latecomers to this list, neither Quebec City nor Montreal **is a stranger** to those who **seek** fine dining. Indeed, travel and food magazines have long affirmed that including these two cities in a Quebec vacation **is** a "must." Montreal is perhaps more international in its offerings, but Quebec City provides exquisite proof that French Canadian cuisine and hospitality **are** second to none in the world. Amid the Old World charm of the lower city **are** to be found some of the quaintest and most enjoyable traditional restaurants, and the newer sections of town **boast** equally fine dining in more contemporary surroundings. The combination of the wonderful food and the charm of the city **is** sure to entice any visitor to return. Either summer, when the city blooms and outdoor cafés abound, or winter, when Carnaval turns the streets into hundreds of connecting parties, **is a** wonderful **time** to visit one of Canada's oldest and most interesting cities.

Exercise 24.10

1. ridden, rode
2. eaten, ate
3. grew, grown
4. hid, hidden
5. wrote, written

Exercise 24.12

1. The umpire stands there, unable to believe what he **is** seeing.
2. Correct.
3. The class had just ended when in **walked** Jason.
4. The rebellion failed because the people **did** not support it.
5. The party was just getting started when Eva **decided** it **was** time to leave.
6. I enjoy my work, but I **am** not going to let it take over my life.
7. Prejudice is learned and **is** hard to outgrow.
8. A Canadian is someone who thinks that an income tax refund **is** a gift from the government.
9. Robert went to Laval for his vacation every summer and **stayed** with his aunt and uncle on a farm.
10. Shahn likes to play cricket with his Canadian friends even though most of them **don't** understand the rules.

Exercise 24.13

For some reason, when mistakes or accidents happen in radio or television, they **are** often hilariously funny. If, in the course of a conversation, someone said, "Here come the Duck and Doochess of Kent," listeners would probably be mildly amused. But many years ago, when an announcer **made** that slip on a live radio broadcast, it **became** one of the most famous blunders in radio history. Tapes of the slip **were** filed in "bloopers" libraries all over the world. This heightened sense of hilarity is the reason that so many people who work in radio **dedicate** their creativity to making the on-air announcer laugh while reading the news. To take one example, Lorne Greene's **was** the deeply serious voice that **was** heard on the CBC news during World War II. He **was** the victim of all kinds of pranks aimed at getting him to break up while reading the dark, often tragic, news of the combat overseas. The pages of his news **script** were set on fire while he **read**. He **was** even stripped naked as he **read**, calmly, and apparently without strain. Lorne Greene **was** a true professional. Many other newscasters, however, **have been** highly susceptible to falling apart on air at the slightest provocation. And there **are** always people around a radio station who cannot resist giving them that little push.

Exercise 24.15

1. The department head called a meeting.
2. The barista will make your espresso in a few minutes.
3. When it gets cold, we plug in the block heater overnight.
4. For many years, professional athletes have used steroids to improve speed and endurance.
5. You may not take photos during the performance.
6. My great-grandfather, who served in the army overseas, wrote these letters.
7. A crew of students made this film for less than $100 000.
8. Thieves broke into our neighbours' house while they were vacationing in Cuba.
9. You made an error in the code you wrote for this program.
10. Teamwork is a valuable concept, especially when we need someone to take the blame for the boss's mistakes.

Exercise 24.16

1. Another Juno was won by Feist. (Active voice is more effective.)
2. The ball was spiked by Jian, after scoring the go-ahead touchdown. (Active voice is more effective.)
3. A bylaw forbidding backyard bird feeders was passed by City Council. (Passive voice is more effective because it focuses on the law rather than on who passed it.)
4. Later that night, the security guard saw a shadowy figure entering the lab. (Passive voice is more effective because it focuses on the intruder rather than on who saw him or her.)
5. Four tickets to the Michael Bublé concert were bought by Courtenay after standing in line all night. (Active voice is more effective.)
6. The truth behind the fake diploma scandal was revealed on the 10 p.m. news. (Passive voice is more effective because it focuses on the scandal rather than on when it was revealed.)
7. People who want to shift responsibility from themselves to others often use passive voice. (Passive is more effective.)
8. After a long debate, Yasmin's idea of a class *Facebook* page was endorsed by the student council. (Passive voice is more effective because it focuses on the idea rather than on who supported it.)
9. Language psychologists have developed a computer program that analyzes speech patterns. (Passive voice is more effective because it focuses on the specific program rather than on the anonymous group who developed it.)

10. After years of research among college students, language psychologists have concluded that people who frequently use passive voice tend to be maladjusted. (Active voice is more effective.)

Exercise 24.18

1. Katie and **I** stayed up most of the night to complete our assignment.
2. There wasn't much **we** could do to rescue it, however.
3. Peng and Yvon were supposed to be in our group, but neither of **them** showed up.
4. When **we** poor, sleep-deprived students submitted the assignment, our professor glared at **us**.
5. Between **us**, **we** had managed to produce barely four pages.
6. After all, what do Katie and I know about the topic assigned to **us**?
7. Both of **us** thought "relative deprivation" had something to do with families.
8. **She** and **I** spent hours writing about being grounded by our parents, forgetting Mother's Day, and suffering our older siblings' bullying.
9. It never occurred to **her** or **me** that the term was a definition of poverty.
10. Katie and **I** have often been late and sometimes absent from class this term, so when the prof adds our class participation mark to the grade we get on our major paper, whose topic we misinterpreted, it's unlikely that **she** and **I** can count on an A in sociology.

Exercise 24.19

1. Correct
2. Jennifer is more into Disney than **I** [am].
3. No one in the class except Lida did as well as **I** [did] on the assignment.
4. Although Sarah, too, likes music, Franco spends more time listening to the radio than **she** [does].
5. The subject of Harry Potter is more exciting to my students than [it is] to **me**.
6. Correct
7. Serge likes to play video games through the night more than **I** [like to].

Exercise 24.20

1. My boyfriend and **I** …
2. I like fast food better than **he** [does].
3. He likes vegetables better than **I** [do].
4. In fact, between you and **me** …
5. … it is difficult for **them** to know where to take him and **me** …
6. The only type of restaurant where **we** [and **they**] can all have what we like is Italian.
7. There, **he** and his friends …
8. We are probably not as healthy as they, but they don't seem to enjoy their food as much as **we** [do].

Exercise 24.21

1. a
2. (no pronoun)
3. a
4. her

5. his (*or* her)
6. an
7. a
8. a
9. the
10. its

Exercise 24.22

1. Everyone I know has a cellphone.
2. Someone has an eye on you.
3. Anyone who writes a generic cover letter can expect not to be taken seriously.
4. No one wants his or her ideas rejected.
5. If you're lost, ask someone for directions. (*Or* If you're lost, ask for directions.)

Exercise 24.23

1. I know that smoking is bad for me and everyone else, but I can't give up cigarettes.
2. If your pet rat won't eat its food, feed the pellets to the kitty.
3. Our cat is a picky eater; her food preferences are inconvenient and expensive.
4. Whenever Stan and Matt played poker, Stan stacked the deck.
5. The gorilla was mean and hungry because he had finished all his food in the morning.
6. Madonna has transformed herself at least five times in her career, an accomplishment that makes her unique.
7. Dani backed her car into a garbage truck and dented her fender.
8. Rocco was suspicious of handgun control because he thought everyone should have a gun for late-night subway rides.
9. Get your ears pierced during this week's special and take home an extra pair of earrings free.
10. Our car is in the shop, but we're still going to the party.

Exercise 24.24

1. The teacher **whom** I had last year liked me so much he made sure I had to take his class again.
2. Broccoli is a vegetable **that** I just don't like.
3. I think movie stars **who** speak up against animal cruelty are cool.
4. I'm someone **who** isn't good to cross.
5. People **who** take long naps are said to live longer lives.
6. Maple Leaf Interiors, **which** redecorated my office, just won an award.
7. Mr. Morales is the teacher **whom** I respect the most.
8. Chefs **who** don't use real butter usually suffer from harsh criticism.
9. The problems **that** we're having at work could drive anyone to quit.
10. We walked across Dead Man's Bluff, **which** he told us would take us to the store, as quickly as possible.

Exercise 24.26

1. you
2. she
3. an
4. you, your
5. one

Exercise 24.27

1. Most people enjoy eating when **they** are with good friends in a pleasant environment.
2. One is never too old to learn, but **one is** never too young to know everything. (*Or* **You are** never too old ..., but **you are** ...)
3. One should always remove **one's** shoes when entering a mosque.
4. Students who don't learn from history are doomed to find **themselves** back in Grade 9 for a second try.
5. When **you visit** Beijing, you must see the Great Wall, the Forbidden City, and the Temple of Heaven.
6. Experience is that marvellous thing that enables us to recognize a mistake when **we** make it again.
7. Middle age is that time of life when you've met so many people that everyone **you meet** reminds **you** of somebody else.
8. The penalties for plagiarism are severe, but most of us don't think about them until after **we've** been caught.
9. Always read through the entire test before **you begin** to answer the questions.
10. **You** can learn another language if **you** have enough motivation; the most effective method is to fall in love with someone who speaks the language you are trying to learn.

Exercise 24.28

When people see a dreadful occurrence on television, such as a bombing, an earthquake, or a mass slaughter, it does not always affect **them**. It is one thing for people to see the ravages of war **themselves** and another thing to see a three-minute newscast of the same battle, neatly edited by the CBC. Even the horrible effects of natural catastrophes that wipe out whole populations are somehow minimized or trivialized when **people** see them on TV. And although viewers may be horrified by the gaunt faces of starving children on the screen, **they** can easily escape into **their** familiar world of Egg McMuffins, Shake'n Bake, and Labatt Blue that is portrayed in commercial messages.

Thus, the impact of television on us is a mixed one. It is true that **we are** shown terrible, sometimes shocking, events that **we** could not possibly have seen before television. In this way, **our** world is drawn together more closely. However, the risk in creating this immediacy is that **we** may become desensitized and cease to feel or care about other human beings.

Answers for Chapter 25: Punctuation (pp. 398–421)

Exercise 25.1

1. My favourite comedians are Curly, Larry, and Moe.
2. If you ignore my terrible accent, poor grammar, and limited vocabulary, my French is excellent.

3. Correct
4. Cambodian food is spicy, colourful, nourishing, and delicious.
5. In Canada, the seasons are spring, summer, fall, winter, winter, and winter.
6. Correct.
7. Regan cannot decide if her bridesmaids should wear black, green, or camouflage dresses.
8. The successful applicant will have computer skills, of course, as well as excellent communication skills, a friendly disposition, a willingness to work hard, and a sense of humour.
9. Both my doctor and my wife agree that I should eat better, exercise more, and stop smoking.
10. Much of the world sees Canada as a land where French is spoken, ice and snow are year-round hazards, and violent hockey is a favourite pastime.

Exercise 25.2

1. I didn't get an A⁺ in that course, but at least I passed.
2. She looked beautiful, yet she also looked quite sad.
3. Omar would have gone to Toronto, but he didn't want to leave Saskatoon.
4. Give me the apple, for I know it's good for me.
5. The cats are acting up, but I still love them dearly.
6. I like only rap music, but I am going to a ballet with my girlfriend anyway.
7. We haven't bought our winter boots, nor have we unpacked our mitts and scarves.
8. Either Magda gets the last piece of pie, or I won't bake one again.
9. I really want to mow the lawn, but I need to go job hunting.
10. I came down with the flu, so I can't make it to work.

Exercise 25.3

1. Remember, a clear conscience is often just a sign of a poor memory.
2. If you think nobody cares, try missing a few payments.
3. When the cannibals ate a missionary, they got a taste of religion.
4. No matter how much I practise, my singing never gets any better.
5. First, cook the noodles in a large pot of boiling water.
6. If Barbie is so popular, why do you have to buy friends for her?
7. Until I had my performance review, I thought my manager had no appreciation of my efforts.
8. No matter how much you push the envelope, it will still be stationery.
9. Ladies and gentlemen, please put away all cellphones, iPads, and any other electronic devices you may have concealed on your person before entering the examination room.
10. In democracy, it is your vote that counts; in feudalism, it is your count that votes.

Exercise 25.4

1. A good day, in my opinion, always starts with a few cuts of high-volume heavy metal.
2. This photograph, which was taken when I was eight months old, embarrasses me whenever my parents display it.

3. Mira's boyfriend, who looks like an ape, is living proof that love is blind.
4. Isn't it strange that the poor, who are often bitterly critical of the rich, buy lottery tickets?
5. A nagging headache, the result of last night's party, made me miserable all morning.
6. Our ancient car made it all the way to Saskatoon without breaking down, a piece of good luck that astonished us all.
7. Professor Repke, a popular mathematics teacher, won the Distinguished Teaching Award this year.
8. We're going to spend the afternoon at the mall, a weekly event that has become a ritual.
9. Correct
10. Classical music, which I call Prozac for the ears, can be very soothing in times of stress.

Exercise 25.5

1. Unfortunately, we'll have to begin all over again.
2. Lord Black, your wife would like a word with you.
3. In college, the quality of your work is more important than the effort you put into it.
4. Hopelessly lost, my father refused to stop and ask for directions.
5. Finally understanding what she was trying to say, I apologized for being so slow.
6. After an evening of watching television, I have accomplished as much as if I had been unconscious.
7. Since the doctor ordered me to walk to work every morning, I have seen three accidents involving people walking to work.
8. That same year, Stephen Leacock bought his summer home in Orillia, Ontario.
9. When an optimist is pulled over by a police officer, the optimist assumes it's to ask for directions.
10. Having munched our way through a large bag of peanuts while watching the game, we weren't interested in supper.

Exercise 25.6

1. Dietitians recommend that we eat at least two servings daily of green, leafy vegetables.
2. Correct
3. Correct
4. Toronto in the summer is hot, smoggy, and humid.
5. St. John's, on the other hand, is cool, sunny, and windy.
6. The dining room table was made of richly stained, ornately carved walnut.
7. This ergonomic, efficient, full-function keyboard comes in a variety of pastel shades.
8. We ordered a large, nutritious salad for lunch and then smothered it in calorie-laden, creamy ranch dressing.
9. For my sister's birthday, her boyfriend gave her a cute, cuddly, seven-week-old puppy.
10. Today's paper has an article about a new car made of lightweight, durable carbon fibre.

Exercise 25.7

1. If it doesn't stop raining soon, we will begin to think we are in Vancouver. (Rule 3)
2. The gates are down, and the lights are flashing, but the train is nowhere in sight. (Rule 2)
3. No words in the English language rhyme with *month, orange, silver,* or *purple.* (Rule 1)
4. At our retirement banquet, instead of the traditional gold watch, we were presented with an Inuit soapstone sculpture. (Rule 4)
5. Dorothy got lost in the Land of Oz, for she had three men giving her directions. (Rule 2)
6. No meal is complete, in my opinion, without a sweet, preferably chocolate, dessert. (Rule 4, Rule 1)
7. My first acting role was as the husband in a school play, but, sadly, it was not a speaking role. (Rule 2, Rule 4)
8. According to my professor, the difference between mechanical and civil engineers is that mechanical engineers build weapons, and civil engineers build targets. (Rule 3, Rule 2)
9. Canadian football, unlike the American version, is full of exciting plays, risky strategy, and frequent upsets. (Rule 3, Rule 1)
10. The optimist sees a glass that is half full while a pessimist sees a glass that is half empty, but an engineer sees a glass that is twice as big as it needs to be. (Rule 2)

Exercise 25.8

1. Whereas the Super Bowl tradition goes back about four decades, the Grey Cup has a history that stretches back to the 19th century. (Rule 3)
2. Otherwise, Mrs. Lincoln said, she very much enjoyed the play. (Rule 4)
3. Our guard dog, a Rottweiler, caught an intruder and maimed him for life. (Rule 4)
4. Unfortunately, my Uncle Ladislaw was the intruder, and he intends to sue us for every penny we have. (Rule 3, Rule 2)
5. Correct
6. We bought a lovely, old, oak dining table at auction for $300. (Rule 5)
7. If there were more people like Gladys, global warming would be the least of our worries. (Rule 3)
8. Correct
9. Deciding on the midnight blue velvet pants was easy, but paying for them was not. (Rule 2)
10. Igor asked, "May I show you to your quarters, or would you prefer to spend the night in the dungeon?" (Rule 4, Rule 2)

Exercise 25.10

2. Correct
4. Correct
6. Correct
7. Correct
10. Correct

Exercise 25.12

1. Juanita was wondering when that book would arrive; after all, she had already waited a month.
2. It really isn't an inconvenience; nevertheless, I will take the compensation.
3. Jamal wasn't the only one who deserved punishment; his brother did, too.
4. Playing video games isn't detrimental to kids' health; they are constantly moving their hands.
5. We were planning to leave on Thursday; however, I am open to leaving earlier if it is possible.
6. You have to stop smiling; otherwise, I think you might get a face cramp.
7. Writing a great résumé isn't easy; I appreciate all your hard work.
8. You should consider applying for jobs in Red Deer, Alberta; Victoria, British Columbia; or Charlottetown, Prince Edward Island.
9. Kathe is the top of our class; everyone wishes for grades like hers.
10. We have important work to do this week; for example, we need to write an email congratulating the boss on his new yacht.

Exercise 25.14

1. Correct
2. Incorrect
3. Incorrect
4. Incorrect
5. Incorrect
6. Incorrect
7. Incorrect
8. Correct
9. Incorrect
10. Correct

Exercise 25.15

1. Right after we moved in, we discovered we had a problem: termites.
2. I have set myself three goals this year: to achieve an 80 percent average, to get a good summer job, and to buy a car.
3. After our bankruptcy, our credit card consultant asked us an interesting question: "Why don't you cut up your credit cards?"
4. Many Canadian writers are better known abroad than they are at home: Carol Shields, Neil Bissoondath, and Michael Ondaatje are three examples.
5. There are a number of inexpensive activities that will improve physical fitness: swimming, tennis, jogging, even brisk walking.
6. Jocelyn is trying to achieve two contradictory goals: significant weight loss and success as a restaurant critic.
7. Several of the animals on the international list of endangered species are native to Canada: the wood bison, the northern kit fox, and the whooping crane.
8. Correct

9. Canada's population is worn out and exhausted at the end of a long, hard winter, but most people are able to console themselves with one comforting thought: spring will arrive sometime in May or June.
10. There are several troublesome implications of biological engineering, but one in particular disturbs most people: the cloning of human beings.

Exercise 25.16

1. Correct
2. The best thing to have for breakfast is *** cereal and a banana.
3. It's an undeniable fact: Canada's trees are truly beautiful.
4. It has always been about only one thing: love conquers all.
5. The most important clothes to have for winter include *** mittens, boots, and a toque.
6. When I am really stressed, only one thing helps: *Star Wars Episode 2: Attack of the Clones*.
7. What it takes is this: perseverance.
8. Correct
9. It isn't nice to critique her: she is just starting out in the business.
10. Correct

Exercise 25.18

1. Pioneer hockey broadcaster Foster Hewitt made famous the words "He shoots! He scores!"
2. Another broadcasting legend, Danny Gallavan, once described a move by Montreal defenceman Serge Savard as "a Savardian spinorama."
3. "All hockey players are bilingual. They know English and profanity," according to the great Detroit Red Wings player, Gordie Howe.
4. Correct (the quotation is indirect).
5. It was Paul Gallico who summed up ice hockey as "a fast body-contact game played by men with clubs in their hands and knives laced to their feet."

Exercise 25.19

1. question mark
2. period
3. period
4. period
5. question mark
6. question mark
7. period
8. question mark
9. period
10. question mark

Exercise 25.20

1. You must be kidding!
2. Turn left! Now!

3. I can't believe I actually passed!
4. Oh, great! We're moving to Backwater, Alberta! (*Or* We're moving to Backwater, Alberta.)
5. Run! It's right behind you!
6. I'm freezing! Turn up the heat!
7. "Workers of the world, unite!"
8. At last! Someone is finally coming to take our order.
9. For the last time, leave me alone!
10. What a great game! I've never seen a better one. (*Or* I've never seen a better one!)

Exercise 25.22

1. Your very angry parents—they are still awake—are waiting for you in the house.
2. If we get to the movie—and we really want to get to the movie—I know you'll enjoy it.
3. Other people have expressed concern over the state of your paper—which really is quite messy. (*Or* Other people have expressed concern over the state of your paper, which really is quite messy.)
4. I am really craving eggs, butter, and toast—foods that are good when I feel sick.
5. What everyone needs to remember—recalling it when appropriate—is that there is usually time to correct past mistakes.
6. Conner has given us a lot to think about—it's almost time for our yearly evaluation.
7. Books like that—and movies too—are so thought-provoking.
8. Applying to relevant jobs can result in only one thing—eventual success.
9. The most we can afford—and it isn't much—is $1000 a month.
10. Science fiction and fantasy—if you like these genres, you'll love watching *Battlestar Galactica*.

Exercise 25.23

1. Five of the students (I was asked not to name them) have volunteered to be peer tutors.
2. The apostrophe is explained in Chapter 26 (pages 432–438).
3. Jason complained that being a manager (he became one in March) was like being a cop.
4. I have enclosed a cheque for one hundred and fifty dollars ($150).
5. More members of the Canadian Forces died in World War I (1914–18) than in any war before or since.
6. Although Mozart lived a relatively short time (he died when he was 36), he composed hundreds of musical masterpieces.
7. As news of her "miracle cures" spread (patients began to come to her from all over the province), the doctor had to move her clinic to a more central location.
8. The new contract provided improved working conditions, a raise in salary (3 percent), and a new dental plan.
9. Ontario and British Columbia now produce award-winning, world-class wines from small estate wineries (Inniskillin, Hillebrand, and Quails' Gate are three examples).

10. "One of the most important tools for making paper speak in your own voice is punctuation; it helps readers hear you the way you want to be heard" (Baker 48-49).

Answers for Chapter 26: Spelling (pp. 422–450)

Exercise 26.1

1. course, affect
2. Are, accept
3. then, dessert
4. you're, losing
5. quite, here
6. whose, conscience
7. assured, number
8. It's, its
9. choose, course, advice
10. Continual, dining

Exercise 26.2

1. Our decorator **chose** a stunning fabric for our **dining** room chairs, in colours that perfectly **complemented** our carpet.
2. My wife is a **woman** who **hears** everything and forgets nothing.
3. She's **quite** hopeful that the committee will **accept** her résumé, even though **it's** late and printed on coloured **stationery**.
4. Other **than** hope and pray that voters will **choose** our candidate, **there** is not much we can do.
5. Blindfolded, my wrists and ankles bound with duct tape, I was **led** to the car and driven out into the **desert**, **where I** was left by the side of the road.

Exercise 26.3

1. b
2. b
3. a
4. b
5. b
6. b
7. b
8. a
9. b
10. a

Exercise 26.5

1. can't
2. she'd
3. he'll
4. we'd
5. who's

6. she'll
7. won't
8. we'll
9. let's
10. you're

Exercise 26.6 **I am** writing to apply for the position of webmaster for BrilloVision.com that **you have** advertised in the *Daily News*. **I have** the talent and background **you are** looking for. Currently, I work as a Web designer for an online publication, Vexed.com, where **they are** very pleased with my work. If you click on their website, I think **you will** like what you see. **There is** little in the way of Web design and application that I **have not** been involved in during the past two years. But **it is** time for me to move on to a new challenge, and BrilloVision.com promises the kind of opportunity **I am** looking for. I guarantee you **will not** be disappointed if I join your team!

Exercise 26.7

1. a woman's role
2. witness's testimony
3. families' budgets
4. children's school
5. the soldiers' uniforms
6. the book's title
7. everyone's choice
8. the Simpsons' cottage
9. the oldest child's responsibility
10. our country's flag

Exercise 26.8

1. you're, your, your
2. Someone's, whose
3. ship's, week's
4. people's, workers', sides'
5. turtle's, turtle's, it's, its, yours

Exercise 26.9

1. Two **silkworms** had a race; they ended up in a tie.
2. When you feel like a snack, you can choose between apples and **Timbits**.
3. **Ted's** career took off when he discovered how easy it was to sell **children's toys** to grandparents.
4. A beginning golfer needs three different kinds of clubs: **woods** for long shots, **irons** for short ones, and a putter for the last four or five shots.
5. Good writing **skills won't** guarantee success in **your** career, but poor writing **skills** are guaranteed to hold you back.

Exercise 26.11

1. I really can't explain why I **co-opted** your look.
2. I really can't stand **big-business** owners.

3. I had a dream I would live to be **ninety-eight**.
4. **Short-term** loans are my bank's specialty.
5. I had to walk up to the **seventh-floor** washroom because ours was broken.

Exercise 26.12

1. A **rubber-band** pistol was confiscated during **algebra class** because it was considered a weapon of math disruption.
2. Please **relay** this message to Mr. Chan: the masons want to **re-lay** the bricks tomorrow.
3. Our **next-door** neighbour teaches **high school**, but she doesn't like being introduced as a **high-school** teacher.
4. We had a presentation by **Atheists Anonymous**, a **non-prophet** organization.
5. Because Angela was an **attorney-at-law** and had once been an **all-Canadian** athlete, no one was surprised when she became **Minister of Recreation**.

Exercise 26.14

1. The man chuckled and said, "Don't quote me on that."
2. Love your sweater! Hate the shoes!
3. "When in B.C. make sure to try the halibut," Mary told Jeff.
4. Interested in seeing a movie? Definitely check out the one I told you about yesterday.
5. Gibson argued, "Testosterone may not accurately predict aggression in the sexes."

Exercise 26.15

1. I don't know, Jim. I hear Canada is a great place to live!
2. The Conservatives let me know that the Liberal candidate wasn't a good choice.
3. Planets such as Jupiter can be seen from McMaster University's observatory.
4. I really don't like Shreddies or Cheerios.
5. If you are going to Victoria, travel up to Nanaimo, too.

Exercise 26.16

1. Don't you think that the authors of this book could have come up with a more imaginative title for this chapter? Why not "Conquering Capitals," for example?
2. C. S. Lewis's books *The Chronicles of Narnia* are being made into a series of films.
3. The producers are hoping these films will be as successful as Tolkien's *Lord of the Rings* movies.
4. Vermeer's most famous painting, *Girl with a Pearl Earring*, became first a novel and then a movie.
5. In his eighties, Leonard Cohen created a Juno Award–nominated album, *Popular Problems*.

Exercise 26.17

1. Next Monday is Valentine's Day, when messages of love are exchanged.
2. By Thursday, I'll have finished my St. Patrick's Day costume.
3. My favourite months are January and February because I love all winter sports.
4. In the summer, big meals seem to be too much trouble; however, after Thanksgiving, we need lots of food to survive the winter cold.
5. A national holiday named Flag Day was once proposed, but it was never officially approved.

Exercise 26.18

1. The review of my book, *The Life and Times of a Hog Rider*, published in *The Globe and Mail*, was not favourable.
2. Clint Eastwood fans will be delighted that the two early movies that made him internationally famous, ***A** Fistful of **D**ollars* and ***F**or a **F**ew **D**ollars **M**ore*, are now available on DVD.
3. Joseph Conrad's short novel *Heart of **D**arkness* became the blockbuster movie *Apocalypse **N**ow*.
4. My essay, "**A B**right and **S**ilent **P**lace," was published in the **A**pril issue of *Landscapes* magazine.
5. Botticelli's famous painting *Birth of Venus* inspired my poem "**W**oman on the **H**alf Shell."

Exercise 26.19

1. Correct
2. After passing Professor Bacchus's course, **I**ntroduction to **W**ine, I registered for **O**enology 200.
3. After studying geography for two years, I began taking courses in ancient **G**reek and modern history.
4. While math is her strong subject, Louisa has trouble with accounting, English, and conversational French.
5. The prerequisite for Theology 210 is **I**ntroduction to **W**orld **R**eligions, taught by Professor O'Connor.

Exercise 26.21

1. It was so cold for the **first half** of winter that hardly anyone was out on the street.
2. He was down **two** strikes in the **eighth** inning, and tensions were running high for the **first** time.
3. We have been waiting **12** months to hear if we are going to get the contract.
4. When I turned **13**, my parents bought me my first computer.
5. **Three hundred and sixty-five** days seems a long time, but **one** year seems so short.
6. I wonder if, by the year **2030** everyone will be able to go to space.
7. Second place is all right, but I would have preferred **first**.
8. **Eighty** people came to my talk even though I had already given it **12** times.
9. Of the **ten** players, nine couldn't catch the ball.
10. **Three-quarters** of a teaspoon is what the recipe called for.

Exercise 26.22

1. Researchers at Cornell University conducted a study that showed that **66** percent of all businessmen wear their ties too tight.
2. More than **10** percent of those studied wore their ties so tight that blood flow to the brain was diminished.
3. **Ninety-nine** percent of the people who read the report wondered why Cornell had conducted such a study.
4. **One** plan is to retire on **December 17**, 2055, when I will be 80.
5. At precisely **8:10 p.m.** on **June 3**, your flight will leave for Whitehorse.
6. You will arrive at approximately **ten o'clock** on **June** 4 if you make all your connections.

7. I won **five dollars** from Ted by proving that February **1865** was the only month in recorded history not to have a full moon.

8. You must be present at **133 West 18th Street** by exactly **seven o'clock** to claim your prize.

9. So far this year, I have spent **$38 000**, or **20** percent more than my anticipated income for the entire year, and it's only **May 15**!

10. At the Indianapolis Speedway, the race cars burn approximately **4 L** of fuel for each lap, while the ship *Queen Mary 2* moves just **15** cm for every 4 L of fuel it burns.

Exercise 26.23

1. The speedboat is powered by **two** 80-horsepower outboard motors.

2. **One** 8-cylinder SUV emits more pollution than two 4-cylinder diesel Volkswagens or **three** Toyota gas–electric hybrids.

3. Because she sold seven **$2-million** homes last year, she topped the agency's earnings list.

4. Correct

5. **Two hundred** people were invited to celebrate my parents' **25th** wedding anniversary on **August 31**, 2013.

6. A total of **ten 15-year-old** girls and **four 15-year-old** boys applied for the commercial acting position we advertised.

7. Our lawyer told us that 38 **percent** of people who die between the ages of 45 and 54 have not prepared a will.

8. Canada's population of about 33 **million** puts us in **36th** place on the list of most populous countries.

9. **Ten** years ago, the average speed on urban freeways was **50 kph**, but it has been steadily declining and is expected to be **30 kph** within the next **five** years.

10. **Seven thousand** ecstatic fans celebrated their team's unexpected **2–1** win in the Memorial Cup final, partying in the streets until **4:30 a.m**.

Index

Note: Page numbers followed by *n* denote material located in footnotes.

B

C

D

E

F

G

J

K

L

Q

R

S

T

U

V

W

Y

Z